The AA **KEY**Guide
Thailand

By Sean Sheehan and Robert Tilley

Contents

KEY TO SYMBOLS

✚ Map reference
✉ Address
☎ Telephone number
🕐 Opening times
👋 Admission prices
Ⓜ Subway station
🚌 Bus number
🚆 Skytrain/train station
⛴ Ferry/boat
🚗 Driving directions
ℹ Tourist office
Tours
📖 Guidebook
🍴 Restaurant
☕ Café
🛍 Shop
🍸 Bar
🚻 Toilets
🛏 Number of rooms
🅿 Parking
🚭 No smoking
❄ Air-conditioning
🏊 Swimming pool
💪 Gym
❓ Other useful information
🛍 Shopping
🎭 Entertainment
🎵 Nightlife
⚽ Sports
✪ Activities
♥ Health and beauty
✿ For children
▷ Cross reference
★ Walk/tour start point

HOW TO USE THIS BOOK

Understanding Thailand is an introduction to the country, its geography, economy and people. **Living Thailand** gives an insight into Thailand today, while **The Story of Thailand** takes you through the country's past.

For detailed advice on getting to Thailand—and getting around once you are there—turn to **On the Move**. For useful practical information, from weather forecasts to emergency services, turn to **Planning**.

Out and About gives you the chance to explore Thailand through walks, drives and organized tours.

The **Sights**, **What to Do** and **Eating and Staying** sections are divided into five regions, which are shown on the map on the inside front cover. These regions always appear in the same order. Towns and places of interest are listed alphabetically within each region.

Map references for the **Sights** refer to the atlas section at the end of this book or to individual town plans. For example, Pattaya has the reference ✚ 316 E10, indicating the page on which the map is found (316) and the grid square in which Pattaya sits (E10).

UNDERSTANDING THAILAND

Thailand is popularly known as the "land of smiles," while the country's tourist board lures visitors with the slogan "Amazing Thailand." Visitors to this Southeast Asian country are struck by the friendliness of its people and by the great variety of its attractions: its islands and beaches, mountains and jungles, exotic culture and temples, and celebrated cuisine. Thailand is a very easy country to explore, with a transportation network that's the envy of its neighbors, and even the most remote villages of the north and east are accessible by local bus. The range of its hotels, guesthouses, restaurants and night spots is unrivaled in Asia, and Bangkok is among the most exhilarating of Asia's capitals.

Rock formation off the coast of Phang Nga in southern Thailand

LANDSCAPE

Thailand is one of Southeast Asia's largest countries, stretching nearly 2,000km (1,200 miles) from north to south, from a mountainous border with Myanmar (Burma) to the Malaysian peninsula. Its terrain conveniently divides the country into four regions: the mountainous north, the undulating central plains, the vast northeastern plateau and the coastal south, with its islands and archipelagos. Bangkok sits like a bulky megalith at its center, at the head of the great bay called the Bight of Bangkok.

POLITICS

When viewed from afar, Thailand appears to be a model of democracy and an area of stability in Southeast Asia, an impression reinforced by the undemocratic forms of government of the two countries that cradle it in the north: militarily-ruled Myanmar (Burma) and Communist-run Laos. Yet it shouldn't be forgotten that democracy came late to Thailand and that for much of the last century the country was ruled by autocratic or military regimes. The last military coup was in 1991, and although the dictatorship was short-lived—brought to an end one year later by a student-led uprising and the intervention of the king—the memory is too fresh for complacency to set in. When the then prime minister, Thaksin Shinawatra, won an absolute majority in the parliamentary election of 2005, political commentators voiced real concern about the return of one-party rule to Thailand.

Thaksin claimed that democracies such as the United States and Great Britain were effectively ruled now by one sole party, but his argument didn't calm the fears of his political opponents.

Thaksin, leader of the Thai Loves Thai (Thai Rak Thai) party, became prime minister in 2001, but had to rule in coalition with the small Thai Nation Party (Pak Chart Thai). Thaksin was so confident of overwhelming victory in the 2005 election that he announced in advance that he wanted to dump Pak Chart Thai.

Bolstered by strong economic factors, a massive injection of funds into rural areas and the positive fallout from his rapid response to the tsunami catastrophe, Thaksin rode to power on a massive wave of popularity, winning 377 of the 500 seats in parliament and dispensing with his original coalition partner. Thailand's oldest political party, the opposition Democrats, garnered only 96 seats and its leader resigned.

Yet, despite Thaksin's spectacular success, he governed a divided country, for his party was wiped out in the mainly Muslim south, where the Democrats took 52 of the 54 seats. The anti-Thaksin mood in the south arose from his clumsy

dropped to below 10 percent of gross domestic product (GDP). Industry's share of the GDP grew to more than 40 percent as export-oriented vehicle assembly increased. Income from tourism also grew steadily during Thaksin's first years in office, accounting for more than 40 percent of national income in 2003—the year that saw a series of crises highlight the vulnerability of this sector.

The SARS epidemic, bird flu and the disastrous 2004 tsunami rang warning bells for the Thai government. The tourism sector proved to be far more vulnerable than anybody thought possible in the heady years of the 1970s and 1980s,

A delicate lotus flower at the Imperial Boat House Hotel, Ko Samui (left). A monk shelters from the sun at Wat Luang (right)

and sometimes brutal handling of Muslim unrest and secessionist fervor. Shortly after the February 2005 election, an embittered Thaksin announced that punitive economic sanctions would be taken against southern communities where anti-government violence occurred. The outcry was so loud and widespread that he backed down and offered to tackle the problems of the south in consultation with opposition parties. In 2006 Thaksin announced his intention to stand down.

ECONOMICS

Thailand was blamed for helping to trigger the disastrous Asian economic crisis of 1997/1998, but ironically it led the regional recovery of the first years of the 21st century. Economic growth slumped more than 10 percent in 1998 after five boom years in which gross national product (GNP) averaged an annual 8.5 percent. By 2006, growth had climbed back above 4 percent annually, a remarkable achievement for which Thaksin Shinawatra claimed credit. He did it after taking power in 2001 with a program of economic measures that became known as "thaksinomics" and that earned him the popular soubriquet "Thailand's Chief Executive Officer."

He promoted privatization, improved higher education and pumped money into the countryside, where subsistence farmers had labored for centuries to make Thailand self-sufficient in agricultural products, particularly rice. Thailand has long been Asia's foremost rice producer, and increasing mechanization strengthened the country's hold on international markets.

Yet Thaksin realized rice was no source of great wealth and he diversified the economy to the point where income from agricultural exports

when resorts such as Pattaya sprung up around the Bay of Bangkok and along the Andaman coast, and previously pristine islands such as Phuket and Ko Samui embraced commercialism.

SOCIETY

The social structure of Thailand has the form of three concentric circles. At its heart are the king and the royal family. They are surrounded by the community of Buddhist abbots and monks. The outer ring is made up of the Thai populace. This structure is supported by a foundation of special forms of behavior and language. The king and his immediate family are so remote from the general public that special terms of language have to be used in talking of them; they command total loyalty and respect, and any form of criticism or ridicule is not only taboo but also a punishable offence. Yet the king is referred to by the simplest peasant as "father"; he is benefactor and protector—not only of the nation but also of the individual. The popular love felt for King Bhumibol, the world's longest-reigning monarch, is palpable and genuine, and Thais talk with true dread of the day when he no longer rules over them. The second circle of Thailand's social structure is populated by representatives of the Buddhist faith, which dominates popular thought and action. Abbots and monks are held in great esteem, but at the same time they lead hard lives of frugal simplicity, supported materially by their congregations. Housewives rise before dawn to fill the begging bowls of monks on their daily rounds. Outside these two formal circles of society is grouped the general populace, which is developing its own rules of social order as the country's increasing prosperity produces a growing middle class.

THAILAND AT A GLANCE

Thailand divides neatly into four distinct regions, each of which developed over the centuries its own separate history and economic structure. The huge metropolitan area of Bangkok is also often regarded as a separate region because of its size. Subdivided into 76 provinces, Thailand occupies a land mass about the size of France, enclosed by mountains in the north and two seas in the south. The distance from the Myanmar border in the north to the southern frontier with Malaysia is nearly as great as the distance between the Baltic and the Mediterranean. It takes at least two days to travel by train or bus the length of the country, and even flying takes up most of the day by the time Bangkok connections are taken into account. Visitors planning to tour Thailand in less than two weeks often underestimate the distances they have to cover, and many holiday itineraries are rapidly rewritten within a few hours of arrival in Bangkok.

Chiang Dao in the north of Thailand (left). A deserted beach at Ko Tao (middle). Gifts for sale in Ao Nang (right)

Bangkok Thailand's capital is classed as a region because of its sheer size: 1,538sq km (600sq miles), home to one-tenth of Thailand's 60 million people. Its center is inland from the great Gulf of Thailand, and Bangkok dominates the urban landscape, industry and economy.

The Northeast The country's largest region is known as Isan. It stretches from the eastern upland reaches of the north to the frontiers of Laos and Cambodia, bordered for much of its eastern length by the Mekong River. Much of the region is a hot, largely arid plateau, where farmers eke out a difficult existence. Yet the food of the Isan is prized highly, and the hospitality of its people is legendary. The towns and villages along the Mekong see few visitors and are true explorer territory. Even more interesting is Isan's southern border with Cambodia, where a string of ruined Khmer castles gives a fascinating insight into a civilization that shaped this part of Thailand.

The North At the other end of the country lie the mountains of the north, including Thailand's highest mountain, Doi Inthanon. From the northern capital, Chiang Mai, the mountains rise in thickly forested ranges to form natural frontiers with Myanmar to the north and west and Laos to the east. The north was a separate kingdom, the realm of Lanna, for nearly 800 years and gave up the last vestiges of its independence to Bangkok only in the 20th century. It still retains a proud sense of nationhood, reflected in the numerous Lanna festivals held. The region's seasons are more pronounced than elsewhere in Thailand, and temperatures can drop to near freezing in the mountains in the cool months from November to March.

Central Thailand Bordered by Bangkok to the north, the Central Plains form Thailand's rice bowl and the country's most densely populated region. The rivers flowing from the mountainous north, tributaries of Thailand's main waterway, the Chao Phraya, feed the vast patchwork of rice paddies that distinguishes the landscape of this largely flat region. Riverside farming communities are grouped around market towns and local administrative centers.

The South To the east and south of Bangkok lie the coastal areas. The eastern seaboard is becoming rapidly industrialized, with vehicle manufacturing plants shooting up around the port of Bang Lamung. But between the industrial zones and the Cambodian border to the south lie such holiday playgrounds as Pattaya and Ko Chang island. The true south is the long peninsula running from Bangkok to the Malaysian border, a tropical region of rainforests, palm-fringed beaches and tourist resorts. On the western side are the Andaman coast and a chain of islands of which Phuket is the biggest. On the east is the gulf coast, with resorts like Hua Hin and Chumphon and the islands of Ko Samui and Ko Pha Ngan. The far south is predominantly Muslim, with some of the most welcoming and interesting Thai provinces.

CHIANG RAI

PHAYAO

NAN

LA

MAE HONG SON

CHIANG MAI

LAMPANG

LAMPHUN

PHRAE

UTTARADIT

NONG KHAI

LOEI

UDON THANI

SAKHON NAKHON

NAKHON PHANOM

SUKHOTHAI

NONG BUA LAMPHU

TAK

PHITSANULOK

KHON KAEN

KALASIN

MUKDAHAN

MM

KAMPHAENG PHET

PHETCHABUN

PHICHIT

CHAIYAPHUM

MAHA SARAKHAM

YASOTHON

NAKHONSAWAN

ROI ET

AMNAT CHAROEN

UTHAITHANI

CHAINAT

LOPBURI

NAKHONRATCHASIMA

SURIN

UBON RATCHATHANI

SUPHANBURI

SINGURI

SI SAKET

KANCHANABURI

ANGTHONG

SARABURI

BURIRAM

AYUTTHAYA

PRATHUMTHANI

NAKHONNAYOK

PRACHINBURI

SAKAEO

CHACHOENGSAO

RATCHABURI

SAMUTPRAKAN

CHON BURI

KH

PHETCHABURI

CHANTHABURI

RAYONG

TRAT

Ko Chang

PRACHUAP KHIRI KHAN

CHUMPHON

RANONG

Ko Pha Ngan

Ko Samui

SURAT THANI

PHANG-NGA

KRABI

NAKHON SI THAMMARAT

Phuket

Ko Lanta

TRANG

PHATTHALUNG

SATUN

SONGKHLA

PATTANI

YALA

NARATHIWAT

MY

THE BEST OF THAILAND

BANGKOK

BedSupper Club (▷ 189) Bangkok's chic symposium, with white linen sheets, food, drink and an air of stylish decadence.

Chao Phraya River (▷ 67) Beat the road traffic and get around by boat.

Chatuchak Weekend Market (▷ 68) Shop at the world's benchmark for street markets.

Chinatown (▷ 68) Take a noisy, sweaty, exhausting and insightful walk through the capital.

Grand Palace (▷ 84) If you visit only one temple in Thailand, make it this one—and bring a camera.

Jim Thompson's House (▷ 71) This traditional house has been gorgeously furnished and decorated by an expatriate connoisseur of Thai art.

May Kaidee's (▷ 248) Feast on Thai vegetarian food, at this restaurant tucked away off the famed Khao San Road.

National Museum (▷ 73) See art and objects from across the country, and the Buddha in all his sublime poses.

The Peninsula (▷ 272) Stay at the best hotel in the capital for views of the Chao Phraya River.

The Sky Bar (▷ 188–189) Sip cocktails on top of the world.

Wat Pho (▷ 83) See the longest reclining Buddha in the world and an authentic massage center.

Wat Suthat (above) in Bangkok, commissioned by Rama I

Ornate doors at Jim Thompson's House (left)

Offerings at the Tao Suranari memorial (above)

Wat Pa Salawan, Korat (below left)

THE NORTHEAST

Ban Khwao (▷ 91) Be amazed by the home-based production process that results in quality silk.

Chiang Khan (▷ 92) Wander through this laid-back little town on the banks of the Mekong.

Khao Phra Viharn (▷ 92) Visit this remote Khmer temple complex just over the border in Cambodia, off-limits for nearly a century, but visitable in a day without a visa.

Khao Yai National Park (▷ 93) See wild elephants and hornbills and take night safaris and treks through the rainforest with knowledgeable nature guides.

Khon Kaen (▷ 94–95) Explore this sophisticated city offering good food and some of the best-quality shopping in the northeast of Thailand.

Lamai Homestay (▷ 275) Stay a night or two in a quiet rice village where you will experience Thai rural life as it is really lived.

Nakhon Ratchasima (▷ 97) Enjoy Thai curries at their most authentic and shopping without the hassle.

Nong Khai (▷ 98) Sit back and relax with a drink on a river cruise along the Mekong River.

THE NORTH

Chiang Mai (▷ 256) Reserve a table at one of Chiang Mai's several *kantoke* restaurants, where a performance of traditional music and dance accompanies the Thai food.

Chiang Mai (▷ 122) Get up before dawn and hike up Chiang Mai's mountain, Doi Suthep, reaching the top before the sun gets too hot and the crowds at the Phra That Doi Suthep temple too dense.

Chiang Mai (▷ 113) Join in the daily "monk chat" in the park-like grounds of Wat Chedi Luang in central Chiang Mai and question the monks about their lives and beliefs.

Chiang Mai (▷ 114) If you're not in town for Chiang Mai's Sunday street market, settle for its nightly bazaar, where the prices are higher but the selection is larger.

Chiang Mai and Chiang Rai (▷ 114 and 118) Browse the night markets of Chiang Mai and Chiang Rai, where you're certain to find just the souvenir or keepsake you've been looking for.

Chiang Rai (▷ 118) Instead of motoring to Chiang Rai, arrive there by boat—there's a daily service down the Kok River from Thaton.

Lampang (▷ 124–125) Switch off for a day's meditation at a Lampang temple.

Lamphun (▷ 126–127) Shop for locally made textiles on Lamphun's covered bridge and then stroll in the twilight through the nearby Wat Haripunchai.

Mae Hong Son (▷ 128) Rent a car and drive the Mae Hong Son loop road, making sure to find time for stops in Pai and Mae Sariang.

Spa towns Soak the day away in the hot springs of one of Northern Thailand's many spas—Chiang Mai (▷ 112–117), Lampang (▷ 124–125), Mae Hong Son (▷ 128) and Pai (▷ 131)—and enjoy a traditional Thai massage.

Tak (▷ 133) Join a houseboat party on any of Northern Thailand's big lakes (the Bhumiphol Dam, for instance) and cruise its waters, stopping for lunch at a floating restaurant.

A naga (dragon-headed serpent) guards Wat Phra Sing in Chiang Mai

CENTRAL THAILAND

Ayutthaya (▷ 135–139) Cruise the canals of Ayutthaya by boat, or amble around the ruins of the old city on the back of an elephant.

Chanthaburi (▷ 140) Tour the jewelry shops of Chanthaburi, Thailand's gem trade center.

Damnoen Saduak (▷ 141) Take an early bus from Bangkok to the Damnoen Saduak floating market.

Kanchanaburi (▷ 142–143) Ride the "Death Railway" from Kanchanaburi to the end of the line, Namtok—but also find time to cruise the famous Kwai River in a longtail boat.

Lop Buri (▷ 144) Throw a few bananas to the monkeys at Lop Buri's Wat Phra Kan, but don't go too close.

Pattaya (▷ 146) Overnight in Pattaya, sample its hedonistic, anything-goes nightlife and vow to return—or to stay away forever.

Phra Chedi Sam Ong (▷ 145) Step across the Myanmar border at the Three Pagodas Pass, then shop for genuine Burmese rubies at the market stalls on either side of the frontier.

Si Satchanalai (▷ 148–149) Seek out the ruined royal city of Si Satchanalai, near Sukhothai, and tour the site on elephant back.

Waterfall at Doi Inthanon National Park (above)

Lounging on the beach at Hat Kamala, Phuket (below)

THE SOUTH

Hua Hin (▷ 156) Visit this seaside resort with a sparkling white beach, an historic hotel, good food and easy access from Bangkok.

Ko Lanta (▷ 159) Chill out on a beach, read a long novel and explore the island's east coast.

Ko Samui (▷ 161) The palm-fringed beaches make this a hugely popular island, but it is large enough for those seeking a quiet retreat.

Ko Similan (▷ 160) Explore these islands that offer the best underwater experience in Thailand.

Krabi (▷ 164) A small and well-provided town that serves as a great base for island trips and water-based activities.

Phetchaburi (▷ 167) Take a walking tour through a town renowned for its historic temples.

Phuket (▷ 168–171) Base yourself at one of the most sophisticated beach resorts in the country.

Phuket Town (▷ 168) Take a break from the beaches and enjoy the photogenic architecture and a spot of shopping.

Big Buddha, Ko Samui (left)

TOP EXPERIENCES

Deepen your knowledge of Thai history by touring the Khmer ruins along the country's southern border with Cambodia (▷ 27).

Get Sporty Rent a mountain bicycle in Chiang Dao and tackle Doi Chiang Dao mountain, one of Thailand's highest (▷ 110).

Join a trekking tour in Chiang Rai or Mae Hong Son to remote hill-tribe villages (▷ 128).

Learn to ride elephants as the mahouts do at the National Elephant Institute's Conservation Center near Lampang (▷ 124).

Master the art of Thai kick-boxing, or Muay Thai, at a martial arts school in Bangkok or Chiang Mai (▷ 187).

Pamper yourself with a day's spa treatment in Bangkok or Chiang Mai (▷ 190–191).

A longtail ferry boat at Ao Nang near Krabi (above)

Take an elephant tour in Ayutthaya (below)

Rent a longtail boat at Chiang Saen on the Mekong River and tell the skipper to take you to the true Golden Triangle, where the borders of Thailand, Myanmar and Laos meet (▷ 119).

Sip wine at Thailand's leading vineyard, Chateau de Loei, in Loei province (▷ 96).

Spend the night in a timber-built cabin at one of Thailand's national parks and rent a guide the next morning to lead you on a trek through virgin rainforest (▷ 93).

Stay overnight in a floating cabin on the Kwai River in Kanchanaburi province (▷ 142–143).

Surprise friends at your next dinner party by serving a complete Thai menu after taking a cooking course at one of Bangkok's many cookery schools (▷ 190).

Tackle the rapids of the Pai River in Northern Thailand in a canoe or, more safely, on a raft (▷ 203).

Try a new water sport at Pattaya or Patong, where instructors in sailing, windsurfing, water-skiing and paragliding operate at the local beaches (▷ 146).

A Khmer Ganesh figure from a museum in Ubon (left)

River in Doi Phu Kha National Park (below)

Living Thailand

An Akha tribeswoman at the Doi Mae Salong morning market in the Chiang Mai Province

Members of a Hmong (or Meo) tribe in a hill village in the Phu Hin Rong Kla National Park (above)

Bank workers leave the office in Salom Road, in Bangkok's business and financial district (right)

People and Society

Thailand's social fabric dictates all the country's actions and the daily routine of its people, from government procedures to the way the humblest farmer conducts his life. At the center stands the monarch, whose picture hangs not only in offices, workplaces and everywhere the public congregates, but also in most homes. The present king, Bhumibol Adulyadej, Rama IX, is genuinely and universally loved, a true father figure. Great reverence is also paid to the community of monks, the Sangha, which is held at a respectful distance by a population that is more than 90 percent Buddhist. Society's third level is taken up by the commoners, increasingly divided into a burgeoning middle class and a peasant majority.

Buddhist monks walk in single file in Chinatown, Bangkok

Despite past demonstrations of student political engagement and fervor, Thailand's youth is quiescent and more concerned with carving out careers than with addressing the political, economic and social problems that beset the country. Thailand even has "yuppies"— a class of young professionals sometimes called "tuppies." Their rapid acquisition of wealth and influence is having a polarizing effect on Thai society, which is in danger of becoming a two-class state, divided between those who control the wealth and the millions of rural peasants.

Women fare best in Thailand

Thailand offers a better life for women than any other country in the Asia-Pacific region. That conclusion was reached by an International Women's Day survey conducted in 2005 by MasterCard International. The survey questioned between 300 and 350 representative women citizens of 13 countries. It rated levels of education, income, labor force participation and access to managerial positions. The survey found that women throughout the region still suffered discrimination in the workplace, but that Thai women fared better than anywhere else.

Japan, Indonesia and South Korea trailed Thailand and the other nine nations when it came to equality of opportunity for women.

Traveling on the Skytrain in Bangkok (above)

A doorman at the Royal Orchid Sheraton Hotel in Bangkok (right)

Wooden huts provide simple accommodation for these hill tribes in the Mae Salong district (above)

A Karen tribesman carrying teak leaves for house roofing (right)

Cynical youth

More than half the students at 30 of Bangkok's top high schools believe that corruption is acceptable if it improves job performance. The finding—which shocked many hardened Thai politicians—emerged from a survey of 4,000 students. The survey also found that more than 40 percent of the polled students had never visited a Buddhist temple. Some people believe that morality is losing its strength in society and that parents are teaching their children less about moral values and more about material success.

A group of smiling local girls in the town of Pattani

Language teaching problems

Thailand is proud never to have been colonized by a Western power. But while neighbors Vietnam and Malaysia are finding their exposure to French and British cultural and linguistic influences is critically important in the age of globalization, Thailand has been relatively sidelined. Until now, non-nationals were barred from teaching foreign languages at state schools, and very few Thai teachers have solid English-teaching skills. The Thai government is now beginning to recognize the need for non-national teachers to help the country learn the international language of business, and in late 2005 legislation was being prepared to admit them to Thai schools.

Thailand's hill tribes

Wherever you travel in northern Thailand you'll encounter hill-tribe people and have the opportunity to visit or stay in their villages. There are nine hill tribes, numbering about half a million people, most originating in remote regions of northeastern Myanmar (Burma) and northwestern China. One, the gentle Akha, traces their origins to Tibet. The Karen are the most numerous, with more than 200,000 people inhabiting most of Thailand's western border with Myanmar. Although the Karen are by tradition animists, many of them are Christian, converted by missionaries. Many of the hill-tribe villages existed for many years on the opium trade, growing poppies on mountainside plots difficult for the police to access. But a government program introducing alternative cash crops is weaning them away from their illegal business.

The practical side of Thai customs

Some of the obscure customs originating in the ancient northern kingdom of Lanna actually serve a practical purpose. Once a year, Buddhists—particularly in rural communities—bring sand to their local temple and seem to the outsider to busy themselves building sandcastles in the monastery compounds. In fact, they are symbolically but also practically replacing the soil, sand and gravel carried away from the temple compound by the feet of monks and visitors. Buddhist belief considers it inappropriate to take anything from a temple, including the soil, sand or gravel. So once a year, at the Songkran New Year festival, people make merit, easing their way to Nirvana, by taking sand to the local temple. In the north, the sand is built into *chedis*, rather like building a sandcastle on the beach, and decorated with flowers, paper flags and money.

One of five traditional raised Thai houses built by Princess Chumbhot in the grounds of the Suan Pakkard Palace

A row of shining gold seated buddhas in a covered gallery in Wat Suthat (above). Colonial-style buildings on the Chao Phraya River in Bangkok (left). A 19th-century temple mural (below)

Culture and
Architecture

Visitors to Thailand's historic cities often ask why virtually the only surviving buildings are temple structures. The answer is that secular homes were normally built of wood, and they have not withstood the ravages of time. Stone and masonry

Devotee wrapping a *chedi* for a festival at Wat Phra That Doi Tung

were reserved for palaces and temples, as if early rulers knew they would be building for posterity. No wooden building in today's Thailand is more than a century or so old, making it difficult for historians to trace a precise line of architectural development. The ruins of temples and royal buildings, however, follow a 1,500-year course that embraces Indian, Sri Lankan, Mon, Khmer, Chinese and Burmese influences within a recognizably Siamese context. Sandstone was the earliest construction material, to be replaced in the 12th century by brick. By the 16th century, stucco was being used more and more. Increasing contact with the outside world in the 19th century brought Western architectural styles to Siam, and neo-Gothic, Victorian and even classical Greek structures arose in Bangkok and royal country retreats. During the late 20th century, renowned architects were employed to give Bangkok a Manhattan look, and soaring skyscrapers now share space with century-old wooden pavilions and shophouses.

Spectacular skyline

Bangkok is not known as a city of architectural beauty, yet the boom years of the early 1990s left it with a collection of spectacular skyscrapers that wouldn't look out of place in Manhattan. More than 700 high-rise buildings, 35 of them taller than 100m (330ft), pierce the skyline of Thailand's sprawling capital, many designed by leading architects. The highest is the Baiyoke Tower II, in Ratchatewi district, which tops 300m (997ft). The 85 floors include a 673-room hotel. When it was built in 1996 it was the tallest building in Southeast Asia and the world's third-highest hotel. Among the most spectacular is the Thai Wah Tower II, a thin wafer that reaches 194m (636ft), with the topmost of its 60 floors framing a graceful arch.

monk
tering a
mple in Mae
ong Son
ight)

spirit house
a beach on
Samet
elow)

Spirit shrine by
the bridge over
the River Kwai
(above)

Le Royal
Meridien Hotel,
downtown
Bangkok (right)

Bangkok's high-rise temple

Thailand has some of Southeast Asia's most distinctive temple architecture, but not all of it is in traditional style. The capital's tallest temple structure, built in 1985, is a modern pyramid-shape high-rise of 10 floors, topped by a traditional stupa or *chedi*, containing relics said to be strands of the Buddha's hair. The temple building, Wat Dhammamongkol (Soi 1, Thanon Sukhumvit), is 95m (312ft) tall and contains the world's largest jade Buddha image.

Banking on architectural award

Thai architect Sathaporn Srikarananda won the country's 1993 award for best work of architectural conservation by converting a temple sermon hall into a boat museum. He found his inspiration in the depiction of the wooden pavilion structure on the back of a rare one-baht banknote from the reign of King Rama VIII. The sermon hall, its high ceiling supported by massive beams and pillars, was built in 1927 and renovated in 1988.

Spirit houses

The building industry in Thailand has a very lucrative offshoot—the construction of spirit houses. Office blocks, condominium buildings, hotels and even petrol stations all have a spirit house for the *pi* (or spirits) who previously lived on the site. The spirits are given food and offerings to ensure that they don't cause problems for the new occupants of their territory. In country areas, when a new house is built, ceremonies are held to appease the spirits who lived in the forest that supplied the timber used in the construction. If a property is enlarged, the spirit house also has to be made bigger to accommodate an increased number of spirits.

Two gold and white beasts guard the entrance to one of the temple buildings of Chiang Mai's Wat Phra That Doi Suthep

Lanna Revival

A new style has entered Thailand's architectural vocabulary—the Lanna Revival. It's not without controversy, however. A conference attended by Buddhist academics and abbots in Chiang Mai complained that the Lanna Revival style increasingly seen in hotel construction was exploiting temple architecture and icons for commercial purposes.

They pointed to the example of a new luxury hotel that had built on its grounds a replica of a famous Lampang temple. Furthermore, the same hotel had built its entrance in imitation of another Lampang temple. Worse still, hotels were displaying Buddha images and statues as decorative items in bedrooms. Stripped of its Buddhist decorations, the Lanna Revival style is actually very ascetic, combining dark teak flooring and paneling with stark white stucco.

Portrait of King Bhumibol in flowers, Chiang Mai Flower Festival (above)

A giant Kratong in the River Ping at Kamphaeng Phet (top)

Photograph of a royal princess giving a dance performance at the Nation Theatre in Bangkok (above

Two girls in formal Thai dress (left)

Royalty and Tradition

Although Thailand's king is now a constitutional monarch and no longer an absolute ruler, he and his family are held in the highest reverence, and any form of disrespect or lese-majesty is a punishable offense. At royal audiences, government officials approach the monarch on their knees and keep their heads below his at all times. The occasional television interviews with the royal family are staged so that the prince or princess sits on a raised dais. Pictures of the king or of earlier monarchs have to be hung above head height. These elaborate displays of reverence are accepted without question by the majority of Thais, who regard the king as the true father of the nation. There have been occasions—notably during confrontations between students and the government in 1992—when he has used this paternal influence to end a crisis. The king is also the guardian of Thailand's customs and traditions, and he is present at all important Buddhist rituals within the palace compound and often attends other temple events. In 1960 he resurrected the ancient Brahman custom of plowing a section of the park adjacent to the palace, the Sanam Luang. The token plowing, held in May, is accompanied by a prediction of how the next rice harvest will turn out. In December, the king and queen review the royal guard in a trooping of the color ceremony very similar to the British one.

The national anthem

First-time visitors to Thailand are often startled to see Thais stop what they are doing and stand stiffly to attention in public places while loudspeakers blare out a stirring melody. Twice a day, at 8am and 6pm, the national anthem is played in open spaces such as railway station concourses and markets. No Thai would ever dare ignore the call to stand in honor of their nation while the anthem is played; foreigners aren't required to follow the practice, but they get approving looks if they do. Theatre and cinema performances are preceded by the royal anthem, and there it's highly disrespectful to sit and munch popcorn while it's played.

Royal guards on Constitution Day Parade, Bangkok (left)

Royal barge (right)

Portrait of Queen Sirikit (left)

Silks in Pak Thong Chai (below)

Eranwan Shrine dancers, downtown Bangkok (above)

Shrine to King Bhumibol Adulyadej on his birthday (left)

Royal dog-lover

King Bhumibol loves dogs, but not just any breed—in fact, no breed at all, but mongrels and strays. He has taken in several, and one of them, Tongdaeng, so captured his heart that he wrote a book about her. Tongdaeng was the offspring of one of a group of stray dogs rescued from the Bangkok pound on the king's orders. The puppy, born in 1998, caught his attention because of her markings, and he named her Tongdaeng ("Copper") after her reddish-brown color. They're now inseparable, and the king takes her with him on most of his travels. His book, *The Story of Tongdaeng*, became a best seller.

"Renaissance man"

King Bhumibol plays saxophone and clarinet, loves jazz and has written 35 registered compositions. His love of jazz developed during the years of his youth that he spent in the United States and Switzerland; he once played saxophone with the great Benny Goodman. Among his jazz compositions are such numbers as "HM Blues" and "Friday Night Rag," but he has also written love songs with titles like "Lovelight in My Heart." He also dabbles successfully in science and technology. His keen interest in agriculture and the environment doesn't stop at theory—he has patented a rain-making idea involving "seeding" clouds over drought areas.

How to *wai*

The *wai* is Thailand's universal form of greeting, and every visitor should get to know the subtle rules governing its use. The height of your palms when brought together before the face or upper body is critical—too low and you may be mildly offending somebody, too high and surprised amusement may be the reaction. Basically, wait for a Thai to *wai* you before returning the gesture. Some Thais welcome foreigners by shaking hands, and in that case a *wai* is not only unnecessary but impossible. Monks and venerable people older than yourself receive the highest *wai*, with the fingertips reaching forehead level. Other adults and young people are the easiest to *wai*—just keep the palms of your hands above chest level. There is no need to return the *wai* of hotel or restaurant staff, or any service personnel.

Queen of silks

Thailand's Queen Sirikit is responsible for putting mudmee silk on the international fashion map. She financed a program to encourage women in rural areas to take up traditional handicrafts as a way of supplementing family incomes and keeping alive age-old skills. In Thailand's northeastern provinces, silk-weaving is a means of livelihood in many villages, and Queen Sirikit launched a project to promote one particularly fine silk, mudmee. She wore mudmee silk on state occasions, at home and abroad, attracting the attention of textile companies and designers. The high point of her campaign came when the French designer Pierre Balmain featured mudmee creations in one of his collections. Now mudmee, once a peasant cloth, is one of Thailand's most fashionable fabrics.

A traffic policeman wearing a respirator in Bangkok (far left)

A Thai farmer leading a pair of water buffalo pulling a cart loaded with harvested rice (left)

Rush hour congestion in the Sukhumvit, Bangkok (left)

Traditional baskets (below)

Urban vs. Rnal

Rural

Nearly 70 percent of Thailand's population of 63 million people live in the rural areas, and one of the problems faced by successive governments in Bangkok has been to maintain their living standards in a booming industrial economy. The latest United Nations report on world poverty levels classes nearly 10 million Thais as "poor"—that is, existing on less than the equivalent of US $1 per day—and most of these are living on the land. A further 5.8 million people are said in the report to be existing on less than 80 cents a day and therefore "ultra poor," while 19 million are listed as being on the poverty line. A parallel report by the UN Development Programme used other factors to measure Thailand's poverty: access to healthcare, housing, education, employment, transportation and environmental considerations. When these factors were considered, the report said, just 5 percent of Thailand's population could be classified as really poor. Nevertheless, most of Thailand's farmers, who form the backbone of the rural economy, exist on little more than $1 per day. City incomes average more than 10 times that, a growing disparity that Bangkok governments have difficulty in combating. Nobody starves in Thailand; subsidized medical services and education and a basic "survival" pension of B600 per month for needy elderly stave off total penury. But many rural dwellers watch in disbelief the antics of Thailand's high-living nouveau riche on TV soap operas.

Clothing the forest

Although illegal logging remains a serious threat to Thailand's vanishing forests, villagers are aware of the problem and have their own way of dealing with it. To protect the teak forests that provide an income to rural communities, most village temples have a festival known as *Wat Pa*—the Holy Forest. Animist beliefs and Buddhist ritual are blended in a ceremony in which the trees are "clothed" in saffron-color monks' robes, to deter thieves from entering the forest and disturbing the spirits that dwell there.

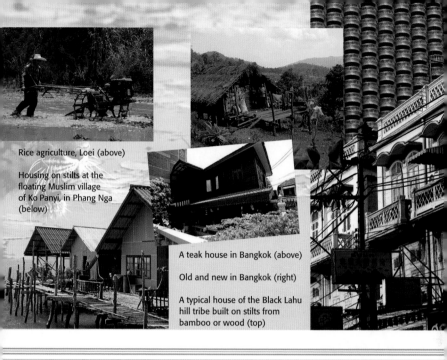

Rice agriculture, Loei (above)

Housing on stilts at the floating Muslim village of Ko Panyi, in Phang Nga (below)

A teak house in Bangkok (above)

Old and new in Bangkok (right)

A typical house of the Black Lahu hill tribe built on stilts from bamboo or wood (top)

Unhealthy Bangkok

Latest statistics confirm what everybody knew anyway: Bangkok is a dangerously unhealthy city. A report by the National Economic and Social Development Board shows that nearly half of the capital's 10 million inhabitants suffer from respiratory ailments. Air pollution regularly exceeds World Health Organization danger levels—on the main shopping street, Silom Road, dust levels are often nearly 10 times the WHO limits. Road accidents account for a huge number of casualties—more than 2,000 people die every year on Bangkok's roads. These statistics contributed to Bangkok's decline in the Mercer Human Resource Consulting list of "liveable cities" in the 12 months to 2005: Bangkok dropped from 102nd place to 106th.

OTOP

A new road sign has appeared at the entrance to most Thai towns and villages: OTOP. It stands for One Tambol One Product and indicates that the local community is specializing in the production of traditional handicrafts. Tambol (pronounced and sometimes written as "Tambon") is the administrative term for a small town or village. The idea of encouraging people in rural areas to supplement their income by starting "cottage industries" was borrowed from Japan, which is now closely involved with Thailand in the OTOP program. Thai communities are actively encouraged to revive traditional skills, from simple basket-weaving to the production of fine teak, bamboo and water hyacinth furniture. There are major OTOP retail outlets in Bangkok and some provincial centers, notably Chiang Mai, and a visit to one of them should be on any foreign shopper's schedule.

The royal projects

In an effort to wean hill-tribe farmers away from cultivating poppies for the production of opium, Thailand's King Bhumibol launched a program of "royal projects" in 1969 to offer them alternative sources of income. Since then, the number of projects has grown to more than 4,000, transforming the nature of Thailand's agriculture, particularly in the far north. The projects have introduced new varieties of crops once unknown in Thailand—temperate-zone fruits such as apples, pears, plums, strawberries and raspberries, and potatoes, artichokes and asparagus. The king called on experts from all over the world to assist in the enterprise: dispossessed white farmers from Zimbabwe helped nurture Thailand's embryonic tobacco industry, French vintners taught Thais to make wine, and German experts discovered soil conditions for growing excellent asparagus.

Thailand's vanishing tigers

Tigers are now so rare in Thailand that when two were sighted northwest of Chiang Mai in July 2005, a general warning not to shoot them was issued. The latest official survey puts the number of wild tigers in Thailand at 250, although the Thai Royal Forest Department says the true number is more like 600. Tigers are a strictly protected species, and severe penalties await any hunter who kills one. Trading in tiger skins or body parts is also a serious offense, but that doesn't prevent villagers in remote areas from offering visitors tiger teeth, claws and even penises. Such wares should not be bought.

A lady selling limes and sugar peas
from a stall in Bangkok (above)

Kaeng matsaman curry (top right)

Red hot chilies (left).
Noodle soup (right)

Food and
Drink

First-time visitors to Bangkok find a
vibrant city that not only never sleeps
but also never stops eating. Noodle
stands line the streets, serving hot
food around the clock, while
restaurants are rarely more than a few
paces apart. One reason given for this
preoccupation with food is that Thais
prefer to eat little and often rather than indulge in large
Western-style meals twice a day. Rice and noodles are the
staple diet, introduced from China more than 1,000 years
ago. There are two kinds of rice: the popular "sticky" variety
and boiled *kao suay*, which is sometimes jasmine flavored.
Sticky rice is eaten with curries and sauces, while *kao suay* is
normally served as a side dish or stir-fried with meat or
vegetables. Sticky rice is also a component of a delicious
dessert: sliced mango and sticky rice soaked in coconut milk.
The coconut milk used to thicken curries and sauces is not
the sweet juice of a ripe coconut (that's served complete with
the coconut, like an exotic cocktail), but is obtained from the
crushed white flesh of the fruit. It was first developed by
French chefs at the 17th-century court of Ayutthaya, where
they shunned the watery sauces and curries prepared by local
cooks. The ample supply of wood in Thailand resulted in an
early development of grilling techniques, while a flourishing
ceramics tradition provided pots for preparing the curries and
soups. Herbs gathered from the forest, chilies and other
spices grown domestically added the distinctly Thai character
and flavor.

"Royal" Thai cuisine

The best Thai restaurants
serve dishes that date
back to the 17th-century
reign of King Narai the
Great, who introduced
many Western influences
to his magnificent court.
Portuguese missionaries
and traders introduced
eggs to the kitchen and
syrups for desserts and
cakes (*kanom*). French
visitors showed the Thais
how to make bread,
which is still called
kanom pang (*pang*
being a transliteration of
the French *pain*). The
first Western ambassador
welcomed to Ayutthaya
was a French diplomat.
The nobleman brought
with him a retinue of
cooks, who transformed
the court kitchens. The
dishes they prepared
became known as "royal
Thai", and can still be
found on restaurant
menus.

Magical lights
illuminate a typical
Thai restaurant (right)

A large tub of eels for sale in Bangkok (right)

Hand-carving fruit is a popular pastime in Thailand (below)

Grilling fish (right)

Eating outside in Chinatown, Bangkok (right)

Herbs and spices

Around 30 herbs and spices are used in Thai cuisine. Three of them are varieties of basil: *horapa* (similar to the kind in Italian pesto), a sweeter version called *gaprao* and *Mangluk*, which has a slight peppery taste. The most important addition to traditional Thai cuisine is lemongrass *(takrai)*, which flavors soups such as *tom yam gong* (spicy shrimp soup). Medicinal powers are ascribed to most Thai herbs and spices. Three varieties of ginger are especially valued: *khing* (young green ginger used as a condiment with meat dishes), *galangal or khaa* (Siamese ginger used to make curry paste) and *grashai* (added to fish curries).

Thai tableware

When you eat at a typical Thai restaurant you'll be presented with a spoon and fork, but no knife. Chopsticks are usually kept in a metal container on the table. All are relatively new additions to the table in a country where people traditionally eat with their fingers. If you're invited to join a family at their meal in a country village, don't be surprised if you're expected to sit on the floor and eat with your fingers from common bowls. Sticky rice was once the staple food of the Thais and is still eaten in country areas in preference to the more refined *kao suay* (or "fine rice"). The only practical way to eat sticky rice is with the fingers, using it to soak up the soup.

Table habits

Etiquette in a Thai restaurant requires you to share your ordered dish with others at the table. The normal practice is for each diner to order one or two items, which should be different from those requested by the others. Each dish should have its own serving spoon, but don't be shocked if your neighbor dips directly into your curry! Rice is usually served from a common bowl. Don't expect dishes to come to the table in the order common in the West—soups and salads are served at the same time as other savory dishes. Only desserts come at the end of the meal. Water is usually drunk, but you'll see Thai businessmen lacing it with whisky.

Learning Thai cuisine

Cookery schools have shot up all over Thailand in response to the increasing international popularity of Thai cuisine. Most are concentrated in Bangkok, Chiang Mai and holiday islands such as Phuket and Ko Samui, but they are also to be found in any city and town on the visitor route. The largest concentration of cookery schools is in Chiang Mai, which has more than 20. Among the more established ones are Gaps House (3 Thanon Ratchadamnoen, Soi 4, tel 053 27 81 40; www.gaps-house.com) and the Chiang Mai Cookery School (47/2 Thanon Moon Muang, tel 053 20 63 88; www.thaicookeryschool.com), which has a restaurant outlet, The Wok (44 Thanon Ratchamanka, tel 053 20 82 87). Courses at all schools last from one day to one week and cost around B990 per day.

Chiang Mai traditional orchestra (left)

Thai women in vibrant costume performing a traditional dance (right)

Pop sensation Tata Young (above). A Thai man, dressed in a woman's costume, performing a traditional dance with candles at the Longan Fair in Lamphun (right)

Arts and
Entertainment

Thailand's struggling theater

The curtain has never risen on a truly contemporary theater scene in Thailand, where the stage is still associated in the public's mind with displays of traditional music and dancing and epic drama. There are only three major annual performing arts festivals, and the chief of these, the Bangkok International Festival of Music and Dance, is dominated by foreign productions. The other two, the Bangkok Theatre Festival and the Fringe Festival, attract only small audiences.

Government or corporate grants are rare, and the country's 10 professional theater companies have difficulty financing more than one or two productions a month between them. Even Bangkok has no theater devoted solely to drama.

After many years in the wilderness, Thailand is beginning to break into the international arts and entertainment scene. The award of a Cannes Film Festival Jury Prize to the Thai avant-garde film *Tropical Malady* in 2004 gave a big boost to a movie industry that had been chalking up some international successes but missing the big prizes. The burgeoning film production infrastructure attracted international producer-directors, and some interesting co-production deals with American studios were being negotiated in late 2005. Thai theater and serious music seem still rooted in tradition, and the few brave attempts at experimenting with new styles and themes have found little popular resonance. The pop music scene, however, is incandescent, thanks to stars such as Tata Young, Bird Tongchai McIntyre and two ground-breaking groups, Carabao and Loso.

Asian pop sensation

Daughter of an American father and a Thai mother, Tata Young has put Thai pop music on the international map. Known as the "Asian Britney Spears," she has cut more than a dozen albums, the seventh of which, "I Believe," launched her on the world stage. Born in December 1980, she made her first album, singing in Thai and English, at the age of 15. It sold 1 million copies within five months of the launch. Tata is also a movie star and won a best actress award in her debut role in the Thai film *Red Bike Story*, which beat box office records when released in 1997.

A musician playing a set of kaen pipes

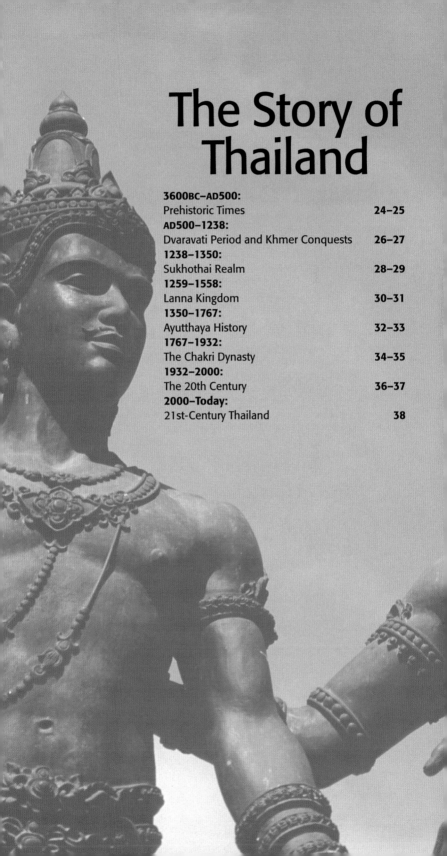

The Story of Thailand

Prehistoric
Times

Scholars still disagree over the true origins of the inhabitants of present-day Thailand, their theories often confounded by new archaeological discoveries. It was long thought that Thai civilization arrived from China, until a Bronze Age settlement was discovered that predated any yet found in China. Yet all agree that migratory patterns and linguistic evidence show that large areas of northern Thailand were settled thousands of years ago by people from Chinese Yunnan. These newcomers, grouped under the generic term "Tai," either absorbed or displaced an aboriginal population who appear to be the ancestors of the hill tribes that inhabit remote areas of northern Thailand. The newcomers introduced agriculture, rearing livestock and cultivating rice that has since formed the basis of Thailand's rural economy and the country's national product. The few records that exist show that these communities formed into ever larger units—called (then as now) Muang—at first for trade but also for mutual defense. Village chiefs rose to become Muang leaders, who formed regional ruling dynasties, assigning sons to take over neighboring Muang. Dynastic realms grew in size and importance, worrying even the emperors of China, who demanded tribute. In the south the Mon and Khmer empires were penetrating deeper into Tai territory, bringing with them Hinduism and Buddhism. The Tai absorbed the religions but resisted domination by the Khmer and Mon, and a struggle for supremacy grew from the sixth century onward.

Bronze Age beginnings

For many years it was thought that the Bronze Age had virtually bypassed Southeast Asia. But then in the late 1960s archaeologists uncovered evidence in a small Thai village that a thriving Bronze Age civilization existed here for up to 4,000 years, until around AD200. The discovery made the village of Ban Chiang world famous and injected money from tourism and scientific research funds into this poor region of northeastern Thailand. The community that settled here some 4,000 years ago on the 8ha (20-acre) site not only mastered the craft of creating implements and ornaments from iron and bronze but also developed a very artistic pottery style, known as the "Ban Chiang Ceramic Tradition." Fine examples of the work are on show at a museum on the excavation site in Ban Chiang.

3600 BC

Early Bronze Age pottery from Ban Chiang on display at the National Museum (right)

Detail of a 2,000–4,000 year-old rock painting depicting an oxen at the Phu Phra Bat Historical Park (above)

Looking across the Mekong River to Laos (right)

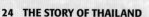

How the world began

A catastrophic flood features in a legend still told in northeastern Thailand to explain the origins of this part of Southeast Asia. The king of the gods, angered by the ingratitude of mortals, inundated the earth with a huge flood. Only three local chiefs survived and lived with the gods until the flood subsided. They returned to earth with a buffalo, which helped them restore the devastated fields before dying. From its nostrils then grew a plant that produced a crop of gourds, which in turn produced two races of people—dark-skinned aboriginals and lighter-skinned Lao. The three chiefs taught the Lao to till the land and raise crops and domestic animals (presumably leaving the aboriginals to their own devices) and the king of the gods sent his son to help them. The son produced seven of his own, whom he appointed to rule over a territory stretching from Yunnan to Myanmar (Burma) and from Laos to northern Thailand.

POW's discovery

One of Thailand's most interesting Neolithic sites was uncovered by chance by Dutch prisoners working on the "Death Railway" near Kanchanaburi in 1943. Japanese troops overseeing work on the railway ignored pleas to protect the site, but after the war Dutch survivors alerted archaeologists to the existence of the riverside site, near the village of Ban Kao, 35km (21 miles) northwest of Kanchanaburi. Among the objects displayed at a small museum (Wed–Sun 9–4.30) adjoining the site is decorative jewelry carved from bone more than 3,000 years ago. Stone axes and clay pots are also among the exhibits.

The evening sky refelected in the Mekong River near Sangkhon (above)

Where dinosaurs roamed

Thailand has some of the world's most spectacular prehistoric fossil sites. Most are in the eastern Isan region, where eight previously unknown species of dinosaurs have been discovered. They include the world's oldest sauropod, *Isanosaurus attavipachi*, which roamed the area 210 million years ago. Remains of the world's oldest tyrannosaur were also discovered in Isan. Two dinosaurs unique to Thailand are the huge plant-eating sauropod *Phuwiangosaurus sirindhornae* and a fish-eating theropod, *Siamosaurus suteethorni*, which lived on the Isan plateau more than 100 million years ago.

More than 800 bones of six different dinosaur species and an almost complete skeleton have been discovered in the Phu Khum Kao National Park, in Kalasin province, where a research center is being set up. There's a small museum at the site, and another in the village of Phu Wiang in Khon Kaen province.

Bones of contention

When archaeologists discovered the remains of prehistoric ancestors of the elephant and crocodile in Thailand's Korat Basin in 2005, they laid bare superstitions nearly as old as the fossils themselves. Their discoveries proved that 10 million years ago this arid region of eastern Thailand was richly forested and teeming with wildlife. The archaeologists ran into trouble when they sought to move their finds to Bangkok—local people regarded the fossils as sacred and imbued with magic powers. One large piece of petrified wood was venerated as a female deity. Among the animal bones were the skulls of two large fish-eating crocodiles, now extinct in Thailand, and of a hyena that has long disappeared from Asia. An incomplete skeleton of a Stegadon, an ancestor of both the mammoth and the elephant, was also recovered from the site—and was thought by locals to have superhuman powers.

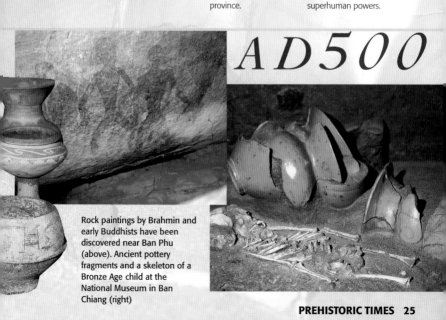

AD500

Rock paintings by Brahmin and early Buddhists have been discovered near Ban Phu (above). Ancient pottery fragments and a skeleton of a Bronze Age child at the National Museum in Ban Chiang (right)

Dvaravati Period and Khmer Conquests

The story of how the Siam region emerged from prehistoric times has been pieced together from the art and architecture of the period. This era is called Dvaravati, from the one decipherable word on a coin discovered from those times. The word Dvaravati is Sanskrit for "doors." Scholars have long mused over the significance of the name, with the most credible explanation being that the "doors" are actually "portals" to a country or territory. Perhaps the name was imprinted on coins used by traders and recognized as legal tender by one region. The portals, according to the theory, must have been the trading centers established along the frontiers of this region. These towns were the one unifying element of the region.

The traders were mostly from India and Sri Lanka, Hindu holy men and Buddhist monks among them. They spread not only their beliefs but also their art and architecture.

The rise of the Dvaravati "empire" coincided with expansionist moves by the Khmer. They established outposts in today's central and eastern Thailand and inevitably came into conflict with local Dvaravati rulers. The end of the Dvaravati era and the retreat of the Khmer followed the formation of regional alliances that were strong enough to challenge both.

Khmer statuary from the Phanom Rung Dvaravati period

Dvaravati palaces

Dvaravati palaces were probably made of wood, so virtually no traces remain of them. A bas-relief found at Muang Fa Daet Sung Yang in Kalasin province gives a good idea, however, of how splendid they must have been. The carved picture shows a scene from a Jataka legend, with prominence given to the palace home of the Buddha's former wife, Yasodhara. The palace compound is entered through an imposing three-tiered gateway, and the princess's home is a handsome mansion with elaborate roof ornamentation. The house was built with each of its four facades facing a cardinal point of the compass, a Dvaravati architectural feature copied by later Siamese rulers.

AD 500

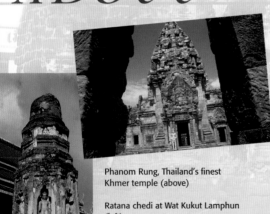

Giant gong at Wat Phrathat Haripunchai, built in 1044 (right)

Phanom Rung, Thailand's finest Khmer temple (above)

Ratana chedi at Wat Kukut Lamphun (left)

Dvaravati art

Dvaravati sculptures found at several sites in central Thailand offer proof that this ancient culture wasn't concerned only with commerce. The important trading center of Nakhon Pathom, for instance, had a highly sophisticated and talented community of craftspeople, judging by the very fine works discovered there. Among them was a remarkable circular stone representing the "Wheel of the Law," the symbol of Buddhist wisdom. The limestone wheel, 95cm (3ft) in diameter, and dating from the seventh or eighth century, incorporates a small statue of a deer as a reminder that the Lord Buddha attained enlightenment in a deer park. The wheel is a central exhibit at the National Museum in Bangkok, where other examples of Dvaravati art include an exquisite Buddha bust, just 20cm (12in) high but as detailed as the greatest Buddha statues.

11th-century lion of the Baphuon style, at Ubon Museum (right)

Queen Chamthewi

The Dvaravati era produced the most glamorous monarch in Thailand's history—Queen Chamthewi of Haripunchai, now the little town of Lamphun. Chamthewi is pictured in history books as a young woman of great beauty and courage, adored by her subjects and feared by her enemies: a female ruler who added grace and glamor to the Haripunchai court but who regularly donned armor and rode into battle on an elephant. Chamthewi was sent to rule Haripunchai by her father, the king of Lopburi. She ruled for nearly 40 years, abdicating at the age of 60 and spending most of her remaining years meditating in a temple she had built on the edge of Haripunchai. When she died, at the age of 92, she was cremated within the temple compound and her ashes were sealed in a *chedi* that still stands—one of Lamphun's most revered monuments. A *chedi* on the other side of town marks the place where her favorite battle elephant was buried.

The unlucky suitor

In the absence of a written Dvaravati history, myths inevitably surround Queen Chamthewi, many of them focusing on her apparent celibacy. Was she a forebear of England's Virgin Queen? Like Elizabeth I, she appears to have had her share of suitors, but none conquered her heart. According to a fable, one smitten chieftain was told that if he could throw a spear from his hilltop home south of Chiang Mai to her palace in Haripunchai she would marry him. His first two attempts fell short and the third throw went totally amiss, the spear rising vertically and then falling into the unfortunate man's heart.

Khmer ruins still cause conflict

The ancient Khmer ruins of Cambodia are still the subject of dispute with neighboring Thailand. The latter nearly broke off diplomatic relations with Phnom Penh in 2003, when its embassy there was attacked: Cambodian protesters feared that Bangkok was resurrecting claims on the ancient city of Angkor. Siamese forces in previous centuries had overrun Angkor three times, and many Cambodians believe present-day Thailand still harbors a territorial claim. Their fears erupted into anti-Thai rioting at the start of 2003 when a Thai actress seemed to remark that Angkor belonged to Thailand. The Thai embassy and other Thai property were badly damaged in the rioting, and Thailand hurriedly evacuated its citizens from Phnom Penh. One ancient Khmer compound on Cambodia's thickly forested northern border, Prasat Khao Phra Vihanalong, is accessible only from Thailand, which has worked out a fragile arrangement with Cambodia to allow for visitors.

1238

Ruins of the Khao Phra Viharn monastery, a Khmer sanctuary dedicated to Siva (below)

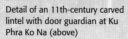

Detail of an 11th-century carved lintel with door guardian at Ku Phra Ko Na (above)

Sukhothai Realm

Although the Sukhothai dynasty lasted less than 150 years, it is regarded as the cradle of today's Thailand. Until the early 13th century, most of Thailand was ruled by weak vassal states and communities controlled by the Khmer from their stronghold in Angkor. It was a vast area to govern from so far away, and disintegration was inevitable. In 1238, two local princes, Phi Khun Pha Muang and Pho Khun Bang Klang Thao, joined forces and marched on Sukhothai, routing the Khmer. Pho Khun Bang Klang Thao, the victor, was proclaimed king and took the royal title Pho Khun Si Indradit, starting a dynasty that was to last until the mid-14th century. He was succeeded by his eldest son, Pho Khun Ban Muang, who died young, vacating the throne for his brother, Pho Khun Ramkhamhaeng. Under Ramkhamhaeng's rule, Sukhothai flourished as no other Southeast Asian realm, and his reign is known as the "golden period" of Thai history. Ramkhamhaeng abolished slavery and most taxes, and he built up a thriving economy. He also extended his realm into today's Myanmar (Burma) and Laos, and into the Malay peninsula. He forged good relations with China. Sukhothai's decline began with Ramkhamhaeng's death and the subsequent rise of the Ayutthaya court. It was annexed by Ayutthaya in 1350 and became a northern outpost of Siam's new center of power.

1238

Birth of the Thai alphabet

Sukhothai gave birth not only to the first Siamese empire but also to the Thai alphabet in use today. The introduction of a truly Siamese alphabet was part of King Ramkhamhaeng's plan to create an autonomous state free from the traces of the Khmer and Mon rulers he had defeated. In the dying years of his rule he developed a script incorporating the original Khmer and the ancient Brahmi script, brought by Buddhist monks and scholars from southern India and Sri Lanka. The new alphabet became known as the "Sukhothai Script," and a famous late 13th-century inscription by King Ramkhamhaeng (now in the National Museum, Bangkok) is the earliest example of its use. The Sukhothai Script was modified over the years, and King Ramkhamhaeng's grandson Li Thai gave his name to one of the embellishments.

Wat Phra Si Ratana Mahathat, Si Satchanalai (top)

Ceramic detail (above)

Sawankhalok kilns museum (left)

Ramkhamhaeng statue in Sukhothai (right)

A green and fruitful city

A stone inscription by King Ramkhamhaeng, now in Thailand's National Museum in Bangkok, gives a vivid picture of the Sukhothai he ruled, indicating that the city really was a haven of peace and plenty. It was a very green city, full of fruit and nut trees—"betel nut and betel-vine woods are all over this city," says the inscription. Groves and orchards of coconut, mango, areca nut and tamarind are listed in a kind of inventory. The trees belonged to whomever planted them. The city was surrounded by orchards, plantations and rice paddies, punctuated by farmhouses ("large and small"), a palace, "residences" and temples. The landscape was so beautiful, says the inscription, that it appeared to be "faked." Fish was abundant, and the water in the city's reservoir was as clean "as the Mekong river in the dry season."

The diplomat king

King Ramkhamhaeng was not only a great monarch but also a skilled diplomat, who recognized the necessity of sealing good relations with his mighty neighbor to the north, China. He undertook two journeys to China, meeting the Mongol emperor Kublai Khan in 1282. On his second visit, in 1300, he persuaded Kublai Khan's successor to allow him to return to Sukhothai with Chinese artisans, who taught the Siamese to make pottery. In no time at all, the kilns of Sukhothai, Si Satchanalai and Sawankhalok were turning out ceramics fine enough to be exported to China and beyond. Examples of Sukhothai ceramics have been found as far away as Japan and the Philippines. The courts of Sukhothai were so proud of the skills their craftspeople had learned from China that they weren't too shy to send examples back to Chinese emperors as tribute.

Ring-the-bell justice

Outside one of the four gates in the city walls of Sukhothai, King Ramkhamhaeng hung a bell, which any citizen with a grievance was encouraged to ring and seek royal redress. Historians have long pondered and argued over this apparent example of the democracy reigning in Sukhothai. But the contemporary inscription now in the National Museum, Bangkok, states quite incontrovertibly: "King Ramkhamhaeng, the ruler of the kingdom, hears the call; he goes and questions the man, examines the case and decides it justly for him. So the people of Sukhothai…praise him."

Kublai Khan, c1215–94 (above)

Souvenirs in a craft shop (left)

Sukhothai art and architecture

Sukhothai produced a style of art and architecture that left its stamp on succeeding centuries and still wields a tangible influence on Thai design. Its greatest contribution was in sculpture, producing Buddha statues of unmatched grace and beauty, with serene, reflective and often gently smiling faces and aristocratic features. Sukhothai craftspeople developed the art of casting in bronze, and they took the then daring step of removing the ancient image of the walking Buddha from its conventional two-dimensional form, in bas-relief, and giving it three-dimensional realism. The "walking Buddha" created in Sukhothai strides confidently, one arm swinging and one raised in the "teaching" pose.

Several Sukhothai architectural features—notably the concave flow of roofs and gables and the cloistered galleries and pillars—persist today. And much of the jewelry you'll find in boutiques and markets has an art nouveau look that dates back to 14th-century Sukhothai.

1350

Wat Chao Chan, Si Satchanalai (right)

The temple of Wat Mahathat in Sukhothai (below)

Lanna
Kingdom

In the mid-13th century, migrating tribes from present-day Laos crossed the Mekong River and established a citadel where the northern Thai river port town of Chiang Saen now stands. Their leader, Mengrai, was proclaimed ruler of a new realm, Annachak Lanna Thai, in 1259. As Mengrai's influence grew, his expanding empire came to be known as Lanna—the land of a "million rice fields." He founded his first true capital south of Chiang Saen, at Chiang Rai, an easily fortified site sitting on a bend of the Kok River. Over the next 30 years he and his followers pushed steadily farther south and built an even larger capital at Chiang Mai, meaning "new city," after overrunning the nearby northern Dvaravati stronghold, Lamphun. Over the following two centuries, Chiang Mai grew into a major religious and cultural center, developing its own distinctive style of art and architecture, which still influences the distinctive appearance of this northern Thai capital. In the mid-16th century, Burmese forces advancing from the south and west lay siege to Chiang Mai and finally broke its defenses, sacking the city and carrying most of the population off as slaves. For almost 200 years, Chiang Mai was a ghost city, until the Burmese were driven out of Thailand in 1774. By then Ayutthaya had laid claim to suzerainty over the north, and a rebuilt Chiang Mai became a provincial outpost, ruled by a prince answerable to the kings of the far-off capital.

The three kings

A remarkable alliance of three provincial rulers is said to have brought about the founding of Chiang Mai in 1296. History records state that when King Mengrai began work on his new capital, two neighboring rulers came to his assistance. Instead of resisting the Lanna advance into their sphere of influence, the ruler of Phayao, Phya Ngum Muang, and the king of Sukhothai, Phra Ruang, offered their support and protection. They are said to have sealed their alliance by opening their veins and mingling their blood in a fraternal bond. Today their statues stand side by side in the "Three Kings Monument" outside the former home of Chiang Mai's last provincial ruler, now the city museum.

1259

Young woman wearing traditional Lanna dress (right)

Wat Lampang Luang, Ko Kha, Lampang (below)

The Viharn Lai Kam, Wat Phra Singh, Chiang Mai (above). Mural of the 19th-century Burmese army (right)

A royal "affair"

The alliance between the three monarchs is said to have nearly foundered on an affair between Sukhothai's celebrated King Ramkhamhaeng and the wife of Phayao's King Ngam Muang. King Mengrai was called on to sit in judgment on Ngam Muang's complaint that the younger Ramkhamhaeng had seduced his wife. The Lanna king had to employ all his legendary diplomacy to reconcile the cuckolded ruler and Ramkhamhaeng, who stood in danger of execution for his adultery. It's said that Mengrai ruled in favor of sparing Ramkhamhaeng's life in the interests of maintaining the alliance between Sukhothai, Lanna and Phayao. The fortunate Ramkhamhaeng got away with an apology and the payment of large damages to Ngam Muang.

Mengrai's "Trojan Horse"

Lanna King Mengrai was a wily ruler, who is said to have conquered the Dvaravati city Nakhon Haripunchai (now Lamphun) by a cunning trick. The Dvaravati realm's northern outpost was too heavily garrisoned and defended for Mengrai to take by sheer force of arms. So he sent one of his cleverest scholars, Ai Fa, to seek employment in the court of the Nakhon Haripunchai ruler, King Yi Ba. Over the following 10 years, Ai Fa consolidated his position in Yi Ba's court, securing the king's favor while at the same time stoking up public opposition to his rule. The ruse worked. At Ai Fa's signal, Mengrai and his army marched on Nakhon Haripunchai and were able to take a demoralized and divided city.

Depiction of Lanna people (below)

Lanna "style"

Although nearly 1,000 years old, the Lanna style of architecture and design is enjoying a renaissance in contemporary Thai hotel and home construction, particularly in Chiang Mai but also in Bangkok. Boutique hotels are shooting up in both cities that employ the traditional Lanna look, which emphasizes simplicity. Dark teak woods and stark white exteriors are combined in a straightforward two-color synthesis where line and form are more important than decoration. Cool whitewashed cloisters enclose hidden gardens and courtyards, where fountains play amid lily ponds and winding walkways. Multi-eaved roofs of red clay tiles reach low to keep out the hot sun, and high, ceilingless living areas keep interiors cool. The only concession to purely decorative color is to be found in the richness of the silk soft furnishings, whose finely interwoven patterns echo the graceful sarongs worn on special occasions by Thai women.

Chiang Mai's calamity corner

The first Lanna monarch, King Mengrai, was killed by a lightning bolt in the exact center of Chiang Mai in 1311. A shrine marks the spot, and terracotta friezes depict his death and achievements. Mengrai's death was the first of three calamities in this corner of the city, earning the area an ominous reputation. An earthquake in the 18th century felled the top of the city's highest *chedi*, in the grounds of Wat Chedi Luang, and in early 2005 a violent storm broke a particularly sacred tree in half. The 46m (150ft) yang tree was planted by a successor of Mengrai, Chao Kawila, and local lore said that if it ever died Chiang Mai would also fall. Religious ceremonies were held in the Wat Chedi Luang grounds to pray for deliverance from any further calamity after the top half of the tree fell.

1558

Detail of Lanna clothing (above right)

Temple wall painting of the Lanna period Thai–Burmese conflict (right)

Old city wall in Chiang Mai, surrounded by the old moat (far left)

Mother and daughter leaving a temple (left)

Ayutthaya History

The rise of Ayutthaya coincided with the decline not only of Sukhothai but of the Angkor-based Khmer empire, the Lanna kingdom in the north and the Lao nation on the Mekong. There had long been a settlement on this fruitful tract of territory at the confluence of three rivers: the Chao Phraya, the Pasak and the Lopburi. Regular flooding enabled the cultivation of wet rice and provided moats for its defense. As the 14th century progressed, another great advantage of Ayutthaya's location emerged; trade between China and India was growing at a staggering rate, and Ayutthaya found itself at the crossroads of the trade routes. Later, explorers and traders from the West arrived, looking for routes that would save them the journey around the Malay peninsula.

Another major factor boosting the growth of Ayutthaya was the arrival of Buddhist monks from India and Sri Lanka. Theravada Buddhism made its base in Ayutthaya and spread from there.

The date of Ayutthaya's founding is officially given as 1350, when a Chinese merchant's son, U Thong, was proclaimed its first king, Ramathibodi I. During his 18-year reign he laid the administrative and legal foundations not only of Ayutthaya but of the future kingdom of Siam. In 1431 Ayutthaya conquered Angkor, and in 1438 it annexed the Sukhothai state. But Myanmar (Burma) remained an intractable foe, and after many wars Ayutthaya was overrun by the Burmese in 1767. The city was destroyed, its inhabitants either killed or carried off into slavery.

Elephant duels

In Ayutthaya's days, kingdoms were won and lost and battles for succession decided in deadly elephant-back duels. King Naresuan the Great earned his grand title—one of only five Siamese rulers to win the addition of "Great" to their names—after (among other courageous feats) killing the crown prince of Burma in a duel fought on the backs of their battle elephants. Naresuan's army engaged a massive Burmese invasion force west of Ayutthaya in 1592. According to contemporary records, he spotted the Burmese crown prince in the middle of the fray and challenged him: "Let us fight an elephant duel for the honor of our kingdoms." Naresuan cut the Burmese leader down with his sword, and the entire Burmese army fled. Burma left Ayutthaya alone for the next 25 years.

1350

Statue of King Narai (1656–88), who was responsible for restoring the city of Lop Buri (left). Memorial to King Taksin the Great (right)

A section of the inner walls of the Narai Ratchaniwet Palace, built by King Narai between 1665–77 in Lop Buri (left). Smaller Buddhas surround the restored Wat Yai Chai Mongkhon in Ayutthaya (above right). Statues representing the Battle of Yuthahathi, in the museum of Muang Boran (right)

Bloody intrigues

The courts of Ayutthaya were hotbeds of intrigue, often fueled by foreign interests plotting to win influence and trading advantages. Thrones were won and lost in schemes hatched behind palace walls and even in the confines of the royal concubines' quarters.

One king, Ekathotsarot, ordered the execution of his young son, Prince Suthat, in 1610 on the flimsiest of evidence. Suthat was accused of plotting a palace coup, denounced by a court official in the pay of a powerful group of Japanese merchants. Ekathotsarot outlived his executed son by only a few months.

A century previously, an Ayutthaya queen-regent, Lady Si Sudachan, had her 11-year-old son poisoned and put her lover, a court official, on the throne in his place. The usurper was assassinated after only six weeks of rule.

Bureaucratic beginnings

Thailand's modern bureaucracy derives directly from the administrative structures created by the early Ayutthaya kings. As the Ayutthaya empire grew and took on ever more important responsibilities, successive rulers built up a compartmentalized structure to deal with policy areas. Departments corresponding to today's government ministries were set up to handle such administrative areas as foreign affairs, trade and taxation. Officials, most of them close to the throne, were given "honor marks" according to their duties, and in time a hierarchical system of government took shape. The officials occupied a middle rank, known as Khunnang (or "nobles"), in a three-tiered system headed by the king and his family. Below the officials was a bottom class of commoners and slaves. The large and powerful community of monks, the sangha, remained outside the class system but held great influence over state affairs.

Women warriors

Women warriors played a key role in protecting the 18th- to 19th-century Ayutthaya realm from outside invasion. When King Anuwong of Vientiane led a large army against northeastern Siam in 1771, the town of Nakhon Ratchasima (Korat) called on the wife of the deputy governor to organize the local defense forces. Madam Mo not only succeeded in breaking a siege of Korat by King Anuwong, but pursued the invader and his army back to the banks of the Mekong River. Taksin the Great rewarded her with the royal title Lady Suranari.

Farther south, on the island now known as Phuket, two famous sisters rallied the islanders in a successful defense against an invading Burmese naval force in 1785. The two, Lady Thepsatri and Lady Srisunthorn, were daughters of the governor of Phuket, then known as Thalang. They are commemorated today by an impressive monument at a highway crossroads in the center of Phuket island.

Ayutthaya's Greek intruder

For a critical period of its 17th-century history, Ayutthaya was effectively ruled by a Greek opportunist and adventurer, Constantine Phaulkon. Son of a hotelier, he came to Asia in 1678 as an official of the East India Company. In Ayutthaya he insinuated himself into the court of King Narai. Phaulkon's influence grew to the point where he was the equivalent of King Narai's prime minister, running the affairs of state. Phaulkon introduced Jesuit missionary priests into the court and was apparently close to converting Narai when the monarch died, in 1688. While Narai lay on his deathbed, a struggle for succession broke out, and the dying monarch's regent arrested Phaulkon and had him beheaded.

Ruins of Constantine Phaulkon's house (above)

1767

European impressions of Siamese officials in the court of King Narai (below)

Objects from the Ayutthaya period (above)

The Chakri Dynasty

With Ayutthaya in ruins and its population either in flight or in Burmese captivity, Siamese unity seemed finally at an end. But a remarkable military leader, Phraya Taksin, took control and within 15 years had founded a new capital, Thonburi, and rid Siam of the Burmese. Despite his remarkable feat, the general took on increasingly fanatical traits, and in 1782 he was deposed and executed. He was succeeded by a fellow general, Chao Phraya Chakri. At his coronation he took the title Rama I, and one of his first acts was to move the capital to a small village called Bangkok, across the river and safe from further Burmese incursions. Rama I laid the administrative and legal foundations of today's Thailand. At his death in 1809 he was succeeded by his son, a highly cultured man who patronized the arts and literature. He and his successor, Rama III, built up Siam's international trade, and established their country's first links with Western colonial powers. The two monarchs who came after him—Mongkut (Rama IV) and Chulalongkorn (Rama V)—performed the delicate balancing act that kept their country free of colonial occupation while ushering their people into the modern world. Road and rail communications were laid, schools and universities founded, civil rights legislation promulgated and, in 1892, Siam's first ministerial government was appointed.

Bronze statue of Muk and Chan, two female warriors who helped repel Burmese invaders on Phuket in 1785

Under Ayutthaya law, a king or queen found guilty of serious wrongdoing or who was just unwanted on the throne was executed in a very bizarre manner. He or she was placed in a velvet sack and beaten to death. This fate, according to contemporary accounts, awaited Taksin, the ruler whose death opened the palace doors to the Chakri dynasty. But rumors persist to this day that an innocent commoner was put in the sack instead of Taksin, who was allegedly smuggled into hiding in the mountains near Myanmar (Burma). He is supposed to have died there in 1825, in his late sixties. Many years later his remains—or those of his unfortunate "stand-in"—were given a royal burial, and the once-reviled ruler was given the title Taksin the Great.

1767

Impressions of early Bangkok: Wat Pho (top left), port and docks (bottom left). French warships anchored at Bangkok after the Pan Nam incident, July 1893 (above). Bangkok's Chao Phraya River (right)

King Rama I, the poet and translator

King Rama I not only oversaw the first blossoming of a vibrant Siamese literature but actively contributed to it as an author and translator. He and a select circle of scribes and academics translated and reworked the Indian epic *Ramayana* and published it in 1797 as the *Ramakien*. The lengthy, colorful story, originally more than 3,000 pages long, is the subject of countless temple frescoes and still features in artistic representations. Works from China, Sri Lanka and Persia were also translated at the behest of King Rama I, and a distinct Siamese literary style arose, in which formal verse gave way to prose.

Palace intrigues

Although the reign of the first Chakri monarch was just and civilized, it was still not entirely free of the palace intrigues and bloody retributions that marked the Ayutthaya period. Tensions frequently surfaced between the king and his younger brother, reaching a head in 1796, when the king ordered his guard to surround his brother's palace after rumors of a coup plot. Only the intervention of the royal princesses prevented a bloody confrontation. The king's brother died in 1803, but the palace intrigues continued, and two of the ruler's nephews were shortly afterward accused with a group of courtiers of plotting against the monarch and were summarily beheaded. Rama I subsequently held fast to the throne, and ruled until his death in 1809.

Mongkut—monk and monarch

King Mongkut is one of the most interesting figures in Thai history. Before taking the throne in 1851, he spent 27 years as a monk, spending most of the time in meditation. He learned English, French, Latin, Sanskrit and the language of Buddhist monks, Pali. He also gained knowledge of the natural sciences and astronomy and successfully predicted a solar eclipse. After his coronation, the 47-year-old monarch abandoned monastic precepts and took 39 wives, fathering 82 children. The youngest of these, Chulalongkorn, succeeded him, although he nearly died from malaria during a trip with his father to southern Siam. Mongkut also fell ill and died from the disease in 1868.

King Mongkut (Rama IV; right)

Anna and the king

King Mongkut hired a governess to educate his children and some of his wives and concubines, but by all accounts Anna Leonowens was nothing like the character portrayed in the movie *The King and I*. Nor did Mongkut at all resemble the autocratic, bare-chested monarch played by Yul Brynner. Welsh-born Anna grew up a lonely child in India, where her soldier father had been stationed. In 1851, the year Mongkut took the throne, Anna married a British officer, Major Thomas Leonowens. He died young, and Anna took up teaching to support herself and her two small children. In 1862 she was hired by the royal court in Bangkok. Anna herself wrote two books on her experiences there, but skepticism has arisen over the truth of her reminiscences. Three movies have been made—the third and latest movie, *Anna and the King*, was released in 1999. Like Anna's books, it has been banned in Thailand.

King Chulalongkorn (Rama V) in European dress (below) and in uniform (left). Anna Leonowens (below right)

1932

The 20th Century

The death of King Chulalongkorn (Rama V) in 1910 ushered in a century of profound social and political change. Chulalongkorn was succeeded by one of his many sons, Vajiravudh, a fun-loving monarch who introduced many Western-influenced reforms and customs. Vajiravudh steered Siam through World War I without conceding any of the country's sovereignty, and he left a successful, viable state to his brother, Prajadhipok. The 10-year reign of Rama VII was much less happy, and in 1932 Siam's last absolute ruler was forced by a group of reformers to agree to the introduction of a constitutional monarchy. The leaders of the coup, Phibun Songkhram and Pridi Phanamyang, dominated the political scene for nearly 20 of the following 25 years. Prajadhipok abdicated in 1935, and a council of regents chose Ananda, then a schoolboy in Switzerland, to succeed him. Phibun became prime minister in 1938 and took a pro-Japanese line during World War II. His former fellow student, Pridi, organized an anti-Japanese resistance and took power from the disgraced Phibun at the war's end in 1945. Ananda returned from Switzerland in 1946 to assume the Siamese throne, but died in mysterious circumstances. His younger brother, Bhumibol Adulyadej, succeeded him, as Rama IX, and is now the world's longest-reigning monarch. Phibun returned from the shadows and overthrew Pridi in 1947, establishing a military dictatorship. He in turn was ousted in 1957. Student demonstrations in 1992 led to a intervention by the king and a period of political calm that persists today.

The railway age

When King Chulalongkorn visited London in 1898 Queen Victoria presented him with a clockwork train set, instilling in the monarch an enthusiasm that laid the foundations of one of Asia's most efficient railway networks. Chulalongkorn returned home determined to give his country the best railway system money could buy. He engaged British and German engineers, who laid track in record time through impenetrable jungle and through mountain ranges. Locomotives and rolling stock were imported from Europe, and by 1920 Bangkok was linked with Malaya and with cities that had previously been remote outposts of the realm, accessible only by unpaved roads or rivers. Chulalongkorn and his successors ordained that railway stations should become architectural features of the landscape, and today even the smallest railway stop in Thailand is a picture-postcard attraction.

1932

Akha people mingle at the Doi Mae Salong morning market, Chiang Rai Province (left)

Portrait of King Bhumibol Adulyadej, displayed during his birthday celebration (right)

Statue of King Ananda Mahidol (Rama VIII), who ruled from 1935 to 1946 (above)

A tragic monarch

King Rama VIII, Ananda Mahidol, was Thailand's most tragic monarch. He was a schoolboy in Switzerland when he succeeded Rama VII, King Prajadhipok, who abdicated in 1935 after confrontations with the military. A council of regents guarded the throne until Ananda's return to Thailand in December, 1945. Six months later, Ananda was dead—found with a fatal bullet wound in the head in his palace quarters in Bangkok. The government at first said he had died accidentally, but a commission of inquiry, which included British and American doctors, concluded he had probably been murdered. But by whom? Suspicion fell on three of the palace staff, and they were put on trial, convicted and executed. Prime Minister Pridi also came under pressure and went abroad, precipitating a government crisis. Ananda was succeeded by his younger brother, Bhumibol Adulyadej, the present King Rama IX.

Chiang Kai-shek soldiers rewarded

The Thai government suppressed a Communist insurgency in the 1970s with the help of Chinese nationalist soldiers who had fled the advancing Red Army of Mao Tse Tung. The refugees, remnants of General Chiang Kai-shek's Kuomintang, were rewarded with Thai nationality and permanent residence in northern Thailand, where they established several communities. The most famous of these is Santikhiri ("Mountain of Peace") in the Mae Salong mountain range near the Burmese border. Visit Santikhiri and you'd be excused for thinking yourself in China—the small town of 20,000, most of them descendants of the original soldiers, has Chinese temples, schools, shops and noodle stands. There's even a home for disabled veteran soldiers, and a museum where the story of Santikhiri is recounted with a display of interesting contemporary pictures and documents.

The *Manhattan* Coup

The most unusual of the several coup attempts that marked Thailand's recent history involved the seizure of an American ship, the *Manhattan*, in the waters off Bangkok in June 1951. Navy rebels took over the ship as Prime Minister Phibun Songkhram, a veteran army officer, was officially accepting it as a gift from the United States. Phibun was taken prisoner and held on the Thai navy flagship *Sri Ayudhya* while negotiations proceeded between the two sides. The talks broke down and the Thai air force bombarded the ship. Phibun jumped overboard and swam to safety—soaked, shaken but still in control of the government. More than 1,000 died in the coup attempt, which was followed by a wave of arrests and drastic cuts in the strength of the navy.

Portrait of King Bhumibol Adulyadej (right). Bronze statue of King Rama VI in Bangkok (below left). View of Doi Mae Salong (below)

When Siam became Thailand

Three name changes occurred before Siam finally became Thailand. The nationalist military leader Phibun Songkhram discarded the historic name Siam in favor of Thailand in 1939, in a controversial move interpreted as an attempt to free the country from its associations with ancient monarchies. Phibun's post-war successor, Pridi Phanamyang, changed the country's name back again to Siam in 1945 in a package of measures intended to repudiate all policy decisions by the now-discredited Phibun. Two years later, Phibun overthrew Pridi—and one of his first acts was to change the country's name back to Thailand.

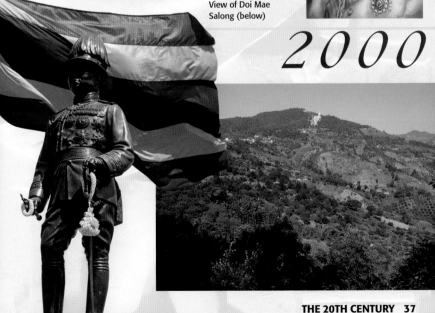

2000

21st-Century Thailand

Thailand recovered rapidly from the 1997/1998 Asian economic meltdown: by 2004 the growth rate was back in double figures. A newly formed political party, Thai Rak Thai (Thai Love Thai), headed by telecommunications billionaire Thaksin Shinawatra, contested elections in 2001 and

won 248 seats in the 438-member parliament. Thaksin introduced successful economic reforms that became known as "thaksinomics," and in the 2005 election he won more than 60 percent of the vote, increasing his party's majority by 127 seats. But skyrocketing world oil prices dented the Thai economy, while

The Thai stock exchange

a wave of separatist violence in Thailand's southern provinces and a slow recovery from the 2004 tsunami added further to Thaksin's problems. By mid-2005, polls showed Thaksin's popularity sinking dramatically. In 2006 he announced his intention to stand down.

Thailand's restive south

Ethnic violence broke out in Thailand's southern provinces in January 2004, and the government has been struggling ever since to bring it to an end. Thaksin at first used strong-arm methods to quell the violence, but after clashes that resulted in the deaths of nearly 200 militant protesters, he tried a more conciliatory approach, including launching millions of paper "doves of peace" over the troubled provinces. But the violence continued, and in July 2005 Thaksin's government assumed emergency executive powers over the provinces.

Thaksin Shinawatra

2000–Today

Beaches in Ko Phi Phi damaged by the tsunami (left)

The Bangkok Bank building on Silom Road (right)

A farm worker harvesting tobacco leaves (above)

On the Move

ARRIVING

Arriving by Air

There are currently seven international airports in Thailand: Bangkok, Phuket, Chiang Mai, Chiang Rai, Ko Samui, Hat Yai and Sukhothai. You are most likely to arrive in Bangkok, even if your final destination is Phuket, Ko Samui or one of the other regional airports, though there are direct flights to Phuket from Europe. Asian airlines, especially from Malaysia, Singapore and Laos, have direct flights to the other international airports, and Krabi is also about to become an international airport in this category. Don Muang was Bangkok's international airport. However, Suvarnabhumi Airport, due to open in 2006, will become the capital's new international airport. Don Muang will continue to be used, although in exactly what capacity remains unclear.

Don Muang Airport (BKK) is 25km (15 miles) north of the capital and has ATMs, 24-hour booths, currency exchange, car rental and hotel desks, official taxi counters, an official tourist information counter (daily 8am–midnight), left-luggage office, post office, internet access points and a number of places to eat and drink, some of which are open 24 hours. There are two international terminals and a third one for domestic routes. A covered walkway connects all three terminals, and the domestic terminal is 0.5km (0.3 miles) away from the two international ones; there are also free bus shuttles every 15 minutes (daily 5am–11pm). For general information about the airport tel 025 351 111.

Phuket Airport (HKT) is on the northwest coast of Phuket island, 32km (20 miles) from Phuket town. There is a tourist office, car rental and hotel accommodation counters, post office, banks, ATMs and exchange booths, left-luggage office, internet access, and places to eat and drink. For general information about the airport tel 076 327 230.

Suvarnabhumi Airport is 30km (19 miles) east of Bangkok. It will have all the amenities and services of Don Muang Airport. There will be one very large terminal, with separate sections for international and domestic routes. For general information about the airport tel 027 230 000 or 023 460 535, or visit www.suvarnabhumiairport.com or www.bangkokairport.info

View of Mae Hong Son airport from Wat Doi Kong Mu

Chiang Mai Airport (CNX) is 3km (1.8 miles) southwest of town. There are booths for currency exchange, two ATMs, car rental and hotel accommodation counters, left-luggage facilities, a restaurant and post office. For general information about the airport tel 053 270 222 (www.airportthai.co.th/airportnew/chmai).

Ko Samui Airport (USM) is in the northeast of the island, 5km (3 miles) from Chaweng, and has booths for currency exchange, ATMs, car rental and hotel accommodation counters, restaurant and bar, and post office. For general information about the airport tel 077 441 230.

GETTING TO THE CITY FROM BANGKOK'S DON MUANG AIRPORT

By taxi: Use only the official taxi counters outside the Arrivals area. Taxis are metered, cost around B300 to B350 into the middle of Bangkok (including the B50 airport pick-up fee and the B70 toll for the expressway) and take from 35 minutes to an hour depending on traffic. Avoid taxi touts, even if they're well dressed and carrying official-looking, photo-ID insignia. Their taxis are unmetered and unlicensed, and robberies are not unknown to have befallen their passengers. A private limousine can be booked online at www.imagelimo.com, and the driver will be waiting for you when you exit customs.

By airport bus: Air-conditioned and comfortable airport buses run one-way from the airport into the city, between 5am and midnight, stopping along the way at designated spots close to many of the big hotels, and taking from 45 minutes to an hour or more depending on traffic. The tickets (B100) are purchased at a counter outside Arrivals. The buses draw up alongside and depart about every half-hour following three different routes: A1 buses go to Thanon Silom; A2 to Thanon Phra Athit for Siam Square and Banglamphu; and A3 to Thanon Sukhumvit. The tourist information office or the staff at the pavement counter will advise you as to which bus goes closest to your hotel and where to get off.

By train: There are trains to Hua Lamphong station in Bangkok, which has its own subway station. The journey takes just under an hour and the 10-minute walking route to Don Muang station is signposted from Terminal 1. Trains from Hualamphong to the north and northeast of Thailand nearly all stop at Don Muang station, so if traveling in that direction you can avoid Bangkok and simply catch a train at the airport.

GETTING TO THE CITY FROM BANGKOK'S SUVARNABHUMI AIRPORT

By taxi: Official taxi counters will handle journeys into Bangkok, and the fare will be around B350 to B400; journeys will take about 30 minutes.

By airport bus: It is very likely that there will be several different routes into Bangkok along the same lines as those operating from Don Muang Airport and taking about the same amount of time.

GETTING TO THE BEACH AREAS OR PHUKET TOWN FROM PHUKET AIRPORT

By taxi: Fares to beaches on the west coast are B400 to B600; to Phuket town about B350.

By airport bus: Mini-vans and buses, booked at counters in the airport, travel to all the hotels: B100 to Phuket town; B170 to Ao Patong; and B200 to Ao Kata or Ao Karon. The journey takes between 25 and 35 minutes.

GETTING TO TOWN FROM CHIANG MAI AIRPORT

By taxi: A reservations system operates at the airport; the fare to the middle of town is around B100. There is a taxi counter at the airport where rates are displayed.

GETTING TO BEACH AREAS FROM KO SAMUI AIRPORT

By taxi: The fare to the beaches is around B250 to B350; taxis are not metered so agree on the fare beforehand.

By airport bus: Mini-vans meet incoming flights for transport to the beach areas. Fares are fixed, depending on the number of passengers; expect to pay around B200 to Chaweng and B250 to Lamai.

MAJOR AIRLINES	
AIRLINE	**WEBSITE**
Air Asia	www.airasia.com
Air France	www.airfrance.com
Bangkok Airways	www.bangkokair.com
British Airways	www.ba.com
Cathay Pacific	www.cathaypacific.com
Emirates	www.emirates.com
Lao Airlines	www.laoairlines.com
Lufthansa	www.lufthansa.com
Malaysia Airlines	www.malaysia-airlines.com
Qantas	www.qantas.com
Royal Jordanian	www.rja.com.jo
Singapore Airlines	www.singaporeair.com
Thai Airways	www.thaiair.com
Tiger Airways	www.tigerairways.com
United Airlines	www.united.com
Valuair	www.valuair.com

ON THE MOVE

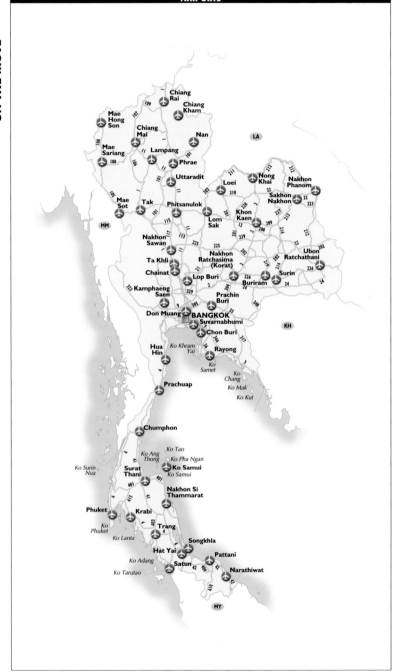

Arriving by Train

The train service connecting Thailand with Malaysia and Singapore is well established. As you are unlikely to have had to obtain a visa in advance for any of the three countries, it is easy and relatively inexpensive to enter or leave Thailand by train. See pages 46–48 for information on Bangkok's Hua Lamphong station, for trains from Malaysia. Afternoon departures from Penang (Butterworth) in Malaysia arrive in Bangkok around mid-morning the next day (B1,200 in a second-class sleeper with air-conditioning).

The State Railway of Thailand (SRT; www.railway.co.th), KTMB (Keretapi Tanah Melayu Berhad; www.ktmb.com.my) of Malaysia and Singapore Railways coordinate the train route between Singapore and Bangkok, via Kuala Lumpur and Penang (Butterworth) in Malaysia. Through travel to Thailand can be reserved in Singapore or Malaysia. However, in Thailand it is only possible to reserve train travel through to either Penang (Butterworth) or Kuala Lumpur, from where a train ticket on to Singapore can be reserved. When crossing the border between Thailand and Malaysia, you will need to get off the train with your luggage and clear immigration and customs before reboarding the train. Coming from Singapore or Kuala Lumpur, you change at Penang (Butterworth) for onward travel to Bangkok, and vice versa.

The international trains to and from Bangkok travel down the east coast of southern Thailand, stopping at Hua Hin, Chumphon and Hat Yai; you can reserve your journey to arrive at or depart from any of these stations.

It is also possible to travel by train between the east coast of peninsular Malaysia and Thailand, although the trains do not actually cross the border. Coming from Malaysia, trains stop at Kota Bahru, from where buses and taxis run to Rantau Panjang, only 1.6km (1 mile) from the international border. Taxis wait to take passengers to the border crossing, as they also do on the other side of the border to take you to Sungai Kolok station on the Thailand side. From here, trains travel to Hat Yai, where you connect with the main train line north to Bangkok. Train schedules work around this arrangement so it is possible to cross the border and pick up a train on the other side without the need for an overnight stay at the Thailand–Malaysia border.

The level of service on trains is high, and on long-distance journeys there is always a dining carriage, with the option of table service. The most stylish and expensive way to travel by train in Thailand is on the Eastern & Oriental Express (www.orient-express.com). There are trips (three days/two nights) from Singapore to Bangkok, costing £990 with all meals and tours included, and round trips (three days/two nights) from Bangkok via Chiang Mai and Ayutthaya for £780.

TIPS

- Trains from Malaysia to Thailand can be reserved online.
- Reserve train travel as far in advance as possible: seats with sleepers are the first to go.
- Peak periods for train travel between Thailand, Malaysia and Singapore are mid-April for the Thai New Year, and late February to early March for the Chinese New Year.
- When planning international train travel to or from Thailand, remember there is a one-hour time difference between Thailand and Malaysia.
- For general information on train travel to and from Thailand from Singapore and Malaysia, visit www.seat61.com

Arriving by train in Bangkok

Arriving by Bus

Buses are comfortable and usually safe; those from Malaysia and Singapore have a better safety record than long-distance, overnight buses within Thailand. Hat Yai in southern Thailand is the transport hub for buses between Malaysia and Thailand. There are buses all the way to Hat Yai from Singapore, but they involve sleeping on board for the 18-hour journey. Buses from Kuala Lumpur in Malaysia take about 12 hours, while the most manageable bus connection is the 6-hour journey from Penang in Malaysia. From Penang, Kuala Lumpur and Singapore, there are also buses to Phuket, Krabi and Surat Thani (for Ko Samui). All these bus routes work both ways should you want to visit Malaysia and/or Singapore from Thailand. With the price of budget air travel so low, though, you may choose to fly instead.

Arriving by Boat

From the Malaysian resort island of Langkawi, there are daily boats to Thammalang in Thailand, 9km (6 miles) south of the Thai town of Satun; the journey to Thammalang, where immigration formalities are conducted, takes just under one hour. From Satun, there are buses to Hat Yai, and to Trang (for Krabi and Phuket). Boats also travel to Thammalang from the town of Kuala Perlis in the far northwest of Malaysia; the journey time is 45 minutes. Note that there are no banks or ATMs at Thammalang, and the opening times of the money exchange facility are sporadic, so make sure you have some Thai currency to hand to pay for a taxi to Satun.

Arriving from Laos

Crossing the Friendship Bridge that spans the Mekong River is both an adventurous and easy-to-organize way to arrive in Thailand. Vientiane, the capital of Laos, is only 24km (15 miles) away from the Friendship Bridge, and taxis and buses make the journey on a regular basis. Minibuses cross the bridge from early in the morning until 9pm, and a Thai visa will be issued to you at the bridge crossing. From the Thai side of the river, a five-minute tuk-tuk ride will take you into the middle of Nong Khai. From here, there are trains to Bangkok, taking about 12 hours; buses to Bangkok take 10 hours. It takes one hour by bus to Udon Thani, from where there are one-hour flights to Bangkok. Another crossing point to the northeast of Thailand is from Khammouan/Tha Khaek to Nakhon Phanom, where there are flights to Bangkok. It is also possible to enter Thailand from Houayxai, a two-day boat ride on the Mekong River from Louang Prabang to Chiang Khong. If traveling from Thailand to Laos, a visa to enter Laos can be purchased at the crossing points for US$30, in cash, plus two passport-size photos. Alternatively, you can organise a visa in advance at the Laos embassy in Bangkok.

A tuk-tuk can bring you from the Mekong riverside into Nong Khai

GETTING AROUND

Getting around Thailand is made easy by an extensive range of transportation options: planes, boats, cars, taxis, buses, coaches, mini-vans, *songthaews*, motorcycle taxis, tuk-tuks and *samlors*. Travel is relatively inexpensive, reliable and efficient, but long-distance journeys can be time-consuming unless you're flying.

BY AIR

Journeys across Thailand that easily take the best part of a day or more by bus or train can be reduced to an hour or so by an internal flight. For example, from Chiang Mai to Phuket takes about two hours by plane as opposed to two days by bus; the journey covered in a one-hour flight from Bangkok to Ubon Ratchathani takes ten hours by train. Internal flights are available through the national airline and a number of smaller airlines, and an internet reservation is the most efficient way to purchase a ticket. See page 41 for further information.

BY TRAIN

The rail network is run by the State Railway of Thailand (SRT), and there are four main lines covering the northern, southern, northeastern and eastern parts of the country. Tickets can be reserved in advance, which is advisable for popular routes like Bangkok to Chiang Mai or Bangkok to Surat Thani (for Ko Samui). Within Thailand, tickets can be reserved in advance in Bangkok or through mainline stations; outside of Thailand, tickets can be reserved online. It is not possible to purchase tickets on the train itself without paying an excess charge. There are no super-fast trains, but for long journeys there are usually comfortable night trains with sleepers.

BY BUS

Buses belonging to the government-run Baw Khaw Saw go mostly everywhere in Thailand, covering short inter-town routes as well as the more obvious long-distance routes. There is also a variety of private companies running buses and mini-vans on all the popular long-distance routes. On the whole, bus travel, whether government-run or private, is reliable with the exception of some budget-price private buses between Bangkok and Chiang Mai, Phuket and Surat Thani. There is often a choice of classes of bus travel, air-conditioning being the most important distinction. Long, overnight bus journeys are not as safe or as comfortable as overnight train travel.

BY BOAT

There are scheduled boat services to all the main islands using a variety of vessels. Popular routes to islands such as Ko Samui and Ko Lanta use large, ocean-going craft with interior seating and air-conditioning, and hovercraft and jetfoils are also in use on some routes. Tickets are either bought on board or, increasingly common, through agents or your island accommodation in advance. Apart from boats to Ko Samui, services are usually reduced during the wet months of May to October.

DRIVING

Outside Bangkok, getting around by rented vehicle is a feasible option. This is especially so in the northeast and southern regions, where roads are pleasantly uncongested. Distances in Thailand are in kilometers and, apart from rural areas off the main network, road directions are in English. Road signs follow easy-to-understand, international conventions.

LOCAL TRANSPORT

Within towns—because walking is an option only for short distances due to the heat—there is always some form of transportation available. Buses and *songthaews* follow set routes with fixed fares, while taxis and tuk-tuks have negotiable rates. Apart from in Bangkok, where metered taxis are the rule, it is essential to agree on the fare beforehand.

Disembarking at the harbor in Chumphon, Southern Thailand

Trains

Trains are not the speediest way to travel across Thailand but they are safe and enjoyable. You can generally rely on the departure times stated in timetables but delays in the course of a journey do sometimes occur. Trains designated as Ordinary are the slowest and are best avoided unless there is no choice. Rapid trains are not rapid at all and only a little faster than Ordinary ones. Express and Special Express are the ones to use whenever possible.

ON THE MOVE

ROUTES
The northern line runs between Bangkok and Chiang Mai, via Ayutthaya, Lop Buri and Phitsanulok. The southern line runs between Bangkok and Hat Yai, via Hua Hin, Chumphon and Surat Thani. At Hat Yai the line branches into two, one heading down to Malaysia's west coast and the other to Malaysia's east coast. The southern line also has a branch that connects Kanchanaburi with Bangkok. The northeastern line splits into two north of Bangkok, with one line terminating at Ubon Ratchathani, via Nakhon Ratchasima (Korat) and Surin, and the other one heading up to Nong Khai via Khon Kaen and Udon Thani. The eastern line branches to connect Bangkok with Pattaya.

CLASSES
Travel in first class provides cabins for two passengers, with air-conditioning, washbasin, small table, and seats that convert into beds. Travel in second class provides comfortable padded seats in cabins, some with air-conditioning and some with fans, with toilet facilities for each carriage. Travel in third class can mean hard seats that are uncomfortable for long journeys but fine for short trips. Trains to Kanchanaburi from Bangkok take about three hours, and only third-class seats are available. Carriages are clean, though, and

with open windows looking out across rural scenes, the journey is very enjoyable.

TRAVELING OVERNIGHT
On overnight journeys the seats convert into lower sleeping berths, and the upper berths fold out from the side of the carriage above the windows. Fresh linen is provided and there is a curtain for each berth that gives a reasonable degree of privacy. Luggage is stored in racks nearby, but keep valuables with you in your berth. In first class you have your own two-bed cabin with a door that locks.

FARES
The basic fare for any journey is subject to supplements determined by the class of seat, type of train and whether air-conditioning is available. Even when these are added you will find fares to be relatively inexpensive, though first-class fares are notably higher. From Bangkok to Surat Thani, for example, the journey of 650km (400 miles) costs approximately B600 in second class with air-conditioning. On overnight journeys, the fare for an upper berth is a little less than that for a lower berth—a difference of less than B100 on the Bangkok–Surat Thani route. Children aged under three and less than 100cm (39in) tall travel free; those aged 4 to 11 and under 150cm (59in) pay half the adult fare.

Rail passes for unlimited travel over 20 days are available for B1,500, or for B3,000 with the inclusion of all supplements (except a sleeper berth). However, unless you are intent on rushing around the country, the rail pass is not an especially economical offer.

BUYING TICKETS
Seats on some short journeys with third-class seating, like the Bangkok–Kanchanaburi route, cannot be reserved in advance. For all other journeys it is advisable to reserve at least a day or two in advance, longer for trains to Chiang Mai and Surat Thani (for Ko Samui), and especially for overnight and weekend journeys. For travel during mid-April, covering the Thai New Year, and over the Chinese New Year period (which changes each year), reserve as far ahead as possible. Tickets are checked on board.

In Thailand tickets can be reserved up to one month in advance from any mainline station: a computerized system issues you with a ticket stating train departure time and seat number. Bangkok's Hua Lamphong station has a special advance reservations office (▷ below).

From outside Thailand, there are a number of agencies that will reserve train tickets for you through their websites (see opposite); a reservation charge will apply.

BANGKOK'S HUA LAMPHONG STATION
In the middle of Bangkok and with its own subway station, Hua Lamphong station is used as the arrival and departure point for

JOURNEY TIMES AND FARES FROM BANGKOK		
TO	JOURNEY TIME	FARE
Chiang Mai	13 hours	B1,253 (first-class air-conditioned sleeper)
Hua Hin	3 hours 30 min	B302 (second-class air-conditioned train)
Kanchanaburi	3 hours	B30 (third-class train)
Ubon Ratchathani	10 hours	B1,080 (first-class air-conditioned sleeper)

A second-class car on a Thai express train

TIPS

- Bangkok's Don Muang Airport has a station on the northern line, between Bangkok and Chiang Mai via Ayutthaya, and on the northeastern line to Nong Khai. If arriving at the airport, these trains can be boarded there without traveling to Bangkok's Hua Lamphong station.
- It pays to check timetables carefully because the difference between a slow and fast train can be anything from one hour to four or more.
- In Bangkok, nearly all trains depart from Hua Lamphong station, but if traveling to Kanchanaburi you need to go to Bangkok Noi station in Thonburi, close to the Thonburi Railway/Bangkok Noi pier, via a Chao Phraya River Express boat.
- At Hua Lamphong station, beware of anyone proffering help and bearing official-looking insignia suggesting they work for the Tourist Authority of Thailand (TAT)—they are touts for private travel agents.

nearly all Bangkok trains. Entering the station from the subway, walk directly ahead, keeping the platforms on your left, for the information booth on the other side of the concourse. To the left of this, parallel with the platforms, is the advance reservations office (daily 8.30–4), where payment can be made with Visa/Mastercard. Take a numbered ticket from the machine just inside the entrance. The ticket windows by the platforms and under the departures display board are for same-day travel, but when the advance reservations office is closed you can use windows 2 to 11. The station has a post office, an ATM and exchange facility, internet access and a left-luggage office (4am–10.30pm).

USEFUL WEBSITES

For reserving tickets online:

Asia-Discovery: www.asia-discovery.com/train.htm

Thaifocus: www.thaifocus.com/travel/train

Traveller2000: www.traveller2000.com/train

Other useful websites:

Seat Sixty-One: www.seat61.com/Thailand.htm

Good information, including pictures of the different classes of travel, timetables and fares.

State Railway of Thailand (SRT): www.railway.co.th

Timetables, seat availability and sample fares, but online reservations are not possible. In Thailand, SRT can be contacted on a 24-hour information line (tel 1690) or at Bangkok's Hua Lamphong station (tel 022 250 300).

Tales of Asia: www.talesofasia.com

Information on train transport scams in Thailand.

THAILAND TRANSPORTATION MAP

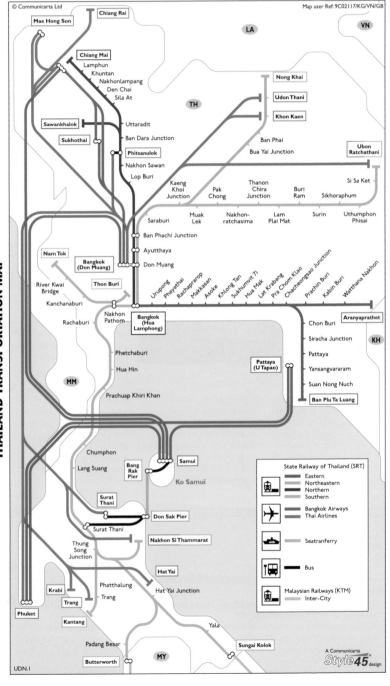

© Communicarta Ltd

Map user Ref: 9C02117/KG/VN/GB

Mae Hong Son

Chiang Rai

LA

VN

Chiang Mai
Lamphun
Khuntan
Nakhonlampang
Den Chai
Sila At

Nong Khai

TH

Udon Thani

Khon Kaen

Sawankhalok

Uttaradit

Ban Phai

Sukhothai

Ban Dara Junction

Bua Yai Junction

Ubon Ratchathani

Phitsanulok

Nakhon Sawan

Lop Buri

Kaeng Khoi Junction

Pak Chong

Thanon Chira Junction

Buri Ram

Sikhoraphum

Si Sa Ket

Saraburi

Muak Lek

Nakhon-ratchasima

Lam Plai Mat

Surin

Uthumphon Phisai

Ban Phachi Junction

Nam Tok

Ayutthaya

Bangkok (Don Muang)

Don Muang

Thon Buri

River Kwai Bridge

Urupong
Phayathai
Rachaprarop
Makkasan
Asoke
Khlong Tan
Sukhumvit 71
Hua Mak
Lat Krabang
Pra Chom Klao
Chacheongsao Junction
Prachin Buri
Kabin Buri
Watthana Nakhon

Kanchanaburi

Nakhon Pathom

Bangkok (Hua Lamphong)

Chon Buri

Aranyaprathet

Rachaburi

KH

Phetchaburi

Siracha Junction

Pattaya

MM

Hua Hin

Pattaya (U Tapao)

Yansangvararam

Suan Nong Nuch

Prachuap Khiri Khan

Ban Plu Ta Luang

Chumphon

Lang Suang

Bang Rak Pier

Samui

Ko Samui

Surat Thani

Don Sak Pier

Surat Thani

Nakhon Si Thammarat

Thung Song Junction

Hat Yai

Krabi

Phatthalung

Hat Yai Junction

Trang

Trang

Kantang

Phuket

Yala

Padang Besar

Sungai Kolok

MY

Butterworth

UDN.I

A Communicarta
Style 45 design

State Railway of Thailand (SRT)

	Eastern
	Northeastern
	Northern
	Southern
	Bangkok Airways
	Thai Airlines
	Seatranferry
	Bus

Malaysian Railways (KTM)
Inter-City

Buses

With the exception of the smaller islands, the chances are that anywhere you want to get to will be served by a public or private bus service. Every town has a bus station of some kind, even if only a stretch of pavement with a ticket office, and they are often used by both government-run and private buses.

GOVERNMENT-RUN BUSES
For short journeys between towns, up to a distance of around 150km (under 100 miles), there are government-run buses that depart whenever there are a sufficient number of passengers. These buses do not usually have air-conditioning if the journey is a short one, and they can get crowded, but you are usually not stuck on one long enough for this to be a hardship. These buses run throughout the day, with the frequency of services always highest in the morning and tending to fizzle out during late afternoon.

For longer routes, the buses are larger, air-conditioned and with a good level of service. For popular routes there is usually the option of a VIP bus that costs more but provides more leg room and a shorter journey time.

Complimentary water, soft drinks and snacks are usually served on longer routes.

PRIVATE BUSES
On longer routes you often won't know whether the bus you have a reserved seat on is a private or government-run one, and most of the time it makes little or no difference. Large towns and cities will have companies competing for business through travel agents: Rival ticket offices are alongside each other at bus stations, but usually there is little variation in their prices. The differences in fares between private and government-run buses running the same route is often negligible, though private buses may be more frequent and offer a slightly higher standard of service. There will be a reason that fares on private buses are noticeably less expensive than rival ones plying the same route, and it is not always prudent to go for the cheapest fare. As well as buses, private mini-vans are often available for mid-length journeys such as, for example, the Bangkok–Hua Hin route.

BUYING TICKETS
For short journeys on ordinary government-run buses, fares are paid on the bus to a conductor, not the driver, and passengers are picked up and dropped off along the route. For longer journeys, on government-run and private buses, tickets are usually purchased before boarding from a ticket office at the bus station, and a seat number is specified. Sometimes your stored luggage will also be ticketed.

In large towns, timetables and fares are clearly displayed for long-distance routes, and you can see the available choices between VIP and regular services.

TIPS
● Some VIP buses have toilets, but do not rely on this. Bus stations have toilet facilities and on long routes there is usually a rest and meal break at a restaurant with toilet facilities.
● Tickets for long-distance routes can be reserved in advance and to be sure of a seat on a popular route it is best to reserve the day before departure; it is advisable to at least confirm timetable details the day before traveling.
● Tourist offices have local bus information and larger ones dispense leaflets listing timetables and fares.

JOURNEY TIMES AND FARES
Fares are based on air-conditioned, first-class or VIP bus services.

FROM	TO	JOURNEY TIME	FARE
Bangkok	Ayutthaya	2 hours	B65
	Chiang Mai	10–11 hours	B500
	Khon Kaen	8 hours	B300
	Korat	3 hours 30 min	B180
	Loei	9 hours	B380
	Pattaya	2 hours 30 min	B110
	Phuket	12 hours	B680
	Ubon Ratchathani	10 hours	B400
Chiang Mai	Chiang Rai	3 hours	B140
	Mae Hong Son	7 hours 30 min	B250
	Sukhothai	5 hours	B175
	Udon Thani	12 hours	B400
Hua Hin	Bangkok	3 hours	B120
Ko Samui	Bangkok	15 hours	B400
Krabi	Hat Yai	4 hours	B170
	Phang Nga	2 hours	B90
	Surat Thani	3 hours	B180
Phuket	Chumphon	7 hours	B300
	Hat Yai	7 hours	B420
	Krabi	3 hours	B117
	Phang Nga	2 hours 30 min	B70
	Surat Thani	5 hours	B220
Surat Thani	Bangkok	10 hours	B600

Flights within Thailand

Long-distance travel within Thailand by train or bus can be time-consuming, but internal flights reach most corners of the country and are not especially expensive. A Bangkok–Phuket flight (85 minutes; about 20 flights daily) costs from B1,000 to B1,500; Bangkok–Chiang Mai (60 minutes; about 25 flights daily) costs from B800 to B1,000; and Bangkok–Krabi (80 minutes; about four flights daily) costs around B2,550.

Thai Airways has an extensive set of domestic routes, reaching most corners of the country, and its timetables can be relied on. Hot on its heels comes Air Asia, with a fleet of Boeing 737-300 planes. Air Asia is gaining a reputation for reliable service, competitive pricing and punctuality. Bangkok Airways has been around for longer and still monopolizes the Bangkok–Ko Samui and Bangkok–Sukhothai routes.

RESERVING TICKETS

All the airlines have websites for online reservations. After payment by credit card you will receive a reference number; turn up at the airport with this number and your passport. Flights with Thai Airways can also be reserved through any Thai Airways travel agent and Air Asia has a call

centre for telephone reservations (025159 999). Check the websites for timetables and fares, and note the luggage limits: on Nok Air it is 30kg (66lb) per person, Thai Airways 20kg (44lb) and AirAsia only 15kg (33lb). The baggage allowances are not generous and it may take some careful planning to avoid having to pay for any excess. Most hotels allow guests to store baggage free of charge and luggage can be left in their locked storage area and picked up days or weeks later.

REGIONAL AIRPORTS

Bangkok's Don Muang Airport (▷ 40, 63) is about to become the airport for internal flights only, with the new Suvarnabhumi Airport serving international routes. It is likely that there will still be a bus service between Don Muang and the city center, and hopefully a bus link with Suvarnabhumi Airport, but you will need to check this with the tourist office.

Thailand's regional airports are usually not far from the city

DOMESTIC AIRLINE WEBSITES	
AIRLINE	**WEBSITE**
Air Asia	www.airasia.com
Bangkok Airways	www.bangkokair.com
Nok Air	www.nokair.com
One-Two-Go	www.fly12go.com
PB Air	www.pbair.com
THAI	www.thaiairways.com

FLIGHTS WITHIN THAILAND		
FROM	**TO**	**AIRLINE**
Bangkok	Chiang Mai	Thai Airways, Bangkok Airways, Nok Air, One-Two-Go, AirAsia
	Chiang Rai	Thai Airways, One-Two-Go, AirAsia
	Hat Yai	Thai Airways, Nok Air, One-Two-Go, AirAsia
	Khon Kaen	Thai Airways, AirAsia
	Ko Samui	Bangkok Airways
	Krabi	Thai Airways, Bangkok Airways, One-Two-Go
	Mae Hong Son	Thai Airways
	Nakom Phanom	PB Air
	Nakhon Si Thammarat	Thai Airways, PB Air, One-Two-Go
	Nan	PB Air
	Phitsanulok	Thai Airways, Nok Air
	Phuket	Thai Airways, Bangkok Airways, Nok Air, One-Two-Go, AirAsia
	Roi Et	PB Air
	Sukhothai	Bangkok Airways
	Surat Thani	Thai Airways, One-Two-Go
	Ubon Ratchathani	Thai Airways, AirAsia
	Udon Thani	Thai Airways, Nok Air, AirAsia
Ko Samui	Bangkok	Bangkok Airways
	Chiang Mai	Bangkok Airways
	Krabi	Bangkok Airways
	Pattaya	Bangkok Airways
	Phuket	Bangkok Airways
	Sukhothai	Bangkok Airways

AIR, RAIL AND FERRY JOURNEY TIMES

This chart gives the duration in hours and minutes (hours are given in the larger number) of journeys between key destinations. As it is not always possible to travel using one single mode of transport, the chart highlights which modes should be used (▷ Key below). See also the transportation map on page 48.

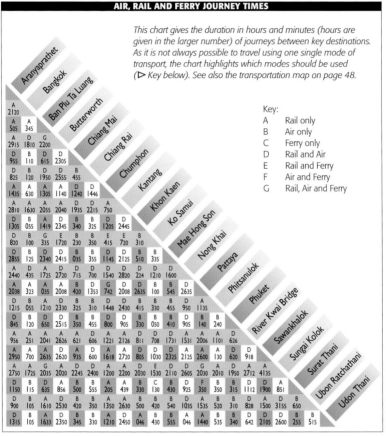

Key:
A   Rail only
B   Air only
C   Ferry only
D   Rail and Air
E   Rail and Ferry
F   Air and Ferry
G   Rail, Air and Ferry

center or the main beach resort area. Chiang Mai's airport is only 3km (1.9 miles) away from the center and Phuket's airport is exceptional in being some 20–30km (12–19 miles) away from the main west-coast beach resort area.

All the regional airports, including Don Muang, have a taxi or minibus service into the local town and for busy destinations this is a well-organized system with fixed rates that are clearly displayed at counters in the arrivals hall. Many resort hotels and the better city center hotels have their own mini-vans bringing guests to and from the airport. If your accommodation is reserved in advance, it is worth checking and confirming the transfer arrangements.

AIR PASSES
There are only two types of air passes. Thai Airways sells a Discover Thailand air pass that covers any three internal routes for US$169 (half price for children aged 2 to 11), with extra routes available for US$59, up to a maximum of eight. All must be specified upon purchase, but dates can be changed. The air pass can only be purchased outside Thailand, through Thai Airways or a travel agent. The Bangkok Airways air pass is more flexible in that only the first route has to be fixed at the time of purchase; it costs US$150 for any three of their internal routes. Currently, it can only be bought through agents.

A Bangkok Air plane at Samui Airport

Taxis and *Songthaews*

Taxis are available throughout Thailand and take different forms, but, with the exception of those in Bangkok, they do not use meters. This means that the fare must be established beforehand. *Songthaews* are a cross between a bus and a shared taxi, but fares for regular routes are fixed.

TAXI FARES

Establishing a taxi fare is more of an art than a science, though it is always easier to handle if you have some idea beforehand of the likely fare for a particular journey. Ask the staff where you are staying, talk to other visitors or check the asking rate with more than one taxi. Sometimes, especially when arriving somewhere for the first time, you simply have to ask the taxi driver what the fare is and use your own judgment. Some degree of bargaining is usually taken for granted, but try to bear in mind, especially with *samlor* drivers, that most of them earn very little and you may be disagreeing over a very small amount in terms of your currency.

TIP
● Carry coins and small notes for paying taxi drivers.

TUK-TUKS

Tuk-tuks are three-wheeled vehicles driven by two-stroke engines. They look attractive, but the name comes from the distinctive noise they make and after a while the charm may wear off. Apart from the noise and exhaust fumes, some drivers resemble kamikaze pilots as they dart in and out of traffic and take right-angle turns with reckless abandon. On a good day, though, they can be fun to ride in and will take you where you want to go with alacrity and little expense.

Samlors are also three-wheeled vehicles; their unmotorized form is the bicycle rickshaw. The ones with motors make as much noise as tuk-tuks.

MOTORCYCLE TAXIS

Motorcycle taxis are found in urban and rural areas and are usually identified by the drivers' conspicuous vests, sometimes bearing numerals, and the tendency for them to gather in small clusters at junctions, outside stations or shopping malls. Thais use them for short journeys. While the driver may or may not wear a helmet, they do not usually carry one for passengers, despite the fact that they are a legal requirement. They are not suitable or safe if you are carrying luggage but in out-of-town locations they are sometimes the only readily available alternative to a long walk. For short hops, their fares are usually fixed at around B10.

SONGTHAEWS

In small towns, rural areas and large islands, public transport takes the form of open-ended vehicles with two rows of seats facing one another. These are *songthaews* (Thai for 'two rows') and passengers can flag them down or be dropped off anywhere along their route. The conventional time for paying the driver varies, either at the start or end of your journey. In Phuket, one *songthaew* runs between the beaches and Phuket town, and the driver stops halfway and collects all the fares. Some *songthaews* are equipped with bells for passengers to press when they wish to alight, but in others you may need to give a shout or tap the railings with a coin to alert the driver. Observe the practice of other passengers.

A more eco-friendly way to travel—a bicycle rickshaw

Bicycling and Walking

Despite the heat, bicycling leisurely around a small town or rural area is one of the most pleasant ways of getting around. The larger and more congested the urban area, the less attractive bicycling becomes, and as a bicyclist you cannot assume that the hard shoulder of a road will not be used by motorists and truck drivers. In Bangkok, of course, bicycling is just not an option, but outside the capital bicycles and tricycles are used regularly by Thais, and motorists are well aware of bicyclists sharing the roadways with them.

BICYCLE RENTAL

Bicycle rental shops are not common but they can be found in areas where entrepreneurs have realized there is a steady demand from visitors. In Chiang Mai, Kanchanaburi and Nong Kai it is not difficult to find places renting out bicycles, usually by the day for around B50 and often with a discount for a longer rental period. They open up the

Rent a bicycle and try out the dirt tracks

local countryside in a way not possible with other means of transportation. In these places, bicycle rental is often also available through guesthouses, and it is not always necessary to be a guest to rent one of their bicycles. In Ayutthaya, where bicycle shops dot the road between the station and the ferry jetty, a bicycle is the ideal way to get around the *wats* (temples) that are too spaced out to reach on foot.

WALKING

Traveling on foot for more than half an hour might prove to be an exhausting and dehydrating experience in the hotter hours of the day. Having said that, longer periods spent walking about are quite feasible if you carry or stop for drinks, maintain a moderate-to-slow pace and use shaded areas as much as possible. The suggested walks in this guide will take well over an hour but are very manageable. Depending on the temperature and time of day, far longer walks are possible. It is a good idea to always carry a supply of water and a hat.

TIPS
● Road and street signs are usually translated into English, but you will find minor differences in the spellings used for maps and brochures.
● *Thanon* means road, so Thanon Sukhumvit is Sukhumvit Road.
● *Soi* means a smaller road branching off a main road. Soi 20 Thanon Sukhumvit, for example, means *soi* number 20 off Sukhumvit Road.

Driving in Thailand

If Bangkok provides your first experience of Thailand's roads and traffic, you are likely to shun the idea of renting a vehicle, but outside of the capital driving is a manageable proposition. Car rental through a reputable company is as uncomplicated as in your home country, and in many areas of Thailand the roads are uncongested and other drivers generally show consideration and drive responsibly. At the same time, expect to encounter some reckless drivers, often behind the wheel of a bus or truck, with little consideration for cars. This is especially so after dark, and long-distance driving at night is not recommended for this reason.

Apart from rural areas off the main road network, road signs are clearly posted in English and Thai, with distances to main destinations indicated in kilometers. On main roads there will be signs warning of sharp bends and/or the need to reduce speed.

In Bangkok the density of traffic and the bewildering mix of traffic directions and lanes—which are subject to constant changes and are not signposted in English—make driving very challenging; it is not recommended. Car rental at Bangkok's Don Muang or Suvarnabhumi airports is feasible if you are not heading into the city, and expressways, signposted in English, connect the airports with routes to other parts of the country.

There is very little vehicle crime, and parking is rarely a problem outside Bangkok.

RULES OF THE ROAD
● Drive on the left.
● All directions and speed limits are in kilometers. In towns and built-up areas the limit is 60kph (37mph), and on other roads the limit varies between 90kph (55mph) and 120kph (74mph).

CAR RENTAL COMPANIES	
COMPANY	**WEBSITE**
Avis	www.avis.com
Budget	www.budget.co.th
Hertz	www.hertz.com
National	www.nationalcar.com

● Military and police checkpoints on roads are not unusual. Usually you will be waved through, unless you have been stopped for speeding.
● You must wear seatbelts in the front seats.
● Large vehicles assume they have priority on roads and drive accordingly.
● Hard shoulders are often used by slower vehicles or by cars yielding to a larger vehicle.
● If the vehicle in front of you is indicating left, the driver may be signaling that it is safe to pass; indicating right may mean it is not.
● A vehicle flashing its lights is **not** giving way to you but rather indicating that it will.
● When it comes to traffic offenses like speeding, common and accepted practice is to hand over some cash (between B200 and B500) to the police officer.

CAR RENTAL
Cars and jeeps can be rented at regional airports or through many hotels and travel agents across Thailand, as well as reserved and paid for in advance through a company's website.

Expect to pay about B1,200 per day for a small, compact car in good condition. Company websites will provide quotes and prices can be compared.

In popular destinations, especially Phuket, Ko Samui and Chiang Mai, there are countless places offering car rental at less expensive rates than the better-known, franchised companies. If you use these then you need to check the insurance cover very carefully to see that the vehicle is actually insured.

It is not advisable to use companies that ask for your passport and expect to retain it until you return the vehicle. The local TAT office should be able to recommend reliable companies, and car rental desks in good hotels will be from reputable and trustworthy companies.

The general rule, and one that is enforced by the larger and more reputable car rental companies, is that the driver is over the age of 21 and able to pay by credit card.

It is normal to ask for pre-authorization for a security deposit from your credit card of B20,000.

A non-Thai driver is supposed to show an international driver's license when renting a vehicle, but in practice it is often sufficient to show your national license.

Vehicles are usually supplied with a full tank of fuel and should be returned with a full tank, and

Watch out for unusual hazards on rural roads

there should be no charge for mileage.

Loss damage waiver, subject usually to a B5,000 charge in the event of a non-recoverable loss or damage to the vehicle, should be included in the car rental price, and you should check this is the case before you rent the car. A drink-related driving offense will invalidate your insurance-covered liability on the vehicle.

Also available is an optional Personal Accident and Effect insurance, which costs around B100 per day. Check your general travel insurance to see if you are covered for accidents while driving a rented vehicle.

Good car rental companies use cars in good condition, but they should have a clear policy in the event of a breakdown. Make sure you know how to contact your rental company if you break down or have an accident.

Before you drive off, check the condition of the car you are renting and ensure that any defects are marked on the rental form.

MOTORCYCLE RENTAL

In Phuket, Ko Samui and Ko Lanta, as well as smaller islands and in the north of Thailand, visitors commonly rent a motorcycle. This can often be arranged where you are staying. Expect to pay around B200 for one day's rental. Insurance is not usually available.

Some of the visitors you see driving rented motorcycles have never driven one before, and as you may yourself be in this category, careful driving is essential. On some islands, roads can be in poor condition, with unexpected potholes.

Always wear a helmet for safety—the police can fine you on the spot if you are stopped without one.

FUEL

Cars usually use unleaded and vans mostly use diesel, but always check before you fill up. Both types of fuel are available at stations across the country and the price for both is currently between B23 and B25 per liter. Larger fuel stations will accept payment by recognized international credit cards, but in rural areas cash may be required.

ON THE MOVE

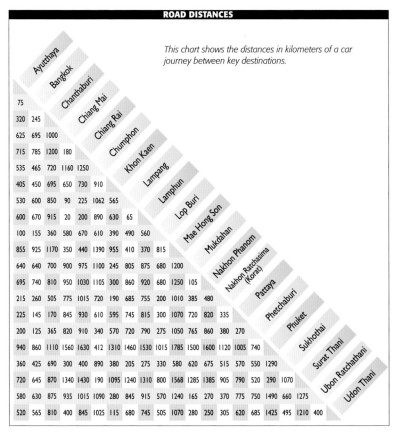

ROAD DISTANCES

This chart shows the distances in kilometers of a car journey between key destinations.

	Ayutthaya	Bangkok	Chanthaburi	Chiang Mai	Chiang Rai	Chumphon	Khon Kaen	Lampang	Lamphun	Lop Buri	Mae Hong Son	Mukdahan	Nakhon Phanom	Nakhon Ratchasima (Korat)	Pattaya	Phetchaburi	Phuket	Sukhothai	Surat Thani	Ubon Ratchathani
Bangkok	75																			
Chanthaburi	320	245																		
Chiang Mai	625	695	1000																	
Chiang Rai	715	785	1200	180																
Chumphon	535	465	720	1160	1250															
Khon Kaen	405	450	695	650	730	910														
Lampang	530	600	850	90	225	1062	565													
Lamphun	600	670	915	20	200	890	630	65												
Lop Buri	100	155	360	580	670	610	390	490	560											
Mae Hong Son	855	925	1170	350	440	1390	955	410	370	815										
Mukdahan	640	640	700	900	975	1100	245	805	875	680	1200									
Nakhon Phanom	695	740	810	950	1030	1105	300	860	920	680	1250	105								
Nakhon Ratchasima (Korat)	215	260	505	775	1015	720	190	685	755	200	1010	385	480							
Pattaya	225	145	170	845	930	610	595	745	815	300	1070	720	820	335						
Phetchaburi	200	125	365	820	910	340	570	720	790	275	1050	765	860	380	270					
Phuket	940	860	1110	1560	1630	412	1310	1460	1530	1015	1785	1500	1600	1120	1005	740				
Sukhothai	360	425	690	300	400	890	380	205	275	330	580	620	675	515	570	550	1290			
Surat Thani	720	645	870	1340	1430	190	1095	1240	1310	800	1568	1285	1385	905	790	520	290	1070		
Ubon Ratchathani	580	630	875	935	1015	1090	280	845	915	570	1240	165	270	370	775	750	1490	660	1275	
Udon Thani	520	565	810	400	845	1025	115	680	745	505	1070	280	250	305	620	685	1425	495	1210	400

Getting Around in Bangkok

Bangkok is a large, sprawling city and getting around efficiently depends very much on establishing, before setting out, the most convenient means of transport for where you want to go. The Skytrain, the subway system and the Chao Phraya River Express boats are most commonly used by visitors to get about, but taxis, plentiful and inexpensive, are sometimes necessary. The bus network reaches every part of the city.

SKYTRAIN

The BTS Skytrain (www.bts.co.th) system offers comfortable, efficient, non-smoking, air-conditioned transportation on two lines between 6am and midnight. Trains run every few minutes. Drinking or eating is not allowed on the trains, and stations have no toilet facilities. The name of each station is announced in English as the train approaches the platform.

Lines

The Sukhumvit Line runs from Mo Chit in the north (station N8), close to the Northern Bus Terminal and Chatuchak Market, to On Nut (E9) on Thanon Sukhumvit; the entire journey takes half an hour. All trains stop at every station, including the interchange at Siam for connecting trains on the Silom Line.

The Silom Line runs from National Stadium (W1), one stop west of Siam, to Saphan Taksin (S6), which is two minutes away on foot from a Chao Phraya River Express boat pier.

Tickets

Tickets are issued by touch-sensitive machines in all stations, with clear instructions in English. Only B5 and B10 coins are accepted. After inserting your ticket into one of the turnstiles to enter the platform area, the ticket is returned to you. Upon exiting through a turnstile, the ticket is retained. Non-turnstile access is available for large luggage and staff will assist.

Fares

Tickets cost between B15 and B40 depending on the distance. There is a useful three-day/four-night Tourist Pass—if purchased in the morning it serves for four days—for B280. The one-day pass for B100 would need a lot of journeys to make it economical. There are also 30-day passes that cover any 10 trips for B250, 15 trips for B300 and 30 trips for B540 (B160, B210 and B360 respectively for those aged under 23). Children under 90cm (35.5in) travel free.

SUBWAY

The MRT subway system (www.mrta.co.th) operates from 5am to midnight, with trains running every 10 minutes on average. Air-conditioned and non-smoking, the subway has one line, running between Hua Lamphong railway station in the middle of the city and Bang Sue in the north, two stations beyond Chatuchak where it connects with the Mo Chit Skytrain station. Subway station Silom also connects with the Skytrain station of Sala Daeng, and subway station Sukhumvit connects with Asok Skytrain station, though the latter connection entails exiting onto the street and walking to the nearby station.

Drinking or eating is not allowed on trains; stations have toilets but no other amenities.

The name of each station is announced in English as the train approaches the platform.

Tickets and fares

Tickets, in the form of a small black, plastic disc, are issued by machines along the same lines as the Skytrain. The disc is used to activate entry through a turnstile and should be inserted into the turnstile, which retains it, when exiting a station. Fares are approximately the same as for the Skytrain.

CHAO PHRAYA RIVER EXPRESS BOATS

The Chao Phraya River Express Boat Company runs boats up and down Bangkok's river every day from 5.30am to 7.30pm (the last boats are an hour earlier on Saturday and Sunday evenings).

Tha Sathorn pier, next to Saphan Taksin Skytrain station and close to the Shangri-La hotel, has been designated Central Pier. The piers north of this are numbered N1, N2 and so on.

You are most likely to use boats between Central Pier and Tha Phra Athit (N13) for reaching places like the Royal Palace, National Museum and Banglamphu. Some of the piers are on the west side of the river, useful for Wat Arun and Thonburi station (for trains to Kanchanaburi).

Types of boats

Boats not flying any flag will stop at piers where people are waiting to board or passengers are waiting to disembark. Boats flying a yellow or orange flag are express boats that do not stop at every pier. A dark blue flag shows that this is the last one of the day.

Special Tourist Boats (▷ 67) run between Central Pier and Banglamphu, and the ticket allows you to hop on and off any of these boats.

Tickets and fares

Tickets cost from B5 to B15 depending on the distance and are bought on board.

The boats get busy and you need to be ready to disembark at the pier you want by making your way towards the back of the boat, which is where you boarded.

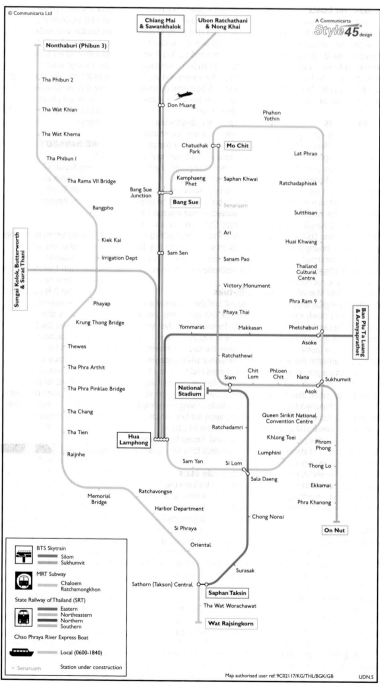

Cross-river boats

These boats ply back and forth across the Chao Phraya River and have their own access and exit points alongside the piers that service the Chao Phraya River Express boats. The fare is B2, which you pay at a booth at the pier; no tickets are issued.

CANAL BOATS

On the *khlongs* (canals), longtail boats operate like the Chao Phraya River Express boats, stopping at piers along their routes. On the Bangkok side of the river, you are most likely to use the route that runs between Tha Phanfa (for Wat Rachanada, Wak Saket and Banglamphu) and Asok (for Thanon Sukhumvit), a useful way of moving between the east and west parts of the city. See also page 69.

The piers are not conspicuous, but *The Official Map of Bangkok* (free from Bangkok airport and tourist offices) clearly shows the course of the canal and the different piers and is useful for monitoring your journey and anticipating arrival at the pier you want. Tickets are purchased from a conductor on board; follow everyone else when they change boats at Tha Pratunam (due to bridge height restrictions).

Fares are between B7 and B15 depending on distance. Have a B20 note ready and state your destination to the conductor. Sitting near the end of each seat row makes it easier to get off; the disadvantage is an occasional light splash from the water.

TAXIS
Metered taxis

Comfortable, air-conditioned taxis with meters, displaying 'TAXI' on the roof, are plentiful, and those available display a red light in the windscreen on the passenger's side.

Fares start at B35. Expect to pay from B80 to B120 for a typical journey across town—from the vicinity of Thanon Sukhumvit around the Asok (E4) Skytrain station, for example, to Central

Pier near the Shangri-La hotel. The meter increases according to distance and time so try to avoid the busiest parts of the day, from 8 to 9.30am and 5.30 to 7pm: traffic jams can be horrendous, the fare will increase and your patience will be tested by sitting for what feels like interminable lengths of time.

A tip is not obligatory but rounding up a fare is customary. There is no charge for pieces of luggage and, apart from journeys to and from the airport, there are no other supplements.

Many taxi drivers speak a little English, but this cannot be taken for granted: do not assume they can read English on a map. Most will know common destinations, and hotel staff will often help by hailing a taxi for you and stating the destination to the driver.

Tuk-tuks

You will find these everywhere in Bangkok and sometimes they are useful for short trips when you may be in a rush. A ride in a tuk-tuk, even the rare one driven in a calm manner, will expose you to traffic fumes and noise to an alarming degree. Two people, three at the very most, can sit comfortably. Having coins helps when paying the fare, which should always be agreed beforehand. Expect to pay from B30 upwards for a short journey.

Motorcycle taxis

Motorcycle taxis are used by Bangkok residents but they can hardly be recommended for visitors, except perhaps for short trips from one end of a long *soi* to your hotel at the other end. A short trip costs about B15. It is against the law not to wear the helmet that should be available.

BUSES

Buses go everywhere in Bangkok, albeit very slowly most of the time, but the difficulty is knowing when to get off for a destination with which you are not familiar—buses are often crowded and you cannot expect the driver to

help or assume a passenger will speak English. Once you have some familiar landmarks and a map, buses can be useful, but to begin with it is best to use a metered taxi or, when appropriate, the Skytrain and/or subway. Bus fares, between B7 and B20, are paid to either the conductor or dropped in a box by the entrance.

LEAVING BANGKOK
By air

Don Muang Airport serves all domestic air routes and will continue to do so when Suvarnabhumi Airport opens.

By bus

There are three terminals for long-distance buses in and out of Bangkok. For buses to northern and northeastern Thailand use the Northern Bus Terminal on Kamphaeng Phet 2 Road, a short taxi ride or 15-minute walk from Mo Chit Skytrain station or Chatuchak subway station. For destinations in southern Thailand use the Southern Bus Terminal on Borommarat Chonnani Road in Thonburi on the west side of the Chao Phraya River. For places in eastern Thailand, use the Eastern Bus Terminal on Sukhumvit Road at Soi 40 and right next to the Ekamai Skytrain station.

TIPS

● *The Official Map of Bangkok*, a fold-out map freely available at the airport, tourist offices and some hotels, shows clearly all the Skytrain and subway stations and river and canal piers. Free Skytrain maps are available at all Skytrain stations.

● Keep a supply of coins to avoid queuing for change at Skytrain and subway stations and for purchasing Chao Phraya River Express boats.

● For returning to your accommodation by taxi, it helps to carry a hotel card with the address in Thai.

Getting Around in Other Major Cities and on Islands

Getting around in cities, towns and on islands is inexpensive. While not always fast, transportation is usually efficient and reliable.

GETTING TO YOUR ACCOMMODATION
From airports

Every regional airport has taxis waiting, and airport staff should be able to give you an idea of an acceptable fare to bear in mind when negotiating a price with the driver. Some airports will have desks for taxis and/or airport buses with fixed prices to your hotel.

If your accommodation has been reserved in advance, and especially if it is a resort hotel, there may be a mini-van waiting for guests at the airport; check this in advance with your hotel.

From bus and railway stations

Bus and railway stations are not usually within walking distance of accommodation, but there will always be tuk-tuks and *samlors* waiting as well as taxis, and some stations will have a *songthaew* service into town.

From island piers

Your place of accommodation may well have its own transport waiting at the pier for guests and this should be checked in advance. On disembarking you are likely to be approached by a variety of touts and/or staff offering accommodation and at busy times of the year, especially between November and February in southern Thailand, these may be worth considering as they will have transport waiting. Usually there will be no shortage of taxis—whether cars, motorcycles or *samlors*—available for transport to wherever you are staying.

GETTING AROUND PHUKET

Airport buses to beach hotels or into town cost from B100 to B200. *Songthaews* run between the beaches and town, a well-organized service with

destinations and fares marked in English. The fare between Phuket town and Kata beach, for example, is B20, while a tuk-tuk from Karon beach to Patong is B100. The bus station is on Thanon Phang Nga, a 10-minute walk from where the *songthaews* congregate. An air-conditioned VIP sleeper bus from town to Bangkok costs B900; a minibus to Surat Thani costs B250. For more details of Phuket transportation, ▷ 168–172 or visit www.phuket-guide.net

GETTING AROUND KRABI

A taxi from the airport into town costs around B300. Thai Airways also runs a minibus service, meeting their flights, for B60. Budget (tel 075 637 913) has a desk at Arrivals. *Songthaews* run from Thanon Maharat to Ao Nang for B20 and to the bus terminal, 5km (3 miles) north of town. A VIP sleeper from Krabi to Bangkok costs B850, while first-class air-conditioned buses to Phuket are B100 and to Surat Thani B150. Reservations for boats include transportation from your hotel to the departure pier. For more details on Krabi transport visit www.yourkrabi.com

GETTING AROUND KO SAMUI

At the airport, where Budget has a car rental desk (tel 077 427

188), minibuses meet flights and charge around B100 to B200 to the beach hotels. *Songthaews* run between the beaches and the pier at Na Thon, with destinations marked in English, while at night they become taxis available for individual rental. For more details on Ko Samui transportation, ▷ 161–163 or visit www.faraway.co.th

GETTING AROUND CHIANG MAI

A taxi system with fixed prices operates at the airport. *Songthaews* and tuk-tuks run between the train and bus stations into town and will take you directly to your accommodation; rates are negotiable, but expect to pay up to B50. Bicycles are a good way of getting around town; there are several rental outlets. For more details on Chiang Mai transport visit www.chiangmai-thai.com

TIP
● Tourist offices and most hotels, guesthouses and restaurants have maps and English-language magazines freely available showing bus stations and other transportation locations, as well as transport timetables and local fares.

The ferry at Ko Phi Phi

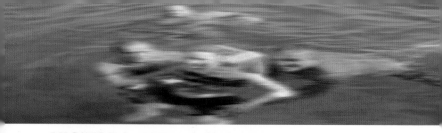

VISITORS WITH A DISABILITY

Visitors with a disability should not be deterred from visiting Thailand, even though the country is not fully geared up in terms of wheelchair access at places of interest and on public transportation. On the plus side, Thai people are usually as accommodating as possible, and it is not too costly to make generous use of taxis and to ask tour guides to arrange access to temples and museums.

PREPARATION AND PLANNING

There are a number of organizations that offer advice and information and some companies that specialize in holidays to Thailand for visitors with disabilities:
www.adventure-holidays-thailand.com A Pattaya-based company that provides tours tailored to people with disabilities. A quote is given on the basis of information you provide, and there is a good range of holidays that can be arranged, including elephant trekking and jungle safaris.
www.asiantraveladventures. com/handicapped Various tours are available for visitors with mobility problems. A nine-night/ten-day tour covering Bangkok, Ayutthaya and Phuket, for example, costs around US$1,000 per person for a group of two or three people. A seven-night/eight-day cultural tour based around Bangkok and Chiang Mai costs US$870.
www.wheelchairtours.com Tours for wheelchair travelers, people with hearing impairments and slow walkers. A four-night/five-day tour of Bangkok, Ayutthaya and Kanchaburi, for example, costs US$1,300 for two people. The website includes a list of wheelchair-friendly hotels in Bangkok, Chiang Mai, Pattaya and Ko Samui.
http://members.chello.nl/ danblokker/index.html Accommodation close to the hub of Chiang Mai.
www.allgohere.com A guide to international airlines and the facilities and services they provide for passengers with disabilities.

ARRIVING BY AIR

Check with your airline about the arrangements they can offer and the facilities at Don Muang and Suvarnabhumi airports. Both airports have elevators to all levels, and wheelchairs are available for passengers. A taxi will take you to your hotel; check with your hotel beforehand about their facilities. The better hotels, especially in Bangkok, Phuket, Ko Samui and Chiang Mai, have experience serving guests with disabilities.

GETTING AROUND IN BANGKOK

Bangkok presents difficulties because of the general lack of provision for people with disabilities and the density of human and vehicular traffic. Sidewalks are often high, uneven at the best of times, and curbs are rarely sloped for wheelchair use. Underpasses with ramps are even more rare, and bridges for pedestrians are accessible only by stairs. The Chao Phraya River Express boats have no wheelchair access, but all the subway stations and many of the Skytrain ones have elevators.

Adventure Holidays will take you places you may never have dreamed of

Bangkok

HOW TO GET THERE

✈ Airport
Don Muang airport, 25km (15 miles) north of Bangkok, is about to be replaced as the city's international airport by **Suvarnabhumi Airport**, 30km (19 miles) east of Bangkok.

🚆 Railway station
Hua Lamphong railway station is in the center of the city at the junction of Thanon Yaowarat and Thanon Charoen Krung.

SEEING BANGKOK

Bangkok is not a city to see in a hurry—the heat and the traffic will defeat you—and it will pay to pace yourself and invest in a little forward planning. The distance from your hotel to a place of interest may not look far on a map but it will take more time than you think. Walking to where you want to go is rarely an option and the best means of transportation will vary from one sight or activity to another. A combination of the Skytrain and the Chao Phraya River Express boats, with the useful connection between the two at Central Pier and Saphan Taksin, will take you to many of the city's cultural highlights, and the air-conditioned comfort of the Skytrain and subway systems will prove a blessing on many expeditions.

If your time is limited, joining a tour is worth considering, if only because the transportation will be included. City tours can be reserved through tourist information offices or any travel agent, and some of the more imaginative ones are offered by Real Asia (▷ 69 and 240). With more than a couple of days at your disposal you can do some exploring on your own, and five days or a week could easily be spent moving about and getting to know something about the city.

BACKGROUND

King Taksin established Bangkok as the country's capital in 1768 on the west side of the river in Thonburi, a response to a Burmese invasion and the destruction of Ayutthaya. Taksin was later deposed by one of his generals, who became Rama I. It was he who in the late 18th century decided, in the interests of defense, to move his palace to the east side of the river.

TOURIST INFORMATION OFFICES

There are tourist information offices at both airport terminals (tel 025 042 703; daily 8am–midnight). In the city, the Tourist Authority of Thailand office (TAT; 1600 Thanon Phetchaburi Mai, tel 022 505 500; Mon–Fri 8.30–4.30) is best reached by taking the subway to Phetchaburi or the canal boat to Tha Asoke.
A more convenient tourist information office may be the Bangkok Information Centre (17/1 Thanon Phra Athit, tel 022 257 612; daily 9–7) at the Pinklao Bridge in Banglamphu (▷ 67). This office is run by the Bangkok Tourist Bureau, which also has an information office on the walkway at Skytrain's Nana and Saphan Taksin stations.

TIP

● *Thanon* is Thai for road, and addresses are likely to use either Thai or English; so Thanon Silom, for example, is Silom Road.

THE SIGHTS

Chinese figures guarding the gate at Wat Pho

DON'T MISS

THE GRAND PALACE
A complex of royal buildings, including temples, rich in architectural design (▷ 84–87)

WAT PHO
The oldest temple in Bangkok and home to the stupendous Reclining Buddha (▷ 83)

CHAO PHRAYA RIVER
A boat trip is the most relaxing way to see the city (▷ 67)

CHATUCHAK WEEKEND MARKET
The mother of all markets—for residents and visitors (▷ 68)

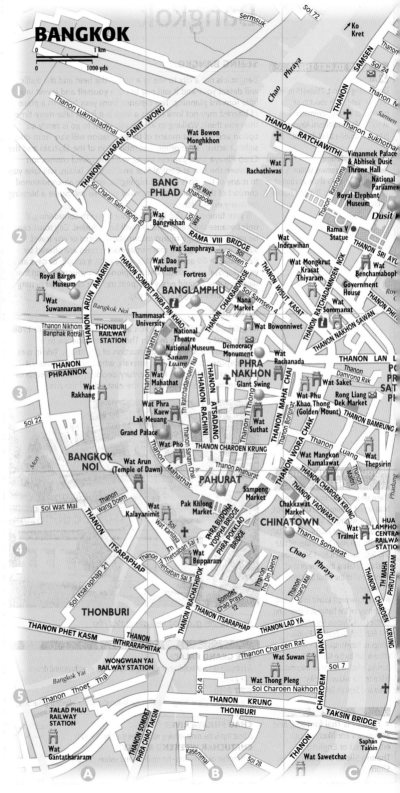

BANGKOK

0   1 km

0   1000 yds

Thanon Lukmahadthai

Thanon Charan Sanit Wong

THANON RATCHAWITHI

Chao Phraya

Sermsuk

Soi 72

Ko Kret

SAMSEN

THANON

Soi 24

Thanon N

Samsen

Thanon Sukhothai

Wat Bowon Monghkhon

BANG PHLAD

Soi Wat Khahabodi

Wat Rachathiwas

Vimanmek Palace & Abhisek Dusit Throne Hall

National Parliament

Thanon Ratchasima

Royal Elephant Museum

Soi Charan Saint Wong 40

RAMA VIII BRIDGE

Wat Bangyikhan

Wat Samphraya

Wat Dao Wadung

Fortress

BANGLAMPHU

Soi Samsen 5

Wat Indrawihan

Rama V Statue

THANON SRI AYU

Wat Mongkrut Krasat Thiyaram

Wat Benchamabophit

Dusit

Royal Barges Museum

Wat Suwannaram

THANON ARUN AMARIN

THANON SOMDET PHRA PIN KHAO

Bangkok Noi

Nana Market

Soi Samsen 4

THANON WISUT KASAT

Government House

THANON RATCHADAMNOEN NOK

Roy

THANON PHI

Thanon Nikhom Banphak Rotfai

THONBURI RAILWAY STATION

Thammasat University

National Theatre

National Museum

THANON CHAKRABONGSE

Wat Bowonniwet

Wat Sommanat

THANON NAKHON SAWAN

THANON PHRANNOK

Wat Rakhang

Sanam Luang

Wat Mahathat

Democracy Monument

PHRA NAKHON

Wat Rachanada

THANON MAHA CHAI

Wat Saket

THANON LAN L

Thanon Damrong Rak

PO PR SAT PI

Soi 22

Wat Phra Kaew

Lak Meuang

Grand Palace

THANON RACHINI

THANON ATSADANG

Giant Swing

Wat Suthat

Thanon Ti Thong

Thanon Boriphat

Wat Phu Khao Thong (Golden Mount)

Rong Liang Dek Market

THANON BAMRUNG

BANGKOK NOI

Wat Pho

Thanon Sanam Chai

THANON CHAROEN KRUNG

THANON WORA CHAK

Thanon Luang

Wat Mangkon Kamalawat

Thanon Maitri

Wat Thepsirin

Wat Arun (Temple of Dawn)

Thanon Mahathat

Thanon Phahurat

PAHURAT

Sampeng Market

THANON CHAROEN KRUNG

THANON YAOWARAT

Phadung

Soi Wat Mai

Thanon Wang Doem

Wat Kalayanimit

Wat Kanlaya

Pak Khlong Market

PHRA BUDDHA YODPHA BRIDGE

PHRA POKLAO BRIDGE

Chakkawat Market

CHINATOWN

Thanon Songwat

Wat Traimit

HUA LAMPHO CENTRA RAILWA STATIO

THONBURI

THANON ITSARAPHAP

Soi Itsaraphap 21

Thanon Thetsaban Sai 1

Thanon Thetsaban Sai 3

Wat Bupparam

THANON PRACHATHIPOK

Somdet Chao Praya 12

Thanon Tha Din Daeng

Thanon Chiang Mai

Chao Phraya

NAKON

THANON CHARGEN KRUNG

PHRUTHARAM

TH MAHA

THANON PHET KASM

THANON INTHRARAPHITAK

WONGWIAN YAI RAILWAY STATION

Bangkok Yai

THANON ITSARAPHAP

Thanon Charoen Rat

THANON LAD YA

Wat Suwan

Soi 4

Soi 7

CHAROEM NAKHON

TALAD PHLU RAILWAY STATION

Thanon Thoet Thai

Wat Gantathararam

THANON SOMDET PHRA CHAO TAKSIN

Wat Thong Pleng

Soi Charoen Nakhon

THANON KRUNG THONBURI

TAKSIN BRIDGE

Kaseml nai

Soi 28

Wat Sawetchat

Saphan Taksin

A   B   C

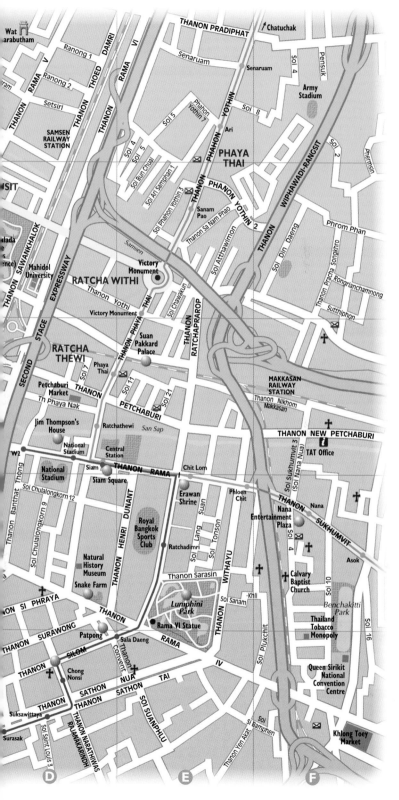

Wat ...arabutham

THANON PRADIPHAT

Chatuchak

Ranong 1

Senaruam

Ranong 2

Senaruam

PENSUK

Setsiri

SAMSEN RAILWAY STATION

Phahon Yothin 7

Soi 5

PHAYA THAI

Ari

Soi 8

Army Stadium

Phemsin

Soi 4

5

Soi Bun Chuai

Soi Ari Samphan 1

Soi Phahon Yothin 3

THANON PHANON YOTHIN

Sanam Pao

PHANON YOTHIN 2

Thanon Sa Niam Phao

Soi 2

WIPHAWADI-RANGSIT

Phrom Phan

Soi Din Daeng

Soi Atthawimon

Phrom Phan

...alada ...ence)

Mahidol University

THANON SAWANKHALOK

Samsen

Victory Monument

RATCHA WITHI

SECOND STAGE EXPRESSWAY

THANON PHAYA THAI

Thanon Yothi

Victory Monument

Soi Chawakun

THANON RATCHAPRAROP

Sutthiphon

Soi Din Daeng

Thanon Pracha Songkhro Rongrianchamnong

RATCHA THEWI

Suan Pakkard Palace

Soi 7

Phaya Thai

Soi 11

Soi 21

MAKKASAN RAILWAY STATION

Petchaburi Market

THANON

Thanon Nikhom Makkasan

Th Phaya Nak

PETCHABURI

Jim Thompson's House

Ratchathewi

San Sap

THANON NEW PETCHABURI

TAT Office

W2

National Stadium

National Stadium

Central Station

Soi Chulalongkorn 12

Siam

Siam Square

THANON RAMA I

Chit Lom

Soi Sukhumvit 3 (Soi Nana Nua)

Nana

THANON SUKHUMVIT

Soi Banthat Thong

Soi Chulalongkorn 9

THANON HENRI DUNANT

Erawan Shrine

Phloen Chit

Nana Entertainment Plaza

Soi 4

Asok

Soi 10

Royal Bangkok Sports Club

Soi Lang

Soi Tonson

Ratchadimri

Natural History Museum

Snake Farm

THANON

THANON RATCHADAMRI

Thanon Sarasin

THANON WITHAYU

Soi Sanam

Calvary Baptist Church

Benchakitti Park

Soi 16

Lumphini Park

Rama VI Statue

Patpong

THANON SURAWONG

THANON SILOM

Chong Nonsi

Sala Daeng

THANON CONVENT

RAMA IV

Soi Plukchit

Thailand Tobacco Monopoly

Queen Sirikit National Convention Centre

NON SI PHRAYA

Suksawittaya

THANON SATHON NUA

THANON SATHON TAI

SOI SUANPHLU

THANON NARATHIWAS RAJAKARINDH

Soi Saint Louis 3

Surasak

Thanon Yen Akat

Soi Si Bamphen

Khlong Toey Market

D   E   F

THE SIGHTS

The latticework veranda of the Abhisek Dusit Throne Hall

Thanon Khao San, in Banglamphu, attracts many visitors

A longtail boat on the Chao Phraya River

ABHISEK DUSIT THRONE HALL

🟥 64 C2 ✉ Thanon Ratchawithi
☎ 026 286 300 🕐 Daily 9.30–4
💷 Part of the B100 entrance ticket to Vimanmek Palace but free with a Grand Palace ticket (valid for one month)
🚢 Tha Thewet pier, then walk or take a tuk-tuk 🚇 Phaya Thai, then take a taxi 🚌 12, 18, 28, 70, 108, 510, 515
❓ Grand Palace dress code applies (▷ 84)

The building of a throne hall for King Rama V was completed in 1904, on a site that is now part of the grounds of Vimanmek Palace (▷ 80), in an architecturally playful style that continues to please the eye. Its interior has been converted into a small exhibition of arts and crafts produced in rural communities under the patronage of the queen. Displays include fine examples of *neilloware*, handmade gold and silverware, textiles from different regions, bamboo basketry, soapstone carvings of animals and people, and wood carvings.

BANGLAMPHU

🟥 64 B2 ℹ Bangkok Information Office, Thanon Phra Athit, under Pinklao Bridge (turn right on Thanon Phra Athit after exiting from boat pier); daily 9–7 🚢 Tha Phra Athit pier 🚌 3, on the boat pier side of Thanon Phra Athit (for the Northern Bus Terminal); 53, on the south side of Thanon Phra Athit (for the Grand Palace); 30 15, 47, 79, on Thanon Ratchadamnoen Klang (for Siam Square)
www.khaosanroad.com

Backpackers have traditionally headed for Banglamphu because it has the highest concentration of budget accommodation in the city. This remains the case, although the area's evolving identity is reflected in the development of mid-range hotels in the heart of what was once solely a backpackers' ghetto. The area deserves a visit, and the idea of staying here for a couple of nights should not be dismissed, because of its self-conscious image as the gathering place for voyagers in search of the Asian experience. There is a multitude of travel shops, internet access points, stands shifting bootleg CDs and DVDs and an array of places retailing hip clothing. The easiest way to reach and experience Banglamphu is by the Chao Phraya River Express boat to Tha Phra Athit. Turn left outside the boat pier and stay on this road, Thanon Phra Athit, as it curves to the right, where there is a quiet park area to your left next to the Phra Sumen Fortress. Stay on what is now Thanon Phra Sumen until you reach the busy crossroads and turn right here into Thanon Chakra Bongse. Walk along here for 300m (330 yards) until you come to Thanon Khao San on your left. This is the nucleus of Banglamphu and at night it boasts a high-pulse atmosphere fueled by bars and restaurants. Tha Phra Athit, the road outside the boat pier, has a more genial atmosphere because it is close to Thammasat University and attracts students to its funky little bars and restaurants.

CHAO PHRAYA RIVERFRONT

🟥 64 C5 (tourist boats departure point) 🚢 Chao Phraya Tourist Boats depart every 30 min 9.30–3, tel 026 236 001 ext. 100/6 💷 B75 (including guidebook)

Sometimes it is easy to forget that Bangkok was built around a river and that the Chao Phraya River is still a main artery that bisects the metropolis. The amphibious origins of the city are best appreciated by taking a boat trip on a Chao Phraya River Express boat. You will see how shops and houses were built on the banks of the river and you will still spot people's homes with boats moored alongside or hooked up by what are now their rear entrances. The famous Oriental (▷ 272), the only hotel with a boat pier named after it, was built to receive its guests from the river, and every day thousands of Bangkok residents use cross-river ferries to make their way to and from Thonburi on the west side. Beyond Banglamphu, the riverfront has its own commercial life, and barges carrying produce are constantly on the move.

Chao Phraya Tourist Boats depart from Sathorn pier, next to the Skytrain Saphan Taksin station, for a tour up the river as far as Banglamphu, stopping at 10 of the main piers along the way. There is on-board commentary. The ticket allows unlimited trips for the day so you can hop on and off and also use their regular boats. See pages 222–223 for an extended tour of the riverfront.

A gardener tidies the park at the Abhisek Dusit Throne Hall

A busy marketplace in Chinatown

Roses for sale at Chatuchak market

CHINATOWN

Chinatown is congested, noisy and smelly but a sensory and cultural experience. A guided walk (▷ 221) minimizes the chances of losing your bearings amid the warren of small streets and narrow, mostly pedestrianized alleyways.

➕ 64 C4 ✉ Streets and lanes around Thanon Ractchawong, Thanon Yaowarat and Thanon Charoen Krung ◷ Best time to visit 8–5; Sat pm especially hectic 🚇 Hua Lamphong

RATINGS	
Cultural interest	●●●●●
Specialist shopping	●●●
Walkability	●●●●

Bangkok's Chinese community used to live in Ratanakosin but in the late 18th century, when King Rama I decided to move his capital to the eastern side of the river and build his palace in Ratanakosin to escape Burmese incursions, the people who were already living there were forced to move downriver. They settled down anew and created their Chinatown situated between Thanon Charoen Krung and the river and bordered by what is now Hua Lampong railway station to the east and the Indian neighborhood of Pahurat (▷ 76) to the west.

First impressions of Chinatown suggest a consumer's nightmare, a chaotic jumble of shops and stands thrown together in a crazy fit, but despite this there is method to the madness. Merchandise is concentrated in different areas according to type. Thanon Yaowarat is full of gold dealers selling jewelry items strictly by weight and with the day's fixed price on show; Thanon Ractchawong is the place to go for household goods; while Sampeng Lane has fabric stalls at its eastern end, followed by hair and beauty items and then clothes. The near-claustrophobic Soi 16 has crammed stalls displaying strange-looking seafood and vegetables, dried fish and freshly killed chickens and ducks.

Chinatown is very much about buying and selling, and the materialistic considerations extend to the afterlife. In the vicinity of Wat Mangkon Kamalawat (▷ 82) there is a multitude of shops selling incense sticks and votive offerings for the temple. The paper replicas of consumer goods, cars, planes, mobile phones and banknotes that you see on sale here are purchased for burning at Chinese funerals as a way of ensuring that the dead have everything they might need in the next world. There is also a landmark Buddhist temple in Chinatown: Wat Traimit.

CHATUCHAK

➕ 65 F1 (off map) ✉ Corner of Thanon Kamphaeng Phet and Thanon Phahon Yothin ◷ Sat–Sun 7–6 (crowds build up from around 11am onwards) ℹ Thanon Kamphaeng Phet 2, inside Gate 1 (closer to the metro station than the Skytrain one), tel 027 246 356; Sat–Sun 8.30–4.30 🚇 Mo Chit 🚇 Chatuchak Park

Situated next to the Northern Bus Terminal, Chatuchak is the weekend home to Bangkok's largest market and a visitor attraction in its own right because of the sheer size of the place and the exuberant diversity of its many thousands of stands. It is spread out over 12ha (30 acres). Maps of the market are posted up at various points throughout the area, and they can also be picked up at the market's information office. There is a systematic and thematic arrangement of the market stands, but if you are arriving here with other people, be sure to identify a meeting point at an early stage and keep your bearings in mind as you head off into the market. There is plenty to consider buying—facilitated by ATM machines near the information office—especially in the way of art and craft items from every corner of Thailand, plus other souvenirs, and clothing and textiles. Some of the best buys include antique lacquerware, traditional musical instruments, silver jewelry and ceramics. Money-conscious Bangkok residents come here for good-value household goods, clothes, plants and pets (including illegal trade in protected species). Fatigue can kick in prematurely at Chatuchak, but there are quite a few places where you can rest up and have a snack or a meal, many of which are squarely aimed at foreign visitors than Thais.

The Democracy Monument

Worshipers at the Hindu Erawan Shrine

A store on Khlong Bangkok Noi

DEMOCRACY MONUMENT

⊞ 64 B3 ✉ Thanon Ratchadamnoen Klang 🚤 Tha Phra Athit pier, then walk through Banglamphu (▷ 67) 🚌 15, 30, 47, 79 on Thanon Ratchadamnoen Klang travel to/from Siam Square and the Skytrain station

This monument was constructed in 1939/40 to commemorate the establishment of the constitutional monarchy, its ideological foundations being the 1932 revolution. This is signified by the 75 cannons buried around it, referring to the Buddhist year 2475 (which is AD1932). The political symbolism of the monument helped make it a gathering point on October 14, 1973, when hundreds of thousands protested against the undemocratic government then ruling the country. Many hundreds were killed by the police and army on that day, and in 1992 there were further killings when protests against another set of military rulers were suppressed. Democracy Monument is a 10-minute walk from Thanon Khao San in Banglamphu (▷ 67), 5 minutes from Wat Saket (▷ 88) or 15 minutes from the National Museum (▷ 73–75). It is also close to a canal pier (▷ Khlongs, right), Tha Phanfa, from where boats plow their way to and from the Tha Asoke pier at the top of Soi 21 off Thanon Sukhumvit.

DUSIT PARK

See page 70.

ERAWAN SHRINE

⊞ 65 E4 ✉ Corner of Thanon Rama I and Thanon Ratchadamri ☎ 022 220 933 🚇 Chit Lom

The Erawan Shrine can be seen from the window of a Skytrain passing overhead, but if you are walking past it on the street,

distracted by the cacophony of traffic and the towering buildings, you could miss it altogether. Bangkok citizens regularly drop by to make offerings of garlands in the hope that their wishes will be granted. A dance troupe is usually standing by to perform at the paid behest of worshipers. This happens frequently, so if you wait a while you may see them in action. It is a surreal and incongruous sight: a Thai dance to a Hindu god in the shadow of smoked-glass edifices and the constant traffic at one of the city's busiest junctions. The shrine was created when a series of accidents accompanying the construction of a nearby hotel was attributed to resident spirits put out by the building work. To placate the spirits, this elaborate shrine was built; there were of course no further mishaps on the site.

JIM THOMPSON'S HOUSE

See page 71.

KHLONGS (CANALS)

🎫 Canal tours B1,800; contact Real Asia (www.realasia.net) or Bangkok.com (▷ 57–58; www.bangkok.com/tours)

When Rama I planned the Grand Palace in his new capital, Bangkok, he chose a site by the river for defensive reasons and constructed a series of canals that would further protect his residence. As the city grew, the river and an increasing number of canals remained the means of travel and it was only very slowly that roads and streets were laid out. For many Bangkok residents, canals (*khlongs*) remain an important means of getting around the city—some mail deliveries are still made using canal networks and for the visitor they provide eye-opening views.

Instead of the façades presented by shops, businesses and hotels, you will see the homes of ordinary citizens, and gain some insight into what lies behind the glitzy exterior that Bangkok presents.

Tours of the canals of Thonburi on the west side of the river are organized by a number of tour companies, but for many of them the canals are only part of the trip: you may find yourself spending time at a less-than-arresting snake farm and a visitor-oriented floating market. Other canal tours include trips to Wat Arun (▷ 81) and the Royal Barges Museum (▷ 77). Alternatively, a longtail boat with a driver can be rented from many of the piers on the Bangkok side of the river. For about B400 (after some bargaining) you can cruise the canals for an hour and get a better idea of why Bangkok, its houses built on rafts and moored on the water, was once called the Venice of the East.

On the Bangkok side of the river, longboats ply their way along a lengthy canal that helpfully connects the west and east sides of the city, from Tha Phanfa near Democracy Monument to a series of piers at the top ends of different *sois* that connect with Thanon Sukhumvit. Useful stops along the way include Hua Chang for Jim Thompson's House (▷ 71) and a Skytrain station. The canal piers are not always clearly marked, especially if you are on board and plonked in the middle of the seat row, so bring a map with you and loose change for the fare. You will feel like an intrepid explorer and, if sitting at the end of a row, be prepared for a slight splashing when the boat gathers speed, even if the plastic wraps are unfolded to shield passengers.

THE SIGHTS

The Suan Bua Residential Hall (above), built by Rama VI. A white rhino at Dusit Zoo (left)

RATINGS	
Cultural interest	● ● ●
Historical interest	● ●
Value for money	● ● ● ●

BASICS

⊞ 64 C2
✉ Thanon Sri Ayutthaya, Thanon Ratchasima and Thanon Ratchawithi
◷ Royal Carriage Exhibition daily 9–5; Dusit Zoo daily 8–6 (tel 022 827 111/3)
💷 Royal Carriage Exhibition free; Dusit Zoo B30
🍴 Food center

DUSIT PARK

Dusit Park, in the northeast of the city, has royal associations that give the area its grand buildings and air of studied elegance.

A statue of Rama V, the king whose interest in European culture shaped Dusit and its distinctive identity, stands in the Royal Plaza on Thanon Sri Ayutthaya. It is possible to enter Dusit from Thanon Sri Ayutthaya, but there are also entrances on Thanon Ratchasima and on Thanon Ratchawithi. Whichever way you enter Dusit, follow the signs for Vimanmek Palace and the nearby information office. A useful free map of Dusit, dispensed by the information office, will guide you around the complex of buildings and exhibition halls that make up Dusit. Vimanmek Palace (▷ 80) and the Abhisek Dusit Throne Hall (▷ 67) are the major sites, but there are other exhibitions and places of interest.

THE ROYAL CARRIAGE EXHIBITION

Close to the Thanon Ratchawithi entrance, the Royal Carriage Exhibition displays over 20 carriages used for royalty over the last hundred years. The earliest ones date from the time of Rama V and include the state coach that was made for him and used for the opening of parliamentary sessions. Many of the carriages are English in origin and the landaus and phaetons you see here look like scenery props from a Jane Austen film set. Quite different in character are the golden palanquins with their ornate roofs.

The other exhibition halls are of less interest. The Royal Paraphernalia Building houses an exhibition of paintings of various royals and assorted items used by them, like a three-tiered umbrella, sedan chairs and a portable throne.

DUSIT ZOO

The entrance to Dusit Zoo is on Thanon Ratchawithi, and children will enjoy seeing the animals and birds that live here. As well as elephants, orang-utans, rhinoceros and other large creatures, there is a reptile house. The area is well shaded and there is a lake with pedalos for rent as well as numerous places to eat and drink. On weekends the zoo can be busy and noisy with Thai families, who come here for a stroll and a meal at the food stands.

You can reach Ko Kret using a Chao Phraya River Express boat

KO KRET

➕ 64 C1 (off map) 🚤 90-min cruise from Sathorn Pier at 9am Sun with English-speaking tour guide, returning from Ko Kret at 1.50pm, tel 026 236 143 💰 B300, child (under 100cm/39in) B250

A visit to Ko Kret (also called Koh Kred) can make a welcome change from the general mayhem of central Bangkok. With an area of only 10sq km (4sq miles), this tiny island provides something of a haven for a very un-metropolitan way of life. One of its attractions is the chance to observe Mon potters at work. Mon people, whose origins are Burmese, have been here for centuries, and earthenware pottery work is their specialty. Allow yourself two hours for a leisurely walk around the island, observing the potters at work and looking at the completed pots and jars exhibited in the Ancient Mon Pottery Centre. There are no cars on the island, and although motorcycle taxis are available, it is much more relaxing just to wander along the tracks. The least troublesome way of reaching Ko Kret is by joining the Chao Phraya River Express cruise on a 40-seat boat from Sathorn Pier in downtown Bangkok on Sundays. This tour includes a visit to a Mon temple, Wat Poramaiyikawas, a lunch break near Baan Kanom, where sweet-making is observed, and a short canal ride, which takes in a small floating market. The alternative to the Sunday cruise is to take any Chao Phraya River Express boat to Nonthaburi and then charter a longtail boat out to the island, but this will be expensive unless you can make up a small group to split the cost.
Don't miss The murals in Wat Poramaiyikawas are essential viewing.

Vernacular style at Jim Thompson's House

JIM THOMPSON'S HOUSE

You'll find traditional Thai domestic architecture, a discriminating collection of fine Thai arts and antiques, and a mystery surrounding the man responsible for it all.

➕ 65 D3 ✉ Soi Kasem San 2, Thanon Rama 1 ☎ 022 167 368 🕐 Daily 9–5 💰 Adult B100, under 25 B50 🚇 National Stadium (Exit 1) 🚤 Hua Chang canal boat pier 🎫 30-min tours (up to 13 people) every 20–30 min 🍴 Café, bar and restaurant
www.jimthompson.com

RATINGS			
Cultural interest	●	●	● ●
Specialist shopping	●	●	
Value for money	●	●	● ●

Jim Thompson was an American, born in Delaware in 1906, who first came to Bangkok as an intelligence officer in World War II and returned to live there after the war. He was largely responsible for introducing Thailand's silk industry to the West and resuscitating its importance within the country. Inside the entrance, there is an exhibition on Thai textiles above the shop that sells Thai silk. Thompson built his home in Bangkok, close to where silk weavers lived, by transporting and reassembling a number of traditional teak houses from the outskirts of the city and filling them with his personal collection of Thai art. He disappeared in mysterious circumstances in 1967 after setting off for an afternoon walk while on holiday in the Cameron Highlands in Malaysia. His body was never found, and various conspiracy theories have emerged as a result. Tours of the house begin in a rice storage barn, brought from Ayutthaya and filled with Thai paintings, and proceed past a precious headless Buddha statue from the seventh century before entering the main house, where Thompson lived in the 1960s. He imported Italian marble for the floor, but nearly everything else you see—porcelain, 17th- to 19th-century cotton paintings, a 13th-century sandstone Buddha, and furniture—was bought or acquired by Thompson in Thailand. In his dining room he entertained visiting celebrities and a guestroom was built for overnight guests. Photography is not allowed inside the house. Be aware that touts linger outside and occasionally dupe people by claiming the house is shut and offering a shopping tour instead.

Don't miss Look out for the eighth-century limestone Buddha in Jim Thompson's study.

The white and gold pavilion of Lak Meuang shrine

Lumphini Park is the largest inner-city park in Bangkok

The neon lights of Soi Cowboy

LAK MEUANG

🕂 64 B3 ✉ Corner of Thanon Ratchadamoen Nai and Thanon Lak Meuang 🕘 Daily 24 hours 🚤 Tha Chang pier

Every Thai city has a foundation stone, and Bangkok's was laid down in the form of a pillar by Rama I in 1782 at the precise time of 6.54 on the morning of April 21, pinpointed by the court astrologers as the most auspicious moment for such an important event. The associated shrine is believed to facilitate people's wishes, and this brings worshipers to the spot every day; as with Erawan Shrine (▷ 69), a troupe of dancers is at hand to perform for those who want to express their gratitude for a wish granted. A visit to Lak Meuang could be taken in before or after seeing the nearby Grand Palace (▷ 84–87) or as part of a walkabout in Sanam Luang (▷ 78).

LUMPHINI PARK

🕂 65 E4 ✉ Thanon Rama IV ☎ 022 527 006 🕘 Daily 4.30am–8pm 🎟 Free 🚇 Sala Daeng 🚇 Si Lom or Lumphini 🚌 2, 4, 5, 7, 15, 47 🍴 A food court within the park opens in the evening ❓ Boat and pedalo rental B30 per half-hour

A small town in southern Nepal where the Buddha was born gives its name to this large park in downtown Bangkok. It is a vast expanse of green where the sound of traffic is rarely intrusive, encircled by concrete paths—a place to seek some respite from urban blues and enjoy some moments of peace and quiet. Rowing boats and pedalos are available for rent on both of the park's two lakes, and youngsters will enjoy feeding breadcrumbs to the resident carp. There is also a children's playground. Lumphini is a relaxing place,

dotted with picnic tables, pavilions and shaded areas so that even in the heat of the day you will see Bangkok residents whiling away some time here. As the sun begins to go down, and very early in the morning also, small battalions of both sexes take up their positions for sessions of t'ai chi. Joggers of all ages pound their way around a running track and there is an open-air gym and a public swimming pool. Between early February and the end of April, kite-flying is a popular activity in the park. The statue in the southwest corner of the park near the main entrance is of Rama VI, the king who owned the parkland before donating it to the city in 1925.

NANA ENTERTAINMENT PLAZA

🕂 65 F4 ✉ Soi 4, Thanon Sukhumvit 🚇 Phloen Chit or Nana

Along with Patpong (▷ 76) and a small area known as Soi Cowboy on Thanon Sukhumvit,

between *sois* 21 and 23, the Nana Entertainment Plaza completes an unholy trio of street locations dedicated to the darker side of Bangkok nightlife. Patpong can at least offer a bustling night market, but Nana Entertainment Plaza and Soi Cowboy have no such redeeming feature. Nana Entertainment Plaza is an open-air, neon-lit amphitheater off Soi 4 with three levels of sleazy bars fronted by bored young women whose job is to cajole passing males to step inside, buy an expensive beer and stare at girls dancing perfunctorily. Soi Cowboy consists of one street packed with about 40 bars, indistinguishable from those in Soi 4. It is named after an American, T. G. Edwards, who ran the first bar here in the early 1970s after he left the army. The women in the bars in Soi Cowboy and the Nana Entertainment Plaza are mostly prostitutes who come mainly from the poverty-stricken northeast of Thailand.

Peace and quiet in Lumphini Park

National Museum

The country's foremost museum, full of treasures from prehistoric times onward. Rock art, spectacular funeral chariots and rare Buddha images from across Asia are only some of the many rich exhibits.

Traditional figures (left and middle) at the National Museum

The oldest parts of the museum date back to the late 1700s

SEEING THE NATIONAL MUSEUM

An easy way to reach the museum from the boat pier is by walking straight ahead after disembarking, crossing the first intersection and turning left at the next intersection on to the signposted Thanon Na Phrathat. The museum is along this road on your left. A map of the galleries is issued with your ticket and, although it is not cross-referenced with the room numbers, it is not difficult to find your way about the various exhibitions. Just by the ticket office, the Gallery of Thai History provides an overview of the historical periods that are represented by the exhibits; this makes a useful start point.

HIGHLIGHTS

THE NORTHERN WING

The first room at the entrance side of the museum houses ornate funeral chariots that make the average European royal funeral carriage seem tame by comparison. The most resplendent one was built in 1799, first used for the funeral of a princess in 1923 and last wheeled out in 1985 for the queen of King Rama VII. The museum's café is next door. On the upper floor of the next gallery, in rooms eight to ten, Sukhothai (13th to 15th centuries) and Ayutthaya (14th to 18th centuries) art is displayed. The walking Buddha, an innovation of Sukhothai art with no known precedent, is represented by an unusual example in room eight; it looks fine from the front but viewed from the side lacks the graceful curves of Sukhothai art.

THE SOUTHERN WING

The Asian Art gallery goes beyond Thailand's borders for gems of Asian art with absorbing examples from early Indian culture, including a Buddha that reveals the influence of Alexander the Great and his Greek army in the northwest of India. Here too is an exquisite standing Buddha, with the thumb and first finger of the right hand touching in the Vitarkamudra manner to represent the spinning of the Wheel of Law.

Upstairs, the Dvaravati Art gallery covers the Thai Mons kingdom of the 6th to 11th centuries, influenced in its sensuality by Indian art,

RATINGS	
Cultural interest	● ● ● ● ○
Historic interest	● ● ● ●
Value for money	● ● ● ● ●

BASICS

✚ 64 B3
✉ Thanon Na Phrathat
☎ 022 241 370
🕐 Wed–Sun 9–4
💷 B40
🚢 Tha Chang pier
🚌 80, 82, 91, 503, 506, 507
🎧 English Wed and Thu 9.30; French Wed and Thu 9.30; German 1st and 2nd Wed of month 9.30
🍴 Café, and an ice-cream parlor by the ticket office
📖 Good selection of books on sale covering most aspects of Thai art

www.thailandmuseum.com
A comprehensive website covering all of the major museums in Thailand.

Topiary pruned in the shape of clouds, outside the museum (above). An image of the Buddha (opposite) on display

TIP

● The Museum café, serving simple but adequate lunchtime meals and drinks, is often more relaxing than the hectic food scene between the pier and the museum.

with some very ancient Buddha images. The centerpiece here is a Wheel of Law. The adjoining Gallery of Prehistory has a terrific example of prehistoric rock art.

BUDHHAISAWAN CHAPEL

Housed between the northern and southern wings, the central galleries begin at the museum's entrance and end with the Budhhaisawan Chapel, home to the revered Phra Sihing Buddha. There is a legend about its magical arrival from Ceylon, but experts regard it as a Ceylonese-influenced example of early Sukhothai art. There are also two other images in Thailand that claim to be the original miraculous one. What cannot be disputed is the outstanding quality of the 200-year-old murals that surround the chapel, depicting moments in the life of the Buddha.

CENTRAL PALACE BUILDINGS

The maze of galleries in the central palace buildings has a large collection of artistic and ethnographic items where visitors will discover their own favorites. The Transportation Gallery is enlivened by a selection of elephant seats and a royal palanquin that took 56 men to carry one passenger. Room 11, Old Weapons, contains an awesome model of an elephant equipped for war.

BACKGROUND

Wang Na, now the central palace buildings, was built in 1792 as a palace for the person officially designated as the heir to the throne. King Rama V abolished this position of the 'Second King' in 1887 and used the palace to house the collection of antiquities his father, Rama IV, had built up and left to him. Rama V had already established a museum of sorts in 1874 when he first made these antiquities open to the public, keeping them in a pavilion inside the Grand Palace.

A shop selling religious items in Pahurat

Bags for sale in a market in Patpong

A snake handler at the Queen Saovabha Memorial Institute

PAHURAT

64 B4 Thanon Chakrawat and Thanon Pahahurat Tha Saphan Phut pier 25, 40 (to/from Thanon Sukhumvit and Siam Square) Grand Palace dress code applies (▷ 84)

The west side of Chinatown comes to an end at Khlong Ong Ang, and on the other side of the canal lies the Indian quarter of Pahurat, separating the old city of Ratanakosin from Chinatown. An urban ramble in Pahurat is not as rewarding as a stroll through the streets of Chinatown, but it does have a distinct ethnic identity and a visit here could be enjoyably combined with a meal at one of the Indian restaurants (▷ 242). There are many shops retailing fabrics and clothes, an above-average number of shops selling guns, and along Thanon Pahurat the Old Siam Plaza department store is worth browsing.

PATPONG

65 D4 Patpong 1 and Patpong 2 Sala Daeng Si Lom

Patpong 1 and 2, two small streets that run off Thanon Silom, gave their name to a red-light area of Bangkok that began attracting such a multitude of visitors, many of them curious peeping toms, that street traders moved in and turned Patpong 1 into a thriving night market for fake designer watches, branded clothes, designer bags and the like. By day, Patpong is a desultory place of no interest, but every night it bustles with human traffic. The go-go bars are still there, a legacy of the Vietnam War, when off-duty American servicemen used Bangkok as a recreation center, and some very sleazy joints operate in the vicinity. Nowadays, the majority of people come to Patpong to shop (▷ 184–186),

but as street markets go the place is seriously overrated as there are no bargains to be had and time-consuming bargaining is necessary before reasonable prices come into play. Having said that, Patpong is unlikely to lose its popularity and you may well find yourself coming here just to see what all the hype is about.

QUEEN SAOVABHA MEMORIAL INSTITUTE (SNAKE FARM)

65 D4 Corner of Thanon Rama IV and Thanon Henri Dunant 022 520 161 Snake milking sessions Mon–Fri 10.30 and 2, Sat–Sun 10.30 B70 Sala Daeng Sam Yan

Though popularly known as the Snake Farm, its official title is a reminder that this is a professional herpetological institute. It was founded in the 1920s as the Pasteur Institute, and the Thai Red Cross now runs the place. It came up with the clever idea of attracting public interest in snakes by organizing shows around the milking of snakes. The sessions begin with a half-hour slide show presenting practical information about how to deal with a snake bite, followed by a live demonstration involving some highly venomous creatures. The venom that is milked from the snakes is used in the production of serum for use across Thailand. Children love the Snake Farm, but bring them in time to be at the front of the audience.

Sign for the Royal Elephant Museum

ROYAL BARGES MUSEUM

See page 77.

ROYAL ELEPHANT MUSEUM

64 C2 Thanon Ratchawithi 026 286 300 Daily 8.30–4 Price included in the entry to Vimanmek Palace (▷ 80) Tha Thewet pier Phaya Thai, then a taxi 10, 56, 70, 72, 510

Alongside Vimanmek Palace, the two stables that once provided a home for the royal white elephants now make up a museum devoted to the role of elephants in Thailand's history and society. There are displays of elephant equipment and information on the contribution elephants have made to the country's economy and folklore. The importance of white elephants is explained: The animals are albinos (more brown than white) whose rarity made them sacred and, de facto, the personal property of the king. When a white elephant was spotted in the wild, and its authenticity accredited by a team of experts, an elaborate ceremony accompanied its presentation to the king prior to it being received into the royal stables. Photographs of the proceedings, which no longer take place, are on show in the museum, but the one white elephant that is still housed in Dusit is not shown to the public.

THE ROYAL ELEPHANT NATIONAL MUSEUM

The instantly recognizable Suphannahongsa *(above) features a prow 15ft (5m) high*

ROYAL BARGES MUSEUM

Take a trip across the Chao Phraya River to view a visually stunning collection of barges. Elaborately carved and exquisitely decorated, these are the Rolls Royces of the marine world.

When Thai kings made a journey along the Chao Phraya River, they impressed and dazzled their subjects by traveling in specially crafted and brightly decorated barges. They plowed through the water in as stately a manner as the rhythmic rowing of up to 50 oarsmen could make possible. Royal processions occurred annually until the late 1960s, and there are still odd occasions when the barges in this museum are put to use. Just seeing them in their dignified boatyard will give you a good idea of how spectacular a show these gilded vessels must make when decked out with uniformed crews and carrying a band of choral singers. The design of the barges is based on representations of those used when Ayutthaya was the capital; they were first built for Rama I (1782–1809), and restored and partly rebuilt by Rama VI in the early part of the 20th century.

THE *SUPHANNAHONGSA*

The signature barge, extravagantly and elegantly decorated, is the *Suphannahongsa*, first winced out in 1911 after being carved from one piece of teakwood. It is nearly 50m (164ft) in length and the golden canopy makes it obvious where the king and queen had their seats. The gleaming prow is ornately decorated and ends in the shape of a mythical bird-like creature associated with Brahma, the Hindu god. The prow on the *Anantainagaraj*, the barge that comes closest in size and magnificence to the *Suphannahongsa*, is equally distinctive, with its traditional multi-headed serpent, the *naga*. A new royal barge was built for the king's golden jubilee celebrations in 1996 and is also in the museum.

SEEING THE ROYAL BARGES MUSEUM

Many of the city's canal tours (▷ 69) include a visit to the Royal Barges Museum, but it is easy to get there by yourself from the Bangkok side of the river by boat. Traveling by bus is also straightforward because you hop off at the first stop over the Pinklao Bridge.

RATINGS	
Cultural interest	●●●○
Historic interest	●●●○
Value for money	●●●○

BASICS

✚ 64 A2
✉ Khlong Bangkok Noi
☎ 024 240 004
◷ Daily 9–5
💵 B30
🚤 Tha Phra Pinklao pier, or a cross-ferry boat from Tha Phra Athit pier to Tha Phra Pinklao; either way, walk up the road from the boat pier and take the first left, signposted Soi Wat Duistaram, and follow the signs to the museum
🚌 3, 7, 9, 11, 503, 507, 509, 511

The prow of the Anantainagaraj

Kite-flying at Sanam Luang

Siam Square has the best shops and entertainment venues

The financial and entertainment district of Silom Road

THE SIGHTS

SANAM LUANG

✚ 64 B3 ✉ Thanon Ratchadamoen Nai ⏰ Daily 7am–8pm 🚤 Tha Phra pier 🚇 Phaya Thai, then a taxi 🚌 3, 6, 7, 8, 9, 12, 25, 30, 32, 47, 53

A large green area was created close to the Grand Palace for the purpose of conducting royal cremation ceremonies. This is still the case—the last such occasion was in 1996 for the mother of the present king—and the green is also used for the annual Plowing Ceremony in May. The actual day of the Plowing Ceremony, determined by astrologists for its auspiciousness for farmers to set about a new rice season, attracts large crowds that come to watch the symbolic plowing by a team of oxen and the sprinkling of blessed rice. The rest of the year Sanam Luang is frequented by city dwellers who enjoy the open space and the cityscape of buildings that lend grandeur to the location. Weekends are a good time to enjoy the social side of Sanam Luang, particularly between late February and the end of April, when kite-flying is popular and you can buy kites from vendors. During the evenings, hawkers use the adjoining street space to peddle peculiar concoctions that promise cures for ailments. The statue at the northern end of the green is the Hindu god Mae Thorani, marking the spot of an ancient temple.

SIAM SQUARE

✚ 65 D3 ✉ Thanon Rama I 🚇 Siam 🚌 15, 47, 79 (for Banglamphu); 25 (for Eastern Bus Terminal and Chinatown); 29 (Victory Monument); 8, 508 (for Grand Palace, Sukhumvit)

There is no square as such, but the concentration of interlocking *sois* and the swanky buildings on one side of Thanon Rama I classify themselves as Siam Square. The Siam Skytrain station, where the two train lines meet, reinforces this sense of being at the heart of the metropolis. A covered walkway from the station leads westwards to the MBK Center (▷ 185), a major shopping destination, while a longer walk in the other direction leads to the spacious interchange of Thanon Rama I and Thanon Ratchadamri. This junction looks more like the heart of the city than Siam Square, but appearances are deceptive: Central World Plaza is disappointing, and it is back at Siam Square where you will find the best mix of shops and entertainment outlets. At street level you can escape the ubiquitous and oppressive awareness of the Skytrain's concrete in the Siam Center, with plenty of inexpensive clothes shops, and the more swish Siam Discovery Center—where each of the six stories has a theme of sorts and where, on the top level, you'll find the most exclusive cineplex in Asia (▷ 186). The other side of Thanon Rama I is a grid of connected streets, popular as a teenagers' hangout, with small shops, bars and restaurants and the Novotel hotel (▷ 272).

SUAN PAKKARD PALACE

See page 79.

THANON SILOM

✚ 65 D5 ✉ Thanon Silom 🚤 Tha Sathon pier 🚇 Saphan Taksin (for the Chao Phraya River Express); Chong Nonsi (the middle of Silom Road); Sala Daeng (top end of Silom Road) 🚇 Si Lom (top end of Silom Road)

Running from near the Chao Phraya River to its junction with Thanon Rama IV and Lumphini Park (▷ 72), Silom Road (Thanon Silom), along with the *sois* running off it, is a hive of activity day and night. The lower end has a number of airline offices, mid-range places to stay, shops and restaurants, including the Silom Village Trade Center (▷ 183), and the area between the river and the Skytrain at Chong Nonsi makes for a nice stroll. At a midway point along this stretch of the road, on your left if walking down from Chong Nonsi, is the Sri Mariamman Hindu temple. The exterior, with its vibrant display of Hindu deities, makes it hard to miss. There is usually a stall outside selling garlands for devotees who come here regularly to worship, especially around midday. The *sois* at the other end of Silom Road are home to Patpong (▷ 76) and a busy commercial and entertainment district where a number of top-notch hotels boast their own shopping arcades. Here, too, is the Silom Complex department store, as well as others in the immediate vicinity (Central Department Store, Robinson Department Store and Thaniya Plaza). The *sois* numbered 2 to 8 connect this end of Silom Road with Thanon Surawong; they are packed with nightspots that range from the seedy to the salubrious.

The benevolent face of a statue, Wat Arun

A stained-glass window at Wat Benchamabophit

VIMANMEK PALACE

See page 80.

WAT ARUN

See page 81.

WAT BENCHAMABOPHIT

🔲 64 C2 ✉ Thanon Sri Ayutthaya and Thanon Rama V ◷ Daily 7–5 💵 B20 🚢 Tha Thewet pier, then walk; or walk from the zoo (▷ 70) or from Vimanmek Palace (▷ 80) 🚇 Phaya Thai, then take a taxi 🚌 10, 56, 70, 72, 510

Rama V commissioned a close relation, the architect Prince Naris, for the building of this temple, completed in 1911. It is a distinctive structure because of the way it blends innovative design ideas, borrowing elements of European architecture with traditional Thai concepts. The building material is white Carrara marble, hence the "White Marble" epithet it has acquired, and you will also discover stained-glass windows that would not be out of place in an English country church were it not for the Asian mythological scenes they depict. The ashes of Rama V are inside the temple, as is a well-executed copy of the very holy Phra Buddha Chinnarat image in Phitsanulok (▷ 145). In a courtyard at the back of the temple is a large collection of Buddha images from different parts of the country showing the various ways in which the Buddha has been depicted over the ages. For a real-life display of Buddhism in action arrive at Wat Benchamabophit early in the morning, between 6.30 and 7, when monks from the temple line up on Nakorn Pathom (which runs parallel with Thanon Rama V) to receive alms from citizens of the city. It is a sight that not many visitors have ever experienced.

The Lacquer Pavilion, built on stilts

SUAN PAKKARD PALACE

Traditional Thai houses filled with fine art and set in a restful garden with an exquisite Lacquer Pavilion.

🔲 65 E3 ✉ 352–354 Thanon Sri Ayutthaya ☎ 022 454 934 ◷ Daily 9–4 💵 B100 🚇 Phaya Thai 🚌 14, 18, 38, 72, 74, 77, 204 🎧 Optional guided tours in English www.suanpakkad.com

RATINGS	
Cultural interest	●●●○
Historical interest	●●○○
Value for money	●●●●○

The name Suan Pakkard, which translates as "cabbage farm," serves as a reminder of the homely origins of the superb landscaped garden around this royal palace. A royal couple, now deceased, had a number of old houses moved here from northern Thailand to serve as their residence in the early 1950s, and they guided the transformation of the original cabbage patch into the marvelous garden you see today. They also built up a collection of art and objects, and these now make up the content of the houses.

In the modern Chumbhot–Pantip Centre of Arts building there are exhibits of painted pottery, spearheads, axes and other finds from the Bronze Age site of Ban Chiang (▷ 90). There are also first-rate examples of Khmer art from the seventh century onwards and figures of the Buddha dating from the 14th century. A garden footbridge leads across to two houses where the exhibits include a howdah (a seat that is placed on the back of an elephant or camel), betel nut boxes, musical instruments and European drawings from the Renaissance period.

The Lacquer Pavilion, serenely posed on stilts, dates back to the mid-17th century and was originally part of a temple in the region of Ayutthaya. It was reassembled here in 1959 and, more recently, renovated to its present condition. Inside, the walls are filled with delicate murals of gold and black lacquer narrating the life of the Buddha and depicting scenes from the *Ramayana*. The paneled pictures are worth examining close up because of the wealth of detail they contain and, in the case of some of the *Ramayana* panels, the glimpses of social life of the period they portray. Look for the depiction of European gentlemen riding horses, reflecting the presence of Western traders and suggesting that the work was completed before the fall of Ayutthaya in 1767.

Don't miss The remarkable bronze jewelry and ceramics from Ban Chiang are particularly rare.

THE SIGHTS

Vimanmek Palace (above, and detail, left) is the largest golden teak building in the world

RATINGS

Cultural interest	◕ ◕ ◕ ○
Historic interest	◕ ◕ ◕ ○
Value for money	◕ ◕ ◕ ◕

BASICS

✚ 64 C2
✉ Thanon Ratchawithi
☎ 026 286 300 ext 5120–5121
◷ Daily 9.30–4
💷 B100, or free with Grand Palace ticket (valid for one month)
☛ Free guided tours are obligatory and take place every half-hour (first tour at 9.45, last at 3.15)
🚢 Tha Thewet pier
🚇 Phaya Thai, then take a taxi
🚌 10, 56, 70, 72, 510
❓ Grand Palace dress code applies (▷ 84)

www.vimanmek.com
Attractive, easy-to-use website.

TIP

● Time your visit to take in the traditional Thai dance show at 10.30am and 2pm each day.

VIMANMEK PALACE

Graceful and airy, this well-crafted house was designed on a grand scale, amid landscaped gardens, and conveys a calm and cultured feel that would have pleased its royal patron.

HISTORY

Vimanmek Palace lies in the Dusit Park area of the city (▷ 70), away to the north of the Grand Palace quarter of Ratanakosin, and the European tone of the district seems quite in fitting with the character of this teakwood mansion. It was erected here in 1901 by Rama V, who visited Europe on two occasions and employed a large retinue of foreign advisers to further his ambitious plans to modernize the country and add some sophistication to Siam's image in the world. Vimanmek Palace was first built on Ko Si Chang as part of a royal resort but was dismantled and rebuilt in Dusit, where it blends in very nicely with the manicured lawns and lotus ponds. It became a favorite getaway for Rama V, who lived here for extended periods of time until 1906, and royals continued to use the place until 1935. It was restored and opened as a museum in 1982 as part of Bangkok's bicentennial celebrations.

Despite aspects of the exterior and interior that are reminiscent of Victorian architecture and design, tried and tested Thai methods were used in its construction. The three stories are built of teak, naturally resistant to tropical heat, and the task of rebuilding was made easier by the fact that nails had not been used in its original construction.

GUIDED TOURS

There are over 80 rooms in the mansion and the guided tour takes you through 30 of them, drawing attention to some of the items that now fill them. Ironically, while the American Jim Thompson (▷ 71) wanted to furnish his Bangkok house with Thai arts and crafts, Rama V, king of Thailand, was keen to add items of European provenance to his collection. The private apartments have been carefully restored to show some of the modern inventions brought to the country by the king. His bathroom was very modern at the time, the first one to have a shower, and innovative for being situated inside and not outside the house.

The rooftops of Wat Arun (above and right)

WAT ARUN

This towering temple on the cityscape offers views across the river and images from Khmer mythology; it's an architectural marvel.

Wat Arun is in Thonburi, on the west side of the Chao Phraya River, where King Taksin first set up his new capital in 1768. It is also called the Temple of Dawn because this was the time of day when King Taksin selected the spot for a new palace. There was already a temple on the site that dated back to the 17th century, and it was here that Taksin housed the Emerald Buddha until his successor Rama I moved it across to Wat Phra Kaew. Rama II and Rama III rebuilt and enlarged Wat Arun, creating the monumental structure that you see today.

PILES OF PORCELAIN

When you first see Wat Arun from the river it is the elongated *prang* (tower) that first strikes you. Rising higher than any other *prang* in the city, its soaring shape has helped make it a familiar logo for Bangkok's Thai identity. The chief *prang* is bordered by four smaller ones and they all glitter and gleam in the sunshine. It is only when you get closer that you realize that the sparkling effect is caused by the light catching countless thousands of pieces of porcelain that have been embedded into the stucco and painstakingly patterned to represent a floral display. The porcelain was provided by local people, pleased to contribute to the building of a shrine, and came in bulk form from merchant ships from China that used discarded porcelain as ballast.

KINARI, *YAKSI* AND *MONDOPS*

The temple design as a whole is a representation of Mount Meru, and includes individual figures of various mythical life forms from Khmer legends. It is not difficult to identify the half-human and half-bird creatures called *kinari* and the devilish-looking characters that are *yaksa* (demons). The four square-shaped structures on the first terrace are *mondops*; they house statues of the Buddha in different postures. On the second terrace are four images of the Hindu god Indra and, in the niches of the smaller *prangs*, statues of Phra Pai, the god of the wind.

RATINGS	
Cultural interest	● ● ● ● ○
Historic interest	● ● ● ○
Photo stops	● ● ● ○

BASICS

➕ 64 A4
✉ Thanon Arun Amarin
☎ 024 663 167
🕐 Daily 7–10
🖐 Free
⛴ Tha Thien pier, then a cross-river ferry
❓ River tours (▷ 67) invariably include a visit to Wat Arun

TIP

● Boat tours restrict your time at Wat Arun but the cross-river ferries are frequent and give you more freedom.

People gather around the Lucky Sara Tree at Wat Mahathat

Wat Mangkon Kamalawat in Chinatown

Visitors at Wat Rachanada

WAT MAHATHAT

✚ 64 B3 ✉ Thanon Mahathat ☎ 026 235 685 (026 235 685 for meditation classes) ⏰ Daily 7–8 ⛴ Tha Chang pier 🚌 3, 6, 8, 12, 39, 508, 512 www.mcu.ac.th

In an area where the Grand Palace acts like a magnet for purposeful visitors and pilgrims, Wat Mahathat goes about its own business. The temple itself, occupying a cramped space, is fairly undistinguished, but the monastery here dates back to the early 18th century and is older than the city around it. The monks you see around the place belong to a Buddhist university that is attached to Wat Mahathat. Also established here is a respected meditation center that conducts courses in English. Across the road from the main entrance on Thanon Maharat there is a religious amulet market that is always busy.

WAT MANGKON KAMALAWAT

✚ 64 C4 ✉ Thanon Charoen Krung ⏰ Daily 7–6 ⛴ Ratchawongse pier, then walk 🚇 Hua Lamphong, then a taxi ride or 25-min walk ❷ Photography is not allowed inside the temple

This busy temple can be taken in while exploring Chinatown on foot (▷ 221), but it justifies a journey on its own merit. Also known as Wat Leng Nee Yee, this is the most popular temple for Bangkok's Chinese, and the place is never empty. Arrive here on a Saturday afternoon and the atmosphere is like a busy beehive, with some devotees departing after making their offerings of incense and flowers and others just arriving to do the same. Although this is a Buddhist temple, some of the deities represented in statues vividly painted in shades of red and yellow are more evocative of a

Chinese Taoist temple. So too is the behavior of those devotees, whom you may see kneeling to rattle hollow tubes of bamboo. When chance rolls out a piece of paper, it is studied for what it portends.

As you enter the temple there are four gigantic statues of sagacious-looking bearded men, two on each side of the passageway, looking down on you. Each is holding a different object—a pagoda, the head of a snake, a mandolin and a parasol. Beyond them lies the main chapel, a large, airy space filled with images of large and small Buddhas and, hanging from the ceiling, attractive lanterns that subdue the amount of light and help create a hushed and devotional atmosphere. Again, the mixture of gold and deep reds is redolent of a Chinese place of worship. Sometimes, the main chamber is filled with the sound of group chanting as a choir of Buddhists dressed all in white read from their hymn sheets.

WAT PHO

See page 83.

WAT PHRA KAEW AND THE GRAND PALACE

See pages 84–87.

WAT RACHANADA

✚ 64 B3 ✉ Corner of Thanon Maha Chai and Thanon Ratchadamnoen Klang ⏰ Daily 9–5 ⛴ Tha Phra Athit pier, then walk through Banglamphu (▷ 67) to Democracy Monument; Tha Phanfa canal boat pier (▷ 69) 🚌 15, 30, 47, 79 on Thanon Ratchadamnoen Klang travel to/from Siam Square and the Skytrain station

From Democracy Monument, walk along Thanon Ratchadamnoen Klang to the large junction where The Queen's Gallery stands and cross

where pictures of the king decorate the roadway. The grouping of edifices across the road is called Wat Rachanada (variant spellings are common). To reach the entrance to the most peculiar of these religious buildings walk down Thanon Mala Chai for 100m/110 yards (the sign on the corner points to Wat Ratchanatdaran). You enter a courtyard/parking area; the pink-tone structure in front with the black spires is Loh Prasat (the 'Iron Monastery'). There are 37 spires, representing the number of stages on the journey to enlightenment. Having deposited your footwear, you enter a strange interior—a cross between a scene from a Kafka novel and something from Gormenghast—where narrow passageways criss-cross in every direction and tiny meditation cells remain eerily empty. A tiring climb up a spiral staircase eventually brings you to the top level (save your legs if you're going on to see nearby Wat Saket—the views from there are far better). When leaving through the courtyard, it is worth heading over to your right for an indoor amulet market, the sign overhead identifying it as the temple's Buddha Center. It is packed with stalls and shops selling religious paraphernalia, with the tiniest Buddha image alongside ponderously large and hideously painted statuettes of assorted Hindu deities.

Worshipers at Wat Mangkon Kamalawat

The stark, white walls of Wat Pho (above). A saffron-robed monk crosses the courtyard (right)

WAT PHO

See a gigantic reclining Buddha in shining gold, with feet decorated with mother-of-pearl, a large *bot* elegantly decorated with artwork and assorted statuary and *chedis*, all set in a working temple.

The gilded reclining Buddha is what everyone comes to see in Wat Pho, known also as Wat Phra Chetuphon since Rama I gave it this name at the beginning of the 19th century. The temple is far older than this, dating back to well before Bangkok became the capital, and it also functions as a center for the study and teaching of traditional medicine. Thai massage training courses are conducted and day visitors to the temple can experience for themselves an invigorating massage. There are *chedis* all around the temple grounds but the ones that will catch your eye are the four largest ones, clad in garish ceramic tiles. Two of them contain the remains of Rama III and Rama IV.

THE RECLINING BUDDHA
There are various buildings and *chedis* (monuments housing a Buddhist relic) inside the temple compound, and the chapel with the reclining Buddha is only one of them: follow the crowds and it cannot be missed. The Buddha is 45m (148ft) in length—behind the gold leaf are plain old bricks and plaster—and because of the size of the chapel it is impossible to stand far enough back to take in the figure as a whole. So what you experience, instead, as you file past, is an intense close-up of a sublimely happy Buddha with inordinately long earlobes about to enter the state of nirvana. The soles of the feet are intricately inlaid with mother-of-pearl depicting the 108 *lakshanas*, the auspicious signs of the Buddha.

THE *BOT*
The *bot*, or *ubosot* (main temple chapel), is on the eastern side and accessed from the outside by the Soi Chetuphon entrance, although you can also get there from the Reclining Buddha inside the temple. It is reached via galleries of nearly 400 assorted Buddha images and entered by teak doors superbly decorated with scenes from the *Ramayana*. The interior, lavishly adorned with pillars and an ebulliently decorated ceiling, holds the remains of Rama I.

RATINGS
Cultural interest	●●●●●
Historic interest	●●●●
Value for money	●●●●●

BASICS
✚ 64 B3
✉ Entrances on Thanon Thai Wang and Soi Chetuphon
☎ 022 219 911
🕐 Daily 8–6
💵 B20; foot massages B300 per hour
🚤 Tha Tien pier, then turn right onto Thanon Maharat and then left for Soi Chetuphon; Thanon Thai Wang is straight on from the pier
🚌 1, 6, 7, 8, 12, 44, 508, 512
👤 Guides can be hired inside the temple for B200 for two people

www.watpho.com
Very thorough website, packed with information.

TIP
● If you use the Soi Chetuphon entrance you will avoid the tour groups congregating around the main entrance on Thanon Thai Wang.

Wat Phra Kaew and the Grand Palace

The royal temple of Phra Kaew and the Grand Palace should not be missed.

Mural at Wat Phra Kaew

The gleaming exterior of the Grand Palace

The shrine in the temple of Wat Phra Kaew

RATINGS

Cultural interest	●●●●●
Historic interest	●●●●
Value for money	●●●●

BASICS

✚ 64 B3

✉ Thanon Na Phra Lan

☎ 026 235 500

🕐 Daily 8.30–3.30

💷 B250 for Grand Palace and the buildings open to the public inside, including Wat Phra Kaew

🚌 4 from Siam Square

🚢 Tha Chang pier

🎫 Free English-language tours from 10 onwards; 1-hour personal audioguide B200

❓ Dress code: no T-shirts or sleeveless vests, shorts, short skirts, flip-flops or slip-on sandals; shoes and some allowable garments are available for day use if ID or a deposit is left

TIP

● Ignore anyone around the Grand Palace who, telling you that it is closed for the day, offers what will turn out to be a shopping tour of the city.

SEEING WAT PHRA KAEW AND THE GRAND PALACE

Highly theatrical in appearance, these buildings are frequented by Thai pilgrims as well as sightseers. The dress code for all visitors signifies the respect and reverence accorded this sacred site. You will never be alone on your visit: tour groups mill around the entrance and ticket office. There is only one gated entrance to the palace and the driveway leads to the ticket office. The psychedelic tones and the sheer variety of shimmering shapes will overwhelm you at first, but the map that comes with the ticket can help guide your walk. There are separate entrances for Wat Phra Kaew, Dusit Maha Prasat and the museum, but most of your time is likely to be spent looking around the temple. The guided tours are a useful way to glean information about what you see because it can be difficult to make sense of it all amid the bewildering array of stupas, mosaics, glittering roof tiles, fabulous images, statues, pillars and pediments that make up the palace and Wat Phra Kaew.

HIGHLIGHTS

ENTERING WAT PHRA KAEW

The temple, Thailand's major Buddhist site, is home to the venerated Emerald Buddha. The *bot* (chapel) that houses the Buddha image is therefore suitably guarded by a series of garishly painted demons. You will be confronted by these devilish-looking figures immediately after entering the temple. There are more statues and structures to contemplate outside the *bot* itself, including a lotus-topped pillar which was a gift to the king by the city's Chinese.

THE EMERALD BUDDHA

The size of the tiny image of the Buddha bears no relation to the enormous reverence in which it is held. Credited with miraculous powers, it was discovered by accident inside a *chedi* (monument housing a Buddhist relic) in the 15th century and kept in Laos for 200 years. The prince who would become Rama I expropriated it in 1779 and constituted it as the symbolic and religious heart of his new capital and the nation.

A shimmering gold mural

UPPER TERRACE

On the upper terrace there stands the glamorous Prasat Phra Thep Bidorn. It is known as the Royal Panetheon because inside, which is rarely open to the public, there are life-size statues of all the kings since Rama I established Bangkok as the capital. The outside is a blaze of different hues, with floral patterns enlivening the gables, a green *prang* (tower) and tiles of shining blue and red. A row of eight *prangs* makes up the east side of the temple. The other buildings visible from the terrace are not open to the public: the royal mausoleum, a library and a *mondop* (a square-shaped building housing a sacred object), as well as a scale model of Angkor Wat, a renowned temple in Cambodia that was under Thai rule in the mid-19th century. The building of the model was commissioned at that time, when Rama IV was king.

THE *RAMAYANA* MURALS

Shaded in arcades along the walls, the paneled murals date back to the late 18th century, but all of them have been repainted at various times over the years. They tell the story of Rama and his wife Sita, an epic adventure story that originated in India and spread into other parts of Asia under the influence of Hinduism. The narrative begins on the side where the palace entrance is situated, with a panel depicting the baby Sita floating down a stream, Moses-like, and being discovered by a stranger. Without a guide it is impossible to follow the whole story (which ends happily), but the intricacy and fine detail of the panels can be appreciated in isolation.

DUSIT MAHA PRASAT

This building, outside Wat Phra Kaew and one of the oldest of all in the Grand Palace, was built as an audience hall and is now used to hold the corpse of a royal before the cremation ceremony. The tiered roof is eye-catching, with its gold, green and red tiles. It's crowned by a golden spire and each part of the stepped roof is decorated with stylized birds *(chofas)*.

MORE TO SEE

WAT PHRA KAEW MUSEUM

✉ Thanon Na Phra Lan

🕐 Daily 8.30–3.30

Close to the Dusit Maha Prasat, the museum collection consists of objects relating to the Emerald Buddha and the restoration of the palace in 1982. The scale models of the Grand Palace show it has developed over the years.

The Grand Palace by night (above). The temple is well guarded (left and opposite)

CHAKRI MAHA PRASAT

Another part of the Grand Palace, recognizable by the portrait of Rama V over the entrance, is a large hall, the Chakri Maha Prasat, that is not open to the public except for a small and less-than-arresting weapons museum occupying part of the ground floor. The unusual exterior is what catches the eye. It was designed by an English architect in 1882, which explains the neoclassical features that reach as far as the roof. The story goes that members of the monarch's family persuaded him to have traditional Thai spires added so as to redeem the structure's foreignness; hence the epithet 'the *farang* with a Thai crown' that has been given to the building.

BACKGROUND

After the fall of Ayutthaya, Rama I decided to move across Chao Phraya River from the site of the first palace on the west side. He wanted a base that would be more able to withstand an attack, and work began in Ratanakosin constructing the Grand Palace with its own temple. An open field, Sanam Luang, was created in front of the palace as a royal cremation site. The palace is still an official residence for the royals and although their day-to-day home has moved to Dusit, a number of buildings inside the palace remain in use and are closed to the public. On certain occasions, like the ordination or death of a royal, important ceremonial events take place here.

The Phu Khao Thong (Golden Mount) at Wat Saket

A row of identical gold Buddhas housed in a covered gallery in Wat Suthat

WAT SAKET

✚ 64 C3 ✉ Thanon Boriphat ☎ 022 237 430 🕐 Daily 7.30–5.30 🚶 Free to climb the hill. B20 to enter the temple 🚢 Tha Phanfa canal boat pier (▷ 69)

From Wat Rachanada walk back to the junction of Thanon Maha Chai and Thanon Ratchadamnoen Klang and turn to your right for Wat Saket and the Golden Mount. The route is signposted. At the Tha Phanfa canal boat pier you turn right and the entrance is on your left. Wat Saket was built outside the city walls by Rama I, and it served as a crematorium before Rama III decided to build a *chedi* (monument housing a Buddhist relic) here. This collapsed before completion and it was left to Rama V to finish the project with the shining monument you see today. It is a short but steep climb to the top of the 80m-high (262ft) hill, passing evidence of the collapse, the retaining walls of concrete built in the 1940s and an information panel about the *chedi*. From the spacious summit you are rewarded with fine views over the city. You can enter the *chedi* at the top of the hill. The relics are said to be some of the Buddha's teeth discovered in an urn in 1899, and the interior murals are of some interest, though you may spend longer on the open terrace identifying landmark buildings on the skyline. If you have just come from Wat Rachanada, or are going there next, the aerial view from here helps make sense of its layout.

WAT SUTHAT AND THE GIANT SWING

✚ 64 B3 ✉ Corner of Thanon Ti Thong and Thanon Bamrung Muang ☎ 022 226 935 🕐 Daily 9–9 🚶 B20 🚌 15, 30, 47, 79

Within walking distance of Democracy Monument (▷ 69)

and Wat Saket (▷ left), the building of Wat Suthat, an archetypal Thai temple, was started in the late 18th century under Rama I but not completed until Rama III was on the throne. The lavish endowments that three monarchs could afford show themselves in the grand style of the main chapel, the *viharn*, which is exceptionally tall in order to accommodate its 8m-high (26ft) Buddha figure. This 14th-century Buddha was brought to Wat Suthat by river from Sukhothai, a journey of over 400km (248 miles), signifying its importance as an object of reverence. It sits on a gleaming dais in the aisled interior, and all around it are impressive paintings depicting innumerable incarnations of the Buddha. The courtyard area outside the *viharn* is filled with a variety of statues of Chinese sages and not-so-sagacious Western sailors.

Lofty teak posts, painted a bright red, are all that remain of Sao Ching Cha, the Giant Swing. In an annual Brahmin ceremony, teams of men would stand on the now-missing seat, which was nothing more than an open board, and swing dangerously high in order to try and catch between their teeth bags of silver coins that hung from a post nearly 25m (82ft) in height. Accidents were common, sometimes fatal, and the event was banned in 1932.

Between Wat Suthat and the Giant Swing, especially along Thanon Bamrung Muang, every other shop is selling Buddhist-related merchandise. You will see monks attentively window-shopping as well as secular Buddhists looking for offerings and accoutrements for their shrine at home.

Don't miss Check out the elaborate carvings on the colossal doors of Wat Suthat.

WAT TRAIMIT

✚ 64 C4 ✉ Thanon Traimit, at the junction of Thanon Yaowarat and Thanon Charoen Krung ☎ 026 231 235/40 🕐 Daily 9–5 🚉 Hua Lamphong 🚌 25, 53

With a Buddha figure over 3m (10ft) high and made of solid gold, this temple is bound to attract visitors in large numbers—hence the signs warning of the danger of pickpockets. The Buddha is an example of Sukhothai art and was probably cast in the 13th century, though it was not until 1955, when a Buddha in stucco was being moved, that it saw the light of day. The stucco figure was accidentally damaged, something shining was detected below the surface and then all was revealed. It seems likely that the plaster cover was a ruse to deceive robbers or the invading Burmese during the Ayutthaya period. The security in its present location seems remarkably lax for an object of such huge value, and it is open to view in a very ordinary building. Although the Buddha's face is not especially serene, there is a viscous quality about the gold surface that makes it seem very special.

Don't miss Try to time your visit to coincide with the fair at Wat Saket in the first week of November.

Three images of Buddha on the gable of Wat Suthat

THE NORTHEAST

Thailand's best-kept secret is its northeast, known as Isan. It's an enticing mix of culture and countryside: wild elephants and gibbons in Khao Yai National Park; the mighty 4,022km (2,494-mile) Mekong River wending its way around the region; Khmer temples and other cultural riches; and Isan arts and crafts—gorgeous silk, especially—at prices lower than anywhere else in the country.

MAJOR SIGHTS

A king cobra at Ban Khok Sa-Nga

View the excavations close up

BAN KHOK SA-NGA: KING COBRA VILLAGE

🕂 310 G6 ✉ Ban Khok Sa-Nga
☎ 019 749 499 🕐 Daily 9–5
💷 Donation to look around the village and see the snakes; the admission cost for a performance depends on the number of visitors. Ask the tourist office in Udon Thani to telephone the venue and establish the payment for a performance 🚌 From Khon Kaen take Route 2 to Udon Thani, turning right at kilometer stone 33 onto road 2039. At kilometer stone 14, signs point the way to a turning on the right for the village

Ban Khok Sa-Nga, a farming village 50km (31 miles) northeast of Khon Kaen with a population of around 700, breeds king cobra snakes and raises them as pets. This allows them to be tamed and trained for the "boxing" performances that take place on demand. The shows begin with children performing their own "boxing" acts with non-poisonous snakes. The main acts get under way when adult king cobras are released from their boxes. You will be either fascinated or repulsed by the spectacle that follows, depending on the degree to which you think the snakes are being goaded simply for the sake of entertainment. It becomes clear that the snakes want to be left alone—they have no wish to attack, and will only adopt aggressive postures under duress. Whatever your feelings about this, there is no doubting the dangers involved—look carefully, and you'll notice that some of the snake handlers have missing fingers. The performances are dramatic and involve the handlers getting dangerously close to the king cobras, looking them straight in the eye and even occasionally putting a snake's head in the mouth.

BAN CHIANG

Archaeological excavations at the village of Ban Chiang in the 1960s completely repositioned Southeast Asia in the history of human civilization.

🕂 311 H5 ✉ Ban Chiang ☎ 042 208 167 🕐 Daily 8.30–5 💷 B30 🚌 From Udon Thani take a *songthaew* to Ban Chiang or take a bus heading to Sakon Nakhon, get off Route 2 at Ban Palu and take a *samlor* from there to the village. There are no afternoon *songthaews* back to Udon Thani so take a *samlor* back to Route 2 and wait for a bus from Sakon Nakhon bound for Khon Kaen

RATINGS				
Cultural interest	●	●	●	●
Historic interest	●	●	●	●
Value for money	●	●		

Ban Chiang, 50km (31 miles) east of Udon Thani, is the site of a human settlement that dates back to around 3600BC. The people lived in huts, made pottery and conducted funeral ceremonies. Their food came mostly from the wild, but some domesticated animals were kept and a primitive form of rice cultivation was in use. From these beginnings, the people began to make bronze tools and ornaments. By 1700BC there is clear evidence of a Bronze Age culture emerging in Ban Chiang, challenging the long-held idea that the Bronze Age started in the Middle East around 3000BC and only reached Southeast Asia some 2,500 years later. The significance of Ban Chiang in overturning this view led to UNESCO declaring it a World Heritage Site in 1992.

The story of Ban Chiang, and the accidental way in which the excavations got under way, is told in the village's national museum. There are two stories to the museum. Downstairs has a metallurgy room and a ceramics room, devoted to the early culture that began around 3600BC. The more interesting Ban Chiang Exhibition is upstairs, beginning with a skeleton, dated 1500BC, of a man who was buried with a bronze axe at his shoulder and wearing four bronze bracelets. Other exhibits include infant burial jars and red-painted pottery that was placed over corpses. Upstairs, there is also a Ban Chiang Today exhibition that consists of tools currently used by the villages.

Ban Chiang village has a number of craft and souvenir shops selling attractive reproductions of the pottery unearthed by archaeologists. Unfortunately these are quite difficult to pack in your luggage!

Don't miss The locally made cotton fabrics, heavy enough for winter wear, available in the village shops are good buys.

A silk weaver at work in Ban Khwao

Beautiful blooms at the Ban Nong Samrong Orchid Nursery

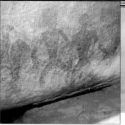
Prehistoric paintings at Ban Phu

BAN KHWAO SILK-WEAVING VILLAGE

➕ 310 F7 ✉ Ban Khwao ◷ Daily 7–7
🚌 From Chaiyaphum, buses to Ban Khwao depart every half-hour between early morning and 6pm 🚗 From Chaiyaphum head west on Route 225 for 13km (8 miles) to Ban Khwao village

Around Chaiyaphum (▷ 92) there are a number of communities that specialize in silk-weaving, and Ban Khwao is one of the more accessible villages. Here you will see the whole process that begins with the breeding of silkworms using mulberry leaves and finishes with the distinctive, tie-dyed *mutmee* silk. The production process takes place under village houses, and you will see the silkworms being fed and covered under large saucer-shape trays of rattan. When the silkworm has created its silk cocoon from a fiber secreted from the mouth, and just before the moth will emerge from inside it, the cocoon is boiled to help release the silk fiber. The dead silkworms are not discarded, and you may be offered one of them as a quick snack. The silk fiber is then carefully unraveled and reeled onto threads. The silk is then dyed in preparation for weaving on the handmade looms. Children and adults alike find it a fascinating and educational experience to observe, and village shops sell some of the fabrics that are made here.

BAN NONG SAMRONG ORCHID NURSERY

➕ 310 G5 ✉ Soi Kamon Watthana on Route 2024 at Ban Nong Samrong ☎ 042 242 475 ◷ Daily 8–6 🚌 From Udon Thani, a tuk-tuk to Ban Nong Samrong will cost about B70 each way 🚗 From Udon Thani, head northwest out of town on Route 2024 and look for signs to Udon Sunshine Orchid Garden

Known also as Udon Sunshine Orchid Garden, this nursery grows and sells a new species of orchid that has been cultivated for its fragrance. Known as Miss Udon Sunshine, it is unique because it is the first perfume to be extracted from an orchid. If you arrive at the nursery between early morning and early afternoon, the scent from the orchid is unmistakable. The orchids and the perfume can be purchased at the nursery. Also worth seeing here is a hybrid of *gyrants* that has become known as the "dancing plant" because of the way some of its leaves move in response to particular rhythmic sounds.

BAN PHU

➕ 310 G4 ✉ Phu Phra Bat Historical Park ☎ 042 910 107 ◷ Daily 8–6 🚌 From Nong Khai, take an early bus to Ban Phu and check the time of the last bus back, usually departing around 3pm; from Ban Phu a *songthaew* and then a motorcycle will take you to Phu Phra Bat Historical Park 🚗 From Udon Thani or Nong Khai, turn off Route 2 onto Route 2021 for 42km (26 miles) to Ban Phu. At Ban Phu, continue for another 12km (7 miles) on Route 2348 to Phu Phra Bat Historical Park

The region around Ban Phu, best reached with your own transportation from either Nong Khai or Udon Thani, is characterized by a strange landscape of odd-shape rock formations and a number of caves and cliffs with traces of prehistoric paintings. The peculiar geology of Ban Phu is thought to have been caused by river erosion working on the rock of a glacier's terminal moraine. The area has been turned into the Phu Phra Bat Historical Park. It is worth arriving when the information center is open (daily 8–4.30) to study the displays relating to the prehistoric paintings and the legends associated with some of the outcrops of rock. An easy-to-follow set of footpaths connects many of the outcrops, and you should give yourself at least two hours to reach some of the more interesting rock formations. It is worth walking to the mushroom-shape Hor Nang Ussa, a bizarre pillar of rock topped by a flat stone and chiseled by human hands to form a shrine or shelter. Legend has it that a princess named Ussa, imprisoned here by her father, was visited by the faithful Baros, who climbed to the top and eventually rescued her. It is thought that Hor Nang Ussa was sculpted into its present shape about 1,000 years ago. There are other examples of such grottos in the park, though none as photogenic as this one. There is also a natural viewpoint at Pha Sadej from where you can gaze northwards across the Thai landscape to the mountains of Laos, 70km (43 miles) away.

Be sure to visit the strange rock formations at Ban Phu

Prang Ku Khmer tower at Chaiyaphum

Monks delivering alms in Chiang Khan

The Khmer temple of Khao Phra Viharn

CHAIYAPHUM

➕ 310 F7 🚌 Daily from Mo Chit station in Bangkok, as well as regular local services to/from Khon Kaen and Nakhon Ratchasima (Korat) 🚗 From Nakhon Ratchasima (Korat) or Nong Khai, turn west off Route 2 onto Route 202

A Laotian named Phraya Lae founded a town in the area around Chaiyaphum in 1819, seeking to escape from the court politics of Vientiane. Seven years later, when the Laotian king decided to go to war with Bangkok, Phraya Lae chose to ally himself with Siam and alerted officials in Korat about the invading army. He was rewarded by King Rama II but was captured in battle by Laotian soldiers and executed outside the town he had founded. A statue of Phraya Lae stands in the center of town on Thanon Banakran. About 3km (2 miles) west of town, on the banks of the river on Route 225, a large tamarind tree marks the spot where he was executed. Each year, between January 12 and 20, a festival featuring an elephant parade to the tree commemorates his loyalty. Geographically, Chaiyaphum is in the exact center of Thailand, yet it remains one of the least-known and least-visited towns in the country. Tad Ton National Park (▷ 105) makes a pleasant day's excursion from town.

CHIANG KHAN

➕ 310 F4 🚌 *Songthaews* and buses travel throughout the day between Loei and Chiang Khan; coming from Nong Khai, *songthaews* travel between Chiang Khan and Pak Chom 🚗 Chiang Khan is 50km (31 miles) north of Loei on Route 201; Route 211 connects Nong Khai with Chiang Khan

Chiang Khan has more character than most small Thai towns, due partly to its setting on the banks of the mighty Mekong River, but also because its old wooden-built houses along the two long narrow streets evoke an earlier age. The town is on the backpackers' trail and there are a number of budget guesthouses and places to enjoy a meal or coffee. Boat trips up and down the Mekong can be arranged through guesthouses whether you are staying there or not. Chiang Khan has a number of temples that are not typically Thai in the way they incorporate colonnades, shapely arches and shutters—stylistic features that suggest a French influence originating from across the Mekong in Laos. A good example can be found opposite *sois* 11 and 12 on the inland side of the main street, Thanon Chiang Khan, that is part of Route 211. Another temple like this can be seen by turning down *soi* 20 at the eastern end of town.

KHAO PHRA VIHARN

➕ 315 J8 🕐 Daily 8–5 💲 Entry to the park B200; border crossing B5; entry to the temple (to the Cambodian authorities) B200 🚗 From Ubon Ratchathani, take Route 24 and turn onto Route 221 near Kantharalak. From Si Saket, take Route 221 through Kantharalak 🚗 A car and driver can be arranged through the tourist office in Si Saket (▷ 103) 🍴 Food and drink stands at the temple parking area, but bring a picnic or eat at Kantharalak

With your own transportation it is easy to reach this well-preserved Khmer temple from Ubon Ratchathani, and it makes a rewarding and adventurous journey; the temple complex is just inside Cambodia but can be visited without a visa. Khao Phra Viharn is dramatically perched on a clifftop and, after crossing the border into Cambodia, you will soon find yourself at the bottom of a broad stone-built avenue that makes its way up the cliffside through a series of four *gopuras* (pavilions) decorated with scenes from Hindu mythology. One of the best examples, depicting Vishnu as a tortoise alongside *nagas* (magical serpents), can be found above the last door of the second *gopura*. In this Hindu version of the Big Bang, the universe is shown being created by stirring the cosmic sea with a large churning stick.

The building of Khao Phra Viharn, dedicated to Shiva, began in the ninth century and was completed by the twelfth. It would have been an arduous journey reaching the temple, a retreat for Hindu priests and a pilgrimage site for devotees. Today, the main sanctuary and its Buddha image are watched over by Cambodian monks on the clifftop, and there are stunning views of the Cambodian plain from the summit if you clamber through one of the stone windows.

Khao Phra Viharn was off-limits for most of the 20th century—because Thailand and Cambodia disputed ownership of the site. To make matters worse, the whole complex was occupied by the Khmer Rouge during the Pol Pot years and mines were laid around the site. It finally reopened in 2003 after international arbitration. It is now safe to visit, but do not stray into the areas where warning signs indicate areas still with mines. Note that Thai baht is accepted by all the Cambodian vendors at Khao Phra Viharn.

Bats in flight at Khao Yai (above). A rope bridge over a pool in the National Park (right)

KHAO YAI NATIONAL PARK

Thailand's oldest and best national park is easily reached from Bangkok, and the availability of decent accommodation and knowledgeable nature guides makes Khao Yai one of the most enjoyable destinations in the northeast.

About 120km (74 miles) from Bangkok, the park was established in 1962. Covering an area of over 2,000sq km (780sq miles), its diverse habitats include mountains and forest, and there are short- and long-distance walks that provide an opportunity to experience wildlife at close quarters. Accommodation is available at the park headquarters, but it is geared towards large groups. It makes more sense to stay at one of the private lodges that are dotted along the 20km (8-mile) stretch of road that connects the town of Pak Chong with the entrance to the park. As well as offering more appropriate accommodation, the best of these lodges have their own experienced guides who will accompany you on half- and full-day tours around the park.

The park headquarters has displays about the park's wildlife, including the dwindling number of tigers. After dark you can take a night safari, where you sit in the back of an open truck and hope that the park ranger and his spotlight will pick out some interesting creatures. Civet cats and barking deer are usually seen, and a herd of elephants is not uncommon.

PARK TOURS

The full-day tours offered by the lodges, which include the night safari, begin early in the morning with a view to catching sight of the white-handed gibbons. Their whooping duets claiming territorial rights are an unforgettable sound, and just as memorable is the sight of any of the four species of hornbills that inhabit the park. The birdlife varies with the time of year, but dollar birds, white-crested laughing thrushes, black-crested bulbuls and trogons are commonly seen. Half-day tours include a visit to caves in the vicinity and, at evening time, an opportunity to observe thousands of birds flying out in wave upon wave for their nightly food trips. Come prepared with suitable footwear for forest walks, long trousers and insect repellent; a pair of binoculars is useful, but your guide will have some and will supply leech socks if necessary. Opportunities for nature photographs abound.

RATINGS

Outdoor pursuits	●●●●●
Photo stops	●●●●
Walkability	●●●●●

BASICS

✚ 313 E8

✉ Park Headquarters: Thanon Thanarat, Pak Chong

☎ 037 319 002, 060 926 531

🕐 Daily 6am–11pm (information center closes at 6pm)

💰 Entrance to national park: adult B200, child B100

🚉 From Bangkok to Pak Chong (2.5 hrs)

🚌 From Bangkok's Northern Bus Terminal to Pak Chong; *songthaews* travel between the park entrance and Pak Chong, but your accommodation will pick you up at Pak Chong

🍴 At park headquarters

www.thaiforestbooking.com/
nationalpark-eng.htm
For reserving bungalow accommodation in the park.

TIP

● It's possible to get lost on the longer walking trails so it is safer to have a guide.

Khon Kaen

A university town in the heart of Isan, Khon Kaen has good hotels and restaurants, excellent shopping for silk and cotton fabrics, and a fine museum. There is an easy-going, confident feel to Khon Kaen that makes it a refreshing place for a sojourn or a base for excursions into the countryside.

Market life in Khon Kaen   *The city museum*   *Ornate balustrade at Wat Nongwan Muang Kao*

RATINGS

Good for food	●●●○
Specialist shopping	●●●●
Value for money	●●●○

BASICS

➕ 310 G6

🏠 15/5 Thanon Prachasamosorn, Khon Kaen, tel 043 244 498; daily 8.30–4.30

🚉 Khon Kaen Station (tel 043 221 112)

🚌 From Bangkok's Northern Bus Terminal to Khon Kaen's bus station (tel 043 237 300)

✈ 10km/6 miles northwest of town (tel 043 246 305); hotel buses meet arriving flights

❓ Budget (tel 043 345 460) car rental at the airport

www.khonkaen.com
Good source of information about the province, including attractions, history and maps.

TIP

● The silk shop next to the Hotel Sofitel Raja Orchid (▷ 275) is one of the very few places where you can buy unstuffed axe pillows.

SEEING KHON KAEN

With daily flights and trains to and from Bangkok (450km/279 miles away) and with buses traveling up and down the northeast's major road, Route 2, as well as connecting with Phitsanulok in northern Thailand, Khon Kaen is well placed to receive visitors. The tourist office has a good range of literature on local attractions and dispenses a city map showing the transportation links, places of interest and the hotels and restaurants. *Songthaews* ply their way up and down the main streets, and tuk-tuk rides around town average B35. Cars can be rented at the airport, and Khon Kaen is an easy city to drive around and find your way. Unlike Korat and Udon Thani, the city's air does not feel polluted.

HIGHLIGHTS

NATIONAL MUSEUM

✉ Thanon Lang Soon Ratchakan, 3 blocks north of the tourist office ☎ 043 242 129 🕐 Daily 9–4 🎟 B30

Khon Kaen's branch of the National Museum has a notable collection of Bronze Age finds from Ban Chiang (▷ 90), pottery and jewelry, and is well worth seeing if you do not have time to visit Ban Chiang itself. The boundary stones exhibited are from the Dvaravati period (seventh to eleventh century) and one in particular is finely carved, with a picture of the Buddha's feet being cleaned by Princess Bimba with her hair. Upstairs, there is an interesting gallery devoted to local crafts, with a specialist collection of the trays used by betel nut-chewers, and a small but choice collection of Buddha statues and ceramics.

WAT NONGWAN MUANG KAO

✉ Thanon Klang Muang 🕐 Daily 8–7 🎟 Free

While the museum is off the north end of Thanon Klang Muang, the city's most visually arresting temple is at the south end of the same long road. Its nine tiers, completed in 1997, are painted in vivid red and gold and shine gloriously in the sunlight. Walk inside the pagoda

A Chinese temple in Khon Kaen

to admire the murals on the first level before climbing to the top for panoramic views of the city. The lake you see, Bung Kaen Nakhon, is a good 10-minute walk away, and the pathway around it is dotted with restaurants and food stands.

SHOPPING

One of the best reasons to visit Khon Kaen is the quality shops selling local silk and cotton as well as Isan arts and crafts. Prices are fixed at the huge Prathamakant Local Goods Center (▷ 194), and in the private shops expect a discount of around 15 percent. A gratifying aspect of shopping here is the fact that you do not need to indulge in prolonged bargaining to get a decent price. As well as the shops, there are vendors on the street—many congregate opposite the Hotel Sofitel Raja Orchid—and every year a Silk Festival takes place at the end of November and early December. The focus of the festival takes place around the Provincial Hall on Thanon Na Suan Ratchakan.

BACKGROUND

Khon Kaen began to emerge as a city of some importance only in the 1960s, when the Thai government injected some capital into its development and the US made it a base for their air force in the Vietnam War. Now the fourth-largest city in the country and home to Isan's most prestigious university, Khon Kaen is emerging as an attractive commercial and cultural center, as reflected in the development of sophisticated hotels and restaurants.

A statue at Wat Nongwan Muang Kao (right)

MORE TO SEE
PHU WIANG NATIONAL PARK
➕ 310 F6 ☎ 043 291 393 🕐 Daily 8–4.30 🐾 B10 (B30 for a car) 🚌 Route 12 from Khon Kaen for 48km (30 miles), as far as Nong Rua, then a right turn onto Route 2038 for 39km (24 miles) to Phu Wiang www.thaiforestbooking.com/nationalpark-eng.htm (for reserving bungalow accommodation in the park) You need your own transportation from Khon Kaen to reach the park, where fossils of dinosaurs were first found in 1981. The prize exhibit is in Site 9: the fossil remains of a new species of dinosaur regarded as the ancestor of *Tyrannosaurus rex*. Bring with you the brochure on Phu Wiang, available from the tourist office in Khon Kaen; it has useful information and a map of the various sites.

CHONNABOT
➕ 310 G6 🚌 Khon Kaen–Korat buses stop at Ban Phai, then take a *songthaew* for 10km (6 miles) to Chonnabot 🚌 Route 2 south from Khon Kaen to Ban Phai, then a right turn on Route 229 to Chonnabot Like Ban Khwao (▷ 91), this town specializes in the production of silk, and you can see women working on different stages in the process in their wooden homes. The silk they produce can be purchased from vendors along the street.

The misty silhouette of the mountains in Loei Province (above).
A butterfly in the Phu Kradung National Park (left)

RATINGS

Outdoor pursuits	● ● ● ● ●
Photo stops	● ● ● ● ○
Walkability	● ● ● ● ●

BASICS

➕ 310 F5

ℹ Loei tourist office, Thanon Charoenrat, tel 042 812 812; Mon–Fri 8.30–4.30

Phu Kradung National Park
➕ 310 F5 ✉ Phu Kradung National Park ◉ Oct–end May; visitor center Oct–end May daily 7–2 ☎ 042 871 333 💷 Adult B200, child B100 🚌 Loei-Khon Kaen buses stop at Phu Kradung village; take a *songthaew* to the visitor center 🚗 Take Route 201 south to Phu Kradung, then turn right onto Route 2019 for 8km (5 miles) 🍴 Restaurant at the first visitor center
Phu Rua National Park
➕ 310 E5 ✉ Phu Rua National Park ☎ 042 801 716 ◉ Visitor center daily 7–4 💷 B200 🚌 Loei-Phu Rua buses travel throughout the day but there is little public transport to the visitor center 🚗 Take Route 203 to Phu Rua village, then right for 4km (2.5 miles) www.thaiforestbooking.com/ nationalpark-eng.htm (for accommodation)

TIP

● If you're not staying in Phu Kradung, you need to reach the first visitor center before 10am to have time to get to the plateau and back.

LOEI

Forming a border area between northern and northeastern Thailand, and 50km (31 miles) south of the border with Laos, Loei makes a pleasant base for visits to national parks.

Loei's transportation links with Udon Thani and Phitsanulok make it your most likely arrival and departure point for visits to the national parks. Although it has a distinctly frontier feel, the town also has a friendly atmosphere. There are no special sights but there is good accommodation in the town, and Loei's dusty streets and shops selling agricultural tools and products are worth wandering around. Internet access can be found at PA Computer (139 Thanon Charoenrat) on the main road that runs parallel with the nearby Loei River. If you are in the region around the end of June, it is worth traveling to the town of Dan Sai, 80km (50 miles) southwest of Loei, for its three-day *Phi Ta Khon* Festival. It is a very distinctive event, where young people dress up in bizarre ghost masks and bright clothes, and a carnival atmosphere prevails. Rockets are set off and live bands perform in the evening.

PHU KRADUNG NATIONAL PARK

The park, 80km (50 miles) south of Loei and closed during the rainy season (June to September), has a trail that leads for 8km (5 miles) from the first visitor center to a viewing area on the plateau of Phu Kradung, three hours away. Here there is another visitor center, places to eat and accommodation in park bungalows (best reserved in advance; go to www.thaiforestbooking.com/nationalpark-eng.htm). There are shorter walking trails that begin from the plateau's visitor center.

PHU RUA NATIONAL PARK

Some 50km (31 miles) west of Loei, Phu Rua National Park is best visited with your own transportation. Having paid the entrance fee, a paved road leads to the summit of a picturesque mountain at 1365m (4,477ft). Before reaching a second visitor center, there are a number of guesthouses that offer more suitable accommodation than the bungalows for rent at the second visitor center. At the summit there are a number of walking trails that provide birdwatching opportunities.

Wat Pa Salawan in Korat (above). Offerings at the Thao Suranari Shrine (right)

NAKHON RATCHASIMA (KORAT)

Thailand's second-largest city, known as Korat, is a transportation hub for the northeast and a base for visits to major Khmer ruins at Phimai and Phanom Rung.

Nakhon Ratchasima lacks obvious charm, and its sprawling size makes it a difficult city to get to know in a short space of time, but when the traffic dies down a little and you gain a sense of direction it becomes less daunting. The old part of the city is still encircled by a moat, and the city gates have been rebuilt and serve as useful reference points.

If arriving at the large, well-organized bus station, on the main Route 2, you need a tuk-tuk to get into town. The train station and the tourist office are at the eastern end of town, while the city center is represented by the landmark Thao Suranari Shrine. The commercial heart of the city is to be found in the streets around the shrine; here you will find a modern shopping complex and a shop selling quality Isan silk (▷ 195).

A MONUMENT, MUSEUM AND CERAMICS

The Thao Suranari ("Courageous Lady") Shrine by the west gate is a monument commemorating Khun Ying Mo, the wife of the provincial governor who saved the city when it faced an invading army from Laos in 1826. The story goes that she gathered together the town's womenfolk, and they offered alcohol and sensual inducements to the Laotian soldiers; once inebriated, the soldiers were slaughtered. The monument has become a shrine and is venerated as a source of good luck and marital harmony. Each year, at the end of March, a festival celebrates the memory of Khun Ying Mo, and there are pageants and parades though the streets, dancing at the shrine and fireworks in the air.

The Maha Wirawong National Museum, on Thanon Ratchadamnoen in the grounds of Wat Sutchnida (tel 044 242 958; Wed–Sun 9–4; B10) has a modest collection of Khmer and Hindu woodcarvings and sandstone images, including an eighth-century statue of Ganesh.

With your own transportation an interesting excursion can be made to the pottery village of Dan Kwian, 15km (9 miles) south of Korat on Route 224.

RATINGS
Good for food	● ●
Historic interest	● ●

BASICS

➕ 314 F8

ℹ Thanon Mittaphap, tel 044 213 666; daily 8.30–4.30

🚉 Nakhon Ratchasima Station (tel 044 242 044; Thanon Mukkhamontri)

🚌 Served by buses (tel 044 256 006) to/from Bangkok, Chiang Mai, Khon Kaen, Ubon Ratchathani and smaller towns like Pak Chong (for Khao Yai National Park) and Phimai

🚗 Budget (tel 044 341 654) car rental

A riverside wat *in Mukdahan*

The lively Indochina Market, Mukdahan

View from Nakhon Phanom across the Mekong River

THE SIGHTS

MUKDAHAN

➕ 311 J6 🚌 To/from Ubon Ratchathani, That Phanom, Nakhon Phanom, Bangkok, Udon Thani

You will feel like an intrepid explorer when you reach Mukdahan, an out-of-the-way and attractive town on the Mekong River, some 170km (105 miles) north of Ubon Ratchathani. Trade links with Savannakhet, the second-largest town in Laos and directly across the river from Mukdahan, fuel the lively Indochina Market by the pier (▷ 195). To appreciate the town's scenic location, climb to the top of Mukdahan Tower (daily 8–6; B20) for stirring views of the river and the rice paddies of Laos. For US$30 you can cross the river and visit Savannakhet on a 15-day visa. Staying in Thailand, Mukdahan National Park is 15km (9 miles) south of town, reached by taking Route 2034 and turning off between kilometer stones 14 and 15. The park is characterized by unusual rock formations and a viewpoint reached after a 2km (1.2-mile) walk from the park headquarters. There is the usual B200 entrance fee.

NAKHON PHANOM

➕ 311 J5 ℹ️ 184/1 Thanon Suntorn Vichit, tel 042 513 490; daily 8.30–4.30 🚌 To/from Nong Khai, Mukdahan, Bangkok, Udon Thani ✈️ Nakhon Phanom Airport for flights to/from Bangkok with PB Air (www.pbair.com)

Nakhon Phanom's claim to fame is its location, on the banks of the Mekong with the best views of the river and the jagged mountains of Laos of anywhere in the northeast. It is worth wandering along the streets of the town for its interesting old buildings: the old Vietnamese-style temple by the pier, the Clock Tower and Custom House,

and the French-style National Library on Thanon Apiban Bancha. With your own transportation, there are places to visit in the vicinity, and at That Phanom (▷ 105) there is the village of Renu Nakhon, where silk and cotton is woven and available for purchase at good prices.

NAKHON RATCHASIMA (KORAT)

See page 97.

NAM NAO NATIONAL PARK

➕ 310 F5 ☎️ 056 729 002 🕐 Daily 6am–11pm 💲 B200 🚌 Signposted off Route 12 at kilometer stone 50, 145km (90 miles) west of Khon Kaen, 160km (99 miles) southwest of Loei 🚌 Buses from Phitsanulok, Khon Kaen and Loei will drop you off at the turn-off on Route 12 www.thaiforestbooking.com/nationalpark-eng.htm (for reserving bungalow accommodation in the park)

Covering about 1,000sq km (390sq miles), this is one of the country's least visited national parks, although it offers pleasant walks and a variety of habitats. Circular trails that are easy to follow begin from the visitor center and vary in length from 1km to 6km (0.5 to 4 miles). There are also longer trails of up to 25km (15.5 miles), although for these it would be advisable to hire a guide from the visitor center. Mammals, including elephants, thrive in the park, and you are most likely to spot barking deer or hear gibbons in the morning. More than 200 species of bird have been identified in the park.

NONG KHAI

➕ 310 G4 ℹ️ On the road leading to the Friendship Bridge, tel 042 467 164; daily 8.30–4.30 🚌 Buses from Udon Thani, Khon Kaen, Loei and most other

towns in the northeast; long-distance buses to and from Bangkok 🚉 Nong Khai station is 4km (2.5 miles) outside of town, near the Friendship Bridge 🚌 Tours to Vientiane and day tours of Nong Khai through Holiday Puyfay at Pantawee Hotel (www.pantawee.com)

Of all the border towns in the northeast, Nong Khai has the most developed infrastructure for visitors and an appealing charm that warrants a stay of more than just one night. There is a fair choice of accommodation and places to eat, an evening boat cruise on the Mekong (▷ 196) and some good places to shop for clothes, arts and crafts and souvenirs. The absence of heavy traffic and a laid-back atmosphere make Nong Khai an enjoyable town to walk around (▷ 224–225) and relax in. Bicycles can be rented from some of the guesthouses by the river front.

The Friendship Bridge, 3km (1.9 miles) out of town, opened to Thai–Laos traffic in 1994. You can obtain a visa for Laos at the bridge for US$30 and a photograph. From the other side it is only 24km (15 miles) to Vientiane, and taxis and *songthaews* are readily available at the border.

The Pantawee Hotel is a good source of local information and, in addition to internet access, there is a travel desk for

Nam Nao National Park

The leafy backstreets of Nong Khai

Silk-weaving in Pak Thong Chai

The main entrance at Phanom Rung

arranging car rental and tours in the area. If you are here in June ask about the dates for the Rocket Festival—it varies each year—and if it is on then arrange for transport to take you there. A tuk-tuk on the street will take you to Sala Kaeo Kou, a temple 5km (3 miles) east of town with an interesting sculpture garden.

PAK THONG CHAI

🚩 314 F8 🚌 Buses from Nakhon Ratchasima (Korat) 🚗 30km (18.5 miles) south of Nakhon Ratchasima (Korat) on Route 304; the village is 2km (1.2 miles) off the road

Pak Thong Chai is a silk-weaving village with a commercial awareness that has resulted in a number of shops retailing the silk by the meter. It is worth taking a look if you have your own transportation and are traveling along this stretch of Route 304, but a special trip hardly justifies itself because prices are high and there are no bargains to be had.

PHA TAM

🚩 315 K7 ✉ Kong Chiam 🕐 Daily 5am–6pm 💰 B200 🚌 From Ubon Ratchathani take Route 217 and then Route 2222 to Kong Chiam, from where Pha Tam National Park is signposted

Inside Pha Tam National Park there is a section of cliff-face, protected from the elements by an overhanging ledge, with prehistoric rock paintings in red that date back at least 3,000 years. You can make out human shapes, huge catfish and fish traps, elephants, and geometric symbols, the significance of which can only be guessed at. The park opens at 5am because it is the first place in Thailand to receive the rising sun, and on weekends Thais arrive very early in the morning for this reason.

PHANOM RUNG

🚩 314 G8 ✉ Prasat Phanom Rung 🕐 Daily 6–6 💰 B40 🚌 From Nakhon Ratchasima (Korat), Route 226 to Buriram, then Route 219 to Prakhon Chai and straight over, then right

Phanom Rung, only reachable with your own transportation, was built between the 10th and 13th centuries using sandstone and laterite. Over a period of 17 years its majestic remains were restored to make it the most impressive and important Khmer temple in Thailand. The quality of the carvings is on a par with those at Angkor Wat in Cambodia.

Phanom Rung stands on the top of an inactive volcano—Phanom Rung means "big mountain"—and is approached by way of a grand stone avenue over 150m (163.5 yards) in length and bordered by small pillars topped with lotus-bud finials. This processional way was completed in the 12th century. At the end of the avenue you walk across a bridge, representing the journey into the world of the gods, with balustrades formed by five-headed *nagas*. A second bridge, with *naga* heads spouting water from the mouth of a monster, accesses the eastern *gorupa* (Khmer doorway), where you will find a pediment depicting Shiva and female consorts. The eastern *gorupa* was the formal entrance to the sanctuary.

In the sanctuary itself there is an even more remarkable pediment with a dancing Shiva and, on the lintel below it, a reclining Vishnu framed by two neatly carved parrots. The Vishnu lintel was stolen from the temple but turned up in the Art Institute of Chicago in 1973 and was finally returned to Thailand in 1988. Other pediments depict battle scenes, thought to refer to

the 12th-century Khmer ruler Narendraditya, who retired to the temple.

The north side of the sanctuary is decorated with scenes from the *Ramayana* that have been beautifully restored; the level of detail is extraordinary. Over the west door Sita is shown being abducted in a chariot.

A visit to the information center (daily 9–4) is recommended before exploring the site because the exemplary display panels provide the historical context for understanding the significance of the temple. Less than 8km (5 miles) southeast of Phanom Rung is another temple complex, Prasat Muang Tam.

PHIMAI

See pages 100–101.

ROI ET

See page 102.

SAKHON NAKHON

🚩 311 J5 🚌 On Route 22 from Udon Thani or Nakhon Phanom

The agricultural town of Sakhon Nakhon is known in Thailand as the town where eating dog meat is relatively popular. A better reason to visit is to view its very sacred and ancient temple, Wat Phra That Cheong Chum, beside the town lake. The white, Lao-style *chedi* (monument housing a Buddhist relic) is 24m (79ft) high, and monks will allow you access if you ask. Northwest of town, off Route 22 and 3km (1.9 miles) past the airport at the village of Ban That (turn left at kilometer stone 156), there is another noted temple, Wat Phra That Narai Jaeng Weng. It boasts some lovely carvings depicting Hindu motifs like a dancing Shiva, a reclining Vishnu and a *naga* engaging two lions.

Phimai

This major Khmer temple was built in Phimai in the late 11th and early 12th centuries to face Angkor and was connected to the Khmer capital by a direct road. Restored in the 1980s, Prasat Hin Phimai is the biggest and most complete Khmer temple in Thailand.

Remains of the Khmer sanctuary at Phimai

Detail of the preserved relief carvings

Stone statues adorn the ruins of the sanctuary

RATINGS	
Cultural interest	●●●○
Historic interest	●●●○
Walkability	●●●○

BASICS

🔲 314 G7

🚌 From Nakhon Ratchasima (Korat) throughout the day; coming from Khon Kaen, get off any Korat-bound bus at the turn-off for Route 206 and wait for a Korat–Phimai bus for the remaining 10km (6-mile) journey to Phimai

🚗 From Nakhon Ratchasima (Korat), 54km (33.5 miles) on Route 2 then 10km (6 miles) on Route 206

TIP

● Bicycles for bicycling between the temple and the banyan tree can be rented from the *Bai Teiy* restaurant on Thanon Chomsudasadet, the road that runs south into town from the entrance to the temple.

SEEING PHIMAI

The restored sanctuary is in the small town of Phimai, and buses from Nakhon Ratchasima (Korat) stop close by the temple. As the last bus back to Korat departs at around 6.30pm, a day trip is quite feasible. Sai Ngam, 2km (1.2 miles) to the northeast of the temple on Route 206, is a single banyan tree that has grown to such an astonishing size that it looks like a small forest of trees. You can stroll among the myriad of branches that have taken root in the ground. Vendors sell small birds in cages that are released for good luck, and the open-air restaurants opposite the banyan tree are ideal for lunch. *Samlors* will take you between the sanctuary and Sai Ngam.

HIGHLIGHTS

PRASAT HIN PHIMAI

🔲 314 G7 ☎ 044 471 167 🕐 Daily 9–6 💵 B40

Be sure to collect the English-language brochure when you buy your ticket as it contains a map of the temple complex and without it you may find sorting out the different elements confusing.

The sandstone sanctuary has a 28m-high (92ft) *prang* (tower) but when you first enter through the main gate to the southeast your attention is taken by the stone staircase and the decorative *nagas* (snakes) on the raised terrace. Passing along a sandstone passageway and through a *gorupa* and the outer walls, the inner sanctuary is reached. It is flanked on each side by a minor *prang*. The one on the right, Prang Bhranmathat, is made of laterite; inside it was found an armless sandstone statue, the original of which can be seen in the museum. The statue of a cross-legged man is thought to be King Jayavarman VII, who ruled in the 12th century. Prang Hin Daeng, on the left (southwest) side, dates to the 12th century when Hinduism began to give way to Buddhism.

The main five-tiered *prang*, made of white sandstone, has fine carvings on the pediments and lintels that depict scenes from the *Ramayana*, while those on the southern side show the dancing Shiva. The pediment on the eastern side depicts Hindu deities. The

Visitors head toward the main five-tiered prang *at the sanctuary*

one on the western side was never finished, but you can make out the figure of a *garuda* (a half-man and half-bird creature) flying to the rescue of Rama and Lakshmana. Other carvings on the inside, though, depict scenes from the story of the Buddha, and what adds to Phimai's uniqueness is the way it represents the cultural transition from Hinduism to Buddhism in Thailand.

PHIMAI NATIONAL MUSEUM

✉ Behind, to the northeast of, Prasat Hin Phimai and just before the bridge
☎ 044 471 167 ◷ Daily 9–4 💷 B30

The single rarest exhibit in the museum is the statue of King Jayavarman VII, but there is a lot more to see relating to Khmer culture. In addition to background information on the history and architecture of Phimai, there are interesting displays relating to contemporary religious beliefs—you will find a clear explanation of the spirit houses that you often see in Thailand. Hindu-inspired art is well represented by statues of Shiva and Ganesha, and there are finds on show from excavations at Phanom Rung (▷ 99). In the museum grounds, and open to view after closing, there are some ancient milestones decorated with representations of the Buddha.

BACKGROUND

The town of Phimai developed on the banks of the Mun River, a tributary of the Mekong, and there is evidence of settlements dating back to Neolithic times. The Angkor empire in the 12th century included large parts of Thailand as well as Cambodia, and Phimai was part of this empire, 240km (149 miles) away from the capital at Angkor. It is thought that the sanctuary at Phimai was built before work was completed on Angkor Wat. It remained an important sanctuary until Thai forces under an Ayutthaya king defeated the Khmer empire in the 14th century.

<table>
<tr><td>MORE TO SEE</td></tr>
</table>

BAN PRASAT

✚ 314 G7 ◷ Daily 8–4.30
💷 Donation box 🚌 From Nakhon Ratchasima (Korat), off Route 2 to the northeast before reaching the turn-off for Route 206 for Phimai

The village of Ban Prasat, where burial grounds dating back 3,000 years were excavated in the early 1990s, has three excavation pits open to the public. A small museum exhibits some of the grave goods: pottery, bronze objects and ornaments made from shells. Village shops sell art and craft items.

Walking Buddha at Wat Buraphaphiram

A food stand in Si Chiang Mai

ROI ET

This attractive small town is built around an artificial lake and an island with a large walking Buddha. An even larger walking Buddha, one of the tallest in Thailand, dominates one of the town's temples.

⊞ 311 H6
🚌 The bus station (tel 043 511 939) is outside the middle of town, served by tuk-tuks

RATINGS	
Cultural interest	● ●
Photo stops	● ●
Walkability	● ● ●

The tourist office in Khon Kaen dispenses a brochure on Roi Et that includes a map showing the town's lake, Bung Phalan Chai, in the center of town. On the lake's island, reached by footbridges, is a large walking Buddha. Rowboats can be rented on the lake. The best place for a meal is along one of the roads surrounding the lake.

The oldest temple in town is Wat Klang Ming Muang, off Thanon Padung Panit, a 10-minute walk northeast of the Buddha statue. It dates back to the Ayutthaya period, before the town was founded, and around the outside of the *bot* (main sanctuary) there are murals, some showing their age, depicting the story of the Buddha.

Wat Buraphaphiram, farther along the same road but to the east of Wat Klang Ming Muang, has an especially large walking Buddha. Its height is around 60m (197ft) and you can walk up one side of the statue for views of the town.

With your own transportation, a short excursion can be made to a late 11th-century Khmer sanctuary called Prang Ku. Take Route 23 east of town for 8km (5 miles), turning right at kilometer stone 8. The ruins of the three-tiered *prang* are less than a kilometer down this unpaved road. To appreciate a more substantial example of Khmer architecture, you need to travel 60km (37 miles) south of town on Route 214 and make a right turn between kilometer stones 6 and 7. This leads to Ku Phra Ko Na, also 11th-century but partly restored in the 1920s. Lintels on the northern side carry depictions of Hindu deities, a reclining Vishnu, and Shiva on a *garuda*, a half-man and half-bird creature.

Stone tortoise at Wat Neua, Roi Et

SI CHIANG MAI

⊞ 310 G4 🚌 From Nong Khai throughout the day; connections to/from Chiang Khan, Loei, Udon Thani and Bangkok

This small town by the Mekong River is renowned throughout Thailand for its production, using rice flour, of spring-roll wrappers. You will see them drying in the sun below people's village houses. Route 211 passes through the town, with a quieter road running parallel to it but closer to the river. There are Lao and Vietnamese families living here as well as Thais, and the French influence from Laos shows itself clearly in the town's bakery, which churns out row upon row of fresh baguettes each morning. The bakery is at the Nong Khai end of town, while the backpackers' traditional port of call, Tim Guest House, overlooks the river and is reached by turning down soi 17—on your left if you're coming into town from the western end. This is the best place to go for a coffee, have a meal or just get some information on the area. Bicycles can be rented and boat trips along the Mekong River can be arranged, though the price only becomes economical if you can make up a small group of people to share the cost between you.

To the west, halfway between Si Chiang Mai and Sang Khom and clearly signposted off Route 211, Wat Hin Mak Peng is a famous and well-endowed temple by the banks of the Mekong. On display here are effigies of Luang Phu Thet, the temple's founder, an ascetic who died in 1994; the figure you first see on entering the temple is an alarmingly lifelike reproduction. The number of visitors to the *wat* drove him to relocate to a quieter temple near Sakhon Nakhon.

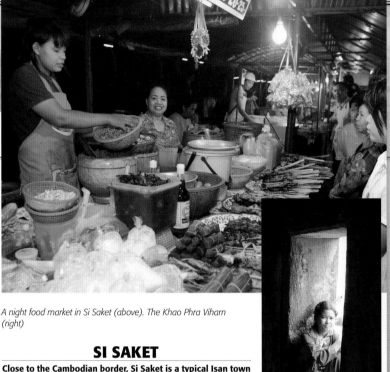

A night food market in Si Saket (above). The Khao Phra Viharn (right)

SI SAKET

Close to the Cambodian border, Si Saket is a typical Isan town where visitors are few and far between. Good transportation links make it a convenient base for an excursion to the remarkable Khao Phra Viharn (▷ 92) and to another less well-known Khmer ruin in the vicinity.

The capital of Si Saket province, with a population of around 135,000, is easy to reach by bus or train from Surin or Ubon Ratchathani, or direct from Bangkok (570km/353 miles away), and a night spent in town before or after visiting the Khmer sites lets you experience small-town life in Isan at an unhurried pace.

Each evening at around 6pm, food stands take up their positions close to the railway line and station, and as the place begins to fill with diners there is a buzz of activity that enlivens the scene, making it the town's social center. Little English is spoken here though: It's a matter of finding something that looks tasty and pointing at what you want. If you can't find anything here to whet your appetite, the town's main concentration of restaurants is along Thanon Kukhan, perpendicular to the rail line. There are also several handicraft shops along this road, selling locally produced silk.

PRASAT HIN WAT SRA KAMPHAENG YAI

To reach this Khmer ruin, take Route 226 west of Si Saket for 40km (24.8 miles), turn off at kilometer stone 81 and the temple is 1km (0.6 miles) down the unpaved road. The site is thought to date back to the late 10th or early 11th century, before the influence of Buddhism made itself felt in this region, and it is thought to have converted to a Buddhist temple sometime in the 13th century. It is an impressive ruin, with the main stupa surrounded by a gallery—made from laterite and restored in places—a grand ceremonial gateway and brick structures adjoining the central stupa. The style of the gallery is architecturally similar to the gallery on the summit at Khao Phra Viharn (▷ 92). The detailed figures carved out of sandstone on the lintels and pediments are very well preserved, and you can clearly make out Shiva with his wife Uma seated in his lap, both sitting atop the bull Nandin. Look too for the lintel in the brick structure on the east side of the stupa that shows Vishnu reclining on a *naga* (serpent) in the company of his wives.

RATINGS

Cultural interest	●●●
Value for money	●●●
Walkability	●●

BASICS

✚ 315 J8

ℹ Thanon Lak Muang (tel 045 611 283; Mon–Fri 8.30–4.30)

🚌 Bus station (tel 045 612 500) is in the town, with regular services to Ubon Ratchathani, Surin and Bangkok

🚆 Si Saket Station (tel 045 613 871) in the center of town and Bangkok–Ubon Ratchathani trains stop here

TIP

● There is nowhere to eat at Prasat Hin Wat Sra Kamphaeng Yai so plan your excursion to take this into account.

RATINGS	
Cultural interest	● ● ●
Photo stops	● ● ●
Walkability	● ●

BASICS

✚ 314 H8

🐘 Elephant shows during the festival B200–B500

🚌 Bus station (tel 044 511 756) in the middle of town, with daily services to/from all the big towns in Isan as well as Bangkok and Chiang Mai

🚂 Surin Station (tel 044 511 295); several of the daily Bangkok–Ubon Ratchathani trains stop in Surin

🚗 Saran Travel (tel 044 513 599; sarentour@yahoo.com), with a desk at the Thong Train Hotel on Thanon Suit near the bus station, for car rental and tickets for elephant shows. Local tours to silk-producing villages through Pirom's House (tel 044 515 140)

TIP

● Accommodation during the Elephant Roundup Festival should be reserved a month or more in advance.

SURIN

A provincial capital town, with a rich Khmer inheritance, Surin is famous for its annual Elephant Roundup in November, and a retail center for locally produced silk.

More than 450km (279 miles) from Bangkok and 200km (124 miles) east of Nakhon Ratchasima (Korat), Surin is close to the border with Cambodia—visas are issued at the border crossing—and Angkor Wat is only 150km (93 miles) away. Prasat Ta Moan, an evocative Khmer sanctuary built on the ancient road that connected Angkor with Phimai (▷ 100–101), lies 70km (43 miles) to the south of Surin and makes the most obvious excursion from town. Many of the villages in Surin province weave silk, and you will find women vendors selling their produce around town as well as through shops.

ELEPHANT ROUNDUP FESTIVAL

Surin erupts into life over the third weekend of each November when festooned elephants parade the streets and mock battles and soccer games using elephants amuse the large crowds that flock to the town. Tickets can be reserved though travel agents in Bangkok and Surin. The village of Ban Ta Klang, 60km (37 miles) north of Surin on Route 214, is the traditional home for the Say people who used to make their living out of training elephants. There is an Elephant Museum (daily 8.30–4.30; free), and occasional elephant shows take place in the village.

PRASAT TA MOAN

To reach this Khmer chapel and resting place, travel south on Route 214 and turn right at kilometer stone 35 for the final 12km (7.5 miles). Small but finely proportioned and typically Khmer in its design, Prasat Ta Moan (daily 7.30–6; B30) has doorways at the four cardinal points in the gallery that encircles the main *prang* (tower), with minor *prangs* adjoining at the sides. Part of the attractiveness of the site is attributable to the four ponds that are part of the overall design, the need for water being part of the cleansing ceremony for travelers in addition to its sacred quality for the priests. Prasat Ta Moan was built in the early 12th century when Jayavarman VII adopted Mahayana Buddhism as the official religion of the Khmer empire. The site has a small tourist center (daily 9–4; free) that provides background information on the construction of the chapel complex.

Elephant statues (top) in Surin, also home to the Prasat Ta Moan (left)

Nam Took Tad Ton, best in the rainy season

TAD TON NATIONAL PARK

➕ 310 F6 ☎ 044 853 333, 044 853 293 (information) 🚌 B200 🚗 21km (13 miles) north of Chaiyaphum on Route 2051
www.thaiforestbooking.com/nationalpark-eng.htm (for reserving bungalow accommodation in the park)

One of Thailand's smallest and less well-known national parks—217sq km (85sq miles) in size—Tad Ton can nevertheless boast some superb scenery. The highland landscape is characterized by dipterocarp and evergreen forest. With your own transportation it is easily reached on a day trip from Chaiyaphum (▷ 92), and outside of weekends or public holidays you are likely to have the place to yourself.

At the entrance to the park there is a track that leads to Nam Tok Tad Ton, a robust waterfall that is seen at its best between June and November during the rainy season. The water pours down from a large platform of stone and it is possible to swim in the basin below the waterfall. The nearby shrine, Chao Pho Tad Ton, is named after a hermit who lived in the area before it became a national park.

There is another smaller waterfall in the park, Pha Phuong, which is also signposted. Walks through the forest with a pair of binoculars reveal a rich birdlife, and you may also spot some barking deer and wild pigs. If you are here during the rainy season, when leeches are plentiful, you should come prepared with insect repellent and wear long trousers and suitable footwear.

Accommodation is available in two-bedroom bungalows with a fan. There is a small grocery shop for campers but no restaurant or food stands.

The seated Buddha at Wat Phra That Phanom

THAT PHANOM

The small town of That Phanom, with a delightful setting by the Mekong River, is home to a shrine revered by the inhabitants on either side of the river.

➕ 311 J5 🚌 Buses to/from Ubon Ratchathani, Udon Thani, Mukdahan, Sakhon Nakhon and Nakhon Phanom. *Songthaews* from Nakhon Phanom pass by Phra That Phanom

RATINGS	
Cultural interest	● ● ●
Photo stops	● ●
Walkability	● ●

TIP

● Try to plan your visit so you are in That Phanom between 8am and noon on a Monday or Thursday to coincide with the market.

Tucked away in the far northeast of Isan, 50km (31 miles) south of Nakhon Phanom, That Phanom has always enjoyed close links with the Laotian communities on the other side of the river. For centuries the villagers of both countries have worshiped as one at Wat Phra That Phanom. Every February, when the town celebrates a religious festival at the temple, Lao people arrive in large numbers to participate. Every Monday and Thursday morning, the Mekong River also serves to bring the nationalities together when Laotian farmers cross the river in boats laden with their fruit, vegetables, pigs, animal skins and exotic herbal remedies from the forest, all of which they hope to sell to Thais. You may not buy anything, but these markets are lively affairs and take place by the riverside.

The legend of Phra That Phanom is that a monk came to the area in the eighth year after the death of the Buddha (535BC), and five local rulers shared in the establishment of a simple brick shrine to house the Buddha relics in the monk's possession. The temple you see today, shining white and covered with gold leaf, was the result of restoration and rebuilding work in the 17th century and then again in the 1940s. Too high for its own good, the stupa collapsed in 1975 during a rainstorm and was rebuilt to its present height—still over 54m (177ft)—four years later. It's modelled on the That Luang in Vientiane, Laos. Devotees make offerings to the temple throughout the year.

A roadway connects the temple with the pier and passes under a Lao arch of victory—a version of the large one in the center of Vientiane. As is the custom, the temple faces both water and the rising sun. This old part of town has a number of old houses that combine characteristics of both Laotian-French and Chinese architecture.

Ubon Ratchathani

Built on the north bank of the Mun River, Ubon Ratchathani is the best base for exploring out-of-the-way attractions in this eastern corner of the country close to the Cambodian border.

A frieze at Wat Supatanaram (left). Smiling children on a school visit to Ubon Ratchathani (middle). A town monument (right)

RATINGS	
Cultural interest	● ● ●
Historic interest	● ●
Specialist shopping	● ● ● ●

BASICS

✚ 315 K7

ℹ Thanon Khuenthani, tel 043 243 770; daily 8.30–4.30

🚆 Ubon Ratchathani Station (tel 045 321 004), on the south side of the Mun River, is served by tuk-tuks and bus from the middle of town

🚌 The main bus station (tel 045 491 689–90), too far to walk to and best reached by tuk-tuk, is on Thanon Chayangkun and serves Korat, Roe Et, Si Saket, Surin and other local towns. Long-distance private buses to Bangkok, Chiang Mai and Phitsanulok use a separate terminal south of the river

✈ Just north of the middle of town (tel 045 244 073); flights to/from Bangkok

🚗 Budget (tel 045 240 507) car rental at the airport

SEEING UBON RATCHATHANI

The tourist office provides a useful town map that shows the location of the train and bus stations and the main hotels. It also shows the main bus routes within town, very useful for getting around because Ubon Ratchathani (usually called just Ubon) is spread out across a large area and some places are too far apart for walking. It makes sense to base yourself around the middle of town and the landmark Thung Si Muang Park. This keeps you close to the tourist office and the best places to eat.

Ubon vies with Khon Kaen as the best place in the northeast for quality shops selling local silk and cotton. The shops worth visiting are listed in the Shopping section (▷ 196–197).

HIGHLIGHTS

NATIONAL MUSEUM

✉ Thanon Khuantani, one block south of the park and three blocks west of the tourist office ☎ 045 255 071 🕐 Wed–Sun 9–4 💰 B30 🚌 City bus 2
Ubon's branch of the National Museum uses the old city hall building, an attractive one-story edifice built in 1918, with exhibits housed in the rooms around a central courtyard. The region's prehistory is introduced with displays of cave paintings, iron and bronze tools and bracelets. Dvaravati culture of sixth to tenth centuries is represented by some rich finds from the Ubon province, ninth-century boundary stones in particular. Pre-Angkor and Angkor civilization, from around the eighth to the thirteenth centuries, account for the museum's most important exhibits, including an exquisite Khmer lintel depicting a series of nine Hindu deities and a tenth-century statue of Ganesh. Other rooms are devoted to displays of local crafts and folk music and worth admiring is the wooden sugarcane press with a finely crafted gear mechanism.

MONUMENT OF MERIT

✉ Thung Si Muang Park, in the middle of town 🕐 Daily 7am–9pm 💰 Free
What will catch your eye in the park is the elongated and brightly painted Candle Sculpture, but it is worth seeking out a less

Colourful shrine at Wat Supatanaram in Ubon Ratchathani

conspicuous monument in the northeastern corner. Here you will find a simple, brick-built obelisk and an explanation of its purpose provided nearby. The notice explains how it was put there by a group of men who were prisoners of war, held in an Ubon camp by the Japanese in World War II. The men, who erected the obelisk after the war, wanted to express their thanks to those residents of Ubon who secretly provided them with provisions despite the risks involved.

WAT NONG BUA

✉ Off Thanon Chayangkul ⏰ Daily 7am–8pm 💲 Free 🚌 City bus 2 or a tuk-tuk 🚏 4km (2.5 miles) north of town on Route 212

This *wat* (temple), built in the mid-1950s, is modeled closely on the *wat* at Bodh Gaya in northeast India, the place where the Buddha achieved enlightenment. The lower part of its white tower is decorated with gold leaf, as is the *chedi* (monument housing a Buddhist relic) at the top, and the base is carved with fine reliefs from the *Jataka* tales. The niches at ground level are home to four standing Buddhas.

BACKGROUND

The Mun River, one of the major Mekong tributaries that cuts through Isan, meets the Mekong River just to the east of Ubon at Kong Chiam, and the prehistoric rock paintings there testify to the ancient origins of human development in this area. Dvaravati and Khmer cultures flourished around Ubon, followed by a strong Laotian influence that is still evident. The town became an important US base during the Vietnam War. Today, Ubon is a prosperous urban center and continues to develop.

TIP

● The time to be in Ubon is early July, when the city celebrates the start of a Buddhist retreat with festive parades of giant decorated candles. In early October, at the end of the retreat, there are more parades, fireworks and boat processions on the river.

A Chinese temple, Yasothon

Time for a drink in busy Udon Thani

YASOTHON

➕ 311 J7 🚌 Bus station is on Thanon Rattanakhet, with daily services to/from Ubon Ratchathani

The principal sight in Yasothon is Wat Mahathat, situated off the main road, which dates back to the foundation of the town itself. The La-style reliquary is thought to be from the seventh century, making Yasothon an ancient settlement.

If you are in Isan around the middle of May it is worth going out of your way to witness Yasothon's rocket festival, which is intended to encourage the gods to produce rain. Called Bun Bang Fai, it is the most exuberant of the rocket festivals that punctuate the skyline at the end of the dry season, and you will be astonished at the size (up to 8m/27ft long) and power (more than 20kg/44lb of gunpowder) of the bamboo rockets. They are fired from launching pads, made of concrete and wood, with local villages competing to see whose can ascend the highest and make the most impressive display. A panel of judges is involved and bets are laid amid the festive atmosphere. When you see spectators moving back from the launch pad, retreat even further back because the explosive charge is potentially dangerous and fatalities do occur.

Just over 20km (12 miles) to the east of Yasothon, reached by turning off Route 202 to the right between kilometer stones 18 and 19, the village of Ban Si Than is worth an excursion. It is a center for axe pillows production and you can observe villagers making them. They can be bought at very competitive prices.

If you miss Yasothon's rocket festival, try to catch Nong Khai's pyrotechnic display in June (▷ 197).

UDON THANI

A busy commercial city, with good transportation links, and a likely resting stop while journeying through Isan or visiting nearby Ban Chiang (▷ 90).

➕ 310 G5 ℹ️ 16/5 Thanon Mukmontri, tel 042 325 406; daily 8.30–4.30 🚌 The central bus station is on Thanon Tikattanon; local buses use another bus station at Talat Rungsina on the north side of town
🚆 Udon Thani Station, with daily trains to/from Bangkok ✈️ Daily flights to/from Bangkok with Thai Airways, AirAsia and Nok Air; the airport is 3km (1.9 miles) outside town and the main hotels meet all incoming flights and shuttle guests to the airport for departing flights ❓ Budget (tel 042 246 805) car rental at the airport
www.udonmaps.com

RATINGS	
Good for food	● ●
Value for money	● ● ●
Walkability	● ●

Udon Thani is a city with two centers; they're too far apart to comfortably walk between them but tuk-tuks are plentiful and a fare from one to the other is B30. The city is a manufacturing center for tuk-tuks and you will see some splendidly upmarket versions, far larger than normal ones and looking like giant motorcycles with posh seating attached.

The train station and the main bus station are both on the eastern side of town. They are close to a modern shopping mall, the Charoensri Complex on Thanon Prachak (▷ 197), which has a Robinsons department store, a cinema, a food center, plus banks and ATM machines. Next door is the Charoensri Grand Royal (▷ 277), the city's main hotel and one of the best places in town to eat. Internet access is available from the small shops opposite the Charoensri Complex.

The town's tourist office is on the northwest side of town, by the side of the landscaped Nong Prajak Park and adjoining lake. Too hot during the day, the paths around the park come alive in the cool of the evening, when lakeside restaurants open for business.

Three main roads—Thanon Wattana Nuwong, Thanon Prajak and Thanon Phosi—run parallel to one another and link the park with Thanon Tikattanon. Adjacent to the tourist office is Lak Meuang, the city's shrine, where daily offerings are made. At first you are more likely to notice a large and garish Chinese shrine, Pu Ya, with a huge statue of a golden dragon inside.

During the Vietnam War, Udon province was home to a number of US Air Force camps and the city became a popular rest-and-recreation center for servicemen; the plethora of pubs with bar girls is partly a legacy of this era.

THE NORTH

Thailand's highest mountains mark the boundaries of the country's northernmost region and ring its moated capital, Chiang Mai. The jungle-covered heights are challenging terrain, while the deep valleys are cut by fast-flowing rivers. Upland trails lead to remote hill-tribe villages where visitors receive a warm welcome.

MAJOR SIGHTS

Mountain view from Chiang Dao (above). The entrance to the caves (left)

CHIANG DAO

Famous for its caves, the village of Chiang Dao sits in the shadow of Thailand's third-highest mountain.

RATINGS

Good for kids	● ● ● ○
Outdoor pursuits	● ● ● ○
Photo stops	● ● ● ○

BASICS

⊞ 308 C2
ℹ TAT Northern Office, Region 1, 105/1 Chiang Mai–Lamphun road, Amphoe Muang, Chiang Mai 50000, tel 053 248 604/7; daily 9–5
🕐 Caves: Sat–Sun 8.30–4.30
💰 Caves: B5

The small market town of Chiang Dao, 75km (45 miles) north of Chiang Mai, is famous for its caves, among the most spectacular in Thailand, which wind deep into the interior of the jungle-clad mountain that broods over the area. The caves penetrate up to 15km (9 miles) into the remarkable mountain, Doi Luang, that leaps straight up out of the rice paddies surrounding the town. Doi Luang stands at 2,225m (7,450ft) and is Thailand's third-highest mountain and perhaps its most spectacular. Its steep, jungle-covered sides are a challenge for the hardiest hiker, but the rewards of a two-day slog up the narrow access path to the summit and back down again are immeasurable, including views to die for. Several species of wildlife, including deer and wild boar, have their home in the impenetrable, forested slopes.

A SPECTACULAR DRIVE
The drive to the caves from the main Chiang Mai–Chiang Dao road is spectacular, a 1.5km-long (about a mile) avenue lined by high yang trees and fronted by the sheer face of the mountain. Like all caves in Thailand, these come with their own mythology, based on the fable of a local hermit who is said to have lived and meditated in them for 1,000 years. The gods rewarded him by constructing within the caverns a collection of fantastic images, presumably the stalactites, stalagmites and crystallized calcium deposits you'll find within them to this day. The first two caverns—Tham Phra Nawn (Cave of the Sleeping Buddha) and Tham Phra Seua Dao (Leopard Cave)—are lit, but you'll need to hire a guide with a lantern (B100 per group of eight) to explore further.

ELEPHANT RIDING
There's much else to keep the visitor in Chiang Dao for a day or two, including an elephant training center (daily 8–5) in the nearby village of Mae Tang. The elephants demonstrate their logging skills and play football (shows daily at 9 and 1), and give rides through the jungle and across a river where raft trips (B800) are also offered.

The view from Wat Phra That Pha Ngao (above). Try the noodle soup at one of Chiang Khong's markets (right)

CHIANG KHONG

Sitting on a broad sweep of the Mekong River, Chiang Khong is the major border crossing between northern Thailand and Laos and is a favorite staging post for visitors traveling through Southeast Asia.

It's hard for the first-time visitor to believe that this rather rundown riverside town, consisting of little more than one main street, was once the capital of a realm that stretched across northern Laos and into China. It was founded at the start of the eighth century and grew into a powerful city state and important trading post between the east and west.

There's little evidence of the town's grand past now though, apart from one 13th-century *chedi* (monument housing a Buddhist relic) at the riverside Wat Luang. There are ambitious plans to restore the town to its earlier economic importance; eventually it will become a vital element of the great Asian Highway project, linking East and Southeast Asia with a bridge currently being constructed across the Mekong. Large flatbed ferries now carry traffic across the river from a jetty on the edge of Chiang Khong to the small Laotian port town of Ban Xouay. Visitors cross on perilously narrow motor-driven canoes, but you'll need a visa to enter Laos on the other side.

Chiang Khong is jammed for most of the year with backpackers from all over the world on their way to or from Laos, Vietnam or China. They give the place a cosmopolitan air quite out of proportion to its size, and the modest guesthouses that cater to them party deep into the night.

The town's markets, strung out along its dusty main street, are awash with goods from Laos and China, mostly textiles and cheap electronic gadgetry, but hill-tribe handicrafts can also be found and are a much better buy.

A LAST RESTING PLACE

On a hill overlooking the river is a reminder of Chiang Khong's more recent history—a cemetery containing the graves of more than 200 Nationalist Chinese soldiers who ended up here after fleeing from Mao Tse Tung's victorious Communist army in 1949. Their graves all face in the direction of China.

RATINGS	
Activities	● ● ●
Good for kids	● ● ●
Photo stops	● ● ●

BASICS

309 D1

TAT Northern Office, Region 2, 448/16 Thanon Singhaklai, Amphoe Muang, Chiang Rai 57000, tel 053 744 674/5; daily 8.30–4.30

TIPS

● If your guesthouse gets too crowded and noisy with the backpackers who throng high-season Chiang Khong, take an evening stroll along the riverbank path and watch the locals cast their lines into the dark waters of the Mekong in the hopes of hooking something for the family pot (the catfish in these parts are the world's largest).

● Even if you don't intend to visit Laos, take a ferry ride across the Mekong and at least step on to Laotian soil before heading back. Boatmen at the ferry crossing will take you over and back for B20 or so. A longer trip on the Mekong by longtailed boat costs between B400 and B500.

Chiang Mai

Northern Thailand's regional capital is dubbed the "Rose of the North" because of its natural beauty and the profusion of flowers that drapes its ancient walls and lines its moat and river bridges.

The entire family on a single moped!

Fairy lights at the Night Bazaar

A pickup gets a dousing at the Songkran (Water Festival)

RATINGS	
Cultural interest	●●●○
Good for food	●●●●●
Historic interest	●●●●●
Specialist shopping	●●●○

BASICS

✚ 308 C3
ℹ TAT Northern Office, Region 1, 105/1 Chiang Mai–Lamphun road, Amphoe Muang, Chiang Mai 50000, tel 053 248 604/7; daily 8.30–4.30

SEEING CHIANG MAI

Chiang Mai's old city is a maze of narrow streets and brick-paved lanes leading to ancient *wats* (temples), quiet monastery gardens, hidden bars, restaurants and boutiques. Although the old city is ringed by an efficient one-way traffic system, the roads and lanes are often as clogged as Bangkok's, and the pollution is only slightly less heavy. Only the most daring visitors rent a car for city sightseeing, so stick to tuk-tuks and red-covered *songthaews*. They are responsible for much of the pollution but are still the best way to get around. Taxis are gradually replacing the *songthaews* but are still difficult to find. *Samlaws* (tricycle "taxis") are ecologically friendly but slow. Bicycles and motorcycles are easily and cheaply rented, but by far the best way of exploring the old city is still on foot. The old city is about one mile square (2.59sq km), and most of the major attractions are to be found within its walls and moat.

HIGHLIGHTS

WAT CHIANG MAN
✚ 117 D2 ✉ Thanon Ratchaphanikai 🕐 Daily 6am–9pm 💰 Donation box
Chiang Mai's oldest temple is also its most interesting. Built in 1297–98 by the first Lanna king, Mengrai, on the site of his Chiang Mai palace, Wat Chiang Man was restored to its present state by the 18th-century monarch, Gawila. The main *viharn*, its beamed ceiling supported by 10 massive teak pillars, is an absolute masterpiece of gold and crimson decoration, but a neighboring, smaller and more modern hall contains the temple's true treasures: the Phra Sila, a carved stone Buddha figure that is said to have originated in India, and the Phra Setangamani, a crystal Buddha reputed to be 1,800 years old. They were placed here by King Mengrai himself and are now contained within a gold and crimson cage, behind three sets of iron bars. At the rear of the main *viharn* is a square, Sukhothai-style *chedi* (monument housing a Buddhist relic) supported by 17 elephants, which was constructed here in Mengrai's time and is said to contain a lock of the Buddha's hair.

The ancient temple complex of Wat Chiang Man, built in the 13th century

WAT CHEDI LUANG

✚ 116 C3 ✉ Corner of Prapokkloa and Rachadamnoen roads ⏰ Daily 6am–9pm
💰 Donation box

Towering above the park-like monastery grounds of Wat Chedi Luang are the bulky remains of an enormous stupa which 15th-century King Saen Muang Ma ordered to be built in the exact center of the old city to safeguard a relic of the Buddha. The king died before it was completed, which was just as well, because an earthquake later destroyed the top of the 86m (282ft) monument— a very bad omen, indeed. One of the carved elephants on the stupa's massive base (the most weather-beaten one) dates from those times. Sinuous *nagas*, or mythical serpents, border the remains of steep flights of steps that lead up to golden images of the Buddha sitting in three loges of the stupa. The fourth, east-facing loge, has a replica of the Phra Keo Emerald Buddha which was once safeguarded here on its long journey to Bangkok. Monks once climbed the steps of the stupa to anoint its Buddha images in holy water. Now they employ an ingenious pulley system that carries the water up to the top of the stupa and then tips it over the structure. You're encouraged to do the same—it's a way of earning merit, avoiding bad luck and easing your journey through the hereafter. The leafy temple grounds contain a 10.5m-long (35ft) reclining 15th-century Buddha, his face contemplating the *chedi*, and a handsome 19th-century *viharn*, or assembly hall. Among the neat little chapels that dot the grounds of the temple is one containing the 13th-century city pillar and another housing a jolly 15th-century golden Buddha, his hands clasping his ample belly and an expression of sheer bliss on his broad face. If you visit at 6pm you'll see and hear the monks at evening prayer and, on fine evenings, witness the sun set brilliantly beyond the *viharn*'s mountain backdrop—an unforgettable sight.

Devotees at Wat Chedi Luang

TIPS

THE SIGHTS

• Chiang Mai's top tourist draw is its celebrated Night Bazaar (⊞ 117 D3), which lines central Thanon Chang Klan for a mile (1.6km) every night from 7pm. There's been a bazaar here for centuries, and although fake watches and fashion accessories, pirated CDs and DVDs now dominate the wares on offer, some of the goods haven't changed a great deal: silks, textiles and hill-tribe handicrafts. The bazaar is held in all winds and weathers, although there's also a permanent building, the Night Market, on this section of Thanon Chang Klan. Some of the stalls and shops here sell genuine antiques. You're expected to bargain—offer half the demanded price and then work toward an acceptable compromise. If you find the Night Bazaar and the Night Market a touch too commercial and if you're in town on a Sunday, make for Thanon Rachadamnoen, which is closed to traffic for the day and turned over to street traders, musicians, artists and craftspeople. In the evening, it becomes a "magical mile," drawing Thais from their homes for a Mediterranean-type "corso" (promenade).

• The English-speaking monks of two Chiang Mai *wats* are happy to meet visitors and discuss their cloistered lives, Buddhism and Thai culture. You can find the monks sitting beneath the trees in the compound of Wat Chedi Luang, Thanon Prapokkloa, every afternoon, or on the campus of Mahachulalongkorn Buddhist University, behind Wat Suandok, Thanon Stuep, on Monday, Wednesday and Friday afternoons.

• Chiang Mai can get oppressively hot, particularly in March and April. If the heat gets too much to bear, take a tip from the Thais and spend a few hours at the city ice-rink, on the top floor of the Central department store on Thanon Huay Kaeow. If you're skating, entrance and skate rental cost B70.

You can fish in the moat surrounding Chiang Mai's old city

WAT PHRA SINGH
⊞ 116 C2 ✉ Thanon Singharat ⏰ Daily 7am–9pm 💰 Donation box
Chiang Mai's principal temple ensemble dominates the western side of the old city, and its high white walls embrace a collection of centuries-old buildings and *chedis* within tree-shaded park-like grounds. Its oldest structure is a *chedi* built in 1345 to contain the remains of the Lanna ruler Pha Yoo. A modern *viharn*—an airy synthesis of white, red and gold—houses a magnificent gilded Buddha, while the temple's true treasure—a 14th-century Buddha said to have originated in Sukhothai—sits in an older, more modest but exquisitely decorated chapel at the rear.

CHIANG MAI TRIBAL MUSEUM
⊞ 116 C1 (off map) ✉ Ratchanangkla Park, Thanon Chotana (the Mae Rim road) ☎ 053 210 872 ⏰ Daily 9–4 💰 Free
The history, culture and way of life of the hill tribes that inhabit the mountains of northern Thailand are explained and illustrated in this comprehensive museum on the outskirts of Chiang Mai. Since many of the villages closest to the city have become little more than small theme parks, crowded with tourist groups and tour buses, a visit to the museum is perhaps the best way to get to know these fascinating but marginalized and often ill-treated people. The handicrafts on show demonstrate their aestheticism, imagination and skill with textiles, basketwork, bamboo, rattan and tropical woods.

NATIONAL MUSEUM
⊞ 116 B1 ✉ Chiang Mai–Lampang road ☎ 053 221 308 ⏰ Daily 9–4 💰 B30
The history of the Lanna kingdom and its culture are well documented and displayed in Chiang Mai's premier museum, a large Lanna-style building on the edge of the city. Among the exhibits, distributed in six sections over two floors, is a fine collection of local San Kamphaeng porcelain dating back to the 14th century.

WAT CHET YOT

✚ 116 B1 ✉ Chiang Mai–Lampang road 🕐 Daily, no fixed hours

One of Chiang Mai's most attractive temple compounds sits on the busy "superhighway" that rings the city. In the center of lawns and paved walkways is the seven-spired *chedi* (Chet Yot) after which the temple is named. It was built in 1455 as a local memorial to the temple in Bodhgaya, India, the village where the Buddha was said to have gained enlightenment.

WIANG KUM KAM

✚ 117 E4 (off map) ✉ 5km (3 miles) south of Chiang Mai on the Chiang Mai–Lamphun road ☎ 053 222 262 🕐 Daily sunrise–sunset

Only in 1984 did archaeologists discover that King Mengrai's first Chiang Mai capital was downriver from the present city. He first chose a site on a bend in the Ping River, but discovered the folly of his choice in the first rainy season, around 1293, when floods inundated the new settlement. Nevertheless, at least six temples were built there, and their ruins have now been laid bare. You can tour them in a horse and carriage (B200) or by tram (B250).

BACKGROUND

Chiang Mai was founded in the 13th century by the Lanna King Mengrai, who at first built his citadel slightly south of the present city, before being forced to move to higher ground by persistent flooding. His new city (Chiang Mai means "new city") grew within a wide moat and stout defensive walls and bastions. The moat still exists, and many of the ancient fortifications have been reconstructed, giving Chiang Mai much of its charm. Despite its stout defences, Chiang Mai was overrun in the 16th century by Burmese invaders, who sacked the city and carried most of its people off to slavery. Lanna became a Burmese vassal state for nearly 200 years, before the Burmese were driven out in 1774. The Lanna kingdom retained its independence for nearly another century before being absorbed into the Siam state ruling from Bangkok.

The old city is compact enough to walk everywhere, even for little legs

The intricately carved façade of Wat Phra Singh

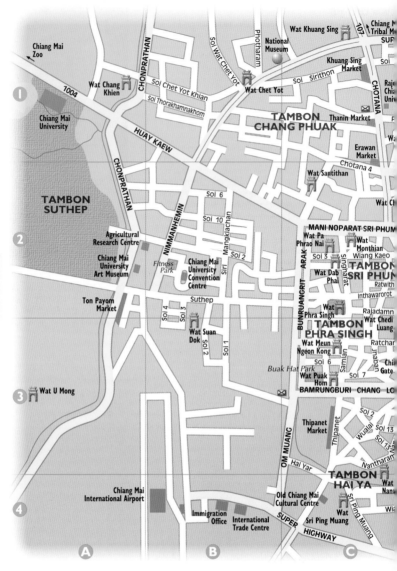

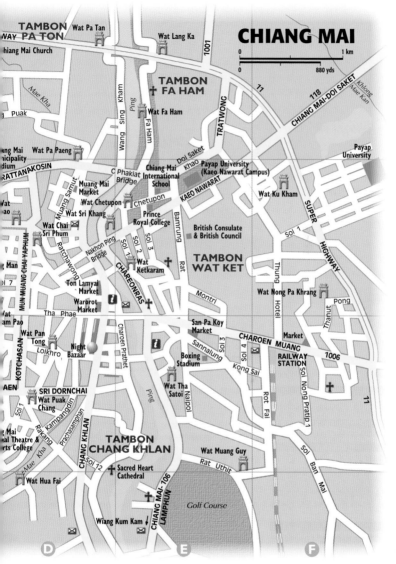

Buddha statue at Wat Phra Singh (top). Serpents guard the temple of Wat Phra Kaew (above)

CHIANG RAI

Chiang Rai possesses three of the region's most historic temples. Thailand's northernmost city is also an ideal center from which to tour the Golden Triangle and the mountains that border Myanmar (Burma) and Laos.

RATINGS

Cultural interest	●●●
Historic interest	●●●
Specialist shopping	●●●

BASICS

➕ 309 D1

ℹ️ TAT Northern Office, Region 2, 448/16 Thanon Singhaklai, Amphoe Muang, Chiang Rai 57000, tel 053 717 433, 053 744 674/5; daily 8.30–4.30

TIP

● Chiang Rai's night market rivals Chiang Mai's for size and variety of goods on sale. It's open every evening from 6–11.

HISTORIC TEMPLES

Chiang Rai is older than Chiang Mai, founded in 1256 by King Mengrai, who moved his capital progressively southward from its original site on the Mekong River. One of its temples, Wat Phra Kaew (daily 6am–8pm), sheltered the fabled Emerald Buddha on its long journey to Bangkok. A modern copy, donated in the late 1990s by a Chinese millionaire, now sits in the main *viharn* of the temple. Chiang Rai's oldest temple, Wat Doi Tong (daily 6am–8pm), built before the arrival of King Mengrai, commands a hilltop site above Wat Phra Kaew. The climb there, through shady woodland, is well worth the effort for the view of Chiang Rai and the Kok River that embraces the city. It's said that King Mengrai also made the climb and planned the layout of his future capital from this vantage point.

Chiang Rai's third temple of note, Wat Phra Singh (daily 6am–8pm), dates from the 14th century and has a handsome Lanna-style *viharn* with some very fine wood carving, bronze Buddha images and murals. It once boasted one of northern Thailand's most beautiful Buddha statues, the Phra Buddha Singh, which was carried off to Chiang Mai by King Mengrai. It's now the finest feature of Chiang Mai's Wat Phra Singh, and the one you see in Chiang Rai's temple of the same name is a later copy.

SHOPPING BARGAINS

Chiang Rai has a night bazaar to rival Chiang Mai's. It's also well stocked with hill-tribe handicrafts, brought down from the nearby mountains every evening by women of the six hill tribes of the region: the Akha, Yao, Meo, Lisu, Lahu and Karen. The bazaar, just off Thanon Phaholyothin, is the place to eat authentic northern Thai food, from any of the stalls that line the road.

Don't miss Khun Kon Forest Park (daily 9am–6pm), 29km (18 miles) south of Chiang Rai, has the highest waterfall in Chiang Rai province—Nam Tok Tat Mok—which plunges more than 60m (200ft) into jungle-fringed pools. The park also has some picturesque hill-tribe villages.

Decorative sa-paper umbrellas

BO SANG

⊞ 308 C3 🛈 TAT Northern Office, Region 1, 105/1 Chiang Mai–Lamphun road, Amphoe Muang, Chiang Mai 50000, tel 053 248 604/7; daily 8.30–4.30

Umbrellas are the specialty of this village 8km (5 miles) northeast of Chiang Mai. The story goes that some 100 years ago a local monk was traveling in Myanmar and asked a craftsman there to mend his umbrella. The monk, Phra In Tha, was surprised to see him use *sa* paper, made from mulberry tree bark. Phra In Tha took the technique home to Borsang and showed Thai villagers how to make *sa*-paper umbrellas. The largest workshop, the Borsang Umbrella Centre (tel 053 338 466; daily 8–5) is in the center of the village. For a fee of B50 upwards you can have your own design painted on the umbrella.

DOI ANGKHANG

⊞ 308 C1 🛈 The Royal Agricultural Station, Tambon Maengon, Amphoe Fang, tel 053 450 107/9

Tucked away in the northwestern corner of Thailand, Doi Angkhang is a delightfully remote upland range, reminiscent of the former colonial hill stations of Asia. Most of the jungle-clad range is a royal agricultural station, worked by the inhabitants of nearby hill-tribe villages. These villages are totally unspoiled and include a community of Chinese descendants of Kuomintang Nationalist Chinese soldiers who fled the advancing forces of Mao Tse Tung. More than 1,000 bird species populate the area, which is criss-crossed by mountain trails that visitors can travel on a hired mule. Bungalows can be rented at the Royal Agricultural Station and there's a luxury hotel, the Angkhang Nature Resort.

Monks in saffron robes beside the Mekong at Chiang Saen

CHIANG SAEN

Destined to become one of the major ports of the Mekong River, ancient Chiang Saen hums with activity as construction workers expand its harbor facilities and archaeologists lay bare its 800-year-old foundations.

⊞ 309 D1
🛈 TAT Northern Office, Region 2, 448/16 Thanon Singhaklai, Amphoe Muang, Chiang Rai 57000, tel 053 744 674/5; daily 8.30-4.30

RATINGS	
Good for kids	● ● ●
Historic interest	● ● ● ●
Photo stops	● ● ●

This neglected Mekong River town is being restored to the important status it once held in Thai history. Harbor installations are being modernized and enlarged to create a port that will handle freighters and barges from Myanmar (Burma), China and Laos. Between the harbor and the town center, work is going ahead on excavating the ancient citadel of Chiang Saen. It was founded in the 13th century by Mengrai, who used it as a stepping stone to creating the Lanna kingdom, setting up his royal residences first here, then in Chiang Rai and finally in Chiang Mai.

Invading Burmese forces laid waste to ancient Chiang Saen in 1588, and a disastrous fire two centuries later gutted the rebuilt city. But the foundations and walls of the old city are now being laid bare, and many finds from Chiang Saen's early history are in the local museum (702 Thanon Phahonyothin, tel 053 777 102; Wed–Sun 9–4; adult B30, child under 14 free).

Established nearly 50 years ago, the museum is one of the most important in northern Thailand, tracing not only the origins of the Lanna kingdom but the prehistory of this region of the Mekong Valley. Among the museum's treasures is a very beautiful 16th-century bronze depicting the emblematic Lanna flame, found in the Mekong. A graceful 19th-century Burmese receptacle attests to the influence Burma once wielded.

Dating from Mengrai's time is Wat Pa Sak and its stepped *chedi*, said to contain holy relics brought here from across the Mekong when the city was founded. The temple's name, Pa Sak, means "teak forest," referring to the hundreds of teak trees planted to provide wood for construction. Nearby is an octagonal temple, Wat Phra That Luang, dating from the 14th century.

Don't miss Longtail boats berthed below the customs post on the main riverside boulevard take visitors across the Mekong to an island that is Laotian territory, although you don't need a passport. The boatmen charge B200 to B500 for the trip.

THE SIGHTS

Doi Inthanon National Park

**Doi Inthanon is Thailand's highest mountain, named after
Chiang Mai's last ruler, Inthawuchayanon, and it dominates
a national park where tigers still roam.**

View from the summit of Doi Inthanon at dusk

*The floral display at Queen
Sirikit's chedi*

RATINGS	
Good for kids	●●●
Photo stops	●●●●
Walkability	●●●●

BASICS

✚ 308 B3

ℹ TAT Northern Office, Region 1,
105/1 Chiang Mai–Lamphun Road,
Amphoe Muang, Chiang Mai 50000,
tel 053 248 604/7; daily 8.30–4.30

www.thaiparks.com
An extensive listing of national parks,
searchable by location and activity.

SEEING DOI INTHANON NATIONAL PARK

The direct route up Doi Inthanon winds gradually through thick
forest that obscures any view of the summit. For an impression of
the height and sheer magnitude of the Doi Inthanon massif turn
left just before the summit onto Route 1192, which leads to the
isolated weaving village of Mae Chaem. From the valley floor you
have a breathtaking view of this grand mountain.

HIGHLIGHTS

PLANT LIFE

Giant rhododendrons and delicate varieties of roses grow in
profusion on the park's upper slopes, and wild orchids cling to the
massive trees of the impenetrable jungle. Thick rainforests and
towering stands of bamboo clothe the mountain's tropical zone,
while teak and pine grow under close Forestry Department
supervision and are hence untouched by illegal loggers.

ANIMAL LIFE

Tigers have been spotted on Doi Inthanon, but they're a very rare
sight. You're much more likely to see deer, gibbons, wild boar and
Siamese hares. The national park is home to more than 300 bird
species (bird-watchers can hire knowledgeable guides at the park
headquarters).

WATERFALLS

Doi Inthanon National Park has some of the highest and most
beautiful waterfalls in Thailand. They are all well signposted and
relatively easy to reach. The highest of them is also the most remote:
the 250m (820ft) Mae Ya waterfall, in the southern section of the
park. It's a 5km (3-mile) hike but well worth the effort to see this
mass of water, higher than Niagara Falls, plunge over a series of steps.
    The easiest to reach are the Watchiratan Falls, 22km (13 miles)
from the national park turn-off on Route 108, and the Mae Klang
Falls, 8km (5 miles) on the same road. Mae Klang, a favorite picnic
spot for Chiang Mai families, has a small market and food stands.

Among the most beautiful of the park's falls is the Namtok Siripum. It plunges more than 100m (300ft) over a high cliff towering above a valley where the royal family support an agricultural project, 11km (6.5 miles) from the edge of the park.

Queen Sirikit's chedi *at Doi Inthanon*

THE ROYAL PROJECT

The Siripum Falls feed trout-breeding tanks, which are one of the most successful enterprises of the national park's royal project. The trout raised here find their way onto the menus of Thailand's leading hotels and, of course, the royal palace. You can enjoy a grilled trout at the simple restaurant that welcomes visitors to the royal project. The trout dishes come in six varieties, including incongruously hot and spicy sauces. The horticultural gardens and greenhouses that make up most of the royal project are a gardener's dream (daily 6–8; free).

A GOOD HIKE

Doi Inthanon National Park is true hiker's territory, and the area is criss-crossed by trails connecting the many hill-tribe villages. Hikers can stay in the villages for a modest fee (negotiable with the village elders); the easiest route to the summit of Doi Inthanon involves three overnights with Karen communities en route. The route to the summit starts at the Mae Klang Falls and takes the hiker through three conveniently located villages: Mae Aeb, Pa Mon and Pang Somdet.

BACKGROUND

The nature-loving ruler Inthawuchayanon was so enchanted by this mountainous region, just 80km (50 miles) from his Chiang Mai palace, that he ordained his ashes to be buried on its 2,330m (7,642ft) summit. A modest white *chedi* in a forest clearing contains his remains at a spot called "the roof of Thailand." The serpentine route to the top winds through two distinct climatic zones, from tropical jungle to deciduous oaks and evergreen firs. In just 30km (18 miles) the average night-time temperature drops in winter from a pleasant 21°C (70°F) to near freezing, with a record of -8°C (17.5°F). Spectacular waterfalls—including Thailand's highest—are easily accessible, either on foot or by vehicle, and hill-tribe villages welcome overnight visitors. Just below the summit and Inthawuchayon's grave are two other, larger *chedis* erected in honor of the present king and queen.

> **TIP**
> ● For the best views of Doi Inthanon avoid the most direct route (Route 108 until Chom Tong, then the country road to the summit)—drive farther on Route 108 until Hot, then take the country road to Mae Chaem and from there to the summit of the mountain. From the valley floor, the Doi Inthanon massif is displayed in all its majesty.

The compound at Wat Phra That Doi Suthep (above). The national park (left)

DOI SUTHEP/ DOI PUI NATIONAL PARK

Chiang Mai's "guardian" mountains, 1,544m (5,000ft) Doi Suthep and Doi Pui, rise steeply to the west. Their forested slopes, waterfalls, ponds and lake form the Doi Pui National Park. The park's entrance is a 10-minute drive from the city.

Doi Suthep's mountaintop temple is one of northern Thailand's most revered places of pilgrimage. It's said that an elephant carrying a Buddha relic was led up the mountain, and on the ridge where it first stopped a *chedi* was built to contain the sacred object. A community of monks later built a temple there.

Until 1935 the only way to reach the temple was along a steep jungle path. Today it's a 10-minute journey on a well-paved road.

WAT PHRA THAT DOI SUTHEP
The broad, leafy terrace of the temple complex sits like a shelf below the summit of the 1,080m (3,542ft) Doi Suthep and commands a spectacular view of Chiang Mai below. The extensive temple ensemble of chapels *(bot)*, assembly halls *(viharn)*, chedis (the main one covered in gold leaf), Buddha images and frescoed cloisters took shape over the past seven centuries. Don't leave without striking one of the sonorous bells that border the terrace. *Songthaews* (B50) set out on the steep mountain road from parking areas on Thanon Huay Kaew, Thanon Sri Poom and outside the Wat Prasingh on Thanon Samlan. From the Doi Suthep parking area it's a long but pleasant climb up a broad flight of steps to the temple, but if that seems too daunting then an ugly funicular also makes the journey.

PHUPING PALACE
The king's summer residence near the summit of Doi Suthep is more like an alpine lodge than a palace. The house itself is closed to the public, but the grounds are worth visiting for the rose garden alone.

DOI PUI MEO
From the parking area below Phuping Palace a road leads 4km (2.5 miles) to a Meo hill-tribe village. The main street is lined by makeshift shops and workrooms where Hmong women create handicrafts.

RATINGS

Cultural interest	●●●○
Photo stops	●●●○
Walkability	●●●○

BASICS

✚ 308 B3

🛈 TAT Northern Office, Region 1, 105/1 Chiang Mai–Lamphun road, Amphoe Muang, Chiang Mai 50000, tel 053 248 604/7; daily 8.30–4.30

Wat Phra That Doi Suthep
✉ Doi Suthep 🕐 6am–7pm 💶 Adult B30, child (under 12) free
Phuping Palace
✉ Doi Suthep 🕐 Daily 8.30–4.30, except when the royal family is in residence, usually from mid-Jan to early Feb 💶 Palace grounds B20

TIP

● A pleasant, shady path leads from the national park entrance on Thanon Huay Kaew about 5km (3 miles) up the mountain, emerging on the main road, where you can flag down one of the many red *songthaews* that cruise the route.

Hill-tribe children from Doi Mae Salong

Doi Phu Kha National Park

Wooden and straw huts in Fang

DOI MAE SALONG

🕇 309 C1 🕇 TAT Northern Office, Region 2, 448/16 Thanon Singhaklai, Amphoe Muang, Chiang Rai 57000, tel 053 717 433, 053 744 674/5; daily 8.30–4.30 🚌 Regular bus services from Chiang Mai and Chiang Rai

Drive to this remote mountain community in the far north of Thailand and you'd be forgiven for believing you'd arrived at a Chinese border town. It was settled some 50 years ago by a Nationalist Army regiment fleeing from Mao Tse Tung's Communist forces in China's civil war. Thailand's government allowed the refugees to stay provided they helped in its own efforts to suppress Thai communists. The Chinese integrated well into the local community and became farmers and opened small businesses, including a restaurant—the Villa—which is today one of the best in the area. Their descendants keep alive many Chinese traditions, however, and the town has a distinctly Chinese character, with its own Buddhist temple, cemetery and specialty shops. It sits atop a 1,700m (5,600ft) mountain range, with magnificent views that some elderly nostalgic residents will tell you stretch as far as China.

DOI PHU KHA NATIONAL PARK

🕇 309 E2 ✉ Tambol Phu Kha, Amphoe Pua, Nan Province 55120 ☎ 054 70 10 00 💰 B200 🕇 Tourist Information Service, 46 Thanon Suriyapong, Amphoe Muang, Nan 55000, tel 054 710 216; Mon–Fri 8.30–4.30

Northern Thailand's largest national park is also the most remote, covering 1,704sq km (650sq miles) of mountainous terrain bordering Laos. From the 1872m (6,140ft) summit of Doi Phu Kha, there are breathtaking views deep into Laos, although it's a long trek there from the park headquarters. The rocky outcrops of the mountain are home to the rare "ancient palm," while oaks and other deciduous trees grow at this altitude. Caves riddle the limestone uplands, and a mountain river flows directly through one, Tham Lot. The waterfalls are spectacular, and one of the pleasures of a stay at the park is a day's trek to either Phufah or Fah Shee Nok cascades for a cooling swim and a picnic in the shade of their jungle settings. Rooms or chalets can be rented at the park headquarters for B800 to B3,200 per night. The headquarters is reached on the Nan–Pua road. A signpost 60km (36 miles) from Nan indicates the 25km (15-mile) side road to the park.

DOI TUNG

🕇 309 D1 ✉ Doi Tung Development Project, Mae Fah Luang, Chiang Rai 57240 ☎ 053 767 015/7 🕐 Daily 6.30–6 💰 Royal villa: B70; gardens: B80; Princess Mother Commemoration Hall: B30; ticket for all 3 attractions: adult B150, child half price 💰 B200, child B100

The Doi Tung mountain southwest of Chiang Rai is the site of a unique royal project to wean hill-tribe farmers away from opium cultivation by encouraging them to engage in profitable handicrafts. The project was begun by the king's mother, the revered "Princess Mother," and is now run successfully by the nonprofit Mae Fah Luang Foundation. The Princess Mother's royal villa (daily 9–5) sits near the summit, overlooking coffee plantations, nurseries and workshops that make up a humming center of commercial activity. The workshops—the "Cottage Industry Center"—turn out traditional textiles, carpets, ceramics, mulberry-paper products and pack the coffee that grows on the mountain. Just below the villa is a lodge with 47 rooms (B2,000 to B2,500). Reservations are essential.

FANG

🕇 308 C1 🕇 Mae Fang National Park, P.O. 39, Fang District, Chiang Mai 50110, tel 053 453 517/8; daily 8.30–4.30 www.dnp.go.th/index_eng

Fang, founded in the 13th century by the Lanna king Mengrai, is the gateway to one of Thailand's newest national parks, Mae Fang. It's a beautiful region of mountains, valleys, waterfalls, hot springs and a rich variety of flora and fauna, including deer, sloth, wild boar—and even bears. About 70km (40 miles) of the park borders Myanmar, a remote highland region rising to Thailand's second-highest mountain, Doi Phahompok (2,285m/7,495ft). The 7km (4-mile) hike to the grassy summit of the mountain is rewarded by a breathtaking view of the border region between Thailand and Myanmar. A circular route takes you past several caves and two waterfalls. Next to the park entrance and headquarters is a natural hot spring with 40m-high (131ft) geysers. Entrance to the park costs B200 (B50 for a vehicle), and bungalows can be rented (B2,000 per night).

HANG CHAT

🕇 308 C3 🕇 Tourist Information Lampang, Tessaban Lampang (Lampang Municipality), tel 054 219 300; 8.30–4.30 www.lampang.go.th

In a forest just off the main Lampang–Chiang Mai highway

Continued on page 129

THE SIGHTS

Lampang

Northern Thailand's second-largest city struggles to maintain its historic role as a major commercia
and cultural center and tends to be bypassed by tourists on their way to Chiang Mai. It has much t
offer, however, including a relaxed riverside lifestyle and one of Thailand's most magnificent temple

Wat Phra That Lampang Luang   Take a carriage ride in Lampang   Young monks at work in Lampang

RATINGS	
Cultural interest	● ● ● ○
Good for kids	● ● ●
Historic interest	● ● ● ●
Walkability	● ● ●

BASICS

✚ 309 C3

🛈 Tourist Information, Tessaban Lampang (Lampang Municipality), tel 054 219 300; Mon–Fri 8–5

www.lampang.go.th
Limited English site listing local statistics and attractions.

TIP

● Lampang's horse-drawn carriages can't be flagged down like normal taxis. There are special carriage stands on several street corners.

SEEING LAMPANG

Lampang is famous for its horse-drawn carriages, the only place in Thailand where this romantic and ecologically friendly mode of transport is used. You'll pay more than the locals, but the fare (B150 to B300 depending on the tour length) is worth it.

The city's mascot is a cockerel, and early in its history it was known as the City of White Roosters (Kukkudnakorn). A rooster decorates the ceramics for which Lampang is famous.

The city's importance as a timber-trading center brought the railway there in the early 20th century, and several trains a day connect it with Bangkok to the south and Chiang Mai to the north. Long-distance buses between Bangkok and the north stop at Lampang's large bus station, which also serves outlying towns. There's also an airport, but the flight schedule is erratic. The compact city center is easy to cover on foot, although you'll need to take a taxi or *songthaew* to visit its top attraction, the lovely Wat Prathat Lampang Luang, 18km (11 miles) to the south.

HIGHLIGHTS

WAT PHRA THAT LAMPANG LUANG

✚ 308 C4 ✉ On highway 1034, 2 miles west of Ko Kha 🕐 Daily 6am–8pm
💰 Free

It's well worth the 18km (11-mile) drive from Lampang to view this large temple complex, one of Thailand's most beautiful *wats*. It stands so far outside the present city because the Haripunchai Queen Chamtewi established her royal residence for a while here in the eighth century, when Lampang itself was an insignificant settlement. The temple compound was built as a fortress, on a mound and surrounded by stout laterite walls. It nevertheless was overrun by the Burmese in one of their forays into northern Thailand. But a local prince drove them out, and the bullet hole marking the spot in a *chedi* (monument housing a Buddhist relic) fence where he shot dead the Burmese commander is a revered memento of those times. The temple museum has a small Buddha image which is said to have been carved from the same stone that produced the Emerald Buddha in Bangkok.

The most curious feature of the temple, however, is a tiny chapel that serves as a camera obscura—a hole in its gnarled door throws a reverse picture of the outside *chedi* onto a screen. Only men may view it, though. Women are denied entry to the chapel, which stands above a hallowed imprint of what's said to be the Buddha's foot.

WAT SRICHUM
✉ Thanon Sichum ⏰ Daily 6am–8pm ✋ Free
The Burmese ruled Lampang for two centuries and built several temples during their time. This is the biggest—and the biggest of all 31 Burmese temples in Thailand. The half-brick and half-timber *viharn*, or assembly hall, has a Burmese-style Buddha image and murals giving a Burmese perspective of the lives of the Buddha.

WAT CHEDI SAO
✉ Tambon Tonthongchai, off Thanon Chae Hom ⏰ Daily 6am–8pm ✋ Free
"Chedi Sao" means "20 *chedis*," and local lore has it that if you can count all of them you're in for good luck. The white *chedis*, of different sizes and topped with gold, pose a tantalizing mystery. It's not clear exactly what purpose they served nor how old they are. The unearthing on the site of amulets from the Haripunchai period indicates that some at least are more than 1,000 years old.

CHINESE QUARTER
✉ Southwest bank of the Wang River
Chinese traders set up businesses in Lampang as it grew in economic importance, and their 19th-century shophouses and homes line Thanon Talad Gae (Old Market). The intricately carved balustrades are fine examples of Chinese craftsmanship.

BAN SAO NAK
✉ 6 Thanon Ratwattana ☎ 054 22 76 53 ⏰ Daily 10–5 ✋ Adult B30, child (under 14) free
This city mansion is Lampang's finest teak house, built in 1895 in a mixture of Burmese and Lanna styles. Its walls contain an intriguing display of Burmese and Thai antiques.

BACKGROUND

Lampang was a major teakwood-trading center, surrounded by thick forest and sitting on a navigable river, the Wang. Although later development did little to beautify the city, some handsome timber-built mansions still stand on its uncongested streets and quiet lanes. In its heyday, the elephants employed by timber companies nearly outnumbered the population.

A gilt painting (top) of thevada (angels) at Wat Phrathat Lampang Luang (above)

Lamphun

Most visitors to northern Thailand head straight for Chiang Mai, bypassing its neglected neighbor, the pretty town of Lamphun, only a half-hour drive to the south and notable for two temples that are among Thailand's finest.

Local basket work for sale

The central chedi at Wat Haripunchai

The shrine to Queen Chamthewi's great war elephant

RATINGS	
Cultural interest	● ● ● ○
Historic interest	● ● ● ○
Photo stops	● ● ● ○
Shopping	● ● ○

BASICS

✛ 308 C3

🛈 Lamphun Information Office, opposite Wat Haripunchai main entrance, tel 053 561 430; Mon–Fri 8.30–4.30

Monument to Queen Chamthewi

SEEING LAMPHUN

Lamphun is a quiet backwater, a pretty town and northern Thailand's smallest provincial capital, with a lazy river, flower-bordered moats and some well-restored remains of the original city walls. There are only a couple of comfortable hotels and few good restaurants, so the town and its outstanding temples are best visited on a day trip from Chiang Mai, 29km (18 miles) away.

HIGHLIGHTS

WAT CHAMTHEWI

✉ Thanon Lamphun–Rimping 🕐 6am–7pm 🖐 Free

The temple that carries the name of the first ruler of early Lamphun, the legendary eighth-century Queen Chamthewi, was built under her instructions and became her home after she abdicated at the age of 60. She spent most of her remaining years meditating within its walls, until her death at the age of 92. She was cremated within the temple compound and her ashes were sealed in a *chedi*, a five-tiered sandstone structure with 60 Buddha figures standing in curved niches. The *chedi* is in good repair, although the original golden top disappeared long ago, giving the temple its alternative name—Wat Kukkut ("broken top pagoda"). The temple's other monument of note, the Rattana Chedi, is almost as old as Chamthewi's, built by the 12th-century King Phaya Sapphasit. It's also decorated with Buddha images standing on ascending platforms. The modern *viharn* is a riot of color, its teak-planked ceiling supported by 10 high columns covered in glass mosaics. In much more restrained taste is a neat little cruciform-shape chapel, with elaborate Lanna-style roof decoration and lifelike bronze statues of revered abbots. The grounds of the chapel, complete with palm garden, offer a peaceful retreat.

WAT HARIPUNCHAI

✉ Thanon Chaimongkol 🕐 6am–7pm 🖐 B40

The center of Lamphun is dominated by this large and immensely interesting temple ensemble, where fact and fable are woven in a fascinating account of the entwined origins of the city and its most

famous *wat* (temple). The Buddha is said to have visited the area in one of his incarnations and to have been fed myrobalan fruit by two hermits. Tradition has it that he was so touched by their hospitality that he ordained a city to be built on the site. Its name was to be Haripunchainakorn—the "city where myrobalan was eaten." The name Haripunchai derives from two ancient words meaning a kind of tropical fruit and the verb "to eat." As a memento of his visit, the Buddha is said to have given the two hermits a lock of his hair, which they placed in a glass urn and buried at the site. Two centuries later, the Haripunchainakorn ruler Artitayaraj transferred the relic to a large golden urn and placed that within a golden *chedi*. That *chedi* still stands, despite the ravages of centuries, which reduced much of the monastery to rubble. The 37m-high (127ft) stupa is the tallest *chedi* in northern Thailand and towers over the monastery compound and its ensemble of 17 temples, chapels and pagodas. Apart from the *chedi*, there's much else of compelling interest to see: the modern *viharn* has a collection of Buddha images, all watched over by towering bronze and gilt statues; the monastery library is a bijou building of stucco and teak with an intricately carved roof; and the belfry contains allegedly the world's largest gong—3m (10ft) in diameter, more than 100 years old and still splendidly sonorous.

Golden dragons on the roof of one of the buildings at Wat Haripunchai

TIP

● Visit Wat Hari Punchai at sunset and marvel at the glow acquired by the temple's golden *chedi*, and the mystery as night falls on the monastery grounds, illuminated by fairy lights.

BACKGROUND

Lamphun was founded in AD680, making it possibly Thailand's oldest city, nearly six centuries older than Chiang Mai. For most of its early years it was ruled by the powerful Chamthewi dynasty, which gave Thailand's history one of its most glamorous monarchs—Queen Chamthewi, who ruled in the eighth century. From the 13th century onward it lost its influence to Chiang Mai.

Chom Kham Lake

RATINGS

Cultural interest	● ● ●
Photo stops	● ● ● ●
Walkability	● ● ●

BASICS

✚ 308 A2

🛈 Tourist Information Centre, Old District Office, Thanon Khunlumphraphat, Amphoe Muang, Mae Hong Son 58000, tel 053 612 982/3; daily 8.30–4.30

www.travelmaehongson.org
Good website with lots of detail regarding transportation, accommodation and activities.

TIPS

● Virtually every hotel, guesthouse and tour operator in Mae Hong Son offers an outing to a village inhabited by the so-called Long-neck Women. The practice of elongating the neck with a stack of rings is an old tradition, but today the women are sometimes paraded like freak-show performers. Many visitors find the sight offensive. The practice seriously shortens the life span of the unfortunate women, whose upper bodies are crushed by the rings they believe are lengthening their necks.

● Take an evening stroll around Chom Kham Lake. The setting sun creates a magically lit mountain backdrop.

MAE HONG SON

Undiscovered by outsiders until about 20 years ago, this remote, mountain-ringed town still has a pioneer feel to it.

Half the inhabitants of Mae Hong Son and the surrounding countryside are ethnic Shan, who have their roots in neighboring Myanmar (Burma). They trade not only at the town's markets but across the nearby border, and not all the goods are legal. Some of the region's most hardened drugs traffickers are based in Shan State, which borders Mae Hong Son province. Thai and international anti-drugs squads work secretly in Mae Hong Son, and although they keep a very low profile there's a tangible atmosphere of intrigue in the rarified mountain air.

For a fine view of Mae Hong Son, nestled around the small lake in the town center, climb Doi Kong Mu, a hill at the southwestern edge of town. At the top is a 19th-century Shan temple, Wat Phra That Doi Kong Moo, with a fine *chedi* containing the ashes of Shan monks.

The town's picturesque lake, Chom Kham, is bordered by a pleasant park and two very pretty Burmese-style temple ensembles—Wat Chom Kham and Wat Jong Klang. Wat Chom Kham was built in 1827 by Shan benefactors, who kept the temple simple, while positioning two Shan maidens as welcoming statues at its white stucco entrance. Neighboring Wat Jong Klang, built about 50 years later, has a museum (daily 8–6) containing a remarkable collection of carved figures depicting scenes from the Jataka legend. The figures, carved in Myanmar, are wonderfully lively representations of local characters.

On the northern edge of town, Wat Hua Wiang has a Burmese-style Buddha that draws pilgrims from throughout northern Thailand.

THAM PLA

Among the many caves in the mountains around Mae Hong Son, the most curious is the Fish Cave, a grotto in a cliff above the main Pai road, Route 1095, some 16km (10 miles) outside the town. A small cistern-like pool just inside the grotto is crammed with mountain carp, while others fight to join them from a river outside. The attraction the dark, dank pool holds for the fish is a mystery that has never been explained. Thais hold the pool in mystical reverence and it's a favorite local excursion destination. The cave (free) is on the edge of the Tham Pla Pha Sua National Park and is reached by a riverside path from the park headquarters.

The elephant hospital at Hang Chat

Wat Phra That Doi Wao, Mae Sai

A wooden carving at Mae Sariang

Continued from page 123

and 16km (10 miles) north of Hang Chat is Thailand's National Elephant Institute and Conservation Center. This is where the king stables his white elephants, although you'll have to sign up for an elephant-training course to view them. More than 30 other elephants populate the center, taking visitors for rides and demonstrating their skills. One group was trained to paint pictures, which have fetched big prices at auctions in London and New York. Another group plays a variety of instruments and has cut two CDs. Performances take place daily at 10 and 11 (and 1.30 on Sundays and public holidays) and cost B50 (child under 14 free).

The center rescues neglected and sick elephants, which are treated in its hospital. Among the patients are elephants who suffered hideous wounds when stepping on landmines in Myanmar.

Ten kilometers (6 miles) north of the center is Hang Chat's renowned farmers' market, Kad Tung Khwian. When local villagers established the market 20 years ago it won notoriety for offering live snakes and other exotic animals. Nowadays, it's a much tamer affair but still a shopper's paradise, offering everything from Lampang pottery to hand-forged swords.

MAE SAI

➕ 309 D1 ℹ️ TAT Regional Office, 448/16 Thanon Singhakhlai, Amphoe Muang, 57000, tel 053 717 433; daily 8.30–4.30 🚌 Regular bus services from Chiang Mai and Chiang Rai

This dusty frontier town is the northernmost point of Thailand, connected by a short river bridge with neighboring Myanmar (Burma). Its chief attraction is its easy access to Myanmar, and

most of the foreigners you'll meet here are expatriate residents of Thailand renewing their visas by leaving the country and then re-entering. You can join them by walking across the bridge over the narrow Mae Sai River and paying US$5 for a day's Burmese visa. That allows you to wander around Myanmar's frontier town, run-down Tachilek, and shop for gems and Burmese souvenirs in the riverside market as well as stock up on cheap liquor and cigarettes in the town's duty-free shop.

Mae Sai has a famous temple, Wat Phra That Doi Wao, approached by a broad staircase of 207 steps. It's known as the scorpion temple because of a large sculpture of the poisonous creature, which is common in these parts. If the climb is too formidable then a motorcycle taxi will take you there for B10. Either way, the trip is worth it for the fine view from the temple terrace of the mountainous border region.

Mae Sai's famous temple

MAE SARIANG

➕ 308 A4 ℹ️ Tourist Information Centre, Old District Office, Thanon Khunlumphraphat, Amphoe Muang, Mae Hong Son 58000, tel 053 612 982/3; daily 8.30–4.30 🚌 Regular bus services from Chiang Mai and Chiang Rai

Mae Sariang is a convenient overnight stop on the Chiang Mai–Mae Hong Son loop, but also an ideal center from which to explore an interesting and picturesque Thai–Myanmar (Burmese) border region. It's a pretty town, with a large population of ethnic Karen from neighboring Myanmar. One of its most notable temples, Wat Mandalay, is Burmese in origin, with Buddhist sculptures by Burmese craftspeople, including a Buddha image brought to the town in the late 19th century by a servant of Mandalay's King Thibaw. The servant fled to Mae Sariang when the British conquered Mandalay, capital of the last independent Burmese kingdom, and in 1909 oversaw the construction of Wat Mandalay, which provided a safe haven for his cherished Buddha. The monastery has another claim to fame—a banyan tree reputed to be a scion of the original bodhi tree in India, under which Siddhartha Gautama, the Buddha, attained enlightenment.

MAE SA VALLEY

➕ 308 B3 ℹ️ TAT Northern Office, Region 1, 105/1 Chiang Mai–Lamphun road, Amphoe Muang, Chiang Mai 50000, tel 053 248 604/7; daily 8.30–4.30

The Mae Sa Valley loop skirts the Doi Suthep and Doi Pui mountain range outside Chiang Mai, winding for a circular 100km (60 miles) through thick jungle and farms worked by hill-tribe communities. It is lined for

THE SIGHTS

The landscape around Nan

Girls from the Lisu hill tribe, near Pai

THE SIGHTS

much of its length by resorts, wayside restaurants, orchid farms and tourist attractions. Traveling the route from central Chiang Mai (via Mae Rim) you first of all reach after 20km (12 miles) the Mae Sa Elephant Camp (Mae Rim–Samoeng road; daily 7–2.30, with elephant shows at 8, 9.40 and 1.30; adult B120, child B80), where three times a day elephants present a show of their skills, from rolling logs to playing football. They can paint pictures, too, and their works of art are on show in Gallery Maesa.

Farther on lies the Queen Sirikit Botanic Garden (Mae Rim–Samoeng road; daily 8.30–5; adult B20, child B10, vehicles B30), a 1,000ha (2,470-acre) stretch of mountain forest and parkland opened in 1993 and now under royal patronage. A 6km (3.6-mile) road through the park passes through a stunning variety of natural flora, from thick stands of bamboo to carpets of delicate lilies. A three-story high hothouse contains a miniature rainforest, while nearby greenhouses nurture more varieties than are listed in the average gardener's manual. Around 350 species of orchid thrive in the park's nursery, which has an excellent English-language explanation of the idiosyncrasies of this exotic plant. Several orchid gardens are also to be found along the Mae Sa route.

Build time into your itinerary for at least a half-day drive along the spectacular Mae Sa route, beginning at the signposted turn-off just beyond Mae Rim (the Chiang Dao road) and ending your tour with lunch or an early evening meal at the lovely Lanna Resort just before the "loop" ends at the Chiang Mai–Hang Dong road. A rented car and chauffeur costs from B1,000 to B1,500 for the day.

MAE SOT

312 B6 TAT Northern Office Region 3, 193 Thanon Taksin, Tambol. Nong Luang, Amphoe Muang, Tak 63000, tel 055 514 3413; Mon–Sat 8.30–4

The small market town of Mae Sot is an important border crossing to Myanmar (Burma) and a haven for refugees from Burmese oppression in the Karen frontier region. Karen refugees and migrant workers give the town a distinctly Burmese character. There are two main refugee camps—Mae La and Mawker—a number of "safe houses" and a famous clinic devoted to treating needy Karen, all of which welcome visitors and material assistance. The town market is full of Burmese goods, particularly gemstones (but caution is advised when buying these). The border is west of the town, where the Thai–Myanmar Friendship Bridge crosses the narrow Moei River. There's a lively market here, too, but be careful when offered obviously contraband goods, particularly cigarettes.

From the hilltop temple Wat Phra That Doi Din Kiu (daily 7–7; free) you have panoramic views of the Moei River and neighboring Myanmar. Mae Sot is also the starting point of one of Thailand's most spectacular mountain routes, the so-called "Sky Highway" to Um Phang, a village so remote it's known as "the end of the world." The 120km (72-mile) highway, Route 1090, winds through and across wild mountain ranges, past waterfalls, hill-tribe villages and two small national parks; the scenery is simply stunning. At journey's end, the mountain-enclosed village of Um Phang, there's a wildlife sanctuary.

NAN

309 E3 Tourist Information Office, 46 Thanon Suriyapong, Amphoe Muang, Nan 55000, tel 054 710 216; Mon–Fri 8.30–4.30 Regular bus services from Chiang Mai

Founded in the 13th century, Nan was once a powerful principality but now slumbers in its isolated corner of northern Thailand, near the Laos border. There are only two roads in and out of the town, and although it has an airport, the flight schedule is haphazard. Nevertheless, it's well worth visiting, time permitting, if only for the spectacular drive there and to visit one of Thailand's most stunning temples, Wat Pumin. The 300km (186-mile) drive from Chiang Mai, on almost deserted modern highways, sweeps and winds through verdant mountain valleys, teak and bamboo forests, rice paddies and past mountainside hill-tribe homesteads. Nan itself has a quiet charm, and if you're seeking peace and quiet, away from the tourist hustle and bustle, then this is the place to be. Even 16th-century Wat Pumin (daily 9–6) is usually deserted, despite its fame. The interest of its 19th-century frescoes lies in their unconventional beauty and historical context. Unlike most other temple murals, these record scenes of contemporary everyday life, populated by caricatures of local characters. They are also a unique historical record, picturing the arrival of French colonial soldiers and Dutch traders in fully rigged sailing ships and an early steamer.

The home of the last ruling prince of Nan, a fine provincial mansion, is now the town museum (Thanon Suriapong, tel 054 710 561; daily 9–5),

A longtail boat moored in the lake at Phayao

The balcony at Ban Prathap Chai

famous for its 1m-long (3ft) black elephant tusk, revered by local people for its supposed auspicious properties.

PAI

🚌 308 B2 ℹ️ Tourist Information District Office, Amphoe Muang, Pai 58000, tel 053 612 982; Mon–Fri 8.30–430 🚌 Regular bus services from Chiang Mai

Pai is a convenient halfway stop on the mountainous road between Chiang Mai and Mae Hong Son, but it's also a pretty spot to spend a day or two. Well-heeled Bangkok businesspeople first discovered Pai, but now the tiny market town is a favorite destination for backpackers and young people seeking an "alternative scene." In high season—November to March— the tiny market town seems to have more visitors than locals, but you can easily escape the crowds by heading off into the nearby hills, either alone or as part of an organized trekking group. Tours into the surrounding countryside and to nearby Shan, Lisu and Lahu hill-tribe villages are organized by most of Pai's several resorts, one of which, the Belle Villa, is among the region's best addresses (▷ 280). The Mo Paeng waterfall, 8km (5 miles) from town, is a delightful picnic spot and has cool pools for swimming. The town has little of intrinsic interest, apart from a couple of small temples—Wat Phra That Mae Yen is worth visiting at sunset for its misty views over the town and the mountains beyond. Most Pai restaurants, bars and cafés line its one main street, Chai Songkram, or border its sleepy river, the Pai—crossed by a bridge "stolen" from Chiang Mai by Japanese forces in World War II and re-erected here to facilitate their advance into Myanmar (Burma).

PHAYAO

🚌 309 D2 ℹ️ Provincial Public Relations Office, Salaklang Jungwat Phayao, Amphoe Muang, Phayao 56000, tel 054 481 704; Mon–Fri 8.30–4.30 🚌 Regular bus services from Chiang Mai

Like so many other small northern Thai towns, Phayao was once a powerful regional center, ruled by a 13th-century monarch so influential that he played a key role in founding Chiang Mai. King Ngum Muang entered into a blood-sealed pact of friendship with Chiang Mai's first ruler, Mengrai, guaranteeing the new city's security, and is honored for his services with statues in central Chiang Mai and on the shores of Phayao's lovely lake, Kwan Phayao. Today's Phayao has little to offer the visitor besides its tranquil lake, northern Thailand's largest stretch of fresh water, whose hyacinth-covered surface is bordered by far-off mountains. It's an angler's paradise; boats can be rented at the waterfront for B300 to B400 per day. The day's catch lands on the menus of the restaurants that line the lake's breezy promenade, a very pleasant spot to take a stroll as the sun sets into the water's western edge. A temple, Wat Sri Khom Kham (daily 6am–8pm) sits on the edge of the lake, a short walk from the promenade. It is reputed—like so many of northern Thailand's temples—to have been founded after a visit to the area by the Buddha during one of his incarnations. The main *viharn* houses Thailand's largest Lanna-style Buddha, 20m (65ft) high and 17m (56ft) broad, so massive that it took Phayao craftspeople 33 years to construct.

PHRAE

🚌 309 D4 ℹ️ Provincial Public Relations Office, Salaklang Jungwat Phrae, Thanon Chaiboon, Amphoe Muang, Phrae 54000, tel 054 511 566; Mon–Fri 8.30–4.30

This busy provincial market town was once a center of Thailand's teak trade, and its former prosperity is evident in many of the late 19th-century timber-built mansions within the remains of its ancient walls. The finest of them lies 1.5km (about a mile) outside the city, though, in the village of Ban Pa Maet. The astonishing building, Ban Prathap Chai (daily 9–5; B20), is an ensemble of antique homes reconstructed on foundations of 130 massive teak columns. It's still a private home, but visitors are invited to wander through its teak-floored rooms, lined with cabinets full of family photographs and mementoes. The ground floor is taken up by a collection of stands selling local handicrafts, most of them (of course) made from teak.

Phrae has several historic temples, the oldest of which, Wat Luang, has a 13th-century, stepped *chedi* (monument housing a Buddhist relic) guarded by well-weathered elephants.

Wat Luang at Phrae

Bridge over the Kok River at Tha Ton

THE SIGHTS

SOPPONG

🔲 308 B2 🏨 Soppong River Inn, Soppong 58150, tel 053 617 107 www.soppong.com

When Pai gets too crowded, nature-lovers make for the village of Soppong, 45km (27 miles) farther along Route 1095 to Mae Hong Son. Soppong, also known as Pang Ma Pha, is a hill-tribe settlement straddling the main road and a center for trekkers heading out into the surrounding mountains. It has about half a dozen guesthouses and simple restaurants with names like "Jungle Guest House" and "Little Eden." Two local caves are of interest: Tham Lot, which has a weird collection of stalactite and stalagmite formations, and "Coffin Cave," named after a number of prehistoric wooden coffins found in its labyrinths.

THA TON

🔲 309 C1 🏨 TAT Northern Office, Region 2, 448/16 Thanon Singhakhlai, Amphoe Muang, Chiang Rai 57000, tel 053 717 433; daily 8.30–4.30

Sitting prettily on a bend of the Kok River, almost next to the Burmese border, Tha Ton is one of the most appealing little towns in this remote northwestern corner of Thailand. Its hilltop temple, dominated by a revered "white Buddha," is a place of pilgrimage and draws people of all nationalities for its meditation sessions. The courses in vipassana meditation, as well as accommodation and food, are free, although a donation is expected. Even if you're not participating in the courses, it's well worth the effort to climb to the terraced temple for a fine view of the mountains of neighboring Myanmar (Burma).

Boats set out here for the four-hour river trip to Chiang Rai,

Where the Mekong and Ruak rivers join

SOP RUAK AND SAM LIAM THONG KHAM

An undistinguished frontier town on the banks of the Mekong River, Sop Ruak claims to be the gateway to Thailand's fabled Golden Triangle and has two museums devoted to the cause of its fame: opium.

🔲 309 D1
🏨 TAT Northern Office, Region 2, 448/16 Thanon Singhakhlai, Amphoe Muang, Chiang Rai 57000, tel 053 717 433; daily 8.30–4.30

RATINGS	
Good for kids	●●●
Photo stops	●●●●
Special interest	●●●●

Sam Liam Thong Kham (the Golden Triangle) has no defined borders and can refer to a large region covering border areas of Thailand, Myanmar (Burma) and Laos or to the point where the frontiers actually meet, at the confluence of the Mekong and Ruak rivers. About 1.5km (a mile) downstream lies the small, one-street town Sop Ruak, once a stronghold of the renegade Burmese drug baron Khun Sa. Although he and his Mong Tai Army controlled the opium trade, Thailand has effectively put an end to his operations on Thai territory, and Khun Sa is now semi-retired.

OPIUM MUSEUMS
A magnificent narcotics museum now stands where opium poppies once grew. A second museum competes for visitors in the center of Sop Ruak; look for the green tin-roofed pagoda above the entrance gate. On the riverbank where smugglers once plied their trade, a large, gilded Buddha statue stands watch.

Two of the region's finest hotels overlook the Golden Triangle: the Golden Triangle Imperial and the Anantara (▷ 278). From the terraces of each hotel there are magnificent views of the Mekong and the uplands of Laos and Myanmar beyond.

Across the road from the Anantara is the Hall of Opium (tel 053 784 444/5/6; Thu–Sun 8.30–4; adult B300, child under 14 free), a spectacular edifice dominating a small valley above the Mekong. You enter through a tunnel where weird music and the simulated smell of opium fill the air and phantasmagoric bas reliefs adorn the walls. The tunnel ends in a lobby filled with blinding light where the story of opium is related on illuminated panels. Subsequent rooms explain the history of opium and other drugs—even the history of tea is told here in a fascinating display.

Fishermen at the Sirikit reservoir

where you can catch a bus back to Tha Ton. A longtail boat leaves daily at 12.30 (B300); a whole boat, accommodating six people, can be chartered for B2,800. A covered raft takes two days to make the trip, stopping for the night at a riverside guesthouse en route. The trip, including accommodation and all meals, costs B1,900. A new raft is built for every trip, so reserving one week in advance is required (tel 053 459 427, fax 053 373 224). Boats and rafts leave from the TAT pier in the center of town.

UTTARADIT AND THE SIRIKIT DAM

🔲 309 D4 🔲 TAT, 193 Thanon Taksin, Amphoe Muang, Tak 63000, tel 055 514 341/2/3; daily 8.30–4.30

Uttaradit played a central role in finally ridding northern Thailand of Burmese domination, and its most famous hero, Phraya Pichai, who fought alongside Taksin the Great in the late 18th century, is commemorated with a statue in front of the Provincial Hall. Phraya Pichai, who also played a role in ushering in the Chakri dynasty that followed Taksin's overthrow, is portrayed in full battle dress and brandishing a sword in each hand. One of his ceremonial swords, other weapons and objects from this period, as well as from Uttaradit's earlier history, are exhibited in the Uttaradit Cultural Centre (Thanon Paetwa; Wed–Sun 8–5).

Uttaradit is the gateway to the Sirikit Dam and the Phu Soi Dao National Park, two areas of outstanding beauty. The Sirikit Dam wall, 113m (372ft) high and 810m (2,670ft) long, is the highest in Thailand and blocks the Nan River, forming a large lake dotted with islands that were once mountaintops.

Standing on the Bhumiphol Dam

TAK AND THE BHUMIPHOL DAM

Birthplace of King Taksin the Great, who took his name from his hometown, Tak is not only one of northern Thailand's most historic areas but also the gateway to a very scenic region and the country's largest dam.

🔲 312 C5, B5
🔲 TAT, 193 Thanon Taksin, Amphoe Muang, Tak 63000, tel 055 514 341/2/3; daily 8.30–4.30

RATINGS			
Good for kids	●	●	●
Outdoor pursuits	●	●	●
Photo stops	●	●	●

Tak today has little to remind the visitor of its former glory, except a shrine containing a statue of its most famous son. His portrait hangs on the walls of many homes, shops and restaurants, and a national park on the road to Mae Sot bears his name: the Taksin Maharaj National Park. The original walled city of Tak lies 25km (15 miles) from today's bustling market town on the Ping River, although little remains apart from a 13th-century hilltop *chedi* (monument housing a Buddhist relic) said to have been built by King Ramkhamhaeng of Sukhothai.

WAT MANI BANPHOT
This ancient temple on Thanon Paholyohtin houses a 13th-century Buddha image fashioned in the Chiang Saen style of the early Lanna kingdom.

TAKSIN MAHARAJ NATIONAL PARK
This small national park halfway between Tak and the Thai–Myanmar (Burmese) border town Mae Sot was originally named after the krabak yai tree, Thailand's largest, which grows in profusion in the area. The park is one of northern Thailand's most beautiful nature reserves, surrounded by forested mountains. Hiking trails criss-cross its 14,980ha (37,000 acres).

BHUMIPHOL DAM
🔲 312 B5
Thailand's largest dam, named after the current king, stretches from just north of Tak into neighboring Chiang Mai province. Houseboats make the 140km (84-mile) overnight trip across the dam and then up the Ping River to a jetty where travelers can catch a bus to nearby Chiang Mai; for houseboat reservations tel 055 549 510. Longtail boats make shorter pleasure trips that include lunch at a floating restaurant and stops for swimming or fishing. A small resort below the dam wall has comfortable accommodation in bungalows (tel 055 599 093).

THE SIGHTS

CENTRAL THAILAND

Thailand's most populous region has many unspoiled villages and towns that figured in the country's history but now sit neglected among the rice paddies and orchards that support the local economy. The former Siamese capital, Ayutthaya, although usually crowded with visitors, still retains a quiet charm, while Kanchanaburi, capital of one of the country's most beautiful provinces, is more than just the site of the bridge over the River Kwai.

MAJOR SIGHTS

Ayutthaya

Thailand's capital for more than four centuries (when the country was known as Siam), Ayutthaya is still a vibrant living city and a World Heritage Site. You'll find a glorious history within its weathered ruins.

Buddhas at the restored Wat Yai Chaimongkhon

The Shrine at Wat Mahathat

Ceramics on sale in Ayutthaya

SEEING AYUTTHAYA

Although the old city of Ayutthaya is fairly compact, you'll need to choose some kind of transportation to visit all the important sights. Tuk-tuks charge about B200 an hour, but drivers will settle for less for a half-day or all-day rental. Bicycles are the cheapest option (B30–B40 a day) and can be rented at the rail station or the Chao Phrom Market at the end of Thanon Horattanachai.

HIGHLIGHTS

WAT PHRA MAHATHAT
✚ 136 B1 🕐 8.30–4.30 💰 Free

After collecting your bicycle at the rail station or Chao Phrom Market head down Thanon Horattanachai to the Phra Ram pond. At the edge of the water stands ancient Ayutthaya's most important temple, Wat Mahathat. This served for centuries as the royal temple, where successive rulers worshiped and participated in Buddhist rites. Its Khmer-style stupa towered over the city, but collapsed in the 17th century, leaving only the monumental base to hint at its original size. The stupa was rebuilt but collapsed again in 1911, and archaeologists discovered a hoard of golden objects in the ruined base. The temple grounds are studded with other *chedis* (monuments housing a Buddhist relic) from various periods and contain Ayutthaya's most famous sight: the massive head of a Buddha image, entwined in the roots of a centuries-old fig tree.

WAT RATBURANA
✚ 136 B1 🕐 8.30–4.30 💰 Free

Across the road from Wat Mahathat stands another of Ayutthaya's most interesting temples, built on the site where the 15th-century King Intharachathirat and two of his sons were cremated. The two sons died in a duel fought to decide the succession to King Intharachathirat's throne, and two *chedis* were built on the site where they were killed to contain their ashes. The temple's main stupa, Ayutthaya's best-preserved one, was found recently to contain not only the usual Buddha relics but a priceless collection of royal golden

RATINGS	
Cultural interest	●●●●
Good for kids	●●●
Historic interest	●●●●
Photo stops	●●●●

BASICS

✚ 313 D9
🛈 TAT Central Region 6, 108/22 Moo 4, Amphoe Phra Nakhon Si Ayutthaya, tel 035 246 076/7; daily 8.30–4.30

http://thailand.sawadee.com/ayutthaya
Easy to use site with plenty of relevant information.

TIPS

● Try to avoid the midday sun when touring Ayutthaya's historical sites. Early morning and late afternoon are the best times, particularly for photos.
● The evening hours at Wat Chai Wattanaram are magical, when the setting sun gilds the ancient temple walls.
● An easy way to see the riverside temples is to rent a boat. There are several operators in front of the Hua Ro Market on the Lop Buri River (around B200 per hour for a tour of the old city).
● Free, detailed maps of Ayutthaya's sights and of the Bang Pa-In Palace are available from Ayutthaya's TAT office.

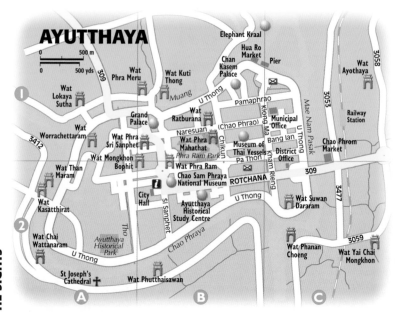

AYUTTHAYA

500 m
500 yds

Wat Lokaya Sutha
Wat Phra Meru
Wat Kuti Thong
Muang
U Thong
Elephant Kraal
Hua Ro Market
Chan Kasem Palace
Pier
Wat Ayothaya
Railway Station
Pamaphrao
(Chao Phrao)
Municipal Office
Bang Ian
Wat Worrachettaram
Grand Palace
Wat Phra Sri Sanphet
Wat Ratburana
Naresuan
Wat Phra Mahathat
Phra Ram Park
Chikun
Museum of Thai Vessels
Pa Thon
District Office
Chao Phrom Market
Wat Mongkhon Bophit
Wat Phra Ram
Chao Sam Phraya National Museum
ROTCHANA
Wat Than Maram
City Hall
Ayutthaya Historical Study Centre
U Thong
Wat Suwan Dararam
Wat Kasatthirat
Si Sanphet
Tho
Ayutthaya Historical Park
Chao Phraya
Wat Chai Wattanaram
U Thong
St Joseph's Cathedral
Wat Phutthaisawan
Wat Phanan Choeng
Wat Yai Chai Mongkhon
Mae Nam Pasak
Khong Ma
Kham Rieng
3058
3053
309
3477
3059
3412
309

A   **B**   **C**

I

2

Hop on for an unusual view of the sights (above)

A Buddha statue at the shrine of Wat Phra Mahathat (opposite)

objects, including 500-year-old votive tablets and containers, now in Ayutthaya's Chao Sam Phraya National Museum. Stairs lead down to the vault where the relics and the gold were kept, within walls still covered with antique frescoes.

THE GRAND PALACE AND WAT PHRA SRI SANPHET
➕ 136 B1   🕐 7–6   🎫 Free

Turn right outside the main entrance to Wat Ratburana and follow the northern edge of Phra Ram pond to the ruins of the former Grand Palace and the royal temple, Wat Phra Sri Sanphet. The palace, described by early Western emissaries as the finest in all Asia, was destroyed by the Burmese in 1767, but the ruins of its six royal halls give an idea of its size and beauty.

The royal temple, Wat Phra Sri Sanphet, was built in 1448, incorporating two large *chedis* for the remains of two early kings. The main *viharn*, Viharn Phra Mongkhon Bophit, built in 1500, contained an astonishing Buddha image, 16m (50ft) high and covered in 170kg (374lb) of pure gold. But the Burmese stripped it of its gold when they sacked Ayutthaya, and the core of the Buddha was later taken to Bangkok and put in a memorial *chedi* there. An immense bronze Buddha image, one of the largest in Thailand, now sits in the *viharn*.

WAT LOKAYA SUTHA
➕ 136 A1   🕐 7–6   🎫 Free

Across the narrow canal behind the Grand Palace ensemble, this temple compound is worth visiting for its huge reclining Buddha, 37m (122ft) long, the head resting on a lotus. It was built of stucco-covered brick in the Middle Ayutthaya period.

AYUTTHAYA HISTORICAL STUDY CENTRE
➕ 136 B2   ✉ Thanon Rotchana   ☎ 035 245 121   🕐 Wed–Fri 9–4.30, Sat–Sun 9–5   🎫 B20

Before setting out on a tour of Ayutthaya, a visit to this very instructive information center is advised. Multimedia technology re-creates the magnificence of ancient Ayutthaya and immerses you in its history.

CHAN KASEM PALACE
➕ 136 B1   ✉ Hua Ro market   ☎ 035 251 586   🕐 Wed–Sun 9–4   🎫 B30

The original palace that stood here was destroyed by the Burmese in 1767, but rebuilt by King Mongkut in the 19th century as a private

• Several monasteries of outstanding interest lie outside the old city, in the southeast corner of town, adjacent to the main highways 3477 and 3059. These include Wat Phanan Choeng and Wat Yai Chai Mongkhon (▷ right).

residence during his visits to Ayutthaya. Today it serves as a history and natural history museum.

CHAO SAM PHRAYA NATIONAL MUSEUM
🗺 136 B2 ✉ Corner of Thanon Rotchana and Thanon Khlong Tho ☎ 035 241 587 ⏰ Wed–Sun 9–4 🚌 B30
Golden objects and a jewel-encrusted sword recovered from the *chedis* of Ayutthaya's royal temples are the highlight of this very interesting museum. Although the collection is impressive, it's still only a portion of what the *chedis* once held—much of the gold placed there by Ayutthaya's rulers as tokens of merit was carried off by looters.

MUSEUM OF THAI VESSELS
🗺 136 B1 ✉ Thanon Bang Len ⏰ 9–5 ☎ 035 241 195
Models of more than 200 traditional Ayutthaya and old Siamese vessels were built by a local historian and craftsman, Phaithun Khaomala, who gives private tours of the museum on request.

ROYAL ELEPHANT PALACE (ELEPHANT KRAAL)
🗺 136 B1 ✉ Thanon Khumkunphan Paton, Phranakhon Si Ayutthaya ☎ 035 211 001, 035 321 982 ⏰ 9–5; www.wangchangayutthaya.com
A palisade of massive teak logs encircles the grounds where wild elephants were trained for warfare in Ayutthaya's heyday. The last round-up was in May 1903 in a presentation for King Chulalongkorn, who took his place in a royal pavilion where early rulers would personally select their war elephants. The pavilion still stands, together with a Buddhist sanctuary for elephant mahouts. Tame elephants now take visitors for rides (B500 per half-hour).

WAT PHANAN CHOENG
🗺 136 C2 ⏰ 7–6 🚌 Free
This temple complex predates the founding of Ayutthaya, and the large gilded Buddha image, the Phra Buddha Trittana Nayok, which sits in its *viharn* was cast 20 years before King Ramathibodi set up his residence there. A popular myth says tears flowed from the eyes of the Buddha when the Burmese sacked Ayutthaya. The 19m (63ft) Buddha statue is so high and the *viharn* so small that no photographer has yet succeeded in capturing the entire figure—you'll find no complete picture of it in any guidebook!

WAT YAI CHAI MONGKHON
🗺 136 C2 ⏰ 8.30–4.30 🚌 Free
This massive structure, with its distinctive octagonal-base, bell-shape stupa, was built by King Naresuan the Great to celebrate his victory in 1592 over Burma's crown prince in an elephant-back duel. It's a suitably proud and flamboyant construction, ringed by seated Buddhas in poses of contemplation. Nearby is a sublime sleeping Buddha.

WAT CHAI WATTANARAM
🗺 136 A2 ⏰ 9–6 🚌 Free
Dominating the banks of the Chao Phraya River opposite the southwestern corner of the old city, this very beautiful temple ensemble was built in 1630 by King Prasatthong in memory of his mother. The main stupa, 35m (120ft) high, and the cluster of smaller ones around it are all built in the Khmer *prang* style, indicating to historians that they might have been constructed to celebrate the king's victory over the Khmer empire.

BACKGROUND
Ayutthaya was founded in 1350 by the U Thong ruler King Ramathibodi I, who recognized the strategic and logistical advantages of the site, which was enclosed by three rivers, giving the city a natural defensive "wall" and providing water for a rapidly growing population. Over the following 417 years, Ayutthaya extended its realm over much of present-day Thailand

The Khmer-style towers of Wat Phra Mahathat

and into Cambodia. It swallowed up Sukhothai and even the Khmer capital, Angkor. Magnificent royal palaces and more than 400 Buddhist monasteries were built, and visiting emissaries from the West compared Ayutthaya at the height of its power in the 17th century to Paris, London and Venice. But the seeds of Ayutthaya's destruction had already been sown; successive rulers were unable to contain the constant threat of invasion from neighboring Myanmar (Burma), and in April 1767 the city succumbed to a 15-month siege and was destroyed by the victorious Burmese.

A Buddha image among the roots of a Banyan tree, Wat Mahathat

The Catholic cathedral in Chanthaburi

The pavilions of Bang-Pa-In palace

BANG-PA-IN

This small village is celebrated for its extravagant royal palace, a slightly surreal blend of architectural styles.

⊞ 316 D9 ⊙ Daily 8–4 ⛟ B100
🛈 TAT Central Region 6, 108/22 Moo 4, Amphoe Phra Nakhon Si Ayutthaya, tel 035 246 076/7; daily 9–4.30

RATINGS	
Cultural interest	●●●○
Photo stops	●●○

Bang-Pa-In, 18km (11 miles) south of Ayutthaya, is famous for its hauntingly beautiful royal palace ensemble, built on and around three river islands. The original palace, built in the 16th century by Ayutthaya King Prasat Thong, was destroyed in the Burmese invasion that wiped out the Siamese capital in 1767. It was then rebuilt by Rama IV as a retreat from the new court in Bangkok and became a favorite country residence of his successor Rama V, King Chulalongkorn. On one of his outings to the palace, the boat carrying his wife capsized and she drowned. The devastated king built a white cenotaph in her memory.

ARCHITECTURAL STYLES

Mongkut and his successor, Chulalongkorn, were influenced by Western styles of architecture, and the structures they built are an eclectic but aesthetically successful mixture. The one truly Thai building, the Isawan Thippa-At Pavilion, a fragile concoction with four porches rising to a delicate spire, appears to float in the middle of one of the lakes. On the riverbank opposite is another ethereal structure, the Krachom Trae Pavilion, an octagonal bandstand-like affair with a domed roof supported by slender pillars. Completing the ensemble in this part of the grounds are three structures that illustrate the regard that Mongkut and Chulalongkorn had for European classical architecture: a graceful bridge with statues of Greek gods and goddesses on its parapets; the Warophat Phiman Throne Hall, an elegant mansion with a classical portico of Corinthian pillars; and the royal temple, Wat Niwet Thammaprawat, with a Gothic interior complete with stained-glass windows. The Rama throne still stands in the Throne Hall, and Thailand's royal family often spends short breaks in the residential section. Behind the Throne Hall is a curious European-style house, the Uttayan Phumisathian Royal Mansion, filled with French furniture from the reign of Napoleon III. Yet another royal mansion, Wehat Chamrun, was built in Chinese style with donations raised by Chinese merchants. Completing the ensemble is a curious observatory, the Withunthatsana Tower, a Legoland-like structure dominating the smallest island.

CHANTHABURI

⊞ 317 F11 🛈 TAT Central Region Office Region 4, 153/4 Thanon Sukhumvit, Amphoe Muang, Rayong 21000, tel 038 664 585; Mon–Sat 8.30–4.30

Chanthaburi is the center of Thailand's gems trade. Its "gem road"—Thanon Sri Chan and Trok Krachang—is transformed on weekends into the country's liveliest gemstone market. Dealers come from as far away as Myanmar (Burma), Malaysia and Cambodia to haggle, and it's been estimated that as much as 10 million baht changes hands on a busy weekend.

The town was an outpost of the Ayutthaya realm in the reign of King Taksin the Great, and remains of his fort can be seen on Thanon Tha Chalaep. Taksin is still highly revered in Chanthaburi, and a blue-domed circular shrine stands in front of one of the restored walls of the fort, with a statue of the king inside. Sturdy cannons from the 19th century reign of Rama III also front the wall. Taksin was a superstitious warrior, and Wat Phlub, a temple built in his honor, has a rectangular stupa where potions were concocted to help in his military campaigns.

Just outside the town is a small national park, Nam Tok Pliew, named after its chief attraction, a waterfall that descends over several steps into a clear pool stocked with fish. Overnight accommodation (tel 039 434 528) is available in the park.

ERAWAN NATIONAL PARK AND SAI YOK YAI NATIONAL PARK

⊞ 312 C8, B9 ⊙ 8.30–4.30 ⛟ B200, child (under 14) B100 🛈 TAT Central Region Office Region 1, Thanon Saeng Chuto, Amphoe Muang, Kanchanaburi 71000, tel 034 511 200, 034 512 500; Mon–Sat 8.30–4.30

One of the Erawan Falls' seven tiers

Market sellers wear traditional wide-brimmed hats

These small national parks, lying on either side of the 323 highway between Kanchanaburi and the Three Pagodas Pass, have two of Thailand's most beautiful waterfalls. The Erawan Falls, on the Kwai Yai River (the "big" River Kwai), are probably the most photographed scene in Thailand. The much smaller Sai Yok Yai Falls, on the Kwai Noi River (the "small" River Kwai), however, are every bit as picturesque. Longtail boats ferry visitors from the Sai Yok Yai National Park headquarters (tel 025 620 760) to the foot of the falls (B300). Houseboats can also be rented for the day (B1,000) or for an overnight trip on the river (B2,000). To rent one, tel 01 85 68 754.

KAMPHAENG PHET

🚉 312 C6 🔢 TAT Northern Office Region 3, 193 Thanon Taksin, Tambol Nong Luang, Amphoe Muang, Tak 63000, tel 055 514 3413; Mon–Sat 8.30–4

An important garrison citadel in both the Sukhothai and Ayutthaya eras, Kamphaeng Phet is today a busy market town. Sections of the old city walls, dating from the 15th century, have been restored and incorporated into the modern urban sprawl, while the most important ruins now form the Kamphaeng Phet Historical Park (daily 9–5; B40), 1.6km (1 mile) from the city center. Three reconstructed statues from the early Ayutthaya period include a gracefully recumbent Buddha. The surviving *chedis* also show Ayutthaya influence. During excavations, many important objects were uncovered, and most of them are on display in the Kamphaeng Phet National Museum (Thanon Pin Damri, Nai Muang, tel 055 711 570; Wed–Sun 9–4; B30).

DAMNOEN SADUAK FLOATING MARKET

This survivor from the days when the Bangkok region was known as the "Venice of the East" is one of Thailand's top visitor attractions but has retained much of its historic character.

🚉 316 D10 🚌 Buses to Damnoen Saduak leave every 20 min from 6am from Bangkok's Southern Bus Terminal; 2-hour journey, B52 🚗 By car, follow highway 4 west from Bangkok and turn left at kilometer stone 80 onto the Bang Phae–Damnoen Saduak road

RATINGS			
Good for kids	●	●	●
Photo stops	●	●	● ●
Shopping	●	●	●

TIP
● Like all Thai markets, Damnoen Saduak's floating version is best visited in the morning—the earlier the better. After about midday it tends to wind down a bit though, and late visitors may find a disappointing number of boats still plying their trade.

Floating markets were the commercial hub of Bangkok in the early days when the city's roads were its waterways—the Chao Phraya River and the canals that feed off it. Early travelers called Bangkok the "Venice of the East." That romantic image has long since faded, but floating markets do exist, although those within Bangkok are disappointingly small and stocked mostly with cheap tourist curios.

The best and biggest floating market in the Bangkok region is at Damnoen Saduak, near Ratchaburi, about 100km (60 miles) west of the capital. Boats have been plying their wares here on the Khlong River and its canals for centuries, and although the market is now geared more toward visitors, locals do still shop there. On a busy day, hundreds of flat-bottomed punts jam the waterways, paddled by market women wearing the deep-blue jackets and straw hats traditionally favoured by Thai farmers. Their boats are piled high with everything you can think of, from fruit and vegetables and household supplies to handicrafts and curios. There are even floating kitchens on some of the boats serving noodles and fried rice, although ordering food from them and keeping your balance on a choppy canal can be a hazardous business. The only way to experience the market firsthand is to rent a boat (B300 per hour) and join the throng. The market women can be importunate, so stay firm but polite—a few words in Thai can help here.

Kanchanaburi

Site of the bridge immortalized by the film *The Bridge Over the River Kwai* (1957), Kanchanaburi is also the capital of one of Thailand's most beautiful provinces.

A museum styled like a prisoner of war hut

A grave at the Allied War Cemetery

Waterside buildings at Kanchanaburi

RATINGS	
Cultural interest	● ● ●
Historic interest	● ● ● ●
Photo stops	● ● ● ●
Special interest (World War II)	● ● ● ●

BASICS

➕ 316 C9

ℹ️ TAT Central Region Office Region 1, Thanon Saeng Chuto, A. Muang, Kanchanaburi 71000, tel 034 511 200, 038 512 500; Mon–Sat 8.30–4
and
TAT and Kanchanaburi Tourist Police, Kanchanaburi Railway Station, 1 Thanon River Kwai, Kanchanaburi 71000, tel 034 512 795, 034 512 668; daily 24 hours

🚌 Regular bus service from Bangkok

SEEING KANCHANABURI

Kanchanaburi's official position as capital of the western province of the same name, one of Thailand's most beautiful regions, is overshadowed by its fame as the site of the World War II bridge built by the Japanese, using Allied prisoners as forced labor. The remains of the bridge and a second, more modern construction stand in the center of Kanchanaburi, where an open, riverside plaza is packed with visitors most of the year. The war cemetery containing the remains of prisoners who died building the bridge is half a kilometer (0.3 miles) away, bordered by an information center explaining the project's dark history. A section of the original line runs from Kanchanaburi to a remote station, Nam Tok, on the edge of the Erawan National Park.

HIGHLIGHTS

WAR CEMETERY

The hideous toll of Japan's conduct of the war in this remote corner of Asia is evident at the cemetery where the remains of nearly 7,000 former Allied prisoners of war lie beneath simple bronze plaques. It's a serene, park-like patch of beautifully maintained land given in perpetuity to Britain, Australia and the Netherlands by Thailand. The cemetery is on a busy two-lane highway, Thanon Saengchuto, about 1km (0.6 miles) from the center of town.

HELLFIRE PASS

About 400 of those who lie in Kanchanaburi War Cemetery died on one stretch of the Death Railway, a series of cuttings known as "Hellfire Pass," 80km (50 miles) northwest of Kanchanaburi, on highway 323. They were literally worked to death, hacking a way for the railway through a rocky mountainside. Under pressure to complete the cuttings in four months of 1943, the Japanese put their slave force of Allied prisoners of war and Asian conscripts to work shifts of up to 18 hours. The work went on through the night, to the light of lanterns, flares and bonfires—giving the scene an inferno-like look and giving the pass its name: "Hellfire." Remains of wooden railway sleepers mark the route through the cuttings, between rocks where broken implements still lie embedded. A museum (daily 9–5; free) at the site tells the story of the construction of the Death Railway and Hellfire Pass in a series of vivid photographs and contemporary documents.

MUANG SING HISTORICAL PARK

✚ 316 C9 ✉ On highway 3085, 20km (12 miles) west of Kanchanaburi 🕐 Daily 6–6 💳 B30

The Kanchanaburi area was one of the furthest outposts of the Angkor-based Khmer empire in the 13th to 14th centuries, and one of the strongest citadels of King Jayavoraman VII was Muang Sing—

"Lion City." Much of it was built in the style of the Khmer Bayon temple complex at Angkor. Siam's first Chakri king, Rama I (1782–1809), discovered the existence of the old city, and his archaeologists uncovered traces of a large and productive community within its earth and brick ramparts. At the center of the site is a tall Khmer *prang*, or tower, in very good condition. A nearby museum has copies of a fine series of bodhisattva images. Bodhisattva was a four-armed god worshiped by the Khmer—a very benign being to judge by the blissful smiles on the handsome faces of the images.

BACKGROUND

Virtually every foreign visitor to Kanchanaburi travels there to view the remains of the bridge made famous by the film *The Bridge Over the River Kwai*. For many it's also a pilgrimage to the sites where more than 12,000 Allied prisoners of war died in 1943 to 1945 while building the "Death Railway" with which Japan hoped to win the war in Southeast Asia. The wooden bridge depicted in the film is now no more than a few wooden stumps, but a more stable

The graves of Allied servicemen, most of whom died building the "Death Railway"

one, built with metal support spans imported from Japanese-occupied Sumatra, has been reconstructed and carries trains running on the original "Death Railway" route. You can walk along the track from one end of the 275m (920ft) bridge to the other bank of the Kwai River. A train service (twice daily; single ticket B100) runs from Bangkok's Thonburi railway station to the end of the line, at Namtok, on the edge of the Erawan National Park some 60km (36 miles) northwest of Kanchanaburi. Beyond Kanchanaburi, the line runs through virgin jungle and inches its way along a long trestle bridge clinging to the side of a river gorge—the journey is not for the faint-hearted.

The railway line's Kanchanaburi station is part of a large plaza adjoining the bridge and lined with souvenir stands and shops. A short walk away is the World War II museum, an eclectic display of dusty mementoes. The museum (tel 034 512 596; daily 8–6; B30) is housed in a riverside temple complex which incongruously also describes the history of Thailand using larger-than-life statues of historical figures. The history of the "Death Railway" is told with a fragmentary collection of exhibits and explanatory labels, some of them guaranteed to raise a few eyebrows with their interpretation of Japan's wartime policies and conduct.

TIP

● The city of Kanchanaburi is the capital of one of Thailand's most beautiful mountain regions, which is well worth exploring. Take Route 323 into the mountains as far the Three Pagodas Pass on the Thai-Burmese border.

THE SIGHTS

Local residents at the Phra Prang Sam Yot

RATINGS

Cultural interest	● ● ● ●
Good for kids	● ● ●
Historic interest	● ● ● ●
Photo stops	● ● ●

BASICS

✚ 313 E8

ℹ TAT Central Region Office 7, Thanon Rop Wat Phrathat, Amphoe Muang, Lop Buri 15000, tel 036 422 7689

🚉 Lop Buri

Lop Buri National Museum

☎ 036 41 14 58 ⏰ Tue–Sun 8.30–4.30 💲 B30, under 14 B15

LOP BURI

Lop Buri has a lot more of interest than the resident tribe of monkeys that have made this ancient city world famous.

The origins of Lop Buri are lost in the mists of prehistory, but by the sixth century it was an important bulwark of the expanding Dvaravati empire. The Khmer took it over in the 10th century and held it until the powerful kingdom of Sukhothai overran it. Ayutthaya succeeded Sukhothai as masters of Lop Buri, and King Narai made it his second capital. Narai welcomed Westerners to his court, and Lop Buri today is an eclectic mixture of Khmer and Ayutthaya ruins and colonial-style buildings.

THE DVARAVATI AND KHMER ERAS

Lop Buri's most famous landmark, the Phra Prang Sam Yot, probably dates from Dvaravati times and was later enlarged by the Khmers, who built its three distinctive *prangs*, or towers, representing the Hindu trinity of Brahma, Vishnu and Siva. The oldest Khmer tower, Prang Khaek, adjoining the market on Thanon Vichayen, is also a Hindu shrine of great beauty. Khmer towers also dot the extensive grounds of Wat Phra Si Maha That.

THE FRENCH INFLUENCE

King Narai constructed an impressive palace ensemble in a mixture of Siamese and French styles. He clearly intended the Phra Narai Ratchaniwat Palace (built 1665–77) to impress visiting Western dignitaries, including the French nobleman Chevalier de Chaumont, King Louis XVI's ambassador to Siam. Three handsome mansions were built, in one of which, the Suttha Sawan Pavilion, King Narai died in 1688. One of his successors, the fourth Chakri monarch, King Rama IV, built his own residence here, the Phiman Mongkut Pavilion. The restored palace now houses government offices and the Lop Buri National Museum.

MONKEY BUSINESS

A famous tribe of monkeys has made its home in one temple compound, San Phra Ghan. The locals not only leave them alone but revere them as a source of good luck and income for the community; once a year a local hotelier treats the monkeys to a party at which they're fed delicacies at trestle tables set up in the temple grounds. They're a favorite visitor sight, but don't go too near—they bite.

Phra Prang Sam Yot

Golden Buddha at Phra Pathom Chedi, Nakhon Pathom

Pim Buranaket Museum, Phitsanulok

Wat Phrasri Rattana Mahathat, at Phitsanulok

NAKHON PATHOM

🗺 316 D9 🛈 TAT Central Region Office Region 1, Thanon Saeng Chuto, Amphoe Muang, Kanchanaburi 71000, tel 034 511 200, 038 512 500; Mon–Sat 8.30–4

Site of the world's largest stupa, Nakhon Pathom also claims to be Thailand's oldest city, with some of the country's most ancient Khmer ruins.
The golden stupa, Phra Pathom Chedi, 234m (417ft) high and taller even than Rangoon's celebrated Shwe Dagon, was built in 1853 over the remains of a pagoda constructed more than 2,000 years ago to enshrine Buddha relics. Within the monastery compound surrounding the *chedi* (monument housing a Buddhist relic) are four *viharn*, each facing a different cardinal point of the compass, and containing a variety of Buddha images. The statues on the *chedi* terrace include an unusual representation of Buddha seated in a chair. Nearby are the ruins of the temple Wat Phra Man, believed to have been built in the same period as the *chedi*. Just outside the town is a former royal palace ensemble, Sanam Chandra, built by King Rama VI in a variety of styles (including English Tudor) as a country retreat and with a shady park reminiscent of European country estates. Within Nakhon Pathom are some attractive European-style buildings that served as backdrops in the film *The Killing Fields* (1984).

PATTAYA AND THE EAST COAST

See page 146.

PHITSANULOK

🗺 313 D5 🛈 TAT Northern Office Region 3, Surasi Trade Centre, 209/7–8 Thanon Boromtrailokanat, Amphoe Muang, Phitsanulok 65000, tel 055 252 742/3; daily 8.30–4.30 🚉 Phitsanulok

Birthplace of Ayutthaya's 16th-century King Naresuan the Great, Phitsanulok served as the capital of Siam from 1448 to 1488. A shrine in the compound of the local Phittayakom school stands on the site of the palace where Naresuan was born. The city is today a busy industrial and commercial center, and a good base from which to tour this region of central Thailand. Pilgrims stream to the city throughout the year to pay homage at what is thought to be the country's finest Buddha image, the Phra Buddha Chinnarat, which sits in a *viharn* of Wat Phrasri Rattana Mahathat (daily 6am–8pm). The official town history records that the Sukhothai-style gilded figure was cast in 1357, although some scholars place its true origins as far back as the 11th century.

An irresistible, nationally famous attraction in Phitsanulok is the eccentric, eclectic Sergeant Major Thawee Folk Museum (26/138 Thanon Wisutkasat; Tue–Sun 8.30–4.30; B50). The museum is a fascinating jumble of arts, crafts and curiosities.

SANGKHLA BURI AND PHRA CHEDI SAM ONG

🗺 312 B7 🛈 TAT Central Region Office Region 1, Thanon Saeng Chuto, Amphoe Muang, Kanchanaburi 71000, tel 034 51 12 00, 038 512 500; Mon–Sat 8.30–4.30

Although this southernmost border crossing between Thailand and Myanmar (Burma) played a vital role in the history of relations between the two countries, most visitors now make the 200km (120-mile) journey to Phra Chedi Sam Ong (the Three Pagodas Pass) from Kanchanaburi (▷ 142–143) to see where the "Death Railway" of World War II passed. Thailand

ripped up its part of the ill-renowned railway after the war, but a rusting section of it can be seen on the Burmese side of the border. On the Thai side, a short, symbolic section of the original track was laid out in front of a "Border Peace Temple." The temple was erected opposite the three pagodas by Japan and Thailand in 2002.

Seven years previously, a group of former Allied prisoners of war who had worked on the railway placed a "time capsule" at the three pagodas site. The capsule—to be opened on April 25 (Anzac Day), 2045—has a large bronze plaque relating the history of the "Death Railway" and plotting its route. It passed just 46m (153ft) from the three pagodas, which in turn marked the route successive Burmese armies took to invade Siam in the 16th to 18th centuries. The pagodas, white *chedis* (monument housing a Buddhist relic) only 6m (20ft) high, are a disappointing sight, standing forlornly in a patch of ragged ground bordered by a market selling cheap Burmese and Chinese goods.

A day's pass for non-Thai visitors to the uninteresting little village on the Burmese side of the border costs B500, payable at the Myanmar immigration office at the border. The crossing is open from 6am to 6pm.

The nearest Thai town to the Three Pagodas Pass is Sangkhla Buri, 10km (6 miles) south, at the head of the vast Wachiralongkon Dam. The outskirts of the town, including a temple, were submerged to create the dam, and a popular outing for Thais is to rent a boat to view the underwater ruins—a ghostly sight. A new, pyramid-style temple was built high above the dam, and a fine view can be enjoyed from its terrace.

Watersports on Pattaya beach (above). Bang Bao fishing village on Ko Chang (left)

PATTAYA AND THE EAST COAST

First-time visitors to Pattaya either hate the resort or love it. It's Thailand's premier playground, unashamedly brash, but also within a short distance of two quiet islands.

Fifty years ago, Pattaya was a quiet fishing village, embraced by long expanses of deserted beaches. Thailand's early boom years attracted the country's newly rich, who built holiday homes on its pristine coast. Then came the Vietnam War and the first aircraft carrying American servicemen for "rest and recreation." Now there's much more recreation than rest, with entire streets of bars, restaurants and karaoke joints. Despite its raunchy reputation, Pattaya has become a popular family holiday destination, with watersports and beachfront diversions. And although much of the town and its surroundings are decidedly downmarket, there is a ritzy side to Pattaya, which boasts luxury hotels, exclusive golf courses and even a pony polo club.

RATINGS

Good for kids	●●●○
Photo stops	●●●○
Special interest (water sports)	●●○○

BASICS

✚ 316 E10
🛈 TAT Central Office, 609 Moo 10, Pra Tumnak, Tambon Nong Preu, Pattaya City, tel 038 42 76 67

TIP

● City transport is by *songthaew*. Just flag one down and name your destination–a city journey usually costs B15–B20.

KO SAMET
✚ 317 F11
This small island off the Rayong coast is a marine national park, a paradise for scuba-divers and snorkelers. Most of the beaches are sandy and less crowded than on the mainland, and the more isolated on the east coast south of Ao Hin Kok are often deserted. Nightlife is found at Hat Sai Kaew (Diamond Beach) on the north eastern side of the island. The sand of its beach is brilliant white.
　　Regular ferries run to the island from the small town of Ban Phe, 16km (10 miles) east of Ranong.

KO CHANG
✚ 317 G11
Thailand's second-largest island (after Phuket) is also a marine national park, offering some of the region's best diving. Despite its size and popularity with visitors, it remains relatively unspoiled, with just one peripheral road that skirts the jungle-clad interior. Half a dozen waterfalls are within hiking distance of the coast. Most of the best beaches are on the west side of the island, which—like Ko Samet—has its Hat Sai Kaew (Diamond Beach), a 5km (3-mile) stretch of glistening white sand fringed with palms and backed by thickly forested hills.
　　Regular ferries run to the island from Laem Ngop, near Trat.

Walking Street in Pattaya, popular with clubbers

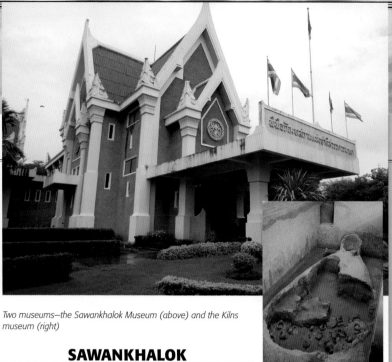

Two museums—the Sawankhalok Museum (above) and the Kilns museum (right)

SAWANKHALOK

A dusty little town with just one main street, Sawankhalok was once the center of a thriving ceramics industry whose products were prized by palaces and wealthy households far beyond the boundaries of ancient Siam.

The special qualities of the soil in the alluvial plain surrounding Sawankhalok were recognized as long as 1,200 years ago. The rulers of nearby Sukhothai and Si Satchanalai prized the locally produced celadon and other ceramics particularly highly and made a royal tradition of presenting tableware and decorative pieces to the imperial courts of China, from where it found its way to Japan. Many fine examples are on display at the Sawankhalok Museum, about 1km (0.6 mile) outside the town on the Phitsanulok road.

Combined ticket for Sukhothai Historical Park, Ramkhamhaeng Museum, Si Satchanalai Historical park and Sawankhalok kilns: adult B150, child (under 14) B100.

CELADON KILN SITE STUDY AND CONSERVATION CENTRE

A huge area of centuries-old kilns is being excavated at the village of Ban Ko Noi, 4km (2.4 miles) north of Si Satchanalai. More than 500 kilns have so far been discovered, although only two are open to the public. A small museum displays some of the wares recovered during the excavations, including celadon pieces in remarkably good condition.

Exhibits from the kilns

RATINGS	
Cultural interest	● ● ●
Historic interest	● ● ● ●
Photo stops	● ● ●

BASICS

🔲 309 D5
ℹ️ TAT Northern Office Region 3, Surasi Trade Centre, 209/7–8 Thanon Boromtrailokanat, Amphoe Muang, Phitsanulok 65000, tel 055 252 743, 055 259 907; Mon–Sat 8.30–4.30

Celadon Kiln Site Study and Conservation Centre
✉️ Ban Ko Noi 🕐 Daily 9–12, 1–4
💰 B20, child (under 14) B10

TIP

● The Sawankhalok kilns are difficult to find and badly signposted. Because of their close proximity to Si Satchanalai it's advisable to include a visit to the kilns in a tour of the area that your hotel can arrange.

Si Satchanalai

An undistinguished, unassuming town, Si Satchanalai is famous for the
nearby ruins of a 700-year-old city that was rivaled in northern
Siam only by mighty Sukhothai.

*Wat Chang Lom in the
Historical Park*

*Cattle grazing near a ruined
monument*

*Visitors explore a rope bridge in
Si Satchanalai*

RATINGS	
Historic interest	●●●○
Photo stops	●●●○
Walkability	●●●○

BASICS

✚ 309 D4
🕐 Daily 8–5
💰 B40, vehicle B50
ℹ Historical Park Information Centre,
tel 055 679 211; daily 8.30–4.30

TIPS

● Although it's a World
Heritage Site, the Si
Satchanalai Historical Park is
difficult to find and badly
signposted. The best way to
visit is to book an organized
tour at your hotel in Sukhothai
or rent a car and driver. The
more adventurous take a bus
from Sukhothai to Si
Satchanalai and persuade a
songthaew driver there to take
them to the historical park
(about B100).
● In front of Wat Chang Lom,
renowned for its carved
elephants, is a real elephant,
which the owner rents out for
rides (B100 for 15 min)
around the historical park.
A trolley train also tours the
park (B20).

SEEING SI SATCHANALAI

The once magnificent city of Si Satchanalai is now a disorderly
collection of mostly ruined brick and laterite reminders of its past
glory. The riverside site ranges over 7sq km (2.7sq miles), the heart
of the original city surrounded by a 12m-wide (39ft) moat. It's a
placid, almost neglected place, lacking the infrastructure of the
Sukhothai Historical Park and consequently not overrun by tourists.

HIGHLIGHTS

WAT KHAO SUWAN KHIRI

For an overview of the site, make your way to the northwestern
corner and climb the small hill to this 14th-century temple, believed
to have been built by Sukhothai's King Ramkhamhaeng. From the
tiered base of its huge *chedi* (monument housing a Buddhist relic)
you have a fine view of the park and surrounding countryside.

WAT CHANG LOM

Immediately to the south of Wat Khao Suwan Khiri is the park's most
impressive temple complex, Wat Chang Lom, with another large,
bell-shaped *chedi* supported by 39 elephants *(chang)* and with a
staircase lined by Buddha figures. Four of the elephants face the
cardinal points of the compass, an important architectural feature in
the Sukhothai period.

WAT CHEDI JET THAEW

The most beautiful ensemble, however, is Wat Chedi Jet Thaew, just
south of Wat Chang Lom. It's named after the seven *(jet) chedis* in
various states of repair that stand in well-ordered rows before the ruins
of the *viharn* where centuries ago monks gathered to pray. The *chedis*
contain the ashes of members of Si Satchanalai's ruling families.

Two other temple ruins are worth visiting: Wat Khao Phanom Phloeng
(next to Wat Khao Suwan Khiri), and Wat Nang Phaya (at the park
entrance), where well-preserved bas-reliefs of flowers on the stone
balustrades are reminders of how artistry and aesthetic imagination
flourished in the Sukhothai period.

The Yom River at dusk

BACKGROUND

Si Satchanalai was traditionally ruled by the crown prince of Sukhothai, 80km (50 miles) to the north and several days' journey by elephant in those times. The greatest of the Sukhothai monarchs, King Ramkhamhaeng, is believed to have built one of the most beautiful of the 134 temples and monuments that make up the Si Satchanalai Historical Park. The park is now (like Sukhothai) a UNESCO World Heritage Site.

Si Satchanalai found itself at the center of a historic confrontation in the mid-14th century, when Siam split into northern and southern realms, placing Sukhothai and its satellite city in a kind of buffer zone. In the century-long struggle that followed, several monarchs tried unsuccessfully to bolster the historic eminence of Sukhothai and Si Satchanalai. In 1438, Sukhothai was annexed by the mightier, southern Siam kingdom of Ayutthaya, and Si Satchanalai faced no choice but to be also absorbed. Its fate was sealed by the renown of its ceramics: they were highly prized by the rulers of Ayutthaya, who grew rich on exporting the ware as far as Japan and the Philippines. The rise of Ayutthaya, and subsequently Bangkok eclipsed both Sukhothai and Si Satchanalai, which faded over the centuries into provincial towns with little political or cultural influence.

TIPS

● Every year, on April 7–8, newly ordained monks are carried through the village of Ban Hat Sieo, near Si Satchanalai, on elephant back. It's a vibrant procession of up to 30 elephants, decorated with traditional trappings and textiles woven in the village.

● Si Satchanalai Historical Park is in one of central Thailand's most remote regions, a rugged, mountainous stretch of virgin forest and tropical jungle. Waterfalls, caves and hot springs are all accessible from the park's headquarters, where timber-built chalets can be rented.

Wat Khao Phanom Phloeng, Si Satchanalai

Sukhothai

The mystical sound of the name alone and its epiphanic meaning—"Dawn of Happiness"—sum up the irresistible attraction of this great historic city, now a World Heritage Site and a must-see destination on any tour of central Thailand.

A herd of elephants bursts out of this wat in Sukhothai

Doing chores, Sukhothai-style

Transport around the Historical Park

RATINGS	
Cultural interest	●●●○
Historic interest	●●●○
Photo stops	●●●○

BASICS
✚ 312 D5
ℹ Historical Park Information Office, tel 055 69 75 27, 055 69 73 10; daily 8.30–4.30

TIPS

• Avoid touring the Sukhothai Historical Park at midday, when the sun can be very hot. Early morning and late afternoon are the best times to visit, particularly for photographers.

• Although the historical park is 12km (7.2 miles) from present-day Sukhothai, consider staying in the new town, where the choice of accommodation is larger and eating possibilities more plentiful.

SEEING SUKHOTHAI

The Sukhothai Historical Park is 12km (7.2 miles) from "new" Sukhothai, a busy but uninteresting market town on the Yom River. There are small guesthouses and simple restaurants near the park, but for an extra few hundred baht, greater comfort and convenience can be found in new Sukhothai. Red *songthaew* pickup taxis run between the new city and the park (B20–B100). The park is vast (70sq km/27sq miles), so rent a bike (B40–B60 per day), either at the entrance or from one of the shops opposite. The entrance fee includes a map. There are a few refreshment stands en route, but it's still best to carry a bottle or two of water, particularly in the hot season (February–end June).

A handsome new information center opposite the park houses fine reproductions of the principal treasures that were excavated at Sukhothai and taken to the National Museum in Bangkok.

HIGHLIGHTS

SUKHOTHAI HISTORICAL PARK AND RAMKHAMHAENG MUSEUM

🕒 Park daily 6–6; museum: daily 9–5 💰 Park: Adult B40, child (under 14) B20; museum: adults B30, child (under 14) B10; combined ticket for Sukhothai Historical Park, Ramkhamhaeng Museum, Si Satchanalai Historical Park and Sawankhalok kilns: adults B150, child (under 14) B100

King Ramkhamhaeng introduced Theravada Buddhism to the region he ruled. The original Khmer and Hindu influences persisted, however, and their imagery is found at many of the 21 sites that make up the historical park. Nearly 200 temples, *chedis* (monuments housing a Buddhist relic) and monuments are scattered over the verdant area of lawns, trees and ponds—fortunately, only about 10 are really worth much study. They are all well marked on the map provided at the entrance booth. Most of the finds from the Sukhothai ruins are in the National Museum in Bangkok, but enough were kept in Sukhothai to make a visit to the Ramkhamhaeng Museum interesting. It contains many examples of temple art from his era, including some fine Buddha statues. The museum is to the left of the Historical Park.

WAT MAHATHAT

Located in the heart of the wall-enclosed center of the old city, this temple compound is the largest and most interesting Sukhothai site. Although probably built at the start of the Sukhothai era, it was enlarged and renovated by King Ramkhamhaeng's son, Loe Thai, whose religious devotion was blamed for the temporal decline of the Sukhothai empire. Although Loe Thai is accused of neglecting matters of state, his artistic and religious energies bequeathed a magnificent ensemble to Sukhothai. He built the Sri Lankan-style lotus-bud *chedi* that still stands as a symbol of Sukhothai. The *chedi* was constructed to contain two Buddha relics brought back from Sri Lanka by a Sukhothai monk. The *chedi* stands at the head of a remarkable collection of 200 smaller ones, ranked like assembled soldiers and each containing the ashes of leading monks and citizens of ancient Sukhothai.

WAT SRA SRI

Here you'll find the famous "walking Buddha," an original Sukhothai creation and—like the lotus-bud *chedi* of Wat Mahathat—a symbol of the city at the height of its creativity and power. The Buddha strides elegantly past the temple's main *chedi*, also in the Sri Lankan style. The temple compound takes up two islands surrounded by a lake swimming with lotuses.

WAT SRI CHUM

An enormous Buddha statue, 15m (51ft) high and 11m (37ft) wide, dominates this temple compound, the most interesting of the 116 that have been found outside the old city walls. The statue is in remarkably good condition, as is a series of frescoes of about the same age that decorates a passageway between the *wat*'s outer walls.

WAT SRI SAWAI

Evidence that the Sukhothai rulers absorbed Hindu and Khmer influences into the architecture of their capital is everywhere to be found in this temple compound of eclectic styles. Even its name derives from the original Thai word for the Hindu god Shiva. Two Khmer-style *chedis* are covered in niches that still contain some original Buddha figures and Hindu deities, exemplifying the strange amalgam of cultural influences that left their mark on ancient Sukhothai.

The remains of Wat Mahathat Sukhothai

Giant Buddha at Wat Sri Chum

WAT TRAPHANG NGOEN

Magically named "The Temple of the Silver Pond," this ruined ensemble also stands on an island in one of the many lakes and reservoirs that must have added greatly to the beauty of the ancient city. Its 13th-century *chedi* is capped with the typical Sukhothai lotus bud and has niches that once held Buddha images.

Buddha image, Sukhothai Historical Park

BACKGROUND

Stand today amid the ruined temples and *chedis* of the Sukhothai Historical Park or stroll through the bustling new city 12km (8 miles) away, and it's hard to imagine that eight centuries ago this small patch of Siam ruled a mighty empire stretching from as far as today's Laos in the north to the Malay peninsula in the south. The story of Sukhothai's astonishing rise to unmatched power in Southeast Asia is much more, however, than an account of battles won and treaties sealed. It's the stirring tale of a people's will to be free, to cast off the domination of a foreign power and to be masters of their own fate. In the 13th century Sukhothai became the heart of a widespread uprising against rule by the Khmer, who had penetrated much of the region from their base in Angkor, in today's Cambodia. Sukhothai was the scene of the decisive victory over the Khmer, when a Siamese prince, Phor Khun Bang Klang Thao, defeated the city's Khmer commander in an elephant duel. The victorious prince, renamed Sri Indraditya, founded a dynasty that ruled the Sukhothai empire for nearly 150 years. Sukhothai reached the height of its power and influence under the rule of Sri Indraditya's youngest son, the great Ramkhamhaeng, who was only 19 when he ascended the throne in 1279. During the 20 years of his rule, Sukhothai flourished as no other Southeast Asian city. Inscriptions found in its ruins tell us that the city was a citadel of freedom and tolerance—its foundation truly was the "Dawn of Happiness." Free trade was allowed, taxes were minimal, slavery prohibited— King Ramkhamhaeng even installed outside his palace a bell that any citizen with a grievance could ring and summon the monarch to sit in judgment.

It couldn't last—Sukhothai declined with the rise in power of Ayutthaya in the south and the Lanna kingdom in the north. It was finally annexed by Ayutthaya in 1438, and faded rapidly in importance.

Wat Mahathat, detail

THE SOUTH

Southern Thailand has lots to offer. You can experience glorious seascapes and sandy beaches, stay in a bamboo hut or a five-star resort. There's diving, snorkeling and rock climbing during the day, and cocktails on the beach and fresh seafood at night. Explore popular destinations like Phuket and Ko Samui, the secluded islands in the Andaman Sea, and spot wildlife in the rainforest of Khao Sok National Park.

MAJOR SIGHTS

ANDAMAN COAST

Lush vegetation and limestone peaks punctuate the landscape with alarming beauty; equally arresting are the dramatic seascapes of turquoise water and tropical islands famed for their beaches and coral reefs.

A longboat sitting off Ao Nang in Krabi (top). Coconut palms at Ko Tarutao

RATINGS

Beaches	● ● ● ● ●
Outdoor pursuits	● ● ● ● ●
Photo stops	● ● ● ● ●

BASICS

✚ 318 B14–320 D19
ℹ 75 Thanon Phuket, tel 076 212 213; daily 8.30–4.30
🚆 To Trang, then a bus
🚌 From Bangkok
✈ From Phuket, Krabi and Ranong
🚗 Highway 4 from Bangkok

TIP

● Find time to watch the sun set over the Andaman Sea, preferably from a beach.

Thailand's Andaman coast begins at Ranong, close to the border with Myanmar (Burma), and stretches south for 550km (342 miles) until it reaches the border with Malaysia. Geographically and culturally constant, it is distinguished by stunning scenery and a human landscape populated by a mix of ethnic Chinese in urban areas and Thai Muslims in the countryside. Fields of rice are less common than plantations of rubber, palm oil and coconut trees. The Andaman coast bore Thailand's brunt of the 2004 tsunami, but recovery programs were speedily implemented.

Weather conditions, due to the impact of the southwest monsoon, need to be borne in mind. When the rain comes in, starting in May and lasting until mid-October, it hits the Andaman coast more persistently than other regions of Thailand, and passenger services to outlying islands are suspended or reduced depending on local conditions. The rainy season, though, is not a barrier to enjoying a successful holiday along the Andaman coast—accommodation is discounted and less advance planning is required.

PLACES TO VISIT

The most visited destination on the Andaman coast is Phuket (▷ 168–171). The beaches are superb and the overall level of services is second to none, but the island can feel busy. The Krabi area to the east, with its own nearby beaches and easygoing character, is an ideal alternative in this respect. So are the excellent white-sand beaches of Ko Lanta (▷ 159), easily reached from Krabi (▷ 164). From Ko Lanta it is easy to island-hop to tiny Ko Jum (Ko Pu; ▷ 158) and Ko Bubu (▷ 157) or the better-known Ko Phi Phi (▷ 158). Diving and snorkeling are always a possibility along the coast, with the outstanding opportunities available around Ko Similan (▷ 160) and Ko Surin Nua (▷ 160) especially popular.

GETTING AROUND

Excellent transportation links make traveling to and along the Andaman coast easy. Other than on Phuket, roads are rarely busy and car rental is easily arranged in the main towns. Boat services to offshore islands are frequent and well organized.

Aerial view of Ang Thong

ANG THONG NATIONAL MARINE PARK

➕ 318 C15 ☎ 077 286 025 🚹 Park entrance B200, child (under 14) B100; day trips from Ko Samui B600
🚢 From travel shops on Ko Samui daily; less frequently from Ko Pha Ngan

The park consists of more than 40 small islands, and a visit to the largest one is a popular day trip from Ko Samui, some 30km (19 miles) to the east. The islands' wildlife is protected, and long-tailed macaques, wild pigs, monitor lizards and langurs, having the run of the place, are not too difficult to spot. There is also a rich birdlife, but bring binoculars to make the best of this. Day trips usually include a climb to the top of the highest point for its views, so bring suitable footwear. Another destination is Tham Bua Bok, a cave where the shapes of stalactites and stalagmites resemble lotuses.

CHA-AM

➕ 316 D11 🚹 Highway 4, a 15-min walk south of the main hub, tel 032 471 005; daily 8.30–4.30 🚃 Tel 032 471 159 for information 🚌 Tel 032 425 307 for information

Between Hua Hin (▷ 156) and Phetchaburi (▷ 167), Cha-am is busy on weekends when families arrive from Bangkok and elsewhere. At other times it lapses into a sleepy beach-based destination. Amenities are condensed into a 3km (1.9-mile) stretch facing the sea. The classy resorts, though, are spread out to the north and south, with beach areas more or less exclusively their own, and a stay here is made easier with your own transportation. The beach in the heart of Cha-am is not perfect but is safe for swimming. Plus, it has a choice of places to eat and mid-range accommodation.

Stock up on essentials at a food stand

CHUMPHON

The town of Chumphon, where southern Thailand begins, has its own nearby beaches and is welcoming to visitors.

➕ 318 C13 🚹 Thanon Paramin Manka, tel 077 511 024; Mon–Fri 8.30–4.30 🚃 Main terminal on Thanon Tao Tapao (tel 077 502 725) 🚌 Call 077 511 103 for information ✈ The airport (tel 077 576 796) is 35km (22 miles) north of town
🚤 Contact Infinity Travel for diving trips (Thanon Taphao, tel 077 501 937 for guided tours; **www.cabana.co.th**)

RATINGS			
Beaches	●	●	●
Good for transport links	●	●	● ●
Outdoor pursuits	●	●	●
Value for money	●	●	●

The main highway from Bangkok splits into two at Chumphon: one branch accessing the Andaman coast to the west and the other heading due south for the Gulf coast in the east. This makes the town's bus terminal, with regular connections to Bangkok and destinations along the east and west coasts, a busy place. Chumphon's train station allows visitors to and from Bangkok to cut down on travel time to the south, and the town is fully geared up for footloose folk on short stays with plans to move on elsewhere. There are plenty of knowledgeable travel agents who can provide useful information as well as reserve transportation and day trips, including the popular route to Ko Tao (▷ 165). Numerous places offer internet access and car and motorbike rental.

ACTIVITIES

The most appealing beach is 12km (8 miles) north of town, known variously as Tha Wua Lan and Thung Wua Laem, and is served by regular *songthaews*. It has a good sandy stretch as well as canoes for hire, a dive center at the large Chumphon Cabana hotel, a choice of accommodation and seafood restaurants. Snorkeling trips to offshore islands can be arranged through the dive center, from the beach-sited hotels or from travel shops in town. In Chumphon town, day trips to Pha To, 100km (62 miles) inland to the southwest, are organized for water rafting on the Lang Suan River. There are many places to stay in Chumphon, quite adequate for a one-night stay but with nothing outstanding. The food scene is more encouraging, with lively food stands set up at night along the main street near the train station and guesthouses with relaxed restaurants and bars.

The gardens at the Sofitel Central Hua Hin (above), formerly the Railway Hotel (left)

HUA HIN

Visited by royalty for over a century and with a good beach and a wide range of amenities, Hua Hin is increasingly popular with visitors from around the world.

RATINGS

Beaches	● ● ●
Good for food	● ● ●
Good for shopping	● ● ●
Outdoor pursuits	● ● ●

BASICS

🗺 316 D11

🛈 Corner of Thanon Damnernkasem and Thanon Phetkasem, tel 032 532 433; daily 8.30–4.30

☎ Tel 032 511 073 for information

🚌 Buses for towns to the north and south, including Phuket and Krabi, depart/arrive at various spots around town. Minibuses to Victory Monument in Bangkok depart from opposite the Esso/Tesco garage on Thanon Damnernkasem

✈ Daily flights to/from Bangkok from airport (tel 032 520 343) 6km (3.7 miles) north of town

TIP

● The finest stretch of sandy beach, safe for swimming, is between Sofitel Central and Hua Hin Marriott.

King Rama VI commissioned the building of a palace in Hua Hin for his family in the 1920s, then Rama VII built another one, and in the same decade the Thailand–Malaysia railway line began running down this side of the coast. Soon after a train station was opened, the grand Railway Hotel followed and guidebooks of that era began referring to the new sedate bathing destination as Hua Hin-on-Sea. It retained a genteel image until the 1980s—and even today it is a far cry from Pattaya (▷ 146)—but high-rise hotels, golf courses, a burgeoning array of bars, nightlife entertainment, fresh seafood restaurants and a jazz festival every June have transformed Hua Hin into a lively beach resort.

The three armed vessels out at sea, rendered innocuous-looking at night when lit up by fairy lights, reflect the fact that Thai royalty still stay in their palace with a private stretch of beach. This leaves 5km (3 miles) of beach for everyone else, and some restaurants have extensions built on stilts over the sand. There are plenty of shops for visitors—souvenir stalls, tailors, artists' studios and a modest department store—as well as travel agents offering various excursions and spas to suit most budgets.

THE RAILWAY HOTEL

A member of the royal family with interests in the State Railway of Thailand commissioned an Italian architect to design the Railway Hotel, built in 1923. Its splendid style appealed to the makers of the film *The Killing Fields* (1984), who used it as a set, but a renovation project in the 1980s transformed it into the Sofitel Central (▷ 285). It is worth visiting for its topiary gardens, open-air lobby and Museum Café, though the renovation may seem too clinical for some people's tastes. The current king reportedly spends time here to escape from Bangkok's polluted air.

Trains to and from Bangkok take over four hours at the best of times and trains back to the capital depart at unhelpful hours, but the teakwood train station itself, a five-minute walk from the middle of town, retains an old-fashioned charm.

Traders at a Muslim market in Hat Yai

Relaxing in a water hole at Khao Sok

Welcome to the Quiet Island

HAT YAI

🗺 321 D18 ℹ 1/1 Soi 2, Thanon Niphat Uthit 3, tel 074 243 747; daily 8.30–4.30 ☎ Call 074 261 290, 074 243 705 for information 🚌 Buses and mini-vans use a variety of points around town; Cathay Tour (Thanon Niphat Uthit 2, tel 074 354 104) reserves tickets and runs its own mini-van services ✈ Daily flights to/from Bangkok from the airport 12km (7.5 miles) southwest of the town with Thai Airways, Orient Thai, Nok Air and One-Two-Go

In the deep south, 933km (580 miles) from Bangkok, Hat Yai is a major-league southern Thailand transport hub. The city bustles relentlessly with commercial life, day and night, and seems more Chinese and Malay in character than Thai. Three long streets, numbered Niphat Uthit 1, 2 and 3, run north–south through the town and parallel to the road with the train station. On and around these streets you will find hotels, guesthouses, places to eat, travel agents and the tourist office. The town is noted for its bullfighting matches, pitching two bulls against each other and involving fever-pitch betting. Regular bouts normally take place on the first Saturday of the month at Noen Khum Thong, a short way out of town on the road to the airport.

HUA HIN

See page 156.

KHAO LAK

🗺 320 B16 🚌 Buses and mini-vans from Phuket, Ranong, Surat Thani, Krabi and Phang Nga

The beaches at Khao Lak, looking out to the Andaman Sea just off Highway 4 and an hour by road from Phuket Airport, were the heart of a thriving and cosmopolitan holiday scene until the tsunami disaster in December 2004. Destruction was widespread, especially to the main hub at Nang Thong, though owners of hotels and visitor-oriented businesses are resolved to rebuilding and reopening. Khao Lak is a base for trips to offshore islands and the hub for dive operators specializing in Ko Similan (▷ 160) and Ko Surin Nua (▷ 160). Travel shops in Khao Lak will all reserve you trips to Khao Sok National Park (▷ below) and day trips into nearby Mynamar (Burma).

KHAO SOK NATIONAL PARK

🗺 318 B15 ✉ Highway 401, east of Takua Pa 💲 Park entrance B200; guided day trip around B1200; overnight trip B1,800–B2,500, night safari B450 ℹ Park Visitor Centre, tel 077 299 150/1; daily 8–6 🚌 Buses from Takua Pa (1 hour); from Bangkok or Hua Hin take a bus bound for Surat Thani but get dropped off 20km (12 miles) before at the junction for buses to Takua Pa which pass the park entrance; from Phuket or Khao Lak take a bus for Surat Thani and get dropped off at the park entrance; mini-vans also run from Krabi and Ko Samui 🚗 On Highway 401, coming from Takua Pa or Surat Thani, the park entrance is at kilometer stone 109 📖 *Waterfalls and Gibbon Calls*, Thom Henley (available in the park)

Accessible from either of southern Thailand's two coasts, Khao Sok National Park is dense in rainforest, rich in wildlife and distinguished by remarkable limestone peaks that dominate the scenery. With over 150 species of bird to identify, a pair of binoculars would be useful. Walking trails lead you from the park headquarters into the interior, and a day's walking would cover the trek to and from the Ton Gloy waterfall with time for swimming. There is plenty of accommodation; visitor amenities spread out along the access road (from the main road to the visitor center) and many of the guesthouses also function as restaurants. Guides can be hired in the park, through guesthouses like the Khao Sok Rainforest Resort, for trips to caves and a lake, with overnight camping trips or accommodation in raft houses on the lake being an adventurous option.

KO BUBU

🗺 320 C17 🚤 Boats depart from Ban Ko Lanta on the east coast of Ko Lanta, and Krabi travel agents reserve tickets for through transport from Krabi

This Robinson Crusoe island is so small that there is only the one place to stay, and with just 30 rooms the island cannot get too crowded. It is the ultimate place to chill out, relax on the 200m-long (218-yard) beach, read a novel or two and take frequent plunges into the warm sea—between May and the end of October, at least, when boats run and accommodation is open.

The beach on Ko Bubu

Wooden bungalows on Sunrise Beach, Ko Pha Ngan

Fishing boats off Ko Phi Phi

KO CHANG

🚩 318 B14 ⛴ Boats depart Nov–end May from Saphan Pla (5km/3 miles outside of Ranong and reached by *songthaew*) to Ao Yai (1 hour) usually twice a day in the morning ❓ Only a few necessities are available at small shops on the island so you should bring items like suntan lotion and insect repellent with you

Not to be confused with the larger island with the same name on Thailand's east coast, Ko Chang is a small, tree-clad island some 7km (4 miles) off the coast in the Andaman Sea, with a scheduled boat service to and from Ranong (▷ 172). The rainy season sees nearly all the island's guesthouses closing down and boat journeys become unpredictable. Ko Chang, inhabited by fishing families and farmers of cashew nuts and rubber trees, has a lovely relaxed pace of life where very little happens—this is what is likely to attract you. Accommodation is all fairly simple, and the best bedrooms have their own bathrooms, fans and mosquito nets; air-conditioning is not available because mains electricity has not yet reached the island. Nearly all the guesthouses serve meals. The best beaches are on the west coast, the one at Ao Yai being especially suited to a couple of days spent lazing about and watching the sun set over Myanmar (Burma). It takes half an hour to walk across to the mangrove-fringed east coast.

KO JUM (KO PU)

🚩 320 B17 ⛴ From Ko Lanta (45 min) or Krabi (1.5 hours), and from Laem Kruat (30 min) on the mainland southwest of Krabi

The island (also known as Ko Pu) is halfway between Ko Lanta and Krabi, and the passenger boats that ply their way regularly between these places are met by longboats that set out from Ko Jum's west coast to pick you up. Mangrove trees cling to the east coast, but the west coast has sandy beaches and a modest selection of inexpensive and mid-range bungalow operations that use generators in the absence of mains electricity. As with Ko Bubu, most accommodation is closed between June and the end of October; at other times there is not a lot to do and nightlife is a low-key affair. To some, Ko Jum is a true retreat from urban blues; to others, it borders on the comatose.

KO LANTA

See page 159.

KO PHA NGAN

🚩 319 D14 ⛴ Boats depart from Surat Thani and from Na Thon on Ko Samui to Thong Sala; speedboats from the north coast of Ko Samui to Ko Tao stop at Thong Sala, plus there are services to Hat Rin; daily services between Ko Tao and Ko Pha Ngan www.kohphangan.com; www.watkowtahm.org

A 45-minute boat trip away from Ko Samui, the island of Ko Pha Ngan possesses many qualities that will endear it to those who find the island of Ko Samui just a tad too developed for its own good. There are superb beaches on the east coast, though they remain remote because there is no surfaced road on this side of the island. Many boats dock at Thong Sala on the west coast, and from here a good road heads north and south to reach most of the accommodation and restaurants. Activities on the island include horseback riding on the beach, meditation courses at Wat Khao Tham and famous full-moon parties on the southernmost promontory of Hat Rin. A plethora of shops and services have turned parts of Hat Rin into a mess and finding a quiet place to stay is becoming more and more difficult. From here, though, a longtail boat runs a taxi service up the east coast for those wanting more relaxing places to stay. The west coast north of Thong Sala has a good mix of accommodation, neither as remote as the east coast nor as noisy as Hat Rin.

KO PHI PHI

🚩 320 B17 ⛴ Boats depart from Krabi; boats also run to/from Ao Nang and Laem Phra Nang Nov–end May; boats also go from Phuket; www.andamanwavemaster.com

Ko Phi Phi consists of two islands but only the larger Ko Phi Phi Don is inhabited, with the smaller island, Ko Phi Phi Le, only visitable on day trips. The tsunami disaster of 2004 wreaked havoc on Ko Phi Phi, hitting the densely packed area of Ao Tan Sai, causing the buildings to collapse and killing hundreds. The northern shoreline of the island, where there are some high-quality resort hotels, was unaffected, and this is where people come for a relaxing few days. The future development of parts of the southern side of the island is unlikely to be as haphazard as it once was; this can only enhance Phi Phi's natural beauty, which was in danger of being spoiled by rampant commercialism and uncontrolled building. What remains unchanged is the first-rate quality of the diving and snorkeling around the island.

The gentle pace of Ko Jum

KO LANTA

Superb beaches and a fast-developing infrastructure that caters to visitors with varying budgets continue to increase this island's popularity. It is best visited between November and April.

Only a few years ago, Ko Lanta was the destination of choice for discerning backpackers. Though readily accessible outside of the rainy season, the island remained relatively undeveloped and there were only a few, fan-cooled bamboo-and-thatch bungalows strung out along the west-coast beaches catering to island-hoppers. Budget accommodation is still available, but so too is an increasing range of middle- and high-priced options. What has not yet changed is the relaxed pace of life, with beach bars and restaurants lighting up along the west coast and beckoning to visitors as night approaches.

EXPLORING THE ISLAND
Shops and amenities, including ATMs, are concentrated toward the north, around Ban Sala Dan, where boats arrive and depart, and along the nearby beach of Hat Khlong Dao, but the entire west coast, served by a good road that skirts the beaches, is continuing to open up with new resorts, restaurants and bars. The east coast has a different character because there are no beaches, but this is where many of the 20,000 or so islanders live and work their farms. Motorcycles and jeeps are easily rented either in Ban Sala Dan or from your accommodation, and a trip down the east coast to the old town of Ko Lanta offers an alternative to beach life. Snorkeling, diving and kayaking is equally easy to arrange. Elephant rides are popular but may also involve trekking so bring suitable footwear.

BEACHES
Sandy Hat Khlong Dao beach is within walking distance of the pier, and its long and broad expanse ensures its popularity without making it seem busy or crowded. The next beach, Ao Phra-Ae, is equally appealing and it is only with Hat Khlong Khong, a couple of kilometers (1.2 miles) to the south and midway down the coast, that rocks begin to pepper the sand at low tide. Unbroken sand continues at the next two beaches, and as you continue south the coves become more secluded until the road ends near the Pimalai Resort & Spa (▷ 285).

The island of Ko Lanta was hit by the 2004 tsunami, but is recovering well

RATINGS				
Beaches	●	●	●	●
Outdoor pursuits	●	●	●	
Photo stops	●	●	●	

BASICS

🔢 320 C17

ℹ️ No official tourist office but information and useful free maps readily available from travel agents on the island

🚢 From Phuket, Krabi, Ao Nang, and Ko Phi Phi outside of the rainy season

🚗 Year-round from Krabi and involving two short ferry crossings

Blue ringed angel fish in the Ko Similan National Park

A ship sails in the turquoise waters off Ko Similan

THE SIGHTS

KO PHAYAM

🔲 318 B14 🛥 Boats depart at 9am from Saphan Pla (5km/3 miles outside of Ranong and reached by *songthaew*); during high season (Dec–Feb) a second or third boat runs daily
🌐 www.a-one-diving.com

This is a trim little island reached by boat in two hours from Ranong, and has no cars, lovely sandy beaches, hornbills flying overhead, a laid-back feel and inexpensive accommodation. Only a few hundred people live on Ko Phayam, making their living from fishing, farming and the small-scale visitor scene. Between June and the end of October, when the boat service from the mainland becomes unpredictable and many of the bungalows close down for the rainy season, they mostly have the island to themselves. There is one village, on the northeast coast, where the main pier is, plus a few shops, restaurants, a solitary bar and narrow roads that lead to the island's two bays. Motorcycle taxis wait at the pier to take visitors to their beachside accommodation. The most attractive, and longest, beach is Ao Yai, 5km (3 miles) away in the southwest of the island. Most of the places to stay are close to this beach, and some rent out snorkeling gear and boogie boards. The other bay is at Ao Kao Fai in the north of the island; parts of it are not ideal for swimming but accommodation is available here. Motorcycles can be rented on a daily basis, but for the short hops between the village and the two bays it is easier to take a motorcycle taxi. All the bungalow operations have restaurants and many of those at Ao Yai set up little beach bars in the high season; there is also Oscar's Bar in the village. Some of the bungalows run trips to Ko Similan and Ko Surin Nua (▷ right) as well as local snorkeling excursions. Travel shops in Ranong (▷ 172) will reserve your choice of accommodation on Ko Phayam and transportation to the boat pier from town.

KO SAMUI

See pages 161–163.

KO SIMILAN

🔲 318 A16 🕐 Mid-Nov to mid-May
🎫 Entrance B200; day trips from Phuket or Krabi B2,900; 2-day/1-night B3,900; 3-day/2 night B4,900
ℹ National Park Office, Thap Lamu pier, 7km/4 miles south of Khao Lak, tel 076 595 045;
www.thaiforestbooking.com
🌐 For guided tours, ▷
www.similanthailand.com;
www.phuketdivers.com;
www.seadragondivecenter.com

Ko Similan, 64km (40 miles) off shore, is the largest of the nine islands that make up the Mu Ko Similan National Park, generally agreed to be one of the most thrilling spots in Thailand for diving and snorkeling. The water is clear to a depth of 30m (98ft), but rough sea conditions close the park in the rainy season. The most convenient way to experience the mesmerizing underwater life is to join one of the many tours available from travel agents in Phuket or reserve a trip with one of the dive operators, mostly based in Khao Lak (▷ 157). A day trip is

Surin Islands

feasible, especially for snorkeling, but the travel time from Phuket is three hours one way; two- to four-day packages involve staying on board a boat or using the park bungalows on Ko Miang, the second-largest island and the park's administration headquarters.

KO SURIN NUA

🔲 318 A15 🕐 Mid-Nov to mid-May
🎫 Entrance B200; day trips from the pier at Kura Buri B1,700 ℹ National Park Office, Tab Lamu pier, 7km (4 miles) south of Khao Lak, tel 077 443 276; www.thaiforestbooking.com
🌐 www.similanthailand.com

Mu Ko Surin Marine National Park is made up of five small islands, 60km (37 miles) off shore; Ko Surin Nua (north) is where the park headquarters is stationed and where accommodation is available. The shallow reefs surrounding 5km-wide (3 mile) Ko Surin, where the water is clear to a depth of well over 30m (98ft), are justly praised for the exceptional quality of marine life on view to divers and snorkelers. Dive operators in Phuket (▷ 168–171), Khao Lak (▷ 157), Ranong (▷ 172) and Ko Chang (▷ 158) all run live-aboard trips, and from Ko Phayam (▷ left) snorkeling day trips are available. Independent travel is also possible, but advance reservation of accommodation through the park office is advisable. The Songkhran New Year in April is celebrated on Ko Surin Tai (south) with a large gathering of *chao ley*, the so-called sea travelers who have lived in this region, ignoring the marine borders between Malaysia, Thailand and Myanmar (Burma), for centuries. During the festivities, longtail boats transport visitors on Ko Surin Nua across the narrow channel that separates the two islands.

Ko Samui

People are drawn to Thailand's third-largest island for its outstanding, palm-fringed beaches. Massages on the beach and visits to spas can be complemented by a more active excursion to the Ang Thong National Marine Park or a wide choice of water sports.

A fruit and sweetcorn vendor on Lamai beach

The Hin Lat Waterfall on Ko Samui

Fishing boats at sunset off Lamai beach

SEEING KO SAMUI

Chaweng has generally expensive accommodation, but this is the place to stay if you want an active time. The beach at Lamai is a delight and quieter than Chaweng, but some find the area's nightlife a little too lively, seeming in places to attract more single men than families or couples. Maenam, popular with backpackers, has budget accommodation, a so-so beach but a laid-back atmosphere and calm nightlife. Choeng Mon, in the island's northeast corner, has a happy balance: a white-sand beach with slingchairs laid out at night around modest bonfires, unhurried restaurants, suitable for families and couples but with buzzing Chaweng not far away. Bophut is pleasantly tranquil as well, with a modicum of shops, watersports facilities and places to stay and eat.

Ko Samui is 25km (15 miles) wide and 21km (13 miles) long, and renting a 4WD vehicle or a motorcycle for a day or two opens up the island using the main 4169 road and the smaller roads signposted off it. During the day *songthaews* run at fixed rates to all the beaches. At night, *songthaews* operate more like taxis and fares are negotiable; regular, unmetered taxis also operate.

Ko Samui can be enjoyed any time of the year, but the weeks between October and mid-April are the busiest in terms of visitors to the island; accommodation needs to be reserved well in advance for this period. Rainy spells are more common from late May to the end of September but rarely last long enough to spoil a visit. It's usually not long before the sun is shining again.

HIGHLIGHTS

ANG THONG NATIONAL MARINE PARK
⊞ 318 C15 🎫 Park entrance B200; day trips from Ko Samui B600 🚤 From travel shops on Ko Samui daily; less frequently from Ko Pha Ngan
This park is easily visited in a day from Ko Samui, and is a great place to see protected wildlife (▷ 155). It consists of many of the 80 islands in the Samui archipelago.

RATINGS				
Beaches	●	●	●	●
Good for food	●	●	●	●
Outdoor pursuits	●	●	●	●

BASICS

⊞ 319 D15
🛈 Na Thon, tel 077 420 504; daily 8.30–4.30
🚤 Boats depart from Pak Nam Tapi pier (tel 077 421 316) east of Surat Thani, and from Don Sak pier (tel 077 426 000) on the coast 70km (43.5 miles) east of Surat Thani; an all-night boat departs from Ban Don pier in Surat Thani; vehicle ferries, which also carry foot passengers, run from Don Sak pier (tel 077 426 000, 077 415 230)
✈ Bangkok Airways flies to/from Bangkok, Phuket, Krabi, U-Tapao (close to Pattaya) and Singapore
🚆 Train–bus–boat combined tickets to/from Bangkok reservable in advance at Bangkok's Hua Lamphong station
🚌 Bus–boat combined tickets to/from Bangkok reservable at the Southern Bus Terminal in Bangkok; travel shops in Bangkok, Hat Yai, Krabi and Phuket all reserve bus and boat tickets to Ko Samui and usually include transport to/from the piers
🛥 For guided tours, ▷
www.ungsafari.com; www.sitca.net;
www.planet-scuba.net;
www.samusawadee.com;
www.samui.org;
www.kohsamui-info.com

Scene from the viewpoint at Laem Nan

TIPS

● Consider pampering yourself with an afternoon spa session at the top-notch Tamarind Resort (www.tamarindretreat.com).
● On a rented motorcycle take extra care navigating the twisting roads and unforeseen hazards and always wear a helmet and suitable clothing; the slightest fall can be extremely painful to bare skin.

Pamper yourself at the Tamarind Resort

CHAWENG

➕ 319 D15 (inset) 🚌 The 4169 ring road has a turn-off for Chaweng that becomes its main street and also accesses the airport

Possessing the longest and loveliest of Ko Samui's beaches, Chaweng on the east coast is the social heart of the island. The 7km (4-mile) stretch of beach, which slopes gently into the sea, can seem busy, but there is space for everyone even with the multitude of available watersports: sailing, windsurfing, parasailing, snorkeling, water-skiing and kayaking. Behind the palm trees, the scene is less idyllic as visitor-oriented developments continue to mushroom; after dark the area's main street becomes a crowded and busy night bazaar with restaurants, bars and discos jostling for your attention. Here too you will find clinics, a hospital (tel 077 230 781; www.sih.co.th), pharmacies, travel agents, internet facilities and a sprawling colony of resorts, hotels, bungalows, spas and massage parlors. Restaurants serve a variety of food, including refined cuisines, but for atmosphere consider leaving the main drag and pick a bungalow-operated place on the beach where you can hear the rhythm of the waves in the background. Chaweng has the best concentration of shops on the island, and as well as the usual stands retailing DVDs and light clothing there are also fashion boutiques and arts and crafts stores.

BIG BUDDHA BEACH

➕ 319 D15 (inset) 🚌 Signposted off the 4169 road in the northeast of the island

The beach gets its name from the 12m-high (39ft) seated Buddha that gazes down on the hedonistic scene below. The Buddha figure, erected in 1972, and temple are reached via a short causeway and, while not especially remarkable, they have become a popular, 'been-there-seen-that' kind of place and can be fun to visit. Souvenir stands are abundant along the way to the ornate, dragon-decorated steps of the temple, and coin-operated machines dispense ready-made amounts of rice as nominal alms for the monks. From the top of the temple steps there are panoramic views of the north coast. The beach itself is not the best that Ko Samui has to offer, but there are places to stay for those seeking a resort-like retreat away from the main action.

Holidaymakers in the surf at Chaweng Beach (above). A giant demon statue (right)

NA MUANG WATERFALLS

➕ 319 D15 (inset) 🚌 Signposted off the 4169 road on its inland stretch in the south of the island

With a rented vehicle, the south coast is worth exploring. The Na Muang Waterfalls, a few kilometers inland, are a pleasant destination along the way, but avoid weekends when visitor overload is a problem. There are two falls, and the first one, close to the road, has a large pool suitable for swimming. The second waterfall is more spectacular, and is 1.5km (about a mile) away on foot along a signposted trail. You have the option of taking an elephant ride there from the first fall, but you will regret the journey if you don't pack a supply of drinking water. From the higher waterfall there are views that stretch away beyond the southern shoreline. The 4170 road, completing a loop that hugs the southern shoreline closer than the 4169, accesses Laem Hin Khom; from here a small road leads to an attractive bay from where there are fine views out to sea. Dotted around the southern coastline are one-off places to stay that provide a sense of privacy and exclusiveness.

BACKGROUND

Fishing families were the earliest inhabitants here; a trade in coconuts came later. The island's interior is still home to forests of coconut trees and, along with tourism, account for Ko Samui's prosperity. Well known only among backpackers until the 1980s, hoteliers and entrepreneurs gradually began moving in, a regular ferry service was established and an airport up and running before the end of that decade. The high season now sees a dozen flights a day landing from Bangkok and the numerous ferries from the mainland are packed full.

Wat Tham Seua temple, Krabi

RATINGS

Beaches	●●●○
Outdoor pursuits	●●●●○
Value for money	●●●○

BASICS

✚ 320 B17

🛈 Thanon Utrakit, north of town on the road to the bus terminal, tel 075 622 163; daily 8.30–4.30

🚌 To/from Bangkok's Southern Terminal (12 hours), Hat Yai (4–5 hours), Ko Samui (bus/boat, 7 hours), Phang Nga (2 hours), Phuket (3–4 hours), Ranong (5 hours), Surat Thani (2.5 hours); the bus station (tel 075 611 804) is north of town, too far to walk, but *songthaews* run regularly into town

🚆 From Bangkok overnight to Surat Thani, then a bus (16 hours)

✈ From Bangkok with Thai Airways, Bangkok Airways and Phuket Air; the airport (tel 075 636 541) is 18km (11 miles) east of town

⛴ Boats to Ko Lanta and Ko Jum mid-Oct to mid-May (2 hours); to Ko Phi Phi Nov–May (1.5 hours); tickets usually include transfer to the pier

📖 *Krabi: Caught in the Spell—A Guide to Thailand's Enchanted Province*, Thom Henley

🛶 One-day snorkeling trips B500–B650; kayaking trips B850–B1,700

🔖 For guided tours,
▷ www.johngray-seacanoe.com; www.yourkrabi.com

TIP

● Pick up one of the useful maps from the tourist office or travel shops around town.

KRABI

Krabi achieves a rewarding balance between visitor-related facilities, excellent transportation links to offshore islands and local beaches, good accommodations and an intrinsically appealing Thai flavor.

The denizens of Krabi (pronounced *gra-bee*) province's eponymous capital are well used to people staying around for a day or two before moving on. This small fishing town is a principal hub for onward travel to some of the region's most popular islands, including Ko Phi Phi (▷ 158) and Ko Lanta (▷ 159). As townsfolk go about their business there is a pleasant air of nonchalance toward visitors. The town's setting is attractive, having expanded mostly on one bank of an estuary, and there is little sense of that rampant, visitor-fueled mania for building that threatens to scar some popular destinations in southern Thailand. Evenings can be pleasant around town, especially on Thanon Kongka and its walkway by the side of the Krabi River. At around 5.30pm mobile food and drink stands are wheeled into place here, powered up from gas canisters; the seafood is unpacked from ice boxes and customers start drifting by as tables and chairs are laid out.

BEACHES, CORAL REEFS AND MANGROVE SWAMPS

There are no "must-see" attractions in Krabi town, but the numerous travel shops around town will book you on a one-day trip to nearby islands that includes snorkeling gear, a packed lunch and transfers to and from your accommodation. Another popular excursion is paddling in a kayak through the slightly creepy world of mangrove swamps or trips to the *hongs* (▷ 166) farther up the coast from Krabi.

The most visited local beach is Ao Nang, a resort area in its own right with plenty of amenities, and easily reached in half an hour by *songthaew* from Thanon Maharat, Krabi's busy main street. Just southeast of Ao Nang is a small, lush-green peninsula, Laem Phra Nang (Railay), where limestone cliffs hover precipitously over the clear emerald water and white sandy beaches. Rock-climbing is a big draw here, as are snorkeling and diving, and bungalow accommodation can be reserved in Krabi or when you arrive. Transportation from Krabi to Railay is easy—by boat in less than an hour from the riverfront pier—but, as with Ao Nang, it is feasible to base yourself in Krabi and make day trips.

A dive boat at Ko Tao

View of the creek at Ko Tarutao

Making shadow puppets in Nakhon Si Thammarat

KO TAO

 319 D14 ⬛ Various companies depart from Chumphon; there are also boats from Ko Pha Ngan, some of which start in Ko Samui 🔷 For guided tours, ▷ www.bigbluediving.com; www.planet-scuba.net; www.on-koh-tao.com

Tiny compared with Ko Samui and Ko Pha Ngan a short way to the south, Ko Tao attracts scuba-divers thanks to the exceptional clarity of the water. There are beaches, though, where non-divers or snorkelers can enjoy themselves, and for such a small island there are a surprisingly large number of places to stay. The south and west sides are where most of the bungalows and resorts are to be found, close to Mae Hat, where boats arrive and depart from, and these can all be full between December and the end of March. Many close down from early June to early September, when sea conditions can be unpredictable. Mae Hat has a healthy cluster of restaurants, bars, dive operators and amenities like ATM machines and internet access, and it serves as the terminus for *songthaews* and motorcycle taxis to the more scattered and remote resorts on the east coast. The best beach for swimming and snorkeling, Ao Leuk, is at the bottom of the east coast, and there is a walkable track connecting it with Mae Hat.

KO TARUTAO

🏛 320 C18 🅷 Park visitor center on Ko Tarutao, tel 074 729 002; park visitor center at Pak Bara, tel 074 783 485; www.thaiforestbooking.com ⬛ Boats depart from Pak Bara (2 daily; 1.5 hours) and from Thammalang pier south of Satun town 🔷 For 3-day trips ▷ www.johngray-seacanoe.com

The single best reason for heading into the deep south on the Andaman coast is to visit Ko Tarutao, the largest of the 50 or so islands that make up the Ko Tarutao National Marine Park and the site of the park headquarters. The only accommodation is in rented tents or park bungalows, which, though fairly basic and lacking hot water, can still fill up around Christmas and Thai holiday periods; try to reserve in advance. Activities you can sign up for include boat trips through the mangrove swamps, hill-climbing to watch the sunset, walks to a waterfall and to sandy beaches where turtles come ashore to lay their eggs, and spotting whales and dolphins off the coast.

KRABI

See page 164.

NAKHON SI THAMMARAT

🏛 320 D16 🅷 TAT office in Sanam Na Muang, in the heart of town, tel 075 346 515; daily 8.30–4.30 ⬛ Buses from Bangkok (12 hours), Hat Yai (3 hours), Krabi (3 hours), Phuket (5–7 hours) ✈ Flights from Bangkok with Thai Airways and PB Air 🚂 Trains from Bangkok

This large town is missing from most visitors' itineraries, not because it lacks interest but simply because it is in the deep south and not a major transportation hub or jumping-off point for one of the offshore islands. One long road, Thanon Ratchadamnoen, bisects the town on a north–south axis and *songthaews* run all the way up and down it throughout the day and evening. At the southern end of Thanon Ratchadamnoen is Wat Mahathat, a stupendous temple that dates back to the 13th century and is the most striking in appearance of any temple outside of Bangkok. A short walk farther south brings you to the National Museum (Wed–Sun 8.30–4.30; B30; www.thailandmuseum.com) and its specialist collection of art and craft items from southern Thailand. Nielloware *(kruang tom)*—a hard-to-find decorative craft that involves rubbing a compound of metals into etched silverware—is a local specialty, and a range of small household items of nielloware can be purchased from any of the handicraft shops on Thanon Thachang, which is close to the tourist office. Thai shadow theater is also kept alive in the town and there's a workshop (south of Wat Mahathat, Soi 3, Thanon Si Thammasok, tel 075 346 394; daily 8–5) which is open to visitors, where the art is demonstrated and puppets are for sale.

PATTANI

🏛 321 E18 ⬛ From Hat Yai and Yala 🚂 From Bangkok to Yala, an hour away by bus

The picturesque town of Pattani is likely to be the farthest south you'll travel unless you're planning to cross over into Malaysia. It's close enough to the border (1,055km/655 miles away from Bangkok) to have been chosen by the Japanese as a landing stage for the invasion of what in 1941 was British-controlled Malaya. Pattani is more Malay and Muslim in character, evidenced by the town's Matsayit Klang mosque (which is within walking distance of where the buses from Hat Yai stop) and the shops selling Malaysian batik. There is strong support in this area of southern Thailand for regional autonomy from the Thai government, and a separatist movement has made itself heard in recent years.

PHANG NGA

The town of Phang Nga is the starting point for trips into the Phang Nga National Marine Park and its breathtaking vista of limestone formations.

Towering limestone rocks in Phang Nga Bay (top and above)

RATINGS	
Good for kids	●●●●
Outdoor pursuits	●●●●●
Photo stops	●●●●●

BASICS

✚ 320 B16

🏛 Park entrance B200; Elephant Belly Cave tours B500; tours of Phang Nga Bay from B200/B550 for a half/full day, plus B300 for overnight stay on Ko Panyi; *hong* tours B2,000–B2,800, overnight *hong* tours B9,000

🚌 From Phuket, Krabi and Surat Thani; the bus station (tel 076 412 014) is in the heart of town

🚤 Tours of Phang Nga Bay depart from Tha Don pier, 9km (5.5 miles) south of town (reached by *songthaew*); www.johngray-seacanoe.com, www.seacanoe.net and, with an office next to the Phang Nga bus station, www.sayantour.com

TIP

● Establish exactly what is covered by a Phang Nga Bay tour before committing yourself.

Highway 4 passes right through Phang Nga and, though the town itself is less than absorbing, everything you might need is usefully gathered around the middle of town and its bus station: hotels, restaurants, banks, ATMs, post office and numerous travel shops. From any of these travel shops it's easy to arrange tours in the bay as well as a local two-hour trip to Elephant Belly Cave. The cave is a natural tunnel through the cliff that stretches for over a kilometer (0.6 miles) and involves some canoeing and sometimes wading as well.

THE BAY EXPERIENCE

Vessels motor their way into Phang Nga Bay and head for the limestone rocks that tower out of the water up to a height of 100m (328ft). You will undoubtedly be taken to the cleft Khao Ping Gan (Leaning Rock), also known as James Bond Island because it provided the set for Scaramanga's headquarters in *The Man With the Golden Gun*. It has inevitably suffered from the hype, and the beach and cave area has souvenir vendors and overpriced seafood restaurants. The standard tour also takes in the Muslim village of Ko Panyi, built on stilts over the water around a mosque-bearing rock. Overnight bay trips involve staying in the village and, like the early-morning trips from town, they improve the quality of the experience by avoiding the crowds that build up from mid-morning onward.

THE *HONGS*

Thai for "room," a *hong* is a tidal lagoon entered by sea canoe through narrow openings in rock. Once inside, you are surrounded by water, dwarfed by vegetation-covered rocks and aware of an eerie silence. The *hongs* of Phang Nga Bay are the focus of day-long trips that are mostly organized from Phuket and Krabi by reputable companies. The tours include lunch and hot drinks and provide time for swimming and sunbathing on a beach. They can be fun as well as educational if you have your own canoe to paddle and if the tour leader is knowledgeable about the *hong's* ecosystem. Best of all are the two-day/one-night trips.

PHETCHABURI

Within day-trip distance of Bangkok or Hua Hin, the ancient *wats* of Phetchaburi are a big draw, and the best of them can be appreciated on a walking tour of the town.

There is no tourist office or obvious town center, but the backpacker's hotel, Rabieng Rim Nam Guest House, is a useful source of information and a central base. It is located at Chomrut Bridge at the junction of Thanon Chisa-in and Thanon Damnoen Kasem. *Samlors* from the train or bus station will bring you here, and the walking tour below begins from here.

A WALKING TOUR

Cross Chomrut Bridge and turn right onto Thanon Phongsuriya, passing the Chom Klao Hotel. Wat Yai Suwannaram is on the right-hand side of the road after 350m (1,170ft). Notice the 18th-century murals decorating the *bot* (main sanctuary) with images of Indra, Brahma and other divinities. There are two other *wats* farther down the street on the other side, but limited time is better spent ignoring these and turning right instead into Thanon Phokarong. After an eight-minute walk down this street, turn right into Thanon Phrasong, where Wat Kamphaeng comes into view on your right. Built to worship Hindu gods in the 12th century, nose your way around the *wat* to appreciate its ancient lineage. Leaving here, continue along Thanon Phrasong and pass two undistinguished *wats* on either side of the street. Cross the river by the main junction, and ahead of you looms the stately Wat Mahathat. This is the town's most visited and most photogenic *wat*, and there is plenty of fine artwork and decorative detail to examine. From Wat Mahathat walk up Thanon Damnoen Kasem to return to Chomrut Bridge and your starting point. The Rabieng Rim Nam Guest House has a good restaurant and makes a suitable place to rest and recuperate.

KHAO WANG

From Thanon Phongsuriya at Chomrut Bridge, a short *samlor* taxi ride will bring you to this hill. It is an exhausting walk to the summit, where the former king's (Rama IV) summer house is now a museum (daily 9–4; B40); there is a cable car (daily 8.30–5; B64).

Don't miss The graceful old library in the middle of the pond in Wat Yai Suwannaram is worth seeking out.

Rama IV's summer house at Khao Wang (top). Detailed carving at Wat Mahathat (above)

RATINGS	
Cultural interest	● ● ● ○
Historic interest	● ● ● ○
Walkability	● ● ● ○

BASICS
✛ 316 D10
🛈 Tourist information from Rabieng Rim Nam Guest House, tel 032 425 707
🚌 Bangkok (2.5 hours), Hua Hin (1.5 hours), Cha-am (45 min)
🚆 Bangkok (up to 8 daily; 3 hours), Hua Hin (1 hour); Cha-am (35 min)

Phuket

Thailand's premier resort, Phuket (pronounced *poo-ket*) has enough diversity to accommodate most tastes. Patong is hedonistic, Phuket town is historical; beaches in the west are long and sandy and those in the northwest are quiet.

Shrine at Laem Phromthep

Sailing at Hat Mai Khao

The Clock Tower roundabout in Phuket town

RATINGS	
Beaches	● ● ● ● ●
Good for kids	● ● ● ●
Outdoor pursuits	● ● ● ● ●

TIPS
● Observe the beach warning flags as riptides and strong currents can occur, especially between May and the end of October.
● The tourist office issues a leaflet setting out the tuk-tuk fares between the beaches and the *songthaew* fares from Phuket town.

SEEING PHUKET

Each beach area has its own character, which affects to some extent the kind of holiday you will experience. Phuket town, on the east coast and without a beach, deserves a visit and is also worth considering as an accommodation base. It has its own identity and appeal, best appreciated on foot (▷ 238–239), and there are regular *songthaews* throughout the day between the town and the west coast beaches. After about 5.30pm the *songthaews* stop running, but tuk-tuks are readily available. Transportation between the beaches is by way of tuk-tuks and taxis and it is easy to rent motorcycles or jeeps (but take care: Motorcycle accidents on Phuket are alarmingly frequent).

HIGHLIGHTS

WEST COAST BEACHES

Ao Patong has a terrific beach and is dense with hotels and amenities—this is the place to arrange a watersport—but while it has an energetic nightlife it has a noticeably seedy side as well and some find the whole place vulgar. Family-friendly Ao Karon offers a better balance of activities and relaxation, though the beach lacks shade, and it's just a short hop north to experience frenetic Patong in small doses. Farther south, the beaches of Kata Yai and Kata Noi benefit from an equally genial air and are home to some good hotels and restaurants. North of Patong, the first beach is the relatively low-key Kamala, which has most amenities close at hand. Once you move farther north, to Bang Tao, you are entering luxury-hotel territory where visitors tend to confine themselves to their resort facilities. The next beach up, Nai Thon, has a sense of privacy due to the lack of hotel developments and public transportation (a taxi from Bang Tao is necessary). Just to the north is Nai Yang, a sedate and shaded beach with accommodations and agreeable restaurants looking out to sea. The last beach on the west coast, just north of the airport, is at Mai Khao; it stretches for a glorious 17km (11 miles), with the J W Marriott hotel the only sizeable development.

KHAO PHRA THAEO WILDLIFE PARK

✚ 321 B17 ✉ Amphur Thalang ☎ 076 311 998 🚍 *Songthaew* to Thalang, turn right and walk the 3km (1.9 miles) to the entrance or take a motorcycle taxi 🚗 Turn right at Thalang on the 402 road, 21km (13 miles) from Phuket town

The tourist office in Phuket town dispenses a useful small guide to the park that describes the Ton Sai Waterfall Nature Trail, which draws your attention to rainforest characteristics like the huge buttresses of the Dipterocarpus species of trees and a particular species of palm (*kerriodoxa elegans* Dransfield) that is only found in Phuket. The waterfall itself is eye-catching only during the rainy months—between June and the end of October when there is enough water to produce a good flow. It is possible to walk along a trail from the waterfall to the Gibbon Rehabilitation Centre, but with your own transportation the center is more directly reached using the directions given in the driving tour (▷ 236–237).

TRIPS AND TOUTS

Phuket has hundreds of small businesses catering to visitors, with watersports and sea-canoeing trips into Phang Nga Bay (▷ 166) being the most popular. Diving and snorkeling trips are highly rated due to the close proximity of spectacular reefs, and packages for novices as well as those with experience are available. Half-day and full-day snorkeling trips to Coral Island (Ko Hai) off the southeast coast are readily arranged in any travel shop. Thai cookery classes are also popular (▷ 178) and good Thai cuisine is served at a number of restaurants. Beware of the food scene in Patong, though, where it is often safer to stick to hotel restaurants.

Part of the Phuket experience is lying on one of the more popular beaches and being offered a massage, cold drinks and sliced fruits, a sarong or trinkets of some kind. Vendors outside tailor shops will suggest you buy a suit or two, and at night the beach roads are awash with stalls selling clothing, DVDs and other items. There are no hard sells, and lots of smiles, but be prepared to bargain. Some of the best shopping on the island is available in Phuket town, with specialist arts and crafts shops as well as department stores and street stalls.

BASICS

✚ 320 B17

ℹ 75 Thanon Phuket, tel 076 212 213; daily 8.30–4.30

✖ Phuket International Airport (tel 076 327 230) is in the northwest of the island, 32km (20 miles) from Phuket town. Airport buses will take you to your hotel, but only taxis are available for the return journey (B400 upwards, but metered taxis charge B55 for 0–2km and B7 for every subsequent kilometer, tel 076 232 192). Airlines flying to Phuket include Thai Airways, Bangkok Airways, Phuket Air, Orient Thai, Nok Air, One-Two-Go and AirAsia

🚍 Regular routes to/from Krabi (3–4 hours) via Phang Nga (2.5 hours), and Chumphon (6.5 hours), Nakhon Si Thammarat (7 hours), Hat Yai (6–8 hours) and Ranong (5–6 hours); bus journeys to/from Bangkok are usually overnight and take 12–15 hours. Phuket town bus station (tel 076 211 977) is at the eastern end of Thanon Phang Nga; *songthaews* to the west coast beaches line up along Thanon Ranong in Phuket town

🚆 To Surat Thani, then a bus to Phuket (6 hours)

💻 www.phuket.com/coralisland (for snorkeling); www.santanaphuket.com (for diving); www.johngray-seacanoe.com, www.seacavecanoe.com and www.andamanseakayak.com (for Phang Nga Bay trips); www.phuket.com, www.phuket.net, www.phuketmagazine.com (for general information)

There are beautiful beaches at Kata Beach (above) and Patong (left)

MORE TO SEE
VEGETARIAN FESTIVAL

Every year, for nine days between late September and November (the dates are determined by the start of the ninth lunar month), a major Vegetarian Festival takes place. Dramatic and noisy processions in Phuket town involve entranced devotees skewering themselves with sharp objects and walking over red-hot coals.

BACKGROUND

Merchants from India and Arab lands were stopping off in Phuket at least as early as the ninth century, but it was another 700 years before the first European traders arrived. Pearls and tin were the valuable commodities, Chinese immigration followed and the English introduced modern methods of tin-mining in the early 20th century. The wealth generated by the tin trade turned Phuket town into the prosperous island capital that is revealed in the lobby museum of the Thavorn Hotel (▷ 238–239). Tin remains important, as does rubber, coconut and fishing, but in recent years tourism has become the main source of revenue. Before the 2004 tsunami, nearly 10 million people a year were visiting the southern provinces on the Andaman coast; Phuket was the major destination. The following year brought financial hardship to all those involved in Phuket's visitor-dependent industries, as hotel occupancy rates plummeted. Patong beach, though, looked more enticing than it had for decades: The quality of the sea water improved and only 13 percent of Phuket's dive sites were found to have suffered damage.

The Ton Sai Waterfall (opposite). The coast at Laem Prom Thep (right)

Mermaid statue on Samila Beach, Songkhla

En route from Surat Thani to Samui

The Friday Mosque in Trang

RANONG

⊞ 318 B14 ⓘ Tourist and tour information from Pon's Place, Thanon Ruangrat, tel 077 823 344 ✈ Phuket Air fly to/from Bangkok 5 days a week; the airport is 20km (12 miles) south of town 🚌 Buses serve Bangkok (10 hours), Chumphon (3 hours), Phuket (5–6 hours), Krabi (6 hours), Surat Thani (3–5 hours), Phang Nga (5 hours) and Hat Yai (5 hours); the bus station is south of town on Highway 4 but many buses will also stop in the middle of town and there are also private bus companies 🚢 Boats to Ko Chang and Ko Phayam depart from the pier at Saphan Pla, 5km (3 miles) out of town and served by songthaews

Only a narrow estuary separates Ranong from Mynamar (Burma) and this gives the town an engaging border atmosphere, where Thais and Burmese mix freely with Malays and Chinese. Day trips into Myanmar are easy to arrange with any of the travel shops around town and Ranong is also the base for trips to Ko Chang (▷ 158) and Ko Phayam (▷ 160). Thanon Ruangrat is Ranong's main street and here you will find shops, hotels, restaurants and internet access.

SONGKHLA

⊞ 321 E18 🚌 Regular services to/from Hat Yai (▷ 157), 25km (15 miles) away, from where there are good road and air links

The most pleasant town on the Gulf Coast south of Hua Hin, Songkhla has charm and character. Bus stops, amenities and places to visit are clustered in a small area around Thanon Jana, the main street that runs from the fishing port on the west side of town. The National Museum (Thanon Jana, tel 074 311 728; Wed–Sun 9–12, 1–4; B30; www.thailandmuseum.com) is housed in an elegant century-old building and displays a collection

of local art and objects. Songkhla is a walkable town and to the north of Thanon Jana there is a forested hill, Khao Tung Kuan, from the top of which the geography becomes clearer, with the Gulf of Thailand to the north and Thale Sap lagoon to the west. Just north of the hill is Hat Samila, an 8km (5-mile) stretch of shaded beach. South of Thanon Jana lies the eye-catching Wat Matchimarat on Thanon Saiburi.

SURAT THANI

⊞ 318 C15 ⓘ 5 Thanon Talatmai, tel 077 288 817; daily 8.30–4.30 🚌 Buses serve Bangkok (10 hours), Hat Yai (4 hours), Krabi (2–3 hours), Nakhon Si Thammarat (2 hours), Phang Nga (3 hours), Phuket (5 hours) and Ranong (4 hours) 🚆 To/from Bangkok (12 hours), including overnight services; the train station at Phum Phin is 13km (8 miles) west of town from where buses and shared taxis travel into town ⓘ Train, bus, plane and boat tickets can be reserved at Phantip Travel (293/6–8 Thanon Talatmai, tel 077 272 230) 🚢 To Ko Samui (▷ 161–163) or Ko Pha Ngan (▷ 158); www.seatranferry.com ✈ Thai Airways flies daily to Bangkok; the airport is 27km (17 miles) north of town, reached by minibus from Phantip Travel

A less-than-arresting town, traffic-choked Surat Thani is where you are likely to find yourself in the course of reaching or departing from Ko Samui or Ko Pha Ngan. Touts congregate around the bus and train stations and you should be circumspect regarding their deals, especially any that involve private buses and accommodation. If you get stuck waiting for a train, the Queens Hotel (tel 077 311 003) has a few good bedrooms. A million miles away from Surat Thani in some respects, but only 60km (40 miles) by road, is the unruffled town of Chaiya, with its ancient wats and 10-day

meditation programs at the International Dharma Heritage (tel 077 431 661; www.suanmokkh.org). Local buses from Surat Thani travel to Chaiya and buses running between Chumphon and Surat Thani will drop you off at the turn off for Chaiya.

Don't miss September/October brings the start of the 11th lunar month and the Buddhist Chak Phra Festival in Surat Thani. It is celebrated with elaborate processions on the town's river and on the streets.

TRANG

⊞ 320 C17 ⓘ Thanon Ruenrom, at the top of the main Thanon Rama VI that starts outside the train station; tel 075 215 867; 8.30–4.30 🚆 Two overnight trains daily between Bangkok and Trang 🚌 Daily to and from Bangkok (13 hrs), Hat Yai (3 hrs), Krabi (2 hrs), Nakhon Si Thammarat (3 hrs), Phuket (4½ hrs) ✈ Daily to and from Bangkok with Thai Airways; tel 075 210 804; www.trangonline.com, www.trangislands.com

There are no "must-see" sights in Trang but the town has good transportation links, a fair choice of easy-to-find hotels and places to eat and a helpful tourist office—all of which increase the appeal of coming here for the superb island beaches that lie some 40km (25 miles) to the west. If you have been to Phuket and found it too commericalized then the islands near Trang will come as a very pleasant surprise. All the travel agent shops in the heart of town offer various packages to one or more island that are easy to arrange. Staying on the mainland, there are opportunities for canoeing, trekking trips and excursions to scenic waterfalls, and the travel shops in town have all the details (from B750 for a day trip to nearly B2,000 for a three-day trek).

This chapter provides information on things to do in Thailand other than sightseeing. In the Bangkok section, entries are listed by theme. Within the other regions, shops, entertainment, nightlife, sports, spas and activities are listed alphabetically by town or area. Festivals and events are listed chronologically at the end of each region.

What to Do

SHOPPING

Your biggest shopping headache in Thailand is likely to be whether you can get everything you purchased into your luggage allowance on the plane. With beautiful handwoven silks of every hue alongside designer ski wear at budget prices, Thailand presents wide consumer choices. One solution to the luggage allowance problem is to post it home.

Shopping in Bangkok can be utterly exhausting if you do not pace yourself. Suan Lum Night Bazaar, the MBK Centre and Chatuchak Weekend Market are dedicated shopping venues well worth visiting. In the south, most of the popular beach destinations have their own night tourist markets. Towns like Hua Hin, Chaweng (Ko Samui) and Phuket town have good shopping possibilities. The central region has no concentrated shopping areas, but Mae Sot, Ayutthaya and Sukhothai have some interesting places to browse. In the north, Chiang Mai is a shopper's paradise for craft goods and clothes, and a visit to the night bazaar may result in you having to buy extra luggage to accommodate your purchases. Chiang Mai is also a hub for contemporary Thai design, fusing traditional materials with modern styles. Shopping for silk, cotton and arts and crafts in the northeast can be very rewarding if you are in Khon Kaen, Ubon Ratchathani or Nong Khai as all three towns have some excellent shops. There are also small silk-weaving and axe pillow villages where you can purchase what you see being made. Prices in the northeast are lower than elsewhere.

A craftsman at work in Ko Samui

Clothing stands in the Indian quarter of Bangkok

BARGAINING

Bargaining is the order of the day in markets and many shops, and it is generally only in modern shopping malls and department stores that fixed prices apply. Bargaining is not always fun—it can be time-consuming and frustrating—and a shop with fixed prices can sometimes be a welcome relief, especially when you are not sure of a fair price. In Bangkok, when shopping for handicrafts, the government-run Narai Phand (▷ 183) is a good place to start because it retails products from all parts of Thailand, and silk can be bought by length. Don't hesitate to bargain in markets or in smaller shops, even if they have price tags. There are no hard and fast rules about how to start negotiating. You'll soon know if you are offering too low a price. Decide what you think the item is worth and start some way below what you are prepared to pay. It helps to check the fixed-price stores first to get an idea of what the shop owner is prepared to accept.

In the northeast, asking prices tend to be reasonable, and a discount of 10 to 15 percent is often the most you should expect. In the night markets of Ko Samui and other beach destinations, initial prices can sometimes be a little outrageous. It is rash, however, to generalize, and every shopping encounter will be different.

FABRICS

Thailand cottons and silks are well worth seeking out. Slightly coarser and with a more comfortable feel than Chinese silk, Thai silk can be bright or subtle with an attractive dull sheen. It is made in small villages, especially in the northeast of the country, by individual craft workers, and a visit to a silk-weaving village to watch its manufacture is a memorable experience.

Cottons are also handwoven in the northeast of the country and can be bought as lengths of cloth or as brightly patterned sarongs, several of which will easily convert to curtains or bedspreads. Look out too for handwoven scarves in rough cotton thread. Another great purchase in Thailand is the wonderfully simple axe pillow, a bright triangular cushion, which is surprisingly sturdy. Bought ready stuffed, they can be a bit unwieldy to get home, but it is possible

to find them without the stuffing, which makes them much more portable.

TAILORED CLOTHES

Bangkok tailors have patterns for you to choose from or they can copy a suit that you have brought or even a photograph. You should make sure you go to a reputable tailor, not one who offers to make up your garment overnight and throw in all kinds of gifts into the bargain. Consider carefully the motives of anyone offering a recommendation for a particular shop because they may be receiving a commission for every potential customer they bring in. Prices

A pile of takran *(woven wicker balls) for sale*

will vary depending on the cloth you choose—imported cloth, especially that of Italian origin, is more expensive—and the amount of time you can give the tailor to make up the suit. Be careful about the number of/absence of vents, buttons, whether it should be single- or double-breasted, what the lapels will look like, the style of the pants (trousers) or skirt. Dressmakers can do similar wonders with a picture or a dress you want copied and in less time.

OFF THE PEG

There is an excellent choice of garments to be bought around Thailand—hippy chic, street-

smart urban wear, clothes by Thai designers, imported European fashions. There aren't many bargains in the imported items, but cheap cotton pants (trousers) and T-shirts are a good buy. If you buy fake items remember that these things are knocked out by the thousand and have a very brief life expectancy—the little crocodiles fall off first, followed by a general unraveling and the occasional dissolution in the washing machine while turning all your clothes green. It is also illegal to import fake goods back to your home country. Locally made shoes and bags are good bargains, and at MBK in Bangkok (▷ 185) you can get a good line in ski wear but check all the zips work.

ARTS AND CRAFTS

Hill-tribe crafts are available in Chiang Mai and Chiang Rai, and in Bangkok, and there are some very pretty woven shoulder bags, clothes and quality jackets to be had. There is also jewelry and basketware. Each tribe has its own pattern for woven cloth, but lots of it is turned out on a large scale these days. Craft items come in a bewildering multitude of forms, and although you will find carved wooded elephants and Buddhas by the thousand, you will also see exquisitely made lacquer vases, celadon and woven accessories for the most sophisticated of homes.

It is hard to beat Chiang Mai for dedicated arts and crafts shopping because there is such a concentration of shops, and it does not take long to get a feel for the value of what you are looking at. Lacquerware items are especially enticing, combining beauty and craft skill and being suitable for packing away in your luggage. Other products, like paper umbrellas, are equally attractive but a little more difficult to transport

home; the beautiful paper stationery on sale is easier to carry and makes a lovely gift. If your luggage space is limited, stick to smaller items like silver-crafted utensils and jewelry.

ANTIQUES AND COUNTERFEITS

If you decide to buy a genuine Thai antique you will have to have a permit to take it out of the country, any reputable dealer can arrange this. Look for the TAT-approval sticker on the door or window of an antique shop. Buddha images are not supposed to be taken out of the country. As in some other Southeast Asian

An antique shop in the River City complex, Bangkok

countries, there is a brisk trade in specially crafted "antiques" that are actually a couple of weeks old and made in large numbers. The faking business extends to designer clothes, watches, DVDs, computer software and music, and Bangkok's Thanon Khao San and Patpong areas are famous for their stands packed with such items. Panthip, a shopping mall in Bangkok, is notorious for its illegal copying of DVDs and CDs. The Thai authorities are trying to crack down on pirating and there are periodic raids on the known outlets, but it is proving an uphill battle.

ENTERTAINMENT

Playing *mah-jong* at a café table, sharing food and drink at a roadside food market or shopping in a market are everyday ways that Thais entertain themselves. Formal cultural occasions are less common, although festivals abound and provide opportunities for more organized activities and celebrations. It is always worth asking in a tourist office about local festivals because they are joyful occasions with an emphasis on fun. Watching Thai boxing is almost more entertainment than spectator sport, with its music and performance, although there is no doubting the seriousness of the bouts. Boxers can use their feet, legs, elbows and shoulders, and the pace is frantic. Watch out also for games of *takraw*, using a woven rattan ball and played around a net like volleyball, wherever a public space allows youngsters the room to organize a game. Traditional Thai dance dramas, if you are lucky enough to come across one, are fascinating in a more subdued manner.

Be aware that while smoking is banned in cinemas and most theaters, some privately-run cabarets will allow it.

DANCE

If you are lucky while in Thailand you may come across

A poster advertising a Chinese opera in Chinatown, Bangkok

a performance of *Lakhon*—an ancient dance drama dating back to the 17th century. The dramas use traditional tales from the lives of the Buddha, from the Indian epic story the *Ramayana* and local fables. They are popular both in Bangkok and in the countryside. Most performers are women who wear elaborate costumes and masks and who dance using highly stylized and symbolic movement, accompanied by a *phiphat* orchestra.

Another form of dance drama is *Khon*—a more sophisticated version of *Lakhon*. All movement is again stylized—the dancers are silent

and accompanied by a chorus which sings and chants the story as it is performed. It can be seen at Bangkok's National Theatre and in cultural shows in restaurants in the main tourist areas. The masks you see in tourist shops are copies of those worn during the *Khon* performances.

Likay is the comic form of dance drama. The stories are more contemporary and are often made up by the troupes. The troupes work on makeshift stages, often wear modern dress and involve improvisation, audience participation and general wackiness, all in Thai of course. Performances last around five hours and you can wander in and out of one without offending anyone. If you come across one, it is well worth watching for a while. In the south of the country you may come across shadow puppet theater, more common in Malaysia. Huge puppets play out traditional stories behind a screen, the audience watching the shadow thrown onto it to the accompaniment of music.

CINEMA

Cinema is very popular in Thailand, far outweighing traditional dance dramas in the public's idea of a good night out. Bangkok has plenty of cinemas, many showing

Chinese movies which depend on car chases, martial arts, romance and comedy, usually

The Barbican, a smart bar in Silom Road, Bangkok

all in one film. Anyone who has taken a long bus ride in Thailand will know the quality of these movies, which are probably more interesting for not knowing what the characters are saying—guessing why they're running around is half the fun. Western movies are also very popular and are usually subtitled rather than dubbed, but you should check beforehand. Thailand now has its own film industry and you should look out for subtitled versions of Thai movies. Every performance of a movie involves the playing of the royal anthem, and the audience stands for the duration.

NIGHTLIFE

In urban areas, upmarket Thai bars have become all glass and steel, with illuminated table tops, designer glasses and huge windows with amazing views. Dance clubs are common in southern Thailand, with local and foreign DJs playing various styles of music. Note that smoking is banned in air-conditioned bars.

BARS AND CLUBS
Theme bars are increasingly popular, ranging from sports bars with large screens to British pubs with beer gardens, and there are also Wild West saloons and antique-filled bars full of red silk and cushions. Many visitors find it more interesting to avoid the dance clubs and enjoy the beach bars which open up at night, after the sunbathers have

given up for the day. Candles flutter in the dark of the evening; you can listen to the waves breaking on the shore or the beguiling rhythms of Buddhist music playing in the background.

DRINKS
Beer in Thailand is taxed relatively heavily. Local beers include Singha, a lighter version called Singha Gold, and Kloster, as well as cheaper beers such as Chang, Cheers, Beer Thai and Leo. While the range of foreign beers is still somewhat limited, Heineken and Carlsberg can also be found in most pubs, restaurants and supermarkets.

Wine in Thailand is mostly imported and relatively expensive although there are a few Thai vineyards; Chateau de Loei is probably the best of these. Thai whisky is popular and inexpensive, and the 35 percent proof Mekong whisky can be mixed to produce a pleasant drink.

OPENING HOURS
Regular bars and clubs generally close at 1am. In some areas this extends to 2am. Live music venues and dance clubs stay open until 2am.

THE GAY SCENE
The gay scene in Thailand, like its straight counterpart, has both a sleaze element and some good places for a night out. In Bangkok, Chiang Mai, Phuket and Pattaya there are many gay bars. Lesbian-oriented venues are far less obvious. There are a few mixed gay bars but in Thailand lesbian women tend to keep a low profile. For information on the gay scene try www.dreadedned.com or www.utopia-asia.com

NIGHT MARKETS
Talat yen is the name for the night markets that open in most towns at around 6pm and which are dedicated to open-air, inexpensive eating. It's one of the least expensive ways to eat in Thailand and the atmosphere is entertainment in itself. Carts with butane heaters set up, deep-frying, barbecuing, stir-frying, and you wander around choosing a few dishes from different stands and then find a place to sit. The vendor will

keep his eye on where you go and bring your food over, and the bill gets sorted out between the various vendors afterwards. This is the place to try out local specialties and to watch Thai families out for a night enjoying themselves.

BANGKOK
Bangkok has the most diverse and organized nightlife scene

Neon signs light up Club 172 in Khon Kaen

in Thailand. A free entertainment magazine, *BK Magazine*, which comes out on the first and third Friday of each month, has a useful nightlife section with up-to-date listings of the kind of music on offer at the various bars and clubs around the city. *BK Magazine* can be found in places like Starbucks, Delifrance and Blockbuster, as well as in bookshops, restaurants and cafés. The two English-language newspapers, *Bangkok Post* and *The Nation*, both have useful weekend editions that contain entertainment and nighttime listings.

SPORTS AND ACTIVITIES

There is a wide range of activities to enjoy in Thailand, whether as a participator or an observer. Depending on how energetic you feel, you can work up an appetite on a rock-climbing course, or chill out at a meditation center.

BICYCLING

Renting a bicycle is possible even in quite small towns, and you can spend a day at your leisure visiting local sights. Bicycle rental is inexpensive, and local motorists are usually careful to avoid accidents, although bicycling may not be advisable in Bangkok or other big cities. If you intend to make a holiday of it, bringing your own mountain bicycle is an option. Roads for the most

A chip shot to the green, near Bangkok

part are paved and have soft shoulders if you need to move over for a larger vehicle. Real aficionados can find plenty of mountain tracks to hurtle along. You should, however, bring spare parts, a medical kit, a bicycling helmet and reflective clothing. Also, make sure your insurance covers bicycling accidents. Bicycles can be taken on trains for a small charge, and there is rarely a charge on buses; ▷ 301 for useful websites.

COOKERY CLASSES

It's a long way to travel just to learn to cook, but when you get home your friends will be seriously impressed by the

wonderful Thai dishes you can put together. Good places to find courses are Bangkok, Chiang Mai, Kanchanaburi, Hua Hin, Phuket and Ko Samui. The farther afield you choose your course, the more unusual ingredients you will encounter. In the northeast this will run to scorpions and silkworms! Courses often include trips to the market (and occasionally the jungle) to collect ingredients. Local markets are a good place to buy those pesky utensils that you can never get back home: bamboo steamers, slotted spoons, and deadly-looking cleavers you will have difficulty getting through airport security. Dried herbs and spices are a good buy in markets.

KAYAKING

Most of the good kayaking centers are on the Andaman Coast, where there are lots of interesting inlets, caves and lagoons to explore. Kayaking is especially suitable for cruising some of the shoreline's fascinating mangrove swamps. Phuket has very good centers with courses and accompanied kayaking trips as well as equipment rental. In the north of Thailand there are river kayaking opportunities. See page 301 for useful websites.

MEDITATION

Thailand has meditation centers and an increasing number of them are offering classes for foreign visitors, chiefly in English. In Bangkok there are lots of centers where you can just roll up and sit quietly for an afternoon but if you want to spend a little more time learning meditation techniques there are centers in more off-the-beaten-track

places. These must be reserved in advance.

Longer meditation retreats are not for the faint-hearted. Many segregate the sexes, insist on white clothing, have a vow of silence and ask you not to leave the center while you are learning meditation techniques. Abstinence from food after noon and from drugs, alcohol and sex throughout, plus a 4am wake up call puts many people off.

Rock climbing at Railay in Krabi

That said, the benefits of a few days spent learning concentration and how to focus your thoughts can be quite life changing. Instruction and accommodation is often free, although the centers expect a donation. For useful websites, ▷ 301.

ROCK CLIMBING

Southern Thailand's Andaman Coast is home to several climbing spots, especially around Krabi, where rock climbing in the limestone rock formations has become popular. On Laem Phra Naeng there are climbing schools all within short distances of both holiday accommodation and

good climbing locations. Courses run from a half-day's instruction to a three-day course, and equipment is available to rent. Rock climbing on the limestone rocks in Railay and Ton Sai in the Krabi area is a popular activity. You are in a harness and roped together. The rope is fixed to metal bolts permanently placed in the rock so if you do slip your fall is safely arrested. Average physical fitness is required, with the mental ability to concentrate more important than muscles. It is a thrilling experience, with every moment focused on the rock and your two hands and legs,

Check out Ko Tao for diving

and an adrenaline rush is guaranteed. For websites for climbing centers, ▷ 301.

SCUBA DIVING

Scuba diving is enormously popular in the warm, reef-filled waters of southern Thailand. It is almost impossible to find a beach resort without a diving school or rental shop, and the huge number of offshore islands offer hours of exploration. Complete novices and expert divers are catered to, and the long coastlines mean that diving is possible all year round. The Andaman Coast offers the clearest waters and safest conditions between December and April, while the

Gulf of Thailand offers favorable weather conditions for diving all year. For your own safety, especially if you are a novice, there are several precautions you should take before choosing a dive course.

It is essential to check on the company's PADI (Professional Association of Divers) certificate and membership of IRRA (International Resorts and Retailers Association). This means checking on their website and asking lots of questions. Don't go for the cheapest course—in order to get customers the school may be cutting corners. Find out what kind of boat is used to take you to the dive sites—you want a nice big one with a radio and a first-aid box and spare equipment.

Check that your travel insurance covers you for accidents while diving and check with the company you book with that insurance is included for the duration of the course.

Look on the Dive Thailand website (▷ 301), which has a forum section where people give accounts of their trips. Anyone who has been badly treated generally lets everyone know about it. The site will also have information on the hundreds of dive sites and companies running courses. Don't break off bits of coral, don't ask your instructor to anchor on a reef and don't buy any coral products.

SNORKELING

Most dive schools and equipment rental places also cater to snorkelers. All beaches have rental equipment and some opportunities for the sport, but it might be a good idea to check the dive centers to see if they will take snorkelers on one of their trips where there will be better opportunities than along the beach where you are staying. If you buy a snorkeling mask

hold it against your eyes without putting on the strap, breathe in and let go. If the mask fits you it will stay in place. If it is the wrong size or shape for your face it will fall off. Bring your own snorkel if you plan to spend some time in southern Thailand.

TAKRAW

A kind of cross between volleyball and basketball without the use of hands, *takraw* is a team game played with a hollow rattan ball. There are several versions of it, one played with teams of three on a volleyball pitch and another with larger teams using basketball-type nets. Other

Scuba-diving courses are popular with holidaymakers

versions have the players standing in a circle simply keeping the ball airborne, and judges award points on the beauty or skill of the hit rather than actually getting goals. Since the players can't use their hands and have to keep the ball in the air, it can be a very acrobatic performance.

THAI BOXING

Muay Thai, or Thai boxing, is extremely popular in Thailand and is the equivalent of soccer in Europe or baseball in the US. Events are regularly shown on TV and there are stadiums dedicated to the sport around the country. Bangkok has two stadiums and is probably the

best place to take in some professional games. The start of the game is a highly ritualized ceremony accompanied by live music from a *phiphat* orchestra. Each boxer follows a pattern of making obeisance to the four quarters of the compass and to his home province. He then performs a dance. When the actual fighting begins, it is less spiritual and more physical. Those of a delicate nature might not want to watch as the bout gets under way, with frenetic betting going on as the match progresses and the wailing *phiphat* getting faster and louder. Some visitors might want to attend a kickboxing school. See page 301 for websites.

TREKKING
If you travel to northern Thailand then a trekking trip may well be the highlight of your stay. November to February is the best time. You need to be fit to undertake a trek since it invariably includes quite strenuous uphill walking in hot conditions and some curious meals. TAT (the Tourism Authority of Thailand) has a list of accredited companies who organize these tours. Do not just go with the people your guesthouse suggests—they get a commission for each person they send. Find out how many people will be on the trek—a large party can make life difficult. A typical trip lasts about four days and includes a trek through the mountains with overnight stays in local villages. When meeting these people, try not to interfere too much with their lifestyle. Do not take valuables with you beyond your camera, unless you are prepared to lose them. Robberies are now rare but still possible.

WHITEWATER RAFTING
Some exciting trips can be had during the rainy season (July to November), when the rivers are full. Most organized and popular are stretches of the Umphang and Mai Khlong rivers. In Pai, in northern Thailand, some excellent trips can be organized—two days along the Pai River through rapids and gorges, camping at night. Less challenging river trips are organized on the Kwai River, near Kanchanaburi. See page 301 for websites.

WINDSURFING
Good windsurfing centers and opportunities are at Pattaya, Ko Samet and Ko Samui. The best winds in the Gulf of Thailand are from February to April and on the Andaman Coast from September to December. Equipment will suit amateurs and beginners, and wetsuits are not necessary.

HEALTH AND BEAUTY

Spas do seem to be located in posh hotels but there are enough affordable places for everyone who wants to have a try. Massages are a Thai specialty, offering the possibility of realigning your *prana* ("life energy")—it has been called yoga for the lazy—using ancient methods first brought to Thailand from India centuries ago and later influenced by Chinese medicine.

SPAS
Most spas include the usual range of facials, aromatherapy, body wraps, baths in exotic substances and general pampering. Many resorts will have at least one spa connected to a five-star hotel, and you do not need to be a guest to book a session.

At some spas you remain fully clothed while others provide disposable underwear or a hospital-type garment. Some massages use aromatherapy oils on the back and others offer a hot stone massage, based on the idea that stones harvested from volcanic lava are rich in energy and release their therapeutic value when heated and applied to the body in a stroking motion by the masseur. Small heated stones are also placed on key energy points of the body, the heat penetrating the body to relax muscular tension.

THAI MASSAGE
A good massage should make you feel refreshed and energized, as blood circulation is stimulated and tension points relaxed. While most forms of massage that Westerners are familiar with tend to manipulate flesh to relieve tension, Thai massage is based on the idea that most problems with the flesh and the mind are caused by the blocking of energy as it flows through the body. The treatment is aimed at relieving these blockage points in order to restore equilibrium. It is a very strange sensation—a kind of pleasant abuse with the massage therapist using her feet, elbows and knees as well as her hands for the workout. The recipient also finds their limbs being manipulated into strange positions. There is a massage therapist on every beach where there are overseas visitors. A massage should last one or two hours and cost around B200 to B300. In Chiang Mai there are several schools that teach these techniques.

WHAT TO DO

FOR CHILDREN

Traveling with children in Thailand can be a rewarding and relaxing experience. Thais love children, and Western ones are still enough of a novelty for regular requests for photographs from smiling locals.

ACCOMMODATION
Hotels rarely charge extra for children if they sleep in their parents' room.

HYGIENE
The normal rules for hygiene apply doubly to children. Make sure their hands are washed regularly, deal with any cuts and scrapes straightaway, and ensure they don't binge on too many mangoes at once. They should also be told to keep away from stray animals—in addition to their poor cleanliness, rabies is not unknown.

SNORKELING
In southern Thailand, snorkeling can be an enthralling experience for children who are able to swim, but adult supervision is constantly required because it is such an absorbing activity that snorkelers can easily lose their sense of distance and direction. There is also the danger of sunburn to the back of the neck and back. Snorkeling packages are usually advertised in resort areas. From Krabi, for example, there are popular four-island day trips that provide masks and snorkels (and life jackets), and children will enjoy the journey by speedboat and the fish-feeding sessions. You may want to consider packing your own gear for children since these may be less readily available in Thailand.

FESTIVALS AND EVENTS

It would be hard to spend any time in Thailand without encountering a festival. Many follow the lunar calendar so they rarely fall in the same week each year. TAT publishes a calendar of events each year, or check out www.thailandgrandfestival.com
    Most festivals have a religious origin, but this is not always apparent. The Rocket festivals that take place in the northeast, for example, are supposed to be a way of reminding a rain god that it is time to release some water from the skies.
    Nationwide festivals are covered here; local ones are listed at the end of each section.

The Chinese New Year, which falls sometime between **mid-January and late February**, is the occasion for celebrations by Thai-Chinese, especially in Bangkok and Phuket.

On a full moon in **February**, Maha Puja is a Buddhist merit-making occasion with nighttime processions to local temples.

Late February to mid-April sees kite-flying contests—Sanam Luang in Bangkok is a popular venue.

The Phanom Rung Festival takes place in the last week in **March**. It celebrates the restoration work at Phanom Rung Historical Park with a procession and sound-and-light shows.

A Buddhist festival in Bangkok

Usually around **mid-April**, Songkhran is the most exuberant national holiday. For visitors, its most conspicuous feature is the dousing of everyone with large amounts of water—be prepared for a soaking.

The most solemn day of the Buddhist year is *Visakha* in **May** when the life, enlightenment and death of Buddha are commemorated.

In **July/August**, a Candle Festival in Ubon Ratchathani brings three days of parades. This marks the Buddha's first sermon and the beginning of the traditional period of retreat for Buddhists.

Around **mid-October to mid-November,** the Kathin Festival marks the time when new monastic garments are offered by the laity to the temples' monks.

Full-moon week in November brings *Loy Krathong*, when small boats made of plant leaves carry blessings of incense, flowers and candles to celebrate the end of the rainy season.

BANGKOK

Most of what you do in Bangkok will require planning, and you will always need to factor in the return journey time. Everything takes longer than you think, and if you try to rush then the heat really kicks in and takes its toll. Shopping, a major draw for most visitors, is probably the easiest activity to organize. Choose a department store or shopping area and work out how to get there with the least amount of walking. Places to eat are never far away from the shops. Entertainment and nightlife is not a problem if you are staying in the same area, but for venues farther afield you may need to return by taxi. To keep up with current events in the capital, look for the free copies of *BK Magazine* and check the entertainment pages of the daily newspapers.

KEY TO SYMBOLS

 Shopping
 Entertainment
 Nightlife
 Sports
Activities
Health and Beauty
For Children

SHOPPING

ANTIQUES

LEK GALLERY
1134 Thanon Charoen Krung (New Road)
Tel 026 395 870
This shop, established in 1975, is on the left side of the street if walking from the Oriental Hotel to the River City shopping complex (▷ 185). The antiques and art come mostly from Thailand, China, Indonesia and Myanmar (Burma), and you could expect to pay B15,000 for a Chinese pottery figure from the Ming dynasty or B50,000 for an 18th-century Buddha.
Mon–Sat 9.30–7 Sri Praya or The Oriental

OLD MAPS & PRINTS
Shop 432, River City, Trok Rongnamkang, off Thanon Charoen Krung (New Road)
Tel 022 370 077
www.classicmaps.com
Maps, engravings and prints of Southeast Asia from before 1900. The shop is run by two German expatriates who know a great deal about their subject, and there is a search facility on their website.
Daily 11–7 Thra Si Phraya

RIVER CITY
See page 185.

ARTS, CRAFTS AND SOUVENIRS

JADE THONGTAVEE
Rm. 202, 2nd Floor, River City
Tel 022 370 077
Jade jewelry and objects carved from jade are the specialty of this shop in River City. Best of all, everything you see is small enough to fit in your luggage. Prices are displayed but expect a discount of around 10 percent.
Daily 12–7 Sri Praya pier

MORAKOT
Rm. 103–104, Ground Floor, River City
Tel 022 370 007
A useful shop for quality gifts and souvenirs, with a large range of Thai, Chinese and Burmese merchandise, reproductions of antique items and a good stock of jewelry.
Daily 10–8 Sri Praya pier

NARAI PHAND
127 Ratchadamri Avenue, off Thanon Ratchadamri
Tel 022 524 670
www.naraiphand.com
Large, government-run craft center, entered next to Gaysorn just across the road from the Erawan Shrine (▷ 69), not to be confused with the private enterprises of the nearby Thai Craft Village. Fabrics and cloth by the meter on the first story, crafts are on the second, and furniture and wood-carved elephants on the third. Fixed prices, shipping can be arranged and internet access on the second level by the café.
🕐 Daily 10–8 🚇 Chit Lom

SILOM VILLAGE TRADE CENTER
286 Thanon Silom
Tel 026 356 816
www.silomvillage.co.th
The most conspicuous visitor-oriented attraction on Thanon Silom is a series of shopping arcades, a hotel, spa, the Ruen Thep Thai dance center (▷ 187) and restaurants. The outlets mostly sell handicrafts and jewelry, and there is also a clothes boutique, two luggage shops and a tailor's shop that also sells Thai silk. It is a convenient cluster of shops, but prices are a bit steep and you need to bargain hard.
🕐 Daily 10–10 🚇 Surasak 🚤 Central Pier

SPAREPART AND ARTSWORKS
Unit A/625 Suan Lum Night Bazaar, Thanon Rama IV
Tel 012 588 132
The delight of Suan Lum Night Bazaar is the variety of inventive and cleverly made craft products for sale. No more so than Sparepart and Artworks, selling imaginative figures of the sci-fi type made entirely from scrap metal. Some are small enough to wrap and easily fit into your luggage, but the models get more fascinating as they get larger in size.
🕐 Daily 4–12 🚇 Si Lom 🚇 Lumphini

TAEKEE TAEKON
118 Thanon Phra Athit
Tel 026 291 473
Turn left after exiting from the Tha Phra Athit pier, cross the road, and this shop is about 200m (220 yards) farther down on a corner. Prices are more or less fixed—expect around a 10 percent discount—and there is a reasonable choice of quality textiles, silk items, axe cushions, jewelry, baskets, stationery and bags. Easy to find if visiting Banglamphu.
🕐 Mon–Sat 9–6 🚤 Tha Phra Athit pier

You'll find plenty of places to buy souvenirs in Bangkok

BEAUTY PRODUCTS
BATH & BLOOM
422 Siam Square, Soi 11
Tel 022 159 325
www.earthfactory.com
A small store packed with bath products, especially handmade, fragrant soaps scented with unusual ingredients like mango, rice and charcoal. A range of detoxifying products use exotic blends of kaffir lime, mint and lemon grass.
🕐 Daily 10–9 🚇 Siam

L'OCCITANE
Central Chidlom, Thanon Ploenchit
Tel 026 557 777
www.loccitane.com
Similar to The Body Shop in its concept—environmentally friendly products with recyclable packaging and no animal testing—but with an Asian accent. Soaps, candles and incense for meditation, fragrances, skin creams.
🕐 Daily 10–8 🚇 Chit Lom

PANPURI
2/F Gaysorn Plaza, Thanon Ploenchit
Tel 012 088 135
www.panpuri.com
A philosophy of holistic well-being underpins Panpuri's bath and beauty products, found in many of the luxury spas in Asia. Everything is hypo-allergenic, using only natural ingredients and plant oils to create the scents.
🕐 Daily 10–9 🚇 Chit Lom

BOOKS
ASIA BOOKS
This is the largest chain of English-language bookstores in Bangkok, and it stocks a good range of maps, guides, coffee-table books, fiction and non-fiction. You can find Asia Books at:

Central World Plaza
3rd Floor, Central World Plaza, Skydome Zone C, Thanon Ratchadamri
Tel 022 556 209
🕐 Daily 10.30–9

Siam Discovery Centre
4th Floor, Siam Discovery Centre, Thanon Rama I
Tel 026 580 418
🕐 Daily 10–9

Sukhumvit
221 (Near Robinson's Department Store), Thanon Sukhumvit, between Sois 15 and 17
Tel 022 527 277
🕐 Daily 9–9

1st and 3rd Floor, Landmark Hotel, Thanon Sukhumvit, between Sois 4 and 6
Tel 022 525 839
🕐 Daily 10–9 (1st), 11–8 (3rd)

WHAT TO DO

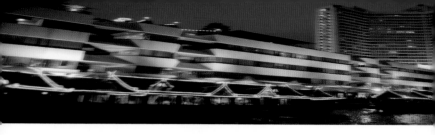

2nd Floor, Times Square Building, Thanon Sukhumvit, between Sois 12 and 14
Tel 022 500 162
🕓 Daily 10–9

3rd Floor, Emporium Shopping Complex, Thanon Sukhumvit, between Sois 22 and 24
Tel 026 648 545
🕓 Daily 10.30–9.30

GOLF EQUIPMENT
GOLF FRIEND
Thaniya Plaza, Thanon Thaniya, off Thanon Silom
Tel 022 312 208
Golfers should head to the top of Thanon Silom, or walk down it from the Skytrain station, and find Thaniya Plaza at the end of Thanon Thaniya. Golf Friend is only one of a number of shops here specializing in golfing gear and selling both new and used items.
🕓 Daily 10–8 🚇 Sala Daeng

MARKETS
CHATUCHAK WEEKEND MARKET
See page 68.

CHINATOWN
See page 68.

KHAO SAN ROAD
Thanon Khao San
In the heart of Banglamphu (▷ 67), Khao San Road was once known only as a place where backpackers came to find dirt-cheap lodging, but it has evolved into a lively street market. It's lined with stands selling inexpensive but iconic items of Thai clothing, CDs and DVDs, jewelry and handicrafts small enough to squeeze into a rucksack. If you wander down the adjoining backstreets where a pleasant Thai atmosphere prevails, you'll find some more individual and characterful shops.
🕓 9–11 ⛴ Tha Phra Athit pier

PATPONG NIGHT BAZAAR
Patpong 1
Bangkok's red-light area (▷ 76) is also the site for a very popular night market. The sidewalks of Patpong 1 and nearby Thanon Silom fill with stands displaying clothes with counterfeit designer labels, counterfeit Rolex watches, bootleg music and movies, leather items, trinkets and assorted other merchandise. There are no bargains to be had here, but it can be fun if you don't allow yourself to get serious about the shopping.
🕓 7–11 🚇 Si Lom 🚇 Sala Daeng

Shopping for bargains in Khao San Road

SUAN LUM NIGHT BAZAAR
Thanon Rama IV
This night market is easy to reach in the southeast corner of Lumphini Park and a short walk from a Skytrain and metro station. In many respects, it is the ideal place to shop for arts and crafts in Bangkok. The atmosphere is a lot less frenetic than Chatuchak Market, and there is far less chance of getting lost in a maze of shop stands. Nor do you have to walk past endless stands selling products you are not interested in. Suan Lum is devoted entirely to Thai arts and crafts, with an emphasis

on quality rather than tourist kitsch. Bargaining will secure a discount of around 10 percent or more. You'll find interesting ceramics at D/643. At B19 lampshades are sold packed down flat, and there's also a nice line here in wooden Buddhas and spa products.
🕓 Daily 3–12 🚇 Suan Si Lom
🚇 Lumphini

SHOPPING MALLS AND DEPARTMENT STORES
CENTRAL CHIDLOM
1027 Thanon Phloenchit
Tel 026 557 777
This is the flagship store of Bangkok's largest chain of department stores. There are seven stories dedicated to quality shopping, including clothes, electronics and a supermarket, all at fixed prices. A trip here can be an exhausting experience, but body fatigue can be relieved on the top floor's Food Loft (▷ 247), where there is also a free internet facility.
🕓 Daily 9am–10pm 🚇 Chit Lom

CENTRAL WORLD PLAZA
Thanon Rama IV
Tel 022 559 400
It is hard to miss this monumental edifice, on the corner of Thanon Rama IV and Thanon Ratchadamri and visible from passing Skytrains, one of the very largest shopping malls in the city. The fifth level is furniture and homeware, and the sixth has a skating rink and cinemas. The other levels have a multitude of various shops and two department stores, Isetan and Zen. Asia Books has a large bookshop here.
🕓 Mon–Fri 10.30–9, Sat–Sun 10–9
🚇 Chit Lom

EMPORIUM
Thanon Sukhumvit between Soi 22 and 24
Tel 026 648 000/5
An upmarket center with a reasonable spread of quality

WHAT TO DO

shops and the flagship Emporium department stores. As well as big-name boutiques like Christian Dior and Armani, there are two bookshops, a Jim Thompson silk outlet, a Boots pharmacy, a gourmet supermarket and some craft shops on the fourth level. Places to eat are on the fifth level, and above that there's a cinema.

🕐 Daily 10–8 🚇 Phrom Phong

ERAWAN BANGKOK

Corner of Thanon Rama I and Thanon Ratchadamri
Tel 022 478 456

Hailed as a "Boutique Mall," this shopping mall offers a less mainstream selection of brand names than the like-minded Gaysorn (▷ below) and is worth a visit if you are looking for chic clothes and fashion accessories. In keeping with the mall's image, there is a Wellness and Beauty Center to indulge the needs of the body beautiful.

🕐 Daily 10–8 🚇 Chit Lom

GAYSORN

Corner of Thanon Ratchadamri and Thanon Phloenchit
Tel 026 561 149

Gaysorn has securely positioned itself at the luxury end of consumer shopping: Louis Vuitton, Fendi, Dior, Celine, Gucci, Prada, Loewe and La Perla are all here, plus many lesser-known but equally pricey stores. Counterfeit versions of some of the branded clothes items can be found in the stands of Patpong. The atmosphere inside Gaysorn, in tune with the overall minimalist style, is more sedate and less busy than your average Bangkok shopping mall.

🕐 Daily 9–10 🚇 Chit Lom (with direct access from skybridge)

MBK

Corner of Thanon Phayathai and Thanon Rama I
Tel 026 209 000

For general shopping and especially for clothes, shoes, leather goods, handbags and luggage, it is hard to beat the seven-story MBK (Mah Boon Krong). Some of the shops have fixed prices, while others allow for some flexibility and you can usually cut quickly to the chase and get their bottom price. MBK is just west of the National Stadium Skytrain station, and a covered walkway takes you directly there. Try to avoid weekends when the place is horrendously busy; the best time is mid-morning on a weekday when most of the shutters are down and your

Fashion-loving travelers can stock up at Siam Square's boutiques

energy levels are high. There are places to eat and drink on the bottom floor.

🕐 Daily 10–9 🚇 National Stadium

PANTHIP

Thanon Petchaburi
Tel 022 549 797

Coming from the Amari Watergate end of Thanon Petchaburi, Panthip is on your left, less than a kilometer (0.6 mile) past the hotel; coming from the Ratchatewi Skytrain station, it is on your right. This is nirvana for computer shoppers or anyone seeking bootleg software, music or movies. Everyone else will find it extremely noisy and a little

claustrophobic, and the places serving food are well below par for Bangkok.

🕐 Daily 10–8 🚇 Ratchatewi

RIVER CITY

Trok Rongnamkang, off Thanon Charoen Krung (New Road)
Tel 022 567 398
www.rivercity.co.th

A sophisticated shopping complex by the Chao Phraya River, next to the Royal Orchid Sheraton hotel, providing free shuttle boats from the other riverside hotels in this area. The shops are mostly devoted to antiques, handicrafts and objects, with an emphasis on items too large to fit in your luggage (they offer a shipping service). There are some exceptions, like Jade Thongtavee (▷ 182), but more typical is the Dragon Gallery, on the third level, specializing in bronze sculptures.

🕐 Daily 9–7 🚤 Thra Si Phraya

THANON SUKHUMVIT

The western end of Thanon Sukhumvit, between Soi 1 and 33, has numerous shops catering to the needs of overseas visitors, but they are not especially good value when compared to MBK (▷ left). Up to Soi 11 the sidewalks are busy with stands retailing fake designer items and the like, but bargaining is essential in order to obtain a fair price. There is a branch of Robinson's department store, one notch below Central (▷ 184) in terms of quality, between Soi 17 and 19, and across the road there is the swish Times Square shopping mall. Near Soi 24 you will find the Emporium (▷ left) while around Soi 71 the less touristy shops are good value for general merchandise.

🕐 Daily 9–11 🚇 Nana for sois 1–13, Asok for sois 13–18, Phrom Phong for sois 18–26, Thong Lo for sois 26–33

TAILOR

GOLDEN WOOL

1340–1342 Thanon Charoen Krung
Tel 022 335 153

A well-established business where men and women can go for a quality, tailor-made suit. There are other reputable tailors along the street that are also worth considering.

🕐 Mon–Sat 9.30–8
💰 US$250–US$800 depending on the material 🚤 The Oriental pier

TEENAGE FASHION

SIAM SQUARE

A series of interlocking *sois* rather than a square, packed with tiny shops and boutiques catering to Bangkok's fashion-conscious youth. Clothes and accessories are reasonable value and often have fixed prices. The nearby Novotel hotel is a useful landmark and rendezvous point.

🕐 10–10 🚇 Siam

THAI FABRICS

JIM THOMPSON'S THAI SILK

Soi Kasem San 2, Thanon Rama 1
Tel 022 167 368
www.jimthompson.com

This shop at Jim Thompson's House is a good introduction to the range of quality Thai fabrics available in the city. Silk is sold by the yard, and there are ready-to-wear dresses as well as cushions and other home furnishings. Jim Thompson shops are also located in the Peninsula, Sheraton Grande, Amari Watergate and Oriental hotels, the Emporium, Central Chidlom department store and Terminal 1 at the airport.

🕐 Daily 9–5 🚇 National Stadium (Exit 1) 🚤 Hua Chang canal boat pier

MUD MEE

L.39, Intercontinental Bangkok, 971 Thanon Ploenchit
Tel 026 519 501

Everything sold in Mud Mee is made from Thai silk, though mostly for women, with silk scarves for around B100, dresses for B250, and skirts, pants (trousers) and tops

averaging around B500. No heavy selling from the staff, reasonable-quality merchandise, and a calm atmosphere are all good reasons for a visit.

🕐 Daily 10–7 🚇 Chit Lom

🎭 ENTERTAINMENT

AFTERNOON TEA

TEA AT THE ORIENTAL

The Oriental, 48 Oriental Avenue
Tel 022 360 420
www.mandarinoriental.com

The full tea set, with a choice of Traditional, Spa for the health-conscious, or the Oriental Thai, comes with a three-tiered platter bearing

Jim Thompson's Thai Silk Shop has a good range of materials

delicacies like vegetable caponata on olive focaccia bread (Spa), cucumber and cream cheese on wheat bread (Traditional) or banana scones and pomela marmalade on pandanus leaf (Oriental). Sit back in what was the original hotel's lobby on white rattan chairs under palm fronds, surrounded by old photographs of famous guests over the years, or explore the Reading Room that was opened by the disgraced English politician Jeffrey Archer in 1993.

🕐 Daily 12–6 💰 B300 for tea/coffee with a choice of cakes and pastries, B880 for the Traditional tea set 🚇 Saphan Taksin 🚤 The Oriental

CINEMAS

Cinemas are not conspicuous because they are usually on the top story of shopping malls, but there are plenty to choose from. Programs are listed in the *Bangkok Post* and *The Nation* newspapers and at www.movieseer.com. First-run releases with original soundtracks and Thai subtitles are the norm. Patrons stand for the national anthem, which is played before each performance. Tickets cost between B60 and B150.

APEX CINEMAS

Siam Square
www.apexsiam-square.com

Apex has a number of locations in and around Siam Square; the Lido Multiplex is at 256 Thanon Rama 1 (tel 022 526 498), Scala at Soi 1 (tel 022 512 861), and Siam at 352 Thanon Rama 1 (tel 022 513 508).

🚇 Siam for all Apex cinemas

EGV CINEMA

6/F Siam Discovery Centre, Thanon Rama I
Tel 028 129 999
www.egv.com

There are cinemas and then there is Gold Class at the EGV cinema, the equivalent of traveling first class. Your reclining seat is electrically adjustable and comes with a footrest, a pillow, blanket and socks. Arrive in time to enjoy the private lounge and complimentary drink. The Gold Class Suite is a double-seat complete with nine kinds of massages. Economy class is on the seventh floor.

💰 B500 and B600 🚇 Siam

MAJOR CINEPLEX

www.majorcineplex.com
7/F, Central World Plaza
Tel 025 155 555

Eight-screen cinema, downtown.

🚇 Chid Lom

WHAT TO DO

SF CINEMA CITY EMPORIUM
6/F, Emporium Shopping Centre,
Sukhumvit Soi 24
Tel 022 609 333
Multiplex in an upscale mall.
🚇 Phrom Phong

SF CINEMA CITY MBK
7/F, MBK Centre, corner of Thanon
Phayathai and Thanon Rama I
Tel 026 116 444
Modern cinema showing the
latest releases.
🚇 National Stadium

DINNER CRUISE
CHAO PHRAYA RIVER DINNER CRUISE
Tel 023 919 634
Check in before departure
time (7.30pm) and take your
seat on the open-air deck as
the boat glides off toward
Pinkaloo Bridge for night
photo shots of Wat Arun and
the Grand Palace. The buffet
dinner, Thai and international
food, begins at 8pm, and you
are back at the River City pier
by 9.30pm. Drinks on board
are extra.
🕐 Daily at 7.15pm 💷 B1,200, child
B750 🚢 River City pier

SUNDAY CRUISES
BANG-PA-IN
Tha Chang Pier
Tel 022 256 179
First stop on this regular
Sunday cruise is an arts and
crafts center at Bang Sai at
around 10.30am. You get a
chance to see craftspeople at
work on miniature wood
carvings and basket weaving.
By noon, 60km (37 miles)
upriver from Bangkok, you have
reached Bang-Pa-In and its
Summer Palace, where royalty
lived during the Ayutthaya
period. The boat departs for
Bangkok at 4pm so there is
plenty of time to have lunch at
one of the many restaurants.
🕐 Departs at 8am, returns 6pm
💷 B430, child (4–10 years) B350;
admission to arts and crafts center
B100; admission to Summer Palace
B100 🚢 Tha Chang ❓ Dress code for
Summer Palace: no shorts or sandals

CHAO PHRAYA RIVER EXPRESS BOAT
Central Pier
Tel 026 236 001
The River Express Boat also
runs a Sunday cruise to Bang-
Pa-In and follows the same
itinerary as the one in the
previous entry. This one is
more convenient if it is easier
to reach Central Pier from your
accommodation.
🕐 Departs at 7.30am, returns 6.30pm
💷 B430, child B350; admission to arts
and crafts center B100; admission to
Summer Palace B100 🚢 Sathon Pier

*Take afternoon tea at the
Oriental hotel*

THAI BOXING
LUMPHINI STADIUM
Thanon Rama IV
Tel 022 528 765
Thai boxing, *Muay Thai*, is fast
and furious and the frenzied
atmosphere has more to do
with the serious gambling that
accompanies the bouts than
appreciation of the finer skills
of the contestants. There is no
need to reserve seats in
advance but turn up at least
half an hour before the first
fights to get the seat you want.
If you want instruction in
Muay Thai, check out
www.muaythai-institute.net
🕐 Tue, Fri 6.30–11, Sat 5pm, 8pm
💷 B1,000–B2,000

RATCHADAMNOEN BOXING STADIUM
1 Ratchadamnoen Nok
Tel 022 814 205
This is the other venue for Thai
boxing in the city and the
quality of the fights is no
different than at the Lumphini
Stadium. The best seats are
always those nearer the
ringside but these are also
most expensive; the cheapest
seats are for the Sunday bouts.
🕐 Mon, Wed–Thu 6pm; Sun 5pm
💷 B220–B1,000

THAI DANCES
ERAWAN SHRINE
See page 69.

THEATER
JOE LOUIS PUPPET THEATRE
Suan Lum Night Bazaar, Thanon Rama IV
Tel 022 529 683
www.joelouistheatre.com
Puppet theater dates back to
the middle of the 19th century
and was almost extinct when it
was resuscitated by Sakorn
Yangkeowsod, who was
nicknamed Joe Louis. The
shows are fascinating for
people of all ages, and as the
puppets act out episodes from
the *Ramakien* a voice-over in
English recounts the narrative.
Arrive early to stroll the night
bazaar, and enjoy dinner on the
terrace in front of the theater.
🕐 Sat–Sun 7.30pm 💷 B500, child
B300 🚇 Ratdamri 🚇 Lumphini

PATRAVADI THEATRE
Soi Wat Rakang, Thonburi
Tel 024 127 287
www.patravaditheatre.com
Over the weekend, visitors are
welcome to come along and
join the classes in Thai dance
and drums or the meditation
and yoga sessions. A busy
program ensures there are
often evening performances.
🕐 Evening performances at around
7pm; meditation and yoga Sun 2pm;
Thai dance and drum classes Fri–Sat
5pm 💷 Thai dance class B100;
meditation and yoga classes take
donations; evening shows vary in price
🚢 Wat Rakhang or Wang Lang pier

RUEN THEP

Silom Village Level 2, 286 Thanon Silom
Tel 026 356 816
www.silomvillage.co.th

Thai classical dance, with or without a set dinner, takes place every evening in the popular Silom Village complex. Shoes are deposited at the entrance, and you enter a low-ceilinged chamber, where everything has a red hue, to watch Thai dancers in elaborate and glittering costumes perform a series of classical dances.

🕐 Show daily 8.30–9.20; dinner 7–9.20
🍴 B600; show only B350 🚉 Surasak
⛴ Central Pier

SUAN LUM BEER GARDEN

Suan Lum Night Bazaar, Thanon Rama IV

The beer garden is part of a self-service food court, but for drinks just take a seat and one of the servers will take your order. Sit at the stage end if you want to enjoy at close quarters the live music that starts up in the evening. The food is mostly Asian and there is a good variety.

🕐 Daily 3–12 🚉 Si Lom 🚇 Lumphini

SALA RIM NAAM

The Oriental, 48 Oriental Avenue
Tel 024 372 918 ext. 3344
www.mandarinoriental.com

Classical Thai dancing at The Oriental (▷ 272) takes place nightly in a teak pavilion on the western side of the Chao Phraya River. The hotel's shuttle boat will bring you over from the hotel's terrace, and the evening's entertainment includes a Thai dinner, served at long, low tables (footwear deposited outside) shared with other guests, making this a sociable rather than an intimate experience. The dancers and their costumes are glamorous and pictures can be taken. The food can be rather bland and drinks are extra.

🕐 Dinner from 7pm, dance from 8.30pm 🍴 B1,850 🚉 Saphan Taksin
⛴ The Oriental

🎵 NIGHTLIFE

BARS

BROWN SUGAR

231/2 Soi Lang Suan
Tel 022 501 826

Not far from the Cambodian embassy, this is a reliably good venue for live jazz and a relaxed ambience. The atmosphere is friendly enough to keep you here all evening, especially with the good food available.

🕐 Fri–Sun 5pm–2am, Mon–Thu 11am–2pm, 5pm–1am; live music Sun–Mon 10pm–1am, Tue–Thu 8.45pm–1am, Fri–Sat 7.45pm–1am
🚉 Ratchadamri 🚉 Si Lom

Movies are often shown in their original language

FACE BAR

29 Sukhumvit Soi 38
Tel 027 136 048

The Face bar and restaurant complex is composed of six buildings that you move between along wooden walkways, surrounded by art; one of them is the oh-so-chic Face Bar. Surrounded by antiques from the Orient, you drop into soft seats and choose drinks from a list of house cocktails. This is one of the *in* places, popular with expats and young professional Thais.

🕐 Daily 5pm–1am 🚉 Ekkhami

MOON BAR

61/F Banyan Tree Hotel, 21/100 Thanon Sathorn Tai
Tel 026 791 200

Up in the sky and open to the night air, the Moon Bar is a cool place to spend the evening, literally and metaphorically. Soft jazz plays in the background, and there is a telescope to view the city landscape. The 61st level is a good place to enjoy a pre-dinner drink and watch the sun set over the metropolis. Compare and contrast this venue with the open-air Sky Bar (▷ below).

🕐 Daily 5pm–1am (weather permitting)
🚇 Lumphini

RE-WIND

2/F, Camp Davis, 88 Sukhumvit Soi 24
Tel 022 603 842

A watering hole with music and food and, as the name suggests, dedicated to retro sounds. There's a casual style to the place, with sofas for comfortable seating and bar stools for those who prefer propping up the counter. The lights dim at around 9.30pm, and a stage area fronts a live band or DJ playing oldies from the 1970s and 1980s. Tuesday is currently hosting a Britpop night.

🕐 Daily 7pm–1am 🚉 Phrom Phong

SKY BAR

64th level, State Tower, 1055 Thanon Silom
Tel 026 249 555
www.thedomebkk.com

Open-air bar some 250m (820ft) above the ground of the State Tower, close to the Chao Phraya River, at the bottom end of Thanon Silom where it meets Thanon Charoen Krung. A strict if idiosyncratic dress code means that if you are wearing shorts—however well pressed and whatever the designer label—or even sandals, you will not be allowed in (but scruffy old jeans are permissible). The Sky Bar vies with the Moon Bar

WHAT TO DO

(▷ 188) as the coolest place to go for a drink before or after a meal. Live music, with a band and singer every night except Monday (band only), and the Sirocco restaurant (▷ 249).

🕐 Daily 6.30pm–1am 🚇 Saphan Taksin

SUNSET STREET

199 Thanon Khao San
Tel 022 822 565
www.sunsetstreet.com

Sunset Street is a square on the busy and bustling Khao San Road (▷ 67) where there are three bars. Sabai is the most relaxing of them, and the music encourages you to linger and lounge around. Sanook Bar is a more hip-hop joint in comparison, while the Sunset Bar is always lively when a live band gets going.

🕐 Sabai Bar 8am–2am, Sanook Bar 5pm–2am, Sunset Bar 12pm–2am
⛴ Tha Phra Athit pier

CLUBS

BED SUPPERCLUB

26 Sukhumvit Soi 11
Tel 026 513 537
www.bedsupperclub.com

With an innovative design and concept that has attracted international attention, this is one of Bangkok's most chic nighttime destinations. Lines form for the bar and reservations are essential for the dining section, where you stretch out and relax on the white linen of sofa beds, eat from bowls, drink and watch a fashion show or whatever event has been planned. Photo ID is required at the door.

🕐 Daily 7.30pm–1am 💰 Sun–Mon B500, including 2 drinks from 10pm, Wed B500, including 2 drinks from 7.30pm, Thu B800, all you can drink from 10pm, Fri–Sat B600, including 2 drinks from 10pm

CONCEPT CM²

Basement Novotel Hotel, Siam Square Soi 6
Tel 022 556 888
www.cm2bkk.com

A well-established nightspot where live international bands are usually playing pop/funk/R&B on Friday to Wednesday in the main stage area. There is also the Boom Room, where DJs play house and techno, a karaoke area and an informal eatery serving pizza and pasta.

🕐 Daily 6.30pm–2am; Ladies night Tue, Thu (free admission) 💰 Sun–Thu B220, Fri–Sat B550; price includes B170 discount on first drink 🚇 Siam

Join the locals at the Radio City bar in Patpong

MOJOS

10/20 Sukhumvit Soi 33
Tel 022 608 429
www.bangkokmojos.com

The top-notch live bands playing blues and jazz can be watched from the floor of the club or from above on the mezzanine. Mojos takes its food seriously too, with popular dishes like smoked ribs and burgers and chips as well as Thai dishes. Decked out in 1950s style, Mojos is deservedly popular.

🕐 4pm–2am 🚇 Asok 🚇 Sukhumvit

MYSTIQUE

71/8 Thanon Sukhumvit, Soi 31
Tel 023 622 374
www.mystique.com

Good music, a dance floor and a hedonistic atmosphere. Tuesday nights are free for women, who also get one free drink. The music on weekends is varied, often hip hop, sometimes calypso and reggae. Weeknights are quieter but never flat, and the quality of the DJs is above average.

🕐 Tue–Sun 8pm–2am 💰 Thu B550, Fri–Sat B650, including two drinks

Q BAR

34 Sukhumvit Soi 11
Tel 022 523 274
www.qbarbangkok.com

One of the most popular clubs in the city, and the big draw is the likelihood of there being a celebrity DJ, usually from the US or UK, in residence. There's a mix of cocktails, and a lively and gregarious atmosphere prevails. The music is usually house, acid jazz, hip-hop or pure chill-out. Photo ID is often required at the door. Food is served until 11.30pm.

🕐 Daily 8pm–1am 💰 Cover charge Mon–Thu B400, Fri–Sun B600, includes 2 free drinks 🚇 Nana

RADIO CITY

76/1–3 Patpong 1
Tel 022 664 567

A surprisingly good place for bands playing familiar rock numbers from the past. The Tom Jones and Elvis impersonations are well known and highly regarded.

🕐 6pm–3am 🚇 Sala Daeng

SAXOPHONE

3/8 Victory Monument, Thanon Phrayathai
Tel 022 465 472

A well-established venue for good music and food. The atmosphere is easygoing, and live jazz is played every night of the week.

🕐 Daily 6pm–1am 🚇 Victory Monument

WHAT TO DO

⊛✪ SPORTS AND ACTIVITIES

WHAT TO DO

BICYCLING

AMAZING BANGKOK CYCLIST
Tel 018 129 641
www.realasia.net
The price of a five-hour bicycle trip includes bicycle, drinks and lunch, and you are taken through backstreets, across main roads and over the river to Thonburi for a fascinating excursion on two wheels with a guide. This gives you an eye-opening perspective on Bangkok life. Trips start from 10/5–7 Soi 26, Thanon Sukhumvit.
⊙ Daily 1pm ⍟ B1500; special weekend tours (10am–4pm) B2000

RUNNING

HASH HOUSE HARRIERS
Tel 028 657 137
www.bangkokhh.com
Visitors are welcome to join the Hash House Harriers for one of their weekly runs, and you do not need to be a speed runner because there is not a competitive spirit; everyone runs, or walks, at their own pace. Each run lasts about 90 minutes and there is always a social drink at the end. Check the website or the sports section of Saturday's *The Bangkok Post* for details of the week's meeting place and contact numbers.
⊙ Sat 5pm ⍟ B350

THAI COOKERY CLASSES

THE LANDMARK
138 Thanon Sukhumvit
Tel 022 540 404 ext. 4305
Using the Nipa Thai restaurant and kitchen (▷ 248), the Thai chefs teach the art of cooking famous dishes like *tom yam goong* (spicy soup with prawns and lemongrass), and green curries with chicken or beef. The course fee includes a cooking class apron, a gift box of Thai spices and herbs and a lunch or dinner (and not the one you've cooked!).
⊙ 10.30–12.30, 2–4 ⍟ 1-day course B1,950, 5-day course B9,000 🚇 Nana

MAY KAIDEE'S VEGETARIAN COOKING CLASSES
123 Thanon Tanao
Tel 022 817 137
www.maykaidee.com
You meet at May Kaidee's restaurant (▷ 248) at 9am and begin the course with a visit to the local market for ingredients. By 10am you are in the kitchen and by 1am you have cooked some 10 dishes. To find the restaurant, turn left at the bottom of Thanon Khao San, cross the road and take the first lane on the right to find the back lane where May Kaidee is situated.
⊙ Daily 9–1 ⍟ B1,000 🚢 Tha Phra Athit (N13)

Improve your Thai cooking skills with a course

♡ HEALTH AND BEAUTY

ABSOLUTE YOGA
14/F Unico Building, Soi Lang Suan, Thanon Phloenchit
Tel 026 521 333
www.absoluteyogabangkok.com
Yoga with a temperature—Bikram yoga of the kind practiced here takes place in a room heated to 37°C. There are full changing facilities, with lockers and towels provided. The other type of yoga available is Power Vinysua yoga. A map showing its exact location can be found on its website.
⊙ Mon–Thu 9–9, Fri 9–8, Sat–Sun 9–5 ⍟ Single class from B500, 5 classes B2,000 🚇 Chit Lom, Exit 4

ANDERSON OF LONDON
Phloenchit Centre Building, Sukhumvit Soi 2
Tel 026 623 000
At prices that should compare very favorably with those back home, this is a smart hairdressing establishment where the professionally trained staff speak English and understand hair. Telephone ahead to be sure of an appointment.
⊙ Daily 10–7 ⍟ Female haircut B600, male haircut B400, shampoo B200, facial massage B1,000, manicure B450, fingernail painting B320 🚇 Nana or Phloenchit

ANNE SEMONIN SPA
4/F Sofitel Silom, 188 Thanon Silom
Tel 022 381 991, ext 1244
www.eurasiacosmetics.com
From Chong Nonsi it is a ten-minute walk to this spa; walk up to Thanon Silom from the station and turn left, and the hotel is farther along on the opposite side of the road. A specialty here is the jet-lag treatment that involves coating your face in a self-heating mud that revitalizes the tired skin and reduces that "economy-class fatigue" that has set in over a long flight. There are lots of other treatments, including waxing and massages, and a private consultation can be booked. Slimming programmes are also available.
⊙ Daily 10–10 ⍟ From B2,000 🚇 Chong Nonsi

BANYAN TREE SPA
Banyan Tree Hotel, 21/100 Thanon Sathorn
Tel 026 791 052/4
www.banyantreespa.com
The whole gamut of treatments is available from just the feet, hands or face to a whole body massage or, the ultimate in spa pampering and soothing the body, the seven-hour Banyan Day. Reduced prices are offered to couples taking the same treatment.

Daily 9–4 🖐 90-min Back Reviver US$95, 2-hour hand, feet and face treatment US$150, 3-hour Thai Ginger Healer US$205, Banyan Day US$380 🚇 Lumphini

GOODWILL

44/16 Thanon Convent
Tel 026 320 626
Goodwill is opposite the BNH hospital and is a neat little place where meals are served, including vegetarian choices like tofu salad, alongside a health and treatment set-up. Treatments include facials, waxing, haircuts and styling, manicures and pedicures, Thai and oil massages and a Thai herbal scrub. The rooftop garden is open for tea and cakes.

Mon–Sat 10–10 🖐 Massages B350–B850; facials B500–B2,200; haircuts and styling B100–B5,000 🚇 Sala Daeng

GOOTA

59/3 Soi Lang Suan, Thanon Phloenchit
Tel 022 553 553
Although oil massages are available, Goota's expertise is nails. Whether painting them or creating acrylic ones, you can leave your nails safely in their hands while watching a movie on a mini-VCD screen. A range of facials is available.

Daily 10–10 🖐 Skin facial B1,300, massage B800, acrylic nails B1,500 🚇 Chit Lom

GRANDE NAIL

63 Soi 63, Thanon Sukhumvit
Tel 027 141 015
www.grandenail.com
Grande Nail's premises, a converted town house with a garden, successfully conjures up the look and feel of a resort so that the pampering factor is satisfyingly high. Acrylic and gel extensions to fingernails are a specialty. A range of hand and foot massages are also offered and nail products are available to buy.

Daily 9.30–7 🖐 B400–B3,400 🚇 Tha Praya Athit

LET'S RELAX

77 Sukhumvit Soi 39
Tel 026 626 935
A homely setting for a spa that pampers a tired body and relieves muscular tension. Sessions begin with herbal tea. The foot massage room has floor-to-ceiling windows looking out on a garden scene, while the main massage room is upstairs on the third floor.

Daily 9–12 🖐 45-min foot reflexology and 90-min hot stone massage B2,200 🚇 Phrom Phong

MOGA INTERNATIONAL TOKYO

3/F The Emporium, Sukhumvit Soi 24
Tel 026 648 890

Excellent spas are situated in the city's finest hotels

Japanese hairdressing salon delivering stylish cuts at good prices, although you pay more for a Japanese hair stylist or for something special. Very popular, and an advance appointment is usually essential.

Daily 10.30–8 🖐 From B750 🚇 Phrom Phong

NAILS UP

Royal Garden Plaza, Bangkok Marriott Resort and Spa, Thanon Charoen
Tel 028 779 971
www.nails-up.com
The ultimate in nail care, with professional attention and high standards of cleanliness from basic polishes to nail extensions. Take the free shuttle, departing every 15 minutes, from Central Pier for the Marriott Resort & Spa and walk through to the plaza.

Daily 10–8.30 🖐 B180–B850

ORIENTAL SPA

The Oriental, 48 Oriental Avenue
Tel 022 360 420, 022 360 400
www.mandarinoriental.com
The hotel's boat will shuttle you across the river to the spa and bring you back invigorated, refreshed and rosy. There is a wide choice of treatments, including manicures and pedicures. The two-hour Essence of Acqa session starts with a 30-minute scrub on a heated table followed by half an hour in the Vitality Pool, a whirl tub, and then the special Rhassoul Bath. Here, clay and herbs are applied to the body and you sit down in the bath and wait for the aromatized steam to trickle down your skin as the lighting changes to resemble a starry night sky.

Daily 7–10 🖐 Essence of Acqa one session US$155, two sessions US$230, traditional 1-hour Thai massage US$70 🚇 Saphan Taksin 🚤 The Oriental

TAMMACHART

Novotel Bangkok Hotel, Siam Square, Soi 6
Tel 022 556 888
A beauty center, managed by the hotel, providing natural therapies for men and women. The available massages include a body slimming one and a Thai–Swedish Sports Massage as well as more traditional Thai versions. Other options include a body exfoliating scrub using milk, coffee and herbs, feet/hand reflexology sessions and a choice of seven facial treatments. You'll need at least one session here if you spend too much time out and about in frenetic Siam Square.

Daily 8–10 🖐 B500–B2,500 🚇 Siam

WHAT TO DO

⊗ FOR CHILDREN

CHERUBIN
Soi 31 (Soi Sawasdee), Thanon Sukhumvit
Tel 022 609 800
A shrine for chocolate lovers and a delightful café where the decor, all chocolate brown and white vanilla, blends with comfortable sofas, teddy bears and a display of English animal books to help create a childlike atmosphere. On the menu are cheesecake, brownies and a Chocolate Shot that delivers instant gratification. If you or your children's taste buds are not satisfied, or you want an overdose, visit the Chocolate Buffet (▷ below).
🕐 Tue–Thu 10.30–7, Fri–Sun 10.30–8
🚇 Prom Phong

CHILDREN'S DISCOVERY MUSEUM
Thanon Kamphaengphet 4, Chatuchak
Tel 022 724 500/1
www.bkkchildrenmusuem.com
This modern-looking building, in the grounds of the Queen Sirikit Park, is a 10-minute walk from Chatuchak's Skytrain station. It is a lively, hands-on type of museum with various experiments, games, computer screens and puppet shows designed to encourage an interest in learning. The Rhythm of the Universe room is especially good.
🕐 Tue–Fri 9–5, Sat–Sun 10–6 🎫 Adult B70, child B50 🚇 Chatuchak

CHOCOLATE BUFFET
The Sukhothai, 13/3 Thanon South Sathorn
Tel 023 448 888
Cocoa from all corners of the world is used to fill cakes, pitas and rolls with cold cuts and croissants—chocolate heaven for children and adults. The warm pudding drenched in a sauce of hot toffee cream is a treat, and there is a choice of over 20 different chocolates, from a diet version to cream white indulgences from Switzerland.
🕐 Fri–Sun 2–6 🎫 B750

DREAM WORLD
Thanon Rangsit–Ongharak, 8km (5 miles) north of Don Muang Airport
Tel 025 331 152
www.dreamworld-th.com
A theme park for children under the age of 12, with rides, parades of cartoon characters over the weekend at 3.45, and on weekdays at 2.30 a show about good defeating bad.
🕐 Mon–Fri 10–5, Sat–Sun 10–7
🎫 B1,000, including transport, buffet lunch and rides 🚇 Mo Chit, then a taxi
🚇 Chatuchak Park, then a taxi

EGV CINEMA
See page 186.

Take the kids kite-flying in one of Bangkok's parks

JOE LOUIS PUPPET THEATRE
See page 187.

KITE-FLYING
Lumphini Park and Sanam Luang
Kite-flying is a national pastime in Thailand and not one confined to children. Contests between rival teams can be quite serious affairs. In Lumphini Park and Sanam Luang, however, the emphasis is on fun. Vendors sell ingeniously designed kites around both parks.
🕐 Daily Feb–Apr, daytime 🚇 Si Lom or Lumphini (Lumphini Park) 🚌 Sala Daeng (Lumphini Park); Phaya Thai and then a taxi (Sanam Luang) 🛥 Tha Phra pier (Sanam Luang)

MBK
Corner of Thanon Phayathai and Thanon Rama I
The sixth floor of this shopping mall (▷ 185) pulsates discordantly to the sound of electronic, coin-fed games of every kind. It is explosively noisy and not suitable for children under the age of 12.

QUEEN SAOVABHA MEMORIAL INSTITUTE (SNAKE FARM)
See page 76.

SIAM SQUARE
See page 186.

FESTIVALS AND EVENTS

MAY

ROYAL PLOWING CEREMONY, SANAM LUANG
A ceremony to commemorate the beginning of the rice-planting season, conducted by Brahmins in Sanam Luang (▷ 78). It is a more formal occasion than usual, but it attracts large crowds in the capital.
🕐 Early May
🎫 Free

BANGKOK INTERNATIONAL FILM FESTIVAL
The month of this festival varies so check the website (www.bangokfilm.org) for details, but it usually takes place around May. It lasts 10 days, with over 150 feature films, seminars, special events and the Golden Kinnaree Awards for excellence in international film.

WHAT TO DO

THE NORTHEAST

The least-visited region of Thailand has the most surprises. There are no beaches or palm-fringed islands, no hill tribes, no "must-see" destinations and relatively little in the way of organized activities. There is a slower pace of life and having your own transportation saves a lot of time and makes a huge difference to getting around. Shopping for silk and cotton and arts and crafts is a rewarding part of any trip to Isan, but you usually need to seek out individual shops, like the ones mentioned here in Khon Kaen or Ubon Ratchathani. Entertainment is not rushed—a slow ride along the Mekong River is characteristic of the lazy pleasures on offer—but there are pleasant bars and cafés to while away the time. Observing cultural life in Isan brings you close to the ordinary lives of Thais, and although less English is spoken in the northeast than elsewhere you will find the people wonderfully patient and helpful.

KEY TO SYMBOLS

- 🌐 Shopping
- 🎭 Entertainment
- 🍷 Nightlife
- ⚽ Sports
- ⭐ Activities
- ♡ Health and Beauty
- ✴ For Children

CHIANG KHAN

⭐ RIMKONG GUESTHOUSE

294 Thanon Chaikong, Chiang Khan
Tel 042 821 125
rimkhongchk@hotmail.com
Rimkong Guesthouse is the place to call in at when in Chiang Khan to ask about any trips or tours that are in the pipeline. Day trips on the river cost around B250 per person, and a cruise at dusk is less than B200. If enough people are interested, boats can be rented for trips up and down the Mekong River, costing from B1,500. Bicycles and motorcycles can also be rented from the guesthouse.

KHON KAEN

🌐 ACT II

14/1 Thanon Pimasoot, Khon Kaen
Tel 019 750 084
Close to First Choice restaurant (▷ 250), this neat little boutique restricts itself to women's tops and jeans, and quality shirts and T-shirts for men. Sizes come in large and extra large, meaning they will fit standard European and North American bodies. There is a changing room. Prices are reasonable for a shop not selling Asian brands.
🕐 Daily 12–6

🌐 CHONNABOT SILK VILLAGE

Chonnabot village
Chonnabot is the best-known silk village close to Khon Kaen and you will easily spot women working away on their looms outside their homes in the shade. Visitors are welcome to linger and observe the fascinating process and vendors sell the women's work on the streets.
🕐 Daily 9-5

⊕ CHOPHAKA

3/12 Thanon Prachasumran, Khon Kaen
Tel 043 228 359

Silk and fabrics, jackets, tops, scarves, ties—more clothes for women than men—and axe pillows sold unpadded so that taking a couple home is quite feasible. Silk is sold by the meter, starting at around B1,000 for 3.6m (about 4 yards). Expect a 15 percent discount off the marked prices. Chophaka is a friendly shop and English is spoken.
🕙 Daily 8–8

⊕ PRATHAMAKANT LOCAL GOODS CENTER

79/2–3 Thanon Ruen Rom, Khon Kaen
Tel 043 224 080

A virtual supermarket of regional arts and crafts, this vast store is a blessing if you want to do a lot of shopping under one roof, and with fixed prices and no hassle from sales staff. There is a wide choice of cotton and silk clothes for men and women, as well as silverware, jewelry and craft goods like carved wooden elephants. If buying silk by the meter, this store offers a wide range of hues to choose from. Prices are reasonable at B240 a meter for two-ply silk, and from B1,350 for *mutmee*—"tied strings"—which gets its name from the method of using dye-resistant string to create patterns in the cotton thread before weaving.
🕙 Thu–Tue 9–8

⊕ RIN THAI SILK

412 Thanon Namuang, Khon Kaen
Tel 043 220 705

A good selection of silk clothes, mostly for women but with some shirts and ties. A meter/yard of plain silk costs from B290, and 4m (4.4 yards) lengths are around B2,700. Prices are more or less fixed, and not much English is spoken. Thanon Namuang is one of Khon Kaen's main

streets, and Prathamakant Local Goods Center, where silk prices can be compared, is a short walk away.
🕙 Daily 8–5

⊕ SILK VENDORS

Thanon Prrachasamran, Khon Kaen

As well as the retail shops in Khon Kaen, individual vendors also congregate on the sidewalk opposite the Sofitel Raja Orchid Hotel and display their produce for sale. The quality varies, but if you are not seeking top-quality silk then these vendors offer good prices for different-size lengths of material. There are no marked prices and you are

You'll find helpful staff at Rin Thai Silk

expected to bargain, but this is not Bangkok and opening prices are not ludicrously high.
🕙 Daily 9–7

⊘ GIK CLUB

Sofitel Raja Orchid Hotel, 9/9 Thanon Prachasumran, Khon Kaen
Tel 043 322 155

A disco and nightclub that benefits from a sophisticated lighting system and a revolving bandstand. The club opens at 9pm, but not much happens until after 11pm, two hours before it closes. There are DJs every night.
🕙 Daily 9pm–1am ⬜ Free admission

⊘ THE UNDERGROUND

Sofitel Raja Orchid Hotel, 9/9 Thanon Prachasumran, Khon Kaen
Tel 043 322 155

The cavernous basement of the hotel is given over to Cleo's Palace, a bar with an Egyptian theme, and Kronen Brahaus, Thailand's first in-house microbrewery. Food can be enjoyed from German, Italian, Chinese or Japanese menus, and each evening (except Monday) a local live band plays from around 7pm to 1am. The Underground is also home to a nightclub, the Gik Club (▷ above).
🕙 Daily 6pm–1am

⊘ ZOLID DISCO

Charoen Thani Princess Hotel, Thanon Si Chan, Khon Kaen
Tel 043 220 400

Sofitel Raja Orchid may be the best hotel in Khon Kaen but it loses on the disco front to Zolid at the nearby Charoen Thani Princess. On the ground floor of the hotel, the disco opens at 9pm but nothing much happens until around 11pm, when the place fills with students from the city's university and the atmosphere livens up. Live bands perform much of the time.
🕙 Nightly 9pm–1am ⬜ Free admission

⊗ KING COBRA VILLAGE

Ban Khok Sa-Nga, northeast of Khon Kaen
Tel 019 749 499

A visit to the King Cobra Village (▷ 90), 50km (80 miles) northeast of Khon Kaen, is more a form of entertainment than a way of finding out about cobras. There is a "boxing" ring with audience seating, a warm-up show by young children handling non-poisonous snakes, and then the main individual bouts between village snake handlers and their cobras. Pose for a photograph afterward, if you wish, with your favorite snake

WHAT TO DO

from the show languidly wrapped around your neck. 🕐 Daily 7–5 💲 To look around the village and see the snakes B10; admission for a performance depends on the number of visitors

⚫ KOSA BOWLING
Thanon Si Chan, Khon Kaen
Tel 043 225 014–17
Situated opposite the Kosa Hotel, this 30-lane bowling alley can get quite busy on weekends—Saturday nights and Sunday afternoon—but most afternoons you will have no trouble finding an empty lane. Shoes are available for rent, and there is also a café in the complex if you want a bite to eat.
🕐 Daily 10.30–2 💲 B59 per game

⚫ LIFESTYLE HEALTH CENTRE
Sofitel Raja Orchid Hotel, 9/9 Thanon Prachasumran, Khon Kaen
Tel 043 322 155
You do not need to be a hotel guest to use the Lifestyle Health Centre. A full range of massages is on offer: traditional Thai, Swedish, Asian blend, sports massage, herbal heat compress and aroma massage, foot, back and shoulder ones. There's also a dozen or so facials and as many body treatments, including a firming aroma lift and G5 cellulite treatment. Special treatments include a hot stone massage and a green tea body treatment that begins with a steam bath before a body scrub using green leaves.
🕐 Daily 10am–11pm 💲 Massages B350–B600, facials B300–B1,050, body treatments B150–B1,200, spa packages B800–B1,350

MUKDAHAN

⊕ INDOCHINA MARKET
The Promenade, Mukdahan
This is one of those markets where making a purchase is less important than just being in the place, and, given that Mukdahan is way off the

regular visitor's trail, you can hardly expect to find what you are looking for. Lao–Thai trade is the genesis of the market, and inexpensive goods are brought over the Mekong River from Vietnam and Laos. Thai cotton and silk make it back across the river to Laos and such fabrics are your most likely buy.
🕐 Daily 7–5

NAKHON RATCHASIMA (KORAT)

⊕ JIRANAI
140/2 Thanon Phokang, Korat
Tel 044 243 819
Jiranai is one of the best shops in Korat for quality silk. Prices

Service with a smile in Nong Khai's market

start at around B750 for a meter/yard of *mutmee* silk, half that for a plain pattern, rising to over B1,500 for more intricate patterns. Silk shirts and blouses are also available, though there is not a wide range. To find the shop, walk along Thanon Phokang from the Thao Suranari shrine in the middle of town; it is on the corner at the end of the first block, on your right.
🕐 Daily 9–6

NONG KHAI

⊕ STREET MARKET
Thanon Rimkong, Nong Khai
This market, encountered on a walking tour around the town

(▷ 224–225), occupies the east end of Thanon Rimkong and it starts at Tha Sadet, the small tower-shape building marking the official crossing point on the river for Thais and Laotians. Spreading eastward from here, the covered market has a multitude of small and large stands selling clothes, arts and crafts, binoculars, toys, household goods and miscellaneous goods from Laos.
🕐 Daily 9–6

⊕ VILLAGE WEAVER HANDICRAFTS
1151 Chitapanya Lane, Thanon Prachak, Nong Khai
Tel 042 411 236
A good place to purchase *mutmee*. Three-meter (3.3 yards) lengths of *mutmee* vary in price from B1,600 to B4,500. Silk and cotton shirts, including free-size silk skirts, tops and skirts are also available. Smaller craft items on offer include woven pencil cases, slippers and purses. Everything has a marked price, but you can expect a 10 percent discount off that. The shop was set up in 1982 as a self-help project for local villagers to help them supplement their meager incomes.
🕐 Daily 8–7

⊕ VILLAGE WEAVER HANDICRAFTS
1020 Thanon Prachak, Nong Khai
Tel 042 422 652
www.weaver.net
This is a branch of the main Village Weaver Handicrafts shop (▷ above) but it is a little nearer to the middle of town, at the corner of Thanon Haisoke and just a little way down from the Pantawee Hotel.
🕐 Daily 8–7

😊 NOBBI'S
997 Thanon Rimkong
Tel 042 460 583
Open as a restaurant from 8am, Nobbi's brightens up with fairy lights at night and is popular with northern Europeans needing a fix on meatballs, home-made sausages, sauerkraut, chicken goulash and smoked ham. With 140 types of beer, especially German imports, and Italian wine at B395 a bottle, the restaurant becomes a late-night pub with a pleasant atmosphere.
🕐 Daily 8am–11pm

⭐ MEKONG BOAT TRIP
Thanon Keawworut, Nong Khai (just beyond the Mut Mee Guest House)
Tel 042 412 211
The boat will not depart for just a couple of passengers, but most evenings it attracts enough people to justify taking off up the Mekong River. Food is served on board if you order it before departure time, but the standard rice dishes are disappointing and it may be more fun to just sit back and relax with something from the reasonably priced drinks list. The boat heads up toward the Friendship Bridge before turning to return along the Laos side, passing fish farms and people washing clothes in the river. You will feel a long way from home.
🕐 Daily at 5.30pm 💶 B30

💆 PANTAWEE HERBAL SPA
Pantawee Hotel, 101–107 Thanon Haisoke, Nong Khai
Tel 042 411 568
Massages at Pantawee come in different forms, from Thai ones by graduates of the Wat Po medical school in Bangkok to a less robust massage with herbal oils. There are other treatments available, and these include a body scrub, leg waxing and an herbal bath. There is also a hair salon.
🕐 Daily, 24 hours 💶 Massages B150–B500, leg waxing B500, hair bleaching B400–B500

PHIMAI
⭐ PHIMAI'S BANYAN TREE
The Khmer temple at Phimai (▷ 100–101) may not excite children as much as adults but Sai Ngam, nearby, will appeal. The single banyan tree is like a small forest, and you can buy small turtles to release into the nearby pond for good luck. Small birds can also be purchased and released.

ROI ET
🏬 ARTS AND CRAFTS
383–385 Thanon Phadung, Roi Et
There is no English sign for this shop, but it is easy to find by following the shophouse numbers; look for the display of

Ubon is a good place to shop for typical Thai gifts

traditional musical instruments in the window. Goods include axe pillows, fabrics, tops, baskets and boxes and a small amount of jewelry. Prices are marked, but bargain hard to secure a reasonable price.
🕐 Daily 9–6

SURIN
NIGHT BAZAAR
Thanon Krungsrinai, Surin
The night bazaar is fun to wander around for its variety of food—grilled locusts are a local delicacy—clothes for the fashion-conscious and general bric-a-brac. Surin is the center of a local silk-weaving industry and during the day there are

usually women displaying silk for sale on the street, where the night bazaar meets Thanon Tannasarn. There are also a number of small shops around town selling silk, mostly to the north of the night bazaar in the vicinity of the roundabout on Thanon Thanon Tannasarn.
🏬 Bazaar daily 6pm–9pm; Street vendors daily 9–5

THAT PHANOM
🏬 RENU NAKHON SILK VILLAGE
Renu Nakhon, That Phanom
Renu Nahkhon is a weaving village that is best visited on a Wednesday when the weekly fair comes alive and there are countless stands displaying cotton and silk for sale. Prices are reasonable.
🕐 Daily 8–8 🚗 Take the inland turning on Route 212, 6km (4 miles) north of That Phanom

UBON RATCHATHANI
🏬 ART HOME
52 Thanon Pichitrangsan, Ubon Ratchathani
Tel 045 254 335
Next to the Laithong Hotel, this modest shop has an interesting selection of skirts, dresses, silk, handbags and axe pillows. The prices are very reasonable—lower than at other shops of this kind in town. Be sure to check out the bargain-price clothes hanging outside on rails.
🕐 Daily 7am–8pm

🏬 MAYBE
124 Thanon Srinarong, Ubon Ratchathani
Tel 045 254 452
Not a large collection of clothes but authentic local cotton woven using traditional designs. Prices are reasonable, less than half what you would pay for quality cotton fabrics in Bangkok or Chiang Mai. To find Maybe, head up past Punchard on Thanon Ratchabut, take the first right onto Thanon Srinarong and walk along here for over half a kilometer (0.3 mile); the shop is on your right.
🕐 Daily 8–7

WHAT TO DO

PUNCHARD
158 Thanon Ratchabut, Ubon Ratchathani
Tel 045 243 433
www.punchard.net
Punchard is the most upmarket arts and crafts store in Ubon, located between the museum and the tourist office, and has a great selection of gift items. There is a second, smaller branch on Thanon Padang. To find the main shop, turn right with your back to the tourist office and take a right turn at the first corner; Punchard is here on your right.
🕐 Daily 9.30–8.30

RAN CHANG THAI
86 Thanon Chawalanok
Tel 045 261 130
Ran Chang Thai is a 10-minute walk from the middle of town, but this friendly arts and crafts shop is worth seeking out if you are looking for souvenirs. Prices are more or less fixed.
🕐 Daily 9–8

UDON THANI
CHAROENSRI COMPLEX
Thanon Prachak, Udon Thani
Tel 042 786 213
The anchor tenant, Robinson's Department Store, adds some substance to Udon Thani's most modern shopping mall. The smaller outlets cover clothes, shoes and accessories, but the department store generally offers better quality. There is a food center on the third level and a cinema on the top level which shows English-language blockbuster movies.
🕐 Daily 10–8

MOJO'S
Thanon Prachak, Udon Thani
Tel 09 516 6129
Around the corner from the Charoensi Complex (▷ above), Mojo's comes alive in the evenings when people call in for cocktails and a meal—chicken wings, 10oz pork chops and 15oz steaks. When the food stops at 10pm the emphasis is on drinking and

conviviality. A big screen drops down for sporting events and there is a pool table.
🕐 Daily 8–midnight

CHAROENSRI HEALTH AND SPA
Charoensri Grand Royal Hotel, 271 Thanon Prachak, Udon Thani
Tel 042 343 555
A menu of massages is on offer, from a traditional Thai one to a special 45-minute anti-cellulite session. Facial treatments range from a half-hour facial brightening treatment to longer detoxifying sessions. There are also jacuzzi bathtubs, herbal saunas, hot compresses and mineral baths.

Thai girls dance during a festival by the Mekong River

🕐 Daily 10–10 💆 Massages B600–B1,600, leg waxing B500, hair bleaching B1,000–B1,500

YASOTHON
AXE PILLOW VILLAGE
Ban Sri Than, Yasothon
Ban Sri Than is a small village, 20km (12 miles) east of Yasothon, dedicated to the production of axe pillows. You can see them being made by villagers underneath their houses, and they can be purchased here at prices a lot lower than those in Bangkok.
🕐 Daily 10–8 🚗 Take Route 202 out of Yasothon, and just after kilometer stone 18 turn right for the remaining 3km (nearly 2 miles)

MID-FEBRUARY–EARLY MARCH

THAT PHANOM FESTIVAL
Phra That Phanom is commemorated and celebrated in a week long event in the small town of That Phanom (▷ 105).

APRIL

PHANON RUNG FESTIVAL
This festival in the town of Phanom Rung (▷ 99) commemorates the Khmer ruins of the town. It begins with a procession through town to the temple and climaxes with a sound-and-light show in the evening.

MAY/JUNE

ROCKET FESTIVAL
Across the northeast but especially in Yasothon and Nong Khai, the Rocket Festival has to be seen to be believed. Homemade bamboo rockets of great size and power are hauled up the launching pad and fired into space to the accompaniment of merrymaking.
🕐 Mid-May to mid-June

PHI TA KHON FESTIVAL
This distinctive festival takes place in the town of Dan Sai, 80km (50 miles) southwest of Loei, and its animist elements suggest origins predating Buddhism. Celebrants dress up in wild and ghoulish costumes, don garish masks and generally have a good time.

JULY

CANDLE FESTIVAL
Ubon Ratchathani is the best place to enjoy this annual carnival although you will see other similar events. Parades of huge carved candles take over the streets.
🕐 Mid- to late July

WHAT TO DO

THE NORTH

Take an empty suitcase with you when you visit northern Thailand—you're sure to return home with it full. The street markets of Chiang Mai and Chiang Rai and the many handicraft villages are among the region's top visitor attractions, and some visitors are there just for the shopping. Golfers buy cut-price Asian clubs and break them in on some of Thailand's finest courses, where green fees are usually a fraction of those in the US or Europe. Sports opportunities are unlimited, from mountain bicycling and upland trekking to whitewater rafting and canoeing. Spas and health resorts are everywhere, and in Chiang Mai you can dump your bags outside the city's main shopping mall and revive aching limbs with a massage on the street. Massage, meditation, yoga, Thai cuisine—all can be learned for a very modest fee and in a few days at any of the schools and academies that dot the north. Festivals such as April's *Songkran* and November's *Loy Kratong* are nowhere as energetically celebrated as in the north. The celebrations make up for the general lack of a sophisticated arts and entertainment scene—a village temple fair can be as wild as the liveliest Bangkok party.

KEY TO SYMBOLS

🏛	Shopping
🎭	Entertainment
▼	Nightlife
🏃	Sports
✪	Activities
♡	Health and Beauty
☻	For Children

CHIANG DAO

✪ BUA TONG WATERFALL

Just off the road between Chiang Mai and Chiang Dao is one of the region's most unusual waterfalls, Namtok Bua Tong. The water flows over the rocks in seven distinct colors, picked up from the calcium carbonate content of the spring water.

It's a beautiful picnic spot on the road north.

 The falls are on the road east from Mae Taeng, 47km (28 miles) north of Chiang Mai, to Mae Khachan

CHIANG MAI

🏛 BAAN TAWAI

Hang Dong, Chiang Mai
Antiques and reproductions provide the sole livelihood of this one-street village, 8km (5 miles) south of Chiang Mai (take the Hang Dong road, Route 108). Whatever you're looking for, you'll find it here, from small carved objects to Chinese medicine chests and ancient armoires. An interesting morning can be

spent prowling around the shops and warehouses.
🕐 Daily 9–6

🏛 BAN MAI KHAM

122 Chiang Mai–Hod road
Tel 040 405 007
Herbal-scented soaps and candles are made in workshops at this Lanna-style crafts center. A collection of small boutiques sells other traditional products, and an adjacent gallery has a good selection of local art.
🕐 Mon–Sat 9–5

GEMS GALLERY
80/1 Moo 3, Chiang Mai–Sankamphaeng road
Tel 053 339 307–10
Claiming to have the world's largest jewelry showroom, the Gems Gallery is certainly impressive. You can also watch jewelry makers busy at their craft in workshops attached to the showroom.
🕐 Daily 8.30–5.30

NORTHERN PARK EMPORIUM
Mahidol Road (the airport turn-off), Chiang Mai
Tel 053 201 911
www.otop-online.com
If your flight's delayed at Chiang Mai airport then fill in the time by visiting the nearby Northern Park Emporium, a government-supported trade center packed with fine local arts and crafts. The imaginatively designed items of furniture may be too bulky to bring home, but the center's showroom and galleries have plenty of fascinating small items of Lanna workmanship.
🕐 Daily 9–5

NORTHERN VILLAGE
Central Airport Plaza, Airport Road, Chiang Mai
Tel 053 281 661
Two floors of this vast shopping mall are devoted to Lanna-style and northern Thai contemporary arts and crafts. The display is arranged like a village crafts center, with individual stands selling anything from handwoven textiles to ceramics and decorative carved items.
🕐 Mon–Fri 10.30–9, Sat–Sun 10–9

ROYAL ORCHID COLLECTION
94–120 Charoenmuang Road, Chiang Mai
Tel 053 245 598
www.siamroyal.com
Rose blossoms and orchid blooms are set in glass and gilt to form original table decorations by the Siam Royal Orchid company. They are available at the company's retail outlet on the second floor of the Northern Village shopping precinct at the Central Airport Plaza.
🕐 Mon–Sat 8–5

SHINAWATRA THAI SILK
18 Thanon Huay Kaew, Amphoe Muang, Chiang Mai
Tel 053 223 264
www.shinawatrathaisilk.co.th
The Shinawatra company is Thailand's oldest industrial silk manufacturer, founded in 1929. Its products range from decorative silk household items and fashion accessories

A glazed orchid from the Royal Orchid Collection

to bespoke silk clothing, even shoes.
🕐 Daily 10–7 🎟 Free

TA-WAN DÉCOR
1 Thanon Nimmanheimin, Soi 1, Chiang Mai
Tel 053 894 941
A small area of upmarket boutiques has arisen in the lane adjoining the Amari Rincome Hotel on Thanon Nimmanheimin. Ta-Wan Décor is on the corner and is probably the best of them, selling an attractive selection of handicrafts and furniture, ranging from chairs to exquisitely carved items.
🕐 Tue–Sun 9–8

TEA HOUSE SIAM CELADON
158 Thanon Tha Pae, Chiang Mai
Tel 053 234 518
More than a dozen varieties of tea and delicious homemade pastries are served in the colonial setting of a century-old restored timber-built mansion on Chiang Mai's busiest shopping street. Celadon and textiles are on sale in the front showrooms.
🕐 Daily 9am–6.30pm

OLD CHIANGMAI CULTURAL CENTRE
185/3 Thanon Wualai
Tel 053 274 540, 053 202 993–5
A visit to Chiang Mai is incomplete without a trip to a *kantoke* dinner and show. "Kantoke" is the word for the trays in which northern Thai food is served. Performances of traditional music and dance are presented on a stage on one side of the restaurant.
🕐 Daily 7–9.30 🎟 Kantoke dinner B300

SIMON CABARET
177 G Building, Chiang Puak road (next to the Rim Ping supermarket), Chiang Mai
Tel 053 410 321–3
www.simonchiangmaicabaret.com
The lavishly dressed (and undressed) "showgirls" who present the dazzling Las Vegas-style Simon Cabaret are actually boys—statuesque Thai transvestites. Although some of the costumes are daringly minimal, the glamorous routines are so tasteful you can take the whole family.
🕐 Performances daily 7.30pm, 9.30pm
🎟 Adult B500, child (under 14) B200

▼ BRASSERIE
37 Charoenrat Road, Chiang Mai
Tel 053 241 665
Thailand's best guitarist, Tuk, performs most nights at this riverside venue. He plays everything from rhythm and blues to reggae, fronting a band that draws a big crowd nightly from 10pm to 2am. Combine a visit with a dinner date on the romantic, lantern-hung terrace overlooking the Ping River.
🕐 Daily 10am–2am 🍴 A la carte menu B50–B250. Bottle of wine B900

▼ CHIANG MAI LAND
Chiang Mai Land is a vibrant 0.8km (0.5 miles) of bars, restaurants, karaoke joints and two of Chiang Mai's best discos. The action starts at 9pm and continues till after midnight.

▼ HUEN SOONTAREE VECHANONT
46/1 Thanon Wang Singkhum, Chiang Mai
Tel 053 252 445
A famous Thai mother-and-daughter combination can frequently be heard at this very ethnic riverside Thai restaurant. Soontaree runs the establishment, while her daughter is often on tour or recording. Other resident singers and instrumentalist also appear nightly on the canopied stage. The northern Thai food is also excellent.
🕐 Daily 5–midnight 🍴 Dinner B250, wine B900

▼ OPEN MIC
U.N. Irish Pub, 24 Thanon Ratchawithi, Amphoe Muang, Chiang Mai
Tel 053 214 554
Read the latest chapter from your travel diary at an "Open Mic" session at Chiang Mai's leading Irish pub. Participants are served free beer and applause and appraisal from other hacks and scribes.
🕐 Tue 8pm

▼ THE PUB
189 Thanon Huay Kaew, Chiang Mai
Tel 053 211 550
Step through the gnarled doors of The Pub and you enter everybody's idea of an English country tavern. Logs blaze in an open hearth on cold evenings, real ales are served at the snug bar and old English movies are shown in a neighboring room. Friday night happy hours are particularly popular.
🕐 Daily 11am–midnight

▼ RIVERSIDE BAR AND RESTAURANT
9–11 Thanon Charoenrat, Chiang Mai
Tel 053 243 239

Check out the Kantoke *dinner at the Old Chiangmai Cultural Centre*

Chiang Mai's "tuppies" (Thai yuppies) pack this sprawling riverside bar and restaurant every night. They love its mix of Thai and Western music, played by live bands. If the bar area gets too noisy you can escape the decibels at an outside table on the riverbank. The food is so-so, but it's the music that draws the crowds.
🕐 Daily 10am–1am 🍴 Lunch B100, dinner B200. Wine B950, other drinks B50–B100

▼ SPICY
Thanon Chayaphum 20, Chiang Mai
Tel 053 246 488
Chiang Mai bars close at 1am, but for some obscure reason

this one stays open until 4am, sometimes later. The "action" is limited to karaoke TV screens, over-amplified music and, for men, the attentions of off-duty servers.
🕐 Daily 9pm–4am 🍴 Drinks B50–B120

⚙ CHIANG MAI SPEEDWAY
254 Moo 11, Chiang Mai–Hod road, Tambol Nong Kway, Amphoe Hang Dong
Tel 053 430 059
Test your racing skills on this fully professional go-cart track on the outskirts of Chiang Mai. An automatic device records lap times and compares them with the day's best. It's an ideal family outing, with baby karts suitable for the kids and competition race models for ambitious moms and dads.
🕐 Daily 9.30–6.30 🍴 B500–B700 for 12 minutes

⚙ CHIENGMAI GYMKHANA CLUB
Chiang Mai-Lamphun road, Chiang Mai 5000
Tel 053 241 035
Chiang Mai is ringed by championship golf courses (the Lanna Golf Club, tel 053 221 911, and the Green Valley Country Club, tel 053 298 249–51, are among the best), but if you only have time for a leisurely nine holes then the century-old Chiengmai Gymkhana Club is a tantalizing 10-minute tuk-tuk ride from the middle of the city. The club itself is worth visiting for its colonial atmosphere and the beauty of the grounds. Clubs and shoes can be rented. There is a restaurant and bar.
🕐 Golf course daily 6–7.30 🍴 B300 for 9 holes, caddy B70

⚙ MAE RIM SHOOTING RANGE
Kilometer stone 2 Mae Rim–Sa Moeng road
Tel 053 112 383, 015 957 113
Try your hand with a rifle or a revolver at northern Thailand's best-equipped shooting range.

Beginners and experts alike are welcomed, and the selection of arms range from a simple air gun to sophisticated rifles.
🕐 Daily 9–6 💰 B100

🧗 THE PEAK
28/2 Thanon Chang Klan (behind the Night Bazaar), Chiang Mai
Tel 053 800 567/8
www.thepeakadventure.com
An artificial rock face in the middle of Chiang Mai gives climbers the chance to practice before tackling the real thing in the mountains of northern Thailand. The Peak also organizes rock-climbing tours.
🕐 Daily 6–10 💰 Adult B200, child (under 14) B100 for half an hour

🧗 VELOCITY
177 Thanon Changpuak, Tambol Sriphum, Amphoe Muang, Chiang Mai
Tel 053 410 665
Mountain bicycles for exploring the uplands around Chiang Mai are available at several city outlets, but Velocity not only has one of the largest selections but also organizes tours of the area. The shop is centrally located on a main road leading straight out of Chiang Mai and into open country.
🕐 Daily 9–8 💰 B50 per day

🎲 CHIANG MAI CHESS CLUB
Kafe Bar & Restaurant, Thanon Moon Muang, Chiang Mai
tedrinquest@hotmail.com
If you're visiting Chiang Mai on a rainy Thursday and fancy a game of chess you'll receive a warm welcome from the city's chess club, which meets once a week at 7pm at the popular Kafe Bar and Restaurant.
🕐 Thu 7pm

🐯 CHIANG MAI NIGHT SAFARI PARK
Kilometer stone 10, Chiang Mai–Hod road
Tel 053 990 000, 053 999 099
Very few tigers now roam Thailand's forests, but you can see them in something like their natural habitat at Chiang Mai's Night Safari Park. They're among more than 100 species of wildlife in the 40ha (100-acre) reserve at the foot of the Doi Suthep mountain range, 2.5km (6 miles) south of town. Other big cats you can catch in your rented car headlights include leopards, jaguars and civets. Restaurant on site.
🕐 Daily 6pm–10pm 💰 Adult B500, child (under 14) B250

🏇 CHIANG MAI RACE TRACK
Chiang Mai–Mae Rim road, kilometer stone 5
A day at the races in Chiang Mai is a great opportunity to see Thais lose their cool and

Live music at the Riverside Bar and Restaurant

their shirts. The track is run by the military authorities with great professionalism. There's a tote, an English-style paddock and the Doi Suthep Mountain as a backdrop.
🕐 Sat 2–6 💰 B10B (B100 for the VIP grandstand)

⛳ GO PUTT PUTT CRAZY GOLF
Chiang Mai Business Park, Chiang Mai
Tel 053 851 643–4
You tour the world in 18 holes at this amusing golf course on the edge of Chiang Mai. The holes each have hazards disguised as national symbols, from the Taj Mahal to a Dutch windmill. There's also a very good restaurant, named (of course) The 19th Hole.
🕐 Tue–Sun 11–11
💰 Adult B120, child (under 14) B90

💆 THE OLD MEDICINE HOSPITAL MASSAGE SCHOOL
Thanon Wualai (opposite Old Chiang Mai Cultural Centre), Chiang Mai
Tel 053 201 663, 053 275 085
This is reputedly the best Thai massage school in the north. The 10-day courses, costing B4,000, include instruction in herbal medicine, and an official government-approved certificate is given to successful students. The school also offers weekend courses in foot reflexology (B2,000).
🕐 Daily 9–6

💆 OASIS SPA
102 Thanon Sirimuangkarajan and 4 Thanon Samlan, Tambol Pra Singh, Chiang Mai
Tel 053 815 000
www.chiangmaioasis.com
There are so many spas in and around Chiang Mai that a visitor could spend two weeks just being pampered. Among the longest established is the Oasis Spa, whose treatments range from a B2,700 "pampering" (aromatherapy, body scrub and massage and facial) to a four-hour complete program costing B5,700. There are two branches on opposite sides of the city.
🕐 Daily 10–10

🐼 CHIANG MAI ZOO
Doi Suthep Road
Tel 053 221 179
Chiang Mai's zoo, on the slopes of Doi Suthep, has the only two giant pandas in captivity in Southeast Asia, on loan from China. It's otherwise not a very spectacular zoo by international standards, but the forest setting of the cages and enclosures has pleasant, shady walks. If you get tired, an electric trolley bus tours the grounds.
🕐 Daily 8.30–5 💰 Adult B30, child (under 14) free; to view the pandas adult B100, child (under 14) B50

❸ RED BULL FAIRGROUND

4 Thanon Huay Kaew (next to Kad Suan Kaew shopping mall), Chiang Mai
This is a great place to entertain the kids before you browse through the adjacent shopping mall. All the usual fairground rides are here, at a cost that won't dig too much into the holiday budget.
🕐 Daily 6pm–11pm 🎟 Rides B10–B20

CHIANG RAI

❹ CHARIN GARDEN RESORT

83 Moo 1, Tambol Mae Suay, Chiang Rai
Tel 053 717 272
Northern Thailand residents traveling between Chiang Mai and Chiang Rai make a point of stopping at this roadside café to stock up on its celebrated homemade cakes and pies. The array of delicious fancy cream cakes, cheesecake and fruit tarts and pies is astonishing.
🕐 Daily 7–7

❹ CHIANG RAI WINERY

160 Moo 7, Baan Tung, Yaow Sri, Chiang Rai
World leaders, including US President George W. Bush, have drunk the fruit wine of Thailand's leading winery. The wine is made from a wide variety of tropical and semi-tropical fruits and herbs. You can buy a bottle or two at the winery retail outlet.
🕐 Mon–Sat 9–5 🎟 Wine B200–B400

❹ HILLTRIBE HANDICRAFT MUSEUM/SHOP

620/1 Thanon Tanalai, Chiang Rai
Tel 053 740 088
www.pda.or.th/chiangrai
Embroidery and woven fabrics made in hill-tribe villages near Chiang Rai are sold in a shop adjoining Chiang Rai's Hilltribe Museum. The handiwork is of a very high quality and remarkable value. Profits from the enterprise go to community development projects.
🕐 Mon–Fri 9–6, Sat–Sun 10–6

❻ WATERFORD VALLEY GOLF COURSE

33 Moo 5, Tambol Wiang Chiang Rung, Chiang Rai
Tel 053 953 425–8
Globetrotting golfers say this magnificent, championship course outside Chiang Rai is among Southeast Asia's finest. It's laid out on a plateau, ensuring cooler temperatures and more breezes than many other northern Thailand courses. Lakes and creeks provide plenty of water; tropical vegetation adds to the hazards; and the mountains furnish an impressive backdrop.
🕐 Daily 8–4 🎟 Mon–Fri B1,100, Sat–Sun B1,650

Children playing in boats on the Kuang River in Lamphun

❸ BAN LORCHA

Thaton–Mae Chan road, Chiang Rai
Chiang Rai's Tourism Development Project is working to prevent hill-tribe villages in northern Thailand from becoming commercial "theme parks," and has started a pilot program at the Akha village of Lorcha, near Thaton. It charges admission, but the money is divided into a village fund for orphans, widows and the elderly. The Hilltribe Tourism Development Foundation aims to expand the scheme to other communities. The small entrance charge covers a tour of the village and a demonstration of traditional handicraft skills.
🕐 Daily 8–5 🎟 B20

❸ THAM PLA

Ban Khunnaam Nangnom, Mae Chan
If you're driving from Chiang Rai to Mae Sai on highway number 1, watch for the sign to Tham Pla, about 12km (7 miles) north of Mae Chan. Although it translates as Fish Cave, Tham Pla is the home of hordes of monkeys.
🕐 Daily, 24 hours 🎟 Free

LAMPANG

❹ SRISAWAT CERAMICS

316 Phaholyotin Road, Lampang
Tel 054 225 931
Lampang has Thailand's richest source of white clay, and its ceramic products are highly prized. Much of it bears the city's cockerel insignia. In mid-December a ceramics festival is held in front of the Big C department store, next to the main bus station.
🕐 Mon–Sat 9–5

LAMPHUN

❹ LAMPHUN'S OLD BRIDGE

Just below the tourist office
Lamphun is proud of its wooden, covered bridge spanning the Kuang River, which is like a local version of Venice's Rialto Bridge. The bridge is lined with stands selling local products.
🕐 Daily 8–6

❸ SERAPEE WINERY AND RESTAURANT

Serapee
Tel 048 031 977
Northern Thailand's only vineyard, in a quiet village between Lamphun and Chiang Mai, produces two varieties of white wine which the German owner serves in his adjacent restaurant. The wines are from hardy European stock and are entirely chemical free. They're light and crisp.
🕐 Fri 6–10, Sat–Sun 11.30–10

WHAT TO DO

MAE HONG SON

✪ WORLD WAR II MEMORIAL MUSEUM
Khun Yuam, kilometer stone 98
Route 108
Roughly midway between Mae Sariang and Mae Hong Son, the World War II Memorial Museum commemorates the hundreds of Japanese soldiers who died here on their retreat from Allied armies in Myanmar (Burma). Local people took the Japanese in, nursing many back to health and burying those who died. A local historian later gathered the belongings they left behind.
🕐 Thu–Tue 9–5 💵 B10

MAE SA

✪ JUNGLE BUNGY JUMP
229 Moo 1, Tambol Mae Rim, Amphoe Mae Rim, Chiang Mai
Tel 053 298 442, 018 851 912
If bungee jumping is your thing, this is the only outfit in northern Thailand. If it doesn't appeal, you can watch the enthusiasts fling themselves into the air.
🕐 Daily 9–6 💵 B1,800

✪ MAE SA BUTTERFLY AND ORCHID FARM
Mae Rim–Mae Sa road, kilometer stone 10
Tel 053 298 605
You can walk through clouds of tropical butterflies at this attractive roadside halt on the way to the Mae Sa Valley. The butterflies live in a netting enclosure, along with a mass of colorful orchids. A shop sells packed kits for visitors to take home and grow their own orchids. There's also an airy terrace restaurant.
🕐 Daily 9–5 💵 Adult B20, child (under 14) B10

✪ MAE SA SNAKE FARM
Mae Rim–Samoeng road, kilometer stone 3
Tel 053 860 719
Snake handlers play with deadly poisonous cobras and vipers in the arena of the Mae Sa Snake Farm. Snakes are also "milked" for their venom in demonstrations.
🕐 Daily 8–4 💵 Adult B200, child (under 14) B100

✪ MAE SA WATERFALL
Mae Rim–Samoeng road, kilometer stone 4
Mae Sa's spectacular waterfall was attracting visitors from Chiang Mai and beyond before any of the other attractions on this mountain route were opened. It descends a mountain slope in eight stages and during the rainy season is a breathtaking sight. The waterfall is in a national park, so you'll be charged to see it.
🕐 Daily 8–5 💵 B200

The tricky process of extracting venom from a king cobra

PAI

⊕ SIPSONGPANNA ART GALLERY
60 Moo 5 Viang Neua, Pai
Tel 053 698 259, 017 351 786
Attached to the charming Sipsongpanna guesthouse is an attractive art gallery showing the work of the many talented artists who have made their home in Pai. Prices are very reasonable and the work on show is impressive.
🕐 Daily 9–9

✆ B-BOP BAR
Highway 1095, opposite the tourist police station
Tel 095 608 561
This is a legendary jazz club, reputedly better than even Bangkok's best. The brick and timber walls and teak rafters ring every night to every kind of beat, from blues to reggae. Thailand's best guitarist, Tuk, is a regular performer.
🕐 Nightly 9–3 💵 Free admission

✪ THAI ADVENTURE RAFTING
73/7 Thanon Charoen Prathet, Chiang Mai
Tel 053 818 844
This Chiang Mai tour company organizes two-day whitewater-rafting trips on the wild Pai River. The expedition leaders are fully qualified and know the region and its rivers so you're in good hands.
🕐 Daily 9–5 💵 B2,000 (2-day trip)

PHAYAO

⊕ BAN SAN PA MUANG
ℹ TAT Northern Office, Region 2, 448/16 Singhakhlai Road, Chiang Rai, tel 053 717 433
This small village 16km (10 miles) from Phayao is famous for the handicrafts made from the fibers of the water hyacinth that grows in the Kwan Phayao Lake. Many locals specialize in the craft.

SAN KAMPHAENG

✪ HOT SPRINGS
San Kamphaeng
Follow the signs from San Kamphaeng or take a *songthaew* to these sulphur springs, set in a valley of flower gardens and woods. Two geysers also feed a swimming pool and baths. Bungalows with private hot tub can be hired for B150 for two hours or rented overnight for B800.
🕐 Daily 7–6 💵 B30 (B50 for use of the pool)

WHAT TO DO

TAK

🌐 HILLTRIBE MARKET

Tak–Mae Sot highway 105, kilometer stone 29

Silverware and textiles made by the Lahu, Lisu and Hmong are sold at this country market on the road between Tak and Mae Sot. Locally grown fruit and vegetables are also piled high on the market stands.

🕐 Daily 6–6

🏌 BHUMIPHOL DAM GOLF CLUB

Bhumiphol Dam, Tak
Tel 055 599 093

The golf club nestled in a mountain valley below Thailand's largest lake claims to be "one of the finest in Asia." It's certainly one of the least expensive—green fees for a day's play on the 18-hole course are B300, and a caddy costs B150. The course is beautifully landscaped in a river valley just below the dam.

🕐 Daily 8–5 💵 Green fees B400, caddy B180

⭐ MYSTERY HILL

Tak–Mae Sot highway 105, kilometer stone 68

If you're traveling by car from Tak to the border town of Mae Sot you can experience a rare phenomenon at a section of the road called "mystery hill." Stop your vehicle at the foot of the hill, switch off the engine and sit back in amazement as the car rolls up the hill. There's no logical explanation for the phenomenon, which attracts travelers from all over Thailand.

UTTARADIT

🌐 LAB LAE

8km (5 miles) east of Uttaradit on Route 1045

Lab Lae got its peculiar name (meaning "Invisible Town"), because it was a forest-hidden refuge for many people in earlier times from wars in the region. Today, it's a lively handicrafts center and a producer of langsad fruit.

⭐ KESANI RAFT TOUR

Sirikit Dam, Ban Tha Rua
Tel 016 056 211

Houseboat rafts ply the still waters of the vast Sirikit Dam, and a cruise on one of them is a great away-from-it-all experience. The rafts can be rented for the day or for an overnight trip. Meals and bedding are included in the cost.

🕐 Daily 9–5 💵 B2,500–B3,000

⭐ SAK YAI WILDLIFE RESERVE

70km (42 miles) east of Uttaradit (Route 1047)
Tel 029 396 200

"Sak Yai" means "large teak tree," and that's the chief attraction of this reserve. The tree is said to be 1,500 years old and the largest in Thailand. Wildlife in the park includes civets and 40 rare bird species.

🕐 Daily 8–6 💵 Adult B200, child (under 14) B100

FESTIVALS AND EVENTS

FEBRUARY

CHIANG MAI FLOWER FESTIVAL

🛈 TAT Northern Office, Region 1, 105/1 Chiang Mai–Lamphun road, Amphoe Muang, Chiang Mai, tel 053 248 604

February is the month when Chiang Mai bursts into bloom, and the first weekend is devoted to a riotous floral display along two sides of the old city moat.

🕐 First weekend in February

STRAWBERRY FESTIVAL SAMOENG

🛈 TAT Northern Office, Region 1, 105/1 Chiang Mai–Lamphun road, Amphoe Muang, Chiang Mai, tel 053 248 604

Chiang Mai's best strawberries come from this nearby mountain community. Punnets of strawberries, wine, jam, jellies, desserts and bonbons are for sale at village stands.

🕐 Second weekend in February

APRIL

SONGKRAN (WATER FESTIVAL) CHIANG MAI

🛈 TAT Northern Office, Region 1, 105/1 Chiang Mai–Lamphun road, Amphoe Muang, Chiang Mai, tel 053 248 604

Songkran is celebrated in even the smallest village, but nowhere as colorfully as in Chiang Mai. The moat surrounding the old city provides unlimited water for festivities in which everyone gets drenched.

🕐 April 13–15

MEKONG BOAT RACES CHIANG SAEN

🛈 TAT Northern Office, Region 2, 448/16 Thanon Singhakhlai, Chiang Rai, tel 053 717 433

Boat races on the Mekong River, featuring crews from Thailand, Laos, China and Myanmar (Burma), are a highlight of the *Songkran* Festival in Chiang Saen. The climax, though, is the crowning of the Queen of the Golden Triangle.

🕐 Middle of April

NOVEMBER/DECEMBER

SUNFLOWER FESTIVAL MAE HONG SON

🛈 Tourist Information Centre, Old District Office, Thanon Khunlumphraphat, Amphoe Muang, Mae Hong Son, tel 053 612 982–3; Mon–Fri 8.30–4.30
www.travelmaehongson.org

The six-week season when the sunflowers bloom on the mountains surrounding Mae Hong Son is celebrated with a seemingly endless program of events, ranging from performances of traditional music and dance to a Miss Sunflower contest.

🕐 November to mid-December

WHAT TO DO

CENTRAL THAILAND

Apart from Ayutthaya and Kanchanaburi, central Thailand isn't a tourist magnet, although the region has much to recommend it, including some of the country's most historic sites, and small towns and villages that have become major craft centers. Ayutthaya alone should be on every visitor's "must-see" schedule, and there are enough attractions within an hour or so of the city to make a week's stay worthwhile. Kanchanaburi and its wildly beautiful border province have much more of interest than the "Death Railway" sites that draw thousands of visitors every year. Kanchanaburi's two rivers—the Kwai Yai ("big Kwai") and Kwai Noi ("Little Kwai")—and central Thailand's many waterways and lakes offer a peaceful alternative to the often crowded beaches of southern Thailand. If you're a night owl, tank up on Bangkok's nocturnal attractions before venturing into central Thailand, where most towns close up early.

KEY TO SYMBOLS

- 🏬 Shopping
- 🎭 Entertainment
- 🍸 Nightlife
- 🎿 Sports
- ✹ Activities
- ♥ Health and Beauty
- 🧒 For Children

AYUTTHAYA

🏬 BAN BANG SADET
A. Pa Mok, Ayutthaya
Women of this small village, 12km (7 miles) north of Ayutthaya (Highway 309), make so-called "court dolls," encouraged by a project launched by Thailand's queen. The finely crafted clay figures depict villagers in poses of everyday life and characters from folk plays.

They are on sale at the village temple.
🕐 Daily 8–6

🏬 BAN RATSADON BUMRUNG
A. Don Chedi, Ayutthaya
This small village, 35km (21 miles) northeast of Ayutthaya (routes 329 and 340), makes fine handicrafts from the water hyacinth that grows in the area. The pliable roots of the plant are made into wickerwork trays, baskets, bags and even hats.

🏬 ROYAL FOLK ARTS AND CRAFTS CENTRE
Tambol Chiang Yai, Amphoe Bang Sai
Tel 035 366 252–3
Local farmers and their families are trained at this

royal project to learn new skills in handicrafts and folk art. On a 5.5ha (14-acre) site, they produce basketwork, hand-woven silk and cotton, wood carvings, traditional dolls, artificial flowers and furniture. The products are sold at the center's own shop.
🕐 Daily 8–5

🏬 WAT SA KAEO
Ban Pa Mok, A. Ang Thong
This 300-year-old temple between Ayutthaya and Ang Thon (Highway 309) cares for needy and orphaned children and has a handicrafts center producing traditional hand-woven textiles, table cloths and bed linen.
🕐 Daily 7–6

✪ BOAT TOURS

Several companies operate one-day boat trips from Bangkok to Ayutthaya. They include: Chao Phraya River Express Boat (tel 022 225 330) and River Sun Cruises (tel 022 669 125). Overnight cruises are operated by Mekhala (tel 022 567 168–9).

✪ BUFFALO VILLAGE

Tambol Si Prachan, Amphoe Si Prachan, Suphan Buri
Tel 035 582 591
A herd of more than 50 buffalo works the fields and rice paddies of this farm museum near the town of Suphan Buri, 40km (24 miles) west of Ayutthaya, demonstrating a way of rural life that is being eroded by the advance of mechanization. Rice-harvesting and threshing methods are demonstrated in a working environment, within a functioning traditional Thai village.
🕐 Daily 9–6 💰 Adult B100, child (under 14) B50

✪ THA SADET BIRD SANCTUARY

Suphan Buri–Don Chedi road (Highway 322), Suphan Buri
ℹ TAT Central Region Office, Region 6, 108/22 Moo 4, Tambol Pratu Nam, Ayutthaya, tel 035 246 076–7
Open-billed storks, painted storks, herons, cormorants, night herons and white ibises have made their home in this watery spot 15km (9 miles) west of Suphan Buri. Visit at sunset to see them return to their nests.
🕐 Daily 8am–4pm 💰 Free

BANG-PA-IN

✪ BOAT RIDES

Bang-Pa-in Palace, Tambol Bang-Pa-in, Ayutthaya
Tel 035 261 673
A catamaran cruiser makes daily pleasure trips around the waterways surrounding Bang-Pa-in Palace. It cruises both banks of the Chao Phraya River and around the islands on

which the palace buildings stand, giving unusual views of this showpiece of eclectic Thai architecture. The boat leaves hourly from the Kho Wat Nivret Tama pier; tickets are sold at the Bang-Pa-in Palace entrance.
🕐 Daily 9–5 💰 B70 (adults and children)

CHANTHABURI

✪ LAEM SINGH BEACH

Chanthaburi is only about 25km (18 miles) from the coast, and its most popular beach is in the Pak Nam district, near the mouth of the Chanthaburi River. Pine trees shade the beach from the afternoon sun, and there are

A water buffalo wallows in the mud

many small bars, restaurants and food stands along its sandy length.

✪ OASIS SEA WORLD

Tambol Pak Nam, Chanthaburi
Tel 039 399 015, 039 363 238–9
Dolphins are the attraction at this marine park on the coast south of Chantaburi. The park is a conservation and breeding center, but the dolphins also present shows for the public, jumping through hoops and playing football (daily at 9, 11, 1.15 and 5, weekends at 7am also). The park gardens are alive with butterflies, and the nearby Laem Sing River has picnic rafts.

🕐 Mon–Fri 9–6, Sat–Sun 6.45–6 💰 B180, swim with dolphins B400 per hour

KANCHANABURI

🌐 KANCHANABURI BLUE DIAMOND

426 Thanon Maenam Kwai, Kanchanaburi
Tel 034 510 172
Thailand's Kanchanaburi province has some of Southeast Asia's most productive sapphire mines. Their blue sapphires are particularly highly prized, and you can find fine examples at this large, reliable jewelry store on the plaza facing the River Kwai Bridge.
🕐 Daily 9–5

✪ THUNG YAI–HUAI KHA KHAENG WILDLIFE SANCTUARY

Tambol Labam, Amphoe Lan Sak, Uthaithani 61160
Tel 078 400 316
Described in the 1980s as Thailand's "largest remaining wilderness," this remote region, bordering Myanmar (Burma) northwest of Kanchanaburi, is still a wild, beautiful stretch of forested mountains, inhabited by 28 endangered species of wildlife. It's the only national park in Thailand that's a World Heritage Site. Although it's very remote, accessible on Route 323 between Kanchanaburi and the Three Pagodas Pass, a visit to the sanctuary is an unforgettable experience.
🕐 Daily 6–6

KO CHANG

🤿 SCUBADIVE THAILAND

Ban Bang Bao pier, Ko Chang
Tel 039 558 028, 071 373 261
www.scubadive-thailand.com
The waters around Ko Chang offer excellent diving possibilities, and Scubadive Thailand knows where they are. The company also organizes courses as well as trips to remote sites for experienced divers.
🕐 Daily 9–7 💰 Prices start at B2,500

WHAT TO DO

✪ SEA ADVENTURES
55/30 2 Ban Bang Bao, Ko Chang
Tel 060 572 715
Ko Chang is the biggest of a cluster of islands off the southern Gulf coast, and on a Sea Adventures catamaran you can tour them all in one day. The company also offers sunset dinner cruises and snorkeling trips in the waters around Ko Chang.
◷ Daily 9–7 Prices start at B2,500

LOP BURI

⊕ BAN THA–KRAYANG BRASS ARTISANS CLUB
168 Moo 1, Tombol Thalay Chup Son, Amphoe Muang, Lop Buri
Tel 036 421 469
The little village of Ban Tha–Krayang has been a center of brass casting for generations and the leading craftspeople have formed themselves into a "club." They turn out works of great skill and beauty, from replicas of famous sculptures to completely original creations.
◷ Daily 9–5

⊕ KHAO PHRA NGAM DIAMONDS
Tombol Khao Phra Ngam, Lop Buri
The Lop Buri area is famous for its sparkling gems, misleadingly called diamonds by the locals. They are in reality highly polished and skillfully cut quartz stones, most of them made at a production center in the Lop Buri district of Tombol Khao Phra Ngam.
◷ Mon–Sat 9–5

⊕ PRACHA SUK SAN ARTS AND CRAFTS CENTRE
84 Moo 4, Tombol Ban Kluai, Amphoe Ban Mi
Tel 036 471 847
Ban Kluai is one of three villages near Lop Buri producing Thailand's coveted *Mat Mi* silk. You can watch it being woven at the village's arts and crafts center, which also has a sales outlet.
◷ Daily 9–5

✪ BEE FARM
Soi 24 Sai Tri, Moo 9, Tombol Phatthna Nikom, Lop Buri
Tel 036 639 292
This country bee farm is a hive of information on Thailand's thriving apiary business. The owners readily show visitors how the hives work and honey is extracted. The bees feed on nearby sunflowers and produce sweet nectar, which is sold in the farm's own shop and throughout the region.
◷ Daily 8–5 Free

View the Summer Palace at Bang Pa-in from a riverboat

✪ BOAT MUSEUM
Wat Yang Na Rangsi, Tombol Talung, Lop Buri
Tel 036 656 402
The timber-built sermon hall at this restored temple, 9km (5.5 miles) south of Lop Buri, has been converted into a museum of boats. Among the array of historic local craft is a single-seat barge typical of those used to navigate the canals in past centuries.
◷ Wed–Sun 9–4 Free

✪ OASIS FARM
85/2 Moo 13, Chong Sarika, Tombol Patthana Nikom, Lop Buri
Tel 017 808 928, 019 941 256
Chicks were imported from South Africa in 2001 to stock one of Thailand's first ostrich farms. Today the farm extends over more than 4ha (10 acres) and supplies other farms with chicks in a burgeoning nationwide agricultural industry. A shop on the premises sells ostrich products ranging from leather handbags to eggs and feathers.
◷ Daily 8.30–5

✪ PA SAK CHONLASIT DAM
Lop Buri train station
Tel 036 411 022
Catch a northbound local train (daily) at Saraburi and ride the single-track line across the 5km (3-mile) wall of the Pa Sak Chonlasit Dam, central Thailand's largest. The railway line runs alongside the Pa Sak River and next to much of the 35km (21-mile) length of the dam, at the northern end of which is a very beautiful waterfall, Namtok Wang Kan Loeng. A special train runs from Bangkok to the dam on weekends and public holidays.
 B200 return

✪ SUNFLOWER FIELDS
Tombol Patthana Nikom, Lop Buri
In November and December, thousands of visitors flock to the sunflower fields of Patthana Nikhom, 45km (27 miles) east of Lop Buri, when Thailand's largest area of sunflowers bursts into bloom, framed by a green upland backdrop.
◷ Nov, Dec

✪ THAM KHANG KHAO
Wat Khao Wongkot, Khao Sanam Chaeng, Amphoe Ban Mee, Lop Buri
Every evening millions of bats turn the sky black above Wat Khao Wongkot, near Lop Buri, as they stream out of the bat cave to feed. The phenomenon lasts at least one hour.
◷ Daily at around 6pm

⊗ LOP BURI ZOO

A. Muang, Lop Buri
Tel 036 413 551

Three tigers sharing an enclosure with four dogs is one of the more unusual arrangements at Lop Buri's excellent zoo. Two inseparable orang-utans are among the animals popular with locals and tourists alike.

🕑 Daily 8–6 💷 B10

NAKHON PATHOM

⊕ AIR ORCHIDS & LAB

Thambon Salaya, Nakhon Pathom
Tel 01 752 6111

Billed as Thailand's only "orchid supermarket," this vast emporium sells more than 40 species. It's an orchid-lover's paradise and a treat for any gardener—and there's no sales pressure. Visitors are given a free cup of coffee or tea and left to wander the paths and shelves that take up nearly half an acre.

🕑 Daily 7–5.30 💷 Free

⊕ DON WAI MARKET

Tambol Nakhon Chaisi, Nakhon Pathom

The riverside community of Nakhon Chaisi plies its wares as it has for centuries in Nakhon Pathom's most vibrant market. Goods of every description are on offer, and traditional food is served at innumerable stands. Get there early to experience the market at its busiest.

🕑 Daily 6–6

⊗ NATURE TREK

Lamphraya Market, Bang Len, Nakhon Pathom
Tel 025 561 225

Cruise the quiet waters of the Nakhon Chaisi River on a tastefully converted 15m (50ft) rice barge. Many interesting temples and wooden homes are on the riverbanks. The barge takes 50 passengers on day trips and 12 on overnight cruises.

🕑 Times vary 💷 B1,600–B2,100

⊗ THE ROSE GARDEN

Thanon Pet Kasem, Tambol Sampran, Nakhon Pathom
Tel 034 322 5893

Thailand's most spectacular garden grew from a small patch of land developed by a Bangkok mayor as a country retreat. His hobby was rose-growing, and roses are still the prime attraction of the extremely beautiful estate that grew from the mayor's relatively modest garden. A nature path through the 28ha (70-acre) estate winds past banks of damask roses, orchid galleries, ponds of lotus and water lilies, a banana grove and topiary and ixora gardens.

🕑 Daily 9–4 💷 Entry B20, show B400

An elephant battle at the Alangkarn

⊗ SAMPHRAN RIVER CRUISES

Samphran District Office landing stage, Tambol Sampran, Nakhon Pathom

Longtail boats leave at 9am every morning from the Samphran District Office pier for two- to three-hour cruises on the Nakhon Chaisi River and its canals. The itinerary includes stops at fruit orchards, orchid farms and a house where traditional sweets are made.

🕑 Daily 9am–11am 💷 B300

⊗ THAI HUMAN IMAGERY MUSEUM

Kilometer stone 31, Thanon Boromarajajonani, Nakhon Pathom
Tel 034 332 607, 034 332 061

Uncannily lifelike sculptures of Thai historical figures as well as ordinary people are exhibited in this version of a Western waxworks. All the kings of the Chakri dynasty are brought amazingly to life in a truly artistic royal pantheon.

🕑 Mon–Fri 9–5.30, Sat, Sun and public holidays 8.30–6 💷 Adult B200, child (under 14) B100

⊗ SAMPHRAN ELEPHANT GROUND AND ZOO

Tambol Sampran, Nakhon Pathom
Tel 034 322 588–93

Although this informal zoo has its share of elephants, the main attraction is its crocodiles, which are, sadly, bred to fight. Other wild animals are kept in enclosures that dot the grounds.

🕑 Daily 8–5.30. Crocodile shows daily 12.45, 2.20, weekends at 10.30 also 💷 Adult B350, child (under 14) B150

PATTAYA

⊕ PATTAYA SHOES DEPARTMENT STORE

109/19 Moo 10, Thanon Phatumnak, Pattaya; 95 Moo 10 Walking Street, Pattaya
Tel 038 423 919, 038 423 959

The two shops of the Pattaya Shoes Department Store back on to each other between two central Pattaya streets and are stocked from floor to ceiling with not only shoes but every kind of leather goods, produced in the first-floor workshop of the main branch, on Thanon Phatumnak. The company, in business since 1980, also makes goods to order.

🕑 Daily 11am–midnight

⊕ ROYAL GARDEN SHOPPING PLAZA

219 Moo 10, Thanon Chai Hat, Pattaya

Pattaya's largest shopping mall has several floors of shops,

selling everything from Thai textiles and handicrafts to brand-name fashions and accessories. There are several restaurants and cafés and, on the top floor, Pattaya's famous Ripley's Believe It or Not Museum (▷ 209).

🎫 Daily 9–9

💎 TOM'S GEMS
239/2 Moo 10, South Pattaya, Pattaya
Tel 038 422 811, 038 429 811
Tom's Gems has been in business since 1975 and has built up a sound reputation for quality, reliability and service. It also prides itself on fashioning jewelry to order from customers' own designs.

🎫 Daily 11–11

💎 WORLD GEMS COLLECTION
98 Moo 6, Thanon Pattaya Nua, Pattaya
Tel 038 412 333
www.worldgemscollection.com
The latest jewelry technology is on display at this immense gems store, where visitors are invited to take part in instruction on the complicated business of gemology. Instruction personnel and sales staff are all highly qualified, and all gems are sold with guaranteed documentation.

🎫 Daily 8.30–6.30

🎭 ALANGKARN CULTURAL SHOW
2/7 Moo 2, Jomtien, Pattaya
Tel 022 161 869
www.alangkarnthailand.com
Reputedly Thailand's biggest entertainment complex, the Alangkarn has an auditorium with a 70m-long (230ft) stage and seating for 2,000, where elaborately costumed performances of traditional music and dance and historical tableaux are presented. The complex also includes cinema screens, surround sound, a shopping mall and restaurant.

🎫 Tue–Sun 6.30–10.10
💶 B1,200–B1,400, including dinner

🎵 BLUES FACTORY
Soi Lucky Star, Walking Street, Pattaya
www.thebluesfactorypattaya.com
Hammond organ enthusiasts crowd the Blues Factory, which has Thailand's only fully functional instrument. The "Factory" also has some of Pattaya's best showbands, and a happy hour that starts at 9pm.

🎫 Daily 6–1 💶 Cocktails from B100

🎵 TIFFANY'S
464 Moo 9, Second Street, Pattaya
Tel 038 421 700
www.tiffany-show.co.th
Tiffany's is famous for presenting the first transvestite extravaganza in Asia. Copied now throughout

The bizarre exterior of Ripley's Believe It or Not Museum

Thailand, it has a stunning cast of transvestites and transgenders, gorgeously costumed and ingeniously choreographed. And it's all tastefully done—you can take the whole family.

🎫 Three shows nightly at 6, 7.30 and 9
💶 B500–B800

🏌 SRIRACHA INTERNATIONAL GOLF CLUB
284–285 Moo 6, Thanon Sukhumvit Soi 7, Sriracha, Pattaya
Tel 038 338 375–8
A crocodile pit is one of the hazards on this entertaining golf course, designed by Gary Player. The club has many other sports facilities, including

a pool, and tennis, badminton and squash courts.

🎫 Daily 6–6 💶 B1,100 (Mon–Fri), B1,500 (Sat–Sun)

🌊 HYNIX OF THE SEA SUBMARINE TOURS
Ticket office: 219/1–3 Tipp Plaza, South Pattaya
Tel 038 711 059–60, 038 711 020
You can admire the marine life off the coast of Pattaya from 30m (100ft) below the surface in the 100-ton submarine *Hynix of the Sea*. The one-hour trips leave regularly from a pier in South Pattaya.

💶 B2,000

🏛 MINI SIAM
387 Moo 6, Thanon Sukhumvit, Pattaya
Tel 038 717 333, 038 727 666
A collection of more than 80 exquisitely crafted miniature replicas of famous structures around the world. The Bridge Over the River Kwai is here, together with the Eiffel Tower, Statue of Liberty, Sydney Opera House and Bangkok's Grand Palace.

🎫 Daily 7am–10pm 💶 Adult B250, child (under 14) B120

🏛 RIPLEY'S BELIEVE IT OR NOT MUSEUM
Royal Garden Plaza, 218 Moo 10, Thanon Chai Hat, Pattaya
Tel 038 710 294–8
www.ripleysthailand.com
You can't miss Pattaya's Ripley's—the fuselage of a Vietnam-era DC3 projects from the building as if it had just crashed. The museum incorporates a cinema with "dynamic motion seating."

🎫 Daily 11–11 💶 Adult B380, child (under 14) B280

🐠 UNDERWATER WORLD
22/22 Moo 11, Thanon Sukhumvit, Pattaya
Tel 038 756 879
A 100m-long (330ft) tunnel takes visitors through schools of sharks and giant rays at this fascinating attraction.

🎫 Daily 9–6 💶 Adult B360, child (under 14) B180

PHITSANULOK

🍷 LADY JANE'S PUB
2/1 Thanon Baromatrailokanart, Phitsanulok

Tel 055 225 280, 016 884 275

Lady Jane is in reality a Thai woman from Chiang Mai who is one of Phitsanulok's most popular landladies, running an English-style pub with uncanny knowledge of how the British like their beer served.

🕐 Daily 6pm–midnight

🍷 PHITSANULOK PLAZA
Phitsanulok Plaza is a pleasure palace of bars, pubs and clubs.

🕐 Daily 9am–midnight

❊ BUDDHA CASTING FACTORY
Thanon Wisutkasat (opposite the Folklore Museum), Phitsanulok

Tel 055 301 668

Buddha images of all sizes are made at this long-established factory, which still uses the age-old method of casting from wax moulds. Most of the Buddhas are in bronze, and you can follow the entire manufacturing process.

🕐 Daily 8–5.30 🎟 Free

❊ THE GREEN ROUTE
Phitsanulok–Nam Nao National Park

Phitsanulok is the starting point of a "Green Route," which follows Highway 12 eastward for 130km (80 miles) through some of the country's most beautiful countryside. It ends at the junction of Highway 21, which leads to Phetchabun and Bangkok. There are plenty of rest stops en route, and Phetchabun has a wide range of hotels and guesthouses.

❊ PHU HIN RONG KLA NATIONAL PARK
PO Box 3, A.Nakhon Thai, Phitsanulok

Tel 055 233 527

www.dnp.go.th

This remote national park, 90km (45 miles) east of Phitsanulok (Route 12), was a stronghold of Thailand's banned Communist Party from 1968 to 1972 and the scene of heavy

fighting between die-hards and government forces. A 3km (1.9-mile) trail from the park headquarters leads to the old Communist headquarters (now a museum), a small café and a shop. The park is now a peaceful, wild region with a weird feature: a huge field of stones, broken by deep fissures.

SI SATCHANALAI

⊕ LUMTAD ANCIENT SILVER
13 Moo 3, Tachai, Amphoe Si Satchanalai

Tel 055 631 589, 055 679 068

Gold and silver jewelry were made in Si Satchanalai and Sawankhalok, as well as ceramics, for the rulers of Sukhothai, and you can buy reproductions of ancient designs at this workshop in the village of Tachai.

🕐 Daily 9–5

⊕ SATHORN CRAFT CENTRE
Uttaradit Road, Si Satchanalai

Locally produced textiles and fine jewelry are sold at a rustic crafts center at the northern end of Si Satchanalai's one main road. There is a small museum at the center, which also includes a coffee shop.

🕐 Daily 9–6

WHAT TO DO

FESTIVALS AND EVENTS

FEBRUARY

KING NARAI THE GREAT FESTIVAL
ℹ TAT Central Region Office 7, Thanon Rop Wat Phrathat, Amphoe Muang, Lop Buri, tel 036 422 768–9

Lop Buri's principal festival honors the Ayutthaya king with sound-and-light shows, theater performances, music and stands selling everything from food to handicrafts.

MARCH

PATTAYA MUSIC FESTIVAL
ℹ TAT Central Region Office 3, 609 Moo 10, Thanon/Phratamnak, Amphoe Banglamung, Chonburi 20260, tel 038 427 667

Pattaya's international music festival takes over the town center for three days, with an emphasis on multicultural and folk music.

🕐 Mid-March

APRIL

LOY KRATONG FESTIVAL
Sukhothai Historical Park

ℹ Sukhothai Provincial Office, tel 055 614 531, 055 611 619

Thailand's *Loy Kratong* celebrations are beautiful, and nowhere more impressive than in Sukhothai, where candlelit floats are launched on the lakes and ponds of the ancient city. Hot air balloons

are also sent off into the night sky above the ruins.

NOVEMBER

MONKEY BANQUET
ℹ TAT Central Region Office 7, Thanon Rop Wat Phrathat, Amphoe Muang, Lop Buri, tel 036 422 768–9

The monkeys are a major tourist draw in Lop Buri and are rewarded on the last Sunday of November with a "banquet" at the Phra Kan shrine and Phra Prang Sam Yot temple. Bananas and other popular fruit, sweetmeats of every kind and even bottles of soft drinks are laid out on decorated tables for the partying monkeys.

DECEMBER

RIVER KWAI FESTIVAL
ℹ TAT Central Region Office, Region 1, Thanon Saeng Chuto, Amphoe Muang, Kanchanaburi, tel 034 51 12 00

The bridge over the River Kwai and the wooden remains of the original structure are the centerpiece of this week long festival. The river is the setting for a spectacular sound-and-light show, and its banks are lined with stands and music arenas.

🕐 Early December

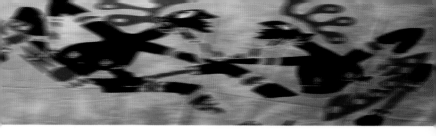

THE SOUTH

You are never far from water in southern Thailand, and water-based activities like snorkeling, canoeing and scuba diving are prime contenders for your leisure time. Innumerable companies offer trips and tours for these activities and their websites are worth consulting. Shopping in the resort areas of Phuket and Ko Samui is dominated by market stands selling similar products, but Phuket town has some interesting individual shops. Outside of Bangkok, southern Thailand has the most sophisticated nightlife in the form of bars, clubs and discos. It also offers the simple but exquisite pleasure of sipping a drink in a deck chair on a beach watching the sun go down or chilling out later at night around a table in a modest beach guesthouse—you do not need to be staying there— listening to the sound of waves in the darkness.

KEY TO SYMBOLS	
⊞	**Shopping**
♪	**Entertainment**
♀	**Nightlife**
⚡	**Sports**
✪	**Activities**
♡	**Health and Beauty**
✖	**For Children**

HUA HIN

♪ SASI GARDEN THEATRE
83/159 Nhongkae, Hua Hin
Tel 032 512 488, 018 804 004
A set Thai meal precedes the show of classical Thai dance, a display of Thai martial arts and a rousing drum dance called *theod theung*. Two episodes from the *Ramayana* are also presented in the form of a masque. After the show, live Thai traditional music continues to be played if you want to linger. Seats can be booked through any travel agent in Hua Hin.
🕐 Daily 7pm–9pm 💶 Adult B750 (excluding drinks), child (5–10) B600

♪ WORLD NEWS COFFEE
33 Thanon Naresdamri, Hua Hin
Tel 032 512 888
On the same street as the Hilton (and under the same management), this is a pleasant and airy café where you can connect to the internet and while away some time reading the international newspapers and magazines—hence the name of the place, presumably— over a coffee and some cake. There are tables outside as well.
🕐 Daily 8am–11pm 💶 From B70

♀ HUA HIN BREWING COMPANY
Hilton Resort and Spa, 33 Thanon Naresdamri, Hua Hin
Tel 032 512 888
Decked out in the style of a Thai fishing village, with a 5,000L (1,100gal) wooden beer barrel, this gregarious pub attracts a good cross section of Hua Hin visitors of all ages. Food is available, as are some interesting micro-brewed house specials: Elephant Tusk, a dark ale; Sabai Sabai, a wheat beer; and Dancing Monkey, a lager. A Thai band provides live entertainment from 9pm onward, and after around 11.30pm a lively atmosphere kicks in.
🕐 Daily 6pm–1am

⚐ ROYAL HUA HIN GOLF CLUB

Hua Hin Prachuabkirikhan
Tel 032 512 475

Five minutes from the middle of Hua Hin, this club—the first golf course in Thailand and designed by a Scottish railway engineer—was opened in 1924. The 18-hole par-72 course length is 6,126m (6,678 yards), and you can rent clubs from B500. Costs are higher on weekends and public holidays.

⊙ Daily 8–8 ⊎ Green fees including caddy and hotel transfers B1,400

⊕ BUCHABUN THAI COOKING COURSE

22 Thanon Dechanuchit, Hua Hin
Tel 032 531 220, 015 723 805

A 9am start, with a pickup from your hotel, and a trip to the local market to shop for the ingredients. The cooking school is a short distance away, and you will learn how to make Thai curry paste, *tom yam* soup, *hor mok* (steamed seafood with fish curry) and Thai desserts. The course finishes at 3pm. You can reserve by phone or at the school itself.

⊎ B950

KO LANTA

⊕ SAME SAME BUT DIFFERENT

Ba Kan Tiang Beach, Ko Lanta

A few hundred meters past the Pimalai Resort in the far south of the island, Ba Kan Tiang Beach is a contender for the ultimate chill-out beach in southern Thailand. Come here to while away an evening and feel a million miles away from home. You'll find wooden tables, lantern lights, cool music in the background and a simple menu of various deep-fried starters and curries. Bring a torch to find your way back to the road in the utter darkness.

⊙ Daily 10am–midnight ⊎ Lunch B150, Dinner B200

⊕ LANTA ADVENTURE

Tel 015 364 507

You can reserve elephant treks direct with this company, through your accommodation or any of the agents in Sala Dan, and there are other companies offering fairly identical trips. An elephant trek can be a little more strenuous than you might think so check the itinerary to see how much walking is involved and wear something sturdier than sandals on your feet.

⊕ TIME FOR LIME

Klong Dao Beach, Ko Lanta
Tel 075 684 590, 099 675 017
www.timeforlime.net

You can rent clubs at the Royal Hua Hin Golf Club

Time for Lime is a well-established cookery school on Ko Lanta with a weekly "menu" of day and evening classes. A typical day covers the preparation of curry paste, *satay* with chicken, spicy prawn soup, seafood with chili paste and barracuda in red curry. A typical evening class covers fresh spring rolls with dips, green curry with chicken and fried rice with vegetables. The course fee includes a Thai meal—not the one you prepare! Vegetarian courses can be arranged, as can babysitting and taxis.

⊙ Daily 12.30–5, 6–10pm ⊎ Day classes B1,800, evening classes B1,400

KO PHI PHI

⊕ HIPPIES

Ton Sai, Ko Lanta

On the beach, just east of the pier and before the PP Villa Resort, Hippies is fairly typical of Ko Phi Phi's nightlife. The food is not the best reason for coming here, but as darkness descends and the fairy lights dimly illuminate the bamboo seats and tables, the laid-back atmosphere can prove enticing. The pace quickens as the night lengthens and soft 1960s music gives way to brasher and more insistent beats.

⊙ 7pm–2am

KO SAMUI

⊕ BLACK JACK

Chaweng Beach Road, Chaweng, Ko Samui
Tel 077 413 214

An English-owned English pub that has been around for 10 years. All the premier league soccer and other major sporting events are shown here. There is a pool table and a nice upstairs terrace. There are snacks and plenty of draught beer.

⊙ Daily 5pm–2am

⊕ COCO BLUES BAR

161/9 Moo 2, Chaweng Beach Rd, Chaweng, Ko Samui
Tel 077 414 354
www.cocoblues.com

Open for breakfast and lunch, this family-friendly bar and restaurant comes alive each evening with a live band playing blues-style, funky music. The full schedule and live broadcasts are listed on the website. You'll find Cajun and creole food—gumbo and blackened chicken are popular—a balcony bar, and a good drinks list that includes some interesting Blues Specials.

⊙ Daily 10am–2am

⊕ FROG AND GECKO

Fisherman's Village, Bophut, Ko Samui
Tel 077 425 248

Away from the hustle and bustle of Chaweng, there are two places of evening

WHAT TO DO

entertainment at the Bophut waterfront called Fisherman's Village. One is an Australian sports bar, the Billabong, and the other is the English-style Frog and Gecko. The busiest night of the week is Wednesday—arrive earlier to get a seat—when a pub quiz gets under way at 8pm. Indian food is served, and there's a large screen for satellite-beamed soccer.
🕐 Daily 10am–2am

🍸 THE THREE MONKEES
Chaweng Beach Road, Chaweng, Ko Samui
Tel 077 422 584
www.3-monkeys.com
A pub and restaurant, between the Beachcomber Hotel and the Silver Sand Resort, with a sociable atmosphere and a sense of fun. There's a pool table, papers to read, food throughout the day (with a free glass of wine), movies and sporting events shown on TV, and a corner with free internet access.
🕐 Daily 10am–2am

🍸 BELLINI
46/26 Soi Colibri (Chaweng Boulevard), Chaweng
Tel 077 413 831
An Italian restaurant with a neat bar where a good wine list competes for attention with some crafty cocktails from well-stocked shelves. The atmosphere is very relaxed for this part of Ko Samui, and Soi Colibri has so far managed to keep a low profile. Come here before or after a meal and consider the menu for a return visit.
🕐 Daily 6pm–1am

🍸 MINT BAR
Soi Green Mango, Chaweng
Tel 070 898 726
www.mintbar.com
One of the top venues in Ko Samui for pulling in international DJs (when the admission price increases) but

reliable for lively music and a crowd most nights of the week. Two levels with space for dancing or sitting.
🕐 Daily 6pm–2am 🍸 B20

🍸 REGGAE PUB
Central Chaweng
Tel 077 413 987
Samui's oldest nightclub has aged gracefully, and when live music makes an appearance it remains a sociable venue for late-night entertainment. There are other bars in the immediate vicinity, but even for a short visit the Reggae Pub holds its own alongside the competition.
🕐 Nightly 7.30pm–2am

Enjoying a kayak adventure with Blue Stars

🍸 SECRET GARDEN
Big Buddha Beach, Ko Samui
Tel 077 245 255
Every Sunday from around 4pm to 8pm, on the beach next to the Ko Phangan ferry pier, there is live music from local bands and the occasional international singer. The event takes place on the beach itself, and there is a lively atmosphere. Thai and European food, including seafood, is on the menu.
🕐 Sun 6–11

🤿 BIG BLUE DIVING SAMUI
Princess Village Resort, Chaweng Beach
Tel 077 456 050
www.bigbluedivingsamui.com

A Swedish company with diving courses starting most days in high season. Big Blue has its own dive yacht and a private pool for learning. Bungalow accommodation is also available. PADI courses are conducted in English, German, French and Swedish.
🕐 Daily 10–10 🤿 Dive trip B3,750–B4,100. Bungalows from B625 per night (B500 when diving)

🤿 BLUE STARS
169/1 Moo. 2 Tambol Bophut, Chaweng Beach Road
Tel 077 413 231
www.bluestars.info
Blue Stars offers adventure trips to Ang Thong National Park, overnight kayaking, and snorkeling among the tidal lagoons of the park.
🕐 Daily 10am–11pm 🤿 Day trips B2,200

🤿 DISCOVERY
Amari Palm Reef Resort, Chaweng Beach
Tel 077 413 196
www.discoverydivers.com
Discovery offers what is probably the least exacting introduction to scuba-diving, with the entire learning facilities available on site. You begin in the training pool, attend lessons in air-conditioned classrooms and finish by using one of the company's on-dive boats. There are one- and four-day courses and advanced courses up to PADI Divemaster status.
🕐 Daily 10–6 🤿 1-day course from B5,100; trips from B3,750

🤿 EASY DIVERS
Opposite Sand Sea Resort, Lamai Beach
Tel 077 231 190
www.easydivers-thailand.com
Easy Divers is one of the leading dive centers on the island, and it has offices on all the main beaches. The European-managed company has been around for over 10 years, and its PADI dive courses are well established.
🤿 Courses from B1,700 (child over 8 B1,000), 4-day PADI courses B12,500

WHAT TO DO

🏃 RED BICYCLE SAMUI

438/7 Moo 1, Tambol Maret, Lamai
Tel 077 232 136
www.redbicycle.org

Bicycling tours to suit all ages and abilities are on offer here, using Cannondale mountain bicycles. A sightseeing tour takes an easy pace to move around the south side of the island with plenty of stops for eating and shopping. The Samui from the Top tour, by contrast, is a mountain route where you travel from 600m (1,968ft) to sea level in 15 minutes. Bicycles can also be rented by the day or week.
🕐 Daily 7–6 💰 B350 per day, B2,000 per week

🏃 SAMUI FRISBEE GOLF

Monkey Theatre Rd, Bophut
Tel 018 942 105
www.samuidiscgolf.com

This sport is a cross between frisbee and golf (using baskets instead of holes), and is the first of its kind in Southeast Asia. It's played over 18 holes and 8ha (20 acres) of land and it takes about two hours to finish the course. Telephone for a free pickup to the course.
🕐 Daily 8–8 💰 B600

⭐ SAMUI INSTITUTE OF THAI CULINARY ARTS

Central Samui Beach Resort, South Chaweng Beach Rd
Tel 077 413 172
www.sitca.net

Daily cooking classes and food-carving courses from a professional institution, SITCA, are on offer here. A culinary shop (and an online mail-order service) is also run by SITCA, where you can purchase ingredients and equipment. The morning cooking class starts at 11.30am, and three dishes are taught by 1am; the afternoon class starts at 4pm and lasts two hours. You eat together with the other participants and can bring along a friend for free.
🕐 Daily 11.30–1, 4–6.30 💰 Afternoon class B1,200, dinner class B1,600

💟 CENTARA SPA

Central Samui Beach Resort, Chaweng Beach, and Central Samui Village, Natien Beach, Ko Samui
Tel 077 230 500 (Chaweng), 077 424 020 (Natien)
www.centaraspa.com

Massages, body wraps and aromatheraphy make up the various packages that come with tempting names like Earthly Pleasures, Seize the Day and Essential Male. Half- and full-day programs.
🕐 Daily 9-6

💟 HEALTH OASIS RESORT

Bang Po, Beachfront, Ko Samui
Tel 077 236 255
www.healthoasisresort.com

Peaceful seclusion at Tamarind Springs

"Relax, cleanse, rejuvenate" is the motto of this resort, which offers a range of fasting, colonic cleansing, and pampering programs. Accommodation is also available, from simple rooms with fans to air-conditioned bungalows. Plus there's a vegetarian restaurant, and a rather special service that claims to establish your vortex location. Full details on the website.
🕐 Daily 9-7

💟 PEACE TROPICAL SPA

17 Moo 1, Bophut
Tel 077 430 199
www.peace-tropical-spa.com

Facial therapies, massage, reflexology and body treatments are on the menu here, as well as packages like a two-hour session that includes a steam room visit before a massage, or a combined body scrub and body wrap. The Happy Hour package is popular—an oil massage followed by facial treatments.
🕐 Daily 10–10 💰 Massages B1,000–B1,500, body treatments B1,500, facials B1,500–B1,700, packages B2,000–B2,300

💟 SPA RESORT MEDITATION

Spa Resort, Lamai Beach, Ko Samui
Tel 077 230 855
www.spasamui.com

You do not need to be staying at the resort (▷ 286) to join any of its courses in meditation or yoga. Every morning at 7.30am free meditation classes are held on the beach by the resort. They are followed by yoga and chi-gung classes. Every month there are also five-day retreats. The website has full details.
🕐 Daily 8.45–10.15 💰 Yoga B250

💟 TAMARIND SPRINGS

205/3 Thong Takian, Tambon Maret
Tel 077 424 221
www.tamarindretreat.com

On the main road between Chaweng and Lamai, with a peaceful hillside setting, Tamarind Springs is one of the island's most sophisticated massage centers. As well as the standard two-hour Thai massage, there is also an oil massage that takes half an hour less, plus separate face, foot and head massages. There are also a number of packages that cater to couples and which begin with a session in the aromatic herbal steam room. Towels and garments are provided.

💟 TONSAI RETREAT SPA

325 Moo 2, Thanon Cherngtalay, Ko Samui
Tel 076 271 250, 098 668 563
www.tonsai-spa.com

Named after the tonsai tree, representing relaxation and serenity, Tonsai Retreat Spa is one of the most glamorous spas anywhere on the island. The treatments are not unusual—massages, facials and body wraps—but the setting is both idyllic and exclusive, and the level of personal service above average. Luxury accommodation is also available at the Tonsai Retreat boutique hotel.

🕐 Daily 9am–7pm 💆 Facials from B1,200, body wraps from B1,850

⭐ SCUBA DIVING
Big Blue Samui Princess Village Resort, Chaweng Beach
Tel 077 456 050
www.bigbluediving.com
Scuba-diving is not just for adults. A professional company with qualified instructors should be able to accept anyone over the age of 10 who is a reasonably good swimmer. Big Blue Samui, for example, runs a two-day course that covers the basic skills and which counts two-thirds of the way toward the Open Water Course certificate, the standard PADI qualification for scuba-diving.

KRABI
🍺 O'MALLEY'S
32 Thanon Chao Fha
Tel 075 612 786
Don't let the name deceive: this "Irish" pub is 100 percent Thai-owned, despite the mural of leprechauns on the wall and a rugby shirt signed by Irish travelers. It is a sociable place for drinkers, with a pool table, darts, football machines and a happy "hour" that lasts all night. While waiting for revelers to turn up, the café two doors down shows a Hollywood movie nightly at 7.30pm. The Asian Rd bar across the road is also worth a visit.

🕐 Daily 11am–midnight

🧗 CLIFFMAN
East Railay Beach
Tel 075 621 768, 016 773 722
www.thaiclimb.com
A well-established rock-climbing outfit based at East Railay beach, halfway between Krabi town and Ao Nang, with courses of varying length available. The rates include medical insurance. There is a climbing wall for absolute beginners to try out before climbing a real cliff.

🕐 Daily 9–8 🧗 Half-/1-/2-/3-day courses B800/1,500/3,500/5,000

💆 CHAO FHA THAI MASSAGE
13/5–6 Thanon Chao Fha
Tel 075 612 958

You could gain a PADI qualification during your stay on Ko Samui

The sunbeds are laid out waiting, and various certificates on the walls testify to the professional training of the massage therapists. All kinds of massages are available—foot, herbal, oil, Thai and face. The herbal treatments are inviting, with lemongrass and kaffir lime and camphor wrapped up and pressed on to receptive parts of your body.

🕐 Daily 10am–11pm
💆 Massages B200 (face)–B500 (foot)

PHUKET
🛍 BIKINI SHOP
Thanon Patak, Kata Beach
Tel 076 333 133

Head here for a wide choice of swimming suits and beachwear, including French designer brands and the latest fashions from Australia as well as less expensive Thai-made products. Mostly aimed at women, there is some beachwear for men. The shop is in front of the main entrance to Club Med.

🕐 Daily 9–8

🛍 PUI FAI SOUVENIR
10 Thanon Rassada, Phuket town
Tel 076 222 263
A lot of merchandise is packed into this small shop, and there are lots of little items that will pack away neatly into your luggage. The picture frames and wooden puppets are especially attractive. All prices are marked up, but negotiation is possible and you should expect around a 20 percent discount.

🕐 Daily 9–6

🛍 RINDA MAGICAL ART
27 Thanon Yaowarat, Phuket town
Tel 066 917 839
The work of two artists in residence, Jay-da and Watcharin Rodnit, who go in for canvases of swirling tones and jazzy motifs. Working in oil and mixed media, they have a very personal style. The gallery does not include the Buddha paintings that feature in most of the other art shops in Phuket.

🕐 Wed–Mon 9–8

🛍 SARASIL ART GALLERY
121 Thanon Phang-Nga, Phuket town
Tel 076 224 532
Watercolor and oil paintings range over a wide subject area, from the ordinary and realistic to the highly abstract. Prices are equally varied, from a few thousand baht to B40,000. You will pass this gallery on the Phuket walk (▷ 238–239).

🕐 Daily 9–6

⊕ SOUL OF ASIA
37–39 Thanon Ratsada, Phuket town
Tel 076 211 133
www.soulofasia.com
This is the most serious antiques and painting gallery in Phuket, with ceramics, lovely paintings in lacquer, sculptures by noted Thai artists, small carpets and big Buddhas. There are two floors of very artful merchandise. You pass this shop on the Phuket walk (▷ 238–239).
🕐 Daily 10.30–8.30

⊕ WOOD AND STONE
55 Thanon Yaowarat, Phuket town
Tel 076 258 022
If looking for a gift or souvenir you should find something here: golden Buddhas and smiling ones reclining gracefully, wooden elephants, carved masks, carved dragons, small decorative boxes. If some of the stock looks similar to the Pui Fai Souvenir shop, that's because the two places are run by a husband-and-wife team.
🕐 Daily 9–8

🎯 PATONG PARK
Soi Kebsap 2, Thanon Sainamyen, Patong
Tel 076 345 185
Bungee-jumping from 60m (197ft) above a pool, the tallest jump in southern Thailand, with professional jumpmasters on hand to uphold safety standards.
🕐 Daily 10–7 💵 B1,400

🎯 PHUKET FANTASEA
Kamala Beach
Tel 076 385 111 (reservations), 076 385 100 (information)
www.phuket-fantasea.com
A nightly dinner buffet followed by a show that defies easy labeling, this claims to be a window into Thai culture via the style of Las Vegas. There is certainly something spectacular about the show. It tells the story of Kamala, the prince of an enchanted kingdom, and it provides the

narrative for a stage spectacular featuring elephants, a tiger, water buffalo, acrobats, plus light and sound effects. Children will love it; adults need to be in the mood for an extravaganza of dancing and set pieces worthy of an epic film. The buffet food is as good as can be expected of a place catering to up to 4,000 diners. Tickets can be reserved at any travel shop in Phuket and transportation there and back for B200 can be arranged.
🕐 Fri–Wed buffet at 6pm, show at 9pm
💵 Dinner and show: adult B1,600, child (age 4–12) B1,200; show only: adult B1,100, child (age 4–12) B800

Catch a show at the Phuket Fantasea

🎯 ROCK & BOWL
Patong Park, Soi Kebsap 2, Thanon Sainamyen, Patong
Tel 076 345 898
This is the largest bowling alley in Phuket, and it attracts a good crowd of locals, expats and visitors. Food, calling itself American-breakfast, is always available. Children will enjoy Rock Bowl as well, with disco music and flashing lights around the place.
🕐 1pm–2am 💵 B80 per game per person, shoes B30

🎵 SPHINX
Thanon Rad Uthit, Patong
Tel 076 341 500
www.sphinxthai.com

The best food at this restaurant is the untamed Thai dishes, and there is a cosmopolitan cocktail list. But the main attraction is upstairs in the theater, where the resident Pharaohs dance troupe features routines from Broadway musicals like *Cats*, reenactments of scenes from classical Thai myths and some comedy as well. The atmosphere is gregarious. Reserve for dinner or show, or both.
🕐 5pm–midnight; performances Wed–Mon 9pm and 10.30pm
💵 Dinner B1,200 (child under 12 B900) for Thai menu; B1,400 and B1,050 for European menu

🍸 BLUE NOTE BAR
Soi Easy, Thanon Bangla, Patong
Tel 076 344 146
In the middle of Soi Easy, a bar and complex on Thanon Bangla, Blue Note is one version of Patong nightlife. A DJ plays mainstream rock and pop, regulars play darts, and major sports events on TV take precedence. Cocktails and beers are both available.
🕐 Daily 10–1

🍸 CLUB MED DINNER AND DISCO
Club Med, Thanon Kata, Karon
Tel 076 330 456
The Half Day Pass provides time for an activity or two and a shower before the buffet dinner, which includes beer and wine, followed by after-dinner live entertainment, either a band indoors or a flying trapeze show outside, and later a disco on a dance floor of sand.
🕐 Half Day Pass valid 3.30pm–1am
💵 Half Day Pass adult B2,700, child (age 4–11) B1,350

🍸 DRAGON DISCOTHEQUE
Soi Easy, Thanon Bangla, Patong Beach
Tel 076 294 231
www.dragondisco.com
The disco is the main focus of entertainment here, but the indoor beer garden can be

enjoyed in its own right as a large pub with pool tables and large screens for sports events. There are three bars and an internet café.

🕓 Beer garden opens daily at 7pm; disco at 9pm

🍸 MOLLY MALONE'S

Thanon Thawiwong (Beach Road), Patong
Tel 076 292 771
Unexciting meals are always available here, but at night a live band enlivens the place considerably and there is a sociable atmosphere. For more of the same, turn right outside and walk around the corner to Scruffy Murphy's.

🕓 Daily 11am–2am

🍸 ZANZIBAR

Royal Phuket City Hotel, 154 Thanon Phang-Nga, Phuket town
Tel 076 233 333
A hotel pub serving food day and night, including ostrich and crocodile meat, and live music from the resident band every night from around 10pm. This is the place not for ballads or old hits but rock and roll with a Thai inflection.

🕓 Daily 6–1

🤿 CORAL GRAND

4/17–20 Soi Vipavadee 32, Vipavadee-Rungsit Road, Jatujak, Bangkok
Tel 077 414 334
www.coralgranddivers.com
This diving company covers Ko Samui, Ko Tao and the Similan Islands. Snorkeling trips to Ang Thong National Park are popular, and their standard scuba-diving Open Water Course takes three and a half days. More advanced courses are also conducted.

🕓 Daily 9–5 🤿 Open water dive course B9,000

🤿 CORAL SEEKERS

16 Soi Teuson, Samkong, Phuket town
Tel 076 354 074
www.coralseekers.com
Coral Seekers has speedboats for snorkeling trips around the island with package deals that

include transport to and from your hotel and snorkeling gear. Half- and full-day trips are organized regularly and water skiing is also an option.

🕓 Daily 9–6 🤿 Day trips B5,550, half-day trips B2,550

🤿 DIVE ASIA

24 Karon Road, Karon Beach, Phuket
Tel 076 330 598, 076 284 117
www.diveasia.com
Dive Asia has been in Phuket for over 25 years and has a good reputation as *the* place to go to learn diving, from Discover Scuba Diving to NITROX courses and IDC/CDC programs for those with previous diving experience.

Recharge your batteries with a Thai massage

One-day dive trips feature alongside cruises that take you to prime locations off the Similan and Surin islands.

🕓 Daily 9–7 🤿 From B2,880

🤿 SANTANA DIVING AND CANOEING

49 Thanon Thaweewong, Patong Beach
Tel 076 294 220
www.santanaphuket.com
Another well-established diving operation in Phuket, this first outfit to establish itself at Patong has its own vessel for live-aboard trips to the Similian Islands and reefs off the coast of Mynamar (Burma). One-day trips around Phuket take place

daily, and beginners are welcomed as well as experienced divers.

🕓 Daily 10–9 🤿 From B2,300

⭐ MOM TRI'S THAI COOKING CLASSES

Kata Beach, Phuket
Tel 076 330 015
www.boathousephuket.com
Every weekend Chef Tamanoon of the Boathouse hotel and restaurant conducts Thai cooking classes to small groups. In the high season you need to reserve a place in advance as these classes are popular. Recipes and apron are yours to keep.

🕓 Sat–Sun 10–2 🤿 2-day course B3,677, 1-day course B2,354

🍳 PHUKET THAI COOKERY SCHOOL

39/4 Thanon Thepatan, Rasada
Tel 076 232 240
www.phuket-thaicookeryschool.com
Northeast of Phuket town and offering free transportation from Patong, Kata, Karon and Phuket town, this is a popular place where courses begin with a visit to a local market for ingredients. Lunch or dinner is included in the fee. A course in Thai vegetarian cooking is also available.

🕓 Daily 10–3 🍳 Mon–Thu B1,900, Fri–Sun B2,200

💜 BODY AND MIND DAY SPA

558/7–12 Thanon Patak, Karon Beach
Tel 076 398 274
www.body-mindspa.com
Hydrotherapy, body wraps and facials are on offer, as well as a range of massages, aromatherapy and sport. Various packages are available, such as a body scrub and aromatherapy massage (two hours; B1,800). The setting is stylish and suitably serene for treatments that leave you calm and revitalized. You'll find it at the end of Karon Beach, before the Central Karon Village resort.

🕓 Daily 11–10 💜 B400–B3,000

○ HIDEAWAY DAY SPAS
137 Thanon Nanai, Patong, Phuket
Tel 076 340 591
www.phuket-hideaway.com
A spa with plunge pools offering traditional Thai aromatherapy (for the body, feet and face), hand massages, hair and skin treatments, body wraps and salt scrubs. There are also Thai aromatherapy cosmetics for sale.
⊙ Daily 9–7

○ P&P OPTIC
6 Thanon Bangla, Patong
Tel 076 340 227
Most kinds of lens and frames—bifocals, plastic, non-reflective ones, contact lens—are available here. Bring your own prescription or have your eyes assessed while you're here. A similar place, Washington Optic, can be found in Phuket town at 52 Thanon Rasada, and both locations should have prices considerably less than those in Europe or North America.
⊙ Daily 9–7 ✋ From B3,800

○ PERFECTION BEAUTY BOUTIQUE AND GALLERY
1/10 Moo 1, Soi Songkhun, Chao Fa Road
Tel 076 264 295
A range of treatments is available, from a hair cut, manicure or pedicure to a complete makeover. There is a mixed spa for men and women and a separate women-only spa room. The gallery attached to the spa displays and sells the work of local artists. Chao Fa Road is just under halfway between Phuket town and Chalong.
⊙ Tue–Sun, 10am–8pm

○ THE SENSE SPA
2/12 Kata Plaza, Thanon Kata, Karon, Phuket
Tel 076 333 014
This is one of Phuket's more tastefully designed spas to be found outside of a five-star hotel. On offer are Thai and Swedish massages, body scrubs, body wraps, hair waxing, facials and a variety of packages that include the Sense of Wellbeing treatment, which takes over three and a half hours to complete. (B4,235).
⊙ Daily 10–10
✋ B1,650–B4,235

○ SILENT SOUND CENTRE
48/17 Moo 9, Soi Ao Chalong
Tel 06 001 5641
www.silentsoundcentre.com
This establishment specializes in Reiki therapy and sound massage. Reiki is a form of hands-on healing designed to increase energy and relaxation levels, while the sound therapy

Relax and rejuvenate at one of the spas on Phuket

makes use of Tibetan "singing bowls" with the aim of restoring the body's energy balance. A two-day Reiki course includes four hours of therapy each day. The sound therapy courses last for three days.
✋ B5,000 (2-day course) and B7,500 (3-day course)

○ TARN TARA SPA
58/11 Moo 6, Thanon Chao Far, Chalong, Phuket
Tel 076 352 062/4
www.tarntaraspa.com
Close to Wat Chalong, off the road between Phuket town and the beaches of Karon and Kata, this is a lakeside spa and a restaurant with a health-conscious menu. The basic three-hour Andaman Sunshine package includes an hourlong oil massage, facial treatment, shampoo or foot massage and a session in a steam bath or pool. You can make reservations online.
⊙ Daily 9am–11pm
✋ B3,000–B5,500

✱ CLUB MED MINI CLUB
Club Med, Thanon Kata, Karon
Tel 076 330 456
A Day Pass includes lunch and a variety of activities, and you do not need to be staying at the resort. Some of the activities, like the bungee bounce and the flying trapeze, are only for children aged over 13. There is also an afternoon package that covers just the activities.
⊙ Daily 10–6
✋ Day Pass child (age 4–10) B1,000, child (over 11) B2,000; activities only package child (4–10) B400, child (over 11) B800

FESTIVAL

SEPTEMBER/OCTOBER

VEGETARIAN FESTIVAL
ℹ Tourist office, 73–75 Thanon Phuket, tel 076 21 22 13
www.phuket.com/festival/vegetarian.htm
This festival of vegetarian delights lasts for more than a week, and Phuket is the place to experience the event at its best. Check with the local tourist office about events happening at different temples around the island. Smaller events take place in Krabi and around Phang Nga.
⊙ Late September to early October

Go out and about in Thailand with these four walks, three driving tours and three river tours. They explore Thailand's varied scenery, from a city walk in Bangkok's Chinatown to a drive along the Mekong River in the northeast. The location of each walk and tour is marked on the map on page 220, where you will also find the key to the individual maps. For both walks and tours it is advisable to use the most detailed map of the area you can find.

Out and About

KEY TO THIS MAP

- **2** Drive
- **4** Walk
- **6** River Tour
- ■ Capital City
- ■ City / Town

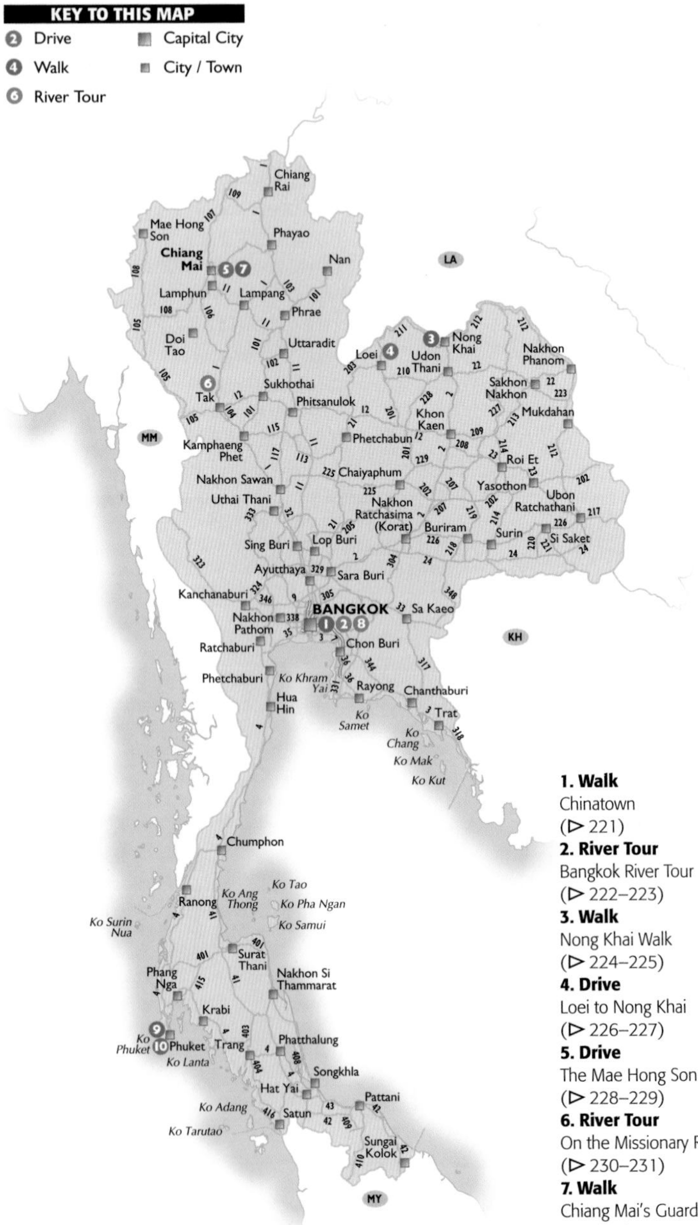

1. Walk
Chinatown
(▷ 221)

2. River Tour
Bangkok River Tour
(▷ 222–223)

3. Walk
Nong Khai Walk
(▷ 224–225)

4. Drive
Loei to Nong Khai
(▷ 226–227)

5. Drive
The Mae Hong Son Loop
(▷ 228–229)

6. River Tour
On the Missionary Route
(▷ 230–231)

7. Walk
Chiang Mai's Guardian
  Mountain
  (▷ 232–233)

8. River Tour
The Slow Boat to
  Ayutthaya
  (▷ 234–235)

9. Drive
Phuket Town to Krabi
(▷ 236–237)

10. Walk
Phuket Town
(▷ 238–239)

KEY TO ROUTE MAPS IN THIS CHAPTER

- ★ Start point
- — Route
- ▶ Route direction
- **2** Walk start point on drive
- **6** Featured sight along route
- ● Place of interest in Sights section
- 🛉 Featured temple
- 🌧 National park / reserve
- 🦌 Wildlife reserve
- 🐟 Marine national park
- 🏔 Waterfall
- ☀ Viewpoint
- 621▲ Height in metres

OUT AND ABOUT

CHINATOWN

This walk will introduce you to Bangkok's Chinatown, its hustle and bustle, shops and stands and everyday life. You may not end up purchasing anything, but more than one of your senses will be stimulated by this walk.

THE WALK

Distance: 3.5km (2 miles)
Allow: 2–3 hours
Start/end at: The Ratchawongse pier
➕ 64 B4

HOW TO GET THERE

Take any Chao Phraya River Express boat to the Ratchawongse pier.

★ The Ratchawongse boat pier is at the end of Thanon Ratchawong; food and drink stands are on hand.

Walk straight up Thanon Ratchawong until you reach a pedestrian crossing (if you reach a set of traffic lights you have gone too far). Turn to the left here, down a congested lane.

❶ **You have entered Sampeng Lane.** This section of the lane was once home to opium addicts and brothels but is now filled with fabric shops.

Continue along Sampeng Lane until you reach a crossroads with a pedestrian crossing and vehicular traffic. Turn right here, for Thanon Wora Chak.

❷ **The very first shop on your right is Eain Nee Kok,** a Chinese medicine store, where some traditional ingredients—gingko leaves, and roselle *(hibiscus sabdariffa Linn)*—are marked in English.

Walk along to the traffic lights and turn right onto Thanon Yaowarat.

❸ **Thanon Yaowarat is a busy thoroughfare.** You will pass pre-World War II Chinese buildings with rickety balconies and enter the hub of Thailand's retail gold trade. Gold shops will become a common sight.

Cross the main intersection with traffic lights, staying on the left-hand side where the Grand China Princess Hotel stands, but

Wat Mangkon Kamalawat temple in Chinatown

stay on Thanon Yaowarat. Look for the signposted Thanon Mangkan on your left and turn down here, past fruit vendors, and turn right at the first crossroad intersection onto Thanon Charoen Krung. Stay on the left side for 25m (27 yards) and look for the Wat Mangkon Kamalawat temple entrance.

❹ **Wat Mangkon Kamalawat** (▷ 82) is one of Chinatown's busiest temples, with lots to look at.

Return to Thanon Charoen Krung, turn left and cross the road at the pedestrian crossing. Go down the lane, signposted Soi 16.

❺ **Along Soi 16 you will pass a smaller temple on your left,** amid the stands selling dried food, fresh lotus fruit, giant sea slugs, hot chestnuts and other delicacies.

Soi 16 brings you to an intersection with Thanon Yaowarat. Turn right, passing Thanon Mangkan again, until you arrive at the intersection with Thanon Ratchawong on your left, just after the Shangarila restaurant. Turn down here to return to the Chao Phraya River Express boat pier.

WHERE TO EAT

Grand China Princess Hotel
215 Thanon Yaowarat
Tel 022 249 977
See page 271.
🄱 Buffet on 10th floor daily
11.30–2.30; Rabiang Pai café on 2nd floor daily 11–9

TOURIST INFORMATION

Bangkok Information Center
Pinklao Bridge, Thanon Phra Athit, Banglamphu
Tel 022 257 612

OUT AND ABOUT

BANGKOK RIVER TOUR

This tour takes you up the Chao Phraya River to Nonthaburi, a town beyond Bangkok's northern boundary, taking in some sights along the way. At Nonthaburi you can take a short walk through the town's market area and cross the river to a little-visited temple on the west side before returning to Bangkok.

THE RIVER TOUR

Distance:	32km (20 miles)
Allow:	4–6 hours
Start/end at:	Central Pier
✚ 64 C5	

HOW TO GET THERE

Take the Skytrain to Saphan Taksin.

★ Central Pier, next to the Saphan Taksin Skytrain station, is designated as N1 on the route traveled by the Chao Phraya River Express boats. Boats travel throughout the day, from early morning until around 5.30pm, and tickets are purchased on board.

Chao Phraya River Express boats with no flag stop at every pier. Boats displaying an orange flag stop at 15 piers and take an hour to reach Nonthaburi. Boats with a yellow flag only make seven stops. The fare to Nonthaburi is B16.

❶ The first stretch of the river, up until the N13 pier, is the busiest, with river traffic and plenty to observe. After the N7 pier, look to the left for fine views of Wat Arun (▷ 81).

Disembark at the N10 pier, Wang Lang (Siriaj). From the pier go straight along Thanon Phrannok to enter the hospital from its side entrance and walk through the hospital grounds for about 300m (330 yards). Turn left just before the sign for the History of Thai Medicine Museum and you'll find the Anatomical Museum on your left.

❷ Visit the Anatomical Museum and see its ghoulish collection of medical abnormalities.

Return to the N10 pier and board a Chao Phraya River Express boat.

❸ After the N13 pier, you approach the asymmetric but

Monks' quarters at Nonthaburi

graceful Rama VIII suspension bridge, completed in 2002. The B20 banknote depicts King Rama VIII standing before the bridge that commemorates his life.

By this stage of the journey you should find that the boat you are in is a lot less crowded. The next pier, N15, brings you to Vimanmek and Dusit's places of interest (▷ 80 and 70).

❹ After the N22 pier and before the railway bridge that crosses the river, you will see glistening temples on your right. After the N25 pier, there is a mosque on the right and houses built on stilts. There are often children playing in the water.

Disembark at Nonthaburi, the terminal pier for Chao Phraya River Express boats.

❺ Outside the pier, the old City Hall by the clock tower is a reminder that you are now outside Bangkok, in the provincial capital of Nonthaburi province.

Outside the pier station, head for the market that you can see ahead of you, keeping to the right-hand side of the road and walking along the covered sidewalk (pavement).

❻ Nonthaburi is a market town, well known for its orchards, and the produce grown in the vicinity is on sale every day of the year in the street market. Among the pyramids of fruit on offer, look for the mangosteen—unattractive on the outside but a delicacy to eat—and the foul-smelling durian. As well as fruit, the market is teeming with inexpensive clothing, watches, wallets and household items.

Continue walking through the market until you reach some traffic lights. Turn right here and continue walking until you reach a pedestrian bridge over the road. Cross over the bridge to the other side of the street.

❼ The view from the bridge may resemble a typical Bangkok street, but you will also see *samlors*, a form of unmotorized transport absent from the capital. The River Plaza shopping center is Nonthaburi's concession to modernity.

Walk back to the traffic lights, turn left and return to the pier on the other side of the street to the covered market. At the pier look for the smaller boats—most of them displaying 120AV on their side—that continuously ply their way across the river. Step aboard and have B10 ready to pay on the other side.

Exiting from the pier on the west side of the river, take a tuk-tuk to Wat Chalerm Phra Kiat. It's a five-minute drive away, and the fare is B10 per person. Ask the tuk-tuk driver to wait for you at the temple.

❽ Wat Chalerm Phra Kiat was built by Rama III, on the site of a 17th-century fortress, in memory of his mother. It is now a restful spot among trees, one that lends the temple a quiet dignity. The

OUT AND ABOUT

roofs and shapely gables are richly decorated with ceramic tiles, revealing a Chinese character in this shrine to Thai Buddhism. The doors and windows, rich in stuccowork, are equally impressive, and the peaceful interior has been carefully restored.

Return to the pier and cross back to the east side of the Chao Phraya River to catch a boat back to Bangkok. Unless you want a long journey back, wait for a boat with a yellow or orange flag. The Rim Fang Floating Restaurant, on the promenade downriver from the pier, is only a few minutes away on foot and is a good place to stop for a cold drink before boarding a Chao Phraya River Express boat. Remember though, that the last boat back to Bangkok departs at around 5.30pm.

WHERE TO EAT

River Plaza
Fast-food restaurants, ice-cream and sorbet parlors by the pedestrian bridge in Nonthaburi.
🕐 Daily 9.30–7

PLACE TO VISIT

Anatomical Museum
Siriraj Hospital, Thanon Prannok
Tel 024 197 000
🕐 Mon–Sat 9–4
💷 B40

TOURIST INFORMATION

Bangkok Information Center
Pinklao Bridge, Thanon Phra Athit, Banglamphu
Tel 022 257 612

A Chao Phraya River Express boat

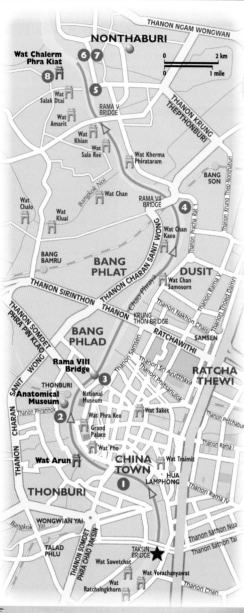

NONG KHAI WALK

This walk takes you through the streets of Nong Khai, where you can visit temples, see examples of how French–Lao styles of building have influenced typical Thai–Chinese architecture, and stroll through a street market. For most of the way you are close to, and walking parallel with, the course of the 4,000km-long (248-mile) Mekong River.

THE WALK

Distance: 6km (4 miles)
Allow: 2–3 hours
Start/end at: Pantawee Hotel, Thanon Haisok

HOW TO GET THERE

The Pantawee Hotel is in the heart of town.

★ In the absence of a tourist information office in town, the Pantawee Hotel with its tour desk and internet access is the best place to visit for travel and local information. The free copy of the hotel's Nong Khai guide includes a town map.

With your back to the hotel entrance, turn to your right and walk to the first set of crossroads and traffic lights. Turn right here onto Thanon Meechai, staying on the right-hand side of the street. Take note of this intersection, as you will return to this point from the other direction at the end of the walk.

❶ Thanon Meechai is one of the four roads in Nong Khai that runs parallel with the Mekong River in a west–east direction, the one furthest from the river being Route 212. Along Thanon Meechai, on the other side of the street, you will see the Danish Baker café with its outdoor tables, suitable for an early coffee or breakfast. Past this at 702/3 you'll find the Silver Antiques shop with old coins and banknotes for sale. A little farther along on the right stands the town's post office.

About 300m (330 yards) past the post office, at the corner with signposted Soi Srimuang, cross the road and go down the lane to Wat Si Meuang temple.

❷ Nong Khai has many temples, but the glittering Wat Si Meuang is one of the most photogenic, distinguished by a black Buddha at the entrance.

Tuk-tuks are a common sight on the streets of Nong Khai

Stay on the left side of Thanon Meechai and continue walking east for another 100m (110 yards). Stop after the signposted Prab-Ho lane on your left, at the Sawasdee Guest House (▷ 276).

❸ The Sawasdee Guest House, and some similar buildings along this stretch of road, is a fine surviving example of the town's vernacular architecture, much of which is inexorably falling prey to modernization. Enter the Sawasdee's lobby, filled with nostalgic objects paying homage to past times, to appreciate its Chinese-style design. Consider pausing here for a cold drink or tea in the breakfast area to the back of the lobby.

As your walk along Thanon Meechai continues, you will see old Chinese–Thai wooden-houses with French touches like slatted shutters and small porticoes—a reminder of when Nong Khai was more influenced by colonial Laos than faraway Bangkok.

Continue along Thanon Meechai for over 1km (about three-quarters of a mile). When you pass a sign pointing right for Luang Pho Phra Sai, next to the Sweet Orchid restaurant, cross to the other side of Thanon Meechai and turn right down

the signposted Phochai Road to Wat Pho Chai, at the bottom on your right.

❹ Wat Pho Chai, perhaps a little too glossy and theatrical for its own aesthetic good, receives more devotees than any other shrine in Nong Khai because it houses the revered Luang Pho Phra Sai, a Buddha image that was brought from Laos to Thailand in 1850 under perilous circumstances. The head of the sitting Buddha image is pure gold, and the body is bronze. Murals tell the story of the image's journey from Laos, including the capsizing of the raft that was carrying it across the Mekong River and its miraculous recovery.

Return to Thanon Meechai, cross the road and walk down toward the river, turning left when you reach the river.

❺ Walking along this quiet riverside setting you will pass a large golden Buddha staring across to Laos. Monks from the temple often stroll along this promenade, shaded from the heat of the sun by their umbrellas. The bridge you can see farther up the Mekong is the 1.2km-long (about three-quarters of a mile) Friendship Bridge, completed in 1994 with the help of funds from Australia. Visas for Laos can be obtained on the other side of the bridge and Vientiane, the capital, is a half-hour taxi ride away.

At the end of the promenade, if the entrance to the main market is closed, turn left and walk through a small covered market that leads to Thanon Prab-Ho and back onto Thanon Meechai. Turn right here, back past the lane that led to Wat Si Meuang, and turn right at the next turning down Soi Srisaget to get back to the riverside. If the entrance to

OUT AND ABOUT

Family life plays out on the street

the main market is open, however, walk straight ahead through the market and avoid the detour.

6 The market is an interesting one, full of clothes and arts and crafts from Thailand. There are also goods smuggled via Laos from former Soviet states in Asia. The market is spread out along Thanon Rimkong as far as Tha Sadet, a pier where only Thais and Laotians can cross the Mekong River.

Continue walking westwards past Tha Sadet, with the Me

Kong Guest House on your right and Nobbi's restaurant on your left. Turn left at the end of Thanon Rimkong, which will bring you to the west end of Thanon Meechai. Turn left here to return to the crossroads where a right turn will take you back to the Pantawee Hotel. If you're feeling hungry, then instead continue along Thanon Meechai where you'll find Danish Baker on the left.

WHERE TO EAT

Danish Baker
Thanon Meechai
See page 252.
⏰ Daily 9–9

You can stock up on silk at the riverside market

A cat eats from a shrine in Nong Khai

LOEI TO NONG KHAI

This drive begins inland at the town of Loei and heads north toward the Mekong River, 50km (35 miles) away. On reaching the river that divides Thailand from Laos, the drive follows its course for 200km (125 miles) to Nong Khai. Vehicular traffic is very light—only the occasional truck or bus is to be seen—and the Mekong is often in view as this scenic route takes you through a very rural region of the northeast.

THE DRIVE

Distance: 220km (138 miles)	
Allow: 4–6 hours	
Start at: Loei	
End at: Nong Khai	

★ The market town of Loei (▷ 96), 50km (35 miles) south of the Mekong River, is a provincial capital and benefits from a university on its northern outskirts. You pass the university on your left as you head out of town.

Leave Loei, heading north on Route 201, signposted to Chiang Khan. You will soon leave the town behind and the traffic will thin out.

❶ The forest-clad hills of Phu Rua National Park (▷ 96) form the scenic background to your left, while nearer to the roadside you will see farmers at work in their paddy fields. Loei is one of Thailand's least spoiled provinces, and the mountain scenery and absence of industry is evident as you head north toward the border.

After 50km (31 miles), turn right at the T-junction (intersection) to drive into the small town of Chiang Khan. You are still on Route 201, which now becomes the main road through the town, but look for the numbered *sois* (small side roads) leading off to your left. Turn down Soi 8, and at the bottom turn right at the T-junction (intersection). Park along this road, Thanon Chai Khong, close to the river.

❷ Chiang Khan (▷ 92), on the banks of the Mekong, has a dry and dusty atmosphere that blends in well with the old wooden shophouses that line Thanon Chai Khong. It is worth calling in at the Rimkong Guesthouse (▷ 274) for a cold drink or coffee. Its rooms overlook the Mekong

and they are fitted with mosquito nets. You will see yellow warning flags along the street alerting people to the problem of malaria-carrying mosquitoes.

Either leave the car and walk eastwards for 1km (about a mile) or drive in that direction, parking just after Soi 20 by Wat Thakhok.

❸ There are fine views of the river from this point, and Wat Thakhok, with balustrades and painted shutters, is a good example of the way Thai architecture in the Mekong region reveals a French–Laotian accent. The first European to explore the Mekong was a Frenchman, Francis Garnier, whose expedition in the 1860s led to the discovery of Angkor Wat.

Drive up Soi 21 to join Route 211 and turn left to continue eastwards toward Pak Chom, 37km (23 miles) away.

❹ The road to Pak Chom is a slow and windy one, passing forested hillside and with the Mekong usually in view as it drifts by on its long journey from Tibet to the south of Vietnam. Pak Chom itself is a one-street town which was the site of a refugee camp for 15,000 Hmong people, displaced here after the victory of the Communist Pathet Lao in Laos in 1975. The refugees have been resettled around the world, and Pak Chom has returned to its quiet, sleepy state.

Drive through Pak Chom continuing on Route 211 and, after 50km (35 miles) and between kilometer stones 97 and 98, look for a sign pointing to Than Thip Falls. Route 211 continues via the large village of Sang Khom.

❺ After Pak Chom, the road improves and stays closer to the river. Water buffalo and big-eared humped cattle lounge by the wayside, banana plants grow on both sides of the road, and the only passing vehicle will be an occasional pickup truck. After 26km (16 miles) you pass a small village where the school has a sign up by the side of the road—"Please Visit Us"— inviting visitors to drop in and give pupils a chance to practice some English.

The sign for the Than Thip Falls takes you off the road for five minutes to the first of two waterfalls surrounded by forest. It is possible to swim here.

Return to Route 211 and after 20km (12.4 miles) on the road past Sang Khom, look for a sign pointing left to Wat Hin Mak Peng. Drive through the temple's entrance—separated by a long, low white wall—and park your vehicle in the compound.

❻ Wat Hin Mak Peng (▷ 102) has a landscaped garden with giant bamboo and remarkably lifelike wax effigies of the monk who founded the monastery. Built close to the river, you can walk down the steps to the riverbank.

Continue on Route 211, heading toward the village of Si Chiang Mai.

❼ Around Si Chiang Mai, look out for the racks of spring roll wrappers drying in the sun (▷ 102).

Keep going along Route 211 for the final 57 km (36 miles) to Nong Khai. There will be more traffic along this stretch of road, and you will lose sight of the river at times. When you are 11km (7 miles) from Nong Khai,

OUT AND ABOUT

ocal produce at a market in Loei

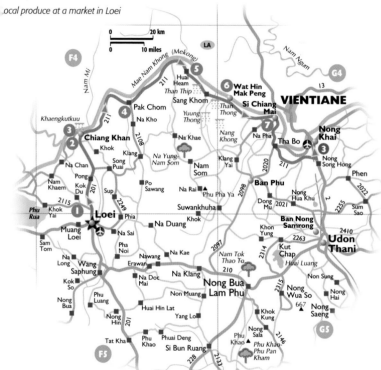

the road joins the three-lane Route 2 for the final drive to your destination.

WHERE TO EAT

Buoy Guest House
Sang Khom
Located on the left-hand side of the road, signposted on Route 211 in the middle of Sang Khom
Tel 042 441 065
If Buoy Guest House is without guests, food may not be available, in which case continue along Route 211 for 400m (437 yards) and eat at the bamboo shack on the left opposite the police station. There is no menu and little choice, but you can be assured that the food is freshly cooked.
🕐 Daily 8–8

TOURIST INFORMATION

Loei Tourist Office
Thanon Charoenrat, Loei
Tel 042 812 812

A stone statue of the Buddha, near the road to Pak Chom

THE MAE HONG SON LOOP

Chiang Mai is the charming capital of northern Thailand and the starting point for many scenic drives through the surrounding mountains. The Mae Hong Son Loop is one of the most spectacular, named after the remote town that marks the drive's halfway point. The road to Mae Hong Son from Chiang Mai has endless hairpin bends, but the drive is punctuated by so many spectacular mountain vistas that it's worth it.

THE DRIVE

Distance:	500km (310 miles)
Allow:	2–3 days
Start/end at:	Chiang Mai

★ With a history stretching back more than eight centuries, Chiang Mai demands a stay of at least three or four days in order to get to know its old town, a warren of lanes enclosed by partly reconstructed defense walls and a wide moat.

Leave Chiang Mai on Route 107, through the one-street suburb of Mae Rim, and after 40km (24 miles), take a left turn at the market town of Mae Malai onto Route 1095, signposted to Pai and Mae Hong Son. The road winds through paddy fields, orchards and hill-tribe villages, gradually climbing to the foothills of the 1800m (6,000ft) Doi Ang Ket mountain range. The province of Chiang Mai ends in a valley 50km (30 miles) from Mae Malai, and the point where Mae Hong Son province begins is also the site of one of the few large villages en route, Mae Sae.

❶ Mae Sae has a predominantly Muslim population, and simple restaurants on either side of the road serve excellent *khao soy* (Burmese-style noodles in a rich meat broth). It's an ideal spot for a lunch break.

Continuing on Route 1095, watch out for the viewpoint on the right, 10km (6 miles) from Mae Sae.

❷ The view from the mountainside wooden terrace is breathtaking, and on a clear day you can see Thailand's third-highest mountain, Chiang Dao's Doi Luang, some 50km (30 miles) to the northeast.

The road descends now into the valley of the Pai River, and as you approach the popular little

A patchwork of rice paddies near Mae Hong Son

resort town of Pai, watch out for a disused multi-span bridge on your right.

❸ The bridge was erected here by Japanese forces as they headed for Myanmar (Burma) at the height of World War II. It's the first of several traces of Japanese wartime presence you'll encounter on this route.

Pai straddles the river of the same name 5km (3 miles) farther on, 130km (70 miles) and a three-hour drive from Chiang Mai.

❹ If you arrive in Pai during the low season you may be tempted to stay overnight, enticed by its laid-back atmosphere, its restaurants, bars and comfortable guesthouses. In high season the small town can be impossibly crowded, and the pull of Mae Hong Son, a further 120km (70 miles), may be stronger.

The Mae Hong Son road (still Route 1095) winds its way through the hill-tribe village of Soppong, past tracks leading to waterfalls and caves.

❺ The most accessible and one of the most mysterious

caves is Tham Pla (Fish Cave; ▷ 128), 8km (5 miles) north of Mae Hong Son. The cave is part of the Tham Pla Pha Sua National Park, and the 20-minute walk to the grotto, with its dark pool packed with fish, is a pleasant riverside stroll. Tham Lot (10km/6 miles north of Soppong) is another interesting cave, but the road there is rough in the rainy season.

Return to Route 1095 and continue onto Mae Hong Son.

❻ Mae Hong Son nestles around a small lake surrounded by mountains. There's enough here—including a cluster of Burmese-style temples—to keep the visitor occupied for several days. If you've driven the six-hour journey from Chiang Mai, then at least an overnight stay is recommended. Walk in the late afternoon up to the hilltop temple Wat Phra That Doi Kong Moo and bask in the sun as it sets over the Burmese mountains to the west of the town.

From Mae Hong Son, Route 108 continues directly south, through forests of teak and conifers. Just beyond the village of Huai Pong, 40km (24 miles) south of Mae Hong Son on the right-hand side of the road, you'll find a cemetery.

❼ This is one of more than 30 wartime cemeteries containing the remains of Japanese soldiers who died in the area during their retreat from Myanmar (Burma) in August, 1945. The next town, Khun Yuam, 30km (18 miles) farther south, has a fascinating little museum with a dust-gathering collection of weapons, uniforms, helmets, personal possessions and photographs left behind in the town by the retreating Japanese. There's

OUT AND ABOUT

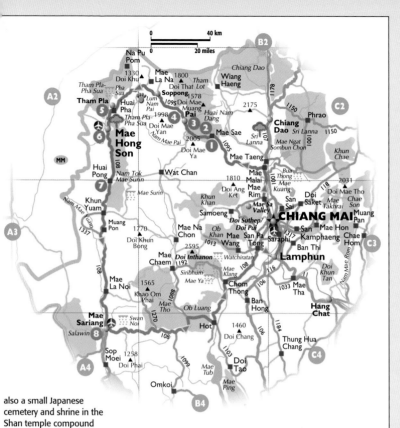

also a small Japanese cemetery and shrine in the Shan temple compound opposite.

From Khun Yuam, Route 108 runs across a highland ridge, through forests and plantations of teak and conifers, to the pretty little market town of Mae Sariang, 70km (42 miles) south.

8 Mae Sariang (▷ 129) is close to the Burmese border and has a large population of Karen refugees and migrants. Some of the local shops and restaurants serve as art galleries for work by Karen artists. Mae Sariang also has two very comfortable hotels if you want to break your journey here.

From Mae Sariang, Route 108 does an abrupt left turn toward Chiang Mai, an easy 190km (115-mile) run, descending from the border highlands to the Mae Ping River valley. The road swings past the heavily forested Ob Luang National Park and through Hot, a rebuilt version of an old town submerged by the waters of the great Bhumiphol

dam. At the village of San Pa Tong, 66km (26 miles) north of Hot, turn right on Route 1013 to Lamphun, then left onto Route 106, which takes you back to Chiang Mai through an avenue of towering *yang* trees, one of the most impressive entrances to any town or city in Thailand.

WHERE TO EAT/STAY

The Belle Villa
Mae Hong Son road, 1.6km (1 mile) from Pai
Tel 053 365 318–21
Pai's leading resort hotel, with an excellent terrace restaurant overlooking paddy fields and the mountains.
🕙 Restaurant daily 6–10

The Riverside
77 Thanon Langpanich, Mae Sariang
Tel 053 681 353
Comfortable hotel with restaurant.
🕙 Restaurant daily 11–11

Rooks Holiday Hotel and Resort
114/5–7 Thanon Khunlumpraprapas, Mae Hong Son
Tel 053 612 324–9

Rooks has almost every modern facility, including a pool and a good restaurant.
🕙 Restaurant daily 11–11

PLACES TO VISIT

Tham Lot
🕙 Daily 9–5
🎫 No admission charge

Tham Pla
🕙 Daily 9–5
🎫 No admission charge

World War II Museum
Mae Hong Son road, Khun Yuam
🕙 Daily 9–5
🎫 Adult B10, child free

TOURIST INFORMATION

Mae Hong Son Tourist Office
Old District Office, Thanon Khunlumphraphat, Amphoe Muang, Mae Hong Son 58000
Tel 053 612 982-3
www.travelmaehongson.org

Pai Tourist Office
Distrct Office, Amphoe Muang, Pai 58000
Tel 053 699 935, 053 699 195-6

OUT AND ABOUT

ON THE MISSIONARY ROUTE

As late as a century ago, missionaries and traders found the easiest and fastest route from Bangkok to the northern outpost of Chiang Mai was by boat, following the network of rivers that lead into the Ping River. You can cover a 140km (84-mile) stretch of this route on board a motorized houseboat, an adventurous way to see one of northern Thailand's wildest regions.

THE RIVER TOUR

Distance:	140km (84 miles)
Allow:	2 days
Start at:	Bhumiphol Dam wall
End at:	Ban Doi Tao

HOW TO GET THERE

The Bhumiphol Dam is 60km (36 miles) north of Tak, a half-hour journey by rented car or *songthaew* pickup taxi (there's a taxi stand at Tak's bus station). If your boat is leaving early in the morning you might want to stay the first night in one of the comfortable bungalows at the base of the dam—it's a very beautiful area in which to spend a day and an evening. The bungalow resort is operated by Thailand's Electricity Generating Authority, and accommodation can be booked by phoning 055 599 093.

You can explore the dam by boat

★ The Bhumiphol Dam, named after Thailand's present king, is the country's biggest and one of the world's top 10 largest dams. It supplies most of Thailand's hydroelectric power.

The houseboat jetties are close to the vast concrete wall of the dam, and the adventure begins as you board one, tottering along a narrow gangplank. Your 'boat' is a plank-floored platform on cylindrical floats (often just empty oil barrels), beneath a thatched roof. There are a few tables and plastic chairs, a rudimentary kitchen and arguably the most important item of all: a karaoke stage, complete with large-screen TV and mega-speakers. You're traveling with Thais as company, and karaoke is an essential item on almost every Thai's holiday itinerary. If the music gets too loud, you can usually escape to a sun-deck.

❶ The first stop is a floating restaurant at the head of the main dam. The menu is understandably dominated by fish fresh from the dam. The tabtim from Bhumiphol Dam are locally famous, and if you can persuade the cook to fry them in garlic you're in for a treat.

❷ If the skipper feels there's time he'll make a stop at one of the dam's few islands, Valentine, where you can swim or just catnap on its sandy beach.

The dam narrows now as its waters wind through a gorge that leads into the Ping River. The northern side of the dam is bordered by the Mae Ping National Park, a wild and mountainous region traversed by just one narrow road. Thick jungle clothes the rocky sides of the narrowing dam, which takes a sharp right turn before yielding to the Ping River. The river, as narrow as 20m (66ft) in places, snakes between the jungle-covered uplands of the Mae Ping National Park and the heights of Doi Mon Chong (1,139m/ 3,730ft) and Doi Lang Muang (1,548m/5,148ft), mountains that dominate one of the wildest regions of northern Thailand.

❸ An overnight stop is made at the tiny river settlement of Kaeng Ko, at the western entrance to the Mae Ping National Park. Supper is served on board, and your bed is on board, too—or, strictly speaking, on boards. You sleep on deck, on thin mattresses. But a glass or two of Thai whisky and an evening of karaoke should guarantee a good night's sleep.

As dawn creeps up the mist-shrouded river, the crew cast off and serve the passengers a Thai breakfast of rice soup. It's now only a 40km (24-mile) chug up river to Doi Tao Lake and the journey's end. Through a break in the mountains on the western bank the Mae Lai River joins the Ping and together, when in full flood, they create a lake 20km (12 miles) long.

❹ Ban Doi Tao lies halfway up the eastern side of the lake. It's a simple village, with a few noodle shops to choose from for lunch and an incongruous modern shopping plaza with souvenir boutiques.

Pickup taxis operate a service from Ban Doi Tao to Hot, 46km (28 miles) north, from where you can catch a bus to Chiang Mai, a further 95km (57 miles) north. Nineteenth-century missionaries and traders completed the entire distance on the Ping River, but of course such temptations as buses didn't exist in those days.

OUT AND ABOUT

WHEN TO GO

The best time to make the trip is at
the end of the rainy season, in
September or October. In the dry
season (Nov–end Feb), the Doi
Tao Lake at the northern end of
the route is liable to dry out so that
only the Bhumiphol Dam can be
navigated, but even a one-day
excursion on its mountain-ringed
waters is a memorable experience.

TOURIST INFORMATION

Tak Tourist Office
TAT, 193 Thanon Taksin, Amphoe
Muang, Tak 63000
Tel 055 514 341-3
🕐 Daily 8.30–4.30

The floating restaurant next to the Bhumiphol Dam

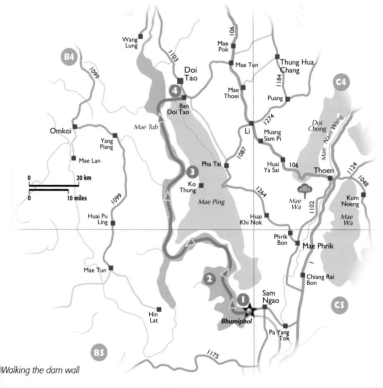

Walking the dam wall

OUT AND ABOUT

CHIANG MAI'S GUARDIAN MOUNTAIN

The vast majority of visitors to Chiang Mai's mountainside temple, Wat Phra That Doi Suthep, travel there by red *songthaew* pickup taxi. However, by doing so they miss out on the spectacular scenery enjoyed by hikers who make the journey on foot.

The rooftops of the Wat Phra That Doi Suthep complex

THE WALK

Distance:	8km (5 miles)
Allow:	4 hours
Start at:	Thanon Huay Kaew, Chiang Mai
End at:	Wat Phra That Doi Suthep temple

★ Start at the entrance to the Namtok Namthatarn waterfall, at 'KM 7' on Route 1004 between Chiang Mai Zoo and Wat Phra That Doi Suthep.

The well signposted and paved minor road to the falls enters the Doi Suthep and Doi Pui National Park, and you'll have to pay B200 admission at the entrance kiosk (this is the fee for entering any Thai national park). The 3km (1.8-mile) walk to the falls, where the strenuous hike up the mountain truly begins, snakes its way through thick forest. Note the way the planners divided the road around one particularly revered tree, a centuries-old *yang* tree that towers majestically over its deciduous companions which stand on either side.

1 A resort-like settlement of national park buildings and a camping ground lies at the foot of the main falls, which plunge 60m (200ft) over granite rocks into deep pools that then feed a narrow mountain river. The *montha* tree is abundant in these parts, and in the winter months it bears beautiful red-and-white flowers. Cool off in the falls or take a break at the refreshment pavilion (daily 9–5).

Venture upwards into the dark green forest, which hangs above the mountain valley like a theater backdrop. The path follows the falls as they plunge over eight separate cascades, each as dramatic as the next. The enclosing forest contains ever more numerous upland evergreens, towering pines and other firs. Young teak fight for space on the mountain with hardy deciduous trees, undergrowth and stands of bamboo and upland palms. Large orchids cling to ancient wood (don't pick any—it's illegal). In the occasional clearing, clouds of butterflies can burst into view—the mountain has dozens of varieties.

2 Keep an eye open for monkeys, wild boar and small 'barking' deer. And keep a very wary eye open for snakes; at least two highly venomous

Taking in the view, Doi Suthep National Park

species—the pit viper and Russell's viper—have made their home on the mountain. Pythons also lurk in the thick brush. If you encounter a 'crocodile salamander,' however, don't be alarmed—they're harmless. Doi Suthep is one of only four locations in Thailand where they are found. The forest teems with birdlife; among the 300 varieties found on Doi Suthep and Doi Pui mountain are pheasants, jungle fowl and parrots. If you're very lucky you might catch a glimpse of an eagle soaring above the mountainside.

About 2km (1.2 miles) from Namtok Monthatarn, another waterfall, Namthok Sai Yai, comes into view.

3 Namthok Sai Yai is another of the mountain's many beautiful waterfalls, and offers an opportunity to cool off before tackling the steepest part of the hike.

A few hundred meters beyond the falls, the trail meets a dirt road skirting the mountaintop. Turn left and follow it for 300m (333 yards) before rejoining the signposted path to the Doi Suthep and Doi Pui National Park headquarters. Shortly after re-entering the forest, watch out for a small white *chedi* (pagoda) on your left. It's one of the mountain's mysteries—no one knows how old it is or who placed it here. Another few hundred meters farther on

OUT AND ABOUT

stands a venerable old fig tree, perhaps the only one this deep in the forest.

❹ The fig tree signals the approach of the National Park headquarters, where a welcome rest and refreshment await you at a simple outdoor restaurant (daily 9–5).

The trail has skirted the hike's goal, Wat Phra That Doi Suthep, which lies through the forest to the left of the National Park headquarters. Head for the park exit, turn left on the paved road and follow it for 1km (0.6 mile).

❺ The fairground-like bustle around the entrance to the temple is a stark contrast to the peace you've experienced on the mountain hike here, but there's no alternative to plunging into the crowds thronging the temple grounds.

There is, however, an alternative to the final stage of the hike, the broad flight of 300 steps that leads up to the main temple compound. A funicular railway now makes that part of the journey easy, and visitors who have braved the 8km (5-mile) hike to get to the temple can be excused for giving in and buying a B20 ticket to ride it.

❻ Red *songthaews* wait at the bottom of the funicular to take visitors the 12km (7 miles) back down the mountain to Chiang Mai.

WHEN TO GO
The best time to tackle this hike is early in the morning, to avoid the midday sun. But even if the journey does get hot, there are waterfalls and wayside pools in which to cool off.

PLACE TO VISIT
Wat Phra That Doi Suthep
🕐 Daily 8–6
💰 Adult B40, child (under 14) B20

TOURIST INFORMATION
Chiang Mai Tourist Office
TAT Northern Office, Region 1, 105/1 Chiang Mai-Lamphun Road, Amphoe Muang, Chiang Mai 50000
Tel 053 248 604 and 053 248 607
🕐 Daily 9–5

Bronze bell at Wat Phra That

The Naga staircase at the temple

A monk in traditional robes at Wat Phra That

THE SLOW BOAT TO AYUTTHAYA

Thailand's former capital and now a World Heritage Site, Ayutthaya is less than one hour's drive from Bangkok on motorway number 1, but travelers with the time (and money) can make the journey the way the Siamese did centuries ago, by riverboat.

THE CRUISE

Distance: 140km (84 miles)	
Allow: 3 days	
Start/end at: Bangkok	

HOW TO GET THERE

Day trips are offered by Bangkok operators, but the most unforgettable journey to and from Ayutthaya is on one of the two luxuriously converted rice barges of Manohra Cruises (www.manohracruises.com). These 100-year-old barges are built of solid teak—from the fat, squat hull to the finely polished decks and feature paneling—with later mahogany and padua wood additions. They are the last word in luxury. Admission to attractions en route is included in the barge fare (approx. US$2,000 per night).

DAY ONE

★ The voyage begins at the Manohra Cruises Chao Phraya river pier, in front of the riverside Marriott Resort and Spa. A steward welcomes you aboard with a fruit cocktail and then shows you to your stateroom, a snug but roomy, luxuriously appointed teak-walled and floored cabin with private bathroom and a river view.

❶ En route to Ayutthaya the barge takes in Bangkok's leading riverside sights, including the Grand Palace ensemble and Wat Arun (the Temple of Dawn). A stop is also made at the Royal Barges Museum, where the King's own barge is kept.

The barge cruises its way past lines of authentic rice barges battling upriver at walking pace behind tiny tugs. Longtail skiffs and outboard dinghies skip from side to side of the busy river. Lunch is served on the open-sided dining deck as the barge leaves central Bangkok behind and heads into the hinterland of Nonthaburi province, past timber-built riverside homesteads and farms, each with their own pier and flat-bottomed boat.

Fine dining on a Manohra cruise

❷ At the first bend in the river, the barge passes the island of Kret, home to a community of ethnic Mon people famous for their pottery kilns.

At 4pm, traditional tea is served on the rear deck: dainty sandwiches, scones and patisserie, accompanied by a choice of teas, some of them from Thai estates.

After tea, a stop is made at Wat Pathum Khon Ka to feed the fish there. This is a traditional merit-making act that is meant to assure travelers of a trouble-free journey, not just to Ayutthaya but throughout life.

❸ The barge ties up for the night a few miles north at Wat Bang Na. This 18th-century temple is famous for its mummified body of an abbot who died in 1988. His perfectly preserved body rests in a glass coffin.

Later, sundowner cocktails are served on the barge, and dinner is served against the beautiful backdrop of the illuminated temple.

DAY TWO

Passengers are taken on a pre-breakfast visit to Wat Bang Na.

❹ At the temple, passengers fill the eating bowls of the monks as they set out on their alms rounds—another merit-making act that helps Thais on their way to nirvana.

As the barge heads nearer Ayutthaya, an Italian lunch is served as a reminder, perhaps, that the Siamese capital was open to all aspects of Western culture, from food to architecture.

❺ The first Ayutthaya stop is Wat Panan Choeng, a 14th-century temple that stood here before the capital was founded. The stucco-covered Buddha in the temple's *viharn* is one of Thailand's oldest.

A stretch limousine picks passengers up for the drive into Ayutthaya and a tour of its ancient monuments and temples. Part of the tour can be made riding on an elephant. After the tour, the limousine carries passengers back to the barge, which is now moored at another temple, Wat Niwet Thamaprawat.

❻ Wat Niwet Thamaprawat is part of the Bang-Pa-In palace ensemble, 18km (11 miles) south of Ayutthaya. The temple was built by King Rama V in European neo-Gothic

OUT AND ABOUT

style, complete with stained-glass windows.

Dinner, served on the barge, features a menu of traditional 'royal Ayutthaya' dishes.

DAY THREE
After a full English breakfast, passengers tour Bang-Pa-In.

7 Bang-Pa-In is an eclectic ensemble of imposing buildings, built on a river island as a summer retreat by Ayutthaya's King Prasat Thong (ruled 1630–55). When the Burmese sacked Ayutthaya in the late 18th century, Bang-Pa-In fell into neglect and disuse, but King Rama IV restored much of it 80 years later. His successors Rama V

and Rama VI carried on his work, adding a collection of royal mansions and pavilions unmatched in Thailand.

The barge now heads back to Bangkok, riding on the swift downriver current, calling at the Royal Folk Arts and Crafts Center at Bang Sai, an hour or so downstream (▷ 205).

8 The center was established as a royal project to encourage farmers and their families to take up ancient crafts, such as basketry, silk weaving and dyeing, wood carving and carpentry. Products can be bought at the center's shop.

Lunch is served as the barge winds through the rice paddies

north of Bangkok, and tea is taken as the skyscrapers of the capital come into view. At 6.30pm, the barge ties up at the Manohra Cruises Chao Phraya river pier.

WHEN TO GO
The sunsets on the Chao Phraya river are one of the attractions of the cruise, and the best time of year to enjoy them is the dry season, from December to the end of February.

TOURIST INFORMATION
Ayutthaya Tourist Office
TAT Central Region 6, 108/22 Moo 4, Amphoe Phra Nakhon Si, Ayutthaya
Tel 035 246 076-7
🕐 Daily 8.30–4.30

A Manohra rice barge at Wat Arun

PHUKET TOWN TO KRABI

While Phuket island can sometimes seem too busy, the town of Krabi is characterized by an easygoing pace. A drive between the two takes in this change of tempo. The drive crosses three of Thailand's provinces, accesses the region's photogenic scenery and also takes you through a rural landscape of rubber and palm oil plantations where Thai Muslims live and work.

THE DRIVE	
Distance:	165km (102 miles)
Allow:	1 day
Start at:	Phuket town
End at:	Krabi

★ Phuket town (▷ 168–171), on the east side of Phuket island, is a workaday community quite different in character from the beach-based life of the island's west coast.

Follow signs out of Phuket town for Route 402, the main highway that will also be signposted to the airport. Go straight ahead at the set of traffic lights where the road to the left is signposted for Patong beach. Stay on Route 402, which leads to the large Heroines Monument roundabout, 10 km (6 miles) north of Phuket town.

❶ The Heroines Monument in the middle of the roundabout (traffic circle) commemorates the defeat of an invading army from Myanmar (Burma) in 1785 and the defiant leadership offered by two women who organized a female army and expelled the enemy.

Turn off to the right onto the signposted Route 4027 for the Gibbon Rehabilitation Center in Khao Phra Thaeo Wildlife Park (▷ 169).

❷ The Gibbon Rehabilitation Center is 2km (1.25 miles) down a signposted turning to the left off Route 4027. Visitors are introduced to the work of the volunteer-run center, helping gibbons rescued from captivity to return to forest life. Gibbons used to freely roam the forests of Phuket and were routinely kept as pets; although this is now illegal the animals remain endangered. A 15-minute walk along a riverside track from the center leads to the scenic Bang Pae Falls.

Continue on Route 4027, which rejoins Route 402 near the turn-off for the airport. Do not take the airport road but continue northwards on the 402, crossing the Sarasin Bridge and the empty beach on your left. After a few kilometers, bear right on the 402, signposted for Phang Nga, along a two-lane highway. Be careful here—slow down for the bends in the road. You are now in the province of Phang Nga.

❸ The province of Phang Nga, separating the provinces of Ranong and Phuket, is noted for its landscape of limestone mountains. Each rock formation rises up in dramatic isolation, though before you see these mountains a more characteristic sight is row

upon row of rubber trees laid out in straight lines with cups attached ready to collect the sap.

After passing through the village of Takua Thung, 10km (6 miles) before Phang Nga, look for a sign on the left pointing to Wat Tham Suwankhuha.

❹ Two caverns make up the temple cave of Wat Tham Suwankhuha, replete with Buddhist images and dominated by a large, awkwardly proportioned reclining Buddha.

Back on the main road, surrounded by an array of limestone peaks, note the right turn at the traffic lights, signposted for Krabi. For a lunch break, though, carry on straight at the traffic lights to enter the main street of Phang Nga town (▷ 166). After lunch, turn around and head back to the traffic lights to take the road to Krabi.

❺ The road to Krabi crosses a small bridge, with views of homes built on wooden platforms in the river, and five minutes later on your left you pass a golden Buddha figure sitting splendidly beneath a towering limestone peak.

When you see a signpost saying 5km (3 miles) to Thap Put take the next right turn onto a small road that runs through a palm oil plantation. This detour will take you through a seemingly endless vista of palm oil trees, a valuable cash crop in this part of the country. This road does eventually rejoin the main Krabi road, or you can return to Route 415 and continue via Thap Put.
   At Thap Put turn right to join Route 4, which leads to Krabi through a Muslim neighborhood and into the province of Krabi.

A resident of the Gibbon Rehabilitation Center

OUT AND ABOUT

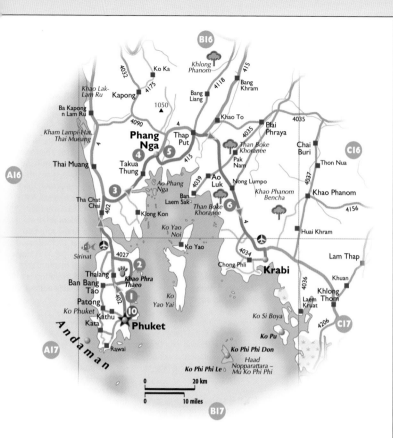

6 The mosque on the right-hand side of the road is evidence of the fact that many of the people living in this area are Muslims, but you will also see *wats* (temples). The province of Krabi, like Phang Nga, is characterized by a karst landscape, and it provides an engaging backdrop for the final leg of this journey to the town of Krabi.

WHERE TO EAT
Phang-Nga Inn
2/2 Soi Lohakit, Phang Nga
Tel 076 411 963
The town's smartest hotel, signposted in the middle of town, has a restaurant on the ground floor.
🕐 Restaurant daily 8–9

PLACE TO VISIT
Gibbon Rehabilitation Center
Bang Pae Wa, Phuket
Tel 076 260 491
www.gibbonproject.org
🕐 Daily 10–4
💰 Entrance to the national park B200

TOURIST INFORMATION
Phuket Town Tourist Office
75 Thanon Phuket
Tel 076 212 213

Krabi Tourist Office
Thanon Utrakit
Tel 075 622 163

Thick cover at a rubber tree plantation

PHUKET TOWN

This walk introduces you to the provincial capital of Phuket, its vernacular architecture, a small local museum and the everyday life of the townspeople. The walk also takes in a wide range of shops where you may be tempted to make a purchase. It will be a hot day, but comfort yourself with knowing that the walk ends at an ice cream parlor in an air-conditioned building.

THE WALK

Distance: 1.5km (1 mile)
Allow: Half an hour, plus time for visits
Start/end at: The fountain roundabout (traffic circle) where Thanon Ranong and Thanon Rasada meet

HOW TO GET THERE

From the east coast beaches, take a taxi or one of the *songthaews* that run regularly into town.

★ The fountain roundabout (traffic circle) can be considered the heart of the old part of town. Look for the street names in English on a blue background. Thanon Rasada is where the *songthaews* to the beaches depart from, but pinpoint the signposted Thanon Yaowarat that heads north.

Walk a short way up Thanon Yaowarat and take the first right turn, with an old-fashioned Chinese pharmacy on the corner, into Thanon Phang-Nga. Pass the On On Hotel (▷ 287) on your left and, before reaching a set of traffic lights, gaze upwards to observe the traditional shophouses along this street.

❶ Some of the shophouses are dilapidated and showing their age; they were built a century ago for Chinese shopkeepers in the economic heyday created by tin-mining on the island. A well-preserved example at No. 90—now the Le Dix clothes shop—is best seen from the left-hand side of the street.

At the traffic lights, turn left into Thanon Phuket and cross to the other side of the street to appreciate the building that is now the Siam City Bank.

❷ The Siam City Bank is a grander example of the kind of buildings constructed in the second half of the 19th century, when the island's capital was rebuilt here to

Robinson's department store

replace the old capital of Thalang, destroyed by the Burmese in 1800.

Walk along to the first crossroads and turn left, at the Honda store, into Thanon Thalang for a street full of fine examples of wooden shophouses built in the Sino-Portuguese style.

❸ The Sino-Portuguese style was brought to Phuket by Portuguese traders and Chinese merchants who were familiar with this architecture from the ex-Portuguese port of Melaka to the south of Thailand. The building style is characterized by shutters, louver windows and decorative carvings on the exterior in stucco and wood. Look for the engraved dragons that reveal the Chinese influence. No. 37, on the right-hand side, is now the Talang Guest House (▷ 287), a good example of how these buildings can be preserved into the 21st century without losing their character. Before reaching the guesthouse, a modern art gallery on the other side of the street is open for business, but Thanon Thalang is full of more traditional shops selling everyday goods and fabrics.

At the crossroads, where Thanon Thalang meets Thanon Yaowarat, turn left to return to the walk's start point but consider a spot of shopping before stopping for lunch.

❹ The Wood and Stone shop at No. 55 (▷ 216) Thanon Yaowarat, on the right-hand side of the street, is worth a browse for gifts. A few doors down at Rinda Magical Art (No. 27; ▷ 215), you may catch the resident artist at work. Close to the fountain roundabout, at 10 Thanon Rasada, Pui Fai (▷ 215) has a large selection of affordable arts and crafts. Here too is a lunch spot suitably named The Circle.

After lunch, walk down Thanon Rasada for an art shop and a small museum.

❺ The Soul of Asia shop (▷ 216) is on the left, and farther down on the right is the Thavorn Hotel and its lobby museum, with old photographs and memorabilia of the town's history.

Continue down the street to a roundabout and turn right onto Thanon Phuket, passing the tourist office on your left. At the clock roundabout, head down the street signposted Thanon Tikok Uthit to the end where there is a Boots pharmacy on the right. Walk straight across the crossroads here and head towards the green-and-white building of Robinson's department store.

❻ You will be surrounded by shops, with clothes stands spilling onto the pavement and the Robinson Ocean Plaza, with Robinson's department store and a cinema. Inside Robinson's, on the ground floor, rest from the heat in the ice cream parlor.

From here, either retrace your steps to the start point or take one of the many taxis or tuk-tuks waiting outside the shops.

OUT AND ABOUT

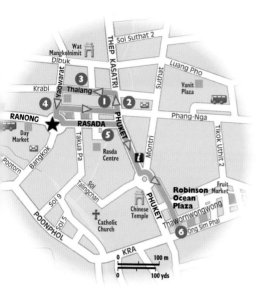

Corner of the Siam City
Bank building

WHERE TO EAT

The Circle
On the fountain roundabout, Phuket
Tel 010 912 187
Daily 8.30am–10pm

PLACE TO VISIT

**Thavorn Hotel Lobby
Museum**
74 Thanon Rasada
Tel 076 211 333
Daily 8am–10pm
B40

TOURIST INFORMATION

Phuket Town Tourist Office
75 Thanon Phuket
Tel 076 212 213
Daily 8.30–4.30

OUT AND ABOUT

A Portuguese-style house in Thanon Thalang

ORGANIZED TOURS

Guided trips and tours can help you explore Thailand, with the added bonus of local knowledge from English-speaking Thai guides. The trips below are all accompanied; the websites should be consulted for further details.

THAILAND

ASIAN OASIS

15th Floor, Regent House, 183 Thanon Rajdamri, Bangkok
Tel 026 519 101
www.asian-oasis.com

Bangkok to Ayutthaya in a restored rice barge and journeys around Chiang Rai featuring visits to villages and the observation of traditional rural life. A three-day/two-night tour to the Akha and Lisa hill tribes costs B17,000.

MEKONG TRAVEL

16 Ledborough Wood, Beaconsfield, Buckinghamshire HP9 2DJ, UK
Tel 01494 681631
www.mekong-travel.com

Adventure trekking, bicycling and diving tours. Tours to Khao Yai National Park, Kanchanaburi, Bangkok and Mae Hong Son. Mountains and Beaches tour and a nine-day trip around northern Thailand.

MORE THAILAND

333/88 Moo 6, Thanon Prachacheun, Tungsaongong, Bangkok
Tel 029 541 688
www.morethailand.com

Beach, cultural and sightseeing trips, "romantic" packages or spa holidays. Reserve online.

BANGKOK

BANGKOK'S SMILING TOURS

403/46 Thai-Asia Condo, Ramkhamhaeng 60/3 Road, Hua-Mark, Bangkapi
Tel 018 273 815
www.bangkoksmiling.com

Grand Palace, Canal, Temple and City and Bangkok by Night tours. Excursions to Kanchanaburi, Pattaya and Safari World.

REAL ASIA

10/5–7 Thanon Sukhumvit Soi 26
Tel 026 656 364, 018 129 641
www.realasia.net

"The Amazing Bangkok Cyclist tour" (▷ 190), a train tour that takes you to the small fishing village of Samut Sakhon, and Thai cookery courses. Some of the best Bangkok-based tours available.

THE NORTHEAST

KHAO YAI GARDEN LODGE AND WILDLIFE TOURS

Thanon Thanarat, Kilometer Stone 7, Pak Chong
Tel 044 365 167
www.khaoyai-garden-lodge.com

Half-day tours (B350) focus on local caves that are home to millions of bats—they fly out en masse at dusk. The full-day tour (B950) takes in a trek through the national park, a visit to a waterfall and a night safari. A one-day trek costs B1,200 and a day's bird-watching B1,300.

LAMAI HOMESTAY

Ko Phet, Bua Yai, near Nakhon Ratchatahni (Korat)
Tel 062 585 894
www.thailandhomestay.com

Trips to the Khmer ruins at Phimai and Phanom Rung. Also activity packages focusing on local crafts.

NORTH BY NORTHEAST TOUR

Mekong Grandview Hotel, 527 Thanon Sunthornvichit, Nakhon Phanom
Tel 042 513 564/70

Environmentally minded tours with a cultural focus such as the seven-day "Allure of the North." Also kayaking, trekking and wildlife tours, bird-spotting and visits to Khao Yai National Park and Phang Nga.

THE NORTH

ACTIVE THAILAND

73/7 Thanon Charoen Prathet, Chiang Mai
Tel 053 277 178
www.activethailand.com

Three- to five-day jungle treks as well as rafting, bicycling and kayaking. The main destinations are Chiang Mai, Chiang Rai, Lampong, Mae Hong Son and Mae Sot.

FOUR LENS

131/6 Moo 13, Sansai, Chiang Rai
Tel 053 700 617
www.fourlens.com

Tours lasting four or five days traveling by air and coach. A Mekong River tour is also available and a Songkram Festival trip.

WAYFARERS THAILAND

20 Thanon Tapae, Soi 4, Chiang Mai
Tel 053 208 271
www.wayfarersthailand.com

One-, two- and three-day treks and tours of Sukhothai and Mae Hong Son. Also day trips to an elephant camp, rafting, cookery classes and handicraft tours.

CENTRAL THAILAND

ASIA DISCOVERY

21 Thanon Silom, Bangkok
Tel 022 313 671–4
www.asia-discovery.com

Tours include a Heritage Tour based around Pitsanulok and Sukhothai using train travel. Also a range of activity tours—rafting, bicycling and treks around Chiang Mai. Lots of half-/full-day Bangkok tours are available; Pattaya is also covered.

THE SOUTH

SEA CANOE THAILAND

367/4 Thanon Yaowarat, Phuket Town
Tel 076 212 172
164/8 Moo 2, Ao Nang, Krabi
Tel 075 695 387
www.seacanoe.net

Sea-kayaking trips in southern Thailand, using their own boats and canoes.

SIAM SAFARI

45 Thanon Chao Far, Chalong, Phuket
Tel 076 280 116
www.siamsafari.com

Tours from Phuket, Krabi and Ko Samui, including nature and jungle tours and a one-day Phuket 4WD adventure that includes a visit to an elephant camp.

OUT AND ABOUT

This chapter lists places to eat and stay, broken down by region, then alphabetically by town or area. Entries in the Bangkok section are listed alphabetically.

Eating and Staying

THAI CUISINE

Bangkok and other big cities in Thailand have their share of restaurants serving international cuisine, fast food joints and trendy Asian fusion places. However, better than this, almost every small town has roadside stands, cafés and restaurants serving freshly made, delicious regional dishes as well as the old favourites of *tom yam*, green curry and fried rice.

Oysters and other seafood are specialties at Glow restaurant in Bangkok (middle)

CURRENT TRENDS

The two eating capitals of Thailand are Bangkok and Chiang Mai, but there are surprises to be had all over the country. Thai cafés and restaurants abound, but there are also the big chains more familiar in the West as well as places serving European cuisine and American-style steakhouses. You don't have to try unusual food if you choose, but the range and variety of cuisines is one of the joys of eating in Thailand. South Indian vegetarian venues are dotted around as are Indian Muslim venues serving *roti* and chicken *biryani*. Chinese food is also well represented and is strongly influenced by Thai elements. Vietnamese food finds a presence in the northeast. Thai food ranges from noodle-based dishes to curry, fried rice, salads and soup.

PRICING

Inexpensive restaurants charge around B60 for a main course, while slightly more upmarket places can charge up to B150 and more. Classy hotel restaurants can charge prices equal to those in similar restaurants in Europe. Service charges only appear in the more expensive restaurants. Street stands are inexpensive and well worth a try for little snacks. Tipping is not necessary where there isn't a service charge but is very welcome.

FRESHNESS

Many of the best and cheapest places to eat, where you will sit down in a real Thai atmosphere and be among Thai people, are the market stands and small, primitive-looking cafés. Most Thai dishes are cooked in minutes and use fresh ingredients picked or slaughtered not too far away from where you are actually eating so freshness of food is rarely a consideration.

Hygiene should never be ignored, though, and you should always check that meat and fish are fully cooked. Also make sure that your own hands are washed carefully before eating, and that your choice of venue is full of happy, healthy-looking customers. If you have a delicate digestive system, work your way up to full-on chili-and-ginger-laden curries and avoid too much exotic fruit at first. Buy unpeeled fruit and peel it yourself. Bottled water is best and avoid salads and homemade ice-cream in risky places.

THAI REGIONAL CUISINES

Thai food is a mixture of indigenous cooking fused with some Chinese and Indian styles. It can be chili fueled or quite bland, depending on the origin of the dish and the region of the country. It typically uses ginger, and galangal, two very similar roots which are chopped and used for flavoring. Galangal in particular gives it that special Thai taste. Coconut thickens the sauce and adds its own rich taste to the blend, while lime leaves, fresh cilantro (coriander) leaves, Thai basil and whole fresh peppercorns usually end up in there too. Lemongrass, chopped or ground, is another essential ingredient. Other ingredients include peanuts for thickening, tiny pea-size eggplants, *nam pla* or fish sauce made from anchovies and occasionally tamarind to add a tangy taste, such as that in *tom yam* soup (▷ 244).

Beyond the typical Thai dishes there are regional variations. Northern Thailand has dishes that are closely akin to those of Myanmar (Burma). Noodles, both fried and boiled, are common, and sticky or glutinous rice is more widely used, primarily because it grows better there. To the south of Thailand, Malay cuisine begins to influence and green curry sauce gives way to Panang curry where cilantro (coriander) root replaces fresh herbs, and peanuts are used to thicken the sauce. Satay—barbecued meats on skewers served with spicy peanut sauce—ubiquitous in Malaysia, is common.

Thai desserts are not desserts as the West have come to know them. Real Thai restaurants tend not to serve them, and the posh ones keep them as a sop to our sugar-fueled palates. Cakes, which can be bought on the street, are often made with sticky rice and coconut cream and bear the hues of pandanus leaves or some other food. Pancakes are made from rice flour and

and the fork used to get the food onto the spoon. Most food is in tiny bite-size pieces so a knife is not necessary. Noodle dishes require chopsticks, and Chinese restaurants always provide them. You can hold your bowl up close to your mouth in your other hand. If you aren't comfortable with chopsticks, no one minds providing a fork and spoon. If you are eating with a group then each person will get their own bowl of rice, while the shared food is brought out in big dishes. Take a little from one dish and then refill. Don't stack up a whole meal at once. Sticky rice and Indian food is often served

So many places to try in Bangkok: Vertigo (left), White Elephant (middle) and Celadon (right)

coconut milk, rolled up around fresh fruit and sprinkled with palm sugar and dried coconut flakes. Look out for coconut custard, often served with fresh lychees or banana, *met kanun* or "jackfruit seeds" (nothing to do with actual jackfruit)—split yellow lentils made into donuts and glazed with syrup, or tapioca and coconut, much nicer than the tapioca that older Brits will remember from school dinners. Fried bananas are everywhere, as is sticky rice served with mangoes.

VEGETARIAN OPTIONS
The more religious Buddhists like to spend at least one day a week being vegan and there are dedicated restaurants serving all kinds of vegetarian food. The trouble is spotting them since they are often run by monks close to a temple and unadvertised. Their name is *raan ahaan jeh*, but this may not help if the words are in Thai. Try asking around.

Tourist areas are aware of the vegetarian market among their *farang* visitors and often have a veggie element to their menus. Most places can take out the meat if you ask them, and since a Thai meal is generally made up of a plate of rice and lots of other side dishes you can easily pick the meat-free ones. Vegetarian fried rice is negotiable in most places, and even vegans can arrive at an arrangement with hand waving, the expression *mai sai* (without) and pointing. The glory of regular Thai cafés and restaurants is that the food is cooked as you order it, so you can choose what goes into it. Cheese and cow's milk are rarely part of Thai cuisine.

EATING ETIQUETTE
Thai food is usually eaten with a spoon and fork, the spoon making the journey to your mouth

without utensils and eaten with the right hand, never the left. Again, if you're not happy ask for a spoon and fork.

STRANGE FRUIT
Custard apples or soursop are round, brownish scaly-skinned fruit with creamy flesh which tastes a little like spicy pears. Durian *(turian)*, the gigantic hedgehog-like fruit, is a definite acquired taste—a little like garlic-flavored custard. It has a distinctive gas-leak smell and is often banned in hotel rooms and on public transport. Thais love it and will spend ages choosing their fruit to get the right degree of softness. Jackfruit *(khanun)* is a spiky fruit whose flesh is like less odorous durian.

Mangosteen *(mang khud)* is like a cross between an eggplant (aubergine) and an apple, with purple skin which breaks into five sweet segments with a bit of a bite to them. Papaya *(malakho)* is better known in the West. Ripe papaya is soft with orange flesh and makes excellent milkshakes. It mixes well with melon and pineapple in many a Thai breakfast. Pomelo *(som-o)* is like a large greenish orange with a sharp taste. Its flesh is less juicy than oranges.

Rambutan *(ngo)* and lychees *(linchi)* are very similar fruits, rambutan being the hairy version. The flesh around the stone inside is very sweet and juicy, nothing at all like the tinned version. They have a short season and don't keep well.

Star fruit *(mafueng)*, shaped like an elongated star, is pale green and tastes very much like a sweeter version of pea pods.

Dragon fruit is not in evidence so much. This shockingly bright cerise, oval scaly fruit, about the size of an elongated tennis ball, has seed-filled flesh which is worth an experimental taste.

In popular destinations menus will come in English but it is a good idea to learn a few basic words in Thai. Spellings of course vary; curry is spelled *gaeng* or *kaeng*, and *popiah* (large spring rolls) sometimes appear as *bapia, paw* or *pia* and so on. If you don't eat some items, learn the expression *mai sai*—"without." Boiled or filtered water is *nam piao*. Condiments are generally on the table, but salt is *kleua* and sugar is *nam tan*.

Try Thai at Celadon (left), or Vietnamese at Saigon in Khon Kaen (middle and right)

Basics
Gai chicken
Muu pork
Neua beef (or generally, meat)
Ahaan ta-lay seafood
Plaa fish
Puu crab
Kung prawns
Kai egg
Kwey teeyo assorted types of rice noodles
Ba-mee (krawp) egg noodles (fried)

Kao rice
Kao neeyo sticky rice
Tahu tofu

Soup
Gaeng jeut curry soup with meat, usually pork, and vegetables
Tom kar gai chicken soup with coconut
Tom yam kung hot-and-sour soup with prawns

Rice dishes
Kao gaeng curry and rice
Kao pat gai/muu/kung fried rice with chicken/pork/prawns
Kao pat sapporot pineapple fried rice
Kao suay steamed rice

Noodle dishes
Ba mil haeng egg noodles fried with egg, meat and vegetables
Kow soi Chiang Mai fried noodles
Kway thiaw mil nam rice noodles in a soup of chicken broth
Kway thiaw rat na rice noodles in thick sauce with vegetables
Pat thai flour noodles cooked with assorted meat and vegetables, bean sprouts and occasionally tofu

The above dishes can be made with either rice noodles (*kway thiaw*) or egg noodles (*ba mil*).

Curry
Gaeng keeyo waan green curry
Gaeng Mussaman Muslim beef and potato curry
Gaeng pet red (in colour but also hot) curry
Gaeng pet gai/neua spicy chicken/beef curry
Gaeng phaneng regular chicken/beef curry

EATING

Meat dishes

Gai tua chicken in peanut sauce
Gai pat bai kraprao fried chicken with basil leaves
Gai pat naw mai chicken with bamboo shoots
Gai yang garlic chicken
Muu preeyo waan sweet-and-sour pork
Neua pat gratiam prik thai beef with garlic and pepper

Phrik chili
Phrik yuak peppers
Taeng kwaa cucumber
Tua lentils (or peas or beans)
Tua ngawk bean sprouts

Phom kin ahaan jay I am a vegetarian (man)
Di-chan kin ahaan jay I am a vegetarian (woman)
Mai sai without (add word for meat/egg)

Kao neeyo mamuang sticky rice with mango
Met kanun sweet glazed lentil dumplings
Sungkeeya fuk tawng steamed custard in pumpkin shell
Sungkeeya maprow on coconut cream custard

Drinks

Bia beer
Chaa tea

A real feast at Sirocco (above and below)

Neua pat naam man hoy beef in oyster sauce
si klok pork and crab sausage

Egg dishes

Kai yat sai omelet stuffed with pork and/or vegetables

Fish dishes

Plaa neung pae sa steamed fish with ginger and vegetables
Plaa pao grilled fish
Plaa preeyo waan whole fish fried with lots of ginger
Plaa rat phrik whole fish cooked with chilies
Tord man plaa fishcakes

Salads

Som tam very spicy salad of green papaya and tomatoes
Yam tang kwa cucumber salad

Vegetable dishes

Pak put ruam mit stir-fried mixed vegetables
Tahu sod sai stuffed soy bean cake

Vegetables

Grathiam garlic
Makeua eggplant (aubergine)
Mekeua thet tomato
Mun farang (tord) potatoes (chips/french fries)
Naw mai bamboo shoots
Pak vegetables
Pat pak lai yang stir-fried veg

Fruit

See page 243.

Desserts

Gluay buat chee bananas in sweet coconut sauce
Gluay kak banana fritters
Kanom beung pancakes stuffed with coconut cream and egg

Chaa rawn hot tea
Chaa yen iced tea
Gluay pun banana shake
Kaafe coffee
Naam kaeng ice
Naam manao lime juice
Naam plao drinking water
Naam som orange juice
Naam yen cold water
Ohliang iced coffee

BANGKOK

There are thousands of places to eat in Bangkok, but the areas with the greatest concentration of quality restaurants with menus in English are to be found around Thanon Sukhumvit and Thanon Silom. Many of the best quality restaurants, especially ones serving non-Thai cuisine, are to be found in hotels, while the best-value places to eat are to be found in food centers and on street stands. In and around Thanon Khao San in Banglamphu there are also inexpensive places to enjoy good food. Eating in shopping areas like Siam Square and the MBK center is best served by food centers, like the Food Loft in Central Chidlom. When it comes to dining out at night, there is a wealth of fine restaurants where a superb meal can be enjoyed.

PRICES AND SYMBOLS

The restaurants are listed alphabetically (excluding Le, La and Les). The prices given for a two-course lunch (L) and a three-course dinner (D) are for one person, without drinks. The wine price is for the least expensive bottle.
For a key to the symbols, ▷ 2.

ANGELINI
Shangri-La Hotel, 89 Soi Wat Suan Plu
Tel 022 369 952
One of the best Italian restaurants in Bangkok, with a chef from north Italy, where the signature dishes include crab cakes with caviar, braised lamb, and a fantastic chocolate soufflé. It is not, though, a quiet or romantic place to dine—the open three-story design, the live band and the open kitchen can add up to a noisy atmosphere.

Daily 11.30–2.30, 6–11
L B700, D B1,500–B2,000, Wine B1,200
Saphan Taksin
Central Pier

AUBEGE DAB
1st Level, Mercury Tower, 540 Thanon Ploenchit
Tel 026 586 222
The style is that of a Paris eatery, with spotless white table cloths, an air of intimacy and waiters hovering in the background. The food aspires to be French, with starters like pan-fried duck liver, though the lamb is imported from Australia. A two-person band plays gentle music from 7.30 each night.

Daily 11.30–2.30, 6.30–10.30
L B400, D B1,500, Wine B1,250
Chit Lom

BISCOTTI
Four Seasons Hotel, 155 Thanon Rajdamri
Tel 022 501 000

An open kitchen by the entrance helps create the informal atmosphere where diners can linger and enjoy the good food; not the place for a quiet romantic meal. Italian menu with pizza and pasta, of course, but also tender beef and lamb dishes and fish like John Dory. Italian wine list.

Daily 12–2.30, 6–10.30
L B580, D B1,000, Wine B1,450
Rajadamri

LA BOULANGE
2–2/1 Thanon Convent
Tel 026 310 355
A cheerful place offering air-conditioned comfort and quiet after a hectic shopping session. Look for house specials on the blackboard and expect to find roasted chicken, steak tartare and smoked ham. Tables indoors and out on the street. Busy at lunchtime.

Daily 7–2.30, 6.30–10
L B300, D B400, Wine B720
Sala Daeng

CELADON

The Sukhothai, 13/3 Thanon South
Sathorn
Tel 023 448 888
www.sukhothai.com
A lovely setting, surrounded by
lotus ponds, and an
uncluttered style to the
restaurant. Appetizers include
mussels steamed with herbs,
and the spicy ones like shrimp
cakes and pickled vegetables
go well with a frozen
margarita. There are varieties
of salads and curries, excellent
seafood choices, including
grilled lobster, vegetables like
shitake mushrooms and bean
curd salad with roasted rice.
The menu covers some
regional specialties from the
north, like spicy sausages with
herbs, and minced pork with
yellow curry from the south.
Set menus for B900 and
B1,200, and a vegetarian one
for B800, serve as a good
introduction to fine Thai food.
🕐 Daily 11.30–2.30, 6.30–10.30
🍴 L B600, D B1,000, Wine B1,450
🚇 Sala Daeng
🌳 Lumphini Park

COCA SUKI

10 Thanon Henry Dunant
Tel 022 516 337
Look for the conspicuous
Central Investigation Unit
building on Thanon Henry
Dunant, and Coco Suki is
facing it on the other side of
the road. A restaurant for the
culinary adventurer, it
specializes in a form of "hot
pot" cooking from northern
China. You choose a
combination of meat, seafood
and vegetables from the
illustrated menu and they are
cooked in a chicken broth.
Choose noodles or rice to
accompany the meal; the
alcoholic drinks are beer and
Chinese saki.
🕐 Daily 11–11
🍴 L B200, D B250
🚇 Siam, take exit 6 and walk along the
elevated walkway to the first set of steps,
leading down to Thanon Henry Dunant;
the restaurant is up on the right

LE DANANG

Sofitel Central Plaza, 1695 Thanon
Phaholyothyhin
Tel 025 411 234, ext. 4041
Vietnamese dishes created by
a Hanoi chef with specialties
like snow fish in tamarind
soup, and smoked duck and
foie gras. Superb dishes
include sautéed prawns in
orange sauce, sea bass in lime
juice and spring rolls filled
with smoked salmon and
herbs. A band plays old
favorites and on Friday nights
there is time for dancing.
🕐 Daily 11.30–2.30, 6–10.30
🍴 L B300, D B400, Wine B1,000
🚇 Mo Chit
🌳 Chatuchak Park

*Angelini restaurant at the
Shangri-La Hotel*

DOSA KING

265/1 Thanon Sukhumvit, Soi 19
Tel 026 511 651/2
Dosa, thin crêpes made from
lentil and rice batter, is the
basis for the vegetarian meals
at this inexpensive eatery off
Thanon Sukhumvit. The
restaurant, brightly lit and easy
to spot from the main street, is
not large but split with a spiral
staircase over two floors.
🕐 Daily 11–11
🍴 L B250, D B350
🚇 Asoke

FOGO VIVO

Ground Level, President Tower Arcade,
973 Thanon Ploenchit
Tel 026 560 384
www.fogovivo.com
The entrance to this carnivore's
heaven, a Brazilian
churrascaria, is next to the
Holiday Inn, and it leads to a
stylish drinks area where a
cigar menu is made available.
A glass stairway leads down to
the dining area and a
sumptuous, eat-all-you-want
buffet of appetizers, salads and
an array of meat and fish that
is being continually grilled in
the open kitchen.
🕐 Daily 11–11
🍴 L B500, D B1,000, Wine B1,000
🚇 Chit Lom

FOOD LOFT

7th Level, Central Chidlom, Thanon
Ploenchit
Tel 026 557 777
For the top story of a huge
department store, this is
positively elegant dining, with
a cool lounge area to enjoy
drinks. Collect a bar-coded
card at the entrance and use it
to choose dishes from a
variety of outlets. Vegetarians
can enjoy meals from the
Indian outlet or try the *laksa* at
the Old Malayan stand.
🕐 Daily 9–10
🍴 L B200, D B250
🚇 Chit Lom

GALLERY ELEVEN

Sukhumvit Soi 11
Tel 026 512 672
An enchanting little eatery,
Gallery Eleven is an oasis of
calm that makes you feel like
you're in rural Thailand. To find
Gallery Eleven, keep on the
left walking down Sukhumvit
Soi 11 and turn left by the
7-11 store opposite the
Ambassador Hotel. The menu
has plenty of Thai appetizers
and traditional dishes. Check
out the mobile bar serving
superb cocktails.
🕐 Daily 9.30–11, 11–1
🍴 L B200, D B300, Cocktails B95
🚇 Nana

EATING

GANJI
Nai Lert Park Hotel, 2 Thanon Withayu
Tel 022 530 123

With comforting views of the hotel's placid gardens, this Japanese restaurant has a sushi bar, two *tempanyaki* counters and a main dining area. The set meals provide a gratifying introduction to Japanese food—appetizers, sashimi or sushi, grilled meat, seafood or tempura, miso soup, *chawanmushi* (a custard) or salad, rice and dessert—and non-novices will not be disappointed either. The à la carte choices are expensive.
Ⓒ Daily 11.30–2, 6–10
Ⓦ L B400, D B650–B850, Wine B1,500
Ⓢ Phloen Chit

GLOW
The Metropolitan, 27 Thanon South Sathorn
Tel 026 253 366

The tone is set upon arrival when you receive a cup of mulberry tea with jasmine. The set lunch offers a choice of one dish and one juice from the menu. The food is organic, created by Chef Amanda Gale, and features raw tuna, spirulina noodles with a sea vegetable salad, or a salad of asparagus, fennel and avocado or tiger prawns grilled with a sesame and tamarind dressing. The same menu is the à la carte one at night. Organic wine, vodka and gin, and desserts like whole wheat pumpkin cake with nutmeg and yogurt.
Ⓒ Daily 11–9
Ⓦ L B400, D B600–B850, Wine B2,500
Ⓢ Sala Daeng

KEANG WANG
77 Thanon Naphralan
Tel 022 265 984

Curries, noodles, herbal coconut soup and prawns are on offer, as well as chicken wings to nibble as an appetizer and a host of one-plate dishes like stir-fried chicken, shrimp and basil. The food is not great, but after a couple of hours out in the open at the Grand Palace

the air-conditioning and convenient location may be enough to draw you in.
Ⓒ Daily 9.30–7
Ⓦ L B160, D B500–B1,000
Ⓢ Tha Chang

MAY KAIDEE'S VEGETARIAN RESTAURANT
123 Thanon Tanao, at the end of Thanon Khao San
Tel 091 373 173
www.maykaidee.com

A small but friendly place, easy to miss because it is tucked away down a lane, parallel to but behind Thanon Tanao. It is worth seeking out for inexpensive but tasty green curry, carrot salad, fried water

La Scala, one of the best Italian restaurants in Bangkok

spinach and other vegetarian delights. The best dessert is the black sticky rice with coconut milk, banana and mango.
Ⓒ Daily 9–11
Ⓦ L B60, D B150
Ⓢ N13 New World Lodge

NIPA THAI
The Landmark, 138 Thanon Sukhumvit
Tel 022 540 404, ext. 4305
www.landmarkbangkok.com

Dimly lit interior with low ceiling, teakwood, polished floor, and live classical Thai music. Taste buds can be challenged by starting with the *koy kung* (hot-and-sour shrimp salad) or the *tom yam* soup—either goes well with the frozen martini—but the spiciness will

be toned down on request. Vegetarians, seafood or meat eaters will all have choices from the menu, and the signature dessert is lemongrass and ginger ice-cream. There is music nightly except Monday.
Ⓒ Daily 11.30–2.30, 6–10.30
Ⓦ L B250, D B390, Wine B1,000
Ⓢ Nana

LE NORMANDIE
The Oriental Hotel, 48 Thanon Oriental (off Thanon Charoen Krung)
Tel 026 599 000

Fine French dining at this very famous Bangkok restaurant, now benefiting from its consultant Guy Martin, chef of the Michelin three-star Le Grand Vefour in Paris. Reservations are essential to enjoy the chandelier-lit splendor. A jacket and tie are mandatory for men.
Ⓒ Mon–Sat 12–2.30, 7–10.30, Sun 7–10.30
Ⓦ L B4,100, D B6,100, Wine B2,500
Ⓢ Saphan Taksin
Ⓔ Oriental

N.P. FOOD CENTER
Off Thanon Ratchadamri

On the other side of the road to Central World Plaza, and looking north towards the Amari Watergate, turn right at the corner where the Aroma Hotel is situated. The entrance to the N.P. Food Center is down this side street on the right after 100m (110 yards). Popular with local office and shop workers, this is ideal for an inexpensive meal in air-conditioned comfort, and there is a wide choice of food stands and fresh fruit drinks. Vegetarians will be happy here as well.
Ⓒ Daily 10–8
Ⓦ L B100, D B150
Ⓢ Nana

LES NYMPHÉAS
4th Level, Imperial Queen's Park Hotel, 109 Thanon Sukhumvit Soi 22
Tel 022 619 000

Global inflections to modern French food at its best. The lunch menu has a choice of six

appetizers and five main courses, and any two courses are B440 (B540 with dessert). The evening menu includes Australian steak and dishes like sea bass with potato salad and citrus-basil sauce or snow fish with saffron. There is one romantic table that can be reserved on a balcony. Check out the life-size Monet paintings—everything can be copied in Bangkok.

🕒 Daily 11.30–2, 6–10
🍽 L from B420, D B1,000, Wine B1,500
🚇 Phrom Phong

LA SCALA
The Sukhothai, 13/3 Thanon South Sathorn
Tel 023 448 888
An open kitchen, muted atmosphere and dark wood and glass make this a restaurant for formal and informal meals. A large buffet is for lunch, while in the evening the menu overflows with pizza, pheasant, beef, pasta and other Italian choices. A popular restaurant that is regarded as one of the best places in Bangkok to enjoy Italian cuisine.

🕒 Daily 11.30–2.30, 6.30–10.30
🍽 L B780, D B600–B1,500, Wine B1,600
🚤 Sala Daeng
🚇 Lumphini

SIROCCO
63rd Level, State Tower, 1055 Thanon Silom
Tel 026 249 555
The tallest alfresco restaurant in the world is waiting for you when you press the button for the 63rd level in the elevator of State Tower. Watch your step when walking down into the balustraded dining area, as your attention will be distracted by the astonishing views of the city. The food, Mediterranean with Asian hints, is expensive, but the setting is tremendous. The Sky Bar (▷ 188–189), just a few steps away, beckons.

🕒 Daily 6–1
🍽 D B2,700, Wine B2,550
🚤 Saphan Taksin
🚢 Sathorn Pier
❓ Dress code: no sandals or shorts

THAI ON 4
Amari Watergate Hotel, 847 Thanon Petchburi, Pratunam
Tel 026 539 000
The jazzy decor distinguishes this swish restaurant, and the walls are decorated with non-figurative art rather than Buddha images and Thai objects. Staff are dressed smartly but anonymously, and the stylish approach is maintained with the artistic presentation of traditional Thai

High-rise dining on the terrace at Sirocco

cuisine with some modern flourishes.

🕒 Daily 11.30–2.30, 6.30–10.30
🍽 L B800, D B920, Wine B1,300
🚇 Phaya Thai

VEGETARIAN FOOD
3rd Level, United Centre, Thanon Silom
Tel 022 893 560
The vegetarian counter in this food center is at the top of the escalator. The usual system applies—buy coupons at the counter and return unused ones for reimbursement. Popular with local office workers; little is in English.

🕒 Daily 11–9
🍽 L B80, D B130
🚤 Sala Daeng

VERTIGO
61st Level, Banyan Tree Hotel, 21/100 Thanon South Sathorn
Tel 026 791 200
www.banyantree.com
"The highest alfresco city hotel restaurant in the world" is Vertigo's claim to fame and, indeed, it may be a hotel restaurant but certainly not a typical one when you are seated 61 stories high, out in the open air gazing down on the twinkling city lights. A tempting menu of grills and Mediterranean flavors, an especially appealing choice of steaks, alcoholic sorbets, a special mini-serving of five different desserts, and a very good wine list. Live music throughout the night.

🕒 Daily 6.30pm–midnight (last orders at 10.30)
🍽 D B2,000, Wine B1,600
🚤 Sala Daeng
🚇 Lumphini

VIMARN THAI
Windsor Suites Hotel, Sukhumvit Soi 20
Tel 022 621 234
On the 32nd story of the hotel, there are spectacular views and dancers fluttering around the tables (nightly 7–9pm). Deep-fried breaded prawns on a taro nest for starters and stir-fried chicken with cashew nuts mixed with dried chili are some of the terrific dishes.

🕒 Daily 6pm–10.30pm
🍽 D B600, Wine B1,000
🚤 Asoke

WHITE ELEPHANT
J W Marriott Hotel, Soi 2, Thanon Sukhumvit
Tel 026 567 700
The buffet lunch is good value and offers a safe introduction to the rich variety of Thai cuisine. At night, Thai music and dance change the atmosphere and there is a more sophisticated mood.

🕒 Daily 11.30–2.30, 6–10.30
🍽 L B465, D B900, Wine B1,500
🚤 Nana

EATING

THE NORTHEAST

One of the benefits of traveling in the northeast is that a meal, whether from a street stand or a quality restaurant, is always less expensive than in other parts of the country. This makes up for the fact that the number and variety of restaurants, especially ones with menus in English, is fewer. The cities of Isan—Khon Kaen, Udon Thani, Nakhon Ratchasima (Korat) and Ubon Ratchathani—all have excellent restaurants and although the emphasis is on Thai cuisine, there are notable exceptions, like the Vietnamese restaurants in Khon Kaen and Nong Khai and the Italian pizza places in Udon Thani. Regional specialties include sticky rice, which comes in its own basket and is dipped into sauces and eaten as an accompaniment to other dishes. Well worth tasting is the spiky papaya salad, *som tam*, useful for vegetarians and a tasty addition to most meals. Isan meat dishes are not to everyone's taste, although you should try some of the spicy sausages.

PRICES AND SYMBOLS

The restaurants are listed alphabetically by town or area, then by name. The prices given for a two-course lunch (L) and a three-course dinner (D) are for one person, without drinks. The wine price is for the least expensive bottle.
For a key to the symbols, ▷ 2.

KHAO YAI NATIONAL PARK

KHAO YAI FOOD CENTRE
Park Headquarters, Thanon Thanarat, Pak Chong
Tel 037 19002
This is the only place to eat in Khao Yai National Park (▷ 93) and the food center has over half a dozen outlets so there is some choice. The menus are similar, though, and not all the places are always open at the same time. The food is inexpensive and unexciting, mostly standard Thai dishes.
◎ Daily 7–8
🍷 L B120, D B150

KHON KAEN

FIRST CHOICE
18/8 Thanon Pimasoot, Khon Kaen
Tel 043 332 374
Not far from the tourist office, this is a bright and airy restaurant and easy to find on Thanon Pimasoot. Breakfasts consist of eggs, bacon and toast and yogurt. Shrimp cakes and bacon sandwiches and a choice of steaks, pizzas and salads. Vegetarians have a sweet-and-sour dish, a curry or omelets to choose from. A pleasant place for a meal or just a coffee.
◎ Daily 8–10
🍷 L B200, D B275

KAEN INN RESTAURANT
Kaen Inn Hotel, 56 Thanon Klangmuang, Khon Kaen
Tel 043 245 420
A comfortable and sociable hotel restaurant, brightly lit and popular with town residents as well as visitors. The Thai food is best enjoyed during the evening when live entertainment—songs in Thai and English—enlivens the atmosphere. The adjoining Wave Side pub is open from 7pm to 1am for pre- or post-dinner drinks.
◎ Daily 10–10
🍷 L B200, D B400

LOONG YUEN
Sofitel Raja Orchid Hotel, 9/9 Thanon Prachasumran, Khon Kaen
Tel 043 322 155
Not really suitable for single dining but two or more people can enjoy a feast of Chinese cooking at Loong Yuen. Roast

duck, deep-fried prawns, boneless chicken with a lemon sauce, and hot-and-sour soup are typical Cantonese dishes on the menu but there are some hotter Sichuan offerings. Authentic Chinese food and etiquette, with your teacup regularly replenished.

🕐 Daily 11.30–2.30, 6–10
🍴 L B400, D B450, Wine B1,350

NAMNUNGRAPLA

51 Thanon Klang Muang, Khon Kaen
Tel 043 236 296

Vietnamese-Thai food and plenty of dishes to choose from the pictorial menu that helps make sense of what is available—starters like shrimp and sugarcane rolls or papaya salad and main dishes like chicken cooked with herbs and pork grilled with spices. Air-conditioned and comfortable.

🕐 Daily 9–9.30
🍴 L B230, D B275

SAIGON

Sofitel Raja Orchid Hotel, 9/9 Thanon Prachasumran, Khon Kaen
Tel 043 322 155

Including Bangkok, this is one of the best places to enjoy authentic Vietnamese cuisine in Thailand; the chef is from Hanoi. The setting is a little public, on the second floor of the hotel, with indoor and outdoor tables. Appetizers include *bo & lon la lot* (beef and pork wrapped in leaves) and *cha gio* (spring rolls deep fried, filled with meat and vegetables), and *pho & chao canh* (a popular Vietnamese soup), roast chicken, stir-fried beef and steamed fish. Great value.

🕐 Daily 6–10
🍴 D B500, Wine B1,000

LOEI

BOTUN RESTAURANT

Loei Palace Hotel, 167/4 Thanon Charroenrat, Loei
Tel 042 815 668

The most comfortable place to enjoy local food in Loei

(▷ 96), and while the restaurant itself suffers from featureless decor, there is a good choice of seafood on the menu. Prices are very good value when compared with hotel restaurants of this kind. The *tom yam* soup with Mekong fish is suitably fiery and the sun-dried fish and mango salad is justifiably popular. Interesting Thai dishes like the omelet with Chinese mushrooms and minced pork. This, of course, is *the* place to drink Thailand's best attempt at wine-making, Chateau de Loei.

🕐 Daily 6–10
🍴 L B220, D B350, Wine B750

A warm welcome at Botun Restaurant

ICE CREAM PARLOUR

Thanon Charonrat, Loei

The best way to find this place, next to the bridge leading to the Loei Palace Hotel, is to walk down Thanon Charonrat from the middle of town to the Loei Vocational College. This modest parlor is wonderful for cooling down with an ice coffee, chocolate sundae or banana split.

🕐 Daily 10–6
🍴 B50

SOR AHARN THAI

Thanon Nok Kaew, Loei
Tel 042 813 436

This large Thai restaurant has tables indoors as well as outside ones under cover. The

English menu presents lots of choices, and there is more than one kind of *tom yam* soup to consider. Mixed seafood salads, curries, boar spicy soup, and sweet-and-sour dishes, all start at around B60.

🕐 Daily 10–11
🍴 L B100, D B200

NAKHON RATCHASIMA (KORAT)

VFW CAFÉ

686 Thaon Pho Klang, Korat
Tel 044 242 831

Close to the railway station and one block south of the Sripatana Hotel (▷ 276), the shabby-looking exterior of the VFW (Veterans of Foreign Wars) is next door to the Sri Hotel. The interior is equally unprepossessing and in need of a facelift, but the menu offers a welcoming selection of Western dishes for anyone needing a break from hot Thai food. A good place for a filling breakfast or brunch.

🕐 Daily 8–7
🍴 L B150, D B350

WAN VARN

101–107 Thanon Mahadthai, Korat
Tel 044 244 509

A short walk from the Thao Suranari shrine in the middle of the city, the dark wood interior offers a calm escape from the heat of the sun. There's an odd style to the place—antique clocks, pictures, posters, tennis rackets, a saxophone and other assorted objects fill the walls. The large menu of Thai dishes (not expensive) includes noodles, salads, stir-fries and seafood, as well as appetizers like spring rolls and grilled spare ribs.

🕐 Daily 10–10
🍴 L B140, D B250

EATING

NONG KHAI

DAENG NAEM–NUANG

1062/1 Thanon Rim Kong, Nong Khai
Tel 042 411 961

The place to enjoy Vietnamese food, even if the choices are limited, in the comfort of a bright and cheerful, air-conditioned restaurant. The specialty is *naem nuang*, which comes to you in the form of barbecued pork, vegetables and a peanut sauce and a set of thin rice sheets with which to roll up the mixture.

🕐 Daily 6–8
🍴 L B100, D B200

DANISH BAKER

Thanon Meechai, Nong Khai

A breakfast of camembert with bread and coffee, a meal anytime from a large Thai and Western menu and a small bar area with stools. On a good day, there is an affable café atmosphere that makes Danish Baker a place to linger with a drink and a book to read or to chat with a fellow traveler on their way to or from Laos. There are a couple of tables outside from which to watch the world go by.

🕐 Daily 9–9
🍴 L B100, D B200

MUT MEE

1111 Thanon Keawworut, Nong Khai
Tel 042 460 717

Tables under bamboo-thatch shade on the banks of the Mekong River provide an atmospheric scene for this popular eatery attached to the guesthouse of the same name. A curry is made fresh each day, and vegetarians have the option of a tofu version. House specials include *gai rat sors som* (chicken in orange), and wine is available by the glass. Breakfast is served, and for a light lunch there are half-baguettes.

🕐 Daily 7.30–9.30
🍴 L B100, D B150

PANTAWEE THAI RESTAURANT

1049 Thanon Haisoke, Nong Khai
Tel 042 411 568

This place has bright lights, whatever the time of day or night, and a pictorial menu to guide you through the options, which include sweet-and-sour papaya salad with deep-fried fish, beef steak with bacon and mushroom sauce, Japanese food and deep-fried oysters. For lunch there are lighter choices like burgers, shrimps and cheese with toast, spicy and sour tuna salad, and pizzas. There's live music at night, a large drinks list, desserts and banana splits. Internet use is

Watch the world go by on the Pantawee Thai terrace

over your shoulder in the lobby of the hotel.

🕐 Daily 24 hours
🍴 L B150, D B250, Wine B750

STEAK HOUSE

403 Thanon Meechai, Nong Khai
Tel 042 460 164

Next to the Sawasdee Guest House (▷ 276), this is a quintessential Thai–Chinese restaurant with swirling fans, tiled floor and tables facing the street and looking across to a Chinese-style temple. Pepper steaks, tempura salad, fish with ginger, omelets and lots of Thai rice dishes make this place more than a steakhouse.

🕐 Daily 8–7
🍴 L B100, D B200

SWEET ORCHID RESTAURANT

550 Thanon Meechai, Nong Khai
Tel 042 460 671

You will pass this restaurant on the Nong Khai walk (▷ 224–225) and it may serve well as a place for a drink and some "Farang Food" as the menu puts it. Specialties include *gaeng Penang gai* (a chicken curry with a Malaysian accent) and *gung chup pang thawt* (fried prawns in batter). Waffles with ice-cream are on the dessert menu. No air-con but fans will keep you cool.

🕐 Daily 10–7
🍴 L B150, D B200

WAN CHING RESTAURANT

120 Thanon Haisoke, Nong Khai
Tel 042 412 558

The Pantawee Hotel (▷ 276) is directly opposite and, although the hotel restaurant would be most diners' first choice, the Wan Ching suggests itself as an alternative if you want a quieter place to eat. The air-conditioned interior is comfortable, but there are also tables outside. The menu consists solely of Thai dishes.

🕐 Daily 9–10
🍴 L B200, B400

PHIMAI

BANYAN TREE RESTAURANT

Sai Ngam, Phimai

Facing the banyan tree, 2km (1.2 mile) from the Khmer temple, this restaurant looks like a food center, but there is just one kitchen. The menu is not in English and little English is spoken so you must look around and point at some dishes that look interesting. Inexpensive but tasty food.

🕐 Daily 11–11
🍴 L B100, D B140

ROI ET

ONE-OH-ONE

220 Thanon Sunthornthep, Roi Et
Tel 043 514 070

This pizza restaurant looks across to the northwest corner

EATING

of the park and the back of the large walking Buddha. Burgers and sandwiches are always available for a light bite and pork and steak appear on the menu, but diners come here for the pizzas, wine by the glass, beers and highballs.

🕐 Daily 10.30–10
🍴 L B120, D B250

SURIN

WAI WAN RESTAURANT

44–46 Thanon Sanitnikhomrat, Surin
Tel 044 515 140

A congenial restaurant that is conveniently located in the centre of Surin; from the train station walk straight down Thanon Tannasarn, the main street heading into town, and Thanon Sanitnikhomrat is the second turning on the left (if you reach the roundabout—traffic circle—you have gone too far). The food is a mix of Thai and Western favourites, including steak and chips, and the service is friendly.

🕐 Daily 8–9
🍴 L B150, D B350

UBON RATCHATHANI

BOON NI YOM UTHAYAAN VEGETARIAN RESTAURANT

Thanon Sri Narong, Ubon Ratchathani

A large, barn-like structure, built entirely of wood, which is hard to miss on the corner of Thanon Sri Narong, though when closed it looks like it might be a country-and-western open-air pub. "Vegetarian Food" is the only sign in English. Leave your shoes by the steps, collect a plate and fill it with any of the food that has been freshly made. There are no appetizers or desserts, but you'll find water and fruit drinks in the cold cabinet. Help yourself and pay at the desk. Good food costing very little.

🕐 Tue–Sun 6am–2pm
🍴 L B20

CHIOKEE RESTAURANT

Thanon Khuenthani, Ubon Ratchathani
Tel 045 241 244

On the other side of the road to the tourist office, in the direction of the museum and just before the Ubon Hotel, this open-fronted little restaurant is always good for a breakfast of the eggs-with-ham-and-bacon kind, as well as sandwiches, soups, salads, curry, chicken with cashew nuts, vegetarian omelet and the usual rice and noodle dishes.

🕐 Daily 6–7
🍴 L B80, D B150

Indochine's upstairs restaurant is dark but spacious

IM AM

23 Thanon Pha Daeng, Ubon Ratchathani
Tel 045 261 897

Superb Isan dishes in this large, air-conditioned, no-smoking restaurant with a menu in English include appetizers like crab or prawn cocktail and oysters on ice. There are lots of Thai salads and curries—try the sour curry with king prawns or the *kang kug* red curry with meat and bamboo shoots. Chinese-style, stir-fried dishes and some steaks are also available, but come here for the fiery Thai food.

🕐 Daily 11–11
🍴 L B160, D B220

INDOCHINE

168–170 Thanon Saphasit, Ubon Ratchathani
Tel 045 245 584

A slightly strange-looking restaurant at night, with a bar and a singer downstairs and the restaurant overhead in a dimly lit but large room. Vietnamese spring rolls are on offer for starters, and grilled beef cooked in wild leaves is one of the popular house dishes. Good-value cocktails.

🕐 Daily 11–11
🍴 L B150, D B300, Wine B800

NICHA GARDEN HOUSE

120 Thanon Saphasit, Ubon Ratchathani
Tel 045 245 990

This modest place, a few doors down from the better-known Sincere restaurant (▷ 254), is recognizable at night by the white and blue neon Pepsi sign on the outside. There is no air-conditioning, but the indoor area has a fan or you can sit sidewalk-side in the evening time. The English menu, bizarrely decorated with an Irish cottage and a snake, features spicy salads, soups, charcoal-grilled fish, sweet-and-sour-chicken, and lots of prawn dishes. In the background there's music from the 1960s.

🕐 Daily 9.30am–11pm
🍴 L B80, D B150

SAKORN

70 Thanon Pha Daeng, Ubon Ratchathani
Tel 045 241 101

There is an English menu here, though very little English is spoken. Persevere, for the food is inexpensive but exceptional. The dining room facing the street has fans but there is also a room indoors with air-conditioning. Try the fried chicken with ginger and onions, or one of the green curries.

🕐 Daily 9.30–11
🍴 L B90, D B160

EATING

SINCERE

126 Thanon Saphasit, Ubon Ratchathani
Tel 045 245 061

A charming and intimate restaurant with a tiny bar, soft music and an appealing menu that includes lobster bisque, appetizers of salmon, snails and clams, a choice of steaks or a fish dish like baked sea bass, and desserts like crêpe Suzette. A French influence accounts for the rich sauces that come with the main meals.

🕒 Mon–Sat 11–11
🍴 L B300, D B1,000, Wine B900

UDON THANI

BELLA ITALIA

1st Level, Charoensri Complex, Thanon Prachak, Udon Thani
Tel 042 343 134

A traditional wood-fired oven delivers fresh and piping hot pizzas from mid-morning onwards. The pizzas and fresh bread are the best reasons for coming here, but there are also pasta meals and steaks imported from Australia. There's also a children's menu of fish fingers and chicken and french fries. The kitchen is spotlessly clean and there is a no-smoking dining room with air-conditioning which is elegant and comfortable. The other dining area has fans and live music from 7.30pm. Bella Italia's main entrance is outside the shopping mall, next to the Sofitel Raja Orchid Hotel.

🕒 Daily 11am–1am
🍴 L B350, D B450, Wine B900

COFFEE CORNER

277/42 opposite Charoensri Complex, Thanon Teekananon, Udon Thani
Tel 017 683 891

Iced cappuccino, latte frappe and fruit blends are good reasons to come to Coffee Corner. It's directly across from the ATM machines outside the Charoensri Complex (▷ 197), and it offers a quieter environment for a coffee or light meal than anywhere

inside the shopping mall itself. Sandwiches and salads are also available, which you can eat either indoors or outside on the sidewalk (pavement) but in the shade.

🕒 Daily 8.30–7.30
🍴 L B130, D B160

FOOD CENTER

3rd Level, Charoensri Complex, Thanon Prachak, Udon Thani
Tel 042 249 222

For a quick and inexpensive meal, the third level of the Charoensri Complex (▷ 197) is filled with food vendors and, although there is little in English, it is not difficult to make out the kind of meals

Pick up a snack at a stand in Udon Thani

being prepared. This is the place to watch a papaya salad being made from scratch. Purchase your coupons at the counter and return any unused ones afterwards for reimbursement.

🕒 Daily 10–7
🍴 L B80, D B120

KRUA TONG LUNCH BUFFET

Charoensri Grand Royal Hotel, 277/1 Thanon Prachak, Udon Thani
Tel 042 343 555

Come here, and come early, for the lunch buffet which is the best-value food spread in the city—sushi, sashimi, Japanese chicken burgers, fried catfish and chili *tom yam* soup, beef in paprika sauce,

fried squid, sea bass and Chinese plum, fish steaks, beef, chicken and pork. Live music in the evening and a menu of mostly Thai food but also some grills in the way of steak, spare ribs and pork chops. The fish deserves a recommendation, either the Mekong fish with a spicy sauce or the snake-head fish. Be sure to make advance reservations at weekends.

🕒 Daily 11–2, 6–11
🍴 L B180, D B300, Wine B500

MAE YA

79–83 Thanon Ratchaphatsadu, Udon Thani
Tel 042 223 889

Not far from the post office in Udon Thani is this modern, three-story and air-conditioned restaurant on the corner of the road. There are two menus to choose from: one for sundaes and other iced delights, the other for grills, burgers, lots of rice and fish dishes such as fried prawn with asparagus or fried serpent fish with leeks. This is a busy place but service is prompt.

🕒 Daily 10–7
🍴 L B130, D B160

VITTORIO PICCOLA ROMA

10/32 Thanon Posri, Udon Thani
Tel 042 327 546

This little Italian restaurant, tucked away in the north of town, brings to your table delicious pizza straight out of the wood-fired oven. It's a long way up Thanon Posri, past the Charoensri Palace Hotel (▷ 277), and too far to walk from the bus and train stations at the other end of town. It's best to take a tuk-tuk.

🕒 Daily 11–3, 5–10
🍴 L B500, D B600, Wine B700

EATING

THE NORTH

Northern Thailand has its own distinct cuisine—spicier and reputedly more imaginative than in other regions of the country. Neighboring Myanmar (Burma) and nearby China have had a very distinctive and positive influence on northern Thai cooking, with the Burmese introducing such delicious curries as *gaeng hang led* (pork and ginger) and the Chinese contributing traditional noodle dishes. One noodle specialty, *khao soy* (two varieties of noodle in a rich meat broth), is unique to the north and has become something of a fetish, spawning debate over its proper method of preparation and the best restaurants to try it. Curries in the north are distinctive because of the generous use of coconut milk used to thicken them. Crispy pork (*kaeb moo*), accompanied by spicy chili and tomato dips (*nam phrik* and *nam phrik ong*), spiced pork sausages (*saikrok*) and vegetarian dishes prepared with such exotic leaf vegetables as morning glory are also prominent on the menus of northern Thai restaurants. A note for wine drinkers: Many Thai restaurants do not stock wine but won't object if you bring your own, imposing just a small corkage charge (usually B50).

PRICES AND SYMBOLS

The restaurants are listed alphabetically by town or area, then by name. The prices given for a two-course lunch (L) and a three-course dinner (D) are for one person, without drinks. The wine price is for the least expensive bottle.
For a key to the symbols, ▷ 2.

BAN SOP RUAK

BORDER VIEW

Imperial Golden Triangle Resort, 222 Ban Sop Ruak (Ban Sop Ruak–Mai Sai road), Chiang Saen
Tel 053 784 001
On the edge of Ban Sop Ruak is a luxury hotel, the Imperial Golden Triangle, with this first-class restaurant. Its name is very apt, because from its broad terrace diners have a breathtaking view of the Mekong and the mountains of Myanmar and Laos. The Thai cuisine is excellent, and the fish comes from the Mekong.
🕒 Daily 6–11.30
🍷 L B180, D B300, Wine B1,500

CHIANG DAO

BAAN KRATING RESORT

63/3 Moo 10, Chiang Dao
Tel 019 520 067, 01 28 92 981
www.baankrating.com
The resort's open-air roadside restaurant, 63km (38 miles) north of Chiang Mai, is an attractive lunchtime stop on the way to Chiang Dao, Fang or Thaton. The resort is a four-star establishment, so its restaurant offers top-quality Thai cuisine. The seasoned chicken wrapped in *pandanus* leaves is a dream.
🕒 Daily 11–9
🍷 L B120, D B150, Wine B800

CHIANG DAO NEST MINI-RESORT

144/4 Moo 5, Chiang Dao
Tel 053 456 242, 060 171 985
www.nest.chiangdao.com
This restaurant has achieved national fame because of the extraordinary culinary skills of resident chef Wicha. Her menus feature such dishes as local buffalo steak in red wine sauce followed by hot chocolate soufflé. She makes her own bread and pasta and uses only locally grown vegetables. Many of her best customers drive from Chiang Mai, 65 km (39 miles) away.
🕒 Daily 11–10
🍷 L B180, D B400, Wine B800

CHIANG MAI

THE ANTIQUE HOUSE

71 Thanon Charoen Prathet, Chiang Mai
Tel 053 276 810

The suitably named Antique House, built in 1870, is one of Chiang Mai's few buildings under an official protection order. The timber-built house is cramped and the main dining area is in a relatively modern extension, but the setting is authentic Lanna. Classical string music is played in the evenings. The menu is also genuine northern Thailand—the pork and ginger curry *(hang led)* is especially recommended.

🕐 Sun–Sat 11am–midnight
🍽 L B200, D B240, Wine B500

GALAE

65 Thanon Suthep, Amphoe Muang, Chiang Mai
Tel 053 278 655

Be sure to arrive at this mountainside restaurant at sunset, then stroll around the outer edge of its centerpiece pond and watch the lights snap on in the city below. It's a spectacular introduction to a very special eating place, where you dine on one of several levels beneath towering yang trees. The Thai food is outstanding; try the pork ribs in a honey glaze or the *hang led* pork and ginger curry, full of lean meat in a peanut-laced gravy.

🕐 Daily 10–9
🍽 L B120, D B200

HUEN PHEN

112 Thanon Rachamanka, Chiang Mai
Tel 053 277 103

Phen's house *(huen* in northern Thai) is two restaurants in one, catering for two distinct classes of clientele. By day, the open-sided street-front dining area caters to a Thai lunchtime crowd with a simple, cheap menu. In the evening, the ancient, cluttered Lanna house at the rear opens up for a more stylish dining experience. The menu then is studded with northern Thai specialties such as delicious *sai uwa* sausage, *nam prik* sauce and *hang led* pork and ginger curry.

🕐 Daily 8.30–3, 5–10; closed last Mon in month
🍽 L B90, D B220, Wine B800

PASTA CAFÉ

21 Soi 5, Thanon Nimmanhaemin, Chiang Mai
Tel 053 357 310

The remarkable thing about this excellent Italian restaurant is that it is run by Thais, who serve pasta that would meet the approval of the most demanding Italian visitor. No

The famous Chiang Dao Nest Mini-Resort

pizza, but every possible variety of pasta, with sauces that are sometimes given a Thai touch of chili. The outside terrace, bordering an elegantly groomed tropical garden, is delightful for a summer evening dinner date. The evening menu extends to include house specialties that change daily, such as *satim bocca*, a succulent veal dish.

🕐 Tue–Sun 11–2, 5.30–10
🍽 L B150, D B400, Wine B700

THA NAM

43/3 Moo 2, Thanon Chang Klan, Chiang Mai
Tel 053 275 125, 053 282 988

Its name means "river pier," and although the original boat jetty has long since gone, this rambling old mansion still sits like a beached teak-built junk on a stretch of the Ping River. The riverside terrace is shaded by vast tropical trees older than the house itself. The upstairs open-sided deck offers refuge on rainy days, and a classical trio performs there nightly. Downstairs there's a small and exclusive art gallery. The food is outstanding, with unusual specialties such as chicken wrapped in pandanus leaves.

🕐 Daily 11–11
🍽 L B120, D B150, Wine B750

THE WRITERS CLUB AND WINE BAR

141/3 Thanon Rachadamnoen, Chiang Mai
Tel 019 282 066

Chiang Mai's unofficial press club is also one of the city's few wine bars. It's a laid-back place to meet the local media people, who include some named foreign correspondents, authors and travel writers. The dark teak bar area leads onto a canopied terrace enclosed by tropical plants. The menu changes daily but often includes local venison and wild boar, and trout from Thailand's highest mountain, Doi Inthanon. Prices are very reasonable, and the house wines are perhaps the best deal in Chiang Mai.

🕐 Sun–Fri 12–12
🍽 L B120, D B240, Wine B900

CHIANG RAI

CABBAGES & CONDOMS

153 Moo 6, Tambon Pangiew, Amphoe Wiangpapao, Chiang Rai
Tel 053 952 311

This rural version of Bangkok's famous Cabbages & Condoms restaurant is just as quirky—an entrance sign welcomes visitors with the words "You have arrived at the rubber triangle," and free condoms are handed out with the after-dinner peppermints. The underlying purpose, however,

is serious, and the restaurants' founder is a respected Thai anti-AIDS campaigner. Oh, and the food is very good, too.
🕐 Daily 7am–10pm
🍽 B120, Wine B450

CHAM CHA

Thanon Singhaklai, Chiang Rai
Tel 053 744 191

Chiang Rai's tourist office is next door to this busy restaurant, and its staff are among its best clients, along with officials from the nearby city hall. Their patronage is a guarantee of the excellence of the Thai food, particularly the kitchen's *pad thai*, a hearty helping of noodles laced with meat or fish. The downstairs dining area gets very crowded, but there are usually spare tables upstairs.
🕐 Mon–Sat 7–4
🍽 L B100

HAWNARIGA

402/1–2 Thanon Banpapragarn, Amphoe Muang, Chiang Rai
Tel 053 711 062

A cool stream, stocked with fish, runs through this thatch-roof, open-sided restaurant. Order steamed *tabtim* with garlic and herbs and it will be served straight from the water. Other northern Thai specialties to try include *sai uwa* sausage with a spicy dip. The restaurant is easy to find—it's next to the city clock tower from which it gets its Thai name.
🕐 Daily 9am–10pm
🍽 L B100, D B140

SALUNGKHAM

834/3 Thanon Phaholyotin, Amphoe Muang, Chiang Rai
Tel 053 717 192

Northern Thai dishes such as *yang ruam* (grilled beef and local sausage) and *khai tun* (steamed whipped eggs) are the specialties of this popular ethnic restaurant. From the upstairs teak-floored terrace you can watch your meal being prepared in the open kitchen below. Non-smokers

have their own area on the ground floor.
🕐 Daily 10.30–10.30
🍽 L B100, D B120

TOKE KHAM

Suanthip Vana Resort, Tambol Takok, Amphoe Mae Suay, Chiang Rai
Tel 053 724 2286–9, 053 724 231–5

From the open-sided terrace of this resort restaurant, 75km (45 miles) south of Chiang Rai on the Chiang Mai road, you have a panoramic view of banana groves and jungle-clad hills. Wickerwork tables and chairs are arranged beneath a traditional Thai beamed roof, supported by massive teak pillars. The food is first class—

The timber-built Antique House, Chiang Mai

try the *pla chon nam tok*, a locally caught fish with a so-called "waterfall" sauce.
🕐 Daily 7am–11pm
🍽 L B160, D B250, Wine B800

KHUN YUAM

BAN FARANG

499 Moo 1, Khun Yuam, Mae Hong Son
Tel 053 622 086

The only restaurant of any standard on the "loop" route between Mae Hong Son and Mae Sariang is roughly halfway, in the village of Khun Yuam. The open-sided, orchid-hung terrace dining area is part of a guesthouse catering to visitors to the nearby World War II museum, and it has an international menu. The pork

or chicken steaks with an herb sauce are very tasty, while the pancakes are a popular local specialty.
🕐 Daily 8am–9pm
🍽 L B150, D B200

LAMPANG

KRUA BANGKOK

Thanon Wiang Khura, Lampang
Tel 054 310 103

The Bangkok "kitchen" ("krua") sits on a quiet stretch of the Wang River, a short walk from the town center. The main dining area, beamed and furnished with rustic tables and chairs, leads out to a small terrace overlooking the river. The menu is as cosmopolitan as the name of the restaurant and Northern Thai specialties, share space with other Southeast Asian dishes. Several Vietnamese dishes are featured—the Vietnamese-style egg rolls are particularly good.
🕐 Daily 11–11
🍽 L B150, D B180

THE RIVERSIDE

328 Thanon Tipchang, Lampang
Tel 054 221 861

From the teak-floored terrace of the Riverside you have fine views of the Wang River and a temple's golden spires breaking through nearby woods. The rambling old building has a collection of dining areas, inside and outdoors, linked by a bandstand where live music is played most nights. Good Thai and Western dishes are served—the snow peas and calf's liver are particularly recommended. So are the excellent pizzas that come from a genuine brick oven.
🕐 Daily 11–11
🍽 L B150, D B200, Wine B750

EATING

LAMPHUN

RIVERSIDE

Thanon Chaimongkol 3, Lamphun

Like Chiang Mai and Lampang, Lamphun has its Riverside restaurant, although it's simpler and homelier than the other two. A plan-floored deck extends out over the riverbank and is an ideal place to enjoy an evening breeze and watch the sun set over the red roofs and golden *chedis* of Wat Haripunchai on the opposite bank. The menu is basic northern Thai fare, mainly fried rice and noodles and spicy soups. There are nightly karaoke sessions on an adjoining terrace.

◎ Daily 8am–midnight

🍴 L B80, D B100

TONFAI

Thanon Chaimongkol 1, Lamphun

Mind your head as you enter this ancient teak-built home on the riverside road a few paces from Lamphun's tourist office. It must have been built for very short people. The upstairs dining room (remove your shoes first) has greater clearance, with high wooden rafters supporting uncovered roof tiles. Unglazed windows look out over the river and are shuttered when the weather gets cool. The northern Thai menu has exotic dishes like curried frog and chicken's innards; the fried rice variations are hearty and tasty.

◎ Sun–Sat 11–11

🍴 L B120, D B150

MAE HONG SON

BAI FERN

87 Thanon Khunlumprapas, Mae Hong Son

Tel 053 611 374

The "Fern Leaf" is one of Mae Hong Son's oldest established and most popular restaurants, well patronized by Thai businesspeople and their families. A live band plays most nights in the larger of the two dining rooms, so if you're looking for peace and quiet

take a table in the smaller, cozier bar area. The menu is full of imaginative variations of northern Thai specialties—the pork ribs and pineapple are especially good.

◎ Daily 11–11

🍴 L B120, D B150, Wine B750

GOLDEN TEAK

Imperial Tara Hotel, 149 Moo 8, Tambol Pang Moo, Mae Hong Son

Tel 053 684 444

Mae Hong Son's top restaurant is in the Imperial Tara Hotel, its large picture windows looking out over lush tropical gardens. Oriental rugs are spread between the wickerwork tables and chairs. The menu is

Try something out of the ordinary!

Thai, Chinese and international, and the vast breakfast buffet is recommended as a good start to a day's touring around Mae Hong Son.

◎ Daily 6.30am–10pm

🍴 L B250, D B300, Wine B900

MAE SAI

SAISHOL

86/2 Thanon Chonlapatan, Mae Sai

This is the northernmost restaurant in Thailand, and from its first-floor dining room you can look over the small border river below and directly into Myanmar. The inexpensive menu has some very tasty northern Thai dishes—try the *khai yat sai* (meat-filled

omelet), and if the weather's hot order a refreshing Thai-style sweet iced tea.

◎ Daily 7am–9pm

🍴 L B100, D B120

MAE SARIANG

RIVERSIDE

85 Thanon Langpanich, Mae Sariang

Tel 053 682 592

The view from the wooden deck of this guesthouse restaurant makes up for the simplicity of its menu. Tables look out over a bend of the Yuam River, flanked by rice paddies and sugarcane fields and backed by the far-off mountains. The menu has mostly Thai rice and noodle dishes, although an "American breakfast" is served until midday.

◎ Daily 8am–10pm

🍴 L B80, D B120

NAN

CHUMPOO-THIP

The City Park Hotel, 99 Thanon Yantarakitkosol, Nan

Tel 054 741 343

www.thecityparkhotel.com

The stylish City Park Hotel's Chumpoo-Thip restaurant serves fresh produce from its own kitchen garden, which diners are invited to stroll around while waiting for their orders. The fish with Thai pepper sauce and the restaurant's own version of the Isan dish *lab* are highly recommended.

◎ Daily 7am–midnight

🍴 L B120, D B250, Wine B1,000

RUEN KAEW

1/1 Thanon Sumondhevaraj, Nan

Tel 054 710 631

The Nan River meanders past the outside terrace of this flower-smothered rustic restaurant on the edge of Nan. Locals pack the place at weekends to listen to its Thai bands and attractive singers, who perform nightly. The excellent northern Thai food is also a big draw—try the honey-baked chicken.

EATING

⏰ Daily 10–11
🍴 L B100, D B120

SURIYA GARDEN
9 Thanon Sumondhevaraj, Nan
Tel 054 710 687
Chinese specialties such as Canton-style pig's trotters feature on the extensive menu of this large, airy restaurant overlooking the Nan River. On warm evenings, take a table on the wood-floored waterfront deck. A Thai band and vocalists perform nightly.
⏰ Daily 11–11
🍴 L B100, D B150

PAI
BAAN PAI
7 Moo 3, Thanon Rangsiyanont, Pai
Tel 053 699 912
The Baan Pai ("Pai Home") is a favorite with locals and visitors alike, serving Thai and Western dishes in the relaxed surroundings of an old timber-built house on one of Pai's two main streets. The Thai menu includes the usual range of rice and noodle dishes, while the Western fare encompasses everything from hamburgers to pizzas. The mashed potato is the best in town.
⏰ Daily 8am–11pm
🍴 L B100, D B150

BEN BENJARONG
Thanon Rangsiyanon, Pai
Tel 053 699 103
From the open-sided main dining room at this popular restaurant you have a fine view of paddy fields and the mountains beyond. The extensive Thai menu includes such favorites as Pad Thai noodles and green and red curries.
⏰ Daily 10–10
🍴 L B100, D B140

PAI BLUES
91/1 Thanon Chai Songkram, Pai
Tel 097 576 997
A charming Swedish–Shan couple run what many visitors say is Pai's best restaurant. The menu is a mixture of Shan and Western food, ranging from curries and basics such as *nam prik ong* to Italian pasta. Wine is served by the glass (B80–B90).
⏰ Daily 9–midnight
🍴 L B100, D B180

PAIRADISE GUESTHOUSE & BAKERY
98 Moo 1, Mae Hee, Pai
Tel 098 387 521
Few guesthouses serve an acceptable breakfast in Pai, so shun what's on offer and head for this Thai-German guesthouse on a hillside just outside town and sample the home-baked breads and

Traditional Thai noodle dishes are on the menu at Baan Pai

homemade jam, with fresh farm eggs and excellent coffee. It will set you up for a day of trekking in the countryside around Pai.
⏰ Daily 8–6
🍴 Breakfast B60–B120

THAI YAI
24 Thanon Rangsiyanon, Pai
Tel 053 699 093
This simple timber-built restaurant serves some of the best coffee in town, a hill-tribe product from the nearby mountains. It goes well with the Thai Yai's full American breakfast. Western dishes share space on the menu with such Thai staples as *pad thai* noodles and fried rice.

⏰ Daily 7.30–10.30
🍴 L B70, D B160

PHAYAO
SANG CHAN
17/4 Chai Kwan Road, Phayao
Tel 054 431 971
The fishing nets draped across the glass façade of this lakeside restaurant signal that this is *the* place to find the best of the day's catch. Tilapia is its specialty, grilled with garlic or chili. The beamed and pillared restaurant has the friendly feel of an Italian lakeside trattoria and it's a favorite weekend destination of local Thai families. There's a flower-bordered front garden for alfresco dining.
⏰ Daily 9am–10pm
🍴 L B140, D B150

PHRAE
NAKHON PHRAE TOWER HOTEL
3 Thanon Muanghit, Phrae
Tel 054 521 321
The Nakhon Phrae Tower Hotel's restaurant is Phrae's top dining establishment and is very popular with the locals. It serves a large variety of Thai and Chinese dishes—try the *lab muang kwa* or *pla kang phad cha*.
⏰ Daily 7am–1am
🍴 L B120, D B250, Wine B750

THA TON
CHANKASAM
209 Moo 3, Tambon Tha Ton, Amphoe Thaton
Tel. 053 459 313
Just 20m (22 yards) from Tha Ton's boat pier, this open-air Thai restaurant is recommended for a good lunch to prepare for the four-hour river trip to Chiang Rai. Fish from the Kok River lands on the restaurant menu and into the excellent *tom yam pla maenam* (spicy river fish soup). The traditional Thai breakfast (*kao tom* rice soup) is also served from 7am.
⏰ Daily 7am–10pm
🍴 L B80, D B120

EATING

CENTRAL THAILAND

Central Thailand is the most fertile region of the country, producing most of its rice and an abundant variety of vegetables and fruit. So restaurant menus here are rich in fresh produce, usually from fields and orchards only a few steps away. Lightly sautéed vegetables are served with the old Thai favorite, *nam prik* (chili dip), which had its origins in Central Thailand. Chili paste is used in many of the curries and the spicy Thai "salad" (*yam*). Lemongrass and kaffir lime leaf add their own distinctive flavors. Central Thailand is famous for its desserts, based on the great variety of fruit that grows in its orchards. The simplest but most delicious is a "cocktail" of fresh fruit in a light, clear syrup, served with crushed ice (*polemai ruam gap nam kaeng*). Apart from Ayutthaya and its surroundings, Central Thailand is not rich in fine restaurants, but the food you'll find in the traditional eating places throughout the region is invariably appetizing and often outstanding.

PRICES AND SYMBOLS

The restaurants are listed alphabetically by town or area, then by name. The prices given for a two-course lunch (L) and a three-course dinner (D) are for one person, without drinks. The wine price is for the least expensive bottle.
For a key to the symbols,
▷ 2.

AYUTTHAYA

CHAINAM
Thanon U-Thong (opposite Chan Kasem Palace), Amphoe Muang, Ayutthaya
Tel 035 252 013
The riverside Chainam is popular for its full Western breakfasts, accompanied by fresh Thai coffee. The menu is a mixture of Western and Thai dishes, in which fried rice and noodles predominate.

Daily 8am–9pm
L B100, D B150

PAE KRUNG KAO AYUDTHAYA FLOATING RESTAURANT
K4 Moo 2, Thanon Authong, Ayutthaya
Tel 035 241 555, 035 243 455
Ayutthaya has several so-called "floating restaurants" bordering its encircling rivers, and this is one of the most attractive, an ancient wooden Thai-style house with a riverside pontoon terrace. The menu is full of well-known traditional dishes.

Daily 11–9
L B120, D B180, Wine B800

PASAK RIVER QUEEN
116 Moo 2, Borpong Nakornluang, Ayutthaya
Tel 035 724 520, 035 724 504, 035 724 519
The big attraction of this waterside restaurant is its riverboat, the *Pasak River Queen*, which makes a nightly

cruise (daily at 6.30pm) around Ayutthaya, with an on-deck à la carte dinner service. Dinner on land, on the restaurant's riverbank terrace, comes cheaper, but is probably not as fun. Fish is, of course, the thing to order; the *tom yam pla mae nam* (spicy fish soup) is delicious.

Daily 10–10
L B160, D B200, Wine B750

PHAE KRUNG KAO
Moo 2, Thanon U–Thong, Ayutthaya
Tel 035 241 555
The dining terrace of this traditional Thai restaurant sits directly on the Pa Sak River, and fresh river fish figures large on the menu. The pork or chicken with pepper and garlic are also highly recommended.

Daily 10–9
L B120, D B160

EATING

SIAM

11/3 Moo 1, Thanon Maharach, Tambol Pratuchai Pranakronsri, Ayutthaya
Tel 035 211 070

Freshwater lobster is the Siam's house specialty. It's expensive (B280) but well worth the outlay. Other traditional Thai dishes are cheaper, and the restaurant also serves a number of Vietnamese specialties. It's right opposite the entrance to Wat Mahathat, ideally located for refreshment after touring the temple compound.

🕐 Daily 10am–10.30pm
🍴 L B120, D B200

CHANTHABURI

CHOMLOM CHOMCHAN

Tambol Tarat, Chanthaburi
Tel 039 323 684

On hot evenings, this open-air riverside restaurant is a delightful place to eat. The food is truly Thai, with an emphasis on fish dishes. The sea bass fishcakes (tod nam pla) and the spicy seafood soup (tom yam talay) are especially recommended.

🕐 Daily 11–11
🍴 L B120, D B150

KAMPHAENG PHET

THREE J GUEST HOUSE

79 Thanon Rachavitee, Tambol Naimuang, Kamphaeng Phet
Tel 055 713 129, 055 720 384

The friendly "Three J" has a rustic terrace restaurant serving Thai dishes of high quality at very reasonable prices. The pad thai are particularly good. The guesthouse is also a good base for touring the area, offering tourist information and a ticket service.

🕐 Daily 8am–9pm
🍴 L B100, D B150

KANCHANABURI

THE FLOATING RESTAURANT

415 Moo 1, Thanon River Kwai, Kanchanaburi
Tel 034 512 595

This is the best of the pontoon restaurants that cluster around the River Kwai Bridge. In fact, it's one of the best dining-out venues of the entire region, with an outstanding 40-page menu encompassing the pick of traditional Thai fare. Six varieties of fish are on offer, besides delicacies such as soft-shell crab and large farmed prawns. Draft Thai and Japanese beer is served.

🕐 Daily 8.30–11
🍴 L B150, D B250, Wine B900

MAE NAM

Thanon Lak Muang, Amphoe Muang, Kanchanaburi
Tel 034 512 811

The waterside terrace at Kanchanaburi's River ("Mae

Guess what the specialty of the house is!

Nam") Restaurant directly abuts both the remains of the original bridge over the River Kwai and the newer structure, also built by the Japanese. Fresh river fish is prepared in a variety of ways. A live band plays in the evenings.

🕐 Daily 8.30am–midnight
🍴 L B160, D B240

RIVER KWAI RESORTEL

55 Moo 5, Tambol Wangkrajae, A. Sai Yok, Kanchanaburi
Tel 034 652 243

The rustic restaurant of the riverside Resortel in the village of Sai Yok, 40km (24 miles) northeast of Kanchanaburi (Route 323), serves excellent Thai dishes in a rural setting.

The green and red curries are particularly tasty, while the fish comes straight from the Kwai Noi River.

🕐 8am–10pm
🍴 L B120, D B180, Wine B700

RIVER KWAI VILLAGE

74/12 Moo 4, Tha Sao, Kanchanaburi
Tel 034 634 454
www.bkk2000.com/rkvh

A gallery of caged tropical birds welcomes you to the River Kwai Village restaurant. The expansive, two-level, open-sided dining room is cooled by breezes from the river below and rows of whirling fans. The menu is an extensive mixture of Thai and Western dishes.

🕐 Daily 7am–10pm
🍴 L B195, D B250, Wine B800

KO SAMET

RIM VIMARN RESTAURANT

Le Vimarn Cottages and Spa, 40/11 Moo 4, Tambol Phe, Ko Samet, Rayong
Tel 026 730 966
www.sametresorts.com

Le Vimarn's elegant restaurant is an open-sided, high-ceilinged pavilion at the edge of the sea on Ko Samet's western coast, an ideal place to watch the sunset. You dine in the utmost comfort, in basketwork or teak chairs at tables set with fine linen and silverware. The menu is a well-conceived balance of Thai and international dishes.

🕐 Daily 8am–11pm
🍴 L B220, D B300, Wine B900

SEA VIEW RESTAURANT

Ao Prao Resort, 60 Moo 4, Tambol Phe, Ko Samet, Rayong
Tel 038 644 100–2
www.samedresorts.com

You dine here in the cool shade of casuarina trees and at the edge of a quiet beach. The seafood couldn't be fresher, and the prawns couldn't be larger. Western dishes predominate but there's also an extensive Thai menu. Cocktails are served at an inviting bar beneath high wooden rafters.

🕐 Daily 7–10
🍴 L B150, D B250, Wine B750

EATING

LOP BURI

BUALANG
46/1 Thanon Pahalyothin, Tambol Thasala, Amphoe Muang, Lop Buri
Tel 036 614 227–30, 036 422 669
Members of the Thai royal family eat at this charming garden restaurant when visiting Lop Buri. You can choose "royal dishes," such as *yam kan ka-na goong krab* (spicy Chinese broccoli with shrimp) or *phoo-nim tod kratiem prik thai* (soft crab fried with garlic and pepper).
🕓 Daily 11–11
🍽 L B120, D B150, Wine B500

LOP BURI STEAKHOUSE
Thanon Sorasak, Amphoe Muang, Lop Buri
Tel 036 420 704
and
Thanon Phahon Yothin, Amphoe Muang, Lop Buri
Tel 036 615 880
The two branches of Lop Buri Steakhouse serve excellent beef steaks with all the trimmings. The salads are also crisp and fresh, and there's an extensive Thai menu.
🕓 Daily 10–10
🍽 L B200, D B250, Wine B300

SANGSAWANG
11–16 Amphoe Muang, Lop Buri
Tel 036 411 632, 036 613 685
This no-nonsense, clean and efficient Thai restaurant, opposite the main entrance to Lop Buri zoo, is very good value for money, serving local fare at very reasonable prices. Try the *yam mamuang* (spicy mango salad), followed by the *pla samlee tod krab* (a grilled river fish).
🕓 Daily 10–10
🍽 L B100, D B150

NAKHON PATHOM

INN-CHAN
The Rose Garden Resort, Thanon Pet Kasem, Tambol Sampran, Nakhon Pathom
Tel 034 322 5893
The Rose Garden Resort's stylish Thai restaurant uses herbs gathered from the resort's own kitchen garden, originally planted here by a mayor of Bangkok. They add aroma and spice to traditional dishes such as *tom yam* soups and the sauces that accompany the fresh river fish. The cool, airy restaurant is an ideal place to end the day after touring the Rose Garden.
🕓 Daily 11–2.30
🍽 L B300, Wine B750

PATTAYA

ART CAFÉ
285/3 Moo 5, Naklua Soi 16, Pattaya
Tel 038 367 652
www.artcafe-thailand.com
Rabbit, lamb and ostrich are some of the more exotic items

Phae Fah Thai, a floating restaurant

on the imaginative menu of this Mediterranean-style eatery. The steaks are enormous, but vegetarians are also provided for, with such specialties as lentil salad with eggplant (aubergine) mousse. Local artists display their works on the walls.
🕓 Daily 11–11
🍽 L B250, D B400, Wine B650

LOBSTER POT
228 Walking Street, South Pattaya
Tel 038 426 083
Lobster is of course the prime dish at this outstanding seafood restaurant at the southern edge of Pattaya. Try the king lobster thermador—expensive but worth a splurge.

The menu is not exclusively seafood; tenderloin steak and cordon bleu share space with traditional Thai dishes and fresh fish. The open-sided restaurant sits on a pier overlooking the bay, an ideal spot for dining on a fine evening.
🕓 Daily noon–1am
🍽 L B200, D B300, Wine B850

PAN PAN SAN DOMENICO
Thanon Thapraya, South Pattaya
Tel 038 251 874
The "Domenico" is one of the region's best Italian restaurants, famous for the flair of its cuisine, which encompasses a big range of imaginatively prepared yet reassuringly traditional pasta dishes. The linguini with seafood is a dream. Portions are large, but try to leave room for the house special—wonderfully creamy and rich tiramisu.
🕓 Daily 9.30am–11pm
🍽 L B200, D B300, Wine B800

PARADISE
215/62–63 Second Road, Pattaya, Chonburi
Tel 038 723 177
You dine in style here beneath a high ceiling that's supported by arched walls covered with hand-painted rainforest murals. Tables are laid with crisp white linen and vases containing fresh flowers. The menu matches the exotic decor, with such specialties as crocodile and lobster. The Thai menu has all the usual favorites, such as spicy shrimp soup and sweet-and-sour pork or chicken, all priced at under B100.
🕓 Daily 10–10
🍽 L B200, D B260, Wine B790

PIC KITCHEN AND JAZZ PIT
255 Soi 5, Pattaya 2 Road, Chonburi
Tel 038 428 387/74
Established in 1984, this elegant Thai-style restaurant and pub is an old Pattaya

favorite, just a few meters from Pattaya's Beach Road and the sea. There are four pavilion dining areas, in two of which diners sit on the polished teak floor, Thai-style. The food isn't cheap, but many of the dishes—the *nam prik khai poo*, for instance—are memorably good. So are the wines, which cost up to B10,000 a bottle. The integrated Jazz Pit Pub serves up some of the best music to be heard in Pattaya.

🕐 Daily 8am–midnight

🍽 L B300, D B400, Wine B800

THAI HOUSE

171/1 Moo 6, Naklua, Bang Lamuang, North Pattaya, Chonburi
Tel 038 370 579–81

The Thai House is really a large mansion—a Thai-style pavilion building with sweeping, multiple eaves and able to seat 800 diners. Performances of traditional Thai music and dancing are given every evening. The menu is suitably large and international, with some original dishes such as *goong pad* "baby corn" (sautéed shrimp with young maize corn).

🕐 Daily 11.30–11.30

🍽 L B200, D B250, Wine B1,050

PHITSANULOK

NA NAM

Thanon 89/4 Wangchan, Amphoe Muang, Phitsanulok
Tel 055 216 404, 055 230 444

From the terrace of this large, open-air restaurant diners have an uninterrupted view of the river, making it a romantic place for an evening out. The Thai menu has such exotic specialties as "flying salty chicken" (*gai khua kem*). The fish dishes are particularly tasty—try *pla neung sea we* (steamed river fish in soy sauce).

🕐 Daily 11–11

🍽 L B120, D B220

PHAE FAH THAI

60 Thanon Wangchan, Amphoe Muang, Phitsanulok
Tel 055 215 674, 055 242 743

Phitsanulok is renowned for its "floating restaurants" which sit directly on the river, their large, airy teak-floored terraces like an ocean liner's promenade deck. The Phae Fah Thai is among the best.

🕐 Daily 11–11

🍽 L B130, D B230, Wine B600

PHAE SONG KWAE

21 Thanon Wangchan, Amphoe Muang, Phitsanulok
Tel 055 242 167

This floating restaurant takes diners out onto the river on

The cozy Dream Café in Sukhothai

dinner cruises, leaving at 6 and 8 every evening. A band plays, on board and also on shore, in the large dining terrace. Fish dishes dominate the menu, and this is *the* place to try barbecued prawns (*goong phao*).

🕐 Daily 11–11

🍽 L B130, D B240

RAYONG

COTE JARDIN

Novotel Coralia Rim Pae, 45/Moo 3, Thanon Pae Klaeng Kram, Rayong
Tel 038 648 008

The Novotel's elegant Cote Jardin restaurant—one of two—is among Rayong's best, serving a very select menu of international and Thai dishes

either in the dining room or on the outside terrace. It's widely known for the quality of its seafood—the *gaeng pet talay*, a seafood curry, is one of its outstanding specialties.

🕐 Daily 6am–midnight

🍽 L B300, D B400, Wine B700

SANGKHLA BURI (THREE PAGODAS PASS)

SONGKALIA RIVER HUT AND RESORT

Sangkhla Buri lake road

From a table at this lakeside resort's open-sided restaurant you can watch fishermen in their shallow-draft boats at work on the vast Khao Laem reservoir, hauling in the catch that lands on the day's menu. The specialty of the lake and the restaurant is *pla red*, delicious in garlic or sweet-and-sour sauce. Traditional "Mon" dishes from nearby Myanmar (Burma) are also on the menu—the pork or chicken *hang led* curry can be very spicy but is nevertheless excellent.

🕐 Daily 11–10

🍽 L B120, D B150

SUKHOTHAI

THE DREAM CAFÉ

86/1 Thanon Singhawat, Amphoe Muang, Sukhothai
Tel 055 612 081

This is no café but a very attractive little restaurant, with wood-paneled walls and polished teak and tile floors, divided up into cozy dining areas and nooks and crannies. Every corner and wall space is filled with bric-a-brac, small antiques and an impressive collection of old clocks. The menu is an imaginative mixture of Thai and Western food. If you fancy staying the night there's a guesthouse extension, the Cocoon—a clutch of neat little rooms bordering the back garden.

🕐 Daily 10am–11pm

🍽 L B150, D B220, Wine B700

THE SOUTH

Southern Thailand has food to suit all tastes, though in resort areas like Ko Samui and Phuket there is a tendency to moderate the fiery character of Thai food and the result can be rather bland. For many visitors, the fresh seafood is the highlight of most menus and it is hard to argue with this. There is a Malay influence on the cooking, which is reflected in the curry known as *mussaman*. It is sweeter than the usual green, red or yellow curries due to the use of brown sugar and coconut, and it's use of these characteristically Malay ingredients that gives this curry its name, the "Muslim's curry."

PRICES AND SYMBOLS

The restaurants are listed alphabetically by town or area, then by name. The prices given for a two-course lunch (L) and a three-course dinner (D) are for one person, without drinks. The wine price is for the least expensive bottle.
For a key to the symbols, ▷ 2.

HUA HIN

CIAO
Marriott Hotel, Hua Hin
Tel 032 511 881
Set facing a superb stretch of Hua Hin's beach, the thatched, open-air Ciao looks its best at night when lit by candles and a cool breeze blows in from the sea. Pizzas and a Caesar salad are always on the menu and expect to find veal, pork or lamb chops and lobster.
🕐 Daily 11–11
🍷 L B500, D B900, Wine B1,200

TAJ-MAHAL
31/1 Thanon Naresdamri, Hua Hin
Tel 032 512 613
To find this cheap little eatery, walk down the street past the entrance to the Hilton and the restaurant is at the bottom on your right. There are *thalis* for vegetarians and most meat dishes are under B100.
🕐 Daily 11.30–11
🍷 L B200, D B300

WHITE LOTUS
Hua Hin Resort and Spa, 33 Thanon Naresdamri, Hua Hin
Tel 032 512 888
High up on the 17th level of the Hilton, the White Lotus has tables inside or out on the balcony overlooking the town and the beach. There's *dim sum* for lunch and a helpful menu, as well as a wine menu that suggests wines for the Chinese dishes which include tempting appetizers like Alaskan scallops and asparagus, and dishes like stir-fried prawns with apple in an orange and lemongrass sauce.

Surprisingly intimate at night, the elevation takes you away from the gregarious street activity 17 levels below.
🕐 Daily 11.30–2.30, 5.30–10.30
🍷 L B250, D B1,100, Wine B1,500

KO LANTA

MR BEAN'S
Klong Dao Beach, Ko Lanta
Tel 015 975 182
English food, with free local delivery, comes into its own on Wednesdays and Saturdays when the place is booked out for the roast lamb dinners. Indian food is available on Friday nights, but the normal menu is one of cottage pie, chili con carne, fish and chips (french fries), shepherd's pie and huge cholesterol-packed breakfasts.
🕐 Daily 8am–midnight
🍷 L and D B200–B300

SEA SIDE
Ban Sala Dan, Ko Lanta
Tel 015 987 340
As Sea Side is next to the pier, with tables over the water, it is

EATING

convenient if you're caught in Ban Sala Dan waiting for a boat. On the menu are chicken and noodles, curries, sandwiches and salads, plus it's open for breakfast of pancakes, toast and eggs. It also has a good line in shakes.

🕐 Daily 8–7
🍽 L and D B100

KO SAMUI

BEETLENUT

Soi Colibri, Central Chaweng, Ko Samui
Tel 077 413 370

Beetlenut is just off the main street, opposite the Central Samui Beach Resort at the south end of Chaweng. It is not a large restaurant and reservations are usually essential because this is currently regarded as the best place to dine on the island. The food is Thai but with a strong Californian twist, which makes the menu an interesting read: dishes include roast duck in a pineapple curry, and prawns with hot *tom yam* soup.

🕐 Daily 6pm–midnight
🍽 D B1,500

CHEF CHOM'S

Tongsai Bay Hotel, 84 Moo 5, Bophut, Ko Samui
Tel 077 425 015

Thai cuisine at Chef Chom's aspires to the exquisite in the luxury setting of the Tongsai Bay Hotel. It is a place to dress up for and a couple of diners is the minimum needed to do justice to the menu. Arrange for a taxi to collect you if you do not have your own transport.

🕐 Daily 11–6, 7–10
🍽 D B1,300, Wine B1,000

THE DECK

Central Chaweng, Ko Samui
Tel 077 230 897

Thai and Western food, quite a few vegetarian choices, and a B99 breakfast available throughout the day—the food is as good as it gets at this price range in Samui. The restaurant is open air, with a bar that sometimes gets too full.

🕐 Daily 8am–2am
🍽 L B250, D B500

THE ISLANDER

Central Chaweng, Ko Samui
Tel 077 230 836

A well-managed pub restaurant with a holiday atmosphere—a place where you can wear shorts. Aside from the Thai and Western food, there is a separate sports area that shows soccer games, and a children's menu.

🕐 Daily 8am–midnight
🍽 L B250, D B500

Dine on the beach at Poppies restaurant

POPPIES

Central Chaweng, Ko Samui
Tel 077 422 419

Poppies comes into its own at night when the place is lit up and people are mingling. It's a popular, longstanding restaurant where you would not feel out of place for having dressed up a little. Try to reserve a table by the sea, under swaying pandan trees, for the full romance factor. Seafood, pizza and meat dishes are on offer, and occasional live entertainment at weekends. Reservations are essential during the high season.

🕐 Daily 7am–11pm
🍽 L B300, D B1,200, Wine B900

SPA RESORT RESTAURANT

Lamai Beach, Ko Samui
Tel 077 230 855
www.spasamui.com

The restaurant at the well-known Spa Resort (▷ 286) is mostly vegetarian, and this is what it does best, but chicken and fish are also an option with many of the dishes. It's open for breakfast and serves all day from a big menu of Western salads, soups, sandwiches, spaghetti and tacos, as well as Thai food like *pla goong* (prawn sautéed with lemongrass, onions and mint leaves).

🕐 Daily 7am–10pm
🍽 L B150, D B300, Wine B430

KRABI

HONGMING VEGETARIAN

4/1 Thanon Pruksa Uthit, Krabi town
Tel 075 621 273

Hongming is an ideal lunch stop situated on the corner with Maharaj Soi 10, which is a turning off the river-facing main street of Thanon Utrakit, and not far from the tourist office. It's a simple Buddhist vegetarian eatery where you simply point to two or three of the dishes prepared that day and they are served to you with rice.

🕐 Mon–Sat 7–5
🍽 L B50, D B50

KOLEE SEAFOOD

Thanon Konk Ka, Krabi
Tel 060 915 523

Along Thanon Konk Ka and facing the river, Kolee Seafood is only one of the many food stands set up each evening in town, but it does have the distinction of an English menu. The *tom yam kung* (shrimp soup with lemongrass and chili) makes a good starter, or tuck straight into fried prawns or squid with curry or mixed vegetables with seafood.

🕐 Daily 5.45–12
🍽 D B120

EATING

TUN GAN
Thanon Utarakit, Krabi
Tel 075 650 876
Connecting with a pleasant little shop, and under the same management, this is a placid little café where relaxing jazz plays in the background. There's a good choice of coffees and teas, shakes and beers, Thai and Western fare (including ostrich steak), and breakfast. Buddha paintings, sold in the hop, adorn the walls.
🕐 Daily 8–8
🍽 L B120, D B160

VIVA
29 Thanon Pruksa Uhtit, Krabi
Tel 075 630 517
Bread at Viva is made fresh each morning for breakfast. On the menu are omelets, crêpes, bruschetta, soup, salads, antipasti, over 30 types of homemade pasta—including unusual dishes like *gamberi piccanti* (spicy garlic prawn)—thin-crust pizzas (you can take away) and imported steaks. It's a friendly restaurant which opens onto the street without being noisy at night. Imported wheat beer from Germany and Italian wines are available.
🕐 Daily 10am–11pm
🍽 L B200, D B450, Wine B900

PHUKET
BAAN KLANG JINDA
158 Thanon Yaowarat, Phuket town
Tel 076 221 777
A 10-minute walk or short ride by *tuk-tuk* from the heart of town to the top of Thanon Yaowarat will bring you to a grand, century-old edifice that was built as the government's revenue-collecting office. It looks best at night when the grounds are lit up and there are outdoor tables on the green. There's live music in the lounge bar Monday to Saturday from 7pm to 8pm before the band shifts to the dining room and then moves back to the lounge from 10pm for another two hours.

🕐 Daily 11–2, 5–12
🍽 L B200, D B400, Wine B950

BAAN RIM PA
Thanon Hat Kalim, Patong, Phuket
Tel 076 340 789
www.baanrimpa.com
Reservations are essential at Patong's most elegant restaurant, set on rocky high ground across from the Novotel Hotel and facing the beach. The royal Thai food includes *yam hua plee gluay* (banana blossom salad) and honeyed chicken in pandanus leaves. There's jazz music nightly except Monday.
🕐 Mon–Sat 12–12
🍽 L B1,000, D B1,000, Wine B1,500

Sophisticated dining at Baan Rim Pa

BEACH HOUSE
6 Thanon Thaweewong, Patong, Phuket
Tel 076 345 639
The Beach House is at the south end of Patong beach, just before the Seaview Hotel, and is managed by a Swedish-Thai couple. You'll find Thai food alongside hamburgers, pork fillet and the like. It's a quiet retreat from the main action, with views of the sea.
🕐 Daily 7am–2am
🍽 L B200, D B450, Wine B950

BOATHOUSE
Kata Beach, Phuket
Tel 076 330 015
Rebuilt after the tsunami disaster of 2004, the

restaurant is as close to the beach as possible and makes for an idyllic scene at night. There are set menus of Thai or French cuisine plus an à la carte menu—the rock lobster with green curry, Armagnac and thermidor sauce is a popular choice and so too is the Australian lamb. The restaurant has an excellent wine list.
🕐 Daily 6.30am–11.30pm
🍽 L B500, D B1,500, Wine B1,500

CAPANNINA
30/9 Moo 2, Thanon Kata, Kata, Phuket
Tel 076 283 418
Capannina is easy to find, being right outside the Phuket Kata Resort and across from the bus/taxi station just up from the beach, and has tables outside on the pedestrianized street or under fans inside. The authentic Italian food includes antipasti, pizzas in two sizes, lots of pasta dishes and tempting desserts.
🕐 Daily 12–11
🍽 L B350, D B800, Wine B550

THE CLIFF
Coastal road between Karon and Patong, close to the Central Karon Village resort, Phuket
Tel 076 286 300
Try to arrive to watch the sun go down over Karon and take your time over the menu of Mediterranean and Asian food, which includes scallop salad, crabs with celery root salad, beef carpaccio, and prawns sautéed in Parma ham. Desserts like crème brûlée and chocolate mousse are also on the menu.
🕐 Daily 6–11
🍽 D B700, Wine B880

CUCINA
J W Marriott Phuket Resort & Spa, 231 Moo 3, Mai Khao Talang, Phuket
Tel 076 338 000
www.marriott.com/hktjw
Cucina has an open kitchen with a brick-built pizza oven, a carpeted dining area and a

EATING

terrace for alfresco dining. A popular dish is *zuppa zio pino*, a kind of bouillabaisse. A solo guitarist plays nightly and the atmosphere can be romantic in a low-key way; reserve a table facing the sea for the best views.

🕐 Daily 6–11
🍴 D B1,200, Wine B1,350

MANI'S GERMAN BAKERY

Soi Bangla, Karon, Phuket
Tel 076 396 882

Between Kata and Karon, at the east end of Soi Bangla, this is the place for rye, wholemeal, malt and onion bread. Pretzels, too. It's open for breakfast sausages, meatloaf and cold cuts, and a smaller outlet of the bakery can be found near the Chalong Circle.

🕐 Mon–Sat 7–4, Sun 7–midday
🍴 L B150

METROPOLE RESTAURANT

Metropole Hotel, Thanon Montri, Phuket town
Tel 076 214 020/9

On the second level of the Metropole Hotel, the menu here is a mixture of Thai and international dishes: curries, grilled pork chops, fried wild boar, and prawns with asparagus. The desserts are uninspiring, but compensation comes in the form of a live band or singer performing most nights on the restaurant's small stage.

🕐 Daily 6pm–midnight
🍴 D B1,200, Wine B1,350

MOM TRI'S KITCHEN

Kata Beach, Phuket
Tel 076 333 568

Head to this restaurant during the day for dream views looking down on Kata Noi beach and, at night, the sound of waves dashing on the rocks below. The sophisticated menu changes regularly, but expect dishes like mango gazpacho, stir-fried lobster and *ped palo* (duck with spices, garlic and peppercorn sauce).

The serious wine list includes organic bottles, and there's a choice of seven high-quality wines by the glass.

🕐 Daily 6.30am–11.30pm
🍴 L B620–B850, D B850–B1,500, Wine B1,500

ORIENTAL SPOON

Twin Palms Hotel, 106/46 Moo3, Surin Beach, Phuket
Tel 076 316 500
www.twinpalms-phuket.com

Just north of Kamala beach, this restaurant attracts island residents as well as visitors so the menu changes every so often and various specials are usually available. Expect good food and familiar dishes like

Listen to the ocean at Mom Tri's Kitchen

Caesar salad, pork spare ribs and grilled chicken.

🕐 Daily 6–midnight
🍴 D B950–B1,250, Wine B900

RICO'S STEAK HOUSE AND PIZZERIA

95/28–9 Soi Bangla Square, Thanon Bangla, Patong Beach, Phuket
Tel 076 342 359

Rico's is a bit Scandinavian, a bit Italian (stone-baked pizzas) and a bit Thai, plus meat from New Zealand and salmon from Norway. The style is informal, with pictures of Hollywood stars on the wall.

🕐 Daily 9am–midnight
🍴 L B250, D B450, Wine B800

RUAMJAI

Thanon Ranong, Phuket town
Tel 076 222 821

A short way past the bus stops for the *songthaews* to the beaches, look for the bright yellow sign displaying Ruamjai's name. Inside is fan cooled, with plenty of tables, a tiled floor and friendly staff, and there's a choice of about a dozen vegetarian dishes at lunchtime. Very clean and very inexpensive.

🕐 Daily 6.30–4.30
🍴 B130 (all-day menu)

SALVATORE'S

15 Thanon Rasada, Phuket town
Tel 076 225 958
www.salvatorestaurant.com

A bright and cheerful restaurant with artwork on the walls and Latin jazz playing in the background. On the menu here are starters such as a shrimp cocktail or Parma ham and salad, pasta dishes such as fettuccine with crab meat, lots of pizzas, more expensive T-bone steaks and tempting desserts.

🕐 Tue–Sat 12–2, 6–11, Sun 6–11
🍴 L B350, D B700, Wine B950

SAWASDEE

65 Thanon Katekuan, Kata, Phuket
Tel 076 330 979

Sawasdee is an Arab-Thai themed restaurant—the shimmering gilded dome as you enter blends aspects of a Thai temple with those of a mosque—but the food is all Thai at night and more European at lunchtime; breakfast is also available. It's easy to find—opposite Sawasdee Village in Kata.

🕐 Daily 6–10.30, 11–2, 6–11
🍴 L B300, D B450, Wine B1,100

EATING

STAYING IN THAILAND

Popular destinations offer a range of accommodation, from exclusive five-star hotels to budget places with dorms, guesthouses and camping sites. Rates at all of them vary according to demand and time of year, falling during the rainy season and escalating in the high season, rising even higher if there is a big festival or event in town. Apart from at quality hotels, it is normal practise to be shown your room before you agree to stay. In cheaper places you should check the shower and hot water and door locks, and if appropriate the availability of mosquito nets and how well the windows close. Note that non-smoking rooms are not common in Thai hotels, and very rarely found in establishments with fewer than five stars.

UPMARKET HOTELS

All the really big names in luxury hotels feature prominently in the big resorts and in Bangkok. There are some home-grown Thai chains too—Amari and Dusit stand out among them. All of these charge much lower rates than their equivalent in the West and if you have the budget for it this would be your chance to experience luxury hotel living for a while. The really exclusive places are small boutique-style hotels with individually furnished rooms, internet access in each room, DVD players and music systems, room service, the ubiquitous spa, a pool, several exclusive restaurants and sometimes a beer garden and bar. Many of these places, especially in the off-peak season, will offer huge discounts if you walk in and ask for a room or email at short notice. They also offer equally big discounts if you reserve via the internet either through a reservations agency or on the hotel's own website. There are reservations agencies in Bangkok airport, and Thai airlines will arrange discounted reservations for their passengers.

RESORT ACCOMMODATION

"Resort" can mean five-star luxury with fitness center, pool, spa, tennis, and golf buggies to drive you around, or just a set of thatched wooden huts on the beach. Most resort destinations in Thailand have their own website with photographs of the various hotels and their facilities so it would be wise to do some research before you make your reservation. If a resort is not on the internet it is probably small with few facilities.

THAI-CHINESE HOTELS

Most small towns have several well-run, clean and efficient Thai-Chinese family-run hotels which offer a range of accommodation with options of fan, air-con, bath and fridge. The cheapest rooms will be fan cooled with a simple shower and double bed. The best rooms will be air-conditioned with a bathroom including a bath, hot water, a fridge, TV and phone in the room. These last few items raise the price considerably. You should ask to be shown the choices of rooms and check that all the facilities

Luxury resort at Chaweng Beach, Ko Samui

are actually working. Ask for a room at the back to avoid the noise of traffic. European-looking visitors may be offered a special high rate so bargain before agreeing to stay. Most of these hotels will be on the main street in town and have a good coffee shop serving Chinese or Thai food.

GUESTHOUSES
Guesthouses of one kind or another are manifold all over

access, as well as good notice boards, other visitors to swap stories with and good traveler information. They rarely take advance reservations so you should turn up before noon to reserve your room for the night.

HOSTELS
These are the cheapest form of accommodation and are really more like the old English youth hostels, fairly primitive with dorm rooms but also some air-

rent a tent then check that the zips work—you don't want to share your sleeping accommodation with some of the park's denizens. You will need a flashlight, a lightweight sleeping bag or sheet and a sleeping mat, plus cooking equipment, drinking water, insect repellent and food. Accommodation in Thailand is so cheap that, unless you love the outdoors, bringing all that equipment seems a little

Sofitel Central, Hua Hin (left). Sheraton Grande, Bangkok (middle). Imperial Boat House, Ko Samui (right)

Thailand and range from budget hotel-type buildings to very simple wooden and thatch buildings with a couple of rooms. They are right at the budget end of Thai accommodation and often run only to a shared bathroom, a fan-cooled room and a double bed. The advantage of the best of them, besides their cheap rates, is that they are run by people who are used to Western tourists, can organize trips and often have internet

conditioned doubles. You need to be a member of Hostelling International to stay at a Thai youth hostel. Membership costs B300 per year or B50 for one night.

CAMPING
Most of Thailand's campsites are situated in the 112 national parks and facilities are basic to say the least. You don't really need your own tent as parks have tents and equipment for rent. If you do

unnecessary. Lots of the parks also have inexpensive bungalows and longhouses, which might make a more comfortable alternative, although they tend to be based around groups of six or more people. You should reserve your park accommodation in advance at www.thaiforestbooking.com/nationalpark-eng.htm. Camping is also allowed on islands and beaches although few people bother with a tent.

More low key, the Lamai Homestay guesthouse

BANGKOK

Accommodation is spread around the city in clearly defined areas and it pays to think about which area best suits your itinerary in the capital. If you want to spend a lot of time shopping and dining out and require good transport connections, then Thanon Sukhumvit and the *sois* that run off it are worth considering. Budgetwise, this is a mid-range area with some top-class hotels like the Sheraton Grande Sukhumvit as well as good-value inexpensive places like Suk 11. For the luxury hotel experience you need to stay by the river or, for chic places like The Met and The Sukhothai, along the top end of Thanon Sathorn Tai. Banglamphu and the Thanon Khao San area is good for budget accommodation, but there are also some good mid-range places here and the area is convenient for the Grand Palace, National Museum and Dusit.

PRICES AND SYMBOLS

Prices are for a double room for one night. Breakfast is included unless noted otherwise. All the hotels listed accept credit cards unless otherwise stated. Note that rates vary widely throughout the year.

For a key to the symbols, ▷ 2.

THE ATLANTA

78 Soi 2, Thanon Sukhumvit
Tel 022 526 069, fax 026 568 123
The lobby is wonderfully old-fashioned, and there is an eccentric charm that makes a stay here quite an experience. Bedrooms with a fan are inexpensive, and the standard rooms with air-conditioning are very good value. There are two pools, a restaurant where above-average consideration is given to vegetarians and a travel desk. No credit cards.

🛏 B590–B750
🛎 49 🗗 Some 🏊 Outdoor
🚇 Phloen Chit or Nana

BUDDY LODGE

265 Thanon Khao San
Tel 026 294 477
www.buddylodge.com
This boutique-ish hotel is in the heart of Thanon Khao San. All the rooms have safe deposit boxes, there is a café, tours can be arranged through a travel agency and the small pool on the fifth floor has a sun deck and bar.

🛏 B1,800–B2,200
🛎 43 🗗 🏊 Outdoor
🚇 Rajdhevee

THE CHINATOWN HOTEL

526 Thanon Yaowarat
Tel 022 250 204/6
www.chinatownhotel.co.th
The photograph in the lobby shows what this hotel looked like before it was completely renovated. Now all the rooms

have bathrooms, satellite TV, minibar and safe deposit boxes, and there is internet access in the lobby.

🛏 B883–B4,500
🛎 75 🗗
🚇 Hua Lamphong

CITY LODGE

Soi 9 and Soi 19, Thanon Sukhumvit
Tel 022 537 705 (Soi 9), 022 544 783 (Soi 19)
www.amari.com
Both these boutique hotels are squarely aimed at visitors to the city who want comfortable and smart accommodation without paying for the frills. At Soi 9 there is a restaurant for casual dining, while Soi 19 has La Gritta, an Italian restaurant open all day. You can use the pool and gym at the nearby Amari Boulevard hotel for free.

🛏 B2,200–B3,200
🛎 28 (Soi 9), 34 (Soi 19) (7 and 14 non-smoking, respectively) 🗗
🚇 Hua Lamphong

GRAND CHINA PRINCESS

215 Thanon Yaowarat
Tel 022 249 977
www.grandchina.com
If you want to stay in Chinatown then this is the hotel to choose. Rooms have all the necessary amenities, including tea- and coffee-making facilities and a fridge, and the hotel has a choice of places to eat, including a revolving restaurant at the top of the hotel. There's also music in the lobby at night, a fitness center and a Thai massage service.

B3,200–B12,000
155 (55 non-smoking)
Outdoor
Hua Lamphong

IMPERIAL QUEEN'S PARK HOTEL

Soi 22, Thanon Sukhumvit
Tel 022 619 000
www.imperialhotels.com
This hotel comprises two 37-story towers and a stupendously large lobby with teak, gold-topped columns and a ceiling inlaid with teak panels, all of which is illuminated at night by glistening chandeliers. The extravagance continues with seven restaurants, a squash court, a spa and a range of rooms—deluxe is the standard, then the premier—and suites.
From B7,200
1300 Outdoor
Phrom Phong, exit 2 and a five-minute walk across the park

J W MARRIOTT

Soi 2, Thanon Sukhumvit
Tel 026 567 700
www.marriott.com/bkkdt
This is one of the best hotels along Thanon Sukhumvit, with a choice of deluxe or executive rooms or a suite. The sports facilities include a spa and a 24-hour gym. There is a Chinese and a Thai restaurant and a New York Steakhouse, as well as a gregarious bar that is usually full. Wireless internet connection and broadband are available in all the bedrooms.

From B7,000 excluding breakfast
400 Outdoor
Phloen Chit

KRUNG KASEM SRIKRUNG HOTEL

1860 Thanon Krung Kasem
Tel 022 250 132
From outside Hua Lamphong railway station, you can see this ocher-color hotel over to your right. Cross the canal bridge and turn right at the first set of traffic lights to reach it—very handy if you need to be up for an early train departure. Rooms are functional but clean. There is a laundry service and a coffee shop.

The Imperial Queen's Park Hotel at dusk

B550
120
Hua Lamphong

THE LANDMARK

138 Thanon Sukhumvit
Tel 022 540 404
This is an ultramodern, 31-story hotel with a range of bars and Thai (Nipa Thai ▷ 248), Japanese, Italian, Chinese and international restaurants. There is a pub—English in its themed decor and with live music—and a 24-hour coffee shop. Two levels, dedicated "Lifestyle Floors," have a more contemporary, less business-like style to the bedrooms, with soft furnishings and

Jim Thompson fabrics, and with broadband internet access.

From B4,200 excluding breakfast
414 Outdoor
Nana

MAJESTIC GRANDE

12 Soi 2, Thanon Sukhumvit
Tel 022 622 999
www.majesticgrande.com
Opened in 2005, this very modern hotel has all the comforts you would expect and with a reasonable discount off the official rates it could be good value. It is down a quiet *soi*, a short walk away from the hustle and bustle of Sukhumvit. There is one restaurant, with live jazz music at night, a café by the pool and smartly furnished bedrooms.

B2,990–B17,000
251 Outdoor
Ploen Chit

THE METROPOLITAN

27 Thanon Sathorn Tai
Tel 026 253 333
www.metropolitan.como.bz
Bangkok's most chic and image-conscious accommodation is to be enjoyed at The Metropolitan, dwarfed in size by the nearby Banyan Tree and Sukhothai hotels but etching out a stylish identity of its own. The design is minimalist, pared down to straight lines, clean hues and an air of sophistication. For dining there is the formal Cy'an restaurant but also healthy, organic cuisine at the informal Glow restaurant, and Asian cuisine at the cool Met Bar. The health and fitness center, Shambhala, has a menu of massage therapies, body and facial treatments, and nail care. Guests receive a free 15-minute head and shoulders massage.

From B7,000 excluding breakfast
171 (79 non-smoking)
Outdoor
Sala Daeng

STAYING

NAI LERT PARK
2 Thanon Withayu
Tel 022 530 123
www.bangkok-
nailertpark.swissotel.com/
This low-rise, five-star hotel, formerly the Hilton, has been transformed by its makeover and given a sophisticated, contemporary identity. The landscaped garden, the most delightful of any Bangkok hotel, surrounds the pool and provides a very relaxed atmosphere in the heart of the city. Three restaurants, including an excellent Japanese one (Ganji ▷ 248), and a lounge bar that could feature in a Star Trek movie.
🛏 From B8,800 excluding breakfast
ⓘ 338 (88 non-smoking) 🔄
🏊 Outdoor
🚇 Phloen Chit

NOVOTEL BANGKOK
Soi 6, Siam Square
Tel 022 098 888
www.accorhotels.com/asia
In the noisy heart of the city, this is a busy hotel where the lobby is so often bustling with people that you should only stay here if you enjoy a constantly convivial scene. There is a Chinese and international restaurant for dining, a health center and a popular nightclub (Concept Cm² ▷ 189). Children under 12 stay for free if sharing their parents' room.
🛏 B5,500–B16,800 excluding breakfast
ⓘ 429 🔄 🏊 Outdoor
🚇 Siam

THE ORIENTAL
48 Oriental Avenue
Tel 026 599 000
www.mandarinoriental.com
The most famous hotel in Bangkok has spread to both sides of the river. The bedrooms, where luminaries like Conrad, Graham Greene and Gore Vidal have stayed, and most restaurants are on the east side; the gym, spa and tennis courts are across the river, reached by shuttle boat. It's a very business-like hotel, and the pool is small and cramped.
🛏 From B14,000 excluding breakfast
ⓘ 393 🔄 🏊 Outdoor
🚤 The Oriental

PATHUMWAN PRINCESS
444 Thanon Phayathai
Tel 022 163 700
www.pprincess.com
If you are planning some serious shopping time in the giant MBK center and Siam Square, then this is the hotel for you. It has direct access to MBK and a Skytrain station is just outside. The atmosphere is a busy one. Japanese and Korean restaurants are just

Alfresco dining by the river at The Peninsula

two of many dining choices, and there's also a lobby bar with live music, a health club, a spa, and tennis and squash courts.
🛏 B6,262
ⓘ 462 🔄 🏊 Outdoor
🚇 National Stadium

THE PENINSULA
333 Thanon Charoennakorn, Klongsan
Tel 028 612 888
www.peninsula.com
On the west bank of the Chao Phraya River and adding a distinctive architectural statement to the Bangkok skyline, The Peninsula excels as perhaps Bangkok's best overall hotel. All the bedrooms look out across the river, but you need to be higher than the first few levels, in a deluxe room, to benefit from a bird's-eye view of the sprawling city. There is a superb pool, first-class Chinese, Thai and Pacific-Rim cuisine in the restaurants, and exemplary levels of service. The hotel's shuttle boat transports you across the river from a small pier next to Central Pier until midnight, after which you can take a taxi across the bridge.
🛏 From B10,400 excluding breakfast
ⓘ 370 (288 non-smoking) 🔄
🏊 Outdoor
🚤 Sa Pan Tak Sin pier

PREMIER TRAVELODGE
Soi 8, 170 Thanon Sukhumvit
Tel 022 251 3031
Decent accommodation in this part of town does not come cheaper than at Premier Travelodge. There's no restaurant, but rooms have safe deposit boxes, cable TV, fridge and telephone.
🛏 B700, excluding breakfast
ⓘ 46 🔄
🚇 Nana

RENO HOTEL
40 Soi Kasemson 1, off Thanon Rama I
Tel 022 150 026
renohotel@dickta.com
The Reno is a good-value, comfortable and friendly hotel. The standard rooms have their own bathrooms, the superior ones come with a TV and safe box and the deluxe rooms have a fridge. The pool is just large enough to swim in, there is internet access in the lobby, and there's a laundry service and a café.
🛏 B890–B1,490
ⓘ 58 🔄 🏊 Outdoor
🚇 National Stadium

SATHORN INN
37 Soi 9, Thanon Silom
Tel 022 381 655, fax 022 376 668
sathorninn@hotmail.com
This is a tidy and well-run establishment, conveniently reached from the airport by the airport bus route that stops

at the top of the *soi*. Standard and deluxe rooms are available, with the latter having balconies, a TV and fridge. There is a coffee shop and internet access in the lobby.
B900–B1,500 excluding breakfast
80
Chong Nonsi

SHANGRI-LA HOTEL
89 Soi Wat Suan Plu
Tel 022 367 777
www.shangri-la.com
Facing the Chao Phraya River, the Shangri-La is in many world lists of top 10 hotels so you will find a spa, two pools, tennis and squash courts, day cruises to Ayutthaya and dinner river cruises. There are also Italian (Angellini ▷ 246), Chinese, Thai, Japanese and Western restaurants.
From B5,500
799   Outdoor
Saphan Taksin
Sathorn Pier

SHERATON GRANDE SUKHUMVIT
250 Thanon Sukhumvit
Tel 026 498 888
www.starwoodhotels.com/bangkok
A 33-story tower hotel, the best on Sukhumvit, fronted by a well-turned-out lobby with a marble floor and high ceiling. Rooms are generously sized and richly furnished. There are two good restaurants, a café and an outdoor eatery by the pool, plus at Riva's there are bands most nights, and a jazz bar that is often packed out. The spa is impressive.
B8,000
429   Outdoor
Asok

SIAM HERITAGE
115/1 Thanon Surawong
Tel 023 536 101
www.thesiamheritage.com
This hotel tries hard to maintain an air of elegance and culture with polished floors, teak furniture and part of the lobby displaying Thai art. There is a spa and fitness center although the pool is not large enough to swim in. Coffee and tea is available in the rooms, plus there's cable TV and a Thai restaurant. This is an interesting hotel with easy access to the Skytrain and the metro.
From B5,200
69   Outdoor
Sala Daeng
Sam Yan

SOFITEL CENTRAL PLAZA
1695 Thanon Phaholyothin, Chatuchak
Tel 025 411 234
www.centralhotelsresorts.com
The ease of access by train and subway, a nearby huge shopping center, the weekend Chatuchak market, and the

Relax in comfort at the Shangri-La

top-class facilities within the hotel—including Vietnamese (Le Danang ▷ 247), Thai, Chinese, Italian and Japanese restaurants—all add up to an attractive proposition.
From B5,500
607   Outdoor
Mo Chit
Chatuchak Park

SUK 11
1/33 Sukhumvit Soi 11
Tel 022 534 525/7
www.suk11.com
Overall, this could easily be the best budget accommodation in the city. There's no restaurant but plenty are located nearby. Reservations are essential.

B250–B1,200
60 (all non-smoking)
Nana

THE SUKHOTHAI
13/3 Thanon South Sathorn
Tel 023 448 888
www.sukhothai.com
Winner of various awards, The Sukhothai is among the world's top hotels. There are two good restaurants and a bar, plus an infinity-edge pool.
B11,200–B84,000
214 (78 non-smoking)
Outdoor
Sala Daeng
Lumphini Park

THE SWISS LODGE
3 Thanon Convent
Tel 022 335 345
www.swisslodge.com
A boutique hotel in the heart of the city. There is a small pool and sun deck, tidy bedrooms with teak furniture, 24-hour room service, a business center and laundry.
B4,900–B8,800 excluding breakfast
46   Outdoor
Sala Daeng

THAI COZY HOUSE
113/1–3 Thanon Tanee
Tel 026 295 870
www.thaicozyhouse.com
Clean and tidy rooms—the more expensive ones have a window and include breakfast. A branch of the admirable May Kaidee's Vegetarian is downstairs.
B700–B950
53
Tha Praya Athit

VIENGTAI HOTEL
42 Thanon Rambuttri, Banglamphu
Tel 022 878 153
www.viengtai.co.th
Rooms are modern, and the Thai restaurant does a daily buffet for lunch and Thai and international food at night.
B1,750–B2,350
200 (49 non-smoking)
Outdoor
Tha Praya Athit

STAYING

THE NORTHEAST

Isan cannot boast the range and variety of accommodation available in the other regions of Thailand, but finding somewhere decent to stay is not a problem. There are also a number of exceptionally good places to suit most budgets. Lamai Homestay is something special, and the Sofitel Raja Orchid is first class and not immodestly priced by international standards. Sugar Guesthouse and the Pantawee are also to be specially recommended. In small towns, travelers will sometimes need to stay in inexpensive hotels or guesthouses, perhaps without air-conditioning, but all the places mentioned here are well-kept establishments where the level of personal attention is high.

CHIANG KHAN

RIMKONG GUESTHOUSE

294 Thanon Chaikon Soi 8, Chiang Khan
Tel 042 821 125
http://rimkhong.free.fr
On the banks of the Mekong River, the best room in this guesthouse is No. 6 overlooking the majestic river. There are mosquito grills on the doors and windows but use insect repellent as well, especially if sitting outside on the balcony at night. Breakfast and good coffee is served.
🏨 B340 excluding breakfast
ⓘ 6

TONKHONG GUESTHOUSE

299 Thanon Chaikong Soi 9, Chiang Khan
Tel 042 821 537
A few doors down from Rimkong Guesthouse, this is a similar kind of setup but with a couple of rooms enjoying air-conditioning. There are soul-stirring views over the Mekong River and a small terrace to watch the sun go down and sip a cold beer in the evening. Food is served all day.
🏨 From B340 excluding breakfast
ⓘ 8

KHAO YAI

GREEN LEAF GUEST HOUSE

Thanon Thanarat, Kilometer Stone 7.5, Pak Chong
Tel 044 365 073
It's budget accommodation, but if you are planning to spend as much time as possible out in the park and with a good nature guide then Green Leaf is worth considering. The restaurant is inexpensive, but the food is tasty and, best of all, the tours into the park are conducted by an expert and full of surprises. Do not confuse the guesthouse with a travel company called Green Leaf in Pak Chong.
🏨 B200–B300
ⓘ 12

KHAO YAI GARDEN LODGE

Thanon Thanarat, Kilometer Stone 7, Pak Chong
Tel 044 365 178
www.khaoyai-garden-lodge.com
Khao Yai is a businesslike bungalow resort that caters for guests of varying ages and budgets. Accommodation starts at shoestring prices and escalates to pricey one-bedroom cabins with air-conditioning and a fridge. The on-site restaurant similarly ranges from standard one-plate rice dishes to German sausages and wine. The best thing about Garden Lodge is its tours (▷ 240) in and around the Khao Yai National Park (▷ 93) and there are various packages

that include different tours. Free pickup from Pak Chong.

🛏 B100–B1,200
ℹ 160 ⟳ Some

KHON KAEN

CHAROEN THANI PRINCESS

260 Thanon Srichan, Khon Kaen
Tel 043 220 400
www.royalprincess.com

A 19-story hotel in the middle of town that would be the best place to stay were it not for the Sofitel Raja Orchid (▷ below). All the rooms have a fridge, and the deluxe rooms have tea- and coffee-making facilities. As well as a café serving international and Thai food, there is a Chinese restaurant and a bar by the pool.

🛏 From B1,500
ℹ 320 (76 non-smoking) ⟳
🏊 Outdoor

KAEN INN HOTEL

56 Thanon Klangmuang, Khon Kaen
Tel 043 245 420

This is a gregarious hotel in the middle of town where you can meet fellow travelers. Plus it's good value for money, with well-kept rooms that come with TV and a fridge. On the premises there's a snooker room, barber shop, massage parlor, 24-hour coffee shop, and a restaurant with evening entertainment (▷ 250).

🛏 B600
ℹ 160 ⟳

KOSA HOTEL

250 Thanon Si Chan, Khon Kaen
Tel 043 225 014/17

The Kosa is a smart and modern hotel, a short distance away from the Sofitel Raja Orchid, with a pool and fitness center and sauna. The only restaurant is a Chinese one, but there is a coffee shop serving European and Isan food and a beer garden outside. The 17-story Kosa can be a busy place, with seminars and mini-conventions taking over the place.

🛏 B1,260–B1,500
ℹ 181 ⟳ 🏊 Outdoor

SAWASDEE HOTEL

177–179 Thanon Namuang, Khon Kaen
Tel 043 221 600
thesawasdee@hotmail.com

In the middle of the city, close to shops and places to eat, this is good-value place in Khon Kaen. The standard rooms have good-size bathrooms; better ones face away from the main road and come with tea- and coffee-making facilities. There is a laundry room with a washing machine.

🛏 B229–B890 excluding breakfast
ℹ 72 ⟳

The impressive Sofitel Raja Orchid in Khon Kaen

SOFITEL RAJA ORCHID

9/9 Thanon Prachasumran, Khon Kaen
Tel 043 322 155
www.sofitel.com

This is a superb hotel in many respects, with local artwork dotted around the lobby and restaurants. The graceful style extends to the bedrooms, where Isan woodcarvings and handwoven silks are to be found. There are Italian, Vietnamese and Chinese restaurants, a microbrewery on the premises, and a basement complex—The Underground (▷ 194)—for evening entertainment. A shuttle bus serves the airport for all flights.

🛏 B2,571–B2,924 excluding breakfast
ℹ 293 ⟳ 🏊 Outdoor 🏋

KO PHET

LAMAI HOMESTAY/GUESTHOUSE

Kok Phet, Bua Yai, near Nakhon Ratchasima (Korat)
Tel 062 585 894
www.thailandhomestay.com

The Lamai offers amazingly good accommodation in a quiet rice village where you will experience rural Thailand up close and for real. Rates include transfer from Korat bus station or Bua Yai railway station, rooms with fan or air-conditioning and a lovely breakfast in the carefully nurtured garden. Lots of activities and excursions are available, including a visit to a local silk village. You can also go on a village market tour, see noodle-making or join a food-foraging trip and see how villagers supplement their diet with scorpions and other insects. Stay here for a couple of nights or make it a base for a longer stay with trips to Korat or Phimai.

🛏 B100–B600; half-board, full-board, and 2- to 4-night packages also available
ℹ 4 ⟳ Some

LOEI

LOEI PALACE HOTEL

167/4 Thanon Charroenrat, Loei
Tel 042 815 668
www.amari.com

Loei does not look the kind of town that would have a comfortable and classy hotel like this one on its doorstep. The open-air lobby and the overall design has a conspicuous lack of decorative features, but photographs behind the lobby show flood water reaching a depth of 2m (6.5ft) in the lobby, when the nearby river flooded in 2002. Bedrooms are spacious and smart, and there's a good restaurant with Thai–Chinese and international food (Botun ▷ 251) and a pub and restaurant with karaoke.

🛏 B2,825–B3,000 excluding breakfast
ℹ 156 ⟳ 🏊 Outdoor 🏋

SUGAR GUESTHOUSE
4/1 Thanon Wisuttitep, Soi 2, Loei
Tel 042 812 982
Typical of the good-value accommodation to be found throughout the northeast, the Sugar Guesthouse is a little out of the way. It is at the river end of town, reached by walking up the top (north) end of Thanon Charoenrat and turning right onto Thanon Pipatmongkol and then left into Thanon Wisuttitep until Soi 2 is reached on your left. There are rooms with fan or air-conditioning, a nice garden, breakfast, laundry service and bicycles and motorcycles for rent.
🛏 B150–B350 excluding breakfast
ℹ 8 🛏 Some

NAKHON RATCHASIMA (KORAT)
ROYAL PRINCESS HOTEL
1137 Thanon Suranarai, Korat
Tel 044 256 629
www.royalprincess.com
The best hotel in the city in terms of facilities, with a good pool, a traditional Chinese restaurant and the Princess Café (6am–midnight), with a Thai-European buffet every night and a Japanese corner. The hotel's location is not perfect, north of the North Gate, and too far to walk into town though *songthaews* run into town along Thanon Suranarai.
🛏 From B1,672
ℹ 186 🛏 🏊 🎾

SRIPATANA HOTEL
346 Thanon Suranaree, Korat
Tel 044 251 652
www.sripatana.com
A good-value hotel, less than 1 km (0.6 mile) from the railway station, with a coffee shop, a 24-hour room service, a fair-size pool, and large bedrooms with bath and shower. If only staying over in the city for a night, this is well worth considering.
🛏 B460–B615 excluding breakfast
ℹ 180 🛏 🏊 Outdoor

TOKYO HOTEL
256–258 Thanon Suranaree, Korat
Tel 044 242 788
Not as good value as the Sripatana but the next best place—the rooms with a fan are especially cheap but they have no hot water; the air-con rooms are the same size, and cost almost twice as much. The hotel is conveniently located in the middle of town.
🛏 B350 excluding breakfast
ℹ 35 🛏

NONG KHAI
MUT MEE
111/4 Thanon Kaeworawut, Nong Khai
Tel 042 460 717
www.mutmee.com

Restful greenery at Mut Mee, Nong Khai

On the bank of the Mekong River, inexpensive accommodation and a good restaurant are two reasons for staying here. The place is kept clean and there is a very relaxed feel to the place. Popular with travelers, it has a small art gallery next door, yoga, reiki and astrology courses, and meditation classes.
🛏 B250–B600 excluding breakfast
ℹ 28

PANTAWEE HOTEL
1049 Thanon Haisoke, Nong Khai
Tel 042 411 568
www.nongkhaihotel.com
The Pantawee wins hands down as *the* place to stay in Nong Khai. The location is convenient—in the middle of town—and there is a choice of rooms, a 24-hour restaurant and bar, internet access any time and friendly staff. Many of the bedrooms have a computer with free internet use. There is also a useful travel desk and information on local tours and bus connections, and a large open-air tub for cooling down in.
🛏 B350–B1,000 excluding breakfast
ℹ 105 🛏

SAWASDEE GUEST HOUSE
403 Thanon Meechai, Nong Khai
Tel 042 412 502
A characterful Thai-Chinese shophouse, carefully restored so as to preserve a sense of times past, with rooms above the back courtyard where breakfast is served. Bedrooms are basic but clean and comfortable, though some of the mattresses lack firmness, and the best rooms come with a fridge. Try to avoid the rooms directly facing the street because in the mornings Thanon Meechai is a busy road and the noise of traffic will wake you up. There is a laundry service.
🛏 B170–B400 excluding breakfast
ℹ 14 🛏 Some rooms

SI SAKET
KESSIRI HOTEL
1102–1105 Thanon Kukhan, Si Saket
Tel 045 614 007
The Kessiri is definitely the best place for a good night's sleep in Si Saket. It is in the middle of town, between the train and bus stations and easily reached from either by tuk-tuk. The rooms are comfortable and there is a restaurant downstairs. Discounts are often available if demand is slack.
🛏 B850–B1,600
ℹ 93 🛏

STAYING

UBON RATCHATHANI

LAITHONG HOTEL
50 Thanon Pichitrangsan, Ubon Ratchathani
Tel 045 264 271
www.laithonghotel.net
Laithong's exterior is unprepossessing, and it is a fair walk from the middle of town, but this is the plushest hotel in Ubon Ratchathani. The restaurant is a mixture of Thai, Chinese and international food, the lobby serves cocktails and there is live music some evenings. There's also a massage parlor and coffee shop, and free transport to and from the airport.
🛏 B1,300–B3,000
🛏 124 🔲 🏊 Outdoor

RATCHATHANI HOTEL
297 Thanon Khuenthani, Ubon Ratchathani
Tel 045 244 388
Close to the museum, on the other side of the street, the Ratchathani is a lot better than the other hotels along this road. All the rooms have showers, and some have baths as well. There are some inexpensive ones with a fan, but the best bedrooms have air-conditioning; when these are discounted they are very good value indeed. A restaurant serves breakfast, lunch and dinner.
🛏 B500–B850
🛏 87 🔲

TOHSANG KHONGJIAM RESORT
68 Moo 7, Ban Huay Tai, Kong Jiam, Ubon Ratchathani
Tel 045 351 174
www.tohsang.com
On the banks of the Mekong River, 95km (60 miles) from Ubon Ratchathani, all the rooms in this resort enjoy views of the magnificent river from their own balconies. Two-thirds of the rooms are called deluxe, and there are eight superior rooms and four villas. Thai massage, spa and a pool, of course, plus evening

kayaking in the river is organized and boat rides from the resort take in a visit to a local village. Local and international food is on offer at the restaurants.
🛏 B8,500–B9,500
🛏 55 🔲

TOKYO HOTEL
360 Thanon Opparat, Ubon Ratchathani
Tel 045 241 739
This is the best-value hotel in Ubon Ratchathani and very adequately equipped. The beds in the clean rooms with cable TV are new and firm, plus there is a little breakfast corner in the lobby and a

The glass façade of the Charoensri Grand Royal Hotel

secure parking area. From the museum, walk north up Thanon Chayangkun and you will see the sign on the left side of the street.
🛏 B220–B800 excluding breakfast
🛏 38 🔲

UDON THANI

CHAROEN HOTEL
549 Thanon Phosri, Udon Thani
Tel 042 248 155
charoenhotel@hotmail.com
Showing its age a little, this is still a decent place to stay for somewhere between the standards of the Charoensri Grand Royal and the Charoensri Palace (▷ below). The rooms are fine—all have a fridge and cable TV. Breakfast

(B153) is not included in the room rate but is available at the restaurant, which also does a lunchtime buffet. There is internet access available in the hotel and a choice of single or double beds. The swimming pool is outside, on your right as you approach the hotel entrance.
🛏 B700–B900 excluding breakfast
🛏 250 🔲 🏊 Outdoor

CHAROENSRI GRAND ROYAL HOTEL
271 Thanon Prachak, Udon Thani
Tel 042 343 555
www.charoensrigrand.com
Close to the train and main bus stations and the city's modern shopping mall, this is Udon's top-class hotel, with a good-value Thai restaurant and professional service. The lobby is bright and airy, however the same cannot be said of the light-challenged interior, and there is a gloomy monotony to the bedroom floors. Still, though, the best place to stay, with a choice of king-size or two queen-size beds in the bedrooms.
🛏 From B1,900
🛏 255 🔲 🏊 Outdoor

CHAROENSRI PALACE HOTEL
60 Thanon Phosri, Udon Thani
Tel 042 242 611
Well, maybe not a palace but very good value for a one-night stay in Udon and just a short tuk-tuk ride (B30 to B40) away from the bus or train station. The bedrooms are large and well kept, with cable TV and fridge, plus there's an attractive little Italian restaurant (Vittorio Piccola Roma; ▷ 254) just up the road.
🛏 From B380 excluding breakfast
🛏 70 🔲

STAYING

THE NORTH

Because of its popularity as an away-from-it-all destination, northern Thailand has a comprehensive range of accommodation, from simple bivouac-style chalets to luxurious resorts to rival those in Bangkok. Trekkers can even stay in hill-tribe villages, sleeping in family homes on floor mats and sharing the household food. A resurgence of interest in the history and culture of the north has spawned a boom in hotels built in early Lanna style, with minimalist combinations of dark-stained teak, white stucco walls and red tiled floors. Boutique hotels of this style are shooting up in and around Chiang Mai.

Between the simple country lodgings and the five-star hotels are thousands of inexpensive guesthouses, ranging from tastefully converted family homes to backstreet, barracks-like buildings, charging as little as B200 per night. Even the cheapest rooms are normally adequately furnished and clean. Rural resorts, particularly those in the mountains, usually offer a wide range of sporting facilities, from access to a golf course and riding stables to canoe and mountain bicycle rental. Many have spas offering beauty treatments and massage. Hotels and guesthouses alike normally have comprehensive travel and tourist information services which are often more informative and helpful than official tourist offices.

STAYING

PRICES AND SYMBOLS

Prices are for a double room for one night. Breakfast is included unless noted otherwise. All the hotels listed accept credit cards unless otherwise stated. Note that rates vary widely throughout the year.

For a key to the symbols, ▷ 2.

BAN SOP RUAK

ANANTARA GOLDEN TRIANGLE

Ban Sop Ruak–Mae Sai road, Chiang Saen 57150
Tel 053 784 079-81
The true "Golden Triangle," where the borders of Thailand, Myanmar (Burma) and Laos

meet, starts at the end of the grounds of this luxurious resort. Top architects and landscapers created a palatial Lanna-style complex, where every room has a view of the Mekong River. A two-story lobby leads to a restaurant and also out to an "infinity" swimming pool. Non-smoking rooms available.
🛏 B3,500
ⓘ 106 rooms, 4 suites 🚭
🌊 Outdoor 🏆

IMPERIAL GOLDEN TRIANGLE RESORT

222 Ban Sop Ruak (Ban Sop Ruak–Mai Sai road), Chiang Saen 57150
Tel 053 784 001
Set high above the Mekong River all rooms have terraces

overlooking the river and the mountains beyond, and the terrace of its Border View restaurant is a splendid spot to watch the setting sun gild the Golden Triangle.
🛏 B2,060–B4,500
ⓘ 74 (20 non-smoking) 🚭

CHIANG DAO

RIM DOI RESORT

46 Moo 4, Muang Ghay, Chiang Dao
Tel 053 375 028/9, 017 066 876
www.rimdoiresort.com
The name of this pretty little resort means "on the edge of the mountain," and that describes its location exactly. The "doi" looms over its cluster of bungalows and chalets. The accommodation is either in simple chalets in the garden or

in more stylish, teak-walled and furnished lakeside rooms. A restaurant and karaoke bar also overlook the water.

🍽 B200–B600 excluding breakfast
🛏 70

CHIANG MAI

PARADISE SPA RESORT

43/1 Moo 6, Tambol Mae Rim, Chiang Mai 50200

Tel 053 860 463–4

Most rooms have spa facilities attached, and rooms are sumptuously furnished in Lanna style. Owner Nina Boomsirithum is a graduate in interior design, and her background is evident in the resort's exquisite ambience.

🍽 B2,200–B7,000
🛏 24

RACHAMANKHA

Thanon Rachamankha, Soi 9, Chiang Mai 50200

Tel 053 904 111

www.rachamankha.com

The spacious rooms are furnished with Lanna, Burmese or Chinese antiques, and open out onto exquisitely designed tropical gardens or onto a secluded courtyard swimming pool. Parking available.

🍽 B6,500–B18,000
🛏 24 rooms, 2 suites (all non-smoking)
📶 🏊 Outdoor

TAMARIND VILLAGE

50/1 Thanon Ratchadamnoen, Chiang Mai 50200

Tel 053 418 898

www.tamarindvillage.com

This is one of the best Lanna-style boutique hotels in Chiang Mai, an understated synthesis of dark woods, whitewashed walls and select antiques. Rooms look out over gardens dominated by the eponymous tamarind tree, while cool cloisters surround a secluded swimming pool, bordered at one end by a small, open-sided restaurant. Non-smoking rooms and parking available.

🍽 B3,000–B4,200
🛏 40 📶 🏊 Outdoor

CHIANG RAI

THE LEGEND RESORT & SPA

124/15 Thanon Kohloy, Amphoe Muang, Chiang Rai 57000

Tel 053 910 400/29

www.thelegend-chiangrai.com

This new hotel, opened in 2004, could become a local legend. It's built in Lanna style on an island in the Kok River, just a short walk from the middle of the city. Rooms are furnished with exquisite antiques and reproductions, while public areas are a Lanna-style mixture of whitewashed walls and teak. The restaurant and pool are on the river bank, with views of the mountains beyond. For

Antiques abound at Rachamankha, Chiang Mai

real seclusion, reserve one of the villas, with their own private pools. Parking available.

🍽 B3,300–B6,700
🛏 78 (all non-smoking) 🏊 Outdoor

THE WHITE HOUSE

789 Thanon Phaholyotin, Chiang Rai

Tel 053 713 427

www.chiangraiprovince.com

Set back from Chiang Rai's main thoroughfare, the White House is a charming villa-style guesthouse with simple but clean, comfortable rooms. Many rooms lead onto a terrace overlooking the pool.

🍽 B350–B1,200, B850 excluding breakfast
🛏 12 🏊 Outdoor

CHIANG SAEN

GIN'S GUESTHOUSE

Sop Ruak Road, Chiang Saen

Tel 053 650 847

The Mekong River practically flows at the end of the garden of this friendly, rambling Thai home, whose owners can arrange boat trips as far as China. Ask for a room on the upstairs floor of the main house, where you'll share a large, comfortable lounge with other guests. Gin, the man of the house, will gladly arrange tours of the region.

🍽 B200–B300 excluding breakfast
🛏 12

DOI ANGKHANG

ANGKHANG NATURE RESORT

1/1 Moo 5, Baan Koon, Tambon Mae Ngon, Amphoe Fang, Chiang Mai 50320

Tel 053 450 110, fax 053 450 120

www.amari.com

The mountains and forests of Doi Angkhang embrace this haven of sybaritis luxury, run by the Amari hotel group. The large and airy rooms, furnished in teak and local fabrics, have huge picture windows. In its fine restaurant, the Camillia, you dine beneath a raftered ceiling. The menu features only organic products from the nearby royal agricultural project.

🍽 B4,150–B5,140 excluding breakfast
🛏 72 rooms (23 non-smoking), 2 suites 🏊 Outdoor 📶

LAMPANG

PIN HOTEL

8 Suandok Rd, Lampang 52100

Tel 054 322 283/4, 054 221 509

www.travelideas.net

The modern, neat and clean Pin is tucked away on a quiet lane linking two of Lampang's busiest streets (parking available). Rooms are furnished and decorated in friendly, pastel shades and light woods. A spacious lounge adjoins a bright breakfast room and restaurant.

🍽 B450–B850 excluding breakfast
🛏 59 (all non-smoking) 📶

LAMPHUN

HOTEL SUPAMIT
204/4 Thanon Jamma Dhavi, Lamphun
Tel 053 534 865
With its grand, Siamese-style porticoed entrance, the functional rooms hardly match the palatial promise of the vast lobby, but most of them have fine views of the city and the *wat*. There's ample parking and a noisy karaoke lounge.
💰 B300–B400
ℹ️ 78 (some non-smoking)

MAE HONG SON

ROOKS HOLIDAY HOTEL AND RESORT
114/5–7 Thanon Khunlumprapas, Mae Hong Son 58000
Mae Hong Son's largest hotel, it also has an efficient tour desk where guests can reserve excursions. The comfortable rooms overlook tropical gardens or the mountains. Parking available.
💰 B2,200–B2,820
ℹ️ 114 (some non-smoking) 🔄
🏊 Outdoor 📺

MAE SAI

PU TAWAN RESORT
414 Moo 10, Tambol Weangpangkhan, Mae Sai
Tel 053 640 727, 069 139 502
Sitting on a hillside above Mae Sai, this romantic little resort is a peaceful retreat from the frontier-town bustle below. Eighteen air-conditioned bungalows are set in lush gardens, half with Bali-style bathrooms open to the sky.
💰 B500–B1,000 excluding breakfast
ℹ️ 18 🔄

MAE SALONG

MAESALONG FLOWER HILLS RESORT
779 Moo 1, Maesalong-Nok, Mae Fah Luang, Chiang Rai
Tel 053 765 496/7
The tea plantations of the Queen Mother's Mae Fah Luang project clothe the mountainsides below this away-from-it-all resort. The 23 bungalow rooms are simple but comfortable; the most

expensive have views of the mountains and gardens.
💰 B1,000–B1,500 excluding breakfast
ℹ️ 45 🔄

MAE SARIANG

RIVERSIDE HOTEL
85/1 Thanon Langpanich, Mae Sariang
Tel 053 681 353
www.riverhousehotels.com
From this attractive hotel you have a fine view of the Yuam River and the mountains beyond. The floors and walls of the rooms are made entirely of wood, so smoking is discouraged. No credit cards, cash only. Parking available.
💰 B200–B700
ℹ️ 12

The exquisite Belle Villa resort in Pai

MAE SOT

CENTRAL MAE SOT HILL HOTEL
100 Asia Road, Mae Sot
Tel 055 532 601–8
www.centralhotelsresorts.com
The sleek exterior of the hotel towers over shabby Mae Sot. The warmly carpeted, bamboo- and rattan-furnished rooms are a comfortable retreat.
💰 From B1,800
ℹ️ 113 (33 non-smoking) 🔄
🏊 Outdoor 📺

NAN

DHEVARAJ HOTEL
466 Sumondhevaraj Road, Nan 55000
Tel 054 751 577
Nan's top hotel is a modern high-rise with rooms clustered

around a chain-style central courtyard where local bands perform most evenings. Parking available.
💰 B1,200
ℹ️ 152 🔄 🏊 Outdoor 📺

PAI

BELLE VILLA
Mae Hong Son Road, Pai
Tel 053 365 318–21
www.bellevillaresort.com
The teak-built bungalows at this resort are furnished and equipped as well as a five-star hotel's suites. The restaurant overlooks a pool, rice paddies and distant mountains.
💰 B3,178–B4,002
ℹ️ 40 🔄 🏊 Outdoor

PHAYAO

GATEWAY HOTEL
7/36 Pratuklong 2 Road, Phayao 56000
Tel 054 411 333–5
The Gateway's pink exterior makes it hard to miss. It's a modern hotel with rooms of international standard. A gym and a pool offer welcome relaxation. Parking available.
💰 B1,000
ℹ️ 108 (all non smoking) 🔄
🏊 Outdoor 📺

PHRAE

MAE YOM PALACE THANI
Thanon Yantra Kritson 181/6, Phrae
Tel 054 521 028
This central hotel is a good base for exploring. Rooms are small but have TV and air-conditioning. Parking available.
💰 B750–B1,000
ℹ️ 104 🔄 🏊 Outdoor

THATON

MAEKOK RIVER VILLAGE RESORT
PO Box 3, Mae Ai, Chiang Rai 50200 (off highway 1089)
Tel 053 459 3556, fax 053 459 329
www.maekok-river-village-resort.com
This resort is an ideal place for a family holiday, with a pool and enough activities to keep children of all ages happy.
💰 B2,625–B4,100
ℹ️ 20 rooms, 8 villas (all non-smoking)
🔄 🏊 Outdoor 📺

STAYING

CENTRAL THAILAND

Central Thailand lacks the range of luxurious resorts of the north but nevertheless can offer a comprehensive variety of accommodation and, in Kanchanaburi province, a unique overnight attraction—river pontoon rooms. The pontoon rooms float directly on the water, mostly the two Kwai rivers, and are often smothered in flowers and jungle creepers. Kanchanaburi and Ayutthaya also have some very attractive riverside resorts, and two luxury hotels opened in Sukhothai in 2004/05 to cater to a steadily climbing number of visitors to the World Heritage Site. New hotels have also sprung up in Phitsanulok, where the city is undergoing a facelift. Elsewhere in central Thailand the accommodation tends to be in conventional city hotels or small guesthouses—one advantage is that room rates are correspondingly low.

PRICES AND SYMBOLS

Prices are for a double room for one night. Breakfast is included unless noted otherwise. All the hotels listed accept credit cards unless otherwise stated. Note that rates vary widely throughout the year.

For a key to the symbols, ▷ 2.

AYUTTHAYA

AYUTTHAYA GRAND HOTEL

55/5 Moo 1, Tambol Tanu, U-Thani, Ayutthaya
Tel 035 335 483/91

The white façade of the Grand dominates the central market area of Ayutthaya. Rooms range from simply furnished ones costing only B500 to spacious, plushly appointed suites. Sports facilities include a large pool, a well-equipped fitness room and a snooker table. Parking available.

🛏 B1,400–B1,800
ℹ 122 💲 🏊 Outdoor 🍴

AYUTTHAYA RIVERSIDE

91/1 Moo 10, Tambol Kamang, Amphoe Pranakorn, Ayutthaya 13000
Tel 035 234 873–7

This modern high-rise with parking sits directly next to the Pasak River. The rooms are furnished in local textiles, and there are five large suites with living areas and work desks. One of the two restaurants is on the river, and dinner cruises embark every evening from its pier.

🛏 B1,800
ℹ 102 💲

KRUNGSRI RIVER HOTEL

27/2 Moo 11, Thanon Rajchana, Tambol Kamang, Ayutthaya 13000
Tel 035 244 333

Rooms are furnished with fine fabrics and drapes and either vast king-size beds or extra-wide singles. Sports facilities include a large pool and bowling alleys. Guests can dine either in the restaurant or on the hotel's own riverboat. Parking available.

🛏 From B1,350
ℹ 212 (60 non-smoking) 💲
🏊 Outdoor 🍴

CHANTHABURI

MANEECHAN RESORT AND SPORT CLUB

110 Moo 11, Thanon Sukhumvit, Tambol Plub Pla, Chanthaburi 22000
Tel 039 343 777/8

The emphasis is on sport at this top-quality resort on the edge of Chanthaburi. Sports and spa facilities include a large pool, a well-equipped fitness room, a snooker table, sauna, steam room and jacuzzi. The modern, comfortably furnished rooms have twin queen-size beds. Parking available.

🛏 B1,500
ℹ 72 (all non-smoking) 💲
🏊 Outdoor 🍴

STAYING

SUANRIMTHARN RESORT
139 Moo 1, Tambol Khoawongkot, Amphoe Khanghang Maew, Chanthaburi 22160

Tel 019 236 332

You'd be forgiven for believing yourself in Switzerland in this neat little resort set in rolling countryside with a mountain backdrop. Accommodation is in Swiss-style chalets, with private balconies overlooking lush gardens, a pool and a fish pond. The restaurant serves Vietnamese, Thai and Western dishes. Parking available.

🛏 B1,250–B3,000
ⓘ 23 (all non-smoking) 🈲
🏊 Outdoor

KANCHANABURI
RIVER KWAI CABIN
28/234 Moo 7, Tham Krasae, Kanchanaburi

Tel 029 678 181–4

From the riverside gardens of this jungle resort you have a fine view of the most spectacular stretch of the "Death Railway," which clings perilously to the side of a Kwai River gorge. Trains from Bangkok, Kanchanaburi and Nam Tok stop at a station nearby. Accommodation is in simple bivouac-style cottages or riverbank cabins.

🛏 2-night package B1,580, includes 5 meals and activities
ⓘ 20 🈲

RIVER KWAI VILLAGE
74/12 Moo 4, Tha Sao, Kanchanaburi 77150

Tel 034 634 455/6

www.bkk2000.com/rkvh

The long-established River Kwai Village sits within several acres of tropical forest bordered by the Kwai Noi River. You can stay in one of the hotel's "raftels," houseboats moored to the riverbank. The "village" has a full entertainment program including a "jungle bar" with live bands and "buggies" for exploring the forest. Parking available.

🛏 B2,000–B2,800
ⓘ 191 🈲 🏊 Outdoor

KAMPHAENG PHET
TECHNO RIVERSIDE RESORT
27/27 Moo 2, Tambon Nakhon Chum, Kamphaeng Phet

Tel 055 722 265

This pleasant riverside resort was probably given the odd name "Techno" because it's a favorite venue for company seminars. Light meals are served in a small, terraced restaurant, with views of the river. Rooms with river views are much more expensive than those without, but well worth the extra. Parking available.

🛏 B450–B1,200 excluding breakfast
ⓘ 45 🈲

The Royal Cliff Beach Resort has a gorgeous location

KO SAMET
AO PRAO
64 Moo 4, Tambon Phe, Rayong 21160

Tel 038 644 100–2

www.samedresorts.com

During the quiet season, this luxury resort has very attractive special offers that cut the room rate by up to half. The rates are then a real bargain for the class of accommodation and services. Rooms are rustic but luxurious; the more expensive of them front the sea, but they are all only a very short walk from the beach.

🛏 B5,100
ⓘ 58 🈲

SAMET VIEW RESORT
88/1 4 Tambon Phe, Rayong 21160

Tel 038 651 681/2

This extensive resort takes up an entire section of coast, including sandy Ao Wai bay and neighboring Ao Hin Klaeng bay. Accommodation is in comfortable, attractively furnished wooden bungalows, many of them directly on the beach, from where boats can be rented for diving and snorkeling trips.

🛏 B2,080–B2,280
ⓘ 30 (all non-smoking) 🈲

LOP BURI
LOPBURI INN
28–29 Thanon Narai Maharach, Amphoe Muang, Lop Buri 15000

Tel 036 412 300, 036 412 609, 036 412 802

www.lopburiinnresort.com

Lop Buri's biggest hotel occupies an entire city corner block. Its six storys have 130 rooms furnished and decorated in international style with some traditional Thai touches, such as paintings of historical scenes. Thai, Chinese and Western cuisine is served in its popular "Lopburi Cafe." Parking available.

🛏 B1,000–B1,500
ⓘ 130 🈲

LOPBURI INN RESORT
144 Thanon Paholyothin, Amphoe Muang, Lop Buri

Tel 036 614 702, 036 420 777, 036 421 453

Each of the 100 rooms at this resort hotel is named after a Thai province and furnished in provincial style—reserve a Chiang Mai province room, for instance, and you're transported to the Lanna north. Facilities include a large swimming pool, sauna and exercise room. The restaurant is one of Lop Buri's best. Parking available.

🛏 B1,200–B1,800
ⓘ 100 🈲 🏊 Outdoor 🈯

STAYING

PATTAYA

GRAND JOMTIEN PALACE

356 Thanon Jomtien Beach, Pattaya, Chonburi 20260

Tel 038 231 405

www.grandjomtienpalacehotel.com

Ask for a west-facing room to enjoy the sunset over the Gulf of Thailand. All rooms have private balconies; those facing inland are cheaper. Two hotel wings overlook the gardens, with their three pools. Parking available.

🏨 B1,510

🛏 52 (all non-smoking) 💳

🏊 Outdoor 🍴

GREEN PARK RESORT

240/5 Moo 5, Soi Pingpa, North Pattaya, Chonburi 20150

Tel 038 426 356–8

www.greenparkpattaya.com

All rooms at this resort overlook its huge, landscaped pool. There are also 16 bungalows set among tropical gardens. The resort's "Park Restaurant" serves Thai and international dishes.

🏨 B1,800–B2,200

🛏 193 (all non-smoking) 💳

🏊 Outdoor 🍴

ROYAL CLIFF BEACH RESORT

Royal Cliff Bay, Pattaya, Chonburi 20150

Tel 038 250 421

www.royalcliff.com

This vast resort is set in 26ha (64 acres) of clifftop parkland with its own beach. There are five swimming pools, ten restaurants and four bars. It's five-star accommodation, with a "presidential suite" costing B55,000 per night. Parking available.

🏨 B5,220

🛏 1,120 (400 non-smoking) 💳

🏊 Outdoor 🍴

PHITSANULOK

THANI HOTEL

39 Thanon Sanambin, Amphoe Muang, Phitsanulok 65000

Tel 055 211 065

www.phitsanulokthani.com

Phitsanulok's top hotel is a high-rise, one block from the river. Rooms are large, airy and

decorated in pastel shades. The elegant restaurant serves Thai and international cuisine. Parking available.

🏨 B980

🛏 105 rooms (7 non-smoking), 5 suites 💳

RAYONG

BAAN PAE CABANA

206/1–2, Moo 3, Tambol Klaeng 21160 Rayong

Tel 038 648 489

If you're catching the boat to Ko Samet island it's worth adding a night or two at this mainland resort, which offers free transfers to the ferry station. Many of the 35 thatched and timber-built

Beautiful furnishings at the Ananda Museum Gallery Hotel

bungalows overlook the sea. The resort offers a wide range of water sports.

🏨 B3,200–B6,000

🛏 35 💳 🏊 Outdoor

SI SATCHANALAI

WANG YUM RESORT

78/2 Moo 6, Si Satchanalai

Tel 055 631 380, 012 834 220

The Si Satchanalai Historical Park is just a short walk from this very attractive resort hotel. Accommodation is in comfortably furnished bungalows. The main building, a substantial teak-built house, has a good restaurant.

🏨 B800–B2,000 excluding breakfast

🛏 10 (all non-smoking) 💳

SUKHOTHAI

ANANDA MUSEUM GALLERY HOTEL

10 Moo 4, Banlum, Muang Sukhothai 64000

Tel 055 622 428–31

Sukhothai's newest luxury hotel, opened in 2004, has luxurious rooms with fine reproductions and local textiles. Original Sukhothai dishes are served in its Celadon garden restaurant.

🏨 B3,200

🛏 32

LOTUS VILLAGE

170 Thanon Ratchathanee, Sukhothai 64000

Tel 055 621 484

www.lotus-village.com

This charming resort-style hotel is tucked away between Sukhothai's new market and the Yom River, with cozy timber-built bungalows. No credit cards. Parking available.

🏨 B1,130

🛏 18 rooms, 2 villas (all non-smoking) 💳

RAJTHANEE HOTEL

229 Thanon Charodvitheetong, Sukhothai 64000

Tel 055 611 031, 055 611 308, 055 612 877

A business hotel, the Rajthanee has all the facilities needed by a traveling tourist. Bathrooms have full-size tubs. The airy terrace restaurant serves Thai and Western food. Parking available.

🏨 B900–B1,200

🛏 84 💳 🏊 Outdoor

THAI VILLAGE HOUSE

214 Thanon Charodvitheetong, Sukhothai

Tel 055 697 583

Just a five-minute bicycle ride from the Sukhothai Historical Park, this guesthouse is within easy reach of the ruined city. Simply furnished timber-built chalets are clustered within an overgrown garden. Parking available.

🏨 B600–B900 excluding breakfast

🛏 100 💳

THE SOUTH

Staying in southern Thailand is usually about being on an island and close to a beach, and nearly all the resorts mentioned here fulfill these needs. Some are five-star establishments where pampering is an art form. Mid-range places vary more in quality, but the best ones are close to a beach, kept spotlessly clean and can arrange most amenities even if they are not directly available. Accommodation during the high season in Phuket and Ko Samui should be booked well in advance. Remember, too, that some resort areas in southern Thailand, in particular Phuket and Ko Samui, can be pricey during the high season when room rates increase significantly. Ko Lanta is growing in popularity as an island with a good range of places to stay that suits most budgets.

PRICES AND SYMBOLS

Prices are for a double room for one night. Breakfast is included unless noted otherwise. All the hotels listed accept credit cards unless otherwise stated. Note that rates vary widely throughout the year.

For a key to the symbols, ▷ 2.

For a key to the symbols, ▷ 2.

HUA HIN

CENTRAL HUA HIN VILLAGE
1 Thanon Damnernkasem, Hua Hin
Tel 032 512 021
www.centralhotelsresorts.com
Almost on the beach and consisting of one- and two-bedroom bungalows with their own raised terrace and very good room facilities. You can use the sports and leisure facilities at the Sofitel Central (▷ 285). The restaurant overlooks the pool. Tours can be booked through the hotel, and car rental is available.
🛏 B5,250 with sea view
🛏 41 bungalows 🛟 🏊 Outdoor 🖳

HILTON HUA HIN RESORT AND SPA
33 Thanon Naresdamri, Hua Hin
Tel 032 512 888
www.hilton.com/worldwideresorts
Every room here has a view of the ocean from its balcony and all the amenities of a five-star hotel. Dining comes in the form of a three-in-one alfresco restaurant that serves Thai, Japanese, Italian and international food, and a Chinese restaurant on the 17th story. There's also a bar with jazz at night. Other facilities include a spa, squash and tennis courts and a children's club.
🛏 B7,560–B9,360
🛏 296 (87 non-smoking) 🛟
🏊 Outdoor 🖳

PATTANA GUESTHOUSE
52 Thanon Naresdamri, Hua Hin
Tel 032 513 393
huahinpattana@hotmail.com
The Pattana is an oasis of calm with attractive and original bedrooms, and with a good kitchen serving up hearty breakfasts. There is a small bar serving coffees and cocktails.
🛏 B325–B550 excluding breakfast
🛏 6 🛟 Some

PUANGPEN VILLA HOTEL AND P.P. VILLA
11 Damnernkasem, Hua Hin
Tel 032 533 785
ppvillahotel@hotmail.com
If you want an affordable but presentable place to stay close to the beach and all the town's amenities, then this may fit the bill. The rooms have a fridge and safe deposit box, the pool is a decent size and the beach is five minutes down the road.
🛏 B1,200–B1,500 excluding breakfast
🛏 296 🛟 🏊 Outdoor

STAYING

SOFITEL CENTRAL HUA HIN RESORT

1 Thanon Damnernkasem, Hua Hin
Tel 032 512 021
www.sofitel.com

Set in 13ha (32 acres) of landscaped gardens and with a glorious beach a few steps away, this remains the classiest place to stay in Hua Hin. Built in 1923 for visitors to King Rama VII's summer palace, preservation work has retained the original structure to an almost clinical degree. Guests can dine in the open air or the air-conditioned Palm Seafood Pavilion, and afternoon tea beckons in the Museum Café.

🍴 From B6,200
① 207 🔄 🏊 Outdoor 🧗

KO LANTA

LANTA CORAL BEACH RESORT

77 Moo 5, Klong Nin Beach, Ko Lanta
Tel 075 618 073

These bungalows have an idyllic setting among swaying palm trees. The immediate beach area is a little rocky but safe for swimming. A small shop sells essential items, plus there is a laundry service, a restaurant and a bar.

⊘ Closed May–end of October
🍴 B400–B600
① 20 🔄 Some

PIMALAI RESORT & SPA

99 Moo 5, Ba Kan Tiang Beach, Ko Lanta
Tel 075 607 999
www.pimalai.com

Occupying 40.5ha (100 acres) of land adjoining a 900m (980-yard) sandy beach at the southwest corner of the island, this is the most luxurious accommodation on Ko Lanta. Rooms have polished teak floors, bamboo curtains, decorative Thai art, and a balcony with a fan. You'll find all the amenities of a five-star resort, including a spa, restaurants, and a dive center with a good reputation.

🍴 B8,500–B14,500 excluding breakfast
① 79 🔄 🏊 Outdoor 🧗

WHERE ELSE!

Klong Khong Beach, Ko Lanta
Tel 015 364 870

Halfway down the west coast, all the bungalows come with a fan and the better ones have hammocks on their balconies. All the beds are equipped with mosquito nets, and there are open-air bathroom facilities. The mood is laid-back and there are good internet facilities, motorcycles and cars for rent, massage, and a pool table.

🍴 B500–B1,500
① 24

The boat-like Hilton Hua Hin Resort and Spa

KO PHI PHI

BAY VIEW RESORT

Laem Hin, Ko Phi Phi
Tel 075 621 1223
www.phiphibayview.com

The bungalows are built atop solid pillars on high ground, with all rooms having a fridge and minibar; the higher-priced ones have tea- and coffee-making facilities. The restaurant is virtually on the beach; the pool is shared with a nearby and pricier resort. This resort emerged unscathed from the tsunami disaster of December 2004.

🍴 B2,700–B4,400
① 110 🔄 🏊 Outdoor

PHI PHI NATURAL RESORT

Moo 8, Leamtong Beach, Ko Phi Phi
Tel 075 613 010
www.phiphinatural.com

This resort is in the northeast of the island, a lot quieter and less eventful than the Tonsai area where you first arrive. The resort is beginning to show its age but it is a well-run and friendly place with spacious bungalows; the standard ones are the least attractive while the seaview deluxe ones with balconies are the most sought after.

🍴 B1,860–B6,000
① 70 🔄 🏊 Outdoor

PP VILLA RESORT

Laem Hin, Ko Phi Phi
Tel 015 706 488

Smart and attractive bungalows with balconies; the more expensive ones are closest to the beach, which is quiet here. The resort was only a little damaged by the tsunami and was able to put itself together relatively quickly.

🍴 From B2,800
① 59 🔄 🏊 Outdoor

KO SAMUI

ANANTARA

B99/9 Moo 1, Bophut Bay, Ko Samui
Tel 077 428 300
www.anantara.com

A wooden walkway leads through gardens and arches to the entrance of this very stylish boutique hotel. There's an Italian restaurant on the pool terrace, a spa with inviting treatments, and the Eclipse Bar, where aquarium fish tirelessly circumnavigate glass vases. The pool is heavenly and there are extensive gardens.

🍴 From B7,000
① 106 (32 non-smoking) 🔄
🏊 Outdoor

CENTRAL SAMUI BEACH RESORT
38/2 Moo 3 Borpud, Chaweng Beach
Tel 077 230 500
www.centralhotelsresorts.com
About 15 minutes from the airport and half an hour from the ferry piers, this large four-level hotel is designed so that every bedroom has a view of the sea. There are lots of leisure facilities—sailing, windsurfing, pool games, sauna, tennis courts, bicycles —and a spa. For dining there are Japanese and Thai restaurants; the Palm Grove does international food.
🍽 B7,500
🛏 208 🅿 ⛱ Outdoor

CENTRAL SAMUI VILLAGE
111 Moo 2, Tambon Maret, Natien Beach, Ko Samui
Tel 077 424 020
www.centralhotelsresorts.com
You'll find this place tucked away in the southeast of the island on the Natien beach near Hua Tanon, a fishing village on the coast about 30km (20 miles) from the airport. Facilities include a spa, snorkeling day trips, bicycles for guests' use and table tennis. The villas with fridge and satellite TV are just minutes away from the beach. There's good seafood and barbecues, and a shuttle bus to Chaweng and Na Thorn.
🍽 From B4,800 excluding breakfast
🛏 100 🅿 ⛱ Outdoor

PALM REEF RESORT
Chaweng Beach, Ko Samui
Tel 077 422 015
www.amari.com
All the rooms, set in tropical gardens on the beachfront, have their own balcony or terrace. Facilities include two bars (one of which is a swim-up pool bar for early evening cocktails), two restaurants, a spa and an air-conditioned squash court.
🍽 B6,800–B11,400
🛏 187 🅿 ⛱ Outdoor

SANTIBURI DUSIT RESORT
Mae Nam Beach, Ko Samui
Tel 077 425 031
www.dusit.com
On the northern tip of Samui at Mae Nam Beach, only 12km (8 miles) from the airport, this resort has a superb location and is amid gardens that seem to go on forever. The Vimarnmek restaurant handles international tastes but the seafood is better. A spa and fitness center are on the premises, as is a reputable dive school.
🍽 From B20,000
🛏 71 🅿 ⛱ Outdoor

You'll find welcoming staff at the Sofitel Central Hua Hin Resort

SPA RESORT
Lamai Beach, Ko Samui
Tel 077 630 976
www.spasamui.com
Bungalows and villas are mostly around the pool; the more expensive ones have a kitchen, lounge and bathroom. The resort runs courses and programs based around cleansing fasts, vegetarian food, yoga and meditation. Reserve online.
🍽 B500–B11,000
🛏 46 🅿 ⛱ Outdoor

KRABI–AO NANG

KRABI THAI VILLAGE RESORT
260 Moo 2, Tambol Ao Nang, Krabi
Tel 075 637 710
www.krabithaivillage.com
Set in 3ha (7 acres) of landscaped gardens, this resort is a walkable distance from the Ao Nang beachfront and has a free shuttle bus service to and fro. The grand lobby of the hotel is high ceilinged and radiates a golden hue. All the bedrooms, with contemporary Thai furniture and polished wooden floors, overlook a pool with swim-up bar. There are four restaurants, and a spa.
🍽 B5,600–B9,900
🛏 120 🅿 ⛱ Outdoor

SABAI MANSION AND SPA
249 Moo 2, Ao Nang, Krabi
Tel 075 637 643
www.sabaimansion.com
There's a good range of rooms here, including ones for families, most of which have air-conditioning; the least expensive rooms have fans. It's just a short walk from the beach, and there's a fridge and safety box in the bedrooms.
🍽 B500–B800 excluding breakfast
🛏 24 🅿 Some rooms ⛱ Outdoor

KRABI TOWN

KRABI CITY SEAVIEW HOTEL
77/1 Thanon Kong Kha, Paknum, Krabi
Tel 075 622 885
www.krabicityseaviewhotel.com
Within walking distance of the heart of the town, this hotel has some rooms facing the river and away from the traffic. The most expensive rooms have the most cramped bathrooms, making the mid-priced ones better value. All the bedrooms have showers (no baths), TV and minibar. There's a breakfast room on the top floor, and a garden between the hotel and river.
🍽 B500–B1,500 mostly excluding breakfast
🛏 29 🅿

PHUKET

CLUB MED
Thanon Kata, Karon, Phuket
Tel 076 330 456
phuccrec01@clubmed.com
A sprawling place dominating the beach, especially appealing

to families with young children. All meals are organized as buffets, mixing Thai, Japanese and Western food, with unlimited beer and wine. There's a terrific range of activities for all ages, including less common ones like archery.

🍴 Adult B5,300 including all meals and activities; child (4–11) B3,180
🛏 304 ❄ 🏊 Outdoor 🍷

FRIENDSHIP BUNGALOW

177/7 Thanon Koktanod, Karon, Phuket
Tel 076 330 499
www.friendshipbungalow.com
This place is easy to reach, being directly across from the *songthaews* and taxi station, and good value because the rooms have hot water and a fridge and the beach is just down the road.

🍴 B1,800; B750 without air-conditioning
🛏 32

J W MARRIOTT PHUKET RESORT & SPA

231 Moo 3, Mai Khao Talang, Phuket
Tel 076 338 000
www.marriott.com/hktjw
A resort in the northwest of the island, close to the airport, and a stroll away from a 17km (10.5-mile) beach that is never crowded. Water features contribute to the prevailing mood of tranquility. The bedrooms are elegant, spacious and come with their own balconies. A spa, Thai cooking classes, a six-hole pitching and putting green are on the hotel grounds, and an ATM machine is on the premises.

🍴 From B11,800 excluding breakfast
🛏 265 (133 non-smoking) ❄
🏊 Outdoor 🍷

KATATHANI

14 Thanon Kata Noi, Kata, Phuket
Tel 076 330 124
www.katathani.com
Stretching for 850m (930 yards) in front of Kata Noi Beach, the rooms are generous in size and, except for the ground level ones, have balconies for watching the

sunsets. Polished wood and stone characterize the style of the resort and there are four restaurants (including a seafood grill on the beach), two tennis courts, cooking classes, five pools and a spa.

🍴 B6,300
🛏 479 ❄ 🏊 Outdoor 🍷

MOM TRI'S BOATHOUSE & VILLA ROYALE

Kata Beach, Phuket
Tel 076 330 015
www.boathousephuket.com
The Boathouse—"a hotel for people who prefer not to stay in hotels"—is on three floors directly overlooking the beach and with great views of the

A villa at the Santiburi Dusit Resort, Ko Samui

sunsets. Villa Royale, 300m (330 yards) away, is even more luxurious, with pavilions, landscaped terraces and interior design inspired by Balinese styles. Facilities include beach chairs and umbrellas, two great restaurants, a spa and a cookery school.

🍴 From B7,500 (B600 excluding breakfast)
🛏 36 (Boathouse), 17 suites and studios (Villa Royale) ❄ 🍷 Outdoor 🍸

ON ON HOTEL

19 Thanon Phang-Nga, Phuket town, Phuket
Tel 076 211 154
A seasoned establishment for budget travelers that offers basic rooms sharing bathroom facilities as well as double rooms with air-conditioning and their own bathrooms. To say it has faded elegance would be charitable, but it's a good base for onward travel, with tours and airport transfers easily arranged and an information desk in the large lobby. *Café*, next door, is a cheerful place to eat, but *Shelter*, a few doors down, serves a better variety of meals.

🍴 B140–B380 excluding breakfast
🛏 49 ❄ Some rooms

PHUKET ISLAND PAVILION

133 Thanon Satoon, Phuket town, Phuket
Tel 076 210 445
www.islandpavilion.com
Not within walking distance of the town center but a pleasant hotel with a spa, a small pool, an outdoor pub at street level and a lounge bar with music at night. Rooms are functional, with a safe deposit box, minibar and tea- and coffee-making facilities.

🍴 From B1,600
🛏 103 (33 non-smoking) ❄
🏊 Outdoor

TALANG GUEST HOUSE

37 Thanon Thalang, Phuket town, Phuket
Tel 076 214 225
This is a clean, three-story guesthouse with character and a choice of rooms with or without air-conditioning. The best rooms are on the top level—the third story—spacious and overlooking the street and roof tops. The best budget accommodation in Phuket town.

🍴 B300–B400
🛏 13 ❄

MAJOR HOTEL CHAINS

Name of Hotel Chain	Description	Number of Hotels in Thailand	Telephone Numbers and Websites
Accor	International hotel chain with hotels in Bangkok, Chiang Mai, Chonburi, Hat Yai, Hua Hin, Khon Kaen, Pattaya, Phuket and Rayong.	20	www.accorhotels.com/asia
Amari Hotels	A Thai hotel group with four- and five-star hotels and resorts in Bangkok, Chiang Mai, Pattaya, Ko Chang, Ko Samui, Phuket, Trang and Loei.	13	Tel 022 553 960 www.amari.com
Central Hotel Resorts	Special savers, deals on children's accommodation, and various promotions at hotels in Bangkok, Ko Samui, Phuket, Hua Hin, Hat Yai, Chiang Mai, Chiang Rai, Mae Sot.	10	Tel 029 372 222 www.centralhotelsresorts.com
Dusit Hotels	Luxury hotels and resorts in Bangkok, Chiang Mai, Chiang Rai, Hua Hin, Khon Kaen, Nakhon Rathasima (Korat), Pattaya, Phuket and Ranong. Video clips on the website show exactly what they look like. The Dusit group includes the Royal Princess Hotels and Resorts, one notch down from five-star luxury.	14	Tel 026 363 333 www.dusit.com
Four Seasons Hotels	Two superb hotels in Thailand: the Four Seasons Resort in Chiang Mai and the Four Seasons Hotel in Bangkok.	2	Tel 1 800 819 5053 (toll free from US); 00 800 6488 6488 (toll free from UK) www.fourseasons.com
Hilton	Another famous chain with two hotels in Thailand, at Hua Hin and Phuket.	2	Tel 1 800 445 8667 (toll free from US); 08705 909 090 (toll free from UK) www.hilton.com
Imperial	One of Thailand's fastest-growing hotel chains, with properties in Bangkok, Chiang Mai, Chaing Rai, Ko Samui, Mae Hong Son and Ch-Am near Hua Hin.	12	Tel 022 619 000 www.imperialhotels.com
Mandarin	Two famous hotels in Thailand: the Oriental in Bangkok and the Dhara Dhevi in Chiang Mai.	2	Tel 1 866 526 6567 (toll free from US); 00 800 2828 3838 (toll free from UK) www.mandarinoriental.com
Marriott	Three hotels in Bangkok, two in Phuket, and one each in Hua Hin and Pattaya.	9	Tel 1 888 236 2427 (toll free from US/Canada); 0800 221 222 (toll free from UK); 001 800 852 2435 (toll free from Thailand) www.marriott.com
Sofitel	An international hotel chain with five top-class hotels in Bangkok, Hua Hin and Khon Kaen.	5	Tel 1 800 SOFITEL (toll free from US/Canada); 0870 609 0964 (from UK); 022 376 064 (from Thailand) www.sofitel.com

STAYING

Planning

BEFORE YOU GO

CLIMATE
● Thailand has three seasons, governed by monsoons but subject to regional variations. See www.climate-zone.com/climate/thailand
● The **cool season** lasts from November to around the end of February, and in the north temperatures can drop low enough at night-time to require a sweater against the chill. During the day, temperatures average 26°C (79°F).
● The **hot season** lasts from around March to the end of May and is felt most in the northeast, where temperatures can reach 40°C (103°F) in the daytime.
● The **rainy season** lasts from June to the end of October and

is the most variable of the three seasons. On the Andaman Coast, in the southern region, the rain is persistent enough to cause some bungalow operations to close down until late October. The choppy water may also affect boat timetables. On the Gulf coast rainfall is most likely between October and January. In Bangkok and the central region, September and October see the heaviest rainfall.

WHEN TO GO
● The cool season is the most pleasant time to visit Thailand and as the demand for hotel rooms and seats on sleeper trains rises there is the most need for planning ahead.
● The northeast will be oppressively hot between March and May, while the Andaman Coast is at its best between November and the end of May.

INOCULATIONS
No inoculations are compulsory for travel to Thailand but it makes sense to consult your doctor about the advisability of some immunizations, especially ones against typhoid and hepatitis, and to ensure that your 10-year polio and tetanus boosters are not out of date. For

information on malaria, ▷ 297. Visit your doctor a month before departure to allow sufficient time for injections. In Bangkok, inoculations are available at the Thai Red Cross (▷ 76; www.redcross.or.th) at the Queen Saovabha Memorial Institute.

WHAT TO TAKE
● Bring with you any necessary prescription drugs but bear in mind that pharmacies have a good range of medicines and English-speaking staff to give advice. You are allowed to bring in up to 30 days' worth of medication without a license from the Thai Food and Drug Administration. Narcotics are forbidden, but certain types of psychoactive substances (categories 2, 3 and 4) are permitted with a doctor's certificate. If in doubt, always carry a doctor's note with you.
● Malaria and other diseases are spread by mosquitoes. You should bring with you and use some mosquito repellent, although it is readily available in Thailand. Mosquito coils, lit and left on a bungalow verandah or bedroom floor, are also available.
● Bring a pair of sunglasses. A hat and prickly heat powder will also help, but both are easily and inexpensively available in Thailand.
● The climate requires the bare minimum of clothing. Some smart clothes are necessary for evening

WEATHER STATIONS

Chiang Mai
14m
46ft

Ubon Ratchathani
121m
397ft

BANGKOK
20m
65ft

Songkhla
4m
13ft

PLANNING

| BANGKOK | CHIANG MAI | SONGKHLA |
| TEMPERATURE | TEMPERATURE | TEMPERATURE |

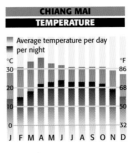

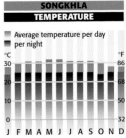

■ Average temperature per day
■ per night

| RAINFALL | RAINFALL | RAINFALL |

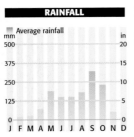

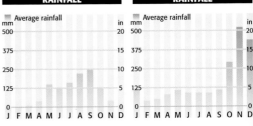

■ Average rainfall

THAI EMBASSIES AND CONSULATES ABROAD		
COUNTRY	**ADDRESS**	**WEBSITE**
Australia	111 Empire Circuit, Yarralumla, Canberra, ACT Tel (02) 623 1149	www.thai-embassy.org.au
New Zealand	2 Cook St, Karori, P O Box 17226, Wellington, Tel 644 4678618	www.thaiembassynz.org.nz
South Africa	840 Church Street, Eastwood, Arcadia 0083, Pretoria thaipta@lin01.globsl.co.za Tel (27 12) 342 5470	www.thaiembpta.co.za
UK (& Ireland)	29–30 Queen's Gate, London, SW7 5JB Tel 020 7589 2944	http://thailand.embassyhomepage.com
USA	1024 Wisconsin Ave, Washington DC 20007 Tel (202) 944 3600	www.thaiembdc.org
Canada	180 Island Park Drive, Ottawa, Ontario KIY OA2 Tel (613) 722 4444	www.magma.ca/~thaiott/mainpage.htm

dining and for visiting the Grand Palace in Bangkok (▷ 84–87). A pair of sandals is essential.

● A money belt is a good idea, especially when wearing shorts. A small shoulder bag or minipack is useful for carrying bottled water and other travel items but is not always the safest means of carrying valuables.

ESSENTIAL ITEMS

● Passport (with at least six months validity)
● Visa (if required; ▷ right)
● Travel tickets and documents
● Travel and health insurance documents
● Credit/debit cards
● Prescription medicines
● Driver's license (if renting a car an International Driving Permit is supposed to be produced, but a national license is usually accepted)

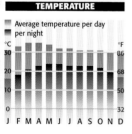

UBON RATCHATHANI
TEMPERATURE

■ Average temperature per day per night

RAINFALL

■ Average rainfall

A FIRST-AID KIT

All these items are easy to obtain in Thailand but an initial supply could be packed in your luggage:
● Sunscreen
● Bandages and lints for cuts
● Antiseptic
● Antihistamine
● Insect repellent
● Imodium or similar for diarrhea
● Aspirin or paracetamol

PASSPORTS AND VISAS

● Your passport must be valid for at least six months from the date of entry into Thailand.
● Most passport holders from Western Europe, North America, Australia and New Zealand do not require a visa and are allowed to stay for up to 30 days after the date stamped in their passport on arrival. Passport and visa regulations can change so always check before you travel.
● Visa requirements can be checked at the website for Thailand's Ministry of Foreign Affairs—www.mfa.go.th/web/12.php—or through your travel agent or Thai embassy.
● Sixty-day tourist visas can be applied for in advance through your country's Thai embassy or consulate, but allow at least two weeks for this. Two photos and a payment are required.
● The normal 30-day tourist visa can be extended for another 10 days at immigration offices in Thailand. Visitors can also make a short visit across Thailand's land borders and obtain a new 30-day visa when re-entering.

CUSTOMS

Visitors entering Thailand have a duty-free allowance of 1 liter of spirits or wine and 200 cigarettes. A license is required to export antiques or Buddha images,

although this requirement is not usually enforced for the mass-produced Buddha images freely available. Any ancient object, religious or secular, requires a license that reputable antique shops will organize for you.

TRAVEL INSURANCE

● Make sure you have full health and travel insurance. If you rent a car or motorcycle, check what your insurance covers.
● If you are planning to go diving while in Thailand, check the terms of the insurance company.
● Make sure you know what to do in the event of the need for a claim arising. Keep details of the insurance policy with you.

TIME ZONES

Thailand is 7 hours ahead of Greenwich Mean Time (GMT), and there is no adjustment for daylight saving.

CITY	TIME DIFFERENCE	TIME AT 12 NOON THAILAND
Amsterdam	−6	6am
Auckland	+3	3pm
Bangkok	0	12 noon
Berlin	−6	6am
Brussels	−6	6am
Chicago	−13	11pm*
Dublin	−7	5am
Johannesburg	−5	7am
London	−7	5am
Madrid	−6	6am
Montréal	−12	12 midnight*
New York	−12	12 midnight*
Paris	−6	6am
Perth, Australia	+1	1pm
Rome	−6	6am
San Francisco	−15	9pm*
Sydney	+3	3pm
Tokyo	+2	2pm

* = the previous day

PRACTICALITIES

ELECTRICITY

Voltage in Thailand is 220 volts. The most common form of socket takes plugs with two round pins, although sometimes they take two flat pins and other times they take both. If you are packing electrical items you need an adaptor plug. American appliances using 110 to 120 volts will need an adaptor and a transformer. Mid-range and more expensive hotels will have 110-volt shaver outlets.

LAUNDRY

Nearly all hotels offer a laundry service, charged either per item or per kilo, but only four- and five-star hotels can be relied on for a dry-cleaning service. Ironing is often included. Thailand's climate makes it easy for visitors to wash their own cotton garments and leave them to dry in the sun. Small packets of detergent are readily available, and some visitors bring a few clothes pegs to hang out their washing on the balcony or veranda of their room or bungalow.

CHILDREN

● There are no special problems bringing children to Thailand and there is plenty for them to enjoy.
● Nearly all restaurants welcome children, although not many will have high chairs or children's menus. When it comes to eating Thai food, a request to tone down the chili for a child's dish usually works and most large hotels have restaurants serving international food that children will be familiar with. In the beach resort areas of southern Thailand, open-fronted restaurants by the sea are ideal in terms of space for young children to play but within sight of parents.
● Accommodation is usually charged by a room rate, not the number of occupants, and children can often be fitted into a double room. Extra beds tend only to be available in the top-end hotels but rooms with three beds are not uncommon.
● Disposable nappies (diapers) are generally available, but some washable ones should be packed as a backup. A changing mat is a useful item to have ready in your shoulder bag. The toilets in four- and five-star hotels are always a

Little ones are usually happy on the beach

good bet when in need of changing facilities.
● Buggies can be difficult to handle because the streets are so bumpy, there are few ramps and beaches are difficult to negotiate. Baby seats are not available in taxis or rented cars.

TOILETS

● Public toilets are not to be found in Thailand, but no one will object to you using the facilities in a hotel or guesthouse. All restaurants, other than the food stands that spring up at night in various towns and cities, will have their own toilets.
● Modern toilets with a seat and mechanical flushing system are found in all hotels, restaurants and places of interest that attract visitors from abroad.
● The alternative to a modern toilet takes the form of a tiled area, level with the floor surface, without a toilet seat and requiring the user to squat. A bucket and scoop will be nearby, with a tap to refill if necessary. Toilet paper is not always provided.

CAR RENTAL

● Driving is not easy and is best avoided in Bangkok because of the complex density of the road network, the difficulty of reading traffic signs in Thai and the challenge of finding somewhere to park.
● Driving a rented vehicle outside of Bangkok is feasible and can be enjoyable. See pages 54–55 for information on driving and car rental.
● Car rental can be arranged in advance through the internet by

using a reputable company like Budget (www.budget.co.th) or through the many agencies that will arrange car rental. Budget will freely deliver and pick up within 30km (about 19 miles) of any of their locations. In destinations like Ko Samui, Phuket and Chiang Mai there are numerous places on the ground offering car rental, but it is advisable to use a reputable company because the less expensive deals may not always provide proper insurance.

LOCAL WAYS

● Visitors to a Thai home are expected to leave their footwear outside the door, and you will be reminded of this by the sight of the family's own footwear collected outside.
● Losing your temper in public does not impress Thai people—they will be embarrassed by such behavior and you will lose respect as a consequence. This is related to the Thai concept of *jai yen*, a "cool heart," which involves keeping calm and avoiding confrontation.
● The royal family is protected from criticism by laws making it an offence to utter derogatory remarks or behave improperly in matters affecting them. Thais stand for the playing of the royal anthem in cinemas and at prestigious occasions, and you are expected to show respect by doing the same.
● Women are traditionally not supposed to touch or hand anything directly to a Buddhist monk. Images of the Buddha are treated with respect.
● Shaking hands is not common among Thais. A familiar form of greeting is the placing of the hands together at chest height with fingertips almost reaching your chin, as if in prayer—a gesture known as a *wai*. Visitors from abroad are not expected to follow the social nuances governing the *wai*, but the general rule is that the junior person in a relationship or encounter initiates a *wai*.
● The term *khun* is used as a mark of respect in addressing people, orally or in writing, and comes before the person's first name. Sirinate Meenakul, for example, would be Khun Sirinate. This accounts for the way in which a foreign visitor,

PLANNING

Respect local customs and remove your shoes

named John Smith for example, might be addressed as Mr John.
• Rules of decorum make it rude to touch another person's head.

DRESS CODES

• Apart from at a very few restaurants in Bangkok (▷ 246–249), formal dress is not required for dining out in Thailand. Better restaurants expect diners to be smartly attired for an evening meal, but this usually means trousers or a dress or skirt as opposed to shorts.
• A dress code does apply when visiting the Grand Palace (▷ 84–87) in Bangkok, and for temples visitors are expected to be modestly dressed. Footwear is always removed and left outside a temple.
• Thai people are modest and dress accordingly and while shorts and short-sleeved tops are fine for beaches and casual situations, it is appropriate to dress more smartly when meeting Thais in non-casual social situations.

SCAMS

Be aware of scams involving smartly dressed people proffering help at Bangkok's railway station or airport. They usually work on commission

for a travel agent or unlicenced taxi company. Around places like the Grand Palace or Jim Thompson's house in Bangkok, do not accept offers of low-priced city tours because this is often an excuse to take you to overpriced shops.

ห้ามผู้หญิงเข้า
โปรดถอดรองเท้า
WOMEN NOT ALLOWED.
PLEASE REMOVE SHOES.

CONVERSION CHART		
From	**To**	**Multiply by**
Inches	Centimeters	2.54
Centimeters	Inches	0.3937
Feet	Meters	0.3048
Meters	Feet	3.2810
Yards	Meters	0.9144
Meters	Yards	1.0940
Miles	Kilometers	1.6090
Kilometers	Miles	0.6214
Acres	Hectares	0.4047
Hectares	Acres	2.4710
Gallons	Liters	4.5460
Liters	Gallons	0.2200
Ounces	Grams	28.35
Grams	Ounces	0.0353
Pounds	Grams	453.6
Grams	Pounds	0.0022
Pounds	Kilograms	0.4536
Kilograms	Pounds	2.205
Tons	Tonnes	1.0160
Tonnes	Tons	0.9842

CLOTHING SIZES

Use the clothing sizes chart below to convert the size you use at home.

UK	Europe	US	
36	46	36	SUITS
38	48	38	
40	50	40	
42	52	42	
44	54	44	
46	56	46	
48	58	48	
7	41	8	SHOES
7.5	42	8.5	
8.5	43	9.5	
9.5	44	10.5	
10.5	45	11.5	
11	46	12	
14.5	37	14.5	SHIRTS
15	38	15	
15.5	39/40	15.5	
16	41	16	
16.5	42	16.5	
17	43	17	
8	36	6	DRESSES
10	38	8	
12	40	10	
14	42	12	
16	44	14	
18	46	16	
20	48	18	
4.5	37.5	6	SHOES
5	38	6.5	
5.5	38.5	7	
6	39	7.5	
6.5	40	8	
7	41	8.5	

PLANNING

MONEY

THE BAHT
● The Thai currency is the baht (B), which comes in denominations of:

B10	brown
B20	green
B50	blue
B100	red
B500	purple
B1000	beige

● The larger the note, the larger the denomination. All notes carry Western as well as Thai numerals.
● Coins come in B10, B5 and B1. There are also 25 and 50 satang/cent coins but these are worth very little and are not used much.
● Some top-end hotels and diving companies quote their rates in US dollars, a legacy of the baht's dramatic fall in value in the late 1990s.

BEFORE YOU GO
● It is sensible to use a combination of traveler's checks and bank cards rather than relying on only one means for making payments and obtaining cash.
● Check with your credit and/or debit card company that your card can be used to withdraw cash from Automatic Teller Machines (ATMs) in Thailand. You should be able to do this without difficulty. It is also worth checking what fee will be charged for withdrawals and what number you should ring if your card is stolen.

TRAVELER'S CHECKS
● Traveler's checks are still a safe and useful way to carry money as you can claim a refund if they are stolen or lost.
● Traveler's checks get a better rate of exchange than cash and as there is a fixed commission rate of B23 per check (some hotels may charge more) avoid carrying too many small denomination checks. Sometimes there is a charge made when you buy the checks, but shop around because this rate varies and sometimes there will be no charge if paying from your bank account.
● Traveler's checks in dollars are the most common and familiar in Thailand, but sterling ones are also accepted; euro checks are less familiar to Thais but are

accepted in the more popular destinations. Traveler's checks can be exchanged in banks, exchange booths and many hotels.

ATMS
ATMs are common across Thailand, including airports, and they all accept Visa and MasterCard, usually with instructions available in English. You will need a four-digit PIN number, but the card does not have to be a chip-and-pin type. There is usually a fixed minimum charge for each withdrawal.
● Not every small island will have a bank and/or ATM but islands like Ko Samui, Ko Chang and Ko Lanta do have them. For ATM locations visit www.mastercard.com and www.visa.com.

BANKS AND EXCHANGE BOOTHS
Banks open Monday to Friday, from 8.30am to 4.30pm, but close on public holidays. In major destinations like Phuket, Ko Samui, Chiang Mai, and areas in Bangkok like Thanon Sukhumvit and Thanon Khao San, exchange booths keep longer hours and are often open seven days a week from 9am to as late as 9pm or 10pm.

WIRING MONEY
● In an emergency, money can be wired to you from your home country, but the agent handling the transaction will make a charge and for small amounts this can be an expensive way of obtaining money. Moneygram (www.moneygram.com) and Western Union

Some Thai banknotes currently in circulation

PLANNING

(www.westernunion.com) are the two major agents.

• Money can also be wired from your home bank to a bank in Thailand but you will need to obtain details from both banks and it will take at least two days to complete a transaction.

CREDIT AND DEBIT CARDS

Credit and debit cards can be used to make payment in many hotels and the more expensive restaurants. Department stores and an increasing number of shops will also accept cards, but some shops will expect the customer to pay the percentage charge made by the card company. Paying in cash can often be an aid in bargaining.

LOST/STOLEN CREDIT CARDS

The following numbers should be used in an emergency to report lost or stolen credit cards.

MasterCard	Tel 022 608 572
Visa	Tel 022 567 326
American Express	Tel 022 735 100
Diners Club	Tel 022 382 920

TIPPING

Tipping is not normal in Thailand, but in hotels and restaurants that cater largely to visitors from overseas a degree of tipping is accepted.

TIPPING GUIDE

Restaurants	Change
Hotel porters	B10–B20
Taxis	Rounded up to the nearest 10 baht

TAXES

• The value added tax (VAT) of 7 percent that is applied to certain goods and services can be reclaimed by visitors to Thailand if the shop operates a VAT refund service. Collect the VAT refund form at the shop at the time of purchase and present it to the airport VAT office before departure with your receipt.

• Top-end hotels will usually add a 10 percent hotel tax plus a service charge that averages around 8 percent. These charges are sometimes indicated by a ++ sign after a quoted room rate.

EXCHANGE RATES

Check current rates of exchange at www.oanda.com or www.xe.net/ucc

PRICES OF EVERYDAY ITEMS (BANGKOK)

These are average prices. Expect to pay around the same in Phuket but less in other regions of the country.

ITEM	BAHT
Petrol	B23–B25 per liter
Lunch	B70–B200
Skytrain or subway ticket	B35
Cup of coffee	B50
Bottled water	B12–B20
International newspaper	B150–B250
Taxi–short ride	B80
Internet access	B1–B2 per minute
Meal for two in mid-range restaurant	B300–B400

ATMs are often the simplest way of getting hold of some bahts

HEALTH

BEFORE YOU GO

● It is essential to have full health and travel insurance arranged before you arrive in Thailand because in the event of a mishap you will have to meet the costs.

● If you have existing home insurance of the all-risks, comprehensive kind, check to see if it includes the loss of personal possessions while traveling abroad.

● Similarly, if you have a private medical policy, check to see if it covers you when in Thailand.

● Before committing yourself to a particular health and travel insurance plan, make sure that you know what it covers in terms of any adventure sports you might be planning, especially diving and trekking, and costs arising from an accident with a rented vehicle. You may have to pay a premium to cover diving or trekking activities.

IF YOU NEED TREATMENT

● If you need to seek treatment for a **non-emergency ailment**, consider in the first instance visiting the nearest pharmacy where there will be a professional, English-speaking pharmacist on duty who can offer advice on possible medicine and/or the advisability of consulting a doctor.

● If you need **to visit a doctor**, check with staff at your place of accommodation for a conveniently located doctor. If you are staying in a four- or five-star hotel there may be a hotel doctor on call. You will need to pay for a doctor's consultation and the cost of any medication that is prescribed. Make sure you get a receipt as this will be needed if you make a claim on your health insurance.

● If you need **to visit a hospital** (▷ 298), check with staff at your place of accommodation for the nearest hospital and arrange for a taxi to take you there. The general standard of hygiene and healthcare at major Thai hospitals is high and English-speaking doctors will be available. Keep receipts for any payments that need to be made.

● In the event of a serious **medical emergency**, get to a hospital as quickly as possible and get someone to contact your

embassy and health insurance company if you have to be transported to a larger hospital, to Bangkok or even back to your home country.

WATER

● It is not advisable to drink water direct from a tap—Thai people do not drink tap water. Bottled water is available everywhere and because of the climate you are likely to find yourself always needing to have a supply ready to hand. In good hotels it is usually safe to use tap water to brush your teeth but if

in any doubt use bottled water.

● In the cheapest restaurants the water that may be brought to your table in a jug will have been previously boiled but if you are unsure ask for bottled water or use your own.

HEAT

● It is important to protect yourself from the effects of the sun, especially if you are fair-skinned. Even if not sunbathing, it is more comfortable during the hot parts of the day to wear sunglasses and/or a hat or peaked cap.

HEALTHY FLYING

● Visitors to Thailand may be concerned about the effect of long-haul flights on their health. The most widely publicized concern is Deep Vein Thrombosis, or DVT. Misleadingly called 'economy class syndrome', DVT is the forming of a blood clot in the body's deep veins, particularly in the legs. The clot can move around the bloodstream and could be fatal.

● Those most at risk include the elderly, pregnant women and those using the contraceptive pill, smokers and the overweight. If you are at increased risk of DVT see your doctor before departing. Flying increases the likelihood of DVT because passengers are often seated in a cramped position for long periods of time and may become dehydrated.

To minimize risk:
Drink water (not alcohol)
Don't stay immobile for hours at a time
Stretch and exercise your legs periodically
Do wear elastic flight socks, which support veins and reduce the chances of a clot forming

EXERCISES

1 ANKLE ROTATIONS	2 CALF STRETCHES	3 KNEE LIFTS

Lift feet off the floor. Draw a circle with the toes, moving one foot clockwise and the other counterclockwise

Start with heel on the floor and point foot upward as high as you can. Then lift heels high, keeping balls of feet on the floor

Lift leg with knee bent while contracting your thigh muscle. Then straighten leg, pressing foot flat to the floor

Other health hazards for flyers are airborne diseases and bugs spread by the plane's air-conditioning system. These are largely unavoidable but if you have a serious medical condition seek advice from a doctor before flying.

PLANNING

• If you are going to sunbathe be sure to use a high-protection sun cream and be careful not to spend too long in the sun, especially during your first few days. It is very easy in Thailand to turn yourself lobster red in a very short time; and as well as looking silly, the experience is damaging to your skin and can prove quite painful. Beware of sunburn on your back and neck while snorkeling; consider wearing a T-shirt and using water-resistant sun cream.

• You will experience dehydration if you do not drink enough water; bottled water should always be at hand.

• Prickly heat and fungal infections can be a minor problem, but prickly heat powder is available everywhere.

MALARIA

• The areas of Thailand most at risk from mosquito-borne malaria are the border areas with Cambodia and Laos and, in the west, the border area with Myanmar (Burma). Urban areas and destinations like Phuket and Chiang Mai are virtually malaria-free.

• Check whether the area you are intending to travel to is at risk. In areas that are at risk, especially during the rainy season, mosquito repellent containing the DEET compound should be used on the body and clothes after dusk when mosquitoes are about. Screens covering windows are usually fitted in bedrooms and a mosquito net is fitted around beds. Mosquito coils are often lit at night and left burning in the bedroom or outside on a balcony or verandah. They are not a fire risk and the very mild smoke keeps mosquitoes at bay. Mosquito coils and nets are inexpensive and readily available in shops and department stores.

• If you are going to an area at risk, discuss with your doctor the use of anti-malarial drugs. They need to be taken before and after your stay in a malaria-risk area.

HEALTH HAZARDS BY THE SEA

• Bites from jellyfish, torn skin from coral and splinters from standing on a sea urchin are risks while swimming or on the beach. It's therefore a good idea to keep your feet covered at all times with rubber soles. The spikes from sea urchins, which are painful and not dangerous, need to be removed one by one from the skin; try to soften the skin first with ointment. Clean and carefully wash any cuts to the skin and apply an antiseptic.

• Seek medical advice if you are unlucky enough to be stung by a jellyfish or bitten by a sea snake. Try to keep calm and still, do not apply a tourniquet, and arrange for transportation to the nearest hospital or doctor.

OTHER HEALTH HAZARDS

• Rabies is prevalent in Thailand, and dogs should not be approached or patted. Worms can be picked up through the feet; wear something on your

Take care in the blazing sun

feet at all times, especially if staying in inexpensive beachside accommodation.

• The most common health complaint experienced by visitors is a bout of diarrhea brought on by unfamiliar or contaminated food. This is best treated by taking lots of fluids and waiting two or three days for your stomach to settle. Medicines like Imodium, which only treat the symptoms, are useful if you have to travel but they do not speed up recovery time. Medication from a doctor may be necessary if the diarrhea persists and your temperature rises.

SPAS, HEALTH CENTERS, PRIVATE HOSPITALS AND CLINICS

• Thailand has plenty of spas and health centers offering a variety of courses and treatments promising physical well-being and mental relaxation. Massages of the head, feet or whole body, facial therapies, aromatherapy, hydrotherapy, body detoxification, meditation and yoga are available. Private hospitals and clinics offer dental treatment, health checks, minor surgery and plastic surgery.

• In every town or city in Thailand you will find small private clinics, often run by just one doctor. Outside of large cities, an appointment is not necessary and it is a matter of showing up and waiting your turn. Such clinics usually dispense any drugs prescribed by the doctor who treats you. Pharmacies are very common, often with an English-speaking member of staff.

• Private dental clinics can be found in every town, and appointments can often be made at short notice.

• See Finding Help (▷ 298) for contact details of hospitals in Bangkok, Chiang Mai and Phuket.

USEFUL HEALTH WEBSITES	
WEBSITE	**DESCRIPTION**
www.who.int/en	World Health Organization
www.tripprep.com	Travel Health Online
www.brookes.ac.uk/worldwise	Basic travel information on countries
www.tmb.ie	Advice and info from the Tropical Medical Board
www.doctorbackhome.com	Doctor Back Home
www.nhsdirect.nhs.uk	Useful guide to illnesses and what to do about them
www.doh.gov.uk and www.fco.gov.uk/travel	Health and travel advice from the British government
www.cdc.gov/travel	Official US site on health information across the globe
www.healthfinder.com	Links to health organizations and medical site, giving a comprehensive range of health advice from the US Department of Health
www.travelhealth.co.uk	Tips and information

FINDING HELP

EMBASSIES AND CONSULATES IN BANGKOK		
COUNTRY	ADDRESS	CONTACT DETAILS
Australia	37 Thanon Sathorn Tai	Tel 023 446 300
Canada	15th Floor, Abdulrahim Place, 990 Thanon Rama IV	Tel 026 360 540
Germany	9 Thanon Sathorn Tai	Tel 022 879 000
Ireland	12th Floor, TISCO Tower, 48/20 Thanon Sathorn Tai	Tel 026 380 303
New Zealand	93 Thanon Witthayo	Tel 022 542 530
UK	1031 Thanon Witthayo	Tel 023 058 333
US	120 Thanon Witthayo	Tel 022 054 000

CONSULAR OFFICES IN CHIANG MAI	
COUNTRY	CONTACT DETAILS
Australia	Tel 053 221 083
Canada	Tel 053 850 147
Germany	Tel 053 838 735
UK	Tel 053 263 015
US	Tel 053 252 629

PERSONAL SECURITY

● Make a list of the numbers of your traveler's checks and keep this with your proof of purchase (necessary for a claim) and the contact number to use in case the checks are lost or stolen. Make sure you keep this information separate from the checks themselves.

● Keep a photocopy of the main page of your passport showing your photograph and personal details and the page with the stamp of your Thai visa, and keep these separate from your passport. Also consider keeping the number of your passport, or a scanned copy of the relevant pages, in an email which can be retrieved if necessary. The same could be done with the details of your travel and health insurance documents and your air tickets.

● Don't keep wallets or purses in back pockets or any open pocket that might be a temptation to a professional thief. The general level of street crime and pick-pocketing is low in Thailand but in high-profile parts of Bangkok—around the Grand Palace, Wat Traimet and on the Chao Phraya River Express boats—pick-pocketing does occur.

EMERGENCY TELEPHONE NUMBERS	
Police	191
Tourist police	1155
Fire service	199

HOSPITALS IN BANGKOK
Bangkok General Hospital, 2 Soi Soonvija 7, Thanon Phetchaburi Mai
☎ 023 103 000; emergency ☎ 023 103 456; 24-hour call center ☎ 023 103 000, 1719; www.bangkokhospital.com. This hospital also has a dental surgery.
Bumrungrad Hospital, 33 Sukhumvit Soi 3 ☎ 026 672 000; emergency ☎ 026 672 999; www.bumrungrad.com
Travmin Bangkok Medical Centre, 8th Floor, Alma Link Building, 25 Soi Chitlom, Thanon Ploenchit ☎ 026 551 024

HOSPITALS IN CHIANG MAI
Chiang Mai Ram Hospital, Thanon Boonreuangrit ☎ 053 224 851/8
Lana Hospital, Thanon Superhighway ☎ 053 357 234
McCormack Hospital, Thanon Kaew Nawarat ☎ 053 241 010

HOSPITALS IN PHUKET
Bangkok Phuket Hospital, Thanon Yongyok Uthit ☎ 076 254 425; www.phukethospital.com
Phuket International Hospital, Airport Bypass Road ☎ 076 249 400; emergency ☎ 076 210 935; www.phuket-inter-hospital.co.th

POLICE
● As well as the regular police you will see in cars and on motorcycles, who you cannot assume will speak English, there are special tourist police whose job is to assist visitors with difficulties. They can be contacted on a special **tourist police 24-hour telephone line** ☎ 1155. In parts of Bangkok, Chiang Mai and Phuket, and some smaller destinations like Hua Hin and Pattaya, the tourist police have their own office or sidewalk cubicle, often stationed near the local tourist office.

● If you have property stolen or lost you will need to report the incident to the police and obtain an official document proving you have lodged a report as this will be needed to make a claim on your insurance. This cannot be done with the tourist police, but they will advise on where to go.

● In the event of a non-criminal emergency, the emergency number for the fire services is ☎ 199 and for police it is ☎ 191. However, the person answering the phone may not speak English and so it is better to use the tourist line number ☎ 1155.

Make a note of emergency phone numbers

PLANNING

COMMUNICATION

TELEPHONES
● The most expensive rates for phoning abroad will be levied by your hotel if ringing from your bedroom. The most economical rates are obtained by using a **Thaicard**, issued by CAT (Communications Authority of Thailand), purchased from post offices and many shops in denominations of B100, B300, B500, B1,000 and B3,000. The cards can be used with the international telephones found near or in a post office as well as dotted around cities and large towns.
● In popular destinations and resorts, including airports, there are also Lenso telephone booths where you can make international calls using pre-paid Lenso cards or your credit card. Lenso phone cards are sold in shops near the payphone.

PAYPHONES
● Payphones will accept either just coins or just phone cards for calls within Thailand. Phone cards in various denominations can be bought from shops, including 7-Eleven, and hotels.
● Payphones in red or a light blue work only for local calls. Payphones in a darker blue work for local and long-distance calls.
● When making a call within Thailand, use the full area code even when you are phoning within the area. Seven-digit numbers preceded by 01, 04, 05, 06, 07 and 09 are mobile or satellite phone numbers and will cost more than landline numbers.

MOBILE PHONES
● Check with your mobile phone company to see if your phone will work in Thailand and for the charges for receiving as well as making calls and text messages in Thailand. You will need to add the international access and country codes, and drop the zero off the area code, if ringing abroad using your mobile.

INTERNET
Emailing from Thailand
● Access to the internet can be found everywhere in Thailand, with rates starting at B1 per minute or with a fixed price for 15, 30 or 60 minutes. CAT sells a CatNet card, which operates like their Thaicards, for use at their

Keeping in touch with those at home has never been easier

computers in a government telephone center. These cards cost B100 and cover three hours of internet use. The most expensive rates, as with phone calls, are charged by hotels.
● Check to make sure that your email provider allows you to access your account from the web and that you know the web address to use. If not, or as a backup, create a new and free email account through www.hotmail.com or www.yahoo.com

Laptops
Only mid-range and expensive hotels and guesthouses will have a phone line in the room; some hotels will have broadband access from your bedroom. You will need an adaptor to plug in your laptop, and American laptops using 110 to 120 volts will need an adaptor and a transformer. For internet access from your laptop using a local access number,

Thai mail boxes are easy to spot

check www.csloxinfo.com for a temporary subscription to a Thai service provider.

CALLING THAILAND FROM ABROAD
The international country code for Thailand is 66, and this is followed by the area code for the region of Thailand with the initial zero missing, then the local number. To ring from the UK, dial 00+66+area code+number; from the US, dial 011+66+area code+number.

CALLING ABROAD FROM THAILAND
To call the UK, dial 001, followed by 44, then the area code with the initial zero missing and then the local number. To call the US, dial 001, followed by 1, then the area code and the local number.

INTERNATIONAL DIALING CODES

Australia	61
Ireland	353
New Zealand	64
UK	44
US	1

For international directory enquiries and operator, tel 100.

MAIL
● Stamps can be bought in post offices. Hotels and guesthouses also sell stamps for letters and postcards, charging a little more.
● Parcels must be packed and sealed at special counters in post offices. The rate for a non-airmail parcel under 5kg is B1650 to the UK and B1110 to the US. Airmail rates are B2420 and B2950 respectively.

PLANNING

OPENING TIMES AND NATIONAL HOLIDAYS

BANKS
- Monday to Friday from 8.30am to 4.30pm, though some may close at 3.30pm.
- Exchange booths, easy to find in resort destinations, Bangkok and Chiang Mai, keep longer hours and are often open seven days a week from 9am to as late as 9pm or 10pm.

POST OFFICES
Most post offices open Monday to Friday, 8.30am to 4.30pm, and on Saturday from 9am to noon. Some may close for lunch and stay open an hour or more longer.

MUSEUMS
Many museums open daily from 9.30am to 4.30pm or 5pm, but when there are exceptions, as with the National Museum in Bangkok, they usually close on Monday and Tuesday.

You'll often find several services available at the same location

SHOPS
Most shops open Monday to Saturday from around 9am to 8pm or 9pm and many keep the same hours on Sunday. Department stores tend to open at 10am. In resort areas and popular destinations, shops catering to visitors will stay open seven days a week.

OFFICES
General office hours are Monday to Friday, 8.30am to 4.30pm or 5pm and on Saturday from 8am to noon.

PHARMACIES
General hours are from 9am to 8pm, including Sunday.

TOURIST OFFICES

TOURIST OFFICES	
TAT (Tourist Authority of Thailand; www.tourismthailand.org) Open daily 8.30am to 4.30pm, unless otherwise stated TAT Helpline Tel freephone 1672 daily 8am to 8pm	**Chiang Mai** 105/1 Thanon Chiang Mai-Lamphun, Chiang Mai Tel 053 248 604, 053 248 607 Email: tatchmai@tat.or.th
Bangkok Head Office 1600 Thanon Phetchaburi Mai, Makkasan, Ratchathewi, Bangkok 10400 Tel 022 505 500 Email: center@tat.or.th	**Kanchanaburi** Thanon Saengchuto, Kanchanaburi Tel 034 511 200
	Ayutthaya 108/22 Moo 4 Tambon Phratoochai, Ayutthaya Tel 035 246 076 Email: tatyutya@tat.or.th
Bangkok Local Offices 4 Ratchadamnoen Nok Avenue, Banglamphu Tel 022 831 555	
Arrival Hall, Terminal 1, Don Muang International Airport Tel 025 042 701 Open daily 8am to midnight	**Khorat** 2102–2104 Thanon Mitraphap, Khorat Tel 044 213 666 Email: tatsima@tat.or.th
Arrival Hall, Terminal 2, Don Muang International Airport Tel 025 042 703 Open daily 8am to midnight	**Phuket** 73–75 Thanon Phuket Tel 076 212 213 Email: tatphket@tat.or.th

TAT OFFICES ABROAD
London 3rd Floor, Brook House, 98–99 Jermyn Street, London SW1Y 6EE Tel (0) 207 925 2511 Email: info@thaismile.co.uk
New York (also covering Canada) 61 Broadway, Suite 2810 New York, NY 10006 Tel (1) 212 432 0433 Email: info@tatny.com
Los Angeles 611 North Larchmont Boulevard, 1st Floor, Los Angeles, CA 90004, USA Tel (1) 323 461 9814 Email: tatla@ix.netcom.com
Sydney (also covering New Zealand) 2nd Floor, 75 Pitt Street, Sydney, NSW 2000 Tel (0) 2 9247 7549 Email: info@thailand.net.au

PLANNING

USEFUL WEBSITES

SIGHT/TOWN	WEBSITE	PAGE
	KEY SIGHTS QUICK WEBSITE FINDER	
Ayutthaya	http://thailand.sawadee.com/ayutthaya	135
Bangkok	www.bangkok.com	63
Chiang Dao	www.chiangdao.com	110
Chiang Mai	www.chiangmai-online.com	112
Chiang Rai	www.chiangraiprovince.com	118
Chumphon	www.chumphon.com	155
Doi Inthanon	www.chiangmai-thai.com/ doi_inthanon.htm	120
Erewan National Park	www.kanchanaburi-info.com/ en/nationalpark.html	140
Hua Hin	www.hua-hin.com	156
Kanchanaburi	www.kanchanaburi-info.com	142
Ko Phi Phi	www.phi-phi.com	160
Ko Samui	www.samui.org	161
Lampang	www.lampang.go.th www.thailandguidebook.com/ provinces/lampang.html	124
Lamphun	http://thailand.sawadee.com/lamphun/	126
Phang Nga	http://phangnga.sawadee.com	166
Pattaya	www.pattayacity.com/pattaya	146
Phimai	www.phimai.ca	100
Phuket	www.phuket.com	168
Mae Sai	www.modernthailand.com/ chiang-rai/mae-sai.htm	129
Sukhothai	www.wayfaresthailand.com/ sukothai.htm	150
Ubon Ratchathani	http://isan.sawadee.com/ ubonratchathani/	106
Udon Thani	www.udonthani.com	108

www.thaimet.tmd.go.th/eng/default.asp
Daily weather updates.

www.travelforum.org/thailand/index.html
Lots of information about the various regions of Thailand.

www.tourismthailand.org
Thai tourist board official website.

www.sawadee.com
Regional information, maps and online hotel bookings.

www.thaifocus.com getround.htm
Deals with forms of transportation with links to timetables, car rental etc.

www.khaosanroad.com
Dedicated to Thanon Khao San, the backpackers' area of Thailand.

www.fodors.com/miniguides/mgresults.cfm?destination= bangkok@21
Fodor's online guide to Thailand, which includes a forum where travelers exchange information.

www.onlinenewspapers.com/thailand.htm
List of links to Thai newspapers.

www.thaiworldview.com/tv/cinema.htm
Database of Thai movies with summaries and reviews of films.

www.thaiwildlife.com
Dedicated to Thai wildlife and the national parks.

www.martialartsphuket.com
A Thai kickboxing camp based in Phuket with history of the sport and details of packages.

www.thailandlife.com
Features on culture, local crafts, a forum for discussion and more.

www.thaipro.com
A Thai search engine offering links to hundreds of Thai sites.

10artscrafts.athailand.com
Dedicated to the many craft forms available in Thailand.

www.onebag.com/home.html
A personal guide to traveling light, aimed chiefly at backpackers.

www.embassyworld.com
Database of every embassy worldwide.

www.cybercaptive.com
Database of cybercafés worldwide, giving street addresses.

www.thaifocus.com/disabledt.htm
Assistance for travelers with disabilities.

www.paddleasia.com
A company based in Phuket which offers kayaking trips and other nature-based holidays.

www.asianbiketour.com
A company based in Chiang Mai which offers motorcycle touring holidays around Asia.

www.railay.com/railay/climbing/climbing_intro.shtml
The website of a reputable climbing school in Krabi.

www.thecrag.com
Accounts of many rock climbing spots in Thailand.

www.divethailand.net
Information on diving in Thailand.

www.activethailand.com/kayaking
Information and links to kayaking organizations, chiefly in the north.

http://johngray-seacanoe.com
A long-established and reputable kayaking tour company in Phuket.

www.activethailand.com/rafting
A company based in Pai that organizes whitewater rafting tours.

www.muaythai.com
Lots of information about kickboxing.

www.cyclingthailand.com
Bicycling routes in Thailand.

www.wfb-hq.org
The World Federation of Buddhists, with listings of meditation centers.

www.onebag.com
The practicalities of traveling light.

www.kropla.com
Useful information on electricity and modem use in Thailand.

PLANNING

FILMS, BOOKS AND MEDIA

FILMS

● Thailand has been the location for many movies. It has stood in on many occasions for Vietnam, particularly in the *Deer Hunter* (1978), and has itself been represented in film by other countries, notably the 1999 movie *Anna and the King* based on the novel by Anna Leonowens (*The English Governess and the Siamese Court*). The movie was filmed in Malaysia since its production and distribution was banned in Thailand—the film and its previous incarnations suggested a romantic involvement between the king of Thailand and the governess, which was considered insulting to the Thai royalty.

● Thailand has been presented to the public in several famous movies over the decades. *Brokedown Palace* (1999) tells the relatively true story of two Australian girls committed to 30 years for a drugs offence. In 2000 *The Beach* was both set in and filmed on Ko Phi Phi, which made the islands enormously popular and no longer a well-kept secret. The opening scenes are set in Bangkok and feature Leonardo De Caprio arriving in Thanon Kao San and viewing the Reclining Buddha in Wat Po.

● James Bond has of course hung out in Thailand a few times. In *The Man with the Golden Gun* (1974) Christopher Lee's secret lair was hidden offshore at Ao Phang Nga, and 1997's *Tomorrow Never Dies* returned to the same spot.

● Thailand has its own movie industry, turning out thrillers, musical comedies and more. Yongyooth Thongkonthun's *Iron Ladies* (2000), based on the true story of how a team consisting mainly of gay men, transvestites and transsexuals won the Thai national volleyball championships in 1996, received a considerable international viewership. In 2001 Wisit Sasanatieng's *Tears of the Black Tiger* won the Dragons & Tiger Award for best new director at Vancouver and was selected for Cannes. The film tells a traditional story in a very up-to-date way, creating images that resemble hand-colored photographs.

● In 1989 Jean-Claude Van Damme's movie *The Kickboxer* brought Thai martial arts to a world audience.

BOOKS

● For the historical background of the country you can do no better than the single volume *Thailand: A Short History* by David K. Wyatt (Yale University Press, 1982). *Southeast Asia* by Mary Somers Heidhues (Thames and Hudson, 2001) is also a usefully concise history of Thailand and the region. *Lords of the Rim* by Sterling Seagrave (Bantam, 1995) remains a popular, albeit exaggerated, tale of Chinese influence in southeast Asia, including Thailand.

● There are a number of interesting and useful books that focus on Bangkok. Nancy Chandler's *Map of Bangkok* (Nancy Chandler Graphics, 2005) is currently in its 23rd edition and comes in the form of a fold-out map of the city center with separate maps of key areas like Sukhumvit, Chatuchak and Chinatown. Only information of possible interest to visitors and expatriates is included, and there is a wealth of local detail assiduously collected by residents of the city. The website www.nancychandler.net has details of other, like-minded publications. *The Grand Palace Bangkok*, by Naengnoi Suksri (Thames and Hudson, 1999) is a richly illustrated guide in color—one of those books you may wish you had consulted before visiting the Palace.

● For those who intend to visit Kanchanaburi *The River Kwai Railway: The Story of the Burma-Siam Railway* by Clifford Kinvig (Conway Maritime, 2005) tells the harrowing story of the prisoners of war and slave workers who worked and died on the construction of the railway line. Along similar lines but in the form of a novel is Pierre Boule's novel *The Bridge on the River Kwai* (Bantam Books, 1990). Best of all on the subject of the Thai–Myanmar railway and its construction is *Railway Man* by Eric Llomax (Jonathon Cape, 1995) who survived the experience and returned to meet the man who brutalized him.

● *The National Parks and Other Wild Places of Thailand* by Stephen Elliott (New Holland, 2006) is an up-to-date guide to Thailand's non-urban attractions.

● Travel literature about the region to look out for includes *Adventurous Women in South East Asia* by John Gullick (OUP), which recounts the adventures of assorted eccentric women travelers of the 19th century. *The Gentleman in the Parlour* by W Somerset Maugham (Vintage Classics, 2001) is a classic tale first published in 1935, of an Englishman abroad, on a journey across Southeast Asia and including Thailand. A more modern and offbeat account of travel in Thailand is *Thailand: The last Domino* by Richard West (Michael Joseph, 1991), who gives a lively account of his journeys across the country, packed with historical and cultural detail.

Don't worry, newspapers come in English too!

• For those who want to understand the cultural mores of Thai society there are several books to choose from. *The Arts of Thailand* by Steve van Beek (Thames and Hudson, 1999) is an excellent, beautifully illustrated account of Thai architecture, sculpture and painting. *Thailand: A Survival Guide to Customs and Etiquette* by Robert Cooper and Nanthapa Cooper (Graphic Arts Center Publishing, 2005) is a new edition of what used to be the *Culture Shock!* series. It is up to date and full of information, though aimed more at the expatriate than the visitor.

• *Phra Farang* by Phra Peter Pannapadipo (Arrow books, 2005) is the story of how a businessman becomes a Buddhist monk in Bangkok. *The Path to Buddha* by Steve McCurry (Phaidon, 2003) is illustrated with photographs from Tibet, but the explanations and account of Buddhism relate to Thai culture also. *The Essence of Buddha: The Path to Enlightenment* by Ryuho Okawa (Time Warner, 2003) offers a general introduction to the philosophy of Buddhism while *An End to Suffering: The Buddha in the World* by Pankaj Mishra (Picador, 2004) manages to do the same but in a more perceptive manner, weaving philosophy, history, biography and politics. One of the best practical manuals for putting the philosophy of Buddhism into practise is *Change Your Mind: A Practical Guide to Buddhist Meditation* by Paramananda (Windhorse Publications, 1999).

• A number of books have been written by Westerners who have been imprisoned for serious drug offences in Bangkok's notorious Bang Kwang prison, dubbed the Bangkok Hilton. The title of Warren Fellows' account, *The Damage Done: Twelve Years of Hell in a Bangkok Prison* (Mainstream Publishing, 1999), leaves little to the imagination; nor does another account, by Sandra Gregory and Michael Tierney, entitled *Forget You Had a Daughter: Doing Time in the Bangkok Hilton* (Vision, 2003). Sandra Gregory, who was caught smuggling heroin at Bangkok airport in 1993, was eventually transferred to a British prison and released in July 2000.

• Thai cooking has to be one of the most fashionable styles around at the moment, and there are any number of good, simple books on Thai food and its preparation. A great start can be made with *Asian Greens* by Anita Loh-Yien Lau (Apple Press, 2001), which has clear illustrations of each and every strange vegetable that you see in Thai markets and Asian stores back home and explains what to do with it. Two books by Jackum Brown, *Thai Cooking* and *Vegetarian Thai Cooking* (Hamlyn, 1999), offer good glossaries and simple instructions on many of the regional variations, from jungle curry to steamed pomfret. In a similar vein is *The Book of Thai Cooking* (Salamander, 2001), which also offers pictures of equipment, basic ingredients and illustrated instructions for over 100 recipes. *A Little Taste of Thailand* (Murdoch Books, 2004) is an affordable book of recipes, from street food to curries. The most comprehensive account of Thai cuisine is *Thai Food* by David Thompson (Pavillion Books, 2002), a doorstop of a book with some 300 recipes, extensive information on ingredients and superb photographs.

• If you experience a Thai massage and want to learn the technique then the best book on the subject is *Step-by-Step Thai Massage* by Mann and McKenzie (Asia Books, 2004). It is a highly practical manual, with photographs illustrating each and every stage, and should be available in most Bangkok or Chiang Mai bookshops.

• Wildlife enthusiasts can look out for *A Photographic Guide to the Birds of Thailand* by Michael Webster and Chew Yen Fook (New Holland, 2002) or *Field Guide to the Birds of Thailand* by Craig Robson (New Holland, 2005).

• There are several good accounts of dive sites in Thailand, including *Diving South East Asia: A Guide to the Best Dive Sites in Indonesia, Malaysia, the Philippines and Thailand* by Kal Muller (Periplus), *Dive Guide Thailand* by Paul Lees (New Holland, 2005) is now in a new and updated edition with practical information, advice and maps on 140 dive and snorkel sites.

• *The Magic of Bangkok* by Sean Sheehan (New Holland, 2003) is an inexpensive book of photographs and text, a reminder of what you saw in the country's capital.

TELEVISION

• Thailand has a plethora of land-based and satellite TV channels. The only cable TV company, UTV, offers several English-language movie channels (all heavily censored), sports channels, Western and Asian imported sit-coms and TV series, CNN, BBC World TV, the Discovery Channel and more. Satellite channels offer a similar range and include Thai variety shows and movies. Land-based TV stations are mostly government owned and show fairly safe run-of-the-mill dramas, documentaries and news.

RADIO

• Thailand has hundreds of radio stations, owned and run by local government bodies. Bangkok has good Thai music stations, and BBC World service, Radio Canada, Radio New Zealand, Voice of America and more can be picked up on short wave bands.

NEWSPAPERS

• There are two English-language daily newspapers available in Thailand: the *Bangkok Post* and *The Nation*. The *Bangkok Post* tends to have rather more international material while *The Nation* focuses on local news. Both are widely available in cities and larger towns. In addition, the Singapore edition of the *International Herald Tribune* is available in Bangkok and the *Asia Wall Street News* can often be found in major bookstores.

Magazines on sale in Sukhothai

FILMS, BOOKS AND MEDIA   303

WORDS AND PHRASES

Thai has its own complex script which is very different from any European language. Here we provide a simple transliteration using the English alphabet.

Courtesy and respect is very important in Thai society, and people consider hierarchy, status and seniority when addressing one another. The safest option is to refer to yourself ("I") as *phom* (if you are male) and *dichan* (if you are female), and address the other person as *khun* (this can be followed by his/her first name). To be polite, men should add *khrap* to the end of sentences and women should add *kha*. Please choose the appropriate alternative indicated in this guide such as *phom/dichan*, etc.

Thai words in this guide have been transliterated as closely as possible to how they are actually pronounced in Thai. However, there are certain characters which should be drawn to your attention. They are:

ua = ou	as in	t**ou**r
bp = p	as in	s**p**are or s**p**ort
dt = t	as in	s**t**op or s**t**ool
uae	as in	**uaggh**

Thai is a tonal language with five different tonal sounds (flat, high, low, rising and falling) denoted by four tonal marks. These tones vary the meaning of a sound. For example, *mai* in a high pitch means "new/again/another," whereas *mai* in a low pitch means "no." The transliteration of Thai tonal sounds has not been attempted in this guide, to keep the notation simple.

Thai verbs do not have tenses. Words or phrases, such as "now," "two days ago," "tomorrow" are used to indicate present, past or future. Articles (a, an and the) do not exist in Thai. Adjectives come after nouns. Thus "a red apple" is "apple red" in Thai.

Learning a few simple words in Thai is easy as many Thai words are monosyllabic. The locals will appreciate it if you can exchange a few words with them in Thai.

NUMBERS

0 soon	6 hok	30 saam-sib	90 gaow-sib
1 nung	7 jet	40 see-sib	100 nung-roi
2 song	8 bpaet	50 hah-sib	1,000 nung-pan
3 saam	9 gaow	60 hok-sib	million lahn
4 see	10 sib	70 jet-sib	quarter nung nai see
5 hah	20 yee-sib	80 bpaet-sib	half khrung

USEFUL WORDS

yes **chai**	you're welcome **Mai pen rai khrap/kha**	where **tee-nai**	who **khrai**
no **mai**		here **tee-nee**	why **tam-mai/pro arai**
please **garunah**	excuse me! **Kor-toht khrap/kha!**	there **tee-nan**	may I/can I? **Phom/dichan kor...dai mai?**
thank you **korb-khun**		when **muae-rai**	

CONVERSATION

I don't speak Thai
Phom/dichan poot pah-sah Thai mai dai

Do you speak English?
Khun poot pah-sah angkrit dai mai?

I don't understand
Phom/dichan mai khao-jai

My name is…
Phom/dichan chue…

What's your name?
Khun chue arai?

Hello, pleased to meet you
Sawatdee khrap/kha. Yin-dee tee dai roojak khun

This is my wife/husband/daughter/son
Nee panraya/sah-me/loog-saow/loog-chai khong phom/dichan

Where do you live?
Khun yoo tee-nai?

I live in…
Phom/dichan yoo tee…

Good morning
Sawatdee

Good afternoon/evening
Sawatdee

Goodbye
Lah-gone khrap/kha, Sawatdee

How are you?
Sabaai-dee rue khrap/kha?

Fine, thank you
Sabaai-dee, korb-khun

I'm sorry
Phom/dichan kor-toht

SHOPPING

How much is this?
Tao-rai khrap/kha?

Where can I buy...?
Phom/dichan ja sue ... dai tee-nai?

I'm just looking, thank you
Dern doo tao-nan khrap/kha, korb-khun

I'll take this
Phom/dichan ao an-nee khrap/kha

Do you accept credit cards?
Chai bat credit dai mai?

Can you measure me please?
Wat dtua hai phom/dichan noi khrap/kha?

MONEY

Is there a bank/currency exchange office nearby?
Taew nee mee ta-nah-kaan/ tee laek-plian ngern taang-bpra-tet mai?

I'd like to change sterling/ dollars into Thai baht
Phom/dichan dtong-garn laek ngern bporn/dollar bpen ngern baht.

Can I use my credit card to withdraw cash?
Phom/dichan ja chai bat credit torn ngern-sot dai mai?

I'd like to cash this traveler's check
Phom/dichan dtong-garn laek cheque dern-taang bpen ngern-sot

GETTING AROUND

Where is the train/bus station?
Satah-nee rot fai/rot bus yoo tee-nai?

Does this train/bus/ferry go to…?
Rot fai/rot bus/ruae-kaam-faak nee bpai…rue bplao?

Where can I buy a ticket?
Sue dtua dai tee-nai khrap/kha?

Please can I have a single/return ticket to…
Kor sue dtua tiew-diew/ bpai-glap bpai…khrap/kha

Where can I find a taxi (stand)?
Ja hah taxi (queue rot-taxi) dai tee-nai khrap/kha?

How much is the journey?
Khah rot tao-rai?

Please turn on the meter
Bpert meter duoy khrap/kha

air-conditioned bus
rot-bus dtid-air

skytrain
rot fai-fah

COLORS

black **see dam**	orange **see som**	green **see kiew**	silver **see ngern**
pink **see chom-poo**	brown **see nam-dtaan**	turquoise **see kiew-om-fah**	gray **see tao**
red **see daeng**	yellow **see luaeng**	white **see kaow**	blue **see nam-ngern**
purple **see muang**		gold **see torng**	

underground
rot dtai-din

airport
sa-naam bin

(longtail) boat
ruae (haang-yaow)

ferry
ruae kaam-faak

bicycle
rot jak-gra-yarn

motorcycle
rot mor-dter-sai

TOURIST INFORMATION

Where is the tourist information office/tourist information desk, please?
Samnak-ngaan kormoon garn-tong-tiew/panaek kormoon garn-tong-tiew yoo tee-nai khrap/kha?

Do you have a city map?
Khun mee paen-tee muaeng rue-plao?

What is the admission price?
Kah kao chom tao-rai khrap/kha?

Are there guided tours?
Mee tour nam-tiew mai khrap/kha?

Can we make reservations here?
Sam-rorng tee tee-nee dai mai khrap/kha?

Do you have a brochure in English?
Khun mee brochure pah-sah angkrit mai khrap/kha?

IN TROUBLE/ILLNESS

Help!
Chuoy duoy!

Stop, thief!
Yut, kamoy!

Call the fire brigade/police/an ambulance
Riak noy-dap-ploeng/ dtam-ruat/rot payah-baan duoy

I have lost my passport/ wallet/purse/handbag
Passport/kra-bpau-ngern/ kra-bpau-sapaai khong phom/dichan haai

I have had an accident
Phom/dichan dai rap u-bat-dti-het

I need information for my insurance company
Phom/dichan dtong-garn kormoon samrap borisat bpra-gan-pai khong phom/ dichan

Excuse me, I think I am lost
Kor-toht khrap/kha. Phom/ dichan kit wah phom/dichan long-taang

I need to see a doctor/dentist
Phom/dichan dtong bpai hah mor/mor-fan

Where is the hospital?
Rong-payah-baan yoo tee-nai?

I feel sick
Phom/dichan roo-suk kluen-sai

I am allergic to…
Phom/dichan pae…

Can I have a painkiller?
Kor yah gae-bpuat noi khrap/kha?

RESTAURANTS AND HOTELS

A table for…, please
Kor dto…tee-nang khrap/kha

Do you have the menu in English?
Khun mee menu pah-sah angkrit rue-plao?

Could we sit there?
Rau nang tee-nan dai mai?

Could I have bottled
still/sparkling water?
**Kor naam-kuat tammadah
(nam plau)/naam-kuat rot
sah duoy khrap/kha?**

The food is cold
Ah-haan yen bpai

The meat is overcooked/too
rare
Nuae suk gern-bpai/mai suk

Is service included?
**Ruam kah borigarn duoy mai
khrap/kha?**

waiter/waitress
panak-ngaan-serve

I am a vegetarian
**Phom/dichan taan
mang-sa-wirat**

I have made a reservation
for...nights
**Phom/dichan jong hong-pak
wai...kuen**

Do you have a room?
Khun mee hong waang mai?

How much per night?
Rah-kah tao-rai dtor kuen?

The room is too hot/too cold/
dirty
**Hong rorn gern-bpai/naow
gern-bpai/sok-ga-prok
gern-bpai**

Double/single room
Hong koo/hong diew

With bath/shower
**Mee aang aab-naam/
naam-fak-bua**

Twin room
Hong dtiang-koo

Please can I pay my bill?
**Phom/dichan kor jaai kah bill
duoy khrap/kha?**

IN THE TOWN		
on/to the right **yoo/bpai taang kwah**	closed **bpit**	beach **haat/chaai-talay**
on/to the left **yoo/bpai taang saai**	monastery/temple **wat**	canal **khlong**
	monument **anusah-waree**	alley **dtrorg/soi**
opposite **dtrong-kaam**	palace **wang/pra-raat-chawang**	embassy **sa-taan-toot**
straight on **dtrong bpai**	town **muaeng**	market **dta-laat**
north **nuae**	street/road **tanon**	police station **sa-tah-nee-dtam-ruat**
south **dtai**	island **ko**	no entry **haam kao**
east **dta-wan-ork**	river **mae-naam**	entrance **taang kao**
west **ta-wan-tok**	bridge **sa-paan**	exit **taang org**
free **free**	village **moo-baan**	men (toilets) **hong-naam chaai**
donation **bor-ri-jaak**	mountain **poo-kao**	women (toilets) **hong-naam ying**
open **bpert**		

DAYS/TIMES/MONTHS			
Monday **wan jan**	night **glang-kuen**	tomorrow **wan-prung-nee**	June **mi-tu-nah-yon**
Tuesday **wan ang-karn**	day **glang-wan**	month **duaen**	July **ga-rak-ga-dah-kom**
Wednesday **wan put**	morning **dtorn-chao**	January **mak-ga-rah-kom**	August **sing-hah/kom**
Thursday **wan pa-ru-hat-sa-bordee**	afternoon **dtorn-baai**	February **gum-pah-pan**	September **gan-yah-yon**
Friday **wan suk**	evening **dtorn-yen**	March **mee-nah-kom**	October **dtu-lah-kom**
Saturday **wan sau**	today **wan-nee**	April **may-sah-yon**	November **pruet-sa-ji-gah-yon**
Sunday **wan ah-tit**	yesterday **muae-waan-nee**	May **pruet-sa-pah-kom**	December **tan-wah-kom**

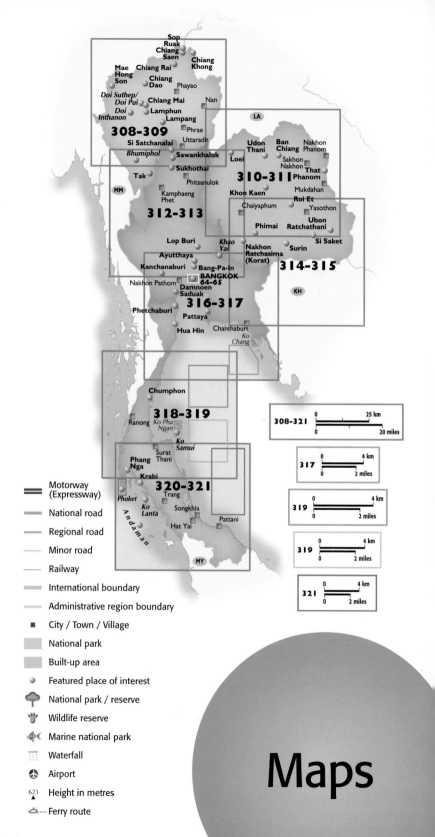

Sop
Ruak
Chiang
Saen
Chiang Rai
Chiang
Khong
Mae
Hong
Son
Chiang
Dao
Phayao
Nan
LA
Doi Suthep/
Doi Pui
Chiang Mai
Doi
Inthanon
Lamphun
Lampang
Udon
Thani
Ban
Chiang
Nakhon
Phanom
Phrae
Sakhon
Nakhon
That
Phanom
308–309
Si Satchanalai
Uttaradit
Loei
Bhumiphol
Swankhalok
310–311
MM
Sukhothai
Tak
Phitsanulok
Khon Kaen
Mukdahan
Kamphaeng
Phet
Chaiyaphum
Roi Et
Yasothon
312–313
Phimai
Ubon
Ratchathani
Si Saket
Lop Buri
Khao
Yai
Nakhon
Ratchasima
(Korat)
Surin
Ayutthaya
Kanchanaburi
Bang-Pa-In
314–315
Nakhon Pathom
BANGKOK
64–65
KH
Damnoen
Saduak
Phetchaburi
316–317
Pattaya
Hua Hin
Chanthaburi
Ko
Chang

Chumphon
318–319
Ranong
Ko Pha
Ngan
Ko
Samui
Surat
Thani
Phang
Nga
Krabi
320–321
Phuket
Trang
Ko
Lanta
Songkhla
Pattani
Hat Yai
MY

Andaman

| 308–321 | 0 | 25 km |
| | 0 | 20 miles |

| 317 | 0 | 4 km |
| | 0 | 2 miles |

| 319 | 0 | 4 km |
| | 0 | 2 miles |

| 319 | 0 | 4 km |
| | 0 | 2 miles |

| 321 | 0 | 4 km |
| | 0 | 2 miles |

━━━ Motorway
(Expressway)

━━━ National road

━━━ Regional road

━━━ Minor road

─── Railway

━━━ International boundary

━━━ Administrative region boundary

■ City / Town / Village

National park

Built-up area

● Featured place of interest

🌳 National park / reserve

🐾 Wildlife reserve

◀✕ Marine national park

▦ Waterfall

✈ Airport

621
▲ Height in metres

⚓— Ferry route

Maps

Page numbers in **bold** indicate the main reference.

ACKNOWLEDGMENTS

Abbreviations for the credits are as follows:

AA = AA World Travel Library, **t** (top), **b** (bottom), **c** (centre), **l** (left), **r** (right), **bg** (background)

UNDERSTANDING THAILAND

4 AA/D Henley; **5l** AA/J Holmes; **5r** AA/J Holmes; **6l** AA/J Holmes; **6c** AA/J Holmes; **6r** AA/J Holmes; **8tr** AA/J Holmes; **8cl** AA/D Henley; **8cr** AA/J Holmes; **8bl** AA/J Holmes; **8/9** AA/D Henley; **9tl** AA/R Strange; **9cl** AA/D Henley; **10tl** AA/D Henley; **10tr** AA/D Henley; **10cl** CPA Media/D Henley; **10cr** AA/D Henley; **10b** AA/J Holmes.

LIVING THAILAND

11 AA/D Henley; **12/3bg** AA/D Henley; **12tl** AA/D Henley; **12tc** AA/R Strange; **12cr** AA/R Strange; **12cl** AA/J Holmes; **13tl** AA/J Holmes; **13tc** AA/B Davies; **13c** AA/J Holmes; **13cr** AA/D Henley; **13bl** AA/R Strange; **14/5bg** AA/J Holmes; **14tl** AA/R Strange; **14tr** AA/R Strange; **14c** AA/J Holmes; **14cr** AA/D Henley; **14cl** AA/D Henley; **15tl** AA/D Henley; **15tc** AA/D Henley; **15tr** AA/D Henley; **15cl** AA/D Henley; **15bl** AA/R Strange; **16/7bg** AA/D Henley; **16tl** AA/D Henley; **16tc** AA/R Strange; **16tr** AA/J Holmes; **16ctl** AA/D Henley; **16l** AA/D Henley; **17tl** AA/D Henley; **17tc** AA/D Henley; **17cl** AA/D Henley; **17cr** AA/J Holmes; **17bl** TAT; **18/9bg** AA/R Strange; **18tc** AA/R Strange; **18cl** AA/R Strange; **18c** AA/J Holmes; **18cr** AA/J Holmes; **18br** AA/J Holmes; **19tl** AA/J Holmes; **19tc** AA/R Strange; **19tr** AA/J Holmes; **19cl** AA/D Henley; **19c** AA/J Holmes; **19cr** AA/ R Strange; **20/1bg** AA/J Holmes; **20tl** AA/J Holmes; **20tr** AA/D Henley; **20ctl** AA/R Strange; **20cl** AA/J Holmes; **20cr** AA/J Holmes; **21tc** AA/J Holmes; **21tr** AA/J Holmes; **21cl** AA/D Henley; **21c** AA/D Henley; **21bl** AA/J Holmes; **22bg** AA/R Strange; **22tl** AA/J Holmes; **22tr** AA/ Strange; **22cl** Getty Images; **22c** AA/R Strange; **22bc** AA/R Strange.

THE STORY OF THAILAND

23 AA/D Henley; **24/5bg** AA/R Strange; **24cl** AA/R Strange; **24br** AA/D Henley; **24/5** AA/R Strange; **25c** AA/B Davies; **25bl** AA/R Strange; **25br** AA/R Strange; **26/7bg** AA/D Henley; **26cl** CPA Media/D Henley; **26bl** CPA Media/D Henley; **26c** AA/B Davies; **26/7** AA/D Henley; **27c** CPA Media/D Henley; **27cl** AA/R Strange; **27br** AA/R Strange; **28/9bg** AA/R Strange; **28c** CPA Media/D Henley; **28cl** AA/J Holmes; **28bl** AA/J Holmes; **28br** AA/D Henley; **29c** CPA Media/D Henley; **29bl** AA/J Holmes; **29bc** AA/D Henley; **29br** CPA Media/D Henley; **30/1bg** AA/D Henley; **30cl** AA/D Henley; **30c** AA/D Henley; **30bc** CPA Media/D Henley; **30br** CPA Media/D Henley; **31cl** Anders Ryman/Corbis UK; **31cr** CPA Media/D Henley; **31bl** AA/R Strange; **31bc** CPA Media/D Henley; **31br** CPA Media/D Henley; **32/3bg** AA/R Strange; **32bl** AA/R Strange; **32c** AA/R Strange; **32cr** AA/R Strange; **32br** AA/R Strange; **32/3** AA/D Henley; **33cr** CPA Media/D Henley; **33bcl** CPA Media/D Henley; **33bcr** CPA Media/D Henley; **33br** Michael Freeman/Corbis UK; **34/5bg** AA/R Strange; **34tl** AA/R Strange; **34cbl** CPA Media/D Henley; **34bl** CPA Media/D Henley; **34cr** CPA Media/D Henley; **34br** Mary Evans Picture Library; **34/5** AA/D Henley; **35c** Mary Evans Picture Library; **35bc** AA/D Henley; **35br** CPA Media/D Henley; **36/7bg** AA/D Henley; **36cl** CPA Media/D Henley; **36cr** AA/R Strange; **36bc** AA/R Strange; **36/7** AA/R Strange; **37bl** AA/R Strange; **37cr** AA/D Henley; **37br** CPA Media/D Henley; **38bg** AA/J Holmes; **38tl** Getty Images; **38cbl** AA/J Holmes; **38cr** Getty Images; **38bl** AA/R Strange; **38br** AA/J Holmes.

ON THE MOVE

39 AA/D Henley; **40/1t** AOT PR; **40b** AA/D Henley; **42t** AOT PR; **43t** AA/R Strange; **43b** Mark Smith, www.seat61.com; **44t** AA/R Strange; **44b** AA/J Holmes; **45t** AA/B Davies; **45b** AA/J

Holmes; 46/7t AA/R Strange; **47c** AA/R Strange; **48/9t** AA/R Strange; **50/1t** AOT PR; **51b** AOT PR; **52t** AA/J Holmes; **52b** AA/R Strange; **53t** AA/D Henley; **53b** AA/B Davies; **54/5t** AA/J Holmes; **54b** AA/D Henley; **56/7t** AA/R Strange; **58t** AA/R Strange; **59t** AA/D Henley; **59b** AA/D Henley; **60t** www.adventure-holidays-thailand.com; **60b** www.adventure-holidays-thailand.com.

THE SIGHTS

61 AA/D Henley; **63c** AA/D Henley; **67tl** AA/J Holmes; **67tc** AA/J Holmes; **67tr** AA/J Holmes; **67br** AA/J Holmes; **68tl** AA/J Holmes; **68tr** AA/D Henley; **69tl** AA/D Henley; **69tc** AA/D Henley; **69tr** AA/J Holmes; **70t** AA/J Holmes; **70cl** AA/R Strange; **71tl** AA/J Holmes; **71tr** AA/D Henley; **72tl** AA/R Strange; **72tc** AA/J Holmes; **72tr** AA/J Holmes; **72b** AA/J Holmes; **73t** Luca I.Tettoni/Corbis UK; **73cl** Doug Steley/Alamy; **73c** AA/J Holmes; **73cr** AA/J Holmes; **74** AA/R Strange; **75** Luca I.Tettoni/Corbis UK; **76tl** AA/J Holmes; **76tc** AA/J Holmes; **76tr** AA/J Holmes; **76b** AA/J Holmes; **77t** AA/D Henley; **77b** AA/D Henley; **78tl** AA/R Strange; **78tc** AA/J Holmes; **78tr** AA/J Holmes; **78br** AA/R Strange; **79tl** AA/J Holmes; **79tr** AA/J Holmes; **80t** AA/J Holmes; **80cl** AA/J Holmes; **81t** AA/R Strange; **81cr** AA/R Strange; **82tl** AA/R Strange; **82tc** AA/J Holmes; **82tr** AA/J Holmes; **82br** AA/J Holmes; **83t** AA/J Holmes; **83cr** AA/R Strange; **84t** AA/R Strange; **84cl** AA/D Henley; **84c** AA/D Henley; **84cr** AA/D Henley; **85** AA/D Henley; **86/7** TAT; **86b** AA/D Henley; **87** AA/R Strange; **88tl** AA/R Strange; **88tr** AA/R Strange; **88br** AA/R Strange; **90tl** TAT; **90tr** Luca I.Tettoni/Corbis UK; **91tl** AA/J Holmes; **91tc** AA/J Holmes; **91tr** AA/R Strange; **91br** AA/R Strange; **92tl** AA/J Holmes; **92tc** AA/B Davies; **92tr** AA/R Strange; **92br** AA/J Holmes; **93t** Dan Sheehan; **93cr** AA/ R Strange; **94t** AA/J Holmes; **94cl** AA/R Strange; **94c** AA/J Holmes; **94cr** AA/J Holmes; **95t** AA/J Holmes; **95b** AA/D Holmes; **96t** AA/B Davies; **96cl** AA/R Strange; **97t** AA/J Holmes; **97cr** AA/J Holmes; **98tl** AA/J Holmes; **98tc** AA/J Holmes; **98tr** AA/R Strange; **98br** AA/J Holmes; **99tl** AA/J Holmes; **99tc** AA/J Holmes; **99tr** AA/R Strange; **100t** Michael Freeman/Corbis UK; **100cl** AA/R Strange; **100c** AA/R Strange; **100cr** AA/R Strange; **101** AA/R Strange; **102tl** AA/J Holmes; **102tr** AA/J Holmes; **102bl** AA/J Holmes; **103t** AA/J Holmes; **103cr** AA/J Holmes; **104t** AA/J Holmes; **104bl** AA/J Holmes; **105tl** AA/J Holmes; **105tr** AA/R Strange; **106t** AA/J Holmes; **106cl** AA/J Holmes; **106c** AA/J Holmes; **106cr** AA/J Holmes; **107** AA/J Holmes; **108tl** AA/J Holmes; **108tr** AA/J Holmes; **110t** AA/J Holmes; **110cl** AA/J Holmes; **111t** AA/J Holmes; **111cr** AA/J Holmes; **112t** AA/D Henley; **112cl** AA/R Strange; **112c** AA/D Henley; **112cr** AA/D Henley; **113t** AA/D Henley; **113b** AA/D Henley; **114** AA/ D Henley; **115t** AA/R Strange; **115b** AA/R Strange; **118t** AA/D Henley; **118cl** AA/R Strange; **119tl** AA/D Henley; **119tr** AA/J Holmes; **120t** AA/D Henley; **120cl** AA/R Strange; **120cr** AA/D Henley; **121** AA/D Henley; **122t** AA/R Strange; **122cl** AA/J Holmes; **123tl** AA/B Davies; **123tc** AA/J Holmes; **123tr** AA/B Davies; **124t** AA/R Strange; **124cl** AA/D Henley; **124c** AA/D Henley; **124cr** AA/D Henley; **125t** AA/D Henley; **125cr** AA/D Henley; **126t** AA/R Strange; **126cl** AA/D Henley; **126c** AA/R Strange; **126cr** AA/D Henley; **126bl** AA/D Henley; **127** AA/R Strange; **128** AA/D Henley; **129tl** AA/J Holmes; **129tc** AA/R Strange; **129tr** AA/J Holmes; **129b** AA/J Holmes; **130tl** AA/J Holmes; **130tr** AA/R Strange; **131tl** AA/R Strange; **131tr** AA/R Strange; **131b** AA/J Holmes; **132tl** AA/J Holmes; **132tr** AA/D Henley; **133tl** AA/J Holmes; **133tr** AA/J Holmes; **135t** AA/R Strange; **135cl** AA/R Strange; **135c** AA/D Henley; **135cr** AA/D Henley; **136** AA/D Henley;

137 AA/D Henley; 138 AA/R Strange; 139 AA/D Henley; 140tl AA/D Henley; 140tr AA/D Henley; 141tl AA/D Henley; 141tr AA/R Strange; 142t AA/R Strange; 142cl AA/D Henley; 142c AA/D Henley; 142cr AA/R Strange; 143 AA/R Strange; 144t AA/R Strange; 144b AA/D Henley; 145tl AA/D Henley; 145tc AA/J Holmes; 145tr AA/J Holmes; 146t AA/D Henley; 146cl AA/D Henley; 146bl AA/D Henley; 147t AA/J Holmes; 147cr AA/J Holmes; 147b AA/J Holmes; 148t AA/R Strange; 148cl AA/R Strange; 148c AA/J Holmes; 148cr AA/J Holmes; 149t AA/D Henley; 149b AA/J Holmes; 150t AA/R Strange; 150cl AA/J Holmes; 150c AA/R Strange; 150cr AA/J Holmes; 151t AA/J Holmes; 151b AA/D Henley; 152cl AA/J Holmes; 152br AA/J Holmes; 154t AA/D Henley; 154cl AA/D Henley; 155tl Michele Falzone/Alamy; 155tr AA/J Holmes; 156t AA/J Holmes; 156cl AA/D Henley; 157tl AA/J Holmes; 157tc AA/D Henley; 157tr AA/J Holmes; 157br AA/J Holmes; 158tl Andrew Woodley/Alamy; 158tr AA/J Holmes; 158b David Halbakken/Alamy; 159t AA/J Holmes; 159cr AA/J Holmes; 160tl Andre Seale/Alamy; 160tr David Sanger Photography/Alamy; 160b David Sanger Photography/Alamy; 161t AA/D Henley; 161cl AA/D Henley; 161c AA/D Henley; 161cr AA/D Henley; 162t AA/D Henley; 162b AA/J Holmes; 163t AA/J Holmes; 163b AA/D Henley; 164 AA/D Henley; 165tl AA/J Holmes; 165tc AA/D Henley; 165tr AA/D Henley; 166t AA/R Strange; 166cl AA/R Strange; 167t AA/D Henley; 167cr AA/D Henley; 168t AA/D Henley; 168cl AA/D Henley; 168c AA/D Henley; 168cr AA/D Henley; 169t AA/D Henley; 169b AA/D Henley; 170t AA/D Henley; 170cl AA/D Henley; 170b AA/D Henley; 171 AA/D Henley; 172tl AA/D Henley; 172tc AA/D Henley; 172tr AA/D Henley.

WHAT TO DO

173 AA/J Holmes; 174t AA/J Holmes; 174cl AA/J Holmes; 174cr AA/J Holmes; 175t AA/J Holmes; 175cl AA/R Strange; 175cr AA/J Holmes; 176t Brand X Pictures; 176cl AA/R Strange; 176/7 AA/J Holmes; 177t Brand X Pictures; 177cr AA/J Holmes; 178t AA/R Strange; 178cl AA/R Strange; 178cr AA/D Henley; 179t AA/R Strange; 179cl AA/J Holmes; 179cr AA/J Holmes; 180 AA/R Strange; 181t AA/R Strange; 181c AA/J Holmes; 182t AA/J Holmes; 182c AA/ R Strange; 183t AA/J Holmes; 183c AA/J Holmes; 184t AA/J Holmes; 184c AA/J Holmes; 185t AA/J Holmes; 185c AA/J Holmes; 186t AA/J Holmes; 186c AA/J Holmes; 187t AA/J Holmes; 187c AA/J Holmes; 188t AA/J Holmes; 188c AA/J Holmes; 189t AA/J Holmes; 189c AA/J Holmes; 190t AA/J Holmes; 190c AA/D Henley; 191t AA/J Holmes; 191c Image 100; 192t AA/J Holmes; 192c AA/R Strange; 193t AA/B Davies; 193c AA/J Holmes; 194t AA/B Davies; 194c AA/J Holmes; 195t AA/B Davies; 195c AA/J Holmes; 196t AA/B Davies; 196c AA/J Holmes; 197t AA/B Davies; 197c AA/B Davies; 198t AA/D Henley; 198c AA/J Holmes; 199t AA/D Henley; 199c Siam Royal Orchid Co. Ltd; 200t AA/D Henley; 200c AA/J Holmes; 201t AA/D Henley; 201c AA/J Holmes; 202t AA/D Henley; 202c AA/D Henley; 203t AA/D Henley; 203c AA/R Strange; 204t AA/J Holmes; 205t AA/J Holmes; 205c Kingdoms Park; 206t AA/J Holmes; 206c AA/R Strange; 207t AA/J Holmes; 207c AA/R Strange; 208t AA/J Holmes; 208c Alangkarn, The Extravaganza Show, Pattaya; 209t AA/J Holmes; 209c AA/D Henley; 210t AA/J Holmes; 211t AA/D Henley; 211c Discovery Dive Center Amari Palm Reef Resort; 212t AA/D Henley; 212c Corbis UK; 213t AA/D Henley; 213c www.bluestars.info; 214t AA/D Henley; 214c AA/J Holmes; 215t AA/D Henley; 215c www.bigbluedivingsamui.com; 216t AA/D Henley; 216c http://phuket-fantasea.com; 217t AA/D Henley; 217c Body&Mind Day Spa; 218t AA/D Henley; 218c www.peace-tropical-spa.com.

OUT AND ABOUT

219 AA/J Holmes; 221 AA/J Holmes; 222 AA/D Henley; 223 AA/J Holmes; 224 AA/J Holmes; 225t AA/J Holmes; 225c AA/J Holmes; 225b AA/J Holmes; 227t AA/J Holmes; 227b AA/R Strange; 228 AA/Strange; 230 AA/J Holmes; 231t AA/J Holmes; 231b AA/J Holmes; 232t AA/Strange; 232b AA/J Holmes; 233t AA/R Strange; 233c AA/D Henley; 233b AA/R Strange; 234 Manohra Cruises; 235 Manohra Cruises; 236 AA/D Henley; 237 AA/ R Strange; 238 AA/D Henley; 239t AA/D Henley; 239b AA/D Henley; 240tl Asian Oasis; 240tc Siam Safari Nature Tours Co. Ltd; 240tr Asian Oasis.

EATING AND STAYING

241 Glow Restaurant; 242cl Glow Restaurant; 242c Glow Restaurant; 242cr Glow Restaurant; 243cl Vertigo Restaurant; 243c White Elephant Restaurant; 243cr The Celadon; 244cl The Celadon; 244c Saigon; 244cr Saigon; 244b Biscotti; 245cl Sirocco; 245c Sirocco; 245cr Sirocco; 245b Sirocco; 246t AA/J Holmes; 246c Biscotti; 247t AA/J Holmes; 247c AA/J Holmes; 248t AA/J Holmes; 248c The Celadon; 249t AA/J Holmes; 249c Sirocco; 250t AA/J Holmes; 250c Saigon; 251t AA/J Holmes; 251c AA/J Holmes; 252t AA/J Holmes; 252c Pantawee Hotel & Panorama Restaurant; 253t AA/J Holmes; 253c AA/J Holmes; 254t AA/J Holmes; 254c AA/J Holmes; 255t AA/J Holmes; 255c AA/J Holmes; 256t AA/J Holmes; 256c Chiang Dao Nest Mini Resort; 257t AA/J Holmes; 257c AA/J Holmes; 258t AA/J Holmes; 258c Chiang Dao Nest Mini Resort; 259t AA/J Holmes; 259c Bananastock; 260t AA/J Holmes; 260c AA/J Holmes; 261t AA/J Holmes; 261c AA/R Strange; 262t AA/J Holmes; 262c AA/J Holmes; 263t AA/J Holmes; 263c AA/J Holmes; 264t AA/J Holmes; 264c AA/D Henley; 265t AA/J Holmes; 265c AA/J Holmes; 266t AA/J Holmes; 266c Baan Rim Pa Restaurant, Phuket; 267t AA/J Holmes; 267c A/D Henley; 268 AA/D Henley; 269cl Sofitel Central, Hua Hin; 269c AA/J Holmes; 269cr AA/J Holmes; 269b www.thailandhomestay.com; 270t AA/J Sawyer; 270c JW Marriott; 271t AA/C Sawyer; 271c Imperial Queen's Park; 272t AA/C Sawyer; 272c AA/J Holmes; 273t AA/C Sawyer; 273c AA/J Holmes; 274t AA/C Sawyer; 274c AA/D Henley; 275t AA/C Sawyer; 275c Sofitel Raja Orchid Hotel; 276t AA/C Sawyer; 276c Mut Mee Guest House; 277t AA/C Sawyer; 277c AA/J Holmes; 278t AA/C Sawyer; 278c AA/J Holmes; 279t AA/C Sawyer; 279c AA/J Holmes; 280t AA/C Sawyer; 280c Phatra Real Estate Plc; 281t AA/C Sawyer; 281c AA/J Holmes; 282t AA/C Sawyer; 282c Royal Cliff Beach Resort; 283t AA/C Sawyer; 283c AA/J Holmes; 284t AA/C Sawyer; 284c AA/J Holmes; 285t AA/C Sawyer; 285c AA/D Henley; 286t AA/C Sawyer; 286c AA/J Holmes; 287t AA/C Sawyer; 287c AA/J Holmes.

PLANNING

289 AA/J Holmes; 292 AA/J Holmes; 293t AA/J Holmes; 293b AA/R Strange; 294 Currency information courtesy of MRI Bankers Guide to Foreign Currency, Houston, USA; 295 AA/J Holmes; 297 AA/J Holmes; 298 AA/D Henley; 299t AA/D Henley; 299b AA/D Henley; 300 AA/J Holmes; 302 AA/R Strange; 303 AA/J Holmes.

Every effort has been made to trace the copyright holders, and we apologise in advance for any accidental errors. We would be happy to apply any corrections in any future edition of this publication.

Project editor
Cathy Hatley

Project management
Cambridge Publishing Management Ltd.

Design
Steve Hawes

Picture research
Liz Allen

Internal repro work
Ian Little, Michael Moody, Sarah Butler

Production
Lyn Kirby, Helen Sweeney

Mapping
Maps produced by the Cartography Department of AA Publishing

Cartographic editor
Anna Thompson

Main contributors
Sean Sheehan, Robert Tilley (authors); Tim and Oi McLachlan (verifiers);
Joanne Osborn (proofreader); Karolin Thomas (indexer)

Copy editor
Emma Sangster

Published by AA Publishing, a trading name of Automobile Association Developments Limited, whose registered office is Fanum House, Basing View, Basingstoke, RG21 4EA. Registered number 1878835.
A CIP catalogue record for this book is available from the British Library.
ISBN 13: 978-0-7495-4976-3
ISBN 10: 0-7495-4976-9

Key Guide is a registered trademark in Australia and is used under license.
Binding style with plastic section dividers by permission of AA Publishing.
Colour separation by Keenes
Printed and bound by Leo, China

Find out more about AA Publishing and the wide range of travel publications and services the AA provides by visiting our website at www.theAA.com/bookshop

A02251
Maps in this title produced from map data © New Holland Publishing (South Africa) (PTY) Limited 2006
Relief map images supplied by Mountain High Maps® Copyright © 1993 Digital Wisdom, Inc
Weather chart statistics supplied by Weatherbase © Copyright 2005 Canty and Associates, LLC
Transport maps © Communicarta Ltd, UK

We believe the contents of this book are correct at the time of printing.
However, some details, particularly prices, opening times and telephone numbers do change.
We do not accept responsibility for any consequences arising from the use of this book.
This does not affect your statutory rights. We would be grateful if readers would advise us of any inaccuracies they may encounter, or any suggestions they might like to make to improve the book. There is a form provided at the back of the book for this purpose, or you can email us at Keyguides@theaa.com

Dear Key Guide Reader

●

Thank you for buying this Key Guide. Your comments and opinions are very important to us, so please help us to improve our travel guides by taking a few minutes to complete this questionnaire.

You do not need a stamp (unless posted outside the UK). If you do not want to cut this page from your guide, then photocopy it or write your answers on a plain sheet of paper.

Send to: Key Guide Editor, AA World Travel Guides
FREEPOST SCE 4598, Basingstoke RG21 4GY

Find out more about AA Publishing and the wide range of travel publications the AA provides by visiting our website at
www.theAA.com/bookshop

ABOUT THIS GUIDE

Which Key Guide did you buy? _____

Where did you buy it?_____

When? _ _ month/ _ _ year

Why did you choose this AA Key Guide?
- ❏ Price ❏ AA Publication
- ❏ Used this series before; title _____
- ❏ Cover ❏ Other (please state) _____

Please let us know how helpful the following features of the guide were to you by circling the appropriate category: very helpful (**VH**), helpful (**H**) or little help (**LH**)

Size	**VH**	**H**	**LH**
Layout	**VH**	**H**	**LH**
Photos	**VH**	**H**	**LH**
Excursions	**VH**	**H**	**LH**
Entertainment	**VH**	**H**	**LH**
Hotels	**VH**	**H**	**LH**
Maps	**VH**	**H**	**LH**
Practical info	**VH**	**H**	**LH**
Restaurants	**VH**	**H**	**LH**
Shopping	**VH**	**H**	**LH**
Walks	**VH**	**H**	**LH**
Sights	**VH**	**H**	**LH**
Transport info	**VH**	**H**	**LH**

What was your favourite sight, attraction or feature listed in the guide?

Page _____ Please give your reason _____

_____

Which features in the guide could be changed or improved? Or are there any other comments you would like to make?

_____

_____

ABOUT YOU

Name (*Mr/Mrs/Ms*) _____

Address_____

_____

Postcode _____ Daytime tel nos _____

Email _____
Please *only* give us your mobile phone number/email if you wish to hear from us about other products and services from the AA and partners by text or mms.

Which age group are you in?
Under 25 ❏ 25–34 ❏ 35–44 ❏ 45–54 ❏ 55+ ❏

How many trips do you make a year?
Less than1 ❏ 1 ❏ 2 ❏ 3 or more ❏

ABOUT YOUR TRIP

Are you an AA member?   Yes ❏ No ❏

When did you book?   _ _ month/_ _ year

When did you travel?   _ _ month/_ _ year

Reason for your trip?   Business ❏ Leisure ❏

How many nights did you stay?_____

How did you travel?   Individual ❏ Couple ❏ Family ❏ Group ❏

Did you buy any other travel guides for your trip?_____

If yes, which ones? _____

_____

Thank you for taking the time to complete this questionnaire. Please send it to us as soon as possible, and remember, you do not need a stamp (*unless posted outside the UK*).

AA Travel Insurance call 0800 072 4168 or visit www.theaa.com

---

Titles in the Key Guide series:
Australia, Barcelona, Britain, Brittany, Canada, Costa Rica, Florence and Tuscany, France, Germany, Ireland, Italy, London, Mallorca, Mexico, New York, New Zealand, Normandy, Paris, Portugal, Prague, Provence and the Côte d'Azur, Rome, Scotland, South Africa, Spain, Thailand, Venice, Vietnam.
Published in May 2007: Croatia   **Published in October 2007:** China

---